KU-242-565

OTHER TITLES IN THE SERIES

The Government of Republican Italy
JOHN CLARKE ADAMS and PAOLO BARILE

The Federal Government of Switzerland
GEORGE A. CODDING, JR.

Government and Politics in Israel
OSCAR KRAINES

Contemporary Government of Japan
THEODORE MCNELLY

The Indian Political System
NORMAN D. PALMER

Contemporary Government of Germany
ELMER PLISCHKE

South Vietnam: Nation Under Stress
ROBERT SCIGLIANO

Norwegian Democracy

JAMES A. STORING
COLGATE UNIVERSITY

GEORGE ALLEN & UNWIN LTD · LONDON

QUEEN MARY
COLLEGE
LIBRARY

To

Edith

CONTENTS

PREFACE

Democratic government is not new in Norway. Even as the Vikings were marauding the continent, the British Isles, and — as is now fairly well established — the coast of North America, primitive lawgiving institutions were being developed. These assemblies or, as they are called in Norwegian, *tinger*, served as the model not only for the Norwegian parliament (Storting), but also for the parliament of Iceland (Alting).

Although the beginnings of Norwegian democracy can be traced to the middle ages, the modern ideological and institutional structure had their origins in the seventeenth, eighteenth, and early nineteenth centuries. The absence of a native nobility and the presence of a vigorous, if not well organized, agrarian group enabled the government established by the Constitution of 1814 to assume a degree of independence in the newly formed Norwegian-Swedish Union which finally led to responsible parliamentarism in 1884.

During the last years of the Dano-Norwegian Union and throughout the period from 1814 to 1905 while Norway was united with Sweden under a common king, nationalism, as well as democracy, became increasingly strong. And in present-day Norway both remain vigorous. Occasionally one is struck by certain conflicts in modern Norway, e.g., the conflict between the extremes of nationalism and the inevitability, due to location and resources, of a high degree of dependence upon other states. Also one discovers an intense type of individualism growing initially out of the very nature of the topography, but this has been tempered by well organized cooperative ventures. Running through all of these — nationalism, individualism, and cooperation — is the thread of democracy.

Much of the institutional fabric and many of the procedural arrangements of Norwegian democracy are not dissimilar from those found in other Western countries, particularly the United Kingdom. But certain institutions, like the parliament (Storting), are unique. And the combination of judicial review and separation of powers with cabinet government has given the Norwegian government a character unlike that found either in the United Kingdom or the United States.

The treatment of Norwegian democracy that follows is reasonably traditional. Introductory background chapters are followed by descriptions of the institutions and practices associated with the legislative, executive, administrative, and judicial functions of the national government. The role of the political parties and the organization of local government are touched upon briefly. Since Norway has pioneered in the fields of social legislation and economic planning, no account of Norwegian democracy would be complete without some reference to these activities. The impact of postwar events on Norwegian foreign policy is examined in the last chapter.

A word should be said about the form of citations made to Norwegian materials. Since changes in spelling and even in rules for capitalization within a title have occurred off and on during the last fifty years, I have made no attempt to secure uniformity, but have rather tried to follow rules in force when the document or book was written. The translation of certain terms has not always been easy, but, whenever possible, I have tried to employ the terms used in English materials published by the government. Throughout the book I have used NK as the symbol for the unit of Norwegian currency (*krone* or crown).

My obligations to Norwegian colleagues are legion; I can only list a few. Professor Frede Castberg was the first Norwegian scholar to open up for me the interesting story of constitutional development in Norway. His counsel throughout my studies in Norway has been most helpful. Dosent Thomas Wyller, Director of the Institut for Statsvitenkap of the University of Oslo, and several of his colleagues (Professor Torstein Eckhoff, Messrs. Tim Greve, Eirik Steinnes, Audun Ervik, and Mrs. Tertit Aasland) read the entire manuscript with the exception of Chapter 11. Much of the material in this chapter was drawn from the writings and lectures given by Professor Ole Myrvoll while he was visiting at Colgate University and Bowdoin College. Mr. Arne Arnesen of the Foreign Ministry was helpful in providing information on personnel procedures in that ministry of the national government. Professor Dayton D. McKean, Mr. Richard N. Clark and his associates on the editorial staff of Houghton Mifflin Company offered invaluable advice and counsel in the final preparation of the manuscript. I am deeply grateful to all of these people but it goes without saying that I alone am responsible for errors and omissions.

I owe a special debt of gratitude to my daughter, Mrs. Susan Storing Maybeck, who typed the manuscript. She was no mere typist; she also played the useful role of critic.

JAMES A. STORING

Hamilton, New York
January 29, 1963

NORWAY
MILES
0 50 100 200
0 100 200
KILOMETERS
NORDKAPP
(North Cape)
Hammerfest
FINNMARK
U.S.S.R.
Tromsø
TROMS
FINLAND
LOFOTEN
ISLANDS
Narvik
Bodø
Arctic Circle
N
Mo
Mosjøen
HELGELAND
SWEDEN
Gulf
of
Bothnia
Namsos
FOSNA
INNHERAD
Trondheim
TRONDELAG
Kristiansund
NORDMØRE
Molde
DOVRE
Ålesund
SUNMØRE
RONDANE
TRYSIL
NORDFJORD
Lillehammer
SOGN
LAND
Hamar
Stockholm
VALDRES
Kongsvinger
HARDANGER
OSLO
Sarpsborg
Bergen
RYEYLKE
Drammen
TELEMARK
Halden
Skien
Haugesund
AGDER
Stavanger
Arendal
Göteborg
Kristiansand
North Sea
S·BRYANT

1

The Land and the People

Natural Resources and the Economy

Every schoolboy in Norway learns at a very early age that his country is poor in natural resources with only about 5 per cent of its area fit for cultivation. He might also be able to pass along an oft repeated, dramatic description of the extreme length of his country by suggesting that if one could rotate it on its southern tip, the extreme northern part would reach as far south as Morocco. Though he may not be able to explain it, the boy may also give implicit expression to the significant impact that location, a jagged coastline, a paucity of natural resources, and a mountainous terrain, unsurpassed even by Switzerland, has had on Norwegian character and institutions.

Norway lies on the same latitudes as parts of Greenland, Siberia, and Alaska (between 58°N and 71°N). Were it not for the moderating influence of the Gulf Stream, the upper one-third of the country, being north of the Arctic Circle, would be a frigid waste. As it is, all of the ports, even in northern Norway, are usable the year around. Along the coast the climate is moderate, much like New England and upper New York State. In the interior, particularly in the mountainous areas, winters are cold and summers are short.

Norway proper[1] has a land area of 124,000 square miles — somewhat larger than Great Britain. Much of this is rugged and mountainous, completely unsuited for agriculture and also for timbering. The mountainous terrain does provide a valuable source of water power, part of which has been harnessed by an expanding hydroelectric industry. In 1959 Norway produced 28.5 million kilowatts but this, it is estimated, is only about one-fourth of the total electrical power-producing capacity of the country. Even today Norway's per

[1] The overseas Norwegian territories include Svalbard, Jan Mayen, two islands and Queen Maud Land in the Antarctic.

capita production of electric power is the highest in the world and double that of the United States. Expanding electrochemical and electrometallurgical industries have been made possible by the availability of cheap electrical power.

Besides water power, the important natural resources of Norway are forests and fish. About one-fourth of the land is covered by forests, but some are not accessible for easy timbering operations. About 90 per cent of the timberland is owned by corporations, private persons, and the municipalities; the balance is owned by the state. The sea around Norway has long provided not only the avenues of communication between separated sections of the country, but also extremely valuable food resources in the form of many kinds of fish. Fishing is carried on all along the Norwegian coast but with especially concentrated activity in the Lofoten Islands in the north. Though much of the fishing takes place in coastal waters, Norwegian fishermen are to be found on the Icelandic and Newfoundland banks as well as the sea around Greenland, where Norwegian sealers are particularly active. Norway leads all European countries and ranks fifth among all countries of the world in the amount of fish caught annually.

Norwegians were among the first to build a really modern whaling fleet. At first whaling activities were carried on principally along the Norwegian coast and in Icelandic waters. Although some small whales are still caught in coastal waters, the really important whaling activity is carried on in the Antarctic with great fleets of catcher boats and as many as eight or nine huge floating factory ships equipped to process and store the meat and oil. Whaling has been a lucrative business, at least until lately. At present, due to the failure in 1959 of attempts to renew the international agreement restricting the catch in the Antarctic, there is a certain understandable pessimism among Norwegians respecting the future of the whaling industry. Some concrete evidence of the uncertainty of the future became obvious in 1961 when one of the largest factory ships in Norway was sold to Japanese interests.

Norway is not particularly rich in other natural resources. Some iron ore and a little copper impregnated ore are to be found in northern Norway and limited deposits of pyrites, lead ore, and sulphur in other parts of the country. There is no coal in Norway proper, and the limited (less than 300,000 tons per year) coal mining operations in Spitsbergen are relatively unimportant. There are as yet no discovered oil resources in Norway. The absence of coal and oil makes necessary substantial imports of these important sources of energy. As the hydroelectric facilities are expanded, imports of coal and oil for industrial use and home heating will be proportionately reduced.

Although the amount of arable land is extremely limited, and the farms are for the most part small, the Norwegians have succeeded in recent years in improving agricultural techniques to the point where the country is now self-sufficient in dairy products, vegetables, meats, and certain fruits. Substantial amounts of grains still have to be imported. Although there are some farms in the southeastern and southwestern parts of the country that run well over 200 acres in size, for the most part Norwegian farms are small — often less than ten acres. As a result, most farmers are forced to find work to supplement their income from the land. In the past many engaged in fishing activities, but mechanization of the fishing fleet has caused many of the small farmers in recent years to take jobs in neighboring industrial plants. Only about 20 per cent of the population of Norway is at present engaged wholly or partly in agricultural pursuits.

While the relative importance of agriculture has declined in recent years, industry has expanded significantly. Industrial production has made steady progress since 1945; the production index for all industries is today nearly three times as high as it was in 1939. The number of workers employed in industry has increased to the point where Norway has now about the same proportion of industrial workers in its population as has Denmark and The Netherlands. The industries employing the most people are transport equipment, food and beverages, clothing and footwear, wood manufacturing, pulp and paper products, and chemicals. Metals and metal products and textiles have become increasingly important in recent years.

The shipping industry stands apart in any consideration of the Norwegian economy, not only because of its size (third largest in the world), but also because of its crucial contribution to the Norwegian balance of payments account. The fact that Norway must import quantities of raw materials, even some foodstuffs, and is limited to exports of fish and related products, timber, wood pulp and paper, a limited number of manufactured articles, and very few other items leads to a constant excess of imports over exports. Were it not for a large merchant fleet, 90 per cent of which never reaches Norwegian waters, the reasonably high standard of living prevailing in Norway would be impossible. The merchant fleet today (1963) totals more than eleven million tons, 55 per cent of which is made up of tankers.

There are definite hazards in the reliance on shipping to make up the imbalance between imports and exports. Shipping is unusually sensitive to fluctuations in business activity, and since, for the most part, Norwegian ships serve industries of other lands, Norway is in a particularly vulnerable position.[2] Also the shipping business is noticeably affected by international political crises and is particularly

[2] In 1960 about 15 per cent of American foreign trade was carried by Norwegian ships. In the same year less than 10 per cent of American trade was carried on American ships.

handicapped in time of war. During World War I 50 per cent of the Norwegian merchant fleet was destroyed and somewhat similar losses were sustained in World War II.

Unlike the situation in many countries, Norwegian shipping is not subsidized by the state. Only by the most efficient type of organization and management is it possible for the Norwegian fleet to compete in a world shipping market against subsidized fleets from other countries. But the Norwegian merchant marine has been able to compete and has not only been an important means of securing sufficient foreign exchange to close, or at least narrow, the balance of payments deficit, but it has also provided substantial tax revenues.

The People

Norway has a small (3,540,000 in 1960), homogeneous population with few large urban centers. Oslo, the capital city, with a population of 465,000, is the largest municipality; only one other city, Bergen, has a population over 100,000. The country is sparsely settled; in 1960 there were 26.5 inhabitants per square mile (the United Kingdom in the same year had 558 and the United States, including Alaska and Hawaii, had 50.5). The population has grown slowly but consistently during the last one hundred years in spite of waves of emigration that saw nearly a million Norwegians move to the United States alone in the period between 1870 and 1930 in search of improved economic conditions. Since World War II emigration has virtually stopped.

The absence of much intermixture between Norwegians and other national and racial groups — at least since the day of the Vikings — has preserved the homogeneity of the Norwegian population. There is really only one minority group: about 25,000 Lapps in the extreme north, some of whom still lead a migratory life with little respect for national boundaries. The small Jewish community in Norway, never really a "minority" group, was severely reduced in size by the Nazis in World War II. There are only a scattering of individuals of the nonwhite races (Negro, Oriental, etc.) resident in Norway at the present time.

Two other factors contribute to homogeneity in the Norwegian population: a common religion, and the absence of a class system based upon an hereditary aristocracy.

The Evangelical Lutheran Church was established by the Constitution of 1814 as the national church of Norway. About 95 per cent of the Norwegian people belong to the State Church; the remaining 5 per cent are divided among other faiths — Free Lutherans, Methodists, Baptists, Pentecostals, Roman Catholics, etc. There is now complete freedom of religion in Norway. The only remaining obstacle to the free exercise of religion was removed in 1956 when the constitutional clause prohibiting Jesuits from entering the country was repealed. In spite of the complete freedom accorded dissenters, Norway has remained a Lutheran country and thus has escaped the dissensions common in countries with strong religious diversities.

Norway has never had a really indigenous nobility; the remnants of nobility found in the country in the eighteenth century were Danish in origin. The absence of an hereditary aristocracy has certainly contributed to a spirit of individualism and to a definite social mobility. Having said this, however, one cannot escape the fact that class stratification has existed and does exist even in present-day Norway. The upper classes in the old days counted membership among the clergy, the intellectuals, and the large landowners; today, significant deference is still accorded the intellectual; but shipowners, whalers, and so-called big businessmen have replaced the clergy and the landowners in the upper levels of the class hierarchy. Though democratic in outlook, the Norwegian is really no egalitarian; he recognizes his position in the class structure of his country and seems content to operate within it. But there are no arbitrary official distinctions of class and no significant bars to social mobility. Also, every attempt is made — through state-supported schools, colleges, and universities and by a comprehensive program of social insurance — to ease the economic burden of all classes, but this, of course, redounds particularly to the benefit of the low-income groups in the society.

The ruggedness of the Norwegian countryside has created a people who are at the same time individualistic and cooperative. Living for years in isolated areas has had a tendency to foster not only extreme individualism but self-reliance and self-sufficiency in the Norwegian which has often been given expression by an announced desire to be left alone. Evidence of this desire can be seen to this day; even in urban communities people make every effort — through the use of fences and other devices — to make sure that their privacy is respected. But, at the same time, the difficult terrain and a sparse, diffused population have made cooperation unavoidable, and this in turn has given rise to a good deal of socialization.

The Norwegian people are proud, patriotic, and present a rather interesting mixture of cosmopolitanism and provinciality. They love their country, not only because they treasure the independence and security it has provided, but also because they appreciate its intense natural beauty. They are well acquainted with the rest of the world, but sometimes give the impression of a degree of inadequacy and naïveté which often does not in any real sense conform to actuality.

Geographical Divisions

Though the population of Norway is homogeneous, the facts of geography have contributed to significant differences among the various parts of the country. These differences have been most marked in language and in certain customs.

There are five distinct geographical regions in Norway: East Norway (*Østlandet*), South Norway (*Sørlandet*), West Norway (*Vestlandet*), the Trondheim Region (*Trøndelag*), and North Norway (*Nord Norge*). East Norway — an area of fairly broad valleys and plateaus — is an agricultural and industrial area extending south and north of Oslo. South Norway is reasonably flat by Norwegian standards; at least the mountains of the area are of moderate height. The region is predominantly rural; Kristiansand, with a population of 28,000, is the largest city in South Norway. West Norway, a large region extending as far north as Bergen and beyond, has a mild climate, a rugged coastline, mountains in the interior, and some reasonably good agricultural land, particularly in the area south of Stavanger. Fishing and fish processing have been the important industries of the region, but in recent years manufacturing has been on the increase. The Trondheim Region partakes of some of the plateau-like characteristics of East Norway and lies between the reasonably temperate area of West Norway and the rugged, sparsely settled North Norway region. All of the Norwegian coastline is marked by deep fjords and dotted with thousands of islands.

Each of the five regions and the subdivisions within them has developed in reasonable isolation. Even today the only means of transportation available to certain of the communities, particularly in the west and north, is by boat. The railroad system does connect all the large population centers in the Eastern, Southern, Western, and Trondheim areas, and it has been extended north as far as Bodø. Air transport has been developed in the years after the war, and at present most of the larger centers of population are connected by an expanding network of airlines. Even remote centers, such as Kirkenes and Hammerfest in the north are served by air transport in the summer months. Without doubt, air transport will make unnecessary costly expansion of the rail network into remote regions now served almost exclusively by boat. The highway system has also been significantly expanded in recent years, and bus travel has become common not only in the more thickly settled parts of the country, but in the farther reaches of the interior and even in the sparsely settled parts of North Norway.

Distinctions of dress, customs, and particularly language have developed as a result of isolation and the difficult modes of travel common until a few years ago. Many of these differences are less noticeable now than they once were, but differences in the spoken language are still quite evident. It is not always easy for a long-time resident of Oslo, for example, to understand the dialect of a farmer from a remote western or northern community.

The spoken dialects, especially in the rural areas, developed naturally from everyday usage. The official written language had, at least in the nineteenth century, a definite Danish character that developed during the 400 years that Norway and Denmark were united under a common king. Not long after Norway became independent (1814) feeble attempts were made to cast off the Danish influence on the language and to make it more indigenous in character. This movement relied on the Old Norse usages, but more specifically on the subsequently developed dialectical forms. The controversy between the people who would retain much of the Dano-Norwegian and those who would change the language to conform with the dialects and with the actual usage in rural areas became extremely heated in the early decades of the present century. This controversy goes on today and has both cultural and political overtones. At present there are two official languages: *Bokmål* (or *Riksmål*), the language which developed from Danish influences, and *Landsmål* (or *Ny Norsk*) which was based in large part on the dialects. Both are official, and both are taught in the schools. As yet, *Bokmål* seems to have a superior position, due in no small part to the fact that its strongest adherents are found in the larger population centers. Also most of the literature is in *Bokmål,* although a vigorous group of twentieth-century writers have employed the medium of *Landsmål.* At the risk of complicating this account, it should be reported that there is a movement to join the two competing Norwegian languages into a kind of compromise tongue called *Samnorsk.* This has had official status since 1958 when it was authorized by parliamentary act.

As indicated above, the language controversy has had political as well as cultural overtones. The Conservatives and the residents of urban areas were inclined to support the early established language while the Liberals and certain Socialists united with the rural elements in demanding that the language take on a more indigenous character. Even today the controversy often becomes heated and intense. To the outsider this may seem, at best, unnecessary, but he must try to understand that the conflict is not only cultural and political but also has a relationship to the deeper roots of national character. A genuine, pure language would give certain Norwegians a sense of cultural security that they do not feel while continuing to use "borrowed" words and phrases.

National Character

There has been a tendency in recent years among certain social scientists to identify certain behavioral traits and ideological backgrounds with what they describe as the national character of a people. In pursuing this approach books have been written describing the American character, the British mind, ad infinitum. The difficulty with such an approach is obvious, but recognizing its limitations one can perhaps identify a certain historical background and a body of common experience that may permit one to speak of a country's national character or, putting it as certain scholars do, its political style.

Two opposing characteristics of the Norwegian people have been noted: homogeneity based upon absence of minority groups and the presence of a common religion; and heterogeneity arising from the geographical situation. Perhaps the differences between the residents of Hammerfest, Tromsø, and Setesdal on the one hand and the man of affairs in Oslo or Bergen are more important than the similarities that may exist among them in outlook and political stance. Recognizing that this may be true, there seem nevertheless to be certain common features of behavior and a common approach to political and social questions that can perhaps be identified as typically Norwegian.

The Norwegian is individualistic, even to the extent of seeming sometimes to disregard the welfare of his fellow citizens. He is often rude, sometimes impolite, though usually in unimportant ways, e.g., in getting on and off street cars. He certainly lacks the courtesy and thoughtfulness so noticeable among his British cousins. On the other hand, like the British, the Norwegians practice a kind of personal individualism that is restrictive in character.

The Norwegians themselves admit to being insecure, perhaps more in their relationships with each other than with people of other lands. This insecurity manifests itself in many ways, but perhaps most importantly in critical attitudes heard expressed on the street and found written in the daily press. Events that in many countries would be dismissed after a single report in the press remain in Norwegian newspapers for days the subject of public scrutiny and debate. If a police officer has made an "improper" arrest, or if a public official has made an error, these infractions are labored long and hard. Perhaps by doing this the critic may be genuinely concerned with correcting a wrong, but he may also be building up his own ego.

Another manifestation of insecurity can be found in the manner in which innovation is accepted. Generally, new products and new ways of doing things are viewed with suspicion. There are many Norwegian housewives who still refuse to accept milk in paper cartons, and many would not buy frozen foods, even if they were more readily available. This conservative attitude extends into the social life of the people; Norwegian dinner parties, though delightful in the extreme, present no surprises to the initiated guests.

A cultural anthropologist could no doubt explain the individualism and the insecurity of the Norwegian by referring to his constant struggle against an unkind physical environment. If he were to survive, not to say prosper, in a rugged country, he had to push himself forward. If he saw others succeed, perhaps by somewhat dubious means, he quite naturally not only blamed himself for not doing likewise, but criticized his neighbors for doing what he himself might have done had he had the wit to think of it. On the other hand, of course, the cultural anthropologist might argue with a certain plausibility that the environment and the ideology that developed among the people facing a hard environment forced a high moral standard which called for criticism of the people who deviated from it.

Whatever the reason, most Norwegians will agree that a certain amount of somewhat irresponsible and perhaps even thoughtless individualism exists among them. To the outsider this is normally not considered nearly as important as the more constructive evidences of cooperation, tolerance, and social concern, all of which have been implemented in an elaborate public welfare program. Most Norwegians would agree that they do have a responsibility to care for their neighbor. Few, even among extreme Conservatives, would reverse the trend toward more and better cooperative ventures in protection against disease and accidents, poverty, hazards of unemployment, and old age.

This paradox between individualism and cooperation is not unique among Norwegians. In fact, in any attempt to define national character, paradox is more apt to be the rule, and consistency of idea and behavior the exception. In the United States, for instance, paradoxical situations and paradoxical behavior can be found in many places and at practically any point of time. For example, Americans worship the law and the Constitution, but at the same time crime rates are higher in the United States than in any other country.

Besides the conflict that exists in Norway between the individual and the group, there are other less striking paradoxes that might be mentioned. The Norwegian is intelligent and literate; less than one per cent of the population cannot read, and the illiteracy that exists is due in large part to physical causes. Not only do the Norwegians read, but they read good books, some of which are written in foreign languages. There are more bookstores in two square blocks in Oslo than there are in many American cities of comparable size. Eighty-two daily newspapers serve a Norwegian population which is considerably smaller than that of Chicago. In addition, there are over a hundred weekly, biweekly, and triweekly newspapers. But this high degree of literacy is accompanied by an occasional manifestation of naïveté that is not always easily explained. Perhaps it may be due in part to the fact that certain Norwegians confine their reading to restricted fields. In certain instances it arises, as was evident in 1961 in the so-called atom bomb protest, among well meaning, intelligent idealists who seemed not to have obtained from their reading a sophisticated political orientation. There is a tendency, among certain individuals at least, to stand on principle, disregarding the necessity of adapting principle to make way for unavoidable political decision. Whatever the cause, the paradox between "literateness" and political naïveté exists in Norway, but perhaps in no higher degree than in some other modern societies.

The Norwegian is friendly, but shy; anxious to become acquainted with other people, but reluctant to take the first step. In certain respects he feels confident and operates individually and socially with care and dispatch. In other respects he admits to inefficiency, a degree of crudity, and a certain lack of concern. Often, at least by American and German standards, he is inefficient. He sometimes works slowly, and his processes are labored and unnecessarily deliberate. But on the ski slope and on the ship his touch is sure and his pace is fast.

The analysis so far pursued in this chapter has had a somewhat negative tone. It would be unfair to allow it to stand without underscoring some of the positive aspects of Norwegian personality, which have been included implicitly in the discussion above. An emphasis on honesty and fundamental integrity, straightforwardness, seriousness of purpose, and an enlightened awareness of domestic and world problems — all can be found in varying degrees, of course, among the Norwegians. If it is true — as is pointed out by the Norwegians themselves — that certain of these qualities are not as obvious as they once were, the fact remains that they have been important in building a mature civilization in Norway as well as contributing to the stability and well-being of an important part of the New World.

A word should be said about the attitude of the Norwegian toward his country; few citizens in the world exhibit greater patriotism and give evidence of such genuine love of country. This is obvious at any time, but was particularly noticeable during the German occupation from 1940 to 1945. Many Norwegians during those years exhibited real courage often at great personal risk. The shock that accompanied the invasion on April 9, 1940, gave way to a campaign of stubborn, determined resistance which became more intense as the Norwegians came to realize the full impact of occupation on the freedom and independence they had enjoyed before the war.

Though it is not easy to identify the ingredients of the Norwegian national character, it is not difficult to state briefly and definitely the policy positions that have in part arisen because the people have certain kinds of ideas and behaviour patterns. In domestic affairs, Norway is a highly developed welfare state with a significant degree of socialized and cooperative enterprise and with a rather high degree of governmental regulation. In international affairs, Norway until 1940 was neutralistic; since World War II she has renounced neutralism by joining forces with the North Atlantic Community. Although committed to the West, Norway still looks toward the possibility of a widened sphere for international cooperation. Because of this attitude, Norwegian political leaders of today are exerting great efforts, as their predecessors did through the League of Nations, to make the United Nations a really effective instrument for peace and security.

2

Historical Introduction

Early Beginnings

Modern constitutional government in Norway had its beginnings in 1814. In that year the Norwegian-Danish Union, in which Denmark had had a predominant position, was dissolved, and the Norwegian Constitution which survives to this day was adopted. Only a matter of months after the Constitution was written, Norway found it impossible to maintain complete independence and joined Sweden in a personal union that lasted until 1905.[1]

Although the modern state was formally organized in the early years of the nineteenth century, the first appearance of an independent Norwegian kingdom antedates 1814 by more than 900 years. In 890 Harald the Fairhaired (*Hårfagre*) had subdued the warring tribal chiefs of the north and obtained for himself recognition as King of Norway. The Saga period that followed Harald's ascension to the first Norwegian throne can truly be called the golden age of old Norse cultural and commercial activity. The art, sculpture, and especially the literature of the period compare favorably with some of the best of the artistic achievements in other older civilizations.

In addition to the general cultural contributions of the period, a body of law and a set of primitive lawmaking and law interpreting institutions emerged. The practice among the people of meeting periodically to make, enforce, and interpret rules had developed by the year 900 to the point that at least two provincial assemblies (*tinger*)

[1] Unless otherwise indicated, the content of this chapter is based upon material drawn from Edvard Bull and others, *Det norske folks liv og historie gjennem tidene*, 11 vols. (Oslo, 1935); Knut Gjerset, *History of the Norwegian People*, 2 vols. (New York, 1915); Karen Larsen, *A History of Norway* (Princeton, 1948); T. K. Derby, *A Short History of Norway* (London, 1957).

were in regular operation (*Gulating* in the west and *Frostating* in *Trøndelag*). In the eleventh century the law of the *Gulating* was "formalized" and put in written form.[2]

Better known than the legal accomplishments of the early Norsemen were their colonial exploits. Colonies in Scotland, Ireland, Iceland, Greenland, and other neighboring islands flourished during the Viking period. Discoveries in other hitherto unknown corners of the earth had been made, and it is certain that the Vikings visited North America in about the year 1000. While exploratory activities waxed and waned after the year 1000, the descendants of Harald the Fair-haired continued many of his rather primitive policies leading to more secure unification within Norway proper. The peak of this development was reached during the years between 1217–1263 under the capable leadership of King Haakon Haakonsson. And his successor — Magnus VI, known as the Law Mender — compiled the first Norwegian code of law. This was in no sense comprehensive, as are modern codes; nor did it make certain obvious differentiations, e.g., between private and public law. It did, however, guarantee certain rights — perhaps even against the King — and can be said to have served as a basis for the law developed in the next few hundred years. It is well established that this was the first attempt at codification made in any European country.

Certain dynastic difficulties throughout the fourteenth century reacted against the external and internal progress made during the two preceding centuries. In 1319, upon the death of Haakon V, the male line of the *Hårfagre* dynasty became extinct and Magnus Eriksson, a grandson of Haakon V, was chosen by a Norwegian council to assume the Kingship. At the same time Magnus Eriksson was also elected King of Sweden by the nobles of that country. Thus began the first of a series of Scandinavian unions.

Magnus Eriksson was beset early by difficulties in both countries. He was forced to agree to a proposal of certain powerful aristocrats in 1343 whereby one of his sons, Haakon, should become King of Norway on coming of age and another son, Eirik, should succeed his father as King of Sweden. This proposal had as its aim the disestablishment of the existing dual monarchy. But in spite of this, the new Norwegian King, Haakon VI, proved strong enough to continue for a time to exercise a considerable measure of control over Swedish affairs. However, by 1371 he had so completely antagonized certain important aristocratic elements in Sweden that he was forced to re-

[2] For a translation of the text of these laws see Laurence M. Larson, *The Earliest Norwegian Laws* (New York, 1935).

linquish any of his remaining rights to the Swedish crown and content himself with the Norwegian Kingship.[3]

Norway United with Denmark

Norway did not remain long an independent kingdom; in 1380 the death of Haakon VI resulted in another union, this time with Denmark. Haakon VI had married Margaret, a Danish princess; and in 1375 their son Olav had been elected to the Kingship in Denmark. Upon his father's death five years later, Olav, who was only ten years old at the time, also became King of Norway. Olav died in 1387, and his death served to strengthen the position of Scandinavian unionism. As he left no lawful heirs, the throne of Denmark reverted to his mother Margaret, who succeeded in enhancing her power over governmental affairs in Scandinavia by getting herself appointed regent for the newly elected King of Norway, Erik of Pomerania. And Margaret's growing influence caused the Swedish nobles to approach her on the possibility of assuming some control over the affairs of the royal house of that country. This finally led to the election of the young Norwegian King, Erik of Pomerania, to the Swedish Kingship. Thus by 1397 another Scandinavian union had been formed, this time including in political fact, if not dynastic perfection, all three countries — Norway, Sweden, and Denmark. This union existed for several years without formal constitutional foundations. But friction soon arose between the union king and his far-flung subjects, and the result was a series of insurrections in both Sweden and Norway. The difficulties in Sweden resulted in its withdrawal from the union in 1448. After that year, with the exception of a short period from 1497–1523, Sweden remained independent of the other Scandinavian countries until the establishment of the Swedish-Norwegian Union in 1814.

The opposition to Danish domination in 1448 was perhaps as strong in some Norwegian quarters as it was in Sweden. But the absence in Norway of capable leaders to direct a strong national independence movement led to the acceptance by the Norwegians in 1450 of a continuation of the Norwegian-Danish Union. To solidify his position Christian I (1450–1481) promulgated a formal act of union following his coronation as King of Norway in Bergen in August, 1450. According to its provisions

> both Kingdoms, Denmark and Norway, shall hence forward be united in brotherly love and friendship, and one shall not lord it over the other, but each Kingdom is to be ruled by native born

[3] For a description of this first attempt at implementation of pan-Scandinavianism, see Gjerset, II, 7 ff.

> magistrates . . . [and] each Kingdom is to enjoy, keep, and use freely its written laws, freedom, and privileges, old and new which they now have, or hereafter may receive, and that both Kingdoms, Denmark and Norway, shall henceforth remain under one king and lord forevermore.[4]

The act of union contemplated two equal and coordinate kingdoms, and there was no indication in the document that Denmark was to have any position of superiority. Norway's experience in the union with Denmark varied greatly throughout the years following the formal establishment of the relation in 1450. The difficulties under Christian II (1513–1524) and Christian III (1536–1559) stand in sharp contrast to the sincere interest manifested in Norwegian affairs by Christian IV (1588–1648). He visited the country frequently and was particularly concerned with the problems of advancing the physical welfare of the land; cities were projected, public buildings constructed, and other improvements were undertaken during the early years of his reign. He rebuilt the capital city which had been destroyed by fire in 1624 and changed its name to Christiania. (The old name, Oslo, was restored in 1925.)

During the closing years of the reign of Christian IV, the opposition in Denmark to the increasing powers and privileges of the nobility had become unmistakably evident. Throughout the years these landed aristocrats had retained the right to choose the King and, as a result, had obtained concessions in the form of tax exemptions and other economic privileges that had become constant sources of irritation to the bourgeois elements in the Danish population. Somewhat the same attitude of hostility toward the nobles existed in Norway. Although the Norwegians had at first objected to the election of the King by the nobles, a procedure agreed to at the Council of Kalmar in 1397, they had become reconciled to it during the years of the Danish-Norwegian Union following the Bergen Agreement in 1450. But 200 years of experience with kings chosen by noblemen, usually Danish, intensified dissatisfaction in Norway to the point where alternative methods of succession to the throne were being actively discussed.

Feudalism had never been as firmly established in Norway as in other parts of Europe. It was weakened further in the fourteenth and fifteenth centuries. This steady decline in the power of the nobility brought an increase in influence to the burgher and farm classes in the centuries that followed. The ruggedness of the topography had a great deal to do with the weak position of Norwegian feudalism; the efficient management of large agricultural estates was not easy although a great deal of land, at one time or another, had come under

[4] Gjerset, II, 69.

the control of the nobles and the church. Though the feudal system was not as firmly entrenched as in Denmark, the Norwegian experiences with their own nobles and, perhaps more important, their contacts with governmental representatives from the Danish nobility had been anything but pleasant. Though the Norwegian middle class was not as large as the bourgeois group in Denmark, there was in Norway an emerging independent farm group (called *bonde*) that favored a sharp curtailment of the powers of the feudal lords.

The opposition in Denmark to the nobility culminated in a rebellion staged by Copenhagen townsmen in September of 1660. With a show of force the burghers compelled the noblemen to abolish the elective kingship and establish in its stead an absolute monarchy based upon the hereditary principle. It might seem strange that a change from a limited monarchy with an elective king to an absolute monarchy with an hereditary king should be forced by a class later to become the most ardent and effective foe of autocratic power. But at that time, the quarrel was not with the king but with the nobles, and the burghers took the step they thought necessary to remove their immediate political enemies from their position of dominance.

The documentary base for the new governmental form was the *Kongelov,* promulgated in November of 1665. By this act the King was given individually all the power he had previously held jointly with the nobles. No uncertainty remained as to the character of the royal power. According to the *Kongelov,* "the King has the highest and most unlimited power, for he is the supreme head here on earth, elevated above all human laws, and he recognizes no other judge, either in secular or spiritual matters, than God Almighty."[5]

The immediate changes brought about by the Copenhagen episode in 1660 applied at first only to Denmark. In order to legalize the transition to an hereditary, absolute monarchy in Norway, it was necessary to secure the approval not only of the Danish Estates[6] but also of the Norwegian Estates (composed at this time of the nobility, clergy, burghers, and farmers). In August of 1661 the King summoned this latter body to meet in Christiania and, without dissent, the Estates approved the change to an hereditary, absolute form of monarchy. Having secured the agreement of the Estates in both countries, the King could promulgate the *Kongelov* which then became the common Danish-Norwegian constitution.

Norwegian nationalists had every reason to be satisfied with the new governmental form. Under the old system, Danish nobles had successfully dominated the administration of Norwegian governmental

[5] Gjerset, II, 229–230.

[6] The Danish Estates had approved the change to an hereditary monarchy on January 11, 1661.

affairs. To their way of thinking, Norway was not in any sense independent but rather a provincial possession of Denmark. The fact that by the close of the seventeenth century the influence of the nobility had been severely reduced and the King had obtained absolute power strengthened the cause of Norwegian nationalism. No longer were the citizens of Norway dependent upon the whims of a foreign nobility; the line of allegiance after 1665 ran directly from the people to the King. It should not be implied from this, however, that Norwegian and Danish leaders of the late seventeenth and early eighteenth centuries were unanimous in conceding to Norway any significant status of independence. Many of the Danish leaders continued to regard Denmark as the overlord, but the prevalence of this view did not discourage the Norwegian nationalists. They persisted in their attempts to force the recognition of Norwegian independence. By the close of the eighteenth century the practical results of these efforts were becoming apparent; some Danes had by this time accepted the idea that Norway was in fact an independent kingdom, united with Denmark under a common king.

The more general acceptance of this view following 1800 may be attributed to two distinct sets of causes. In the first place, nationalistic sentiment in Norway had become definitely crystallized, and organizations designed to advance the cause of undisputed independence, had been established. One of these, *Selskapet for Norges Vel,* attempted to advance Norwegian nationalism on many different fronts. Not content with obtaining more general recognition of the political independence of Norway, this society, in cooperation with other intellectual groups, agitated for the establishment of a Norwegian university. Largely as a result of these efforts, King Frederik VI authorized the organization in 1811 of the national Norwegian university in Oslo, and in 1813 instruction in the new institution began.

Another set of causes giving support to the cause of Norwegian independence had their roots in the existing European political situation. In 1807 Denmark found herself confronted with extremely difficult choices in foreign policy. The Napoleonic decrees and the English Orders in Council made a neutral position impossible, and the situation was complicated further by the formation of an alliance between France and Russia. No longer could Denmark-Norway postpone the decision; she must either ally herself with Napoleon or join forces with England.

Leading Danish statesmen favored cooperation with England, but unfortunate circumstances drove their country into an alliance with Napoleon. England had rushed warships to Copenhagen shortly after the agreement between Russia and France had been announced. English envoys, who accompanied the fleet, suspected that a secret treaty already existed binding the Napoleonic allies to Denmark-Norway. Because of this suspicion, they demanded in return for an alliance with England that Denmark show unmistakable evidence of good faith by turning over the Danish-Norwegian fleet to the English for the duration of the war. The Danish negotiators refused to accede to this humiliating demand, and the English, interpreting this answer as a confirmation of their suspicions, turned their guns on Copenhagen. After destroying vast sections of the city, the English naval commanders attacked the Danish fleet, lying in the harbor, and in short order the seventy vessels were captured by the English. After this episode Denmark-Norway was forced to turn to Napoleon, and on October 31, 1807, a formal Treaty of Alliance between France and Denmark-Norway was concluded. Five days later England declared war on Denmark-Norway.

The war with England brought nothing but despair to both Denmark and Norway. The coasts were blockaded, commerce was disrupted, and foreign trade was reduced to a trickle. The muttering in Norway against the policies of the Danish monarch, Frederik VI, grew louder; the advocates of Norwegian nationalism more outspoken. Not content with attempting to defend his people against England, Frederik VI, persuaded by his French and Russian allies, declared war on Sweden. Norwegian leaders were confident that their country would, of necessity, assume the greater share of the burdens imposed by these new, unpopular hostilities. Such a situation seemed intolerable in the face of the effectiveness of the English blockade. But in spite of serious difficulties, the Norwegian forces, under the capable leadership of Prince Christian August, were, at least in the beginning, highly successful against the Swedes. However, Swedish internal conditions caused the Norwegian leaders to refrain from taking full advantage of their early victories. The war was as unpopular among the Swedes as it was among the Norwegians, but the mentally unbalanced Swedish King, Gustav IV, remained resistant to the demands of his people that peace be concluded. Sweden's military leaders appealed to Christian August for an armistice that they might go to Stockholm and depose their King. Christian August agreed, much to the discomfiture of his father, King Frederik VI. Gustav IV was deposed, but not in time to ward off the pending difficulties with Russia that resulted in an invasion of Swedish territory by Russian troops. When Charles XIII finally replaced Gustav IV on the Swedish throne, he concluded treaties of peace with both enemies, but only after he had agreed to cede Finland to Russia.

Succeeding events in Sweden brought nearer the eventual breakup of the Danish-Norwegian Union. Charles XIII, the newly crowned Swedish King, was childless and of dubious competency. After his ascension to the throne, the Swedish Estates, in an effort to restore better relations with their neighbors, elected Christian August, the popular Danish-Norwegian prince, to the position of heir apparent. His death shortly after his election cut short the rejoicing among the friends of Scandinavian unionism in all three countries. Again the Swedish Estates were called upon to elect a successor to Charles XIII. The advocates of a union with Norway favored the election of a Danish prince, and the proponents of more complete pan-Scandinavianism put forth as their candidate the Danish King, Frederik VI. Another group, favoring an adjustment of the difficulties suffered as a result of the Napoleonic wars, appealed to the French Emperor for his advice on the succession question. In the meantime the feeling in Sweden was growing lukewarm to the Danish candidates, and the demand for an aggressive, militaristic regime was increasing. Consequently, after some further discussion, the Swedish Estates invited Marshall Bernadotte, Prince of Ponte Corvo and high-ranking officer in the Napoleonic military hierarchy, to assume the position of Crown Prince. Bernadotte accepted, came to Sweden in October, 1810, changed his name to Carl Johan, and entered upon his new duties as the Swedish Crown Prince.[7]

It was not a happy situation that faced Carl Johan in 1810. The old King, Charles XIII, had reached a state of complete incompetency, making necessary the assumption by the newly elected Crown Prince of virtually all executive power. His ignorance of Swedish traditions and his inability to speak the Swedish language intensified the difficulty of his task. In spite of these handicaps, Carl Johan lost little time in making the preparations necessary to reach the goals he had set for his adopted country, i.e., the restoration of Sweden's prestige and the acquisition of Norway as compensation for the earlier loss of Finland to Russia. In considering steps to be taken he became convinced that he could not hope to gain his ends through an alliance with Napoleon. Consequently, when the break between France and Russia came in 1811, Carl Johan was prepared to desert his former leader and attempt to negotiate an alliance with Russia. But in this undertaking the Swedish Crown Prince was not supported by many of his country's leaders, who had certain traditional antagonisms toward the Russians. The humiliating defeat at the hands of Russia in 1809, followed by the loss of Finland, had intensified this hatred. At the same time many Swedes were mildly sympathetic with the Napoleonic cause, notwithstanding the fact that their country had failed to observe certain parts of the French Emperor's continental system. Sweden's failure to aban-

[7] For a more detailed account of the establishment of the Bernadotte dynasty in Sweden, see Franklin D. Scott, *Bernadotte and the Fall of Napoleon* (Cambridge, Mass., 1935).

don trade relations with Great Britain in disregard of the Napoleonic dictates culminated in the French occupation during January, 1812, of Swedish Pomerania. This act of aggression marked a turning point in the foreign policy of Sweden; no longer could the nobles justify a course favorable to Napoleon. Carl Johan's desire for a Russo-Swedish alignment was about to be fulfilled.

The treaty of alliance with Russia, concluded on April 5, 1812, was supplemented by a more definite agreement made during the summer of the same year. Sweden was to help Russia in campaigns against France and in return Sweden was to receive Norway and Seeland.

England had at first manifested no great enthusiasm for the deal between Sweden and Russia, but the need for aggressive and certain military assistance in the coming fight against Napoleon caused her to acquiesce later to Sweden's terms. But the English insisted that Carl Johan must show certain, concrete evidence that he intended to fulfill completely his obligations to the allied powers by taking an active part in the military campaigns.

Shortly after the treaty of alliance between Sweden and Russia had been signed, Frederik VI of Denmark received demands from Sweden requesting the immediate transfer of Norway to the Swedish crown. The Danish King refused emphatically and proceeded to strengthen Danish-Norwegian unity by appointing Prince Christian Frederik, heir presumptive to the Danish-Norwegian throne, as viceroy of Norway. This act, it was hoped, would serve notice on England and her allies that the Danish King intended to resist with all possible vigor any attempt to divide his domain. Not many months after Christian Frederik's arrival in Norway, Napoleon was defeated by the allies at Leipzig (October 19, 1813). This event sealed the fate of the Danish-Norwegian Union. Before joining in further operations against the French, Carl Johan made a hurried campaign into Holstein. The Danes offered little resistance and after perfunctory negotiations agreed to the terms offered by the Swedish Crown Prince.

1814: An Eventful Year

The Treaty of Kiel, signed on January 14, 1814, provided that Norway was to be ceded by the "King of Denmark to the King of Sweden" and that it should remain a "kingdom united with Sweden." Whether intended or not, the negotiators neglected to include in the cession the distinctly Norwegian possessions — Iceland, Greenland, and the Faroe Islands — and this omission caused serious difficulties later.[8]

[8] The final phase of subsequent conflicts over the status of the former Norwegian colonies concentrated chiefly on Greenland. Iceland obtained

The Treaty of Kiel was greeted in Norway with mixed emotions. The first incomplete dispatches told only of the cessation of hostilities; the pleasant prospect of peace after years of war with their accompanying economic maladjustments was welcome indeed. But when Frederik VI's official communication describing the treaty bargain with Sweden became known in Norway, contentment and happiness gave way to anger and unrest.

Immediately the leaders in Norway began to consider possible courses of action. They were practically unanimous in agreeing that the act of cession was not legally or morally binding upon their country. Norway, they argued, was a separate, independent state, had been united with Denmark by constitutional means through a common king, and had never been a Danish province or a territorial possession. Consequently, they argued, the treaty must be regarded as lacking in binding force and the subsequent renunciation of the Norwegian throne by Frederik VI viewed as clearing the way for the establishment of a new, completely independent government in Norway. Although a number of outstanding men soon rallied to the cause of Norwegian nationalism, it was the presence of one — the Danish Crown Prince, Christian Frederik — that proved particularly fortunate. He had been appointed viceroy of Norway in 1813 and had won many admirers, who looked to him for leadership in the difficult days ahead.

Christian Frederik lost no time in making his position clear. In answer to Frederik VI's order that preparations be made for the transfer of Norway to Sweden, the Crown Prince dispatched an emphatic refusal. Not long after that (February 16) he met with a group of prominent Norwegians at Eidsvold. Twenty-one of the country's principal leaders, including Christian Magnus Falsen, Professor George Sverdrup, Peder Anker, Carsten Anker, John G. Adler, and Carsten Tank, attended the meeting. Christian Frederik presented his plan

---

a significant degree of self-government in 1874 as a result of agitation for independence that began in the 1830's. In 1918 Iceland became an independent kingdom united with Denmark under a common king. In 1940, as a result of the occupation of Denmark by the Germans, the dual monarchial arrangement was abolished and Iceland became an independent republic unaffiliated with Denmark.

Norway's claim to the Faroe Islands was not seriously pressed, but constant assertion of her claim to Greenland led not only to several diplomatic exchanges but litigation before the Permanent International Court. This body decided in 1933 that Norway's claims to Greenland could not be substantiated and that the island should remain a Danish possession. Needless to say, this was a very unpopular decision in Norway.

For a simple, concise statement of Norway's case, see Frede Castberg, "Det norske standpunkt i Grønlandssaken," *Nordmands Forbundet,* Vol. 24 (August, 1931), pp. 239–241.

for saving Norwegian independence: he would ascend the throne by right of succession. This suggestion encountered determined opposition, and it appeared that the cause of Norwegian independence had struck its first snag, until Professor George Sverdrup convinced the Danish prince that to appropriate the crown without the official approval of the Norwegian people was unjust and perhaps even illegal. After reaching agreement among themselves and with Christian Frederik, the committee decided that a representative convention should be called. Besides electing a king, this assembly should also formulate a constitution. In the meantime Christian Frederik was to serve as regent. On February 19 the prince, acting in his new role, issued a proclamation calling upon all the people to gather in their churches for the purpose of renewing allegiance to their country and naming delegates to the convention. By the middle of March the first Norwegian national election in modern times had provided the membership for the most important conclave in the history of the land — the Eidsvold Convention of 1814.

While Norwegian patriots were engaged in laying the groundwork for an independent governmental structure, the other European countries were preoccupied with the final stages of the Napoleonic struggle. Carl Johan had gone south after his successful campaign into Denmark, leaving the task of subjugating Norway to the old Swedish King, Charles XIII, and his advisers. No one in Swedish official circles had taken seriously the rumor that Norway would refuse to abide by the terms of the Treaty of Kiel. And it was not until after the governor-general, appointed by Charles XIII to administer governmental affairs in Norway, had been curtly rebuked by Christian Frederik for his impudence in attempting to "govern" a free and independent kingdom that the true situation became apparent to the Swedish ministers. But, even then, they were constrained to inaction, principally because Carl Johan, their only effective leader, was absent from the kingdom.

At the same time the English attitude toward the Scandinavian "settlement" generally, and Carl Johan particularly, was growing lukewarm. England had never been enthusiastic about the specific provision calling for the "cession" of Norway to Sweden. The traditional ties of trade between Norway and England, coupled with a growing distrust of the Swedish Crown Prince, caused English sentiment to grow progressively more sympathetic to the cause of Norwegian independence. Diplomatically, however, England was bound to respect her agreement with Sweden. As a result, Norwegian attempts during the early months of 1814 to secure English assistance in resisting the execution of the terms of the Treaty were unsuccessful. But the failure of Carsten Anker, the Norwegian emissary in England, did not serve to discourage Norwegian patriots at home. By April 9 most of the delegates elected at the church meetings held during February and March had assembled at Eidsvold.

Of the 112 delegates to the Eidsvold Convention, fifty-four were from rural districts, twenty-five from the cities and towns, and thirty-three from the army and navy. Fifty-nine of the delegates were from the higher echelons of the government services (*embedsmenn*), sixteen were businessmen, and thirty-seven were farmers. This distribution did not reflect any marked degree of proportional representation of the various classes in Norwegian society, largely because the suffrage rules imposed for the election favored the propertied class.

Most of the kingdom's outstanding men were in attendance at the Constitutional Convention of 1814. Christian Magnus Falsen, Peder Anker, Peter Motzfeldt, Wilhelm F. K. Christie, Severin Løvenskiold, George Sverdrup, Nicolai Wergeland, Herman Wedel Jarlsberg, Gustav Peter Blom, Teis J. T. Lundegaard, and Jacob Aall were among the many leading figures who took prominent parts in the deliberations at Eidvsold.

After the Convention opened it soon became apparent that the delegates were divided on the question of a Swedish-Norwegian union. A determined independence party, led by such thoroughgoing nationalists as Christian Magnus Falsen, Professor George Sverdrup, and Wilhelm F. K. Christie, was opposed by a pro-Swedish group, headed by Count Herman Wedel Jarlsberg (the only nobleman at the Convention), Jacob Aall, Nicolai Wergeland, and others. The group opposing the union with Sweden was the larger and had little difficulty in securing the passage of a resolution on April 15 binding the Convention to respect the independent position of the Norwegian kingdom. In order to clinch their victory, the advocates of independence moved the adoption of another resolution, the aim of which was to avoid, at least for the duration of the Convention, any consideration of future cooperation with Sweden. According to this proposal, the Convention was to concern itself solely with two matters: drafting a constitution and electing a king. No other questions were to be considered. Although considerable difference developed in the course of the debate on this motion, it finally passed on April 19 by the narrow margin of the vote of the President of the Convention.[9]

In undertaking the task of writing a constitution, the Convention relied heavily upon the report of a committee that had been appointed on April 12 and instructed to prepare a preliminary draft of fundamental principles. This group of fifteen men included within its ranks some of the most illustrious members of the Convention: Falsen, Sverdrup, Motzfeldt, Wedel Jarlsberg, Wergeland, and Jacob Aaal. On

[9] *Riksforsamlingens forhandlinger,* I, 24 ff. This is the official documentary account of the proceedings at the Convention of 1814.

April 16 this committee made its preliminary report. To serve as a foundation for the constitution, eleven principles were proposed. Only that section of the committee's report proposing uniform compulsory military service failed of adoption. The other ten were accepted by the Convention in the following form:

1. Norway is to be a free, independent, and indivisible kingdom. Its form of government shall be a limited hereditary monarchy.
2. The people shall exercise the lawmaking power through their representatives.
3. The right to levy taxes shall be exercised by the people through their representatives.
4. The power to declare war and conclude peace shall be vested in the regent (king).
5. The regent shall possess the power of pardon.
6. Judicial powers shall be separated from legislative and executive powers.
7. Freedom of speech shall be maintained.
8. The Evangelical Lutheran Church shall be the State Church. All religious sects shall have freedom of worship. Jews shall be excluded from the kingdom.
9. No further restrictions upon economic freedom shall be imposed.
10. No personal, mixed, or hereditary privileges shall be hereafter granted.[10]

After this set of fundamental principles had been approved, the Convention instructed the committee to proceed with the formulation of a detailed constitutional draft. In this undertaking, as well as in preparing the earlier report, the committee was guided by provisions in the constitutions of certain other countries. It is quite clear that the French Constitution of 1791, the Swedish *Regjeringsform* of 1809, the Batavian Constitution of 1798, the American Constitution of 1787, and the fundamental law (*Kongeloven* of 1665) underlying the Danish-Norwegian Union were all examined carefully by the members of the drafting committee.

Besides the constitutions of foreign states, the committee had available embryonic drafts prepared by certain Norwegian leaders prior to the opening of the Convention. The most important of these preliminary documents was unquestionably the one written by Johan Adler and Christian Magnus Falsen. It had been written shortly after it became apparent that Norway would be in need of a new fundamental law and had been examined by many of the delegates to the Convention prior to their arrival in Eidsvold. Many of them found

[10] *Ibid.*, pp. 15–33, *passim.*

it quite acceptable. Although the final constitutional document approved by the Convention was significantly different from the document written by Adler and Falsen, it is clear that the committee and the Convention used many of the ideas contained in this preliminary draft.

On May 4 the plenary debate began on the individual sections in the draft constitution. The fear that Carl Johan's return from France would interrupt the proceedings caused the members of the Convention to limit discussion to one week. On May 11 the revised draft was submitted to an editing committee, and on May 16 the Constitution was adopted by the Convention. The following day the document was officially signed and sealed. Thus, in a matter of less than two weeks, a constitution was written which not only met immediate needs in the early nineteenth century, but has been flexible enough to adapt to the social, economic, and political changes in Norway during the twentieth century.

The influence of the ideas of at least three political philosophers can be seen on examining the Norwegian Constitution of 1814. Popular sovereignty as enunciated by Rousseau, the separation of powers principle advocated by Montesquieu, and the liberalism of John Locke were influential in helping to shape the ideological base of the Eidsvold Convention.[11] The document also embodied the workable parts of the existing Norwegian legal and political tradition. Samuel Laing, British writer and political observer, emphasized this fact early in the nineteenth century in his oft-quoted opinion on the Norwegian fundamental law:

> There is not probably in the history of mankind another instance of a free constitution, not erected amidst ruins and revolution, not cemented with blood, but taken from the closet of the philosopher and quietly reared and set to work, and found to be suitable without alteration to all the ends of good government. The reason of this apparent singularity is, that all the essential parts of liberty were already in the country. The property was in the hands of the whole body of the people. The ancient laws and institutions affecting property were in full operation, and were conceived and administered in the very spirit of liberty. As far as regards property, these laws and institutions left nothing for the most liberally constituted assembly to legislate upon. As far as regards personal rights, the

[11] The following specific examples of influences exerted by Rousseau, Montesquieu, and Locke are outlined by Frede Castberg, *Norges statsforfatning* (Oslo, 1947), I, 73–79: the suspensive veto is based upon the popular sovereignty idea of Rousseau; the provision for an independent judiciary is illustrative of the influence of Montesquieu, and the guarantee of certain individual rights is based upon the philosophy of Locke.

> mild and enlightened administration of Denmark, although under an arbitrary form, had left few general grievances to be redressed. There was nothing in the condition of the people, the state of property, the civil or religious establishments, which did not fit in with a free constitution in which legislative power was vested in the people. These had all emanated from the people in ancient times; and, there being no hereditary privilege, or power, or property vested in any class of the community, had been handed down unbroken through the ages. The new constitution was but the superstructure of a building of which the foundations had been laid, and the lower walls constructed, eight centures before by the ancestors of the present generation.[12]

On the same day (May 17) that the Constitution was signed by the delegates, the Convention elected Prince Christian Frederik to the Norwegian Kingship. Two days later the new monarch officially assumed his duties as head of the Norwegian state, and on May 20 the Convention adjourned.

The new Norwegian Constitution was launched under extremely trying circumstances. The defeat of Napoleon in the spring of 1814 enabled the European powers to turn more attention to the Swedish-Norwegian problem. During May of 1814 England, Russia, Prussia, and Austria sent emissaries to Copenhagen with instructions to press for immediate and complete compliance with the provisions of the Treaty of Kiel. Frederik VI assented to their demands and ordered his Crown Prince, Christian Frederik, to renounce his Norwegian Kingship and return at once to Denmark. After becoming convinced that the disturbances in Norway were not the result of Danish intrigue, the foreign representatives journeyed to Christiana to lay their demands before the young Norwegian King.

In the meantime Carl Johan had returned to Sweden determined to subdue the rebellious Norwegians. By July 28, 1814, the Swedish forces, augmented by Russian troops, were pushing their way into Norwegian territory. The struggle that followed brought scant success to either side. The willingness of the Norwegian soldier to oppose Swedish aggression was dampened by the desultory tactics of their leader, Christian Frederik. He proved no match, either in technical skill or courage, to the seasoned ex-marshal, Carl Johan. On the other hand, there seemed to be no disposition on the part of Carl Johan and his lieutenants to follow through on the military advantages that seemed to be theirs.

[12] Samuel Laing, *Journal of a Residence in Norway during the years 1834, 1835 and 1836* (London, 1840), pp. 479–480.

Norway United with Sweden

The course of diplomatic and military events during the summer of 1814 had convinced many Norwegian leaders, including the King, that a position of absolute independence for their country was untenable. Consequently, when Carl Johan offered an armistice and certain conditions under which the integrity of the Constitution could be maintained, he found the Norwegians willing to accept his proposals. The terms of the armistice agreement, signed at Moss (Norway) on August 14, 1814, provided for a Norwegian-Swedish union of apparently legal equals leaving to the Norwegian Storting (parliament), established by the Constitution, the solution of certain technical problems associated with the new status of the country. Carl Johan agreed, on his part, to respect the Norwegian Constitution as promulgated by the Eidsvold framers, insisting only on those alterations made necessary by the change from an independent to a union monarchy. In addition, a secret article of the Moss agreement required Christian Frederik to relinquish unconditionally all rights to the Norwegian throne.

The Norwegian acceptance of the Swedish terms was dictated by the realization that they could, by no stretch of the imagination, expect to win the armed conflict with the Swedes. Carl Johan's acquiescence, on the other hand, came as a result of his appraisal, not solely of the immediate situation, but rather of the long-range future. The difficulty of maintaining a union for any length of time based upon force, as well as the growing indifference of his former allies, convinced the Swedish Crown Prince that a peaceful settlement was more desirable than a military conquest. Moreover, he no doubt had in mind the possibility of enlarging Swedish control of Norwegian affairs once the union had been securely established.[13]

The events immediately following the armistice negotiations demonstrated a willingness among Norwegian citizens to accept the terms of the Moss agreement. Christian Frederik's abdication caused little turmoil. By October 20 the members of the extraordinary Storting had approved tentatively the Norwegian-Swedish Union by an overwhelming majority. Final parliamentary action on November 4 joined the two northern countries in a union destined to endure for nearly a century. Charles XIII was chosen King of Norway and Carl Johan was designated as the heir apparent. By August 6 of the following year (1815) a formal Act of Union (*Riksakt*) had been approved by the parliaments of both countries. It was in the nature of a treaty, recognizing by implication and express provision the independent status of each of the kingdoms. Norway had again joined a Scandinavian

[13] Bull, VII, 406–408.

union, but this time with hopes of maintaining her independence and national integrity.

The experiences of Norway in the years immediately following 1814 demonstrated clearly the nature of the newly formed Scandinavian union as seen from the perspective of the Swedish ruling class. Ostensibly the *Riksakt* contemplated joining two equal and independent states under a common ruler. Actually, Carl Johan, who succeeded to the throne in 1818, had no such intentions, but had, in fact, accepted the Norwegian Constitution and the union arrangements of 1814 as temporary expedients. And he did not delay long in considering constitutional alterations that would be consistent with his desire for an enhancement of Sweden's powers in this union of "equals."

A threatened *coup d'état* in 1821 was the first real manifestation of Carl Johan's determination to strengthen his authority over Norwegian affairs. Not long after the Storting approved the disputed debt settlement with Denmark, a matter fraught with great international significance, Carl Johan ordered certain contingents of Swedish and Norwegian soldiers to report for duty near the Norwegian capital city of Christiana. The announced purpose of the King's action was to give his troops an opportunity to execute extensive maneuvers. This explanation was discredited when it was learned that the Norwegian soldiers had been given blank cartridges, while the Swedes were supplied with ball cartridges. The appearance of a part of the Swedish fleet in the harbor at Christiana confirmed the Norwegians in their suspicions that their King intended to give his soldiers something more than target practice. The arrival of Carl Johan, accompanied by a number of high military officials, in the capital city on July 17 served only to increase the apprehension in Norwegian official circles.

Another struggle between Sweden and Norway seemed in the making. But the King, as he had done not many years earlier, decided to abandon the idea of enforcing Swedish domination of union affairs by military might. As before, the fear of incurring the ill will of the other European powers who, after the Danish-Norwegian debt settlement, had no grievances against Norway was undoubtedly a determining factor in Carl Johan's decision. Whether it was the international situation or the impulsive character of the Swedish King that caused the change is immaterial; the fact remains that a military conflict was averted.

Although Carl Johan gave up his militaristic plan in 1821, he did not abandon his objective of securing for himself and his country a dominant position in the Swedish-Norwegian Union. Thirteen distinct constitutional proposals, calculated to have these effects, were submitted to the Storting in 1824. These amendments enlarged greatly the power of the King. He was to have the right of absolute veto, the right to dissolve the Storting and order new elections, the right to appoint the presidents of the Storting, the right to discharge state employees with the exception of judges, and the right to create a new Norwegian nobility. All these proposals for constitutional change were defeated by the Storting in 1824, and at the next session, three years later, the same amendments on reconsideration were once again turned down. They were resubmitted to the Storting in 1830, and again the Norwegian legislators were united in their opposition. Although the amendments reappeared in every session of the Storting until Carl Johan's death in 1844, the royal demands for their passage in the face of continuing resistance grew less insistent with each succeeding parliamentary session.

Hopes for a more powerful union dominated by Sweden did not die with Carl Johan. He had threatened to subjugate Norway by show of force and imposed constitutional changes; his successors hoped to amalgamate the two nations and secure Swedish domination through the operation of social, economic, and political processes. To the Norwegians there was little difference between subjugation and amalgamation. Both processes seemed to call for a strong, arbitrary kingship and greater power for Sweden; both would have had the effect of decreasing the virility of Norwegian nationalism.

Many instances of Norwegian opposition to Swedish domination can be found in the period between 1850 and 1905, the year the union was disestablished. Three movements will serve to illustrate the tendency: the constant war waged by the Norwegians against the office of viceroy, the battle for parliamentarism, and the demands for independent diplomatic and consular services for Norway. By the revised Constitution of 1814 the King was given the right to appoint a viceroy for Norway. This officer acted as the final coordinator of Norwegian administrative affairs and served, for all practical purposes, as chief executive in Norway. Experience with the office was as varied as were the personalities of the several incumbents, but, generally, the viceroy's office was considered by the Norwegians as an instrument of Swedish domination and overlordship. Several attempts were made to abolish the position. As early as 1818 a bill designed to accomplish this purpose was introduced in the Storting, but it received little support, and another legislative attempt in 1848 also failed. In 1854 an act abolishing the office was finally passed, but was promptly vetoed by the King.

The agitation in Norway against the viceroy's position during the years that followed awakened intense interest in both kingdoms. Advocates of amalgamation opposed abolition because they thought it would lead to a weakened union. The proponents of abolition finally prevailed and shortly after the ascension of Oscar II in 1872 the viceroy (now called *statthold*er) was replaced by a minister of state for Norway.[14] The practice of having a part of the Norwegian Cabinet resident in Stockholm during the King's stay in Sweden was continued, but the new arrangement provided for integration of all administrative responsibilities in the office of the minister of state for Norway.

The changes in the administrative structure led to demands for a closer relationship between ministers and legislators and to the eventual installation of a parliamentary system in Norway. A growing liberal faction under the leadership of Johan Sverdrup, Bjørnstierne Bjørnson, and others had for some time recognized the need for some form of ministerial responsibility. The effectiveness of their agitation resulted in the acceptance by the King in 1884 of the principle that the cabinet should have continuing responsibility to parliament. After that date, with the exception of the veto power which he retained, the King's control of policy matters was substantially reduced.

Dissolution of the Norwegian-Swedish Union

While Sweden was willing to accede to Norway's demands in the viceroy issue and in the struggle for parliamentarism, she was not disposed to accept the Norwegian solution to the problem of administering the foreign affairs of the Scandinavian union. Since 1815 diplomatic and consular matters had been handled jointly. This proved to be a satisfactory arrangement until the late nineteenth century when several factors combined to make it increasingly unpopular among Norwegian political leaders. In the first place, the incumbents in diplomatic and consular posts were very seldom Norwegians. Secondly, Sweden's share in determining foreign policy was very definitely on the increase. An amendment to the Swedish Constitution passed by the Rigsdag in 1885, without Norwegian concurrence, brought foreign affairs, which had hitherto been administered by the Union King, more directly under the control of the Swedish parliament. At the same time the membership of the ministerial committee charged with examining and passing upon diplomatic questions affecting both kingdoms was increased from three to four, but Norway continued to have only one representative on the committee. A third factor contributing to dissatisfaction among the Norwegians was based upon the realization that their country's economic interests and those of Sweden did not always coincide. This made it difficult, if not impossible, for union consuls, who were usually Swedish, simultaneously to represent adequately and fairly the economic and commercial interests of both kingdoms in some situations.

By 1891 Norwegian sentiment against the joint system of administering foreign affairs had crystallized into a definite party program. The

[14] The King's legal right to appoint a viceroy existed until 1891.

Pure Liberals, campaigning on a platform favoring an independent foreign service for each country, succeeded in obtaining in that year a majority of the seats in parliament. Although the party had a mandate to work for a completely independent foreign service, the new Liberal Ministry, headed by Johannes Steen, was reluctant to take such drastic action. Rather, it attempted to secure Swedish recognition of Norway's right to establish an independent consular service. A resolution of the Storting embodying this demand was passed on June 10, 1892, but it was promptly vetoed by the King.

The veto by King Oscar II of the consular resolution led to the resignation of the Steen Ministry in the spring of 1893. This was followed by a Conservative government headed by Emil Stang, who resigned after the elections of 1894 gave the Pure Liberals another popular mandate. After some delay and disagreement, a coalition government under Francis Hagerup, a Conservative, was formed in October of 1895.[15]

In the meantime, Swedish sentiment against an independent consular service for Norway had been gaining momentum. Many members of the Swedish parliament had been loud in denouncing Norway's demands as unreasonable and contrary to the Act of Union (*Riksakt*). There was some talk of maintaining the status quo through the use of force. These rumors only served to intensify nationalistic feelings in Norway and to increase the urgency of the consular issue.

The seriousness of the tension in June of 1895 had caused the Storting to recede from its former position and agree to negotiate with Sweden. A committee representing both kingdoms was instructed to study the issue and submit its findings to the parliaments of their respective countries. On March 26, 1898, the report of this committee was filed with the Norwegian Storting. Four distinct plans of settling the problem were suggested, but none of them had any chance of being accepted by the Norwegian parliament. Although the committee failed to develop an acceptable solution to the consular difficulties, its investigations and reports did serve to temper, at least for the time being, the antagonism between the two countries.

During the four years that followed, the demands for an independent Norwegian consular service remained, officially at least, in abeyance. In 1902 the issue was revived, this time on the initiative of the Swedish Minister of Foreign Affairs, Alfred Lagerheim. Another committee was appointed, and by March 24, 1903, another suggested solution to the controversy had been reported. Separate consuls for

[15] Stang offered his resignation in January of 1895, but owing to the difficulties of naming a new cabinet as well as the complicated relationship with Sweden, the effective date of resignation of the Stang Ministry was delayed well into October.

each kingdom were to be permitted and the governments of the two countries were each to designate the administrative department to which consuls were to be responsible. The committee's report was met with favor in Norwegian governmental circles, in spite of the fact that some people thought that Sweden might still continue to dominate foreign affairs even if the suggested change were adopted. But it was generally believed that this might be avoided by further negotiations and through some experience with the plan.

The political situation in Norway during 1903 favored continuation of bargaining on the consular issue. In the parliamentary elections held in that year, the Liberals and Conservatives joined in a coalition party pledged to secure an independent consular service through negotiation and cooperation rather than by more belligerent means. After the election, a new coalition government once again was formed under the leadership of Hagerup (Conservative).

Disagreement within the Swedish Cabinet during the summer of 1904 resulted in a decided setback for the prospects of an amicable settlement of the consular issue. The resignation of Lagerheim, the Swedish Foreign Minister, who was friendly to a lenient policy in settling the dispute with Norway, placed the responsibilities of continuing the negotiations directly in the hands of Boström, the Swedish Prime Minister. He did not favor a separate Norwegian consular service, independent of Swedish control, and began to take steps to implement his proposed policy. Quite expectedly, the Norwegian Cabinet found it impossible to accept the Swedish terms, and negotiations came to an abrupt close.

Re-evaluation by the Norwegians of the new Swedish position as well as the exigencies of the political situation within Norway itself led to the creation of a new coalition government under the leadership of Christian Michelsen. The new Cabinet lost no time in facing the issues. On May 10, 1905, a bill creating a separate consular service for Norway was submitted to the Storting by a special committee. Less than two weeks later the measure passed both branches of the parliament. King Oscar II's veto on May 27, 1905, was followed directly by the resignation of the Michelsen Cabinet. As the King was unable under the circumstances to find any of the party leaders in Norway willing to accept appointment as prime minister, the Storting, by resolution of June 7, declared the union with Sweden dissolved and empowered the Michelsen Government to continue in office for the time being. The die was cast; Norway could not turn back.

The reaction of the Swedish government to the developments in Norway was awaited anxiously by the people in both countries. Sweden could refuse to accept the decision of the Norwegian parliament and attempt to maintain the union by force. A minority in Sweden favored this course, but the Swedish parliament, influenced by an active majority desiring a peaceful settlement with Norway, agreed conditionally to the dissolution of the union, providing that a plebiscite on the issue were held in Norway, and, if the voters favored dissolution of the union, a formal application then be followed by a conference, made up of representatives from the two countries, for the final settlement of problems incident to the separation.

The Norwegian Storting accepted promptly these proposals of the Swedish Rigsdag. A plebiscite had in fact been ordered by the Storting before the Swedish parliament had made its suggestions. The result of the plebiscite, held in August, was overwhelmingly conclusive. About 85 per cent of the eligible voters participated, with 368,208 favoring dissolution and only 184 opposing it.

During the first three weeks of September, delegates from the two kingdoms met at Karlstad to iron out problems related to the dissolution of the union. It was agreed at this conference that neither government should hinder the free movement of goods in transit, that a demilitarized neutral zone on either side of the boundary would be maintained, and that the nomadic Laplanders of the north were to be free to migrate from one country to the other. These provisions and several others more technical in nature were submitted by the negotiators to their respective parliaments. On October 9 the final agreement was ratified by the Storting, and on October 16 the Swedish Rigsdag accepted the provisions and annulled the Act of Union. This was followed on October 27 by the abdication of Oscar II as King of Norway.[16]

Norway in the Twentieth Century

Immediately after the dissolution of the union with Sweden, the Norwegian people were faced with decisions concerning the kind of government best suited for the future. Several political and intellectual leaders considered this an opportune time for the abolition of the mon-

[16] The resolution of the conflict of 1905 without resort to arms demonstrates a high degree of political maturity in both Sweden and Norway. And when considered in the context of earlier difficulties between the two countries dating back to 1814, a peaceful settlement in 1905 becomes even more noteworthy. A great many accounts are available describing the events leading to the dissolution of the union. The official documents are all to be found in J. V. Heiberg, *Unions oppløsning 1905,* 2 vols. (Oslo, 1906. Fairly comprehensive secondary accounts can be found in Yngvar Nielsen, *Norge i 1905* (Horten, 1906) and Bernt A. Nissen, *1905* (Oslo, 1930). The best comprehensive account in English of the problems faced by the Swedish-Norwegian Union is to be found in Raymond E. Lindgren, *Norway-Sweden: Union, Disunion and Scandinavian Integration* (Princeton, 1959).

archy and the establishment of a republic, based perhaps on French or American patterns. A stronger faction, convinced of the durability of Norwegian monarchical traditions, favored the retention of a kingship. Overtures had already been made to the Swedish royal house, suggesting the election of a Bernadotte prince, but these, quite understandably, had been unceremoniously repulsed by King Oscar II. The Norwegians turned next to the Danish royal house, offering the new throne to Prince Carl, a grandson of King Christian IX. Prince Carl agreed to accept the Norwegian Kingship only if the results of a referendum indicated unmistakably both popular approval of the monarchical form and of his candidacy.[17] A plebiscite held on November 12–13 revealed that approximately three-fourths of the voters favored the selection of the Danish prince. The Storting, having elected him to the Kingship, immediately notified Prince Carl, who assumed the distinctly old Norse name Haakon (VII) and took up his duties on November 27 as King of Norway. Finally, after 600 years of involvement in various kinds of Scandinavian unionism, Norway had re-established once more her own royal house.

The years between 1905 and 1963 have witnessed a continuing democratization of political and economic institutions and processes in Norway. Voting rights have been extended and electoral regulations liberalized. The King's powers to exercise any significant veto over parliamentary acts and to negotiate in any personal manner with foreign states were eliminated by settlement of the union question in 1905. At the same time, the power and prestige of the Storting has increased. With certain exceptions, to be noted in the chapters that follow, Norway had by the early years of the present century developed a parliamentary system similar in most fundamental respects to that of the United Kingdom. Democratization also went forward during the period after 1905 in the economic field. Increasingly, the state undertook to provide safeguards against accidents, disease, the hazards of old age, and unemployment.

Since 1935 the Labor party has had complete responsibility for the government except for the period during World War II (1940–1945). In spite of the presence in Norway of a multiple party system,[18] bona fide coalition cabinets have been established only in time of real crises. The normal practice has been to vest total responsibility in one party

[17] Prince Carl was married to Maud, daughter of Edward VII of Great Britain. This connection, as well as the overtures that had been made to the house of Bernadotte, was reassuring to other European dynasties and paved the way for cordial acceptance of the new Norwegian royal line. On the other hand, Prince Carl's insistence on a plebiscite, in spite of contrary advice from his father-in-law, reduced the antagonism toward monarchy among the liberal democratic elements in Norway.

[18] See pp. 135–143.

(usually the largest) even if it does not command a majority in the Storting. Thus from 1935 to 1940 the Labor party provided the Prime Minister and Cabinet without a majority of the parliamentary seats. Though not aligned in a formal coalition with Labor during these years, the Agrarian party had agreed to support the government, but without representation in the Cabinet. From 1940–1945, while the Cabinet was in exile in London, it was truly a coalition, made up of representatives from all significant parties — Labor, Conservative, Liberal, and Agrarian, as well as a special representative from the Home Front. Immediately after the liberation in May of 1945 Einar Gerhardsen, a Laborite, formed a genuine, though temporary, coalition which gave way, after his party obtained a majority in the Storting in the November elections, to a Labor government. At present (1963), though the Labor party does not have a majority in the Storting, it does have a sufficiently large delegation (74 out of 150) to enable it to support its Cabinet without difficulty.

In international affairs, Norway had pursued a neutralistic policy during World War I and throughout the twenties and thirties. Even in 1940 when it seemed inevitable that all of Europe would be drawn into war, the Norwegian government attempted to steer a middle course between the two belligerents. It came as a distinct shock to have this policy upset by a systematic German invasion on April 9, 1940, extending throughout the coastal areas of the country from Narvik to Oslo.

No chapter in recent Norwegian history is more tortured than the occupation period during World War II (1940–1945). But perhaps no other contains comparable evidences of heroism, patriotic dedication, self-sacrifice, cooperation, and effective initiative. Many men and women — from high positions and low — became heroes in the resistance movement at home and in the service of their country abroad. Obviously no list of people can be included in this connection, but mention should be made of the important roles played by certain groups: the hastily organized and inadequately equipped military groups, the fearless, imaginative members of the Home Front, the seamen who kept the merchant marine functioning so efficiently, the clergy, the teachers, the students, and, not least, the members of the Supreme Court, who upheld the law and refused to be intimidated by Hitler's underlings in Norway. And by no means last, the statesmanlike role of leadership played by King Haakon VII should be underscored. He was a tower of strength throughout the war and became the symbol around which all Norwegians — at home and abroad — could rally. Even on the most confusing day in modern Norwegian history — April 9, 1940 — the King's position was clear; he knew that Norway could not capitulate but must resist the Germans whatever the cost. In order to avoid internment, he, his Cabinet, and members of the Storting left Oslo as soon as transportation could be arranged and established a temporary seat of government in nearby Hamar. Besides selected documents and records, they brought with them the country's gold supply which they finally succeeded in getting out of the country.

The German demand that the King appoint Major Vidkun Quisling to the prime ministership was met with emphatic refusal. Quisling, leader of a fascist organization, the Norwegian National Union party, had no significant following; his party had polled less than 2 per cent of the popular vote in the preceding parliamentary election and it had no representation in the Storting. No one in Norway had taken Quisling seriously, although it must have been known, at least in some quarters, that he and his associates had connections with Hitler and other Nazi leaders before the invasion of Norway.

Finding it impossible to induce the King and Cabinet to cooperate, with or without Quisling in the Cabinet, the Germans were forced to set up their own government in occupied Norway. They were handicapped since the *Blücher,* carrying the administrative personnel to be used during the occupation, had been sunk in the Oslo Fjord by shots from the little fort at Oscarsborg. Though Quisling had proclaimed himself head of the government as early as the evening of April 9, the Germans were hesitant to support his regime in the beginning since they had hopes of creating an occupation government based upon "friendship and cooperation." Without German support, this first Quisling government fell on April 15 and the Norwegian Supreme Court, sitting in Oslo, appointed on request of the Germans an administrative council of distinguished Norwegians. But this council refused to cooperate with the occupation forces and was dismissed in September of 1940. An attempt had been made during the summer to convene the Storting and force it to request King Haakon VII's abdication. Failing in this, Josef Terboven, the German commissar for Norway, induced the Presidential Board of the Storting to address a communication to the King asking him to abdicate. To this the King gave an emphatic refusal. After September, 1940, the Germans gave up their attempt to rule by cooperation and installed a full-fledged occupation government. By February, 1942, this regime had been crystallized: the "government" with Quisling as Minister President was made subject to the German occupation authority, headed by Terboven.

On leaving the capital in April of 1940 the legitimate government of Norway faced several serious problems: military, political, and constitutional. Though plagued by inadequate equipment and small forces, the Commander of the Norwegian forces, General Otto Ruge, was able to organize a delaying action which lasted about two months and was strong enough to permit the King and Cabinet to retreat to the north, where they were finally evacuated on June 7 aboard the British man-of-war *Devonshire*.

Before definite plans for the government's withdrawal from the country had been made, certain political and constitutional questions that might embarrass a government in exile had been considered. The Prime Minister (Johan Nygaardsvold) and his Cabinet had, shortly after the evacuation to Hamar, tendered their resignations to the King, who had refused to accept them. Rather than create a new Cabinet, the King, on the advice of C. J. Hambro, President of the Storting, and others, agreed to enlarge the Nygaardsvold Government by appointing ministers without portfolios from parties not represented in the Cabinet. With minor changes the Nygaardsvold Government continued in office for the duration of the war.

The constitutional question created by the need to establish a government in exile in London had been anticipated on April 9 in the last meeting of the Storting held (at Elverum) during the occupation. President Hambro introduced a resolution giving the King in Council power to take the action required to protect the kingdom if the parliament could not be convened. There was difference of opinion concerning the need for this authorization since Article 17 of the Constitution gives the King in Council power to issue provisional orders and Article 41 permits the King to be absent from the country for relatively long periods if he is "in the field." Whether necessary or not, the resolution was approved without dissent, though no record of a vote is to be found.

If the two paragraphs of the Constitution cited above were not adequate, it could be argued, as it has been convincingly by Professor Frede Castberg, that the emergency situation itself gave the King and his Cabinet the powers necessary to protect the country and prosecute the war even though undertaken from foreign soil.[19] Whatever can be said of this and other views, it is sufficient now to say that after the war the Norwegian Supreme Court ruled completely constitutional the actions taken by the government in exile.

Space does not permit any description of the Norwegian war activity at home, in England, and on the high seas. Perhaps the most significant contribution made by Norway was through its merchant marine, at least 90 per cent of which was not in Norwegian waters on April 9, 1940. Though all ships were ordered by the occupation authorities to return to Norway, none did in fact return. As a result, all were free to join in the war effort. Without Norwegian shipping, the allied cause would have been severely handicapped. (Norway had a tanker fleet in 1940 approximately equal to the British.) It was through its shipping that Norway was able to secure the foreign ex-

[19] Castberg, *Norges statsforfatning*, I, 182–189.

change necessary to buy goods during and after the war. But this was not inexpensive since, as had been the case in 1914–1918, about 50 per cent of the Norwegian merchant fleet was lost during World War II.

The history of the post World War II period will be found interspersed in the chapters that follow. But certain of the broad currents might be listed here. The first task facing the Norwegians after the war was rebuilding, particularly in North Norway where many of the towns had been more or less completely destroyed by the Germans when they retreated to the south in 1944. A general rehabilitation of industry as well as an improvement of living standards was greatly aided by the assistance under the Marshall Plan provided by the United States. Improvements were made in the welfare program and urgently needed housing programs were launched.

In the international field, Norway abandoned her former neutralistic position after the war in favor of participating in the North Atlantic Treaty Organization. She continued her activity begun under the League of Nations in support of international cooperation by giving generous, constructive support to the United Nations and related organizations.

3

The Executive: King and Council of State

Nature of the Kingship

The Norwegian Constitution definitely prescribes that the official governmental form shall be "a limited and hereditary monarchy."[1] This provision is followed by rather minute stipulations concerning the King's powers, duties, and privileges and a complete legal base for lines of descent, regency, and other matters directly associated with what might be called a personal kingship. Although many of these items will be more carefully considered in the discussion that follows, it should be pointed out at the start that Norway's modern kingship is a vastly changed institution from that contemplated by the constitutional provisions. The King's power today is titular; his role, symbolic and ceremonial.

With the advent of the parliamentary system in 1884, the significant powers of the King were taken over by a Council of State (cabinet) responsible to the Storting (parliament). Even before 1884 the King's personal prerogatives had been decreasing and the Council's realm of authority had been constantly increasing. At the present time the King has only nominal power; all of the real executive power resides in the Council of State. But, despite this, the Norwegian King, like the British Queen, does play an important role. His is the office around which all elements of Norwegian political life rally; his is the task of

[1] *Constitution of Norway,* Paragraph 1.

molding the various ingredients of Norwegian politics into one unified whole. Professor Castberg has summarized the characteristics of the King's position in the following manner: "The king is in modern state life, first and foremost the personification of the idea of state. He represents the common ideas held by all the component members of the state. He represents the authority of the state." In somewhat the same vein in a subsequent discussion on the advantages of the hereditary features of the Norwegian kingship, the same author contends that the very fact that the office of chief of state is inherited and outside the influence of political factionalism makes it more possible for the King "to symbolize national unity and give expression to the common feelings of the people."[2]

Although Norway has had long experience with monarchy, the country does not really have a strong monarchical tradition. This apparent paradox may be due in part to the fact that though the experience has been long — from the ninth century when Harald the Fairhaired became the first King of Norway — it has been punctuated by significant dynastic interruptions and long periods of foreign domination. For about 400 years prior to 1814 Norway was united with Denmark under a common king. Though this began as a union of equals, the Norwegians soon found themselves not only under the domination of the Danish King, but also subject to the rule of the Danish nobility and Danish civil servants. From 1814 to 1905, it will be recalled, Norway was united with Sweden, but once more under a foreign (Bernadotte) royal house. Only since 1905 has modern Norway been a completely independent constitutional monarchy; and the present ruling house has, at best, only a tenuous, distant relationship to the Norwegian monarchs of the fourteenth and fifteenth centuries. It should be re-emphasized that there was a strong minority favoring a republican form of government in 1905, in spite of the fact that Prince Carl of Denmark was elected King of Norway by a substantial majority.[3]

The new King, who had taken the name Haakon VII, was not genuinely popular during the first years of his reign. There were people in Norway who had some reservations on any one associated with Danish royalty and there were others, particularly those who had favored a republic, who feared that the new monarchy might become a focus of power for conservative or even reactionary forces. The new King's demeanor was correct, if not always exuberantly friendly, and as a result, not only did the controversy over the form of government disappear, but a genuine appreciation of the King's political

[2] Frede Castberg, *Norges statsforfatning* (Oslo, 1947), I, 169.
[3] See pp. 33–34.

neutralism and respect for democracy developed on all political fronts. But, in spite of this, King Haakon failed to generate genuine affection and spontaneous enthusiasm among his people. His manner was formal and, unlike his son Crown Prince Olav, his linguistic and cultural orientation and interest remained Danish. He was respected but not really loved.

The German invasion of Norway in April of 1940 changed all this. Amid hesitations and uncertainties in some official circles, the King remained calm and determined. He refused categorically all offers of compromise put to him by the Germans and summoned his people to offer unanticipated resistance, both before and after he left the country. He not only exhibited great skill and determination as a nonpolitical chief of state during the five years while the government was in exile in London, but great personal bravery during the weeks that he and his Cabinet were fleeing from place to place in Norway. By the end of 1940 Haakon VII had established himself as the rallying point for all Norwegians engaged in fighting the Germans, at home and abroad. But he had done more: he had won the unquestioned affection of his subjects. He died on September 21, 1957, after a record breaking reign of fifty-two years and was succeeded by his son, the present King Olav V.

Despite the overwhelming respect and affection shown Haakon VII and the unquestioned popularity of Olav V, there is no enthusiasm for monarchy in Norway to compare with that existing in Great Britain. As has been indicated, this may be due to lack of monarchical continuity and to Norwegian resistance to domination at the hands of Danish and Swedish kings. No doubt the absence for over one hundred years of a Norwegian nobility has had something to do with the position of the King. There is no court, as in Britain or Sweden, and this gives a certain lackluster aspect to Norwegian monarchy. There is at present only one person in line of succession, Crown Prince Harald. Both the princesses, Astrid and Ragnhild, have married commoners, but even if they had married persons of royal blood, their male offspring would not be eligible to succeed to the throne, since succession is possible only through the male line. Should Prince Harald not have an eligible heir, and should the dynasty thus run out, it is doubtful that a prince from another royal house would be elected to the kingship as was Haakon VII in 1905. Rather than do this, it is quite conceivable that the Norwegian people would agree to install a president as the titular chief of state. But, of course, this is an academic question at present; it is only mentioned here to demonstrate the distinctly "nonmonarchical" view of monarchy which seems to be taken by the Norwegians.

Constitutional Provisions Regulating the Kingship

After prescribing in 1814 hereditary monarchy as the official governmental form, the Constitution continues by outlining the rules governing the King's power and position. In the first place, the fundamental law gives the King absolute power in handling the immediate affairs of the royal household. All members of the royal house are answerable only to him. This restriction applies particularly to Norwegian princes, who may not marry without the King's consent and are restrained from accepting other crowns without his express permission and that of two-thirds of the members of the Storting.

> The order of succession shall be lineal and agnatic whereby only male, born in lawful wedlock, may succeed male; the nearer line shall pass before the more remote, and the elder in the line before the younger.
>
> If there is no Prince entitled to the succession, the King may propose his successor to the Storting, which has the right to decide the election if the King's proposal is not agreed to.[4]

Besides losing his rights to ascend the Norwegian throne by marrying without the King's consent or accepting another crown without securing the necessary approval, the prince may become ineligible to succeed to the kingship by virtue of violation of Paragraph 4 of the Constitution which provides that "the King shall always profess the Evangelical-Lutheran religion. . . ." Should the Crown Prince embrace any other religious doctrine, he would be prohibited from ascending the Norwegian throne. If the King were to refuse to continue as a bona fide member of the State Church, even if he joined no other, the Storting would be forced by the Constitution to declare the throne vacated and proceed to elevate or elect a successor. An interesting, though highly academic, problem of constitutional law might develop if the King who had left the State Church were to be "reconverted" to the official religious faith. The consensus of constitutional opinion seems to hold that this action would not regain the throne for the

[4] *Constitution of Norway,* Paragraphs 6 and 7. Some elaboration should be made on the present position of the royal house. As indicated, both daughters of King Olav have married commoners and, though this was not unanimously applauded at the time by the Norwegian people, there is now no evidence of serious disapproval or dissatisfaction. Quite bluntly put, few people are much concerned either way about the problem of succession. There is some talk, but again not a great deal of real concern, about the marital possibilities available to Crown Prince Harald. It is on the basis of this apparent lack of real interest in the future of the monarchy that one can assume that no turmoil would result if the royal house were one day to be replaced by a presidency.

former ruler, but it would undoubtedly assure him his rightful place in the regular line of succession.[5]

Two other provisions of the Constitution might also cause a King to lose his throne. The first requires that "the King shall reside in the Kingdom and may not, without the consent of the Storting, stay outside the Kingdom for more than six months at a time; otherwise he shall have forfeited, for his person, his right to the crown." Another provision, similar to one previously cited applying to princes, demands that the "King may not accept any other crown or government without the consent of the Storting. . . ."[6] There seems to be no question as to the results of a violation of the provision requiring residence within the country; such an action would lead to forfeiture of royal power. Although no such penalty is written into the prohibition against acceptance of other crowns, it is clear that a violation of that part of the Constitution would also lead to loss of royal power. In fact, a similar restriction upon princes carries with it a specific statement that the acceptance of another crown without parliamentary consent would cause the prince to lose his rights to succeed to the Norwegian throne. It is doubtful that any less serious penalty would be attached to the same violation were it committed by the King.

Besides the possibilities mentioned in the preceding paragraphs, the throne may become unoccupied in case the King's death occurs either before there is an eligible Crown Prince or prior to the time that the latter has attained his legal majority — twenty-one years of age. If the King dies without a male heir, the Storting is empowered to elect a new King. If the King dies and the Crown Prince is under twenty-one years of age, it becomes the duty of the Council of State to summon the Storting into immediate extraordinary session. Before this body is assembled, and before it has made provision for a "guardianship government," the Council shall administer the affairs of the kingdom. After the Storting has convened, it shall at once designate the "guardians who are to conduct the government on behalf of the King during his minority."[7]

At least two other circumstances may make necessary the installation of a substitute or substitutes to assume the executive duties.

> If the King is absent from the Kingdom otherwise than by reason of his being in the field [of battle], or if he is prevented by illness from attending to the government, the Prince next entitled to suc-

[5] Bredo Morgenstierne, *Lærebok i den norske statsforfatningsret* (Oslo, 1927), I, 114.

[6] *Constitution of Norway,* Paragraph 11.

[7] *Lov om Kongens myndighetsalder,* May 13, 1921. See also *Constitution of Norway,* Paragraph 43.

ceed to the Throne shall conduct the government . . . provided that he has attained the age fixed for the King's majority. If that be not the case, the Council of State shall carry on the administration of the Kingdom.[8]

Ordinarily, incidental travel or short periods of illness do not make necessary the operation of this provision for a regency.[9]

The distinction that is made between the conditions outlined in the preceding paragraph and the circumstances resulting in a more permanent "guardianship" in the event the King is not of legal age involves more than a mere difference of duration. To the substitute scheme provided in case the King has not attained his majority, the term "guardianship" is attached; the provisional system established in case of the King's absence from the country or if he should be prevented from discharging his duties because of sickness is usually called "regency." In the first instance, the formal executive powers are removed from the King's councilors and placed in the hands of guardians selected by the Storting; while in the second, perhaps because it is anticipated that the incapacity of the King will be of short duration, the royal prerogatives are allowed to remain as a part of the executive powers of the Council of State.

Powers of the King

Although the Norwegian Constitution definitely grants important executive power to the King, it must be re-emphasized once again that no significant part of this authority can be exercised by the King personally. As will become more apparent in the discussion that follows, the Constitution has been interpreted in such a manner as to insert, by implication, "King in Council" in practically all instances where the grant of power has any real governmental importance, even if, in a specific instance, no definite mention is made of the Council. The Constitution, by express provision, recognizes two separate and distinct classes of executive powers. In the first category are those matters which must be handled by the King in Council according to well established parliamentary usage whether stated or not; in the second is included a much smaller range of authority in which the King is permitted to act without formally consulting the Cabinet.

Any executive act that is explicitly or even implicitly official in

[8] *Constitution of Norway,* Paragraph 41.

[9] It will be recalled that King Haakon VII was out of the country for five years during World War II. The Germans and a few Norwegian Nazis tried to argue that the throne had been vacated as a result of the King's sojourn in the United Kingdom. But, even technically, the King was within his constitutional rights since he was "in the field" conducting the war against the German Reich.

character can only be taken by the King after approval of the Council. For example, the Constitution specifies that it is the King in Council, and not the King alone, who has the power to pardon criminals. Also, it is the King in Council who is empowered to choose "all civil, ecclesiastical, and military officials." Although certain other grants of executive authority are not definitely designated by the fundamental law as requiring action "in Council," it must be assumed that such procedure was intended by the constitutional framers. Thus it is safe to say that all matters of about the same relative importance as the two cited powers, i.e., the pardoning power and the appointing power, must be handled by the King in Council.[10]

There are two kinds of actions — unquestionably official — that may be undertaken by the King personally. The King can decide without the approval of the Cabinet who should assume the office of Prime Minister following a ministerial crisis. Obviously he would do this only after consultations with his staff and certain of the political leaders in the Storting and also within the letter and spirit of the parliamentary principle. Secondly, the King may assume personal command of the armed forces if this is approved by the Cabinet. In the unlikely eventuality that this were done, he could act as commander in chief without submitting his specific decisions on strategy and organization to the Cabinet for approval.

A more satisfactory approach to an understanding of the limits on the King's power might begin with the question: What is *not* included in the phrase "acts of official character"? Ordinarily those personal prerogatives, such as the King's disciplinary authority over the royal household, his right to choose the court attendants and office staff, and other matters directly related to the distinctly personal aspects of his position, can unquestionably be handled by the King without the consent of the Cabinet. But even in this personal area, the King is not *really* free from advice unless the act in question could not possibly have even the most indirect political consequences. And since the nature of his office allows little privacy, sometimes so-called trivial, personal decisions may attract public notice and thus become at least quasi-political in character. Although the King may not always seek cabinet advice on these "trivial" problems, he may often act only after consulting his staff, particularly if questions of precedent and protocol are involved.

In the exercise of one official, as distinguished from personal, function the King is constitutionally independent of the Cabinet. He is given the power by the Constitution to confer decorations "on whomever he pleases as a reward for distinguished services."[11] The only

[10] Morgenstierne, I, 140–143.
[11] *Constitution of Norway,* Paragraph 23.

"knightly order" (*ridderorden*) remaining in Norway is the Order of St. Olav. The honors of this organization are conferred upon those individuals who have rendered outstanding services to the Norwegian state or society. The King, as the Order's *Stormester* (Chief), together with the group's governing board, exercises supreme authority over the affairs of the Order of St. Olav. Neither the Council of State nor individual Cabinet members may participate in the deliberations of the official board of the Order.

Before leaving the general subject of the King's "personal" power, it must be emphasized that although the Norwegian monarch, especially in the nineteenth century, did in fact have a significant field of activity in which he could act without the sanction of the Cabinet, since 1905 the personal power of the King has become seriously restricted. In most cases the King seeks advice even if he is not compelled to do so by constitutional law, and matters that may seem on their face to be private in character are often referred to the appropriate governmental departments. Continued usage of this procedure will naturally make it more difficult for the King to reassert any power that might once have been exercised outside the boundaries of Norwegian parliamentarism.

The Council of State (Statsråd)

Composition of the Council of State

The Eidsvold framers had ample historical precedents to guide them in their deliberations on the nature, composition, and organization of the King's Council. The Privy Council in Great Britain had been a vital instrumentality after the thirteenth century and out of it had grown the British Cabinet. The French *Conseil d'État* had served its king in an advisory capacity until his absolutism was cut short by the popular uprisings of the French Revolution. The Swedish *regjeringsform* of 1809 provided that the king of that state should depend for expert advice upon a group of citizens appointed for the purpose. It was perhaps upon this latter plan that much of the framework for the Norwegian Council of State was originally built.

According to the original provision of the Eidsvold Constitution, the Council of State was to be made up of at least five members. Following the establishment of the union with Sweden shortly after the Constitution had been written, the number was increased to eight, of which one was to serve as Prime Minister. During the period of the Swedish union, the policy was maintained of allowing the Prime Minister and two other members of the Council (alternatingly) to remain in Stockholm during the term of the King's residence in Sweden. In 1905, with the dissolution of the union between Norway and Sweden, the constitutional provision relative to the Council of State was amended, but the number of members remained as before — a Prime Minister and seven others. At present (1963), through changes in Constitution and law, the Council includes fourteen persons besides the Prime Minister.

In addition to the regular members of the Council of State, the Crown Prince is entitled to take a seat in the body on attaining his eighteenth year. The intention of this provision is to acquaint him with the processes of Norwegian parliamentarism and not necessarily to impose upon him any executive duties. He sits with the Cabinet as an observer and auditor only; he has neither "vote nor responsibility."

In certain unusual situations the King is empowered by the Constitution (Paragraph 12) to summon Norwegian citizens, not members of the Council, to take positions in the Council of State. This royal prerogative has never been exercised and would scarcely be consistent with prevailing parliamentary practice. Consequently, it is doubtful whether any practical application of this constitutional power will ever be made.

Qualifications of Members

Constitutional provisions as well as established parliamentary practice have prescribed certain qualifications for members of the King's Council. In the first place, they must be Norwegian citizens not under thirty years of age. Ordinarily they are recruited from the membership of the Storting, although they need not be. If they do come from the Storting, they may not continue as regular voting members of parliament after accepting cabinet positions.[12] Prior to the constitutional changes of 1916, only men were permitted to serve as members of the Council of State. At present women are eligible, but to date there have been only four who have served in cabinet positions.

In addition to the requirements of citizenship and age, the members of the Cabinet must also either have been "born in the kingdom of parents who at that time were subjects of the State or [have] been born in a foreign country of Norwegian parents who were not at that time subjects of another State or . . . [must] have resided ten years in the Kingdom [or have] been naturalized by the Storting."[13] Besides

[12] A member of the Storting who joins the Council of State relinquishes his seat in parliament to the *varamann* (alternate). (For a description of the system of alternate members in the Storting, see pp. 76–77.) Any member of the Cabinet, whether drawn from parliament or not, has a right to debate, but not vote, in the Storting. Unlike the practice in other countries where the cabinet ministers remain members of the parliament and sit with their party group, the Norwegian ministers sit in a semicircle on front benches in the Storting.

[13] *Constitution of Norway,* Paragraph 92.

these qualifications, the Constitution requires that appointees to cabinet posts, as well as to other top governmental positions, must be able to speak the Norwegian language. The original Constitution required that all members of the King's Council must be affiliated with the official State Church. In 1919 this was changed to allow dissenters to become members of the Council. Today only a majority of the members must be affiliated with the State Church (Lutheran). Apparently in an effort to curtail the extreme forms of nepotism, the Constitution has made it impossible for near relatives to hold positions simultaneously on the King's Council. This rule applies to husband and wife, parents and children, brothers, sisters, or brothers and sisters.

Formation and Disestablishment of a Government

The creation of a Norwegian Cabinet[14] is accomplished in much the same manner as it is in most states operating with a parliamentary system. After an election the King usually turns to the leader of the party having the largest number of members in the Storting with the request that he form a Cabinet. In the years immediately prior to 1940, it was usually impossible for any single party to command a majority in the Storting. In every case except during World War II, where a genuine coalition existed, the largest party would form a minority government and secure the support needed for its maintenance from one or more of the other parties.[15] From 1945 to 1961 the Labor party held an absolute majority in parliament and thus needed no continuing support from any of the other parties. As a result of the election held in September of 1961, the Labor party has now (1963) 74 out of the 150 seats in the Storting, but because of a divided opposition it still functions for all practical purposes as a majority party. Although the constitutional power to appoint cabinet members rests with the King, it is the Prime Minister who actually makes the appointments.

Although it might seem that the Prime Minister in Norway, or in any parliamentary democracy for that matter, is free to choose members of his Cabinet, he is in fact bound by certain inescapable obligations. He usually has a limited number of men in high party ranks with the experience requisite for given positions. Also he and his party are particularly indebted to certain men who must be recognized in one way or another. Furthermore, the reaction of the public to cabinet appointments cannot be overlooked. In the last ten years another problem has faced the Norwegian Prime Minister. He has not always been able to find enough qualified politicians and has had to

[14] The terms Cabinet and Council of State, the more formal designation, will be used interchangeably throughout this book.
[15] See pp. 34–35, p. 132.

appoint some men to cabinet posts who have come with academic or administrative backgrounds, albeit with some political experience. To the uninitiated student of politics this might not seem to present any problem. But a man not well schooled in politics has difficulty playing the role of a cabinet minister in two important respects: he is not always disposed by experience to compromise, and he may often find it difficult to take proper notice of public sentiment, particularly if it seems illogical and misinformed. Quite apart from these problems, recent Labor Prime Ministers in Norway have found the younger potential political leaders annoyed and irritated on being passed over in favor of these "experts." This is a two-way problem: the Prime Minister has had difficulty tapping mature leadership among his younger political colleagues and they, on the other hand, have felt shut out, by an appointing policy favorable to the experts, from the prospect of obtaining the experience required.

Much the same procedure is used to unseat a government that has lost the confidence of the Storting as is employed in other states operating under the parliamentary system. Failure of a cabinet proposal to be accepted by parliament or a vote of lack of confidence are the most commonly used devices. Certain variations from standard parliamentary practice are discussed in Chapter 5, and others will be considered in the closing paragraphs of this chapter.

Powers and Duties of the Council of State

Generally speaking, the powers and duties of the Council of State are dual in nature. First, each member of the group, with the exception of the Prime Minister, holds a position as head of one of the administrative departments; there are no ministers without portfolio. Second, the whole group is responsible for making policy, planning programs, and, theoretically at least, serving as the advisory council to the King. A more detailed analysis of the administrative functions of cabinet members will be developed in Chapter 6. At this time only the policy role of the collective Cabinet will be considered.

Before examining the collective responsibilities of the Cabinet, it might be worth while to say a word or two about cabinet meetings. For years the formal meetings have been held on Friday mornings in the King's palace in Oslo. Usually the hour of eleven finds the cabinet members seated around the long, narrow table in the regular chamber reserved principally for such occasions. Before proceeding to the business of the day, the King glances about him to ascertain whether a quorum (one-half of the membership) is present. After the formality of opening the meeting has been completed, the King, acting as the mouthpiece of the Prime Minister, presides over the consideration of formally presented propositions. At any given meeting these may include: (a) proposals to be submitted to the Storting (Royal Propositions), (b) sanction of formal laws passed by the Storting,[16] (c) enactment of provisional ordinances based upon power granted by the Storting or on the authority of Paragraph 17 of the Constitution, and (d) the passage of special church legislation under authority of Paragraph 16 of the Constitution. In addition, the Council in the formal meetings ratifies appointment and dismissal of high-ranking civil servants (*embedsmenn*), passes generalized administrative regulations, and ratifies the more important administrative decisions. In the field of foreign policy, the Council, in its Friday sessions, ratifies treaties, appoints delegations to international conferences, and, as necessary, approves instructions to be given to these delegations.

Since a great many difficult decisions have to be made (perhaps as many as fifty to sixty on each Friday) there is little time for discussion at the formal meetings of the Cabinet. Most of the matters presented have been considered in a "preparatory" meeting of the Council of State not attended by the King. Even these meetings are often hurried, and special cabinet meetings are required at irregular intervals for the examination of both policy and administrative matters. Preparatory work by regular cabinet committees precedes discussion and decision in the plenary sessions of the Council.

Two general classes of policy proposals are handled by the King's Council. In the first place, suggestions of policy are examined and carefully weighed before they are submitted to the Storting for final legislative consideration. Each minister is expected to outline parliamentary programs thought essential for the proper functioning of his department. As a rule, these have been carefully worked out in the department before they are presented for cabinet consideration. The scrutiny by the Cabinet and its committees serves a double function: it offers opportunity for viewing any given policy from the perspective of a total program and permits the political consequences of the proposal to be evaluated. Often proposals are rejected on the ground of political inexpediency or because they are ill-timed or hastily and inexpertly drawn or are inconsistent with other proposals thought to be essential.

Besides acting upon specific legislative proposals, the Council of State also gives serious consideration to broad, general policy questions, both foreign and domestic. In recent years foreign policy, particularly its economic and military aspects, has occupied a good deal of time in cabinet meetings. Although the Foreign Minister is given a

[16] Royal approval of all laws is a juridical requirement; it has had no political significance since 1905. The King (or King in Council) no longer has a functioning veto power in spite of the fact that it has not been removed from the Constitution.

comparatively free rein in the day to day administration of his office, the development of new policy, worked out and implemented through the ordinary channels of diplomatic relations, international conferences, or in treaty negotiations, is, in the last analysis, a cabinet responsibility. Norway, as has been noted, altered its position in international politics after 1945 from one of neutrality to one involving significant commitment to the West through the North Atlantic Treaty Organization. This change was made after careful study in the Foreign Ministry, detailed consideration by the Cabinet, complete consideration in the Foreign Affairs Committee of the Storting, and a full-dress debate in the Storting proper. None of these steps was perfunctory; they were all important.

In addition to policy questions, the Cabinet also handles some matters that may be distinctly administrative in nature. After a legislative action has been taken by the Storting, administrative organization and procedures are, as a rule, outlined by the appropriate department. Insignificant details are always left to the department, but the whole Cabinet may be called upon to express opinions on certain of the anticipated political consequences of administrative decisions. Not infrequently, administrative matters rather than broad questions of policy become the source of criticism from the opposition and from the press. Consequently, it is important not only to have the breadth of advice that cabinet consideration can give, but also to make certain that all cabinet members have some familiarity with any political or administrative problems that may arise.

Distinctive Features of Norwegian Parliamentarism

In order to understand the unusual characteristics in the Norwegian parliamentary system it is necessary to survey briefly the several steps leading to its present form. This development can be divided into three historical periods: the first covers the span of years from the Eidsvold Convention of 1814 to the establishment of the Sverdrup Ministry in 1884, the second from 1884 to the dissolution of the Norwegian-Swedish Union in 1905, and the third from 1905 to the present time.

The Constitution, both as written in 1814 and as amended by 1963, fails to include any provision authorizing the incorporation of a responsible cabinet system as a part of governmental practice in Norway. Quite the contrary, the separation of powers principle remains in the Constitution in much the same form today as it had in 1814. The requirement of the fundamental law that the King be advised by a "Council of Norwegian citizens" and that certain executive actions be taken only after that advice has been obtained can in no way be construed as directly authorizing the prevailing parliamentary arrangements.[17]

Perhaps some support for the idea of cabinet responsibility to parliament can be found in the constitutional paragraph that insists that

> if any member of the Council of State is of the opinion that the King's decision is at variance with the form of government or the laws of the Kingdom, or is prejudicial to the Kingdom, it is his duty to make strong remonstrances against it, and also to have his opinion entered on the record. A member who has not thus protested, shall be deemed to have been in agreement with the King, and shall be answerable in such manner as may be subsequently decided, and may be impeached by the Odelsting before the Constititional Court of the Realm. [*Riksretten*][18]

It was on the basis of this paragraph that one of the first important disputes between the King and the Norwegian parliament arose. Prime Minister Severin Løvenskiold was impeached by the Odelsting (one of the chambers of the Storting) for failure to protest against the King's resolution of July 2, 1836, dismissing the Storting in accordance with Paragraph 80 of the Constitution, which gives the King the right to take such action when parliament has "finished its business." The resolution of impeachment accused Løvenskiold of failing to protest against a royal decree that was unquestionably prejudicial to the kingdom. In the ensuing trial before the Constitutional Court of the Realm the Prime Minister was adjudged guilty. His continuation in office by the Swedish King after he had been declared in violation of the fundamental law indicates that no clear conception of ministerial responsibility had developed by 1836.

In 1845 Minister Jørgen H. Vogt was impeached for failure to advise the King properly relative to a provisional order designed to place a duty on iron imports. Although the action against Vogt failed, largely because it was not well grounded on bona fide constitutional foundations, the case is important because it illustrates the continuing tendency of the Storting to check the ministry.

The years from 1870 to 1884 saw developments that eventually led to the final victory of the Storting in its struggle with the King over the issue of cabinet responsibility to parliament. The immediate question at issue was whether or not the Constitution should be amended to allow members of the Council of State to take part in legislative deliberations. Two unsuccessful attempts had been made by the Storting to obtain royal sanction for such a change. In 1880 the resolution was passed for the third time in identical form, and again the

[17] *Constitution of Norway,* Paragraphs 12, 20, 21.
[18] *Ibid.,* Paragraph 30.

King vetoed the proposition. Shortly thereafter (June 9, 1880), the Storting passed a resolution proclaiming that the legislative act was valid without royal sanction, since it had been passed unaltered by each of three successive parliaments, and, in accordance with constitutional provision (Paragraph 79), it must be considered binding law even though it lacked the signature of the King.

The King refused to be guided by this resolution of the Storting, and the question remained unsettled until after the election of 1882. In that year the Liberal party, which had been largely responsible for the agitation against the King's position in the preceding parliamentary session, won sweeping victories at the polls. Encouraged by this display of popular approval, Johan Sverdrup, the party's capable leader, was able to push through a resolution impeaching the sitting Prime Minister (Christian Selmer) and the members of his ministry. The resulting trial focused the attention of the Norwegian people squarely upon the issue of ministerial responsibility to the Storting. After a judicial hearing that lasted about two months, Selmer and his colleagues were judged guilty of failing to advise the King properly according to the demands of Paragraph 30 of the Constitution. Though King Oscar II did accept the verdict of the impeachment court as well as the resignation of the Selmer Cabinet, he attempted to rule with an "opposition ministry" without conceding the principle of ministerial responsibility. When this tactic failed he accepted the demands of the Liberals by appointing Johan Sverdrup as Prime Minister. Sverdrup was careful to select a cabinet that met with the unquestioned approval of the Storting and, as a result of this action and the acquiescence of the King, parliamentarism was formally established in Norway.

The second period in the development of responsible government in Norway saw one major deviation from recognized parliamentary practice. In 1893, after the Steen Ministry had resigned, King Oscar II selected Emil Stang to form a Cabinet and this government remained in power until October of 1895 in spite of the fact that the Storting had early displayed unmistakable evidences of lack of confidence.[19]

From the break with Sweden in 1905 to the present, the King has not ventured to install a cabinet not acceptable to the Storting. And it is inconceivable that any Norwegian King would in the future interfere with the operation of cabinet government. Were he to do so, this could only result in abdication since the organization of the military services and the temper of the country would preclude the use of force. Any extraconstitutional excursions by the King would most certainly result in the establishment of another type of titular chief of state, perhaps a president.

[19] See *Stortingets forhandlinger, 1893,* VII, 849.

Although the parliamentary idea is definitely entrenched in modern governmental practice in Norway, its application is not without certain distinctive characteristics. The fact has been alluded to that ministers are constitutionally bound to protest against royal resolutions that are at variance with established forms or otherwise are prejudicial to the welfare of the kingdom. Failure to protest or absence from the council meeting at which the resolution was announced indicates acquiescence in the action taken. Moreover, the approval of the minister is accompanied by direct responsibility for the actions taken under the royal resolution. If the consequences demonstrate that the act is "unconstitutional" or extremely harmful to the state, the Storting may not only insist upon the cabinet member's resignation, but also institute impeachment proceedings against him. Since the King no longer exercises any real governmental authority, the constitutional obligation to protest a council decision (in the form of a Royal Resolution) is now applicable, if at all, to decisions of the Council itself. Because the contemporary cabinet ministers' responsibility is primarily political and not related in a legal sense to royal power, as it once was, it is doubtful whether a minister could be impeached for failure to "protest." Of course, there is the possibility that the Cabinet might undertake a willful, unconstitutional, or illegal act, and if this could be established as having occurred, those ministers who had not protested might find themselves subject to impeachment proceedings.

In order to clinch the matter of ministerial responsibility, the Constitution insists that all resolutions emanating from council meetings shall be countersigned. Ordinarily this act is done by the Prime Minister, but if he is unable to do it, another member of the Council may perform the function. The pages of Norwegian constitutional history are filled with accounts of differences engendered by the countersignature rule. It may be said, however, that present-day constitutional authorities continue to agree on the indispensability of the countersignature procedure. It is not merely an indication that the resolution is accurate and complete in all its technical details, but further, it provides formal evidence that the measure is in harmony with the general principles of the party in power.

The presence of the suspensive veto, vested in the King, has been referred to and has occasionally been listed as another of the distinctive characteristics of Norwegian parliamentary government. The mere existence of the King's right to approve or disapprove legislative enactments is not in itself sufficient to cause the Norwegian veto to attain uniqueness. In theory, at least, the same power is to be found vested in chiefs of state in other countries using the parliamentary type of organization. But the practical application of the veto power is different in Norway from that in other states operating under parliamentary systems. The Storting is empowered to employ three distinct legislative methods, the choice in any situation depending upon the nature of the subject matter of the proposed enactment. If it is a formal problem involving rights of citizens, the bicameral procedure must be used. If, on the other hand, the matter does not seriously involve these rights, it may be handled by the Storting sitting as a one-house parliament. And constitutional amendments may also be acted upon in a plenary session of the Storting.[20]

In the passage of laws under the bicameral procedure the King's sanction is essential to make the enactments complete. The Constitution provides that if he refuses to approve the law it may be passed over his veto. Thus, in accordance with a constitutional change made in 1937, if an unaltered bill has been passed in two sessions of the Storting, organized after two separate elections, the bill becomes law without the King's signature. Formerly, to be valid without the King's approval, the measure would have had to be passed three times. Resolutions, passed in the unicameral Storting, both ordinary and those containing suggested constitutional changes, do not require the King's sanction to give them final validity.

One of the persistent questions that arises in connection with any discussion of the veto power is: can it be reconciled with the spirit of parliamentarism and a titular kingship? Professor Castberg answers this query by insisting that there may be possible uses for the veto even in a parliamentary system operating with a monarch excluded from exercising real governmental authority.[21] Once in a while a law reaches the King that is unquestionably "unconstitutional" and it is conceivable that serious drafting errors may have been made by parliament in the course of the law's enactment. Sometimes a parliamentary debate, though resulting in the passage of a law, might have the effect of stirring up determined popular opposition to significant parts of the measure. If any of these situations were to appear in an aggravated form, the King, through his Council, would be justified in exercising the veto power. That such cases will arise infrequently is evident from the very nature of the political and legislative process now in use. Neither of the Kings of the present royal house (in office since 1905) has exercised the veto power. This is some indication that the safeguards of the veto, now in reality only available to the Cabinet, are no longer important. The fact is that most controversies between Cabinet and Storting will have been settled by political negotiations long before any exercise of the veto is contemplated. If they cannot be settled in this manner, the controversy will eventually reach the people through the electoral process. And if significant

[20] See pp. 83–85.
[21] Castberg, I, 464–465.

constitutional questions arise, they will be settled by the courts, not the King in Council.

It should be underscored before concluding discussion of the countersignature requirement and the veto "power" that these procedures are at the present time archaic and devoid of real interest to most contemporary students of Norwegian government. Even Professor Castberg's "case" for the veto is generally conceded to be unduly legalistic and perhaps even somewhat pedantic. If one could assume a situation where the veto would be used by the King in Council, one of two situations would be prevailing: a revolutionary or semirevolutionary condition or a radical, unexpected change in the nature and rules of democratic government. In either case it would be difficult for present-day students to anticipate the way in which constitutional provisions, written in 1814, would be applied.

Another noteworthy feature of the Norwegian parliamentary system that has been alluded to previously is the requirement that members of the King's Council may not be voting members of the Storting. The original Constitution not only prohibited members of the parliament from assuming ministerial positions, but insisted further that no cabinet member could be present at parliamentary sessions. Subsequent amendments to the Constitution gave cabinet ministers the right to be present in parliament and to be heard, without the right to vote. It should be re-emphasized once more that should a member of parliament be appointed to a cabinet position, his district will not be unrepresented in the Storting since his legislative position will be taken over by an alternate (*varamann*).[22]

A Cabinet may be unseated as a result of the passage by the Storting of a lack of confidence resolution. This procedure is seldom used; only once since 1905 has a Cabinet been forced to resign as a result of a positive vote of lack of confidence. This occurred in 1928 when the shortlived (from January 28 to February 15, 1928) Hornsrud Cabinet resigned after the Storting had indicated its lack of confidence by formal resolution. The fact that this ministerial crisis came at an unusually difficult time, both economically and politically, partially explains the action.

Cabinets have occasionally been forced out of office as a result of the failure of the Storting to pass measures designated by Prime Ministers as significant cabinet proposals. In the event the subject matter of a given legislative proposal requires action in both chambers of the Storting, resignation will not follow if the proposal is temporarily disapproved in one of the chambers, but only if it is disapproved finally by both. If the proposal is of the type that can be passed by the Storting in its plenary capacity, a legislative action contrary to a previ-

[22] See p. 76.

ously enunciated cabinet position will usually lead to the resignation of the Cabinet.

Because the Labor party had a majority in the Storting from 1945 to 1961 and has at present a near majority, the situation with respect to cabinet crises differs significantly from that prevailing before World War II when no party could normally muster a clear parliamentary majority. Lack-of-confidence resolutions, never frequent in Norwegian history, are not likely to be much used in the immediate future. It is, of course, still possible for a Cabinet to suffer a legislative defeat serious enough to force its resignation. But for this to occur at present, it would require either serious defections in the Labor party ranks or an unheard of degree of unanimity among a seriously divided opposition. Defection among Labor members is not likely to occur because discipline in the party is fairly strict. Since the opposition parties run the gamut from the extreme left to moderate conservatism, and since, at least for the present, there is substantial agreement on the most important problems facing the country — those relating to foreign policy — it seems unlikely that the necessary degree of agreement could be obtained which would lead to defeat of a crucial part of the present government's program.

Situations other than those showing concrete evidences of lack of confidence have given rise to ministerial shifts in the past. The death or resignation (due to other than political causes) of a Prime Minister has usually made necessary the formation of a new Cabinet. Also a Cabinet will automatically resign if its party has suffered defeat in a national election. This is by now a well established practice; for a Cabinet to continue in office after an electoral defeat could not only lead to trouble in the Storting, but would also be interpreted as undemocratic and a violation of the rules of the game.[23]

One of the most distinctive features of the Norwegian parliamentary system is the fact that it does not provide the King (or Cabinet) with the power of dismissing the Storting in a cabinet crisis. It would seem that the King or Council should have the opportunity of appealing to the people by the application of a procedure similar to the one employed in the United Kingdom. Conflict between the separation of powers idea and parliamentarism has, in this situation, been resolved in favor of separation of powers. It has been argued that to allow the

[23] As has been indicated, the Labor Government did not resign when it lost its majority in the Storting in the election of 1961. It was generally agreed, even by the opposition press, that there was no real alternative to continuation of a Labor Government. Labor controlled seventy-four seats and the five other national parties the remaining seventy-six seats. Also Labor could count on support from several parties for its foreign policy program and could no doubt secure enough votes from among the Socialist People's party or the Liberals to support its domestic program.

King in Council power to dissolve the Storting would for all practical purposes destroy the independent position vouchsafed to the parliament by the Constitution.

Whether or not granting the King in Council power to dissolve the Storting would make any significant difference in the operation of the Norwegian parliamentary system is debatable indeed. Although it might make for clearer issues, it would be at the same time cause the voter greater confusion by increasing the number and frequency of elections. In fact, under present circumstances, the Cabinet does not seem to be hampered by the lack of a power of dissolution. As a rule, the Storting cooperates with the Cabinet and very seldom does it hamstring policy proposals through the use of distinctly political devices.

4

Nominations and Elections

Suffrage Regulations

The original statement of suffrage rules found in Paragraph 50 of the Eidsvold Constitution gave the right to vote in national elections to a restricted group, including high-level government employees (*embedsmenn*), landowners, and a propertied merchant class. Changes in these regulations were slow in coming,[1] but by 1884 the Constitution had been amended giving the franchise to all men with a certain minimum annual income (NK 800[2] for city residents, NK 500 for rural residents). In 1898 the property qualification for voting was removed completely, and the right to vote was extended to all male citizens who had attained the age of twenty-five years. In 1907 certain groups of women were given access to the ballot in national elections; at first only women with a given minimum annual income or those whose husbands had the prescribed minimum income were permitted to vote. By 1913 these income restrictions had been removed and women as well as men were qualified to vote on reaching the prescribed legal age. Another amendment to Paragraph 50 of the Constitution came in 1920, reducing the age requirement from twenty-five to twenty-three years, and this was reduced again in 1946 to twenty-one. In its present form the suffrage provision of the Constitution (Paragraph 50) gives the right to vote to all Norwegian citizens twenty-one years of age and over who are at present, and have been for five years, residents in the kingdom.

Citizenship, one of the principal voting qualifications in Norway, as

[1] In 1821, because the law differentiated between ownership of land in Finnmark and the other parts of Norway, a special law was passed giving the residents of Finnmark the same suffrage rights as the residents in other parts of the country.

[2] Throughout the book the symbol NK will be used to designate the unit of Norwegian currency (crown or *krone*).

in most democratic countries, is defined by the Law of 8 December, 1950.[3] Like most citizenship laws, the Norwegian law is complicated and detailed. In general it gives citizenship to a child whose father is a Norwegian citizen, irrespective of residence. If the mother has Norwegian citizenship and the child is born in Norway but cannot claim citizenship through his father, the child is considered, under the law, a Norwegian citizen. An illegitimate child born to a Norwegian woman, whether or not a resident of the country, has Norwegian citizenship at birth, providing of course the mother is a citizen of Norway. A child born of foreign parents may obtain Norwegian citizenship between the ages of twenty-one and twenty-three if he demonstrates that he has resided in the country since birth and makes application for citizenship in writing. A foreigner may be naturalized if he has reached the age of eighteen, has been resident in the country during the seven years immediately preceding the time he applies for naturalization, gives evidence of having conducted himself properly, and demonstrates that he has the necessary means to care for himself and his dependents. Prior to 1888 citizenship in Norway rested quite generally upon the so-called domicile principle. According to this rule, citizenship is dependent upon residence within the territorial limits of the state. In 1888 and by subsequent amendments (1924 and 1950) the view that citizenship could be determined by the citizenship of one or both parents, irrespective of domicile, was incorporated into Norwegian law. Thus, at present, both rules — *jus soli* and *jus sanguinis* operate.

The residence rule included in the suffrage regulations does not require that the voter must have lived continuously in the country during the five years immediately preceding the election, but he must ordinarily be in residence at the time the election is held. This obviously does not mean that he has to be physically present in his district on election day. He may cast an absentee ballot by delivering it to the proper official in his district, to an official in some other district, or to a designated officer abroad (diplomatic or consular officer or the captain of a Norwegian ship). Anyone voting by absentee ballot is required to demonstrate that he has a legal residence within the country.[4]

A Norwegian citizen may lose his right to vote if he is imprisoned

[3] See *Norges lover,* pp. 2060–2062.

[4] *Lov om Stortingsvalg av 17 desember 1920,* Nr. 1. A special voting rule applies to officials attached to the diplomatic and consular services and to the members of their households. They may vote without having fulfilled the five-year residence requirement in that polling district in Norway where they last resided. Their ballots may be cast at the election proper or in absentia.

for a criminal offense, if he enters the service of a foreign state, if he has been found guilty of certain kinds of misconduct in elections (buying or selling votes, multiple voting, etc.), or if he has been declared legally incapable of handling his affairs.

Electoral Organization and Procedure

Elections: Time and Manner

National elections are held once every four years, usually sometime in September. Because there is no provision in the Norwegian Constitution for dissolution of the Storting, special (called) elections are unnecessary. The fact that only parliamentary candidates are included on the ballot at the national election makes the problem facing the voter comparatively simple.

From 1814 to 1905 the mode of election remained substantially the same as had been outlined by the "framers" at Eidsvold. This was an indirect method of voting whereby electors were chosen from large election districts and they met, somewhat like the members of the electoral college in the United States, though with more discretionary power, to choose the parliamentary representatives for their respective districts. In 1905 a far-reaching change was made in the electoral procedure. In that year the indirect method was abolished; members of the Storting were thereafter to be elected by the people directly with no intervening "electoral college." At the same time, a change was made in districting. The old districts were divided into subdistricts (*valgkretser*) and each one of these smaller areas was allotted a single representative. Elections in the new single-member districts resembled the French system used during many years in the Third Republic (*scrutin majoritaire à deux tours*). If none of the candidates in a given election obtained an absolute majority, a run-off election was held in which all the candidates might participate (not only those who had polled the most votes) and in this second election the candidate who polled the most votes, not necessarily a majority, was elected.

The change back to multiple member districts and the movement away from "plurality elections" came simultaneously in 1919. The constitutional amendment of that year made provision for a list system of proportional representation, abolished the single-member constituency, and established the county (*fylke*) as the multi-member election district for the rural areas. In addition, the two large cities — Oslo and Bergen (counties in their own right) — were constituted as election districts and nine other urban districts made up of towns and cities in one or several counties were established. In 1953 these urban districts were abolished and the cities that previously had not been included in the county election district were incorporated within it. Thus, at present, the county and the election district are conterminous. (There are eighteen rural and two urban counties.)

Registration

The first step in the electoral process is a nation-wide registration of all qualified voters. In the rural districts the *lensmann* (a combination sheriff and rural mayor) assumes responsibility for this undertaking, and in the incorporated cities and towns the function is performed by such officials as the central administration may designate. The registration (*manntallet*) is in reality a census of voters and quite unlike the American process of the same name. The prospective voters in Norway need not concern themselves with the process, at least in its early stages, since the registering official is required to include the names of all qualified voters without prior solicitation at any time on their part. The voters do have the opportunity of examining the records after the enrolling process has been completed to ascertain if their names have been wrongfully omitted from the electoral roll. A rather elaborate machinery of committees is provided by law to which the voter may appeal should he feel the "census taker" has made a mistake. It is important that all such cases be promptly brought, as no citizen may vote who is not properly registered.

The registration process takes place shortly after July 1 of the year in which elections to the Storting are to be held (every fourth year). The work of the registering official must be so nearly finished forty-two days before election day that he can publish a preliminary report of qualified voters which can then be scrutinized by the citizens of the subdistricts for possible errors and omissions. After the deadline for receiving complaints has passed, the committee (made up of the registering official and at least two other persons selected by the local community council) designated to act upon disputed cases meets, and by at least thirty-five days before the election is held its final list must be made public. Between that time and the eighteenth day prior to the election another opportunity to protest is given anyone who feels he has a grievance. This time the complaint must be lodged with the election judges (*valgstyret*), who must pass upon the case well before the election is to be held. In certain instances appeals may be taken from this board directly to the Storting. It should be pointed out that the registration process is not as complicated in practice as it appears in the law. Many of the election districts are small, and the officials are often well acquainted with everyone in the community. Thus the provisions for filing complaints are not as necessary as they might be if the country were more thickly populated. But the procedures are retained in order to make absolutely certain that no one who is qualified to vote loses his right because a government official has not done his job with care.

Included in the final draft of the registration report will be the names of all Norwegian citizens of the precinct (or precincts if there is more than one in the subdistrict) who are qualified to vote in the coming election. In addition, those who have not reached legal age by July 1, but will become twenty-one before the appointed election day, are included. Any person whose residence has changed after July 1 may appeal to the election judges for inclusion on the rolls in the precinct in which he resides on election day.[5]

Election Districts and Officials

As indicated above, the administration of nominations and elections is carried on in twenty electoral districts: eighteen rural counties (*fylker*) and two urban districts, the metropolitan counties of Oslo and Bergen. All of these districts are divided into subdistricts (*valgsogn*) which in turn may be broken up into smaller units (referred to as precincts in this discussion). The number of parliamentary seats assigned to each of the election districts varies from four in Finnmark county to thirteen in the city of Oslo.

The administering agency in the election district is the district committee (*distriktsvalgstyret*), made up generally of members from the county council or, in certain districts, of representatives from the subdistrict committees (*valgstyrene*). This latter committee is composed of the registration official and the members of the local community council. If the subdistrict is divided into smaller units, another committee, the precinct board (*stemmestyret*), is selected by members of the subdistrict committee to administer the affairs in this smallest of electoral units. The precinct board has only the function of supervising the mechanics of the election. The district and subdistrict committees are given the responsibilities of preparing for the election, counting the votes, and officially announcing the result.

Nominations

The nominating procedure for national elections is outlined in the Law on Nominations passed on December 17, 1920, and amended in 1933, 1949, and 1953.[6] The regulations of the law are not mandatory on a political party; if it does not wish to avail itself of the expense allowances provided, it may conduct its nominating procedure without reference to the provisions of the law. But the fact that delegates to

[5] Detailed rules governing the registration procedure can be found in *Lov om Stortingsvalg av 17 desember 1920.* See *Norges lover,* pp. 1128–1142.

[6] *Norges lover,* pp. 1142–1143.

district nominating conventions receive their expenses from the state if the law is observed has been stimulus enough for a rather general adherence to the law among the parties. In order for a party to operate under the terms of the Law on Nominations, it is necessary that it be properly registered in the Department of Justice. This procedure simply requires the central office of the party to satisfy the Department that it intends to nominate candidates for Storting positions. The party name is entered on the official records with the assurance that no other political organization may use it.

The convention system is used to name candidates for parliamentary positions in Norway. Each subdistrict (*valgsogn*) caucus elects delegates to a district convention which, in turn, selects the nominees and places their names in rank order on the party list. Certain definite qualifications are required of participants in the subdistrict caucus and district convention: they must be members of the party, at least twenty-one years of age, and in full possession of their voting rights. No person who has officially taken part in the official convention of one party may participate in a similar meeting sponsored by another party in the same year.

Although the principal responsibility of the subdistrict convention is the selection of delegates to the district meeting, possible parliamentary candidates may be considered and their names submitted — even in rank order — to the district committee. The manner in which delegates to the district convention are chosen is left to the discretion of the party organization, but ordinarily the plurality principle prevails. Written credentials are provided the delegates in order to avoid any embarrassing disputes when they arrive to take their places in the district conventions. The number of delegates to be sent from each subdistrict varies with the number of votes the party polled in the subdistrict in the last parliamentary election. Smaller subdistricts are guaranteed a slightly disproportionate voice in the district convention through the operation of a graduated scale.

The district convention is held at a time and place determined by the district committee. If the party does not have such a set of officers, the national committee may make these decisions. After the credentials of delegates have been examined, the organization of the district convention is set up and the business of selecting candidates for places on the list is undertaken.

Not unlike the situation in most countries, the provisions of the law offer only a skeletal view of the nominating process in Norway. It was no doubt the intention of the framers of the law to give final authority over selection of candidates and the arrangement of the list to the district convention. Presumably it was thought that the delegates participating in this convention would be selected for their skill and political know-how and hence need not come with binding instructions from their constituencies, but the system has not always worked as planned. Specific evidence of deviations from the law is not easy to substantiate since only in the last few years has any really serious study of the nomination and election system been undertaken by Norwegian political scientists.[7] From data that are available it is quite clear that the provisions of the law and the regulations of the parties give a seriously incomplete picture of the Norwegian nominating process. Without doubt, notwithstanding the letter and spirit of the nomination law, the delegates to the district convention do come with instructions to support the candidate or candidates whose qualifications have been given prior consideration in the subdistrict caucuses. Among the qualifications viewed by politicians and laymen alike as essential in a "good" candidate are: strategic residence, previous experience in local government, and active participation in party affairs. Age, sex, and profession or business position also must be seriously considered in selecting candidates and in deciding on their proper placement on the party list. Agriculture, fishing, and the public service, in that order, have supplied the largest number of candidates in the past. The man or woman with experience in communal government is, all other things being equal, in a stronger position to secure nomination than one without such experience. Though something can be said in support of this attitude, certain demands are imposed upon a member of parliament that have little relevance to experience gained in local government.

It seems quite clear that there is a good deal of competition among cities and towns to secure for their residents a favorable position on the party list. This competition continues even though residence in the district was abolished as a legal requirement for candidates in 1953. It should be noted that the elimination of the district residence requirement has not as yet had any noticeable effect on the character of the candidates. Normally nominees continue to stand for election in the district of their residence.[8] The fact that the issues are national, not local, and that the contest is between parties, not individuals, does not seem to reduce the demand among politicians for representation from their localities. Obviously prestige factors, not issues, play a role in the continuation of this kind of pressure.

It is certain that pressure groups such as trade unions, women's

[7] A start was made by Tim Greve, *Nominasjon ved Stortingsvalg* (Bergen, 1953). Henry Valen, Stein Rokkan, and others are undertaking a fairly comprehensive study of the national nominating and election procedures, based upon data from specific geographical regions.

[8] An exception to the residence rule to cover present and former cabinet members was provided in 1913. For latest provision, see *Constitution of Norway*, Paragraph 61.

organizations, employers' organizations, and sports groups have at least an indirect effect on the nomination process. If these groups are large and active in a given election district, the nominating convention cannot avoid being influenced by them. The extent to which the central office of the party has any determining role in the selection of candidates for parliament positions is not always clear, but certainly no candidate would be placed high on a party list without the knowledge and acquiescence of the central office. The Labor party and the Communist party exercise the strongest central control over the nominating process at the present time, but most of the other central offices keep in close touch with the work of the subdistrict caucuses and the district conventions.

The Election Proper

The first step in the actual election process is taken when the lists of nominated candidates are submitted to the district committee. This must be done at least thirty-two days before the election. Each list must have an appropriate heading, indicating which party or political group is sponsoring the candidates, and it must be accompanied by either a petition signed by a group of qualified voters or by an official authorization of a recognized political party submitted by its district or central organization. Practically without exception, the lists come to the district election committee directly from the parties.

Two or more parties may join forces in a given election by presenting a joint list (*fellesliste*) of candidates. To establish such a list negotiations between (or among) the parties must begin well before the nomination deadlines. The parties must first agree that a joint list should be prepared, and secondly, they must undertake the difficult task of arranging the names of candidates from the cooperating parties in acceptable rank order on the ballot. By cooperating in the presentation of a joint list, parties may be able to secure representation that might have been denied them had they acted individually. In calculating the results of an election and in distributing seats,[9] a joint list is treated in the same manner as is an individual party list. Parties particularly of the political center are usually more inclined to consider possibilities offered by joint lists than are parties on the right and left, but there is frequently a great deal more speculation and discussion of cooperation than there is concrete action.[10]

After the nomination proposals have been received, the district

[9] See pp. 68–69.

[10] In the 1961 election the Liberal party and the Center party presented joint lists in five election districts (*Østfold, Opland, Vest-Agder, Aust-Agder,* and *Sør Trøndelag*). In the Bergen district, the Conservatives and the Christian People's parties presented a joint list.

committee gives them its official scrutiny and announces, through the press and by posting publicly, the names and membership of the various party lists. This must be done in ample time so that protests may be filed if errors have been made.

The election proper comprises the second step of the process. The election day (in September) is set by the King in Council several months in advance of the election. Ordinarily one day is sufficient for the conduct of the election, but should weather and road conditions prevail that make it impossible to complete the process in one day, it may be continued on the following day. In case that day happens to be Sunday or a religious holiday, the polls are required to close during the hours that church services are in session. In recent years no elections have been carried over to Sundays.

The present election law in Norway combines a list system of proportional representation with a modified form of preferential voting. According to the law, the voter not only makes his choice of a party list, but may indicate some choice of candidates by striking out names on the list and substituting others. As each party or political group may include on its list as many names as there are members of the Storting to be elected from the district, plus a maximum of six additional names, the voter could — though he seldom does — exercise a considerable degree of discretion in making his selections. (The only practical reason for permitting each party to include more names on the list than there are places to be filled, is to insure enough candidates for the alternate positions [*varamenn*] that are provided in the Norwegian legislative setup. These individuals serve in the absence — temporary or prolonged — of the regular members of the national parliament). If the voter fails to register any preferences by eliminations or write-ins — and this is common — it is assumed that he has voted for the candidates in the order in which their names are found on the party list. Failure to utilize the opportunity given for write-in votes, both from independent groups of candidates and from the lists of other parties, is explained in part by the fact that such procedure would be out of harmony with the list system of proportional representation, founded as it is upon the assumption that elections are contests between parties and not designed to encourage independent candidates.

The third step in the electoral process, namely, the mathematical determination of the outcome of the balloting, is the most complicated part of Norwegian elections and perhaps need not unduly concern the general student of government. Up until 1953 the d'Hondt system was used, but in that year the Lagüe modified odd numbers method was installed. A brief discussion of the process is included here only to show how the system is designed to represent parties proportionately.

The district committee first computes the total vote received by each list by application of the following formula. All ballots are examined to determine how many votes each candidate has received and in arriving at this figure, the committee reckons with that number of preferential choices which is equal to the number of parliamentary places the district is entitled to receive. For instance, if four members of the Storting are to be elected, fourth place choices will be counted. These totals for all members of the list are then added, and this sum becomes the total of votes received by the list. Each list total is then divided by 1.4, 3, 5, 7, etc. The list that has the largest quotient is conceded the first representative. The second is assigned to that list having the next largest quotient, and this process continues until each place has been allocated.

An example may make the procedure more understandable. In the hypothetical case outlined below, there are five seats in the Storting to be filled.

Party	*Total Vote*	*Quotient I* *Total Vote ÷ 1.4*	*Quotient II* *Total Vote ÷ 3*	*Quotient III* *Total Vote ÷ 5*
A	20,000	14,285	6,666	4,000
B	16,000	11,428	5,333	3,200
C	7,200	5,142	2,400	1,440
D	4,500	3,214	1,500	900

As a result of the calculations Party A with the largest quotient (I) will receive the first seat and Party B with the next largest quotient (I) the second. Additional seats will be distributed as follows: A–1, B–1, and C–1.[11]

After the places have been allocated to the parties, the ballots are again examined to determine which candidate on each party list has the most votes for first place. If a second seat has been assigned to the party in question, another count is made to ascertain which nominee received the largest number of votes for first and second place combined (excluding, of course, the individual who had the largest number of first place votes). A third place would be determined by reckoning with ballots marked first, second, and third choice. If a joint list (*fellesliste*) is entitled to a parliamentary member, he is selected by the same method as is used in case of individual party lists.[12]

[11] The d'Hondt system in use between 1919 and 1953 called for division by 1, 2, 3, 4, etc., but in most other respects it was not significantly different from the Lagüe system now in use. Both give some advantages to the larger parties, but perhaps this is less marked in the Lagüe procedures.

[12] Between 1930 and 1949 another kind of interparty cooperation was possible. This was called *listeforbund* or *listesamband* which might be

After the roll of representatives in the Storting has been compiled, it is relatively simple to continue the process in order to determine who the alternate members are to be. Each party is allotted a number of alternates equivalent to the number of seats it has obtained in the district plus two. Thus if the Labor party has four seats, it would be entitled to six alternates. The identity of these persons is determined by continuing the calculations, reckoning, for this purpose, with fifth, sixth, seventh, etc. choices.

As indicated in another connection, absentee voting is permitted if the voter is unavoidably to be away from the subdistrict on election day, is engaged in public business that makes it impossible to reach the voting place, or is unable to go to the polls for reasons of health. The ballot must be delivered in person by the voter to a "vote receiver" normally not more than eighteen days or less than one day before the election. Exceptions can be made to this timing in certain situations. The "vote receiver" in the subdistrict is usually the person in charge of registration of voters; on the high seas and abroad a person is designated, usually by the King, to receive the ballots. Absentee ballots are counted in the appropriate districts after the official polls have closed.

After the final results of the voting have been determined, the district committee is empowered by Paragraph 46 of the National Election Law to issue certificates of election to the successful candidates. Before the newly elected members of the Storting can take their seats, they must present these credentials to the proper parliamentary committee, which examines them and certifies their authenticity to the Storting. Ordinarily the legality of the certificates is unquestioned and the examination is perfunctory. However, if it can be proved that there has been a violation of the election procedure as it is outlined

---

loosely translated "electoral alliance." Under the operation of this system each of the two or more cooperating parties in the *listeforbund* presented individual lists but in addition to the ordinary heading, a subheading was included indicating the nature of the electoral alliance. Each voter used the list of his party and if he did not wish to have his vote count for the *listeforbund* he had only to strike out the subheading. The calculations of the results were made in two ways: (a) as if no *listeforbund* existed and (b) as if the parties in the *listeforbund* were in effect a single party. The method most profitable to the parties in the alliance was to be used. If it developed to the advantage of the parties to consider the *listeforbund* as a single list, the distribution of seats was determined in much the same manner as for single party lists, i.e., the person with the highest number of first place votes would be chosen if one seat is allocated; others were filled by reckoning with second and third choice designations. This was a rather complicated arrangement and offered few advantages not available under the joint list (*fellesliste*) procedure. As a result, it was given up in 1949.

in the law, or if it can be shown that the district committee erred in arriving at the final results, the election involved may be invalidated and the person refused his seat.

Evaluation of Norwegian Electoral System

No electoral system, however fine its rule and theory, is worth much unless it works well in practice. The Norwegians have had over forty years of experience with the present system, and in that period certain strengths and weaknesses have become obvious.

In the first place, installation of the list system did seem to increase voter participation. The three elections before the plan was adopted, 1912, 1915, and 1918, may be taken as typical examples of the popular voting interest under the old plurality system. In 1912, 65.86 per cent of the qualified voters participated in the balloting; in 1915, 61.78 per cent; and in 1918, 60.46 per cent. In the first two parliamentary elections after the list system was installed (1921 and 1924), these percentages had risen to 67.02 per cent and 69.89 per cent respectively. The growth in the number of participants was steady until in 1936 the per cent of qualified voters casting ballots stood at 84.02. By 1957 the percentage of eligible voters participating in the parliamentary election had declined somewhat — to 77.47. Participation throughout the period was generally higher in the cities than in the rural areas.

It is not fair to give the new system all the credit for the high degree of participation in Norwegian elections. At least two other mechanical features operate to encourage the voter to go to the polls. In the first place, the registration system is simple and does not require him to enroll personally as a possible voter. The "registration census" is taken by a government official, and through adequate notice the voter is assured that he is listed among those eligible to take part in the election. In the second place, the ballot is short, being made up only of candidates for parliamentary posts. Consequently, a rather complete knowledge of party proposals and a comparatively intimate acquaintance with the candidates' records is possible. Then, too, the country is small, its population homogeneous, its problems are not as difficult for the voter to comprehend as they would be in a more complicated political community. With improved facilities of communication, an increased interest in political matters might have developed under almost any kind of election system. Moreover, the Norwegian people have been deeply concerned in the last decades with matters that usually elicit voter interest and concern, such as improving social service programs. This, added to a developing degree of civic responsibility among Norwegians in the twentieth century, has stimulated interest in national elections.

If certain reservations can be entertained on the effect of the list system on popular participation in national elections, it can certainly be argued that it did have the effect of apportioning seats in the Storting among the parties more in relation to their numerical strength in the country than would have been possible under a plurality system. In 1957, for example, with an average of 11,941 voters for each representative in parliament in the kingdom at large, the figures for four of the parties deviated from the national average by less than 10 per cent (Labor had 11,099; Conservative, 12,056; Liberal, 11,427; Center, 11,054). Because the Communist vote (60,060) was not concentrated but spread over the country at large and because the party succeeded in electing only one man, the discrepancy between popular vote and the seat won by the Communist was disproportionately large. The Christian People's party lost several close contests and thus accumulated a popular vote (15,270 for each man elected) out of proportion to the twelve seats won.

Another favorable result of the operation of the list system in Norway cannot be as conclusively verified by citing figures. It has been contended, but not without dissent, that the system has provided opportunities for the ablest party members to secure preference in nominations. To be sure, a majority of the party in the district could prevent a recognized and respected party leader from attaining a seat in the Storting, but this occurs very infrequently. Most voters, depending upon the party's judgment, vote the list in the order arranged by party authorities. And, since competition is often keen, the party organization generally nominates the best men it has available.

At least two other results of the operation of the system should be mentioned. In the first place, the list system does make easier the breakup of large political parties into smaller factions and groups and, perhaps paradoxically, the system does seem to favor the larger parties. The comparative simplicity of the nominating procedure, coupled with the ease of obtaining official sanction for an electoral list, increases the temptations for dissenting party members to break from the old party and establish a new organization. Perhaps the viewpoints of a faction are so definitely different from the party in a particular section of the country that to remain within the parent group would mean a complete sacrifice of the minority's political position. Under a plurality system the minority might have no choice but to make this sacrifice, but under the present Norwegian system a break could be made enabling the splinter group to gain national recognition for its cause and perhaps, due to the workings of the proportional system, secure a seat or seats in the Storting.

In 1933 three new political groups prepared lists: the Commonwealth party, which succeeded in polling 18,786 votes (1.5 per cent of the national total), the National Union (Quisling's party) with a vote of 27,850 (2.23 per cent), and the Christian People's group with 10,272 (0.82 per cent). But each of these organizations was prompted to active participation in the election by a certain definite policy and program that did not necessarily involve a clear break with any one single party.[13] In 1957 and again in 1961 small left wing groups broke away from the Labor party, and in 1961 the dissident Socialist People's party did succeed in electing two of its parliamentary candidates, somewhat to the surprise of seasoned political observers in Norway.[14] Although the list system does seem to encourage the birth of small parties, it does not offer commensurate advantages to both large and small parties. The method of distributing the seats generally favors the larger parties, although not to the extent that it once did or as much as a plurality system would.

By way of summary, it can be said that the list system of proportional representation used in Norway has worked well, and there is no serious agitation for change. The nomination and election procedure is well understood and generally favored by the Norwegian voter and this in itself makes it satisfactory. No doubt improvements could be made in this, or in any system, but since other substantive problems may be more in need of attention, the Norwegian is inclined to accept a workable, albeit not completely perfect, arrangement. He may be intelligent in this view since it seems unlikely that agreement on perfect democratic mechanics can be achieved in any country, but it becomes particularly difficult in a community like Norway with a strong emphasis on individuality of opinion and complete freedom of expression.

[13] The Commonwealth party and the Christian People's party each secured one seat in the Storting. Because the vote of the National Union party was widely spread throughout the country, it did not succeed in electing anyone to parliament.

[14] See pp. 142–143.

5

The Norwegian Storting

In one important respect the Norwegian Storting (parliament) defies classification: it is neither unicameral nor bicameral within the ordinary meanings of these terms. The 150 members of the parliament are elected for four-year terms from the twenty electoral districts without reference to chambers or divisions.[1] Only after the Storting has been organized is it divided: one quarter of the members (38) are elected by the whole house to serve as members of the Lagting and the remaining three quarters (112) become members of the Odelsting. For some matters the Storting sits as a plenary assembly, and for others the two divisions are required to convene separately.

Membership

Qualifications, Privileges, and Obligations

Before considering how this unusual type of parliament operates, it might be well to examine first certain details related to membership, beginning with the qualifications of members. In order to serve as a member of the Storting one must have attained the age of twenty-one years, be in possession of full suffrage rights, and have resided in the kingdom for ten years. Residence in the election district was once required, but in 1952 this requirement was abolished.[2] In spite of this, only a very few members of parliament have been elected from districts in which they did not have legal residences.

Besides this positive statement of qualifications, the Constitution also enumerates certain classes of individuals who, because of their po-

[1] In a strict sense the two parts of the Storting should be called "divisions," not "houses" and perhaps not "chambers." Throughout this discussion the term "division" will be used for the most part, though on occasion the word "chamber" is used for emphasis.

[2] See p. 65.

sitions, are not qualified to become members of the Storting. "The officials employed in the Government offices and the attendants or servants and pensioners of the Court are debarred from being chosen as representatives."[3] The same restriction applies to individuals attached to the diplomatic and consular services. Members of the Council of State (Cabinet) may be nominated and elected to the Storting, but if they continue after election to hold cabinet positions they relinquish their rights as regular voting members of the Storting. It will be recalled that all cabinet members, whether drawn from within or outside the Storting, may participate in parliamentary debates, but without the right to vote.

In considering the obligations, rights, and privileges of members of the Storting, it might be of interest to examine first the unusual constitutional stipulation that persons elected to parliament are *required* to serve. In most countries a candidate for an elective position is not forced by law or the constitution to accept the obligations of the office to which he has, by active campaign, aspired. Nor is the "forcing clause" an important part of electoral practice in Norway at present. No doubt the intention of the proposal when it was made a part of the Constitution in 1814 was to emphasize the responsibility of all men to participate in democratic government regardless of personal desire and convenience.

A few individuals were always exempt by law from the operation of the "forcing clause." A person hindered from assuming his responsibilities by an impediment which the Storting judged to be valid might be excused from accepting election. Also, any person who has been in active attendance during each of the legislative sessions of the last four-year term might legally refuse to continue, if elected for another term. In case a successful candidate wishes to avail himself of any of the foregoing exceptions, he must, within three days after he has received notice of his election, notify the district electoral committee of his decision. His place is then filled by calling up the man on the party list who stood next in the vote count.[4]

At least four distinct rights are associated with membership in the Storting, either by direct constitutional provision or by reasonable implication. In the first place, the member of parliament is presumed

[3] *Constitution of Norway,* Paragraph 62.

[4] The obligation to serve if elected applies also in a certain sense to the acceptance of nomination. If a party insists upon nominating a person, he can refuse only if he can claim the exemptions provided by law. But it would be seldom that a party would force the nomination upon a person who was not willing — even eager — to accept. There may once have been reason to resort to law to induce reluctant leaders to assume responsibility, but now that political positions have become more attractive — both in prestige and money — this is rarely necessary.

to be independent of direct constituent control; after his election he is supposed to serve not as a delegate subject to the whims of the people, but rather as a representative with wide discretion in the making of policy. Technically, no ties either of specific instructions or party discipline should force the abandonment of this position of independence. Theoretically, the member is free to act as his best judgment dictates, pledges or party affiliations to the contrary notwithstanding. Also he need not take the view that he is a delegate from a given district; like his counterpart in the United Kingdom, he can consider himself a representative of all the people in the country. But, not unlike the member of the House of Commons, the member of the Storting finds himself in actuality bound by ties to his constituency and most certainly by specific provisions in his party's program. Any other view of his responsibility would be fatal, not only to his own political future, but also to the success of the party program that served as the basis for his election. The alleged independence of the Stortingsman is a holdover from the day when separation of powers was much more evident in practice than it is now that parliamentarism has become well established in Norway.

The second rights of legislative membership, namely freedom from arrest, has always been thought to be based upon a fairly secure legal foundation. The Constitution insists that "the representatives shall be exempt from personal arrest while on their way to and from the Storting, as well as during their stay there, unless they are caught in public crimes. . . ."[5] Earlier writers on Norwegian constitutional law argued that the right protected the representatives from arrest only in civil cases. If this view were accepted, the constitutional protection would have even less meaning at the present time that it in fact has. Prior to 1874, when arrests for debts could be made, the clause might have hindered police officers from employing detention procedure to collect bills owed by members of parliament. If the right is to have any significance at present it must include freedom from arrest in criminal cases. And it certainly can be argued that since the intention of the clause was to assure the Storting of independence in its relation to the executive branch of the government, this purpose would be defeated if criminal matters were excluded. Moreover, the language of the clause itself seems to imply that at least a certain amount of protection from arrest in criminal cases was intended. For example, the constitutional exception to the right allows arrest if representatives are "caught in public crimes." Apparently, according to this provision, the police officer was empowered to arrest a member of Storting if he witnessed the criminal act. However the argument for or against freedom of arrest for criminal acts may have been supported in the

[5] *Constitution of Norway,* Paragraph 66.

past, the fact remains that the "right" has no real force at the present time. The provision of the Norwegian Constitution, like its counterpart in the American Constitution, has now only academic interest.[6] The Norwegian provision remains as another vestigial evidence of the separation of powers thought so necessary in Norway during the period of the union with Sweden.

A third right accorded members of the Storting by the Constitution is less uncertain in application. Legislators may not "be called to account outside the meetings of the Storting for the opinions they have expressed there."[7] This provision also has its counterpart in the Constitution of the United States. The interpretation of most Norwegian constitutional authorities is that the clause exempts members of the Storting from prosecution for slander as a result of opinions expressed in good faith in parliamentary discussion. Like the companion clause in the Constitution of the United States, the parliamentary immunity provision of the Norwegian Constitution confers privileges that are not subject to review and interpretation by the courts.[8]

The representative's right to receive reimbursements for traveling expense and a salary for his services as a member of the Storting is another of his constitutional guarantees. The amount paid has varied throughout the years. In 1963 each member received NK 26,000 ($3,600) in regular annual salary plus travel and expenses allowances varying from NK 20 to NK 40 ($2.80 to $5.60) per day.

Alternate Members

One of the most interesting and unusual figures in the Norwegian Storting is the alternate member or *varamann*. Although this office is not recognized by express constitutional provision, it has been a part of the parliamentary arrangements since the Constitution was established in 1814 and, though the evidence is not conclusive, it is quite certain that the use of alternates for a variety of offices in Norway was practiced long before the Constitution was written. At present, the practice extends not only to government policy-making bodies, but even to private clubs and associations. Most councils — public and private, national and local — have not only regular members but usually an equal number of alternate members available to participate if regular members are forced to be absent for long or short periods.

Many benefits can be credited to the scheme of alternate member-

[6] See *Williamson v. United States,* 207 U.S. 425 (1907). For a discussion of freedom of arrest in Norway, see Frede Castberg, *Norges statsforfatning* (Oslo, 1947), I, 328.

[7] *Constitution of Norway,* Paragraph 66.

[8] Freedom of expression in parliamentary debate is treated in detail in a collection of documents entitled, *Ytringsfriheten i Stortinget etter grunlovens, paragraf 66* (Oslo, 1953).

ship in the Storting. In the first place, a long wait for a successor is unnecessary after the disability or death of a regular member. Under this system there is no need for any vacancy to exist, even for a few days, as it is usually possible for a *varamann* to assume legislative responsibilities on a moment's notice. Then, too, the use of alternates serves to unify the legislative program throughout each session since it is inconceivable that the political viewpoints of the regular member and his alternate will be significantly at variance. Both are members of the same party and both were elected at the same time and on the same political program. On the other hand, if the vacancy were to be filled by special election, the continuity in public policy would not necessarily be so secure. New issues could have arisen, and different views might have come into prominence in the interval between the general and the special elections.

The use of alternate members makes it possible to have a complete complement of legislators, both in plenary sessions and in the committee rooms, at all times. If regular members of the Storting are called away to international conferences or recruited for other special governmental assignments, they can be assured that their legislative responsibilities will not suffer. And since each party in each election district may include on its list substantially more names than there are parliamentary seats to be filled from the district, there is no danger that there will be a shortage of alternates even if a great many regular members are absent at any one time. The pool of alternates also becomes a source upon which parties can draw in filling first-line places in subsequent elections. Many regular members of the Storting have gained valuable experience during the years they sat as alternates.

The constitutional requirements that apply to regular members of the Storting are also applicable to the alternates. They must meet the same qualifications, they have the same privileges, and are as much obligated to accept office as are the persons elected to the primary legislative posts.

Organization of the Storting

Two Houses or One?

It will become apparent as the functions and prerogatives of the two divisions of the Storting — the Lagting and the Odelsting — are more closely examined that the Eidsvold framers were convinced of the validity of the traditional arguments in favor of a two-house parliament. It is clear that the men of 1814 examined carefully the constitutions of practically all the important states of that period and most of the models provided for a bicameral plan based upon some more or less natural division within the state. In England, for instance, the upper house was one made up of peers, and in the United States the Senate was designed to represent the several commonwealths. The absence of an indigenous nobility and the lack of geographical subdivisions that could appropriately serve as constituencies for the members of a second house caused the Convention to adopt an artificial type of organization, combining both unicameral and bicameral features; there was some precedent for this in the Batavian Constitution of 1798.

A number of suggestions had been given careful consideration by the members of the Convention. It was thought particularly desirable by a few, including Adler and Falsen, who, it will be recalled, had written an early constitutional draft, that the Lagting should be given greater permanence and stability than the other division. In order to accomplish this, the proposal was made that the members of the smaller division serve for longer terms than the representatives in the Odelsting, and that only a certain percentage of the members of the Lagting vacate their positions once every three years. As this idea did not harmonize with the desired method of election, the plan was abandoned. It must be noted that, although a bicameral parliament was thought desirable, there was no intention of vesting one of the "houses" with greater powers and privileges than those enjoyed by the other.[9]

It is true that the Constitution did finally give to each division a set of functions to be exercised more or less exclusively. Although, as will be clear in the discussion that follows, the legislative function can be undertaken both in plenary sessions of the Storting proper and through the two divisions meeting separately, if parliament is to act as a bicameral assembly, introduction of bills can take place only in the Odelsting. The Odelsting is given the further exclusive power of examining all public reports and documents emanating from the various administrative agencies. In addition, this division of the Storting has the sole power of impeachment, assigned in much the same manner as it is in the American Constitution. The court for trying cases arising as a result of impeachment proceedings, the High Court of the Realm (*Riksretten*), is drawn from members of the Lagting and the Supreme Court of Justice.[10] This latter function is the only exclusive one assigned by the Constitution to the Lagting.

Although the thirty-eight members of the Lagting are formally elected by the total membership of the Storting, the determining decision on selection of members occurs through the parliamentary party groups, more specifically in the executive committee of each of these groups. The membership of the Lagting is arranged so that each party is represented in that body in roughly the same proportion as it is

[9] *Riksforsamlingens forhandlinger* (Oslo, 1914), I, 150–238.
[10] See pp. 150–152.

represented in the Storting as a whole. A party member who has a preference may make this known to his party committee, and an attempt is made to take this preference into account. There seems to be no serious competition among members of parliament for assignment to the Lagting, and no special prestige is attached to membership in this division. Many Stortingsmen prefer to sit in the Odelsting because — as will become apparent later — the work there offers greater political challenge. Others, who have important responsibilities in the Storting proper or in other public or private positions, prefer assignments in the Lagting because its sessions are not as time-consuming as those of the Odelsting. But since it is important for the parties to be ably represented in the Lagting one would normally find a preponderance of the older, more experienced men in this division. Even this does not appear to give the Lagting any preferred prestige position.

The legislative sessions in each of the divisions are convened annually on the first weekday of October. Neither can be convened independently of the other, as often more business is transacted in the Storting meeting as a plenary body than is transacted in the two divisions. The King (in Council) is constitutionally empowered to call extraordinary sessions, if he deems such action necessary. As a rule, the Storting seldom adjourns its regular session before the middle of June, although it may well have been in recess two or three times before finally adjourning. In extraordinary sessions the King may by proclamation adjourn the Storting when, in his judgment, the work is completed or further progress seems impossible.

Officers and Committees

Each individual division, as well as the Storting proper, elects its own officers. A president, a vice-president, and two secretaries are chosen by the members of each of the three bodies. No person may hold more than one of these offices at any given time. In the election of officers the successful candidates must secure a majority rather than a mere plurality of the vote. If no candidate secures a majority, a second ballot is taken with the two candidates who received the most votes in the first election remaining as possible choices.

The usual duties undertaken by similar officers in other parliamentary bodies are exercised by the Norwegian legislative officials except that a more definite use is found for the vice-president: he shares the job of presiding over meetings with the president on a regular schedule. The two secretaries in each of the divisions and in the Storting divide their work in a similar manner.

The parliamentary members who have been chosen to the presidential and vice-presidential positions in each of the divisions and in the Storting constitute the ex officio Presidential Board; the chairman of this group is the President of the Storting. Besides being responsible for formulation of a general plan by which the Storting will be guided in its consideration of pending proposals, the Board is required to keep the members informed of any new matters that may come up for legislative consideration. Another group with coordinating responsibilities is the Steering Committee, made up of members of the Presidential Board and the chairmen of all the standing committees of the Storting. (There is only one set of committees for the entire parliament.) The Steering Committee is responsible for determining the order of business, setting up calendars, and taking care of such other mechanical matters as are necessary to expedite legislative business.

Besides the ex officio Presidential Board and the Steering Committee, there are at least two other committees that do not fit conveniently into the regular roster of Storting committees. The first of these, at least in point of time of appearance, is the Election Committee (*Valgkomité*). This group is selected by the Storting soon after it has convened and the offices of president, vice-president, and secretary have been filled. Two characteristics should be evident in its make-up: it should represent each political party proportionally and its members should be selected from as many different electoral districts as possible. At present (1963) the Committee, made up of thirty-seven members, meets these specifications reasonably well. Its chief duty is the selection of Stortingsmen to serve on the regular committees, but it also acts as a nominating committee in cases where the Storting is required to select nonlegislative governmental officials. For example, the auditing committee to check the activities of the State Bank, *Norges Bank,* is chosen by the Election Committee, acting in this instance in conjunction with the regular parliamentary committee that handles banking affairs. Like other parliamentary officers and committees the Election Committee serves throughout the regular four-year parliamentary term.

Another group that is more or less independent of the regular committee structure is the Protocol Committee. This ten-man committee is selected by and from those members of the Odelsting who are members of the Election Committee. The Protocol Committee is empowered by constitutional provision to survey "the records of such diplomatic matters and . . . such matters relating to military command as . . . are to be kept secret. . . ."[11] If any member of the committee wishes the Odelsting to become aware of the contents of any such documents, he may force consideration by that chamber. In addition, the Protocol Committee of the Storting acts as a final investigating

[11] *Constitution of Norway,* Paragraph 75. See also Castberg, I, 340.

board in matters of accounting and auditing. As is obvious from its duties, this is an important parliamentary committee.[12]

Before proceeding to an enumeration of the remaining parliamentary committees, it might be well to re-emphasize the fact that the Norwegian parliament acts both as a unicameral and as a bicameral parliament. In subsequent discussion an attempt will be made to show how this unusual system works in practice. But it should be pointed out here that a significant share of the legislative work is done by the Storting sitting as a unicameral parliament. Because of this, and because both divisions when they do act independently work together rather closely, it has not been found necessary to have a set of committees for each, but rather a set of joint committees for the Storting as a whole. If the Constitution or established practice requires the use of the bicameral procedure, it is possible for the members of each division to avail themselves of written committee reports under the prevailing system. Since membership of the committees is so arranged as to give a proportionate number of seats to each division, the members of the Lagting as well as of the Odelsting may rely not only upon formal written committee reports, but also upon the views expressed in debate by members who sat with the committee in its deliberations.

At the present time there are twelve regular committees; special committees may be created if necessary. Every member of the Storting is required to serve on one committee and is limited to that one regular assignment, although he may also serve on a special committee. Members of the Protocol Committee are excluded from serving in any other committee capacity. The President of the Storting may, if he so desires, be excused from all committee services. The average size of the regular committee is eleven, and membership on each is arranged so as to represent the parties in proportion to their membership in the Storting. Some attempt is also made by the selection committee (Election Committee) to secure a reasonable degree of geographical distribution.

A list of the regular committees in the present Storting (1963) and a brief summary of the various matters that come to each in the exercise of its legislative functions are given below.

1. The Committee on Administrative Matters is concerned principally with regulations and appropriations for the royal house, Council

[12] This description of the Protocol Committee is oversimplified. There are in fact two committees: one made up of ten members with general responsibilities including fiscal oversight and a nine-man committee (same membership less one) charged with examining secret documents relating to foreign affairs. See *Stortingets forretningsorden* (Oslo, 1961), Paragraph 9.

of State, and the governmental departments. In addition, it usually surveys legislation designed to supplement or alter existing statutes relating to salaries and pensions of administrative personnel.

2. The Finance and Tariff Committee is perhaps one of the most important groups in the Storting. As the name implies, its sphere includes general matters of finance and taxation, and it plays an important part in budgetary formulation.

3. The Justice Committee handles proposed bills dealing with courts and police. In addition, questions of citizenship, naturalization, elections, domestic relations, and industrial relations come before this group for detailed consideration.

4. The Church and Education Committee is the counterpart of the Church and Education Department in the administrative structure. Bills designed to promote, finance, and regulate the State Church and public educational institutions at all levels are previewed by this committee.

5. The Communal Committee considers matters of municipal regulation and taxation, public works with special reference to housing, fire protection, regulation of hotels, and related problems.

6. The Agricultural Committee has responsibility for examining those bills that are designed to regulate, promote, and subsidize farming in Norway.

7. The Committee on Military Affairs considers problems of defense, organization and regulation of the services, etc. Quite understandably, the work of this committee has increased significantly in recent years.

8. The Communications (and Transportation) Committee handles all matters dealing with communication and transportation not specifically given to any other parliamentary committee.

9. The Ocean Commerce and Fishing Committee has important responsibility in drafting and considering legislation relating to these two crucial sectors of the Norwegian economy. General proposals for promotion and regulation are handled by this committee, but measures concerned specifically with the social and economic security of seamen and fishermen are usually referred to the Committee on Social Affairs.

10. The Lumbering, Water Power, and Industries Committee handles legislative proposals dealing with forests, forest products, hydroelectric installations, and state-owned industry and industry operated by private enterprisers under franchise (concession) from the state. With forests covering about 23 per cent of the area of Norway, it is only natural that the lumbering business should assume a position of great importance. The export of paper, wood pulp, and other timber products has increased greatly in the last two decades. Much of the

impetus given to this section of the Norwegian economy has come from the Storting through the passage of an intelligent and comprehensive set of conservation laws. Excellent natural conditions make possible the generation of millions of kilowatts of electrical energy in Norway. Most of the production of electricity takes place in plants owned by counties and communes rather than by the state, though all regulation rests finally in the hands of the Storting.

11. The Committee on Social Affairs considers all proposals and problems relating to pensions, insurance plans, and other areas of social welfare before legislation is finally enacted by the Storting. Though Norway's social security program had made beginnings even during the last part of the nineteenth century, it was not until after 1915 that many of the laws designed to protect underprivileged and socially depressed groups were passed. Since that time the program has been expanded until it now covers, in one way or another, the entire population.[13]

12. The Committee on Foreign Affairs and the Constitution handles all legislative business dealing with Norway's relations with other states and international organizations as well as proposed constitutional amendments. Norway's membership after World War II in the United Nations, NATO, EFTA (European Free Trade Association), the Nordic Council, as well as expanded diplomatic and consular activities, has caused an increase in legislation related to the organizational and financial aspects of foreign policy. Provision is made for expanding this committee if necessary by adding the President and Vice-President of the Storting, the chairman of the Committee on Military Affairs, and up to eight members of the Election Committee. This expanded group may not only sit during regular parliamentary sessions, but may also advise the Cabinet on foreign affairs during the time the Storting is not in session.

The responsibility of the Committee on Foreign Affairs and the Constitution for constitutional changes, amendments to certain organic laws, and for parliamentary rules of procedure is not strictly in harmony with its role in foreign affairs. The committee was given these extra tasks at a time when foreign affairs were less important than now and retains them for want of a more appropriate arrangement.

Legislative Procedure[14]

The principal question that arises on examining the Norwegian system of parliamentary organization comes down to this: when can the Storting act in a plenary capacity and when does it need to act

[13] See pp. 180–192.

[14] Parliamentary rules are to be found in *Stortingets forretningsorden.*

through its two divisions? The factors that determine which method shall be used are sometimes not completely clear, even to the members of the Storting. But there are certain guidelines that can be identified. Only when "laws" are being considered does the bicameral arrangement come into use; "plenary resolutions" may be adopted by the Storting sitting as a unicameral parliament.

Having identified the two parliamentary vehicles — "laws" and "plenary resolutions" — the task of defining each and determining its limit and scope still remains. It is quite certain that the "law" form must be used if the parliamentary action affects in general all citizens of the country or has anything to do, even indirectly, with their rights, privileges, and obligations. It is also clear that budgetary proposals, even if in a certain sense they can be said to affect *all* the people, can be passed by resolution in a plenary session of the Storting. Proposals that do not have general application, such as those relating exclusively to a given county, may be enacted by the Storting functioning as a unicameral assembly. Also the organization of the public services may be provided for in a plenary session of the entire membership of parliament since this does not affect *all* citizens in any intimate sense.

An example or two may help to clarify the difference between "law" and "plenary resolution." If it is intended to rewrite, amend, or enlarge the criminal code, this without question can only be accomplished by law enacted by the Storting in its bicameral capacity. Such a proposal unquestionably affects directly each individual citizen's rights and duties. If, on the other hand, a bill is presented which would appropriate money to build and maintain a set of highways, such a proposition may assume the form of a "plenary resolution" and be enacted in the unicameral Storting. But if money for this enterprise is to come from regular, well-established tax sources, the legislation authorizing collection will have been passed by both the divisions of the Storting.

The Constitution gives some further clue as to the proper definition of each of the legislative vehicles. According to Paragraph 75 of that document:

> It belongs to the Storting — (a) to enact and to repeal laws; to impose taxes, duties, customs, and other public charges. . . . ; (b) to open loans on the credit of the Kingdom; (c) to control the finances of the Kingdom; (d) to vote the sums of money necessary to meet the expenditure of the State; (e) to decide how much shall yearly be paid to the King for his Royal household, and to determine the appanage of the Royal family. . . .

The paragraph concludes by authorizing the Storting to review minutes of the Council of State and diplomatic transactions, to summon witnesses in legislative hearings, to institute and revise salary schedules and pension lists, to appoint an auditing committee to examine the state's accounts, and to pass naturalization laws. Apparently only the first grant of power, i.e., (a) above, requires the "law" technique and the bicameral treatment; the other functions may be undertaken by the Storting as a whole through the use of plenary resolutions.

The complications of the Norwegian legislative organization and procedure can be observed rather dramatically by noting that legislative enactments organizing the military establishments may take the form of plenary resolutions even though these may be considered to have general application. But it would not be sufficient to stop with such an enactment since rights and obligations of individuals are usually involved in any such organization. Because of this a companion "law," enacted by the bicameral procedure, might be required as a supplement to the action taken by the Storting in plenary session.[15]

At the risk of confusing an already complicated differentiation, one further comment should be made. The enactment of the bicameral Storting is, in a certain sense, a stronger law than that passed in a unicameral session. For example, if there is conflict between provisions of a "law," passed by the two divisions of parliament, and a "plenary resolution," the courts will uphold the law and not the resolution. Also, a "law" may subsequently displace an enactment accomplished through the use of a "plenary resolution," but law enacted by the bicameral Storting could not be superseded by an action taken in a plenary parliamentary session.

Although Norwegian constitutionalists may occasionally refine the definitions, the distinction between laws and resolutions does not cause the practical minded member of the Storting a great deal of concern. To be sure, he is guided in his actions by an adaptation, at least, of the general principles outlined above. Should an occasion arise that might give rise to conflict, he may agree that the subject at hand requires action of both sorts. But this does not occur with great frequency.[16]

[15] Some observers have drawn parallels between "law" and "plenary resolution" in Norwegian practice with public and private bills in the United Kingdom. This is misleading and not particularly useful. Some public bills may be handled by the unicameral procedure in Norway; others require action by both divisions of the Storting. Private bills, as they are defined in the United Kingdom, would always be considered as "plenary resolutions" in the Norwegian parliament.

[16] For a contemporary, scholarly analysis of the problems associated with the unique nature of parliamentary organization in Norway, see Castberg, II, 7–73, and Johs. Andenæs, *Statsforfatningen i Norge* (Oslo, 1945), pp. 138–145, 154–158. For an historical account of the problem of differentiating between law and resolution, see Bredo Morgenstierne, *Lærebok i den norske statsforfatningsret* (Oslo, 1927), II, 86–186. See also James A. Storing, "Unique Features of the Norwegian Storting," *Western Political Quarterly,* March, 1963.

The procedure followed in passing plenary resolutions is not greatly different from that in use in the ordinary one-house legislature. The introduction of the bill occurs in much the same manner as it does under the bicameral plan. Committee consideration is followed by debate in the assembled Storting. The final vote on the proposition need show only a majority of the members present favorable in order to give it the sanction of legal enactment.

The question — important during the time of the union with Sweden — as to whether or not a resolution passed by the Storting in its unicameral capacity requires the official sanction of the King is now academic since the veto power of the King has been nonexistent since 1905. It was well established even before 1905 that plenary resolutions did not require the sanction of the King. Since constitutional amendments call for a special procedure (passage by two successive Stortings with an intervening election) and a two-thirds vote, it was also rather generally agreed during the period of the Swedish-Norwegian union that these, definitely, did not require approval of the King to be valid.

In contrasting the procedure of the Storting acting as a one-house assembly with that used when it functions as a bicameral parliament, one is impressed with the absence of elaborate written regulations covering the first procedure and the presence of minute constitutional rules outlining the second. Perhaps one explanation for the definiteness of the constitutional requirement governing the bicameral procedure can be found in the determination on the part of the framers to prevent the development in parliament of two equal and coordinate branches on anything like the American pattern. Although each division was given certain spheres of action which could not be encroached upon by the other, the Odelsting was always considered to have a superior position since only in it could bills be introduced.

The introduction of a bill in the Odelsting may be by a private member, by the Cabinet, or any of the members of the Odelsting. Occasionally a private person outside of parliament may propose a bill by securing a member of the Odelsting to introduce the measure. Similarly, representatives in the Lagting can secure the introduction of bills by appealing to friendly colleagues willing to sponsor their bills in the Odelsting. In recent years, however, the Odelsting has adopted the policy of granting significant priority to legislation initiated by the Cabinet. As a result, if a bill is introduced by a private member, either as his own or on request, it is referred to the appropriate administrative department for its official consideration before being sent to the appropriate parliamentary committee. The practical effect of this policy has been to give the departments — that is to say, the Cabinet — control over most of the bills introduced in the Storting.

After the bill has been introduced in the Odelsting, it is referred by the President to committee. Occasionally the matter may involve two or more rather separate propositions and, as a result, it may be expedient to join temporarily two or more committees for the consideration of the bill. If the proposal is a distinct departure from ordinary legislation, or if the proposition is extremely important, a special committee may be appointed. All bills, whether proposed by a private member or by the Cabinet, are subjected to committee consideration and, unlike the practice in the United Kingdom, even government measures are subjected to painstaking and careful scrutiny in the parliamentary committees. This procedure may be explained by the fact that, historically, separation of powers has been an important first principle in Norwegian governmental practice. Even today, with parliamentarism and party discipline firmly established, separation of powers in a certain sense continues to operate. The members of the Storting are jealous of their prerogatives, and for that reason legislators continue to insist on reviewing minutely the measures proposed by the administration. They argue that not only is separation of powers still constitutionally in effect, but also that the Storting is more representative from the geographical, occupational, and social standpoints than could possibly be the case in any or all of the administrative departments. This being true, the practical effects of a measure can be more accurately judged by a parliamentary group than by an administrative department. With the present trend away from "genuine" politicians and toward "experts" in cabinet posts, this argument has greater validity than it might have, for example, in the United Kingdom where cabinet members are drawn to a much larger extent from the ranks of practicing politicians of long experience than they are in Norway. Only in very unusual cases does a bill escape the rigors of committee examination in Norway. If the need for immediate action is so desperate as to cause delay to become extremely costly, the Odelsting may consent to action without the customary committee report. But this kind of action can be prevented by a vote of one-fifth of the members present.

The committee examines carefully each detail of the proposed measure. In order to perform this task deliberately and without interruption or distraction, the meetings of the group are usually held behind closed doors. Written evidence may be submitted, witnesses called, excursions taken, and other procedures, designed to give the legislators the information necessary to make an intelligent decision, may be used. Often members of the Council of State are called upon for expert testimony in spite of the fact that they have presumably been consulted before the initial draft was presented to the Odelsting. The committee may report the bill unchanged, change it materially or immaterially by the addition of amendments, or eliminate the measure by refusing to report it back to the house.

Should the Labor party continue to hold a majority or near majority in the Storting as it has since 1945, and as a result should a modified two-party system develop, it is unlikely that the parliamentary committee will remain as strong as it has been in the past. Even today it is not as strong as it was before 1940 when all Cabinets were dependent for their continuation on support from two or more parties.

After the committee's deliberations have been completed, the bill is sent to the Odelsting for that body's consideration. In order to take official action of any kind, that division (as well as the Lagting and Storting proper) must have at least one-half of its members present. Ordinarily, the debate in the Odelsting does not begin until after the written committee report has been placed in the hands of the members and they have had an opportunity to study the proposal. In the meantime, the committee's recommendations are given adequate publicity both in the press and over the radio.

The consideration of a legislative measure by the Odelsting may take a number of different paths. In general, the rules of procedure first allow majority and minority leaders of the committee that considered the measure to express themselves on the bill in its entirety. Should others desire to be heard on the question of the measure's advisability, they are given such an opportunity after the Odelsting has received the advice of the members of the committee. The minister in charge of the department that either has prepared the bill or will administer the measure when and if it is finally approved by the parliament is given an opportunity to be heard. If the proposition is important to the Cabinet's program, or if there are significant political ramifications associated with it, the Prime Minister will take an active part in the discussion. Although debate is limited, the rules are designed to allow a complete and careful consideration of the measure.[17] In the end, however, the Odelsting depends very largely for its final decision upon the committee's report and expert ministerial advice. Questions without serious political significance are often addressed spontaneously during the course of the debate to members of the Council of State. Formal interpellations concerning matters of government policy are not considered in the Odelsting, but in plenary sessions of the Storting.

After the debate on the general aspects of the bill has been closed, consideration is given to the individual provisions of the measure. Amendments may be presented, paragraphs may be completely rewritten or removed, and other internal changes may result from this minute examination of the measure's contents. Here again, the limits

[17] *Stortingets forretningsorden,* Paragraph 32.

of debate are only designed to give every member an opportunity to be heard.

As a rule, the balloting that follows the Odelsting's consideration of the measure is divided into two phases. First, the bill is voted upon provision by provision; second, the question of the adoption of the proposition in its entirety is submitted to the membership. An interesting regulation should be mentioned in this connection. "A representative that is not in the legislative chamber when a matter is submitted to balloting, must not vote, and one that is present and qualified to vote, may not leave . . . until the balloting is completed."[18] Ample time is given to allow absent members to find their places in the legislative chamber, but should they fail to appear until after the balloting has commenced, even though they might yet cast an effective vote, they will not be permitted to do so. Those members present in the hall when the announcement of the balloting is made may not leave until the final vote has been taken. Although this latter regulation does not expressly demand that the members present actually cast ballots, it has been interpreted practically as having the effect of requiring members present to vote, either affirmatively or negatively, on a pending proposal. There is apparently no opportunity for them to refuse to vote if they are present in the chamber when the vote is taken.[19]

Three different balloting methods are commonly used in the Odelsting. A simple call for the yeas and nays is sometimes sufficient. If the measure is deemed to be sufficiently important, or if one-fifth of the members present demand it, a roll-call vote is taken. In cases involving the selection of individuals to offices a secret written ballot is used. In practically every situation a simple majority determines the issue.

If the bill passes the Odelsting, it is sent to the Lagting for its consideration. Procedures similar to those outlined above are employed by this body in its deliberations on the measure. About the same kind of debate, the same limits on discussion, and practically identical balloting methods are followed in the Lagting as were used in the Odelsting.

If the Lagting accepts the proposal without amendment and in the same form as it was passed by the Odelsting, the bill goes to the King for his official sanction. If he signs the measure it becomes an accepted part of Norwegian law after certain technicalities concerned with promulgation have been satisfied. If the bill is not passed by the Lagting in exactly the same form that received the official approval of the Odelsting, it must return to the latter division for further con-

[18] *Ibid.*, Paragraphs 37–41.
[19] Vilhelm Haffner, *Stortingets voteringsordning* (Oslo, 1960), p. 83.

sideration. Two alternatives are open at this time to the Lagting. It may send the bill back asking that the Odelsting eliminate the measure completely from the legislative program. This may be accomplished by a request for indefinite postponement, or it may take the form of a proposal to recommit the proposition to the government for further study and consideration. In any event, the Lagting cannot itself eliminate the law or send it back to the government, but must request the Odelsting to do it.[20]

The second alternative that the Lagting may elect is to amend the measure and send the changed version back for consideration by the Odelsting. Technically, the Lagting is restricted in its amending power within the limits of the spirit and general subject matter of the original measure. But this limitation has not been unduly confining in practice; in fact, it has been so liberally interpreted as to permit the smaller division to substitute virtually a new measure for the one submitted originally by the Odelsting.

When the legislative proposition has been returned to the Odelsting, this chamber may drop the bill or send it back to the Lagting, either unaltered or with amendments. If the matter is dropped by the initiating division, the other chamber is unable to revive it. On the other hand, if the Odelsting agrees to the Lagsting's amendments, the bill is immediately sent to the latter division, which in turn submits it to the King for his official consideration. At this stage the Lagting is not permitted to reconsider, but must promptly exercise its ministerial function of relaying the bill directly to the King.

The Odelsting may not wish to eliminate the bill, but cannot agree completely with the amendments that have been suggested by the Lagting. In such a situation, the larger division may change the amended provisions and return the bill in this form to the Lagting for its final examination. Ordinarily, a compromise between the two differing positions may develop before a final revision is accepted by the Odelsting.

After the Odelsting has taken action on an amended bill it goes back to the Lagting for its final, formal consideration. Accepted practice has decreed that the question before the division at this stage of the legislative process is the simple one leading to approval or disapproval of the proposition last submitted by the Odelsting. It is not possible for the Lagting to refuse to accept the amended measure by agreeing to approve the bill as originally drawn. Nor can it change any detail of the second proposal sent to it by the Odelsting. If the vote indicates that the majority of the members of the smaller division favor the amended proposition, it is straightway submitted to the King.

[20] Ragnar Knoph and others, *Loven og lovgivningsmakten* (Oslo, 1935), p. 113.

If the Lagting fails to approve, "the whole Storting shall meet in a joint sitting, and the bill . . . [be] disposed of by a majority of two-thirds of the votes."[21] The proposition to be considered by the plenary session of the Storting is the one last disapproved by the Lagting. According to established Norwegian parliamentary practice (since 1839), the Storting is excluded at this stage from adding any amendment to the measure. It must follow much the same procedure as was used by the Lagting in its second consideration, except that greater freedom of debate is allowed in the Storting than was permitted in the smaller division. If the bill is approved in the assembled Storting by a two-thirds vote — and if past experience holds, this is quite unlikely — it is recommitted to the Lagting whose duty it is to send it to the King for approval or disapproval. Here again the Lagting is not given any discretionary power in the exercise of this function, but must immediately submit the proposed law to the King.

Since the veto power of the King, although still provided for in the Constitution, has not been used since 1905, it has, for all practical purposes, atrophied from lack of use. Certainly the King could not reassert a veto power independent of his Cabinet, and it is extremely doubtful that any Cabinet would "advise" a royal veto. Rather than do this, the Cabinet would choose to resign if defeated on a crucial issue by the Storting.[22]

After a matter has been definitely settled either in the form of an enactment or through failure to summon a legislative majority favorable to the bill, the rules of the Storting prohibit a revival of the issue during the current session. Only in case of exceptional need not present at the time of the original consideration, may the Storting reconsider a previously adopted action. And should this develop, the proposition must be subjected again to a complete committee examination.

Official promulgation of a law that has successfully passed the Storting and been given the required approval of the King must be accomplished in accordance with definite provisions outlined in Paragraph 81 of the Constitution. All new laws are published in *Lovtidende* and, unless otherwise specified, become effective four weeks after publication.

Relation of the Council of State to the Storting

Although a more complete description of the several characteristics of responsible parliamentarism in Norway was given in the chapter on the Council of State, it might be appropriate to summarize briefly

[21] *Constitution of Norway,* Paragraph 76.
[22] See pp. 55–56.

here the policy-making role of the Cabinet. It has already been mentioned in an earlier discussion that members of the Council of State, unlike members of the British Cabinet, are not active voting members of parliament. The members of the Norwegian Cabinet, however, whether or not they are chosen from the Storting, do have access to the sessions of that body and do join in the debate and discussion.

The official rules of the Storting permit interpellations and provide a definite system for handling them. If a member of the Storting wishes to confront the Cabinet or an individual minister with a formal interpellation, he must file a written copy of it with the President of the Storting. This officer determines, through consultation with the Prime Minister, when the matter can be considered. Interpellations are usually of interest to all the representatives and consequently are answered in a plenary session of the Storting. If the cabinet member wishes to avoid discussing the issue for the time being, he may so inform the President, who in turn notifies the members of the Storting that the interpellation is to go unanswered. It is obvious that no cabinet member can afford to use this delaying tactic with great frequency.

A second method of securing information from members of the Council of State is through the question period. Questions, as distinct from interpellations, are less formal and often more specific. While interpellations are occasionally used to embarass cabinet officers, questions are most often employed as a genuine means of securing information on a particular aspect of governmental policy. Usually a series of questions are grouped together and a part of a daily session is given over to hearing the answers. Occasionally in the course of parliamentary debates, a question comes up that requires an immediate answer. Any such question may be put and answered without delay, but only after the President has been assured that the query is strictly germane to the subject under discussion.

There has been a great increase in the use of questions and interpellations since 1945 and particularly during the last five or six years. During the parliamentary session of 1961 it was obvious that the opposition groups in the Storting were attempting to embarrass the Labor Cabinet by an unusually large number of questions on a wide range of subjects in the hope that these might have some effect on the fall elections. This use of questions and interpellations, though perfectly understandable, was deplored at the time even in some quarters of the opposition press as wasteful of the time and energy of the Storting. In some respects, this type of criticism is naïve since one of the major purposes of a question hour is to allow the opposition to embarrass the government in power by pointing out its real and even fancied mistakes.

Besides furnishing information, the Council of State also performs the important function of preparing legislative proposals. In the last two or three decades this part of the Norwegian Cabinet's work has been increasing steadily both in scope and in importance. Practically all significant proposals are now drafted in the offices of the administrative departments. The advisability of such a procedure is apparent when one considers the need for control over legislation essential to the smooth functioning of any parliamentary system. Most states operating under the system permit members of the administration to retain their positions of leadership and control in parliament. The fact that in the Norwegian system cabinet members are not full-fledged members of the Storting makes it even more necessary to allow them to take an important part in the drafting and presentation of legislative programs.

As can be noticed from the foregoing discussion, the position of the cabinet member in the Storting is one characterized by influence rather than by the possession of significant control over legislation once it has been introduced. Although he may not vote, he does, by virtue of his very presence in the Storting, exert a good deal of pressure upon the members of the parliamentary body, particularly since the individual holding a cabinet position is often selected from among the leaders of the major party in the Storting. The fact that legislative proposals are normally organized and presented as a part of a general party plan makes the position of these leaders vitally important, even though they are without the usual powers granted to working representatives in parliaments of other countries.

6

National Administration

Effective administration of the public services is important in any country, but particularly important in a highly socialized country like Norway. Several matters deserve attention even in a brief account — as this must be — of the organs, principles, and practices of Norwegian public administration. Some, including the principles underlying division of responsibility between the state and the local subdivisions as well as a brief sketch of the machinery of local administration, are included in the chapters on local government and social legislation. In this chapter the emphasis will be entirely on national administration with an outline of the chief organs and a summary account of certain of the personnel procedures.

Organization of National Administration

There are four chief kinds of organs of administration in Norway: the regular departments (all Cabinet level and sometimes called ministries), independent agencies of which the Bank of Norway (*Norges Bank*) is a good example, agencies which are partly independent and partly under the administrative supervision of the regular departments (State Railways), and public corporations such as the State Liquor Monopoly (*A.S. Vinmonopolet*). The emphasis in the discussion that follows will be focused on the departments and, to a limited degree, on the independent and quasi-independent agencies.[1]

[1] There is no comprehensive account in English or Norwegian of the work of public corporations. A listing and some statistical data can be found in *Statistikk årbok for Norge* (published annually by the Central Bureau of Statistics in Oslo). The administrative relationship between public corporations and other administrative units is referred to throughout the pages of *Norges statskalender* (Oslo, 1962). Scanty references can also be

Before sketching the functions undertaken in each of the fourteen regular departments, mention should be made of two offices, the Prime Minister's office and the Cabinet Secretariat, which are not strictly speaking administrative in character, but do undertake functions of coordination that have some effect on administration. The Prime Minister's Office was organized in its present form in 1955 and has eight professional employees who undertake coordination and planning activities for the Prime Minister in three fields: juridical-administrative, economic, and foreign affairs, including defense. The staff of the Office is concerned mainly with the policy questions facing the Prime Minister and his Cabinet, but since policy and administration are sometimes difficult to keep separated, the Office does play at least an incidental role of coordination in administrative matters.

Much less significant as an administrative agency is the Cabinet Secretariat. In a very restricted sense provision was made for this agency shortly after the Constitution was written in 1814; it was reorganized in its present form in 1909. Its staff is small — two professional officers — and its activities are limited to general record-keeping; the preparation of cabinet reports; serving as a communica-cation link between Cabinet and parliament; editing certain governmental publications, notably *Norsk Lovtidende* in which the laws passed by the Storting are published; and serving as the "office staff" for the collective Cabinet. Obviously, its relation to the line activities of administration is strictly incidental.

The outline of the organization of the regular administrative departments which follows will give at least a superficial view of the functions undertaken by each.[2]

Department of Defense

First organized in 1814, organized in its present form in 1945.

1. Personnel and Organization Division: All personnel matters including recruitment, promotions, dismissals, pensions, health and social programs, organization of military units, and military education are handled by this division.

2. Administrative Division: Internal organization of the Department and its subdivisions, construction and administration of buildings and camps, legal matters — domestic and international — and contracts come within the jurisdiction of this division.

---

found in *The Norway Year Book* (Oslo, 1962). Preben Munthe, "Some Structural Changes in Norway's Economy Since the War," *Norges Handelshøyskoles Særtrykk-serie,* No. 23 (Bergen, 1959), contains some references to problems facing nationalized industries.

[2] For a more complete account of the organization of the departments, see *Norges statskalender.*

3. Division for Cooperation in NATO
4. Budget and Accounting Division
5. Materiel Directorate
6. Press Bureau

Church and Education Department

First organized in 1818, organized in its present form in 1845.

1. Church Division: All matters such as personnel, property, ritual, religious education, missionary programs, and any other activities that have any bearing on the State Church are handled in the five offices of this division.[3]

2. School Division: Eight offices in this division exercise significant control of all levels of elementary and secondary education from the folk school through the *gymnasium* (secondary school which is roughly equivalent to junior college in the United States). Though the Department is ultimately responsible for many educational matters, the Norwegian system is not as highly centralized as the French. Local school committees have an important area of responsibility for primary and secondary schools.

3. Cultural Division

(a) Office of Higher Institutions of Learning and the Sciences: Besides exercising control of all institutions of higher learning, the office supervises many other cultural and educational institutions and activities, including the National Broadcasting System, state research funds and organizations, certain museums, and the like. As is the case in the lower schools, the role of the Department in higher education is curcumscribed sufficiently so as to leave complete academic and substantial curricular freedom to the faculties of the universities and other collegiate institutions.

(b) Cultural Office: This office deals with all cultural institutions not included in the Office of Higher Institutions. Painting, sculpture, architecture, music, and films, as well as organizations related to these and other art forms are supported and supervised.

(c) Library Office

(d) Youth and Sports Office: The emphasis in this office is on organized and unorganized athletics, occasionally connected with school programs, but for the most part independent of the schools.

Department of Justice and Police

First organized in 1818 and last reorganized in 1953.

1. Administrative Division: This is a large, heterogeneous division

[3] Sometimes even complicated theological questions, such as the obligation of a clergyman to believe in a literal hell, come to the Department for adjudication and settlement.

which includes several offices dealing with both substantive law and procedure. The bulk of the *Justice* part of the Department's task is handled in this division.

2. Division of Prisons
3. Law Division: This division is concerned chiefly with proposed changes in the Constitution, the civil and the criminal codes.
4. Police Division: From January 1, 1937, the state has had complete control of the police. The administration of police is in the hands of this division.
5. Office of Civil Defense

Department of Finance

Organized in 1818

1. Division of Customs and Excises
2. Administrative Division: This division is in charge of internal administration of the Department as well as certain other miscellaneous functions and offices, including the Central Statistical Bureau, state loan program to certain organizations, the insurance carried by the state, and related matters.
3. Ordinary Tax Division
4. Finance Division: Preparation of the state budget and the administration of accounting and disbursement procedures are the chief responsibilities of this division.
5. Tax Law Division: This division prepares reports and drafts legislation for the use of the Cabinet and parliament in preparing new or amended tax laws.
6. Economic Division: This division is concerned with economic planning and, in this connection, with preparation of the national budget which contains a set of economic objectives and, incidentally, should be distinguished from the state budget which is a finance plan containing estimates of anticipated income and expenditures necessary to support the government programs for the fiscal year. Questions involving the effect of currency management and credit on the economy generally, and on the national budget specifically, are handled in this division.
7. Division of Administrative Planning (*Rasjonaliseringsdirektorat*)
8. Public Printing Office
9. Office of the Treasurer

Department of Agriculture

Organized in 1900.

1. Division of Agriculture
2. Division of Forestry
3. Division of Veterinary Affairs

4. Administrative Division
5. Crop Rotation Division
6. Other related agencies, including offices dealing with international matters, agricultural laws, land concessions, and sport fishing and hunting.

Department of Foreign Affairs

Organized in 1906.

1. General Division: This is the largest division and has jurisdiction over general internal administrative matters in the Department, personnel within the Department and in the foreign service, relations with other departments, the departmental budget, fiscal accounting, the archives and library of the Department, and other matters that are not included in other divisions.
2. Political Division: The five offices of this division handle relations between Norway and the United Nations, NATO, other international organizations, and also relationships between Norway and the countries in the Sino-Soviet bloc.
3. Trade Policy Division: Commercial and economic relations with all states not under the jurisdiction of the Political Division and all other commercial and economic matters, whether covered by multilateral or bilateral arrangements, are handled by this division.
4. Protocol Division: All matters of protocol relating to the royal house, Norwegian and foreign diplomats, and the administration of passport and visa regulations come under the jurisdiction of this division. Arrangements for conferences and visitations of foreign dignitaries are also made by the division.
5. Law Division
6. Press Bureau
7. Office for Cultural Relations with Foreign Countries

Department of Social Affairs

Organized in 1913 and last reorganized in 1951.

1. General Division: This is a large division concerned with a great many things, chief among them being: internal administration, child welfare in the general sense, alcoholism and related problems, and relations with other states and international associations in the field of social legislation.
2. Pension and Social Insurance Division (*Trygdeavdeling*): This division supervises all the pension and insurance programs discussed in Chapter 10. In addition it has certain fiscal and auditing responsibilities for special funds under the supervision of the Department.
3. Health Directorate: This is the agency responsible for the Pub-

lic Health Program and the Health Insurance Plan.[4] The names of the offices in the division describe the range of its activity: Budget and Personnel, Tuberculosis, Psychiatry, Hygiene, Drugs, Dentistry, and Hospital.

Department of Industry and Crafts

First organized as part of the Department of Commerce (or Trade — *Handelsdepartement*) in 1916 and reorganized last in 1958.

1. General Division: This division is concerned, as the name implies, with general matters, but also has jurisdiction over rules respecting crafts, mining, and whaling. It also safeguards the state's interests in iron, aluminum, and hydroelectric works (*A/S Norsk Jernverk, A/S Årdal og Sundal Verk, Norsk Hydro A/S*), and in such other establishments as the state may have ownership or concession interests.
2. Industrial Division (divided into offices for the several categories of industry).
3. Waterpower and Hydroelectric Division
4. Planning Division

Department of Commerce

Organized in 1885 as part of the Labor Department. Established as a separate department in 1946.

1. Road and Railroad Division
2. Post and Telegraph Division
3. Coordination Division: Besides coordinating routes of the several transportation services, this division has a legal office to care for problems relating to taxis and trucking companies.
4. Civil Aviation Division
5. Hotel and Tourist Directorate

As could be evident from even a superficial view of the range of functions performed, the Department of Commerce is one of Norway's largest administrative units.

Department of Fisheries

Organized in 1946.

1. Division of Fishing and Hunting (*Fangst*): General problems related to the fishing, whaling, and sealing industries are the concern of this division. In addition, it has jurisdiction in certain related areas, such as harbors and pilots.
2. Division for Processing Fish and Fish Products

Department of Trade and Commerce

Organized in 1947 and last reorganized in 1959.

1. Trade Division: This division has a wide array of functions.

[4] See pp. 182–185.

Among the most important are: preparation and administration of legislation affecting markets, stock exchanges, business practices, competition, weights and measures; assisting with trade fairs, etc. Mediation services in connection with disputes over property rights are also provided by this division.

2. Foreign Exchange Division: Most matters related to foreign exchange, not under the jurisdiction of the Bank of Norway (*Norges Bank*), are handled in this division.

3. Division of Trade with Other Countries: All problems of foreign trade not related to foreign exchange questions come within the jurisdiction of this division.[5]

4. Navigation and Seamen's Division
5. Ocean Shipping Division
6. Directorate for Economic National Defense
7. Directorate for Regulation of Exports and Imports

Department of Communal and Labor Affairs

Organized in 1948.

This is a joint department, as the name indicates. All supervision of local government is under the Department. In addition, labor legislation is drafted and administered by the Department, and it has major responsibility for housing (through *Boligdirektoratet*).

Department of Wages and Prices

Organized in 1955.

Through its two divisions, the Department administers laws and regulations affecting wages and salaries of all public servants and the laws regulating prices and rents.

Department of Family and Consumer Affairs

Organized in 1956

This is the newest and smallest of the administrative departments. Its sphere of activity is evident from its name.

Internal Organization of the Departments

There is some variation in organization in the several departments depending on size and the nature and extent of activity undertaken. Large units like the Department of Commerce and the Department of Social Affairs have rather elaborate structures, while a small department like the one dealing with Family and Consumer Affairs is simple and compact. As in other countries, the administrative activities of the central government expanded significantly in the years following

[5] Foreign exchange regulations are generally administered through the Bank of Norway (*Norges Bank*).

World War I and, as new functions were undertaken, a serious attempt was made to incorporate them into the regular departmental structure. Where this was not feasible and a quasi-independent agency had to be established, as a rule it was placed under the supervision of one of the regular departments. Also, as new departments were established, they were given control of related semi-autonomous enterprises. For example, when the Department of Commerce was created in 1946 it was given a rather wide range of authority over the State Railway System and civil aviation.

In spite of variations, there is a certain amount of symmetry and uniformity of organization in the administrative departments. As should be clear from the outline given below, each of the departments, except the very newest, Family and Consumer Affairs, is made up of two or more divisions with an *ekspedisjonssjef* heading each. The division in turn is subdivided into bureaus and a *byråsjef* is in charge of each of these units. As a rule the breakdown terminates with the bureau, although for operational purposes the bureau may occasionally also be subdivided. In some departments directorates, headed by a director, who is on the same (sometimes higher) level as the *ekspedisjonssjef*, are also included. The difference between a division and a directorate is sometimes insignificant; in certain cases the directorate has a limited degree of autonomy.

At the very top level, besides the minister who is the political chief of the department, there are often two other officers: the undersecretary (*statssekretær*) and the counsel (*råd*), who may or may not be the chief legal advisor of the department. The undersecretary is a political appointee and as such serves at the pleasure of the minister and gives up his position if the Cabinet resigns. The counsel, on the other hand, is a high-ranking civil servant not subject to the same uncertainty of tenure as are political appointees. The responsibility of each of these officers is determined in each instance by the minister. Normally, the undersecretary acts as a channel of communication to the minister, and if the latter is unable to discharge the responsibilities of his office for limited periods, the undersecretary becomes acting head of the department for the time being. Like the undersecretary, the counsel also has general supervisory authority, but may, in addition, have specified counseling functions, e.g., on legal or financial questions. His office, too, serves as one of the last links in the chain of command culminating in the office of the cabinet minister.

The remaining parts of the chain of command are clear and relatively simple in Norwegian national administration. Proposals are first discussed and decisions taken in the bureau. If the matter is simple or of a routine nature, the decision at the bureau level will be final. A more complex question is passed up to the chief of the division (*ek-*

spedisjonssjef), who in turn may make a final decision or transmit the matter to the undersecretary (if there is one) or the counsel or, in some instances, to both. These latter officers, as has been indicated, report directly to the minister. Each officer at every level — bureau, division, directorate — is responsible for the work of his unit and is expected not only to supervise administration, but give leadership to his subordinates and at the same time provide the minister with information and advice.

Independent and Semi-independent Agencies

It is perhaps incorrect to call any administrative agency in Norway "independent." In a certain sense all agencies are responsible in one way or another to the appropriate departments. And, most certainly, complete independence from cabinet control would be inconceivable. But some establishments do have a wider area of discretion than others, and it is with these in mind that the terms "independent" and "semi-independent" are used. It is impossible and perhaps unnecessary to consider in any detail all the agencies that have, in greater or lesser degree, a sphere of independence. But in order to understand the position occupied by "independent" organs generally, three have been singled out for at least perfunctory examination: the Bank of Norway, the State Railway System, and the National Insurance Institution (*Rikstrygdeverket*). Of the three the Bank of Norway is perhaps most independent of departmental control, and the National Insurance Institution, though in many respects self-governing, is perhaps the least independent.

The Bank of Norway was organized in 1816; since then a great many laws and administrative ordinances have changed both its structure and its functions. Present-day regulations are based on a rather comprehensive set of rules laid down in 1922 and amended in subsequent years. The last law to affect the Bank was passed in 1949.[6]

The governing organs of the Bank are: a board of directors of fifteen members, an executive council (*direksjon*) of five members, and an administrative staff headed by the chairman of the executive council. The members of the board of fifteen are elected by the Storting for six-year terms with seven or eight elected every third year. The chairman and vice-chairman of the executive council are chosen by the King in Council after the members of the board of directors have had opportunities to make suggestions. Both chairman and vice-chairman serve for indefinite terms; they may be removed or they may resign, but in each case six months' notice must be given. The three remaining members of the executive council are elected by the Storting for six-year terms. Each of the branches of the Bank of Norway

[6] *Lov om statens overtakelse av aksjene i Norges Bank av 8 juli, 1949.*

(twenty at the present time) has its own executive council made up of three members elected by the Storting. At both branch and national levels alternates (*varamenn*), who serve when the principals are absent for one reason or another, are selected in the same manner as are regular members of the boards and councils.

It may be sufficient to say that the Bank of Norway performs much the same functions as does the Bank of England, and that its scope is somewhat wider than the Federal Reserve Bank System of the United States. It issues all the paper currency in Norway, serves as the banker's bank, sets the discount rates, and is the chief channel of foreign exchange between Norway and other countries. At present, with more liberal foreign exchange regulations, this latter function is less important than it was for several years after World War II when severe restrictions on the availability of foreign currencies were in force.

Turning to the second of the "independent" agencies under examination, the State Railway System, the first thing to note is that with the exception of a few miles, the entire railway network in Norway is state-owned. The board responsible for the State Railway System is made up of seven members with an equal number of alternates. Three of the members are elected by the Storting for four-year terms, two are appointed by the King in Council for four-year terms, and two are elected by the railroad workers for three-year terms. The Director General of the Railway System is appointed by the King in Council and serves an indefinite term. This is one of the highest paid positions in the Norwegian public service (NK 53,000).

Generally speaking, the State Railway System operates independently, but planning is carried out in consultation with the appropriate division in the Department of Commerce. It might be emphasized that, though the Director-General of the Railway System has operational independence, since the services rendered come within the daily scrutiny and understanding of people generally, the Cabinet is quite sensitive to criticism of the operation. This sensitivity, coupled with the planning role played by the Department of Commerce, justifies the conclusion that the Railway System is, at best, a "semi-independent" agency.

The State Railway System is generally considered to be quite efficient. The service is good although the equipment is not up to the British or German standards. Although highways have improved greatly in the last ten years, many communities rely heavily upon the railway system for transportation of both goods and people. Because of the topography, roadbeds are very expensive to build and this, coupled with sparse traffic in some areas, causes the State Railway System to lose money. The deficit, made up from public revenues, has run between 160 to 175 million *kroner* annually during the last several years, or to put it another way, about one-third of the cost of the system is provided by subsidies from the state.

Perhaps the independent agency that is most dependent upon other sectors of administration in Norway is the National Insurance Institution (*Rikstrygdeverket*). This is the central office of all the state and communal insurance plans (health, unemployment, accident, old age pensions)[7] with responsibility for fiscal and general supervision of all local insurance funds (*trygdekasser*). This supervision is exercised not only on a regular schedule, but also includes announced and unannounced special investigations. The governing board of the National Insurance Institution is composed of five members (with alternates) appointed by the King in Council for four-year terms. One of the four is designated by the King to serve as chairman.

The Department of Social Affairs devotes a great deal of its time to planning and supervising social legislation generally and the insurance and pension programs specifically. Of the three subdivisions within the Department, two are occupied much of the time with such matters. And it is to one of these, the Pension and Social Insurance Division, that the National Insurance Institution is responsible, not only in the area of planning, but operationally as well.

Personnel Administration

The Ordinary Civil Service

In spite of the expanded bureaucracy made necessary by the increased activities undertaken by the Norwegian state during the last two decades, the administrative structure has been sufficiently integrated to provide fairly well-defined lines of responsibility. Although departments and offices have increased and new services have been added, a fairly high degree of centralized supervision has been achieved. Also, through the recent efforts of the Division of Administrative Planning (*Rasjonaliseringsdirektoratet*) in the Department of Finance, organizational arrangements no longer thought suitable have been replaced. This process of modernization and streamlining has not as yet been extended to public personnel administration in Norway. For the most part civil servants are recruited, examined, promoted, and given tenure in accordance with the provisions of the Law on Public Servants passed in 1918. Only in the last few years have plans been projected to update the procedures.

There is, as yet, no central agency responsible for personnel matters in the Norwegian central government, nor are there any centrally administered civil service examinations. The Department of Wages and Prices has, since its establishment in 1955, assumed certain plan-

[7] See pp. 180–192.

ning responsibilities in the area of personnel, but it exercises no operating control, except on salary scales, and has no supervision of the actual processes of hiring, promoting, or dismissing civil servants. Each department and semi-independent agency is in complete control of these processes, subject of course to general laws and their judicial interpretations.

In the discussion that follows a brief description will be given of personnel policies and procedures with special reference to: the establishment of positions with attached qualifications, recruitment of candidates, examination of candidates, appointments, probationary periods, dismissals, training programs, and fringe benefits. But before considering these matters, a word should be said about the various classes of Norwegian civil servants. Based upon law and practice extending as far back as the Dano-Norwegian Union (before 1814), civil servants are divided into two main classes, the names of which unfortunately have no satisfactory English equivalents: *embedsmenn* and *bestillingsmenn.* The distinction between the two is concerned mainly with grade and official status. The *embedsmann* is in the higher rungs of the service; usually all officers of the government with the rank of bureau chief or above are in this category. All other civil servants, with the exception of nonclerical manual workers, are *bestillingsmenn. Embedsmenn* are "named" by the King in Council (somewhat in the same manner as certain officers are "commissioned" by the President of the United States) while other civil servants are appointed by the head of a department or independent agency. Except for the fact that by definition *embedsmenn* occupy the higher positions and by tradition certain prestige has been attached to the title, the distinction between the two classes of civil servants does not in itself have great importance at the present time.

Perhaps a more significant and useful classification permits differentiation of activity through the establishment of the following categories: (a) leadership (or supervisory) class, (b) expediters, (c) clerical personnel, and (d) manual workers. A fifth class should no doubt be added — scientific and technical personnel — although this class is sometimes subsumed within one or the other of the first two groups.

All positions in the Norwegian civil service must have been established by act of parliament and most often by specific provision in the state budget. As in other countries, the need for new positions must be justified in the preparatory stage of budget-making through negotiations between the line departments and the Department of Finance. If a conflict becomes irreconcilable in these negotiations, the Cabinet will make the final decision. Before the position is authorized by law, the qualifications for the position and its placement on the salary scale will have been determined. As a rule, the salary attached to the position will be more or less fixed by past practice, but if no precedent exists, a decision on salary will be worked out by the appropriate departments — the department which is to have the new position, the Department of Finance, and lately the Department of Wages and Prices.[8]

The formal qualifications that attach to a given position have special significance in Norway since they must serve as a substitute for the examinations used in selecting civil servants in Great Britain and the United States. As a rule, the qualifications will be determined by the department in which the position is placed. In setting these up the bureau chief will recommend, in a preliminary way, the specific credentials he thinks incumbents should possess. In the final stages of the process, the minister will make the decision, but most often in accord with the original recommendation. Usually the qualification requirements are stated in such terms as will correspond with degrees or certificates granted by universities, technical institutes, special higher educational institutions, the *gymnasia,* and, for the very lowest positions, the elementary schools. For example, a position as Secretary II in the Commerce Department might call for a degree in economics with a particular emphasis on statistics. Or, as is quite general even for certain nonlegal positions, the qualification requirements might call for a law degree.

Once the position has been established with qualifications specified and salary attached, the appropriate administrator can proceed to the recruitment stage. The vacancy is announced in *Norsk Lysingsblad,* which is published daily and contains mainly notices of vacant positions in the state and communal civil services. Usually the announce-

[8] The salary scale for Norwegian civil servants can be found in *Norges statskalender,* pp. 42–43. The scale runs from a low of NK 8,532 for beginning clerical personnel to a high of NK 44,598. A breakdown of beginning salaries by rank follow:

Departmental Counsel	NK 42,834*
Departmental Undersecretary	39,306
Ekspedisjonssjef and Director	37,542
Underdirector	32,250
Bureau Chief	27,014
Consultant I (*Konsulent*)	24,382
Consultant II	22,972
Consultant III, First Secretary	18,037
Secretary I	15,552
Secretary II	13,358
Clerical	From NK 9,068 to 13,358

* To find rough dollar equivalents divide by 7.

It should be noted that the title "Secretary" as used in Norway does not usually place the holder in a clerical position. Rather it is a designation for administrative personnel at the lower levels.

ment is also inserted in the newspapers. The notice states clearly the title of the position, its location, qualifications required, nature of the work, salary, deadline for applications, and the name of the officer to whom the application should be sent. For positions in the lower echelons an attempt is made to give as much publicity as possible to the vacancy, often using other means than the two mentioned above. Openings at the higher levels of the civil service are not so well advertised; occasionally they may only be announced in the department in which they occur. This restricted kind of recruitment is not used if it seems obvious that an insufficient number of qualified candidates will be found by this method. When used, the restricted announcement is designed chiefly to give capable people within the department opportunity for promotion. Though at first this might seem a dubious procedure, since it limits the range of choice, there does seem to be convincing evidence that it has worked not only to the satisfaction of the civil servants, but of the public as well.

The officer who usually receives the application for employment in the civil service is the bureau chief. He checks the credentials, letters of recommendation, and, as a rule, he interviews some (not necessarily all) of the applicants. He then indicates his first, second, and third choices and sends this recommendation with the candidates' papers to a personnel committee (*innstillingsråd*) in the department. Besides the bureau chief, this committee is made up of the counsel, all the division chiefs (*ekspedisjonssjefer*) in the department, and two representatives from the appropriate civil service union or association.[9] If the department is large, the committee need not include all of these officers, providing eliminations have been approved by the Department of Wages and Prices, but in no case can the two representatives from the civil service be eliminated from the committee. If all members of the committee agree (in writing) to the bureau chief's recommendations, all appropriate documents are forwarded to the minister who, in nearly every instance, will appoint the person standing first on the list. If any member of the committee disagrees with the bureau chief's choices, a meeting of the committee must be held and a decision taken by majority vote. Although the minister will usually appoint the number one man on the list, he can appoint any one of the three recommended by the committee. If he should insist on naming an applicant not on the list of three, he must seek the advice of the committee and, should this group disagree with him, the controversy must be settled and the appointment made by the King in Council. In perhaps 90 per cent of the cases the

[9] The civil service representatives are chosen usually for a term of years — two or three — although this may vary from department to department. No one may sit as a representative if he has an immediate personal interest in the outcome of the deliberations.

committee and minister will agree with the bureau chief's recommendations.

For positions at the bureau chief level or higher (*embedsmenn*) the recommending process is somewhat more simple. Since these people are "named" by the King in Council, the recommendation of the appropriate minister becomes the basis for decision, this time by the Cabinet. The minister need not submit his recommendation to a committee, but as a rule he seeks the advice of the division chiefs as well as the departmental counsel. In practically every case a bureau chief would be appointed from within the department.

Whether an appointee is an *embedsmann* or a *bestillingsmann,* he will receive formal, written notice of his appointment, the only difference being that the former will be given a document signed by the King, while the latter will get a letter from the appropriate cabinet minister.

Although there is no specific provision in the law or the regulations that a three-year probationary period is required, other legal provisions, not necessarily related to the civil service, and well-established usage support the practice. During the three-year period the public employee may be discharged without cause on three months' notice. After the probationary period he can be discharged only for cause or if continuation of his position becomes unnecessary or is not in the best interests of the state. If the employee is dismissed for cause, he must be given six months' notice and may appeal the dismissal to the minister, and, if dissatisfied with this decision, to the Cabinet. If the employee is removed from his job because it has become unnecessary or for reasons other than for cause, he will receive in a lump sum 60 per cent of his annual salary to tide him over until he secures another position. If in such a situation he refuses to accept another position in the civil service for which he is qualified, he loses the right to receive this severance compensation.

Before considering one or two of the problem areas in the public service that are now under discussion in Norwegian governmental circles, reference should be made to fringe benefits and working conditions. In general, civil servants are paid entering salaries higher than those received by comparable employees in private employment, but the salaries at the higher levels of the government service are definitely lower than those paid outside the government. As is the case in other countries, this difference is offset in part by the security of tenure enjoyed by civil servants. And of course the motivation of the public servant is different; he normally places salary secondary to opportunity to render a social service consistent with his professional training and experience. As far as fringe benefits are concerned, differences between those received by private and public employees are not great.

All Norwegians are protected against hazards of illness, accidents, and unemployment, and all are covered by an old age pension plan. The civil servants do have their own independent pension program which is supported by annual contributions by the employee of 6 per cent of his current base salary plus additional contributions by the state up to 12 per cent of salary. The employee, on reaching the compulsory retirement age of seventy years, may receive a pension equal to 66 per cent of his last salary if this is no more than NK 28,100 (Class 20) plus an additional amount if his salary is higher. An employee who retires at seventy at the present time with a base salary of NK 33,500 (considered substantial in the Norwegian civil service) would receive an annual pension of about NK 22,000 (a little more than $3,160). This would be slightly lower than the absolute maximum permitted under present (1963) laws and regulations.[10] In addition to the pension program for ordinary civil servants, there are other systems covering special classes such as manual workers, employees on limited tenure, and employees in the State Railway System. Other public servants, such as cabinet members, are also covered for pension purposes by special legislation.

In addition to retirement benefits, civil servants receive two-week vacations with pay annually. Sick leave is granted on certification of a doctor, normally for two weeks, but under certain circumstances it can run for as long as three months. Leave with pay for a few days at a time can also be given to employees who have special problems with family and close associates and are forced to be absent from work. General state laws regulate conditions of work and special rules set up maximum hours (thirty-eight and three-quarters hours per week in winter and thirty-five hours per week in summer) and, under certain conditions, allow for overtime compensation. For the most part these rules apply only to clerical and manual employees.

Recruitment and Appointment Practices in the Foreign Service

The personnel policy of the Department of Foreign Affairs is sufficiently different from the other departments to warrant special consideration. As has been the practice in many other countries, foreign service officers are selected in a manner different from the other employees of the Department of Foreign Affairs.

In one important respect the Department of Foreign Affairs has lagged behind the other units of administration in personnel policies

[10] There are other benefits allowed for widows and children and opportunities are given for early retirement. All of these supplementary provisions and exceptions to the general procedure are outlined in the law, *Lov om statens pensjonskasse av 28 juli 1949,* and described in Dorothy Burton Skårdal, *Social Insurance in Norway* (Oslo, 1960), pp. 132–142. A condensed description can be found in *Norges statskalender,* pp. 43–47.

as they relate to the nonforeign service civil servants. Selections in this department are for the most part made by the bureau chief without any consultation with a personnel committee. He determines qualifications (with advice from his administrative subordinates), advertises vacant positions, evaluates applications, and makes appointments. Only in recent years has there been significant agitation, both within the ranks of departmental employees and from the Department of Wages and Prices, for a modernization of recruitment and appointment procedures. It seems likely that in the future the reasonably uniform policies now applying in other departments will also be followed in selecting nonforeign service officers and employees in the Department of Foreign Affairs.

Compared with the simple procedure used in selecting personnel for the Department, the regulations governing the appointment of foreign service officers seem somewhat complex. In order to be eligible for consideration for a post in the foreign service, the applicant must be a Norwegian citizen, at least twenty-one years of age, but no older than thirty, in good health, and able to meet one of the following educational qualifications:

1. Graduation with *embedsexamen*[11] from a Norwegian university or graduation from one of the several specialized institutions of higher education in engineering, agriculture, business administration, military affairs, or from some other comparable institution.

2. Graduation from *gymnasium* or from *handelsgymnasium* (business school), followed by at least three years of successful practical experience in some job related to foreign trade or other external relations.

3. Possessed of specially needed background not covered in 1 and 2 above.[12]

The responsibility for accepting and evaluating applications received as a result of published announcements (similar to those used to attract other applicants for government positions) rests with a special committee, the Aspirant Committee (*Aspirantnevnd*), appointed by the King on recommendation of the Department. At present the members of the committee serve for three years. The committee consists of one representative from each of the following: the Department of Foreign Affairs (Chairman), the University of Oslo, the national trade union movement, the shipping industry, trade and commerce, industry, and fishing. In addition to the regular committee of seven, an equal

[11] A university examination — or to use the Anglo-Saxon equivalent, a degree — entitling the graduate to admission to certain professions in public and private life.

[12] *Reglement om rekruttering og utdannelse i utenrikstjenester* (Oslo, 1948, revised 1956).

number of alternate members is appointed. The administrative and clerical work of the committee is handled by a paid secretary.

Written applications with supporting documents are filed with the secretary, who in turn sends them to members of the committee. Normally all members will not examine all applications, although this was the intention when the rules were first written. Some screening will have been done by the secretary, who usually submits only about one-third of the applications for committee consideration. Certain candidates eliminate themselves, other are so unquestionably superior that they merit much more serious consideration than others. Usually there are as many as ten applications for every opening available.

All candidates who are given serious consideration are interviewed by the committee, usually in plenary session. After the interviews, selections are made, based not only on the number of foreign service officers needed in the coming year, but also on the kinds of positions candidates may be called upon to fill.

Before they are given definite job assignments, all successful applicants (with the rank of aspirants) are enrolled in a training program that may run from a year to eighteen months. The course of study provided in this program includes courses and lectures in diplomatic and consular practice; accounting; economic theory and practice, especially as it relates to domestic problems and international trade; constitutional, administrative, and international law; history and practice of Norwegian foreign relations and Norwegian relations with international organizations; and foreign languages. A supervisor is responsible for each of the subject areas, and the Aspirant Committee provides overall supervision. The instructional staff is drawn from the Department, the University, other institutions of higher education, and from business and commerce. The course of study is demanding, and each aspirant is periodically checked to determine whether or not he is making satisfactory progress. After the training period is completed, the aspirants are given both oral and written examinations. The severity of the screening process and the diligence of the aspirants have resulted in an enviable record of accomplishment: No aspirant has failed this examination during the last five years.

After completing the training period, the aspirant enters upon a two-year assignment as an attaché. He may be given a position abroad — this is quite unusual — or he may serve in the Department in Oslo. During this period he may be dismissed without cause. At the close of the two-year term a report on the officer's experience is filed with the Department by his supervisors, and, interestingly enough, this is not confidential, but must be shown to the officer. Whether there is any relationship between this procedure and the fact that practically no one on a probationary appointment has failed to achieve permanent status is not clear. But, as is the case after the training period, people who leave the service after the probationary years do so in almost every case on their own volition.

Within the Department itself (and, as appropriate, in the foreign service) the rank order of positions from lower to higher are: Secretary II, Secretary I, First Secretary, Consultant II, Consultant I, Bureau Chief, and *Ekspedisjonssjef*. Beyond this there is the Consul, Undersecretary, and Minister. Foreign service officers rotate between assignments in the field and the Department in Oslo, but not on a rigid, mandatory scheme. Normally they would not serve longer than five years abroad on any single assignment.

Promotions are based completely on seniority in the lower ranks. Though the responsible leadership positions (bureau chief, ambassador, etc.) are practically always filled from the ranks, the Foreign Minister may, if he wishes, bring in outsiders, but this happens very seldom and never for partisan, political reasons. If he should do this he must be able to demonstrate to his ministerial subordinates, his colleagues in the Cabinet, and to the public generally that no qualified person was available within the Department.

If one can trust subjective evaluations, the Norwegian foreign service (with a total membership of about 200) has a good reputation at home and abroad. Despite the fact that salaries are low,[13] foreign service officers enjoy other compensations in the form of status and prestige. Morale in the service is good, since, though advancement may be slow, it is reasonably certain. Because there are no political appointments at the ambassadorial level, career officers can aspire to the very highest positions.[14]

Evaluation of Norwegian National Administration

It is not easy to assess the work of any set of public administrators since objective criteria are often difficult to apply. It is made more

[13] The net beginning salaries for 1963 were:

Chief of Mission, First class	NK 42,834
Chief of Mission, Second class	35,778
Counsellor of Embassy and Consul	25,698
First Secretary and First Vice-Consul	18,037
Second Secretary	15,552
Attaché	13,358

In addition to salary, foreign service personnel receive housing allowances and sometimes representation and other allowances besides comprehensive social security coverage.

[14] For a brief account of the history and immediate post World War II operation of the Norwegian foreign service, see Reidar Omang, *Utenrikstjenesten* (Oslo, 1954).

difficult in Norway than in certain other countries because study and research in the field of public admiinstration has not as yet been well developed. Only in recent years have some small beginnings been made in this field of inquiry at the University of Oslo and in the School of Business Administration in Bergen. Certain studies have been made in the area of business administration which may prove helpful to the Norwegian students and practitioners of public administration, but there are definite limits to the usefulness of any such comparative analysis. Public administrators have different objectives, different values, than their counterparts in business, and consequently similar sets of criteria do not apply. To state this difference in its simplest form: the business administrator is interested in showing a profit, while the government administrator should be concerned almost solely with providing service.

Perhaps the best method of determining the effectiveness of the public administrator is to analyze the attitudes he invokes in the public and in the press. In the absence of empirical data it seems safe to say that generally the Norwegian citizen is satisfied with his national administrative arrangements. He complains about alleged inefficiency, delays, undue amount of red tape, and the like, but these are complaints that the very best of administrations find inescapable. And in Norway, as in many democratic countries, the complaints are often petty and not well grounded in the facts, and they are often not based upon substantial experience. It seems doubtful that public administrators are really any less efficient or any less alert than are men and women employed in private enterprise.

If Norwegian public administrators come in for more criticism than do their fellow nationals in private business, it may be explained in part by the size and extent of state undertakings in Norway. It is clear that some of the criticisms of public administrators come as a result of the immensity of the job undertaken by the Norwegian state; if nongovernmental organizations were faced with the same wide and burdensome assignment, they might well be subject to the same complaints. Red tape, undue delays, and bureaucratic attitudes are caused more by the size of the enterprise than by its ownership whether in Norway or in any other country.

Most of the complaints thus far referred to, though occasionally irritating, are not really important or fundamental. The thoughtful Norwegian, being aware of the problems facing a civil servant in a democratic society, is not unhappy with the management of his government. Nevertheless, there are certain weaknesses or problems in the system which cause him some concern.

One of these has been referred to before and has been most noticeable during the last five or six years of Labor party government. The problem is concerned with political leadership in general, and for purposes of this discussion it can be put simply: there are too few politicians and too many experts in the top ministerial positions. Of the fourteen men in the present Cabinet, only two or three can be classified as working politicians; the remainder are experts, some of whom have come up through the civil service ranks. To the casual observer this may not seem to be a serious difficulty. But if one recognizes the role and function of the cabinet minister as being, in large measure, political in character it does take on a certain significance. Without question, the minister, as head of his department, must have administrative leadership ability of a high order. But even more important, he must be able to interpret his department to the public and to his colleagues in the Cabinet as well as to translate the mood and needs of the public to his departmental subordinates. He has also an extremely important part as a member of the top planning board of the country — the Cabinet. All these tasks require a kind of political skill which can best be obtained through practical political experience. It may well be that the problem associated with political inexperience in certain cabinet quarters is transitory and will be solved whether or not the Labor party continues its cabinet responsibility. In any event it should be clear that the difficulty is not related to the structure of the government or the program of the Laborites, but rather to the difficulty of obtaining a steady flow of adequate leadership material in any party like the Norwegian Labor party that has been in power a long time. And this is a problem that assuredly is not confined to Norway.

A second problem is more closely related to structure and organization, particularly those aspects related to government personnel. As a matter of fact, there are two problems: one concerning the organization of the personnel services of the national government and the other relating to pre-induction and in-service education and training programs for civil servants. Both are under study at the present time, and certain solutions are being proposed.

It is doubtful that a centralized personnel agency, comparable to the United States Civil Service Commission or the personnel section of the British Treasury, is needed or contemplated in Norway. But a greater degree of overall control would certainly improve procedures and the efficiency of the service. Beginnings in this direction have been made through the establishment of a Directorate for Personnel in the Department of Wages and Prices. Two related questions have been discussed seriously in governmental and academic circles in Norway in the last several years: is the educational background of civil service applicants adequate and what can be done to improve in-service training?

Without doubt, the educational qualifications of applicants, though usually sound, have been limited, since most job specifications have called for preparation principally in two fields — law and economics. A course of study in these two areas will provide admirable backgrounds for lawyers and economists in the public service, but certainly may not guarantee competence or suitability for supervisory responsibilities in administration. There is no necessary relationship between the study of law or economics and the procedure and mechanics of administration. Public administrators require a much broader type of training than can be offered in any fairly restricted discipline.

It was in the hope of improving the educational qualifications of civil servants and the in-service training programs in the departments that a special committee (*oplæringskomite*) was established in March, 1956; it made its report some two years later.[15] The committee was headed by Professor Rolf Waaler, an internationally recognized authority in administration and Rector of the School of Business Administration in Bergen, and composed of outstanding representatives from academic circles, the Department of Finance, and from the several associations of civil servants. The report was submitted to the Storting formally by the newly established (1956) Department of Wages and Prices in February, 1961.[16]

In brief, the committee recommended that a new course of study combining law and administration be established at the University of Oslo and that another combining economics and administration be set up at the School of Business Administration in Bergen. It stopped short of recommending a special school to train national civil servants modeled on the one recently established for communal employees.[17]

Regarding in-service training, the committee insisted that adequate indoctrination in his job should occupy the major share of the newly appointed civil servant's time during the first several weeks after appointment. This should not be hastily or perfunctorily undertaken by underlings in the departments, but rather taken seriously and participated in by top-level supervisors. In addition, the committee proposed a special course of study on the theory and practice of state administration for new inductees in civil service positions with eighty hours devoted to lectures and fifty hours to the preparation of papers and other written assignments. Other proposals for stipends, leaves of absence for study, the improvement of promotion procedures, an increased emphasis on qualifications and less on seniority were made

[15] *Innstilling om oplæringsproblemene i statsforvaltningen av 30 juni, 1958.*

[16] See *Stortingsmelding number 49,* 1960–61.

[17] See p. 178.

by the committee. To supervise both the in-service training program and the preparation of adequate pre-induction education, the committee recommended that a permanent office in the national government be established.

As could be expected, the report was accorded a mixed reception. The Department of Finance and the Department of Wages and Prices approved the proposals rather enthusiastically. Other reactions varied from hostile (Justice and Police, Trade and Shipping) to friendly but cautious (Church and Education, Industry and Crafts, and Social Affairs). Other departments and agencies were uninterested; some felt themselves not directly affected by the proposals. In the years to come the new program will no doubt be pressed forward in the Storting by the advocates in the two key departments, Finance and Wages and Prices. But expectations for early and complete acceptance of the committee's recommendations are not high.

This reluctance to accept change and the fear of innovation and fundamental reorganization are not unique to Norwegian administrators. But perhaps because of the emphasis on individuality, a pride in the standing of established curricula in institutions of higher learning, and confidence in their long-term democratic practices, the Norwegians may be less inclined to accept change than are fellow democrats in other countries. This is not to say that the presence of vested interests and an emphasis on the status quo do not also play a part in opposing change in Norway.[18]

[18] As this was being written a new institution (with old roots) — the *Ombudsmann* — was being established to provide safeguards to individuals who think their rights have been invaded by administrative action or inaction. In the absence of a set of administrative courts, the *Ombudsmann* should play a role of protecting the citizen against the irresponsible bureaucrat. He may serve the Norwegian citizen in somewhat the same manner as the Inspector General serves the American soldier. For background material see: *Instilling fra Komiteen til å utrede spørsmålet om mer betryggende former for den offentlige forvaltning,* 1958 and Odelsting Proposition No. 30 — *Om lov om Stortingets ombudsmann for forvaltningen,* 1960.

7

Political Parties

Historical Introduction

The beginnings of political factionalism were evident in Norwegian politics even before the adoption of the Eidsvold Constitution on May 17, 1814. Although Denmark's rule, especially after 1800, had been severely condemned by a great many Norwegians, there was nonetheless a definite pro-Danish group in Norway which viewed some of the appeals of the nationalists among their fellow citizens as inflammatory and ill-advised. This group practically disappeared after the terms of the Treaty of Kiel (January 14, 1814) became known. The opposition in Norway to the attempted "transfer" of their country from Denmark to Sweden was nearly unanimous, at least at first. But a minority soon became reconciled to the union with Sweden, and by early spring of 1814 it had enlisted the aid of a number of prominent political leaders, among whom were Herman Wedel Jarlsberg, Nicolai Wergeland, Peder Anker, Jacob Aall, Severin Løvenskiold, and Gustav Peter Blom. The members of this group argued that a union with Sweden would be a definite improvement over the ills suffered under Danish domination. But this "pro-Swedish" group was unsuccessful in convincing the majority of the members of the Eidsvold Convention that the Swedish union should be accepted without resistance.

On most other questions before the Eidsvold framers there was virtual unanimity of opinion. The Convention, not unlike the Philadelphia Convention of 1787, was dominated largely by representatives from the upper strata of Norwegian society. But this fact did not cause any serious differences of opinion and, because of the essential democratic nature of the Constitution, no significant rift over the proper sphere of governmental authority persisted after the constitutional debates were concluded. But the relations with Sweden were not so easily settled. Although the pro-Swedish advocates won the initial engagement and succeeded in getting established a peaceable union based securely upon provisions of the new Constitution, the chapter was not closed. In a certain sense the dispute continued to plague Norwegian politics throughout the years and was not settled finally until the union between Norway and Sweden was terminated in 1905.

The beginnings of the present-day Conservative party can be traced to the differences engendered by the union question. The defense of the status quo, including of course the prevailing relationship between Sweden and Norway, by this early conservative group was certainly not unpatriotic or anti-Norwegian. Rather, the men who favored cooperation instead of conflict with Sweden and the Swedish King believed that only through such a course could the best interests of Norway be effectively served.

Opposition to the status quo position of these early conservatives was slow in arising. Though economic conditions in Norway were particularly bad in the years immediately following 1814, there were no leaders on hand to advocate change and adjustment of government programs which might possibly have alleviated the difficulties. Even if new programs had been proposed, it is unlikely that they would have been given any popular support, since the view that government should concern itself with economic problems had not emerged by 1815. To be sure, individual instances of opposition to the established government, which was dominated, administratively at least, by civil servants of high rank (*embedsmenn*), did appear. Even before 1814, while Norway was still ruled from Copenhagen, an incipient farmers' revolt clearly demonstrated dissatisfaction with the dominating position of these high-level civil servants. But this did not lead to the organization of any opposition party. In 1816 a serious attempt by Hans Barlien to organize an agrarian opposition in the Storting met with failure and two years later a similar venture engineered by Teis Lundegaard, who had been a member of the constituent assembly at Eidsvold in 1814, was no more successful.

It was not until 1833 that a really great leader appeared to direct the energies of a growing agrarian political movement. Ole Gabriel Ueland, a vigorous peasant from western Norway, unimposing in appearance but possessed of many capabilities, was a skillful tactician, an eloquent speaker, and an expert parlimentarian. His program was not built upon a well-articulated set of political principles, but rather upon immediate demands for definite policies. It was impossible at this time to secure agreement on any theoretical basis for an agrarian party, but it was not difficult to unite the farmers on specific issues. Increased powers for self-governing communities, opposition to special privileges and monopolistic practices injurious to the farming community, and a reduced state budget were the principal parts of Ueland's platform.

While Ueland was championing the cause of a distressed agriculture, Henrik Wergeland, another great Norwegian, was directing political opposition in other fields and on a much wider front. Wergeland was a poet who sensed the injustice and unfairness inherent in the prevailing system dominated by "foreigners and aristocrats." His father, Nicolai Wergeland, had been one of the signers of the Eidsvold Constitution. The son's early life had been deeply influenced both by his father's political experience and by his own deep-rooted realization that many aspects of Norwegian life were in need of comprehensive readjustment.

Knut Gjerset in his classic *History of the Norwegian People* evaluates in the following words the political opposition and the literary and ideological upheaval that took place in the 1820's and 1840's:

> Long cherished literary views were challenged, and old social ideas were given a rude shock. It was a storm which electrified and cleansed the atmosphere, and stirred the germs of life into new growth. . . .
>
> Wergeland laid no new foundations, but he was the chief architect who reared the cultural structure of Norway on the foundations laid by the Eidsvold men, and continued to work in their spirit. They had adopted the liberal and progressive ideas which had their origin in English political institutions and scientific thought, and which found their full development in the revolutionary struggles of America and France; he made these ideas the living force in the new national development. They made the people supreme in theory; he would make them supreme in practice. They had acted for the people; he taught the people to act for themselves. . . .[1]

Wergeland's political agitation did not long remain unchallenged. Another poet, Johan Sebastian Wellhaven, seized the gauntlet thrown down by Wergeland and a series of poetic and literary duels between the two men followed. To Wergeland's cry that a political, social, and literary revival must soon take place in Norway, Wellhaven responded favorably. But, he argued, this cannot come from the lower strata of society, nor can it with certainty come from within the kingdom itself. It would be far wiser, according to Wellhaven, to depend upon the upper classes and perhaps even on foreign leaders to show the way.

[1] Knut Gjerset, *History of the Norwegian People* (New York, 1915), **II**, 466, 468.

An earnest young university student, Marcus Thrane, followed with interest this conflict between Wergeland and Wellhaven. Thrane was the son of a bank functionary who had misappropriated funds and, as a result, had been reduced to a position of poverty and disgrace. After spending some time abroad, Marcus Thrane returned to Norway and entered the University to study theology, but he did not remain to take a degree. Thrane's great interest was not academic, but practical and political. He had witnessed the operation of the European revolutionary movements of 1848 and, as a result, had become convinced of the need for tight solidarity among and between laborers and farmers. He thought this could be developed only through some kind of socialist society. But Thrane's socialism — unlike that of Marx, which was to follow — was supplemented by an intense agitation for a revival and rebirth of Christian principles. Theoretical speculation did not appeal to Marcus Thrane, though he had read widely and learned a great deal from the experience of people in other countries. He was predominately a leader and political agitator, and it was he who first encouraged the laboring elements in Norwegian society to organize and form an effective opposition to the King and his supporters among the Norwegian *embedsmenn.*

On December 27, 1848, Thrane succeeded in organizing the first Norwegian "laborers' society" in Drammen (*Drammens arbeiderforening*). The movement — not unlike the Knights of Labor in the United States — spread rapidly until by June of 1850 there were 273 such societies with a total membership of 20,854. This phenomenal growth caused the workers to realize their potentialities and the gains that might be made through cooperative efforts to secure more adequate representation of their class in the Storting. Also they began to appreciate that a strong labor organization would greatly improve their pressure group position. But neither of these approaches was employed successfully by labor in the first half of the nineteenth century due in no small part to the fact that many members of laborers' societies were not eligible to vote. To be sure, Johan Sverdrup, the eventual leader in the battle for parliamentarism and liberalism in Norway, was elected to the Storting in 1850, largely by the concentration of votes friendly to labor and small landholders. Other candidates, allied with the agrarianism of Ueland or the intellectual liberalism of Wergeland, were also able to obtain seats in the Storting. But Thrane did not consider the cause of labor secure in the hands of these rather diverse anti-conservative groups and counted his agitation among the voters as definitely unsuccessful.

Labor societies operating as pressure groups were also ineffectual during this period. On May 19, 1850, Thrane presented a petition to the King signed by over 1200 people demanding, among other things, removal of discriminatory qualifications for voting, better educational facilities, and reforms in court procedure. All of the demands were refused by the government. These rebuffs, coupled with dissension within the ranks, as well as the arrest of certain leaders of the movement, caused the socialists of the forties and fifties to join forces with the rather heterogeneous liberal groups opposing conservatism.[2]

The more important of the mid-century liberal groups was the one headed by Johan Sverdrup. Though effective at times, Sverdrup found his "party" disorganized and lacking in discipline. Such a situation was distasteful to a man of Sverdrup's temperament, and he made several attempts to unify and solidify the divergent liberal elements in the Norwegian parliament. As early as November of 1850 Sverdrup proposed that a liberal group be organized in the Storting to promote definite policies: democratization of the administrative and judicial branches of the government, expansion of the suffrage, greater independence in communal affairs, and improvement of the workingman's position. By 1858 Sverdrup had become convinced that not only must the "new" liberalism be supported by an organized group in the Storting, but that real progress could not be made unless the liberals also organized on a country-wide basis. It was with this end in view that he appealed to Ole Ueland, the former leader of the agrarian political revolution in 1833, but neither he nor Sverdrup wanted to take the first step and, as a consequence, no organization was developed in 1858.

In the following year another meeting of members of the Storting favorable to the liberal cause was held. A party name, Reform Society (*Reformforeningen*), was adopted and a political program outlined. The question of group discipline again became one of the obstacles to harmony in the meeting of 1859. Sverdrup was determined that the minority in the party must be bound by the decisions of the majority. Needless to say, his suggestion caused wide divergence of opinion, both in the meeting, in the press, and among the people. But in spite of this and the early failure of the Reform Society, the decade of the sixties saw the ideas germinated in the liberal parliamentary group unite with those of a new country-wide liberal farm group, the Farmer's Friend Society (*Bondevennforening*). This organization was not unlike the Thrane movement of the 1840's. It was a mass move-

[2] The movement led by Thrane was important, not so much for its socialist foundations, but rather because it was the first well-organized mass organization of "little" men in Norway.

ment with no formal connections in the Storting, although it did have as one of its objectives putting pressure on parliament. It grew to a membership of about 20,000 during the late 1860's, but died out in the following decade.

In the years between 1869 and 1884 the liberal movement continued to flourish; it was during this period that many reform measures received their first enactment by the Norwegian parliament. Basic to these policies and others advocated by Sverdrup and his liberals was the demand that the Storting be recognized as the central, final source of authority in the Norwegian government. This idea had been growing steadily, and finally, in 1884, the Liberals (then a political party in the modern sense) were able to force the acceptance of parliamentarism on the King.

The Conservative party remained, after 1884, reasonably well knit, but the Liberals suffered a good deal from internal strife.[3] Even as early as 1887 argument over a church reform bill split the party into two groups: Moderate or National Liberals, and Pure Liberals. By 1903, the Moderate Liberal group had for all practical purposes gone to the camp of the Conservative party. In the same year (1903) another liberal group appeared, headed by Christian Michelson, who was to play a leading role in the break between Norway and Sweden.

The same year (1887) that saw Norwegian liberalism torn by party strife witnessed the birth of another political organization, the Labor party, which since the late 1920's has been the leading party in the kingdom. Organizational activity among Norwegian workers had continued intermittently from the time of Marcus Thrane's agitation in the 1840's down to 1887. After the Thrane movement disappeared philanthropic workmen's associations were established in the 1850's and 1860's. In the 1870's the first group of trade unions was organized, but many of these were weak and short-lived. It was not until well past 1880 that the trade union movement had become firmly established. By the spring of 1887 the demand for building a genuine labor party on a national scale led to a convention held at Arendal.[4] The early leaders of this new labor movement were the socialists, Carl Jeppesen and Christian Holtermann Knudsen. Although a modified socialist program was adopted not many years after the organization meeting at Arendal, it was not until 1903 that the party perfected

[3] Although "Liberal" is not in any sense a translation of the Norwegian party name *Venstre,* it is used in this book because it seems to be more meaningful than "Left," a literal translation of the Norwegian term. The party is not leftist, at least at present; it is more nearly centrist.

[4] The objective of this meeting was not clear-cut. Some delegates favored the organization of a federation of unions; others thought that a single organization could serve both as federation *and* political party.

its organization and program to the point where it could expect any serious support from the voters. By that year the party had a fairly well-defined socialist program which had been developed under the influence of a new leader, Alfred Eriksen, and the party succeeded in electing a five-man delegation to the Storting.[5]

Although three political parties — Conservative, Liberal, and Labor — were operating on a national scale by 1905, the events of that year were not conducive to much internal political conflict. To be sure, some differences of opinion over certain unimportant particulars in connection with the union controversy did exist, but most Norwegians, of whatever party, were united in their opposition to the Swedish position on the consular question.

The years between 1905 and the close of World War I witnessed a steady growth in party activity. The Liberal party again suffered from internal dissension, this time caused by disagreement over the "concession laws," which aimed to prevent foreign capitalists from gaining control of the country's natural resources. Two factions appeared in 1909 as a result of this argument: the Radical Liberal element under the leadership of Gunnar Knudsen favorable to a strict conservation program and the Liberal Leftists (*Frisindede venstre*) who advocated less extreme solutions to the problem.

The period saw also increased activity among the farm classes, leading to a strengthened position for the National Agrarian Society (*Norsk bondelag*), an agricultural organization which had attempted from its beginning in 1896 to influence both parliamentary and administrative decisions affecting agriculture. The growing importance of this Society, coupled with the distressing conditions among Norwegian farmers after World War I, caused the establishment of a new political party, the Agrarian party (*Bondepartiet*), in 1920. Its strength then, as well as later, lay chiefly in the farming sections of the kingdom.

Other interesting political developments transpired in the postwar period. After the Russian Revolution of 1917 the more radical elements of the Labor party demanded an open alliance with the Bolshevik party as a means of advancing the cause of the Norwegian proletariat. Communistic propaganda flooded the country, and many of the leaders among Norwegian Laborites argued for closer relationships with their Russian brethren. Finally, in 1919, the Labor party severed its relations with the old Socialist International at Amsterdam and attached itself to the Communist International in Moscow.

[5] Perhaps the chief reason for lack of support of the Labor party in the early years of its existence may be ascribed to the central role being played by the Liberals in working toward expansion of the suffrage. Naturally,

Needless to say, this action was followed by a serious cleavage in Labor's ranks. The communist faction, for the moment, dominated the Labor party, while the less radical elements seceded and formed the Social Democratic Labor party. By 1921 the split had left twenty-nine parliamentary seats in the hands of the communistically controlled Labor party and eight with the dissenting Social Democrats.

The experience of the Norwegian Labor party with the Moscow alliance was not happy. The Labor party had agreed to many of the earlier requests of the Communist International, but later demands met with serious resistance. For example, many Norwegian Laborites opposed the Russian demand for a complete structural reorganization of their party. The demand that Norwegian communism embrace atheism and the order requiring laborers to affiliate with the Bolshevik Trade International precipitated an open break in the fall of 1923. A large faction, which became the Norwegian Communist party, remained loyal to Moscow. When the Norwegian workers went to the polls in 1924, they found three parties bidding for labor's vote: the Norwegian Labor party, the Communist party, and the Social Democratic Labor party.

By 1927 the Social Democrats had rejoined the parent group. Greatly strengthened by this union, the Labor party was able to increase its membership in the Storting from twenty-four in 1924 to fifty-nine in 1927. At the same time the Communists were fast losing ground. Their representation in parliament was reduced from six in 1924 to three in 1927. Many members of the Communist party had gone over to Labor, and this trend continued until by 1930 the Communist party was unable to elect a single member to the Storting. Since then, except for the four-year period immediately following World War II when the Communist party had eleven seats in the Storting, representation of the party has been confined to one or two.

A definite fascist movement appeared in Norway after World War I as a reaction to the expansion of socialism and communism. Two separate political groups championed the fascistic cause on two different fronts. The Patriotic Society (*Fedrelandslaget*) attempted to advance along lines of established governmental practice and appealed to the so-called liberal elements of the bourgeois. A second organization, the National Union (*Nasjonal Samling*), established in 1933 under the leadership of Vidkun Quisling, advocated abolition of parliamentarism and urged the installation of a government based upon

---

many of the workers, anxious to expand voting rights, gave their support to the Liberals, since their program in the Storting had a good chance of passing. After the establishment of manhood suffrage in 1908, the Labor party, no longer dependent on a Liberal program of enfranchisement, could stand more securely on its own feet.

economic respresentation. This party, though never represented in the Storting prior to the outbreak of war in 1940, was given dubious governmental responsibilities by the Germans during the occupation. Since the close of the last war there has not been any evidence of organized or unorganized fascism in Norway.

The noteworthy developments in Norwegian politics after the war are the following: the increase in support given the Labor party (in 1957 Labor had 78 of the 150 seats in the Storting, but by the election of 1961 this had been reduced to 74); the reinvigoration of the Christian People's party, first organized in 1933, but up to this time without much of a following and only the remnant of a "Christian centrist" type of program; and the decreasing significance of the Communist party.

Party Membership

A sharp distinction should be made between Norwegians who vote a party ticket in a series of elections and regular dues-paying party members. Only a small part (under 20 per cent) of the eligible voters in Norway are continuing, bona fide members of a party, and of the actual voters in any given election, perhaps only about one in four holds membership in the party of his choice.[6] Membership may be individual (the rule in most parties except the Labor party) or collective. Trade unions and other associations join the Labor party en masse, automatically committing to formal affiliation all their members unless some of them have taken steps to exclude themselves.[7] There are about 100,000 members of the Labor party who at present hold membership through their organizations and not as individuals. Membership in all parties is open to anyone willing to declare that he is in accord with the party's principles. Strictest in enforcement of this requirement is, of course, the Communist party, but the Labor party also insists, at least at the time petition for membership is made, that the applicant subscribe to its party principles. Only the Liberal and Christian People's parties have no requirements in their bylaws of commitment to ideology. Within those parties having the requirement, commitment is not always easy to enforce after a person has once joined, but it is doubtful that one would continue long to pay party dues unless he was reasonably sympathetic to the party's objectives. It is possible for a party to expel members who become disloyal to party principles or who for other reasons are no longer considered suitable. In 1961 the national convention of the Labor party sustained

[6] These figures and certain other facts in this section are taken from a study undertaken by Henry Valen which will be published soon.

[7] It should be noted that in Norway the local trade union affiliates with the party and not the national union, as is the case in the United Kingdom.

the expulsion by the national committee of certain party members who had become active in the *Orientering* movement which had been working contrary to accepted party principles by advocating defense and international programs completely in opposition to those being pursued by the Labor government.

Each party can count on substantial support from nonmembers who have identified themselves with the party. In a recent survey undertaken by Mr. Henry Valen it was discovered that about two-thirds of the Norwegian voters considered themselves definitely affiliated with a given party for election purposes, if not through hard and fast membership. About one-fourth replied that they were independents, and the remainder either were politically indifferent or failed to respond to the question. It seems obvious from election results that the Labor party has the greatest number of reliable nonmember supporters.

Each of the parties levies annual dues on members in varying amounts from a low of NK 2 to NK 15. The Communist party apparently counts on gifts in addition to dues because it reports that annual per capita contributions by members vary from NK 12 to NK 60 annually. From 10 per cent (Communist) to 100 per cent (Conservative) of the membership dues remain in the treasury of the local unit; the remainder is divided between district and national treasuries.

Other sources of income are obviously essential, but the parties generally consider annual dues extremely important, not only for morale reasons, but also for their financial well-being. This is particularly true of the smaller parties, e.g., the Center (formerly the Agrarian party) and Christian People's parties. Nonetheless, contributions from individuals, from organizations and, lately, from political auxiliaries make up the largest part of the parties' income. There has been no official report on party finances since 1950, and the figures for that year are no doubt very much out of date. On the basis of these figures, party dues account for about 80 per cent of the total income of the Communist party, 70 per cent for the Liberal party, 50 per cent for the Conservative party, 65 per cent for Center, 50 per cent for Christian People's, and 37 per cent for Labor. The Labor party and the Conservative party have considerably larger budgets than the other parties and are most successful in securing large contributions; the former from its associated trade unions and the latter from businessmen and industrialists.

Party Organization

Viewed geographically, the primary unit in all of the Norwegian parties is the party society (*partilaget*) made up of all members in a given locality. In cities and in large rural communes these primary units are often joined together in a communal organization which is governed by a committee or board elected by the several party societies. Only in the Communist party is the local society broken down into smaller subdivisions (cells). The membership in the primary political unit in all parties is usually small, and consequently many of its decisions can be made in meetings of the entire membership. To care for details which come up between meetings a small committee is elected by the group.

Each of the local societies and communal groups are joined together in a county-wide (*fylke*) representative assembly. Since the twenty counties serve not only as governmental units, but also as parliamentary election districts, the party machine in these areas is largely responsible for making parliamentary nominations and for conducting the campaign that follows. Since the party representative assembly in the county meets usually only once a year, most of the day-to-day matters are handled by a county (election district) party committee chosen by the assembly.

The highest governing organ in Norwegian political parties is the national convention held by each party at varying intervals. The Liberals have an annual convention; Labor, the Center party, and the Christian People's party meet biennially, as does the Conservative party, but the latter holds an additional national convention in the years immediately following national elections; and the Communist party convention meets every fourth year. All of the major party conventions meet in March or April some six months before the parliamentary election.

The delegates to the national convention are chosen by the representative assemblies in the counties in accord with varying formulae which take into consideration membership, the number of votes cast for the party in the last election, and the number of representatives in parliament last elected by the party from the district. In addition to these regular delegates, certain other people have seats in the convention, with or without voting rights. All of the parties include as special convention members their representatives in the Storting, either the entire group or a selected number of representatives. In the Labor party convention the parliamentary delegation is represented by one-tenth of its membership, but in addition members of the national committee, party members who hold cabinet posts, representatives from affiliated groups, such as youth organizations, women's organizations, and trade unions, and other specially invited guests are regularly included.[8] In the bourgeois party conventions, the party press is usually

[8] Most of these special delegates to the Labor party convention do not have the right to vote.

singled out for representation, but in the Labor party and the Communist party no special representative status is given to the party press.[9] The parties vary in their evaluation of the need for representation of affiliated groups. The parties also vary in the privileges given to delegates not regularly elected; in all parties these delegates have the right to debate and in most parties the right to propose resolutions and motions. In the Conservative, Center, and Christian People's parties they also have a limited right to vote.

The most important task facing any national convention is preparing the party program. Past, pending, and future problems facing the national government are discussed and party positions are agreed upon. Usually a draft program has been prepared in advance by the national committee and this has been discussed in the county assemblies and often in the local societies. Thus the delegate comes to the convention with some background and sometimes with proposals for alterations, additions, or deletions. Generally, these suggestions, if out of harmony with the views of the national committee, are not approved or, if approved, much watered down by the convention. This is not to say that the debate on the program in the convention is not serious and often protracted since the delegates take the matter of program writing very seriously. They not only hope to win votes as a result of the appeal made by the several parts of the program, but they are also prepared to implement them if the party is given a mandate from the people. In this respect, the Norwegian party program is a more serious document of commitment than is the party platform in the United States. Perhaps the best reason for this difference can be found in the homogeneity within each of the Norwegian parties and in the vigor with which the press, the significant part of which is partisan, criticizes deviations from agreed-upon party policy.

The extent to which the party program, particularly in detail, affects the outcome of elections is as hard to measure in Norway as it is in most other democratic countries. It can be assumed that the Norwegian citizen casts his vote for the party which most closely represents his interests and, except for persons who are unusually concerned with specific issues, details of the program are often not given careful scrutiny. Significant exceptions to this generalization can be noted. In 1949, the issue of Norway's adherence to NATO perhaps alone caused the Communists to lose their eleven seats in the Storting and to suffer a 40 per cent reduction in popular vote. On the other hand, campaigning in 1961 on two planks in their platform thought to

[9] This can be explained by the fact that the Labor party and the Communist party own outright the two chief party organs: *Arbeiderbladet* and *Friheten,* while the bourgeois organs are usually owned and operated by individuals or corporations.

be "popular" — prohibition of nuclear weapons on Norwegian soil and a greatly extended old age pension system — the Liberals did little better than hold their own.

Besides preparing the party program, the convention has two other important functions: selecting the national party leaders and settling any internal problems affecting the organization, discipline, or general welfare of the party. All changes in the bylaws and rules of procedure must be made by the national convention. Occasionally, in the parties which have reasonably tight disciplinary control over their members, such as the Labor party and Communist party, the convention is called upon to take disciplinary action. This, it will be recalled from a previous discussion, was done by the Labor party convention of 1961, when it sustained the dismissal of certain nonconforming members of the party. In each of the parties the convention selects a representative national committee varying in size from seventeen to fifty which meets at infrequent intervals (Center party once a year, Labor party at least twice a year, Conservative party two or three times a year, Christian People's party five times a year, and Liberal party eight times a year). This committee has final responsibility for implementing the party program, making decisions for change of program if made necessary by changed situations, providing aid to district committees during political campaigns, and supervising the general and financial administration of the party's affairs. In the Labor party, the Liberal party, and the Christian People's party the national convention selects all members of the national committee; in the other parties some are elected by the convention and the remainder, usually including the country chairmen, serve in an ex officio capacity. A smaller executive committee which meets frequently — three times a month on the average — is also selected by the convention. This committee prepares matters for the national convention and the national committee and assumes the day-to-day job of executing and supervising party affairs.[10]

One of the key figures in the Norwegian political system is the national party chairman. He is elected along with a vice-chairman by the national convention for terms varying in length with the parties from two to four years. With few exceptions the party chairman presides over both the national committee and the executive committee. Often, if he is a member of the Storting, he also serves as the party's parliamentary leader. This has been the practice in the Liberal, Labor,

[10] In the Labor party all thirteen members of the executive committee are elected by the national convention. In the Conservative party, six members of the executive committee are chosen by the national committee (*landsstyret*) and in addition, representatives from the party youth movement, woman's organization, press, and the Chairman of the Committee on Finance sit on the executive committee. Selection in other parties vary somewhat from these models.

Center, and Communist parties in the last several years. At the present time (1963) the national chairman of the Labor party, Einar Gerhardsen, serves as Prime Minister, and the leader of the party's parliamentary group is Nils Hønsvald.

The role of the national party chairman, joined as it often has been in recent years with leadership responsibilities in the parliament, is an important one in Norwegian political affairs. As a rule, tenure in this office has been long and the power and the responsibility associated with it large enough to attract really able men to the job. The roster of men who have served as party chairmen includes such distinguished names as Gunnar Knudsen, Johan Mowinckel, and C. J. Hambro. Uniting leadership positions in party and parliament has been fortunate in that it has made easy the communication between the party's parliamentary group and its national committee whether the party has been responsible for the government or in opposition.

The general secretary, the head of the administrative office of the party, is chosen by the national committee in all parties except Labor and Communist. In the Labor party he is chosen by the national convention and in the Communist party by the executive committee. Of all of the general secretaries the one in the Communist party is perhaps most powerful. In the other parties the power of the general secretary over party affairs varies with the stipulations in the bylaws, the extent to which committee members take active roles, and the background and status of the incumbent in the secretariat. Not unlike similar officers in other countries, both in politics and in other fields, the Norwegian party general secretary can usually find within his sphere of authority sufficient power and responsibility to build for himself a position of commanding significance. He is responsible for the budget, the propaganda and information services; has charge of planning the agenda for meetings, preparing documentation and proposals; and communicates with the several party groups in the communes and the election districts. There is obviously some danger because of the nature of this position that a degree of overcentralization, bureaucracy, and even autocracy will develop. But, perhaps because of the smallness of the country, the genuine interest of most members of party committees, and the scrutiny of the opposition press, this danger has not grown great in Norway. It is true that there is evident among some of the voters an apathy that could give rise, if not to domination by the general secretary, at least to overcentralization in the party mechanism generally. But this type of threat to democratic politics is unquestionably not confined to Norway.

The national party headquarters in Norway are modest indeed when compared to those in Great Britain and the United States. The Conservative party has the largest staff at present and the Christian People's party the smallest; the average number of full-time employees in a headquarters office is nine.

Party Activities: National and Local

Political parties in Norway, as in all democratic countries, are engaged in the following activities: (a) preparation of the party programs, (b) nomination of candidates and campaign activities, (c) education of the electorate on issues and proposed solutions of pending problems, (d) installation of their programs if elected to power, and (e) criticism of the other parties. Since some consideration has been given above to the framing of party program, no elaboration of this activity will be undertaken in this connection.

As has been indicated in Chapter 4, nominations for parliamentary positions take place at a meeting in the election district, *fylke* (the county). Though the extent of supervision by central party authorities varies, the district meeting is usually left fairly free to choose the candidates it wishes. Most of the party central offices insist on being kept informed, but would interpose a veto only if a proposed nominee were suspected of party disloyalty or possessed of other disabling qualifications not known to the district meeting. But the district organization generally has sufficient power over the nominating process to enable it to oppose any excessive domination by the central organization. Occasionally, the nature of the nominating process also gives the member of parliament who is strong in his district a degree of independence from certain kinds of party discipline, since he owes his nomination not to the central authorities, but to the party members in his district. But it should be underscored that, for obvious reasons, this is a weapon that the actual or potential member of parliament would seldom be inclined to use.

Besides naming candidates for the Storting, the parties also nominate candidates for the elective positions in the communes. Before the last war the national parties evidenced less active interest in communal elections than they have in the last fifteen years. At present, most of the parties nominate separate lists for most of the communal elections. Labor has perhaps been most active in local elections and nominates separate lists in about 90 per cent of the communes. Only the Center party, which was and still is a class interest party (agrarian) and consequently does not operate in all districts, deliberately fails to enter many local electoral contests. The parties have found in recent years that they must keep the local party societies strong and occupied between national elections if they are not to become ineffective. Consequently, in spite of the fact that most of the significant political decisions are made in the national Storting, serious attempts have been made by each of the parties to capture control of the communal councils, perhaps as much to stimulate party activity as to carry out a party program at the local level.

To attract interest in its program and support for its candidates the party carries on educational and propaganda activities at all geographic levels. Usually local committees have responsibility for this in the communes or the counties and their work is supplemented by the central office, which prepares party literature, guides, and study manuals; provides speakers; and gives advice to the local organizations. The best developed central information services are to be found in the Conservative and Labor parties, perhaps for the obvious reason that these two parties seem to have the most money to spend.

Since 1945, and in a certain sense since 1935, only the Labor party has had the satisfaction of implementing its party program through parliamentary action. The other parties have had to be content with forcing minor amendments and serving as critics of the Labor Government. Unlike the situation in Great Britain where the opposition in parliament is united, the function of criticism in Norway is divided and consequently is not as strong as it might otherwise be. Cooperation between the bourgeois parties in criticism is informal and sometimes disorganized. But it is supported by an active opposition press which brings to light, in one way or another, the more serious mistakes of the government. Though it seems impossible to build a bourgeois coalition for the positive purpose of opposing Labor in parliamentary elections, it is not quite as difficult to get agreement to take a united negative position respecting a parliamentary proposal of the Labor Government.

The Party Press

There are eighty daily newspapers in Norway with a net circulation of 1,300,000. In addition, there are 117 weeklies and biweeklies which have a circulation of 400,000. In a country of about three and a half million people this would provide one newspaper for every other person in the population. Oslo, with less than a half million people, has ten daily newspapers.[11] Perhaps few newspapers in any part of the world are *really* nonpartisan, but Norwegian papers are, as a rule,

[11] *Aftenposten* (Conservative), *Dagbladet* (Liberal), *Morgenbladet* (Conservative), *Verdens Gang* (has been Independent, now leaning Conservative), *Morgenposten* (Conservative), *Nationen* (Center), *Vårt Land* (Christian People's), *Handels og Sjøfarts Tidende* (Independent Conservative), *Arbeiderbladet* (Labor), *Friheten* (Communist).

avowedly partisan. To be sure some may call themselves "Independent Conservative," but it requires no close reading to discover the bias to be much more conservative than independent.

Newspapers for the most part are owned by individuals or by families (*Aftenposten*) and corporations (*Dagbladet* and most of the rest of the Oslo press). The Labor party and the Communist party own their own Oslo newspapers. Both of these, Labor's *Arbeiderbladet* and the Communist *Friheten,* are finally controlled, as are other party activities, by the respective national conventions.

The entire Norwegian press carries on rather constant partisan activity and this is not confined to election years. Conservative and Liberal dailies (particularly *Dagbladet*) have not been slow at any time to point out the mistakes of the Labor Government. And *Arbeiderbladet* and the other Norwegian Labor papers have always been ready to provide defense and explanations. There is a fairly constant political bicker going on in the Norwegian press and sometimes the issues involved may be quite inconsequential. This tendency to bicker and the fact that no newspaper is really independent makes it difficult for the neutral observer to obtain completely objective information.

One can with justice raise serious questions concerning the importance of newspapers — whether in Norway or elsewhere — in shaping political opinion. It is generally agreed that Norwegian readers choose the paper that best fits their political views, and they seldom read the paper which supports their political opponents. This situation, not uncommon in other countries, would lead one to query the real political effectiveness of the papers.[12] Though the press may have little effect on the mill-run voter, does it not exercise significant influence on the opinion leader, who in turn may influence the average citizen? This is the hypothesis, as yet unproved, advanced by certain contemporary social scientists in Norway and the United States.[13]

Pressure Groups

Norway, being a small homogeneous country, has few pressure groups in the American sense of the term. And the pressures they do exert are more often on the party than on the policy-makers and the public administrators. It is the party that usually takes responsibility for promoting the projects supported by the pressure groups falling within their respective areas. For example, the trade unions need not

[12] It will be recalled that Franklin D. Roosevelt won the presidency in the United States four times with about 75 per cent of the press opposing him most of the time.

[13] See Henry Valen, *Partienes organisasjon,* Mimeographed (Oslo, 1960).

maintain a lobby in the Storting; the Labor party promotes labor's interests in parliament, and as required, in administrative circles. The farmers also have been represented in the Storting since the 1920's by their own class interest party (Center, formerly Agrarian, party). The position of large and small businessmen and industrialists is not as clear-cut as that of labor and agriculture; the Conservative party represents business in most respects and the Liberals have been active, at least in the past, in promoting certain segments of the Norwegian economy, notably shipping and, to some extent, fishing. Often certain groups have felt themselves inadequately represented by one or more of the regular parties and have set up parties of their own. Norwegian fishermen have done this on occasion. Professional associations such as medical, dental, and legal societies seem more concerned with internal problems of their profession and less with the promotion of friendly legislation than is true in many other countries, especially in the United States. But these groups do make their contributions in the shaping of public policy by providing expert advice and suggestions. It is not impossible that in undertaking this function, the representatives of the group also try to make certain that the position of members of their craft are protected economically. But the chief emphasis seems to be not so much on selfish interests as on the more general problems affecting all the people which are of particular concern to the group in question. The political activity of these professional associations is confined largely within the parties; their representatives would not think of making a political appeal to the parliament and people at large. And without question, whatever politics they may pursue, it does not begin to compare with the intense political activities of, for example, the American Medical Association or the American Bar Association.

It should not be assumed from what has been said that the Norwegian pressure groups are nonpolitical and have no interest in improving their positions through political activity. They not only work through the parties, but often exert indirect pressure through the press and from the public forums. Though these are the chief modes of attack, more direct tactics are also employed. For example, in the immediate postwar period it was not unheard of for businessmen and industrialists, obviously not members of the Labor party, to secure from the Labor Government certain concessions, particularly in the allocation of scarce materials. The complaint often made by young men who were trying to get established in business at that time was that the large, well-established enterprises were able, through the use of influence and persuasion, to secure concessions not available to all. Though this policy of the government no doubt made sense economically, it is cited here to show that even in a country where pressure group activity is not blatant it does nevertheless operate, albeit on a smaller scale and with less intensity than in a larger country like the United States.

Party Programs

It is obvious that in a multiple party system, such as that found in Norway, each of the parties can be more homogeneous and can have a more secure and consistent foundation of principle and philosophy than is possible in a two-party system. One would expect to observe, and in fact one does observe, significant differences in principle between *each* of the seven or eight parties now operating in Norway. But in some respects the differences between the parties are not as great as one would expect, and the Norwegian system has, from a basic philosophical point of view, some of the earmarks of a two-party arrangement. The fact is that the real difference in principle exists between the three (or four if one counts the small Social Democratic party) parties who espouse a greater or lesser degree of socialism on the one hand (Communist, Labor, and the Socialist People's parties) and the nonsocialist or bourgeois parties (Conservative, Liberal, Center, and Christian People's parties) on the other. Certainly it is between these two groupings — socialist and nonsocialist — that the really significant difference of principle lies. But the influence of history, tradition, and the memory of past political conflicts, coupled with genuine disagreement on certain immediate aspects of public policy, keep alive some real, and many fancied, cleavages between the nonsocialist parties as well.

Labor Party

The Labor party has since 1927 been the strongest party in Norway.[14] From 1935 to 1945 Labor was responsible, with the support of the Agrarian party, for the government, and from 1945 to 1961, with an absolute majority in the Storting, it was solely responsible for creating and maintaining Cabinets. Though the election of 1961 eliminated the clear majority of the Labor party, it continues in power by virtue of having 74 of the 150 seats in the Storting.

The party's foundations are socialistic; it adheres to the principles of the Second Socialist International. It will be recalled that in the early 1920's it was for a brief time affiliated with the Third International in Moscow, but in the last thirty years it has become a moderate socialist party similar in many respects to the British Labor party. It

[14] See pp. 120–125 for a brief sketch of the party's history.

should be unnecessary to enumerate socialist principles in this connection but, suffice it to say, that in the years before and after it came to power the Norwegian Labor party advocated the public ownership of the essential means of transportation, production, and communication, in addition to educational, recreational, and certain cultural facilities. On paper its program has never deviated from these socialist objectives. But a long period of political responsibility has had the effect of forcing some compromise, if not with the objectives, at least with the timing of their implementation. Because of this, the critics, especially on the extreme left, are now saying that the Labor party is no longer active, not to say militant, in its prosecution of socialist aims. This criticism has resulted in some minor disaffection in the party from time to time and also has led to the establishment of more orthodox socialist parties. In 1957 the Social Democrats entered the parliamentary campaign; in 1961 the Socialist People's party — which not only advocated increased socialization, but demanded a revision of current Norwegian foreign policy — also ran candidates.

The most significant general objectives in the 1961 platform of the Labor party were the following: (1) continued planning to insure full employment, adequate economic growth, and just distribution of income and wealth among classes in society; (2) significant expansion of facilities for education and research; (3) increased resources to be made available for expansion of transportation (especially roads) and communication facilities; (4) planned industrial development for the more economically insecure sections of the country; (5) new policies to improve the position of older people in the society; (6) significantly increased aid of several kinds to the underdeveloped areas of the world with the eventual total goal for this aid to be one per cent of the gross national product;[15] and (7) complete support of the United Nations, North Atlantic Treaty Organization, disarmament, abandonment of nuclear testing, economic cooperation in Europe, and the Atlantic community.

The Conservative Party

The Conservative party is the oldest of the present-day Norwegian parties.[16] It has a tradition and a set of principles not unlike the Conservative party in Great Britain. It has rather generally supported the status quo, the interests of the so-called "established" class, economic as well as political, and has viewed with skepticism innovations and the expansion of certain aspects of the state-supported social security pro-

[15] All parties stressed aid to underdeveloped countries in 1961 and direct reference was also made by the Liberals to the one per cent quota.
[16] See pp. 117 ff.

grams. Like conservatives in other countries, it has supported the well-born and aristocratic classes and has been prepared to use the state to protect commerce and industry through trade restrictions, subsidies, and high tariffs. It had reservations, at least in the nineteenth century, on expanding democracy, and though now agreeable to wide suffrage and broad political participation, it still has doubts concerning the wisdom and efficacy of unlimited mass democracy. It has generally been on the side of the State Church in the few instances when controversy between this institution and dissident groups became significant.

Though dubious at first concerning the wisdom of a broad social security coverage, the party now accepts this without serious reservation. In this respect, and perhaps in many others, the Conservative and the Laborite differ not so much in principle as in attitude and particularly in method. The Conservative would expand the social security program, if at all, certainly at a much slower pace than would the Laborite. In fact, he would be more cautious in almost every respect, but particularly in increasing the services now provided the individual by the state. His critics say, justifiably or not, that he shows no similar caution when the question of aiding big business is under consideration. He certainly is honest in the conviction that the individual must stand or fall on his abilities, ambition, foresight, etc.

The program of the Conservative party for the period 1961–65 contains the following proposals: (1) in international affairs: support the United Nations, work to unite the European Free Trade Association with the European Economic Community, even if this may result in closer political association with other European countries, aid underdeveloped countries, support NATO and Norwegian defenses (use of atomic weapons to be decided by the government and Storting); (2) in domestic economic affairs: encourage capital accumulation through savings which would be possible by revising tax laws, no manipulation of discount or interest rates, encourage private investment, protect private property against expropriation and other types of state intervention, insist that state sell its interest in quasi-public economic enterprises, simplify the entire tax structure, eliminate government controls, etc.; (3) in social security: increase old age pensions, expand hospitals and other similar facilities, decentralize administration of the social security programs; (4) culturally: expand education at all levels, inaugurate a second radio program (there is now only one) and expand television programming, improve all cultural and recreational facilities; (5) governmentally: protect commune against state encroachment, encourage Storting to reassert its power against Cabinet; and (6) give aid and support to all sectors of the economy: fishing, agriculture, transportation, etc.

The Liberal Party

Before World War I the two dominant parties in Norway were the Conservative and the Liberal. While the Conservatives supported the status quo, the Liberals agitated for change and innovation, not solely through state intervention, in the early stages at least, but through an emphasis on freeing the individual from all restraints whether imposed by government or by the ruling economic classes. The Norwegian Liberal believed (and still believes) in the dignity and rights of man, and he has always had an optimistic view concerning the possibilities of man's perfectability. To achieve his destiny man must be free; the state should support no class against any other class, but should only provide essential protection to all. Trade should be unrestricted and commerce unfettered, and to achieve these ends democratic government, a broad electorate, and responsible parties are first essentials. With these objectives in mind the Norwegian Liberals fought successfully for the principle of parliamentary responsibility which was established in 1884 through the efforts of the party under the able leadership of one of Norway's outstanding statesmen, Johan Sverdrup.

Modern Liberalism has been under fire in recent years and like their associates in other parts of the democratic world, Norwegian Liberals have had difficulties adapting certain elements of their nineteenth-century philosophy to the changed economic and social conditions of the 1950's and 1960's. Along with the high priest of early liberalism, John Stuart Mill, Liberals in Norway as well as those in certain other countries changed their views on state intervention and came to accept social security programs and other forms of amelioration calculated to improve the lot of the individual. Before the Labor party espoused these programs in the 1930's, the Liberal party had made important beginnings with old age pensions, protection of seamen, etc. As a result of these changes, though the party still stands today as the champion of individualism, it accepts state authority as the best method of ensuring freedom for the individual. In doing this the Norwegian Liberal party is faced with some of the same problems confronting similar groups, notably the British Liberals. It is caught between the socialists with whom they agree on many objectives, if not on means, and the conservatives who have taken over some of the zeal for individual liberty which was previously the exclusive stock in trade of all liberals. Notwithstanding this, the Norwegian Liberals continue to support a maximum freedom, although certainly of a different kind from that favored by their predecessors in the nineteenth century.

The Liberal party was always strong in Western Norway among farmers, fishermen, small businessmen, and certain shipping interests, but some of this strength was lost in the twenties and thirties both to

Labor and to the Center (then Agrarian) party. There is now a noticeable cleavage in the Liberal party between the rural districts in Western Norway and the cities, particularly Oslo. The party in Western Norway has had a kind of religious orientation and has, for example, generally favored the curtailment of the sale and use of alcoholic beverages. The urban element in the party has put less emphasis on religion and has generally disagreed with their party colleagues in the west on the temperance issue. At the moment, although there are no immediate issues involving religion or control of the liquor traffic, the difference between the two wings of the party remains. Perhaps the very nature of the liberal assumption, based as it is on individualism, is the cause of some of the differences of opinion to be found in the Liberal party.

The main elements in the Liberal position can be found summarized in the party program for 1961 in the following statement:

> 1. The condition for all progress is satisfactory economic development and full employment in our country. The sixties will offer large problems through expansion of markets, reorganization of domestic economic life and through the use we make of our economic possibilities. The new situation promises much. It will be important to secure our welfare and promote economic growth.
>
> 2. Our democracy has created good conditions for many groups in society, but not for all. Welfare programs must be made available to those groups not now sharing in this development. It will be important to obtain like conditions for all.
>
> 3. Our society is only a small part of western civilization, which in turn is only a small part of the world. One of our important tasks is to work for economic and political progress in those parts of the world where people meet hunger and need daily and where political rights are yet unknown. This task must carry with it the abolition of colonialism. We must recognize our responsibility and accept our share of the economic obligations involved. It will be important to secure freedom and welfare for all people.
>
> 4. Our fourth objective points to new forms of freedom. The rights of individuals are established and the foundations for economic and social rights are laid. Therefore [it is now important that] education and cultural problems be given a much greater consideration than ever before.[17]

The Center Party

The Center party since it was started in 1920 (then called Agrarian party) has been a distinctly class-interest party with little or no follow-

[17] *Fremgang i frihet, Arbeidsprogram for venstre, 1961–65* (Oslo, 1961), p. 2.

ing except in agricultural districts. Only in the last two or three years has it made serious attempts to enlarge its scope and expand its appeal. To date it seems not to have made significant progress in widening its base, although the experience with the new approach has not been long enough to predict future results.

One significant difficulty faced by the party is the lack of a really distinctive political philosophy. It shares many principles with the Conservatives and in some respects, especially in its attitude towards the rights and obligations of individuals, it has a certain kinship to the Liberals. The emphasis placed in rural areas on religion and temperance makes difficult any serious divergence on these matters between all of the nonsocialist parties, particularly in their direct appeals to the so-called "farm" vote.

Disregarding immediate political appeals and the program similarities and turning to an examination of the essential philosophy underlying the program of the Center party, one finds this to be a kind of agrarian conservatism. Like farmers the world over, the Norwegian farmer has normally been prepared to leave things as they are except when faced with great economic strains, occasioned usually by depressed prices. Under such circumstances farmers have a tendency to become radical, sometimes violently so. When conditions are favorable and prices are good they generally favor the status quo and individualistic efforts, but when conditions are unfavorable they champion government intervention and cooperative enterprises. This has been the experience of the Norwegian farmer. He has at times opposed state intervention and state control not only in economic affairs but in other areas as well, while at other times he has gladly accepted the paternalism and support of the state.

A hasty summary of the central core of the philosophy — such as it is — of the Center party could be put as follows: It has been generally conservative on economic, social, and religious matters, but it has been radical in the demands on the state when agriculture has been in a depressed condition. With this kind of background, which has given the party no really independent position in relation to the other bourgeois parties, it seems doubtful that the Center party can rid itself in the near future of its class interest character. It has served too many years as a kind of pressure group for agriculture to have much of a chance to win votes from the other bourgeois parties or from Labor on anything like a national scale. But, nonetheless, serious steps are being taken to generalize its appeal and certain items in its 1961 program show evidence of this change. The present platform insists that the state should be so organized as to best serve the individual citizen; full employment should be accompanied by an equitable distribution to all classes; as far as possible the administration of social services should be decentralized; Norway should have strong defense establishments and should cooperate fully with her allies in NATO; the United Nations, disarmament, and aid to underdeveloped countries should be adequately supported; provision should be made for popular referenda on certain questions; all parts of the educational system should be expanded and improved; grants under the old age pension should be increased and the various pension schemes coordinated; transportation facilities, especially roads, should be improved, and private contractors given real opportunities to obtain contracts; the cost of living index should be revised; foreign capital should not be given preferential position and, where possible, new industry should be in private hands and not owned and administered by the state. In addition to these general objectives, the party program contains special provisions for the support of agriculture, forestry, and fishing.

The Christian People's Party

This party was organized in 1933. There seems to be some difference of opinion as to why it was started, but, in spite of the fact that there may have been some strictly personal causes built upon the frustration of one or two of its leaders, it has developed into a right-wing group which actively fosters and protects a conservative religious position, theological as well as social. The party has no unique political philosophy beyond what might be called Christian conservatism. It has its chief support in rural areas, particularly in Western Norway where it has been quite successful. In 1957 it ranked third (after Labor and Conservative) among the parties in popular vote, although, because its strength was concentrated in limited geographic areas, it obtained only twelve seats in the Storting, while the Liberal and Center parties with smaller popular votes were each able to elect fifteen members of parliament.

Some excerpts from the introduction to the party program of 1961 will give an indication of the principles supported and the direction pursued by the party.

> The times are uncertain and tense. . . . It seems clear more than ever before that the only chance people have for peace is to build their society and their international relations on the fundamental ideas of Christian belief and morals. If God is not allowed to guide people, what forces will then be used? . . . This — help to underdeveloped countries — is a great challenge to all Christendom and also to our country . . . From our view of life, the expansion of schools is a central political problem. . . . [It should] be a Christian

school and religious instruction should have a central position . . . Economically, the situation in the future will be marked by new and increased cooperation in Europe. . . . Norway's membership in E.F.T.A. opens new perspectives and makes new demands not only for cooperation but also competition. [The party will continue] to work so as to allow Christianity, with its life-giving power, to influence our people.[18]

The Communist Party

When the Labor party broke away from the Communist International in 1923 a certain segment of it refused to withdraw and thus was born the present Norwegian Communist party. It adopted an orthodox program and remains to this day closely affiliated with the Communist parties in the rest of the world. Never large — it achieved its highest vote in 1945 (176,535 — 11.9 per cent of the total) when eleven Communists were elected to the Storting — and never really militant, the party has been considered no real threat to orderly democratic processes in Norway. It has followed not only the orthodox Communist party line, but has defended without reservation Soviet foreign policy before and after World War II. This defense has not always been easy, particularly during the Soviet-Finnish War in 1939 and during the Hungarian Revolution in 1956. Less difficult for the Norwegian Communists was its role of opposition to Norwegian membership in the North Atlantic Treaty Organization in 1949. At the present time the party conducts a quiet campaign advocating complete socialism and a more aggressive fight against NATO, atomic weapons for Norway, and economic cooperation in Western Europe.

The Socialist People's Party

The Socialist People's party is a left-wing socialist party organized in the spring of 1961. This is the second attempt made by dissident socialists since 1945 to break away formally from the Labor party. In 1957 a Social Democratic party was organized, but it made a disastrous showing in the election of that year (2,855 votes, 0.16 per cent of the total). The present dissident group seems better organized and is making serious efforts to be recognized as a going political concern and not merely as an angry socialist minority.

The philosophy and the specific program of the party is simple and easily understood. It calls for a reinvigorated socialism and a neutralistic foreign policy for Norway. It argues, with some justification perhaps, that the Labor party is no longer socialistic and demands increased socialization all along the line, beginning with banks and in-

[18] *4 år med Kristelig Folkeparti* (Oslo, 1961), p. 2–3.

surance companies. Like the left-wing socialists in Great Britain, it advocates in uncompromising terms not only complete socialization of the whole economy but a much expanded public welfare program.

In foreign policy the immediate objective of the party is to make certain that no atomic weapons are stationed in Norway. For the long run it advocates Norwegian withdrawal from NATO and the return to the neutralism practiced prior to the German invasion in 1940. The party would not only disassociate Norway from Europe politically and militarily, but also protest against any proposal which might bring Norway into closer economic alliance with the rest of Europe, particularly through membership in the Common Market.

Though generally not conceded much chance for success in the parliamentary election held in September of 1961, the party upset the calculations of the pundits by winning two seats in the Storting. Though this was not a triumphant victory for intensified socialism and a neutralistic foreign policy, it did give the Labor party cause for concern. And the victory of the Socialist People's party caused the Laborites to lose their clear majority in the Storting.

8

The Courts

The judicial system in Norway is organized with much the same structure as in other democratic countries. Ordinary criminal and civil matters are adjudicated by the regular courts, and impeachment cases are tried before the special High Court of the Realm (*Riksretten*). Questions that are distinctly technical in nature, such as disputes over eligibility for pensions, are settled by administrative boards and committees acting in quasi-judicial capacities.

The hierarchy of ordinary courts is at present arranged as follows:

1. Supreme Court of Justice (*Høiesterett*)
2. Courts of Civil and Criminal Appeals (*Lagmannsrettene*)
3. Local Courts (*Herredsrettene og byrettene*)
4. Conciliation Councils (*Forliksrådene*)

Organization of the Judiciary

Conciliation Councils

Each organized municipality (city, town, or rural governmental area) has a conciliation council composed of three members elected for four-year terms by the communal council (*kommunestyret*). All residents of the community that have attained the age of twenty-five, except the chief executive (*fylkesmann*) of the county (*fylke*), officers employed in the indictment office of the Department of Justice and Police, and practicing attorneys, are required to serve as members of the conciliation council if so designated by the communal council. Exceptions to this rule may be claimed by persons over sixty-five years of age, nonresidents domiciled in the community, and individuals who have served as conciliators during the last two terms. The members of the council serve without salary, but they do receive a small fee for each case handled. At present there are approximately 750 such councils in the country. The organization and jurisdiction of the conciliation councils as well as of the regular courts, original and appellate, are provided for by law.[1]

With certain exceptions, a dispute that seems likely to lead to court consideration must be submitted to a conciliation council for mediation before it can be taken to the ordinary courts. Matrimonial disputes, proposed actions against the state, cases involving rights under patents and copyrights, certain disputes between landlords and tenants concerning rights under leases, and some other specific matters are not submitted to scrutiny by the conciliation council before action begins in one of the regular courts. But even in some of these cases, mediation of some sort is attempted; divorce actions, e.g., are generally preceded by attempt at friendly settlement, usually initiated by the parish priest or by some other individual.

The procedure of conciliation is simple. The plaintiff requests a hearing of his complaint before the council in the district where the defendant resides. Both parties must, as a rule, appear in person; they may not be represented by lawyers, nor may lawyers be present in a counseling capacity at the hearing. The parties to the controversy explain their respective positions and advance their arguments. The members of the council have, particularly in small communities, an intimate acquaintance with the disputants and perhaps even with their present problem. Often the council is able to suggest a settlement that is acceptable to both parties. If this happens, a formal minute of the agreement is entered in the council's records, and the case is closed. If the conciliators fail to secure agreement between the parties, the controversy may be taken to the local court for more formal judicial consideration.

The aim of the conciliatory system is threefold: to secure settlement of disputes in a friendly manner; to decrease the burden of business carried by the ordinary courts; and to offer opportunity for all people, regardless of station and economic position, to obtain settlement of disputes with a minimum of expense. Of the estimated 25,000 cases handled annually by the conciliation councils, somewhat less than 40 per cent are settled either by mediation or through judgment by default in the event the defendant fails to appear. Slightly more than 25 per cent of the controversies are submitted to the courts for trial.[2]

Local Courts

Local courts are of two kinds: the *herredsrett* is the judicial agency in the rural areas; the *byrett* is the formal court of first instance in the

[1] *Lov om domstolene av 13 August 1915.*

[2] Royal Ministry of Justice, *The Administration of Justice in Norway* (Oslo, 1957), p. 31.

towns and cities. At present there are eighty-seven local courts in the country districts (*herredene*) and seventeen in as many cities and towns. In each of these courts, except the ones in Oslo, Bergen, Trondheim, Kristiansand, and Stavanger, there is usually only one permanent professional judge. Temporary deputy and assistant judges are appointed to assist under the direction of the senior judge. On occasion these young judges hear cases which have been assigned to them by the permanent judge of the court, but normally the junior judges would not finally decide cases or deliver judgments except as specifically authorized to do so by the *fylkesmann* and then only if the young judge in question had had significant judicial experience. After completing their two-year terms of service many of these deputy and assistant judges go into civil service positions that have certain adjudicatory character; some of them return to positions in the permanent judiciary.

All permanent judges in the ordinary division of the Norwegian judiciary are "named" by the King in Council. Practically speaking, the advice of the Minister in charge of the Department of Justice and Police largely determines the selections. All permanent judicial appointees are in the highest class of public servants (*embedsmenn*) and, as a result, have secure tenure and well respected status. Even the King (in Council) is unable to remove them by arbitrary action; they can only be dismissed by court decree. Deputy and assistant judges are appointed by the Minister of Justice and Police and are not given permanent tenure.

The local courts have complete original jurisdiction in civil cases and limited jurisdiction in criminal matters. Generally their jurisdiction in criminal cases extends to all misdemeanors and what might be called minor felonies in the United States. The line of demarcation between the jurisdiction of local courts and the courts of civil and criminal appeals is determined by the extent and nature of the possible punishment. Normally, if the crime calls for imprisonment for five years or less, the local court has jurisdiction. But irrespective of punishment, these courts hear certain classes of cases in the first instance, e.g., cases involving larceny, embezzlement, or fraud, and, in addition, all cases involving an alleged criminal under the age of eighteen. All serious felonies (*forbrytelser*) are heard in the first instance by the court of civil and criminal appeals and, as the name implies, this court also hears appeals in criminal and civil matters from the local courts.

A single professional judge presides in the local court, although in certain classes of cases (maritime disputes and real property cases) or if requested by one or both of the parties, two lay judges sit with the regular judge to help determine questions of both law and fact. Also, the judge of the court may, on his own initiative, call in lay judges — always two — to serve with him on a given case. The position of these individuals at this level of the judicial structure is quite different from the juries in the English and American systems. There is also a measurable distinction in Norwegian judicial institutions between the lay judges of the local courts and the juries used in the courts of civil and criminal appeals. Lay judges in the local courts do not merely attempt to determine the true status of the facts, but they act with the professional judge on an equal footing in surveying all other aspects of the case. Obviously, in discharging their responsibility the laymen will not disregard the legal background of a respected professional judge, but they are nonetheless in a real sense equal partners with the judge in making the final decision. The lay judges are selected by lot from a panel, the members of which are chosen by the communal council for four-year terms. In criminal actions two lay judges always serve as members of the court, except in very minor cases. Here again the lay judges stand on an equal footing, at least legally and formally, with the professional judge since they share in the total decision-making process involving both law and fact.

Intermediate Court

The court on the middle echelon of the Norwegian judiciary, called for want of a more accurate name, the court of civil and criminal appeals, was last reorganized in 1936.[3] Prior to that time the intermediate court (*lagmannsretten*) had been concerned exclusively with criminal cases, both originally and on appeal. In 1936 this court was given jurisdiction over civil appeals and the older civil appellate tribunal (*overretten*) was abolished. Thus at present the five courts of civil and criminal appeals[4] have original jurisdiction in serious criminal cases and both criminal and civil appellate jurisdiction.

For the hearing of any given civil case the personnel of the court of civil and criminal appeals includes a senior judge, who serves as president, and two associate judges, all of whom are professionals. If the parties insist, or if the professional judges find it advisable, two to four lay judges, selected from a panel recruited in the same manner as in the local courts, are added. The professional judges are appointed by the King in Council, usually from candidates who have passed their University law examination with a "superior" rating. Some of the as-

[3] The Norwegian name *lagmannsrett* literally translated would be less descriptive. The court is called court of civil and criminal appeals in the English version of the Ministry of Justice publication, *Domstolene og rettsplein i Norge* (Oslo, 1955).

[4] In Oslo, Skien, Bergen, Trondheim, and Tromsø.

sociate judges are recruited from the membership of the local courts; others are permanently appointed to the appellate court by the King.

When the court of civil and criminal appeals considers a criminal case, whether originally or on appeal, it is made up of the three professional judges and, as a rule, a ten-man jury.[5] The jurors (men or women) are selected by lot from a panel chosen by the communal councils in the district. Unlike the lay judges, the jury in the criminal section of the court of appeals only decides whether the defendant is guilty or not guilty. Seven of the ten must agree on a verdict.

Besides jurymen and lay judges, the Norwegian judicial system makes provision for another representative of the people to be present at some of the court sessions. This officer, the *rettsvidne,* is chosen by the registrar of voters or, under certain circumstances, by the court and bears some resemblance to the party watcher often found in American polling places on election day. His chief job is to observe whether or not the legal processes have been consistently and conscientiously followed. In cases tried before a single judge, a *rettsvidne* is always required to be present and in certain special actions, including disputes over fishing rights, an attempt is made to name a lay observer who has at least a general knowledge of the subject in controversy. The duties of the *rettsvidne* in preliminary hearings for law violators are especially significant. Although the police in Norway are unusually careful in maintaining dignity and decorum in all their relationships with alleged offenders, the possibility of "railroading" a person by a perfunctory preliminary hearing is made more difficult by the presence in the court of an impartial "watcher." Normally, the *rettsvidne* serves only for a short time, sometimes only a day. He is called upon, before final decision is reached, to make whatever comment he wishes on the proceedings as far as he has followed them and his remarks become a part of the official court record.[6]

The Supreme Court

The Supreme Court of Justice (*Høiesterett*) is the only Norwegian tribunal specifically provided for in the Constitution. At present its total membership includes a Chief Justice (*justitiarius*) and seventeen other judges, appointed by the King in Council and removable only through impeachment proceedings. The Court is divided into two sections without reference to subject matter of litigation, but rather for the purpose of expediting the business of the Court; these sections may

[5] Juries are not used in treason trials and in cases involving certain economic regulations.

[6] *Lov om domstolene av 13 august 1915,* No. 5, Paragraphs 101–105.

sit simultaneously. Normally only five judges sit on any one case and the membership of the group is determined by the Chief Justice.[7]

Although not strictly speaking a third division of the Supreme Court, the Judicial Committee on Appeals (*kjæremålsutvalget*) does perform many of the functions often associated with an intermediate appellate court. It is composed of three members of the Supreme Court appointed by the Chief Justice. It hears all petitions for appeals and decides on the validity of the appellant's plea for a Supreme Court review of his case. The Committee may refuse to certify the case for a hearing by the Supreme Court if it finds serious errors in the appeal proceedings or if it knows that the appeal will fail.

The jurisdiction of the Supreme Court of Justice is completely appellate. In matters of civil law the power to review the judgments of the lower courts extends to all aspects of the case, but cases involving a monetary dispute can be appealed to the high court only if the amount in controversy is at least NK 8,000. Exceptions to this rule can be made by the Judicial Committee on Appeals. If the actions are not concerned with money, but involve questions of divorce or domestic relations, changes of names, and other matters of similar nature, they may be appealed to the Supreme Court with the permission of the Judicial Committee on Appeals.

Although the details of appellate procedure are too technical for consideration in a limited discussion of this kind, it should be reemphasized that the Norwegian Supreme Court has, in some respects, a wider range of appellate authority than does the Supreme Court of the United States.[8] The Norwegian high court can review *all* the evidence, can take into account new evidence, and can conduct its own investigations; it is in no sense restricted to a consideration of the factual matters transmitted to it from the lower courts. But generally the Supreme Court will not lightly disregard the evidence considered in the lower courts. Whatever it considers, the Norwegian Supreme Court does have the power to dispose of the case finally without remanding it to a lower court for a retrial.

Criminal cases come to the highest court both from the courts of civil and criminal appeals and also directly from the local courts. If the appellant contends that an error has been made by the local court in method of procedure, interpretation of the laws, or meting out of punishment, he may bring his complaint directly to the notice of the

[7] In some instances when it becomes obvious that dubiety exists among even a minority of the five-man section on the constitutionality of a law or ordinance, the entire court will be called together to decide the case.

[8] See *The Administration of Justice in Norway*, pp. 42–52, for a brief review of procedure governing appeals.

Supreme Court. On the other hand, should he assert that the error of the lower court was connected with the finding of the facts, he must bring his case on appeal first to the court of appeals. The findings as to the facts in the latter courts must, as a general rule — both in cases of original and appellate jurisdiction — be considered final and not subject to review by the Supreme Court. But the demarcation between law and fact is not always completely clear, and consequently the Supreme Court is allowed a certain latitude in dealing with the facts.

As in civil proceedings before the Supreme Court, the appeal in a criminal case comes first for scrutiny to the Judicial Committee on Appeals. Generally, appeals are brought by the accused person, but they may also be brought by the state, particularly if it can be demonstrated that defense evidence may have been based upon forged documentation or other types of misrepresentation. This is somewhat at variance with British and American practice which considers acquittal by a lower court as completely final. It should be noted that very few appeals are settled to the detriment of the accused as a result of appeal proceedings initiated by the state.[9]

The High Court of the Realm

The High Court of the Realm is a specially constituted tribunal authorized to hear impeachment trials. The Odelsting is empowered by constitutional provision (Paragraph 86) to prefer the charges and the High Court of the Realm is given responsibility for conduct of the trial and for making the decision.

Precedents for the impeachment procedure adopted by the Constitution of 1814 were numerous. Britain had had years of experience with a somewhat similar idea. The House of Commons had the power to bring the charges; the House of Lords the authority to hear the evidence. The American Constitution had given more explicit expression to the British model. Meanwhile, Sweden had made provision in its Constitution of 1809 for a variation on the Anglo-American impeachment process. An impeachment court, made up of officials in high governmental positions, replaced the Swedish upper house as the agency to hear evidence and testimony in support of charges of malfeasance. A combination of the Anglo-American and Swedish systems was finally adopted by the Norwegian framers. A part of the membership of the impeachment trial court was to be recruited from the smaller legislative division (*Lagting*) and a part from the Supreme Court of Justice.

The personnel of the High Court of the Realm is selected for each case by a rather elaborate system of elimination. All the members of

[9] For a brief account of appellate procedure in criminal cases, see *The Administration of Justice in Norway,* 79–88.

the Lagting and of the Supreme Court are potential members of the High Court of the Realm, and provision is made for each party, accuser (Odelsting) and accused, to strike from the lists an equal number of legislators and an equal number of Supreme Court Justices. This procedure may continue until the personnel of the impeachment tribunal is made up of fourteen members of the Lagting and seven justices from the Supreme Court. Occasionally the parties do not avail themselves of their complete authority to eliminate members, and in that event the number is reduced by lot to the constitutionally designated figure. In no case does the President of the Lagting, who is the ex officio chairman of the High Court of the Realm, and the Chief Justice of the Supreme Court retire from the impeachment tribunal.

It is conceivable that so many prospective members of the High Court of the Realm would be ineligible to serve in a particular case as to make it impossible to have a final panel of fourteen legislators and seven Supreme Court justices. Ineligibility results if it can be shown that the legislators or judges have had previous connections with the case under consideration. For instance, if an individual had been a member of the Odeslting when the impeachment resolution was discussed or passed, he would not be qualified to serve as a judge in the hearing of the case. If ineligibility of potential members is great enough the High Court may be constituted with fewer than the minimum number prescribed by the Constitution, provided that at least ten persons who are eligible can be found in the two bodies. But should either the Lagting or the Supreme Court have so many ineligible members as to make it impossible to recruit from each fourteen and seven respectively, it is not permissible to make up the difference by recruiting extra members from one of these bodies which may have a surplus of eligibles.[10]

> A person sitting in the High Court of the Realm as a member of the Lagting does not vacate his seat in the Court if the period for which he is elected a member of the Storting should expire before the High Court of the Realm has terminated the trial of the case. If, for some other reason, he ceases to be a member of the Storting, he shall resign as a judge of the High Court of the Realm. The same rule shall apply if a judge of the Supreme Court of Justice, sitting as a member of the High Court of the Realm, retires as a member of the Supreme Court of Justice.[11]

In other words, unless the legislator ceases to be a member of the Storting through other causes than failure at the polls, he con-

[10] *Lov om rettergangsmåten i riksrettssaker av 5 februar 1932.*
[11] *Constitution of Norway,* Paragraph 86.

tinues to serve on the impeachment tribunal until after the case under consideration is decided. Thus, if he should become ineligible to a parliamentary seat due to loss of voting rights, or if he accepts a position on the Council of State, he is obliged to resign from the High Court of the Realm. Supreme Court jurists must vacate their places on the impeachment court if, during the course of the trial, they resign from their regular judicial positions.

The procedure to be followed in trying impeachment cases is defined by law. Ordinarily the court sessions are open to the public, but, if the matter should be fraught with international complications, secret sessions may be ordered. Customarily, oral testimony, rather than formal, written briefs, form the basis for the final decision. Usually the witnesses appear in plenary court sessions, but should circumstances require, a committee of the Court may hear certain classes of evidence. In most other regards the procedure in impeachment cases is similar to the process outlined by law for the settlement of civil disputes.

After the testimony has been heard and the parties have closed their respective arguments, the case goes to the Court for its decision. Although twenty-one judges usually make up the membership of the Court for hearing the evidence, only fifteen remain to make the final decision. These jurists, ten of whom are members of the Lagting and five are justices of the Supreme Court, are selected by lot. The verdict of the High Court of the Realm is final and may not be appealed. Nor may the King pardon an individual adjudged guilty by the impeachment tribunal, unless the punishment imposed is the death penalty. If the offender is found guilty, he may be removed from office and, if the gravity of the offense warrants, a fine or prison sentence may be imposed. Constitutionally the Court could go so far as to demand the death penalty.

Judicial Independence

Judicial independence was established by the Eidsvold Convention as one of the fundamentals underlying the contemplated governmental framework. In one of the principles adopted by that body on April 16, 1814, it was declared that the power of the courts should be separate and distinct from the spheres of authority enjoyed by parliament and the executive. This was another manifestation of the separation of powers principle so definitely a part of the political philosophy of many of the members of the Eidsvold Convention.

In order to maintain the integrity of the idea of judicial independence, the Convention placed certain safeguards in the fundamental law. In the first place, the members of the bench are secured permanent tenure by the Constitution, limited only by retirement regulations and can be removed from office only through impeachment procedures. In the second place, the courts are given complete and final power in the adjudication of disputes, and this process cannot be interfered with by parliament or the King in Council.[12] To be sure the King does have the pardoning power, but this can be exercised only after the courts have finally and definitely disposed of the case.

A number of weaknesses in the case for judicial independence could be mentioned. In the first place, the Storting may establish, abolish, and alter various parts of the kingdom's court machine. The parliament could, at least in theory, go so far as to eliminate all judicial agencies except the constitutionally established Supreme Court of Justice. The Storting also has the power to prescribe judicial procedure and jurisdictional limits. This authority is expressly granted by constitutional provision (Paragraph 88) as far as the Supreme Court is concerned, and it may be reasonably implied that the Storting can exercise a similar final authority over the other branches of the court system.

Perhaps the most serious encroachment upon the judicial independence is made by the Storting when it creates and enlarges the judicial authority of certain administrative agencies. On establishment many administrative units, particularly in the last two decades, have been given a body of discretionary quasi-judicial power. To be sure, appeals to the courts are usually possible from these administrative agencies. Another control over the courts available to Cabinet and parliament is fiscal, but since the part of the budget devoted to judicial administration is small, this is a power that would normally not have important effects. One can scarcely envision a situation in which the parliament would deliberately and seriously set out to cripple the courts through its power over the purse.

Notwithstanding certain controls that can be exercised by the Cabinet and parliament over the courts, and recognizing that a pure form of separation of powers is not only impossible, but perhaps undesirable, the fact remains that the Norwegian judiciary retains a substantial degree of independence. This is supported, as has been pointed out, by constitutional provisions, but perhaps equally important by strong traditions and an alert public opinion. It can be argued that in a parliamentary government the courts, like other governmental agencies, should be responsive to political change and adjust to the policies being pursued by the government in power. And that this does occur, not only in parliamentary governments, but also in certain states operating other forms of government, is quite obvious. One has only to

[12] *Constitution of Norway,* Paragraphs 88 and 90.

examine the history of the United States Supreme Court to obtain evidence to support this conclusion. But in Norway there are fewer strictly "political" questions that come to the courts, and this accounts for a degree of judicial independence at least as large as that found in the United States and certainly larger than that ordinarily found in a parliamentary governed state.

Judicial Review

All regular courts in Norway have the power to declare legislative and administrative acts unconstitutional. This authority of the courts (not only the Supreme Court of Justice) was definitely not anticipated by most of the members of the Convention of 1814. In fact, one of the particularly noteworthy constitutional drafts (Adler-Falsen) expressly prohibited any form of judicial interference with the powers granted to parliament and the executive.[13] The early years of constitutional government in Norway saw little change in this general appraisal of the proper sphere of judicial authority. It was not until the latter part of the nineteenth century that judicial review became permanently established in approximately its present form.

In order to understand the results of this development and the contemporary practice in Norway, it is important to differentiate between the procedural and substantive aspects of legislative enactments and administrative orders and decrees. By procedural, in this connection, is meant those formal aspects of the policy-making process that are concerned largely with the technical questions of method. Was the law passed according to the constitutional prescriptions with the proper observance of quorum requirements, procedure, sanction, etc.? The answers to queries of this kind will establish the law's validity or invalidity from the procedural point of view. The substantive aspects of the law, on the other hand, are concerned not with form and technical requirements, but rather with the content of the measure.

In reviewing the actions of either the legislative or executive branches of the government, the Norwegian courts are unquestionably able to invalidate laws or decrees that violate constitutionally outlined rules of procedure. If the proposition under scrutiny is a law, it may have been passed without proper regard for the intricate rules established by Paragraph 76 of the Constitution. Or possibly it was enacted by each house in slightly different forms, or without awaiting the required three-day period that the constitutional provision insists must elapse between legislative considerations. Similarly, a unicameral (plenary)

[13] For an account of judicial review in Norway, see G. J. Hallager, *Norges Høiesteret, 1815–1915* (Oslo, 1915).

resolution could be set aside if its passage was effected by disregarding constitutionally outlined procedures.

If the act under review is a provisional order or an administrative decree, it also must have been issued in accordance with legally prescribed rules of procedure. For instance, certain types of actions require consideration by the Council of State; others may become effective only after due notice and publication.

The competence of the Norwegian courts to invalidate a law or resolution because of its substantive content has until recently been open to some question. Most Norwegian constitutional authorities now agree that the right does exist. But, they contend, it may be exercised only if parliament has ignored the prohibitions of the Constitution so as to make reconciliation between legislative enactment and fundamental law impossible. The Storting must be acknowledged to be the policy determining body and, as such, it, and not the courts, has the final power to decide *what* is to be done. The fact that the judicial organs might consider the course adopted by the Storting unwise or inexpedient is not enough to prompt the courts to invalidate a measure that is procedurally constitutional.

The older view of the court's power to invalidate laws on substantive grounds was more limited. A distinguished authority on Norwegian constitutional law sums it up in a few words. "If the law has been [passed by the Storting and] signed by the King it can only be invalidated if there has been a wilfully apparent, unquestionable, presumptive and intentional disregard for the provisions of the Constitution."[14] Though this rule is now relaxed, the burden of proof still rests with the party who is attempting to establish the unconstitutionality of the law. The content of unicameral resolutions must also be examined with the same care. It is conceivable, however, that substantively this type of enactment might more often violate constitutional dictates than would an action by the two chambers of the Storting. Certain matters cannot be handled by unicameral resolutions, but must be enacted by the Storting in its bicameral capacity. Consequently, the courts might declare that, although the Storting was within its rights in passing the measure, the subject matter was such as to require bicameral action. At this point the line between procedure and substance becomes fine indeed.

Obviously constitutional amendments cannot be invalidated as a result of judicial examination of content. It would be ridiculous, and certainly undemocratic, to allow the courts the right to review proposals for changes in the fundamental law. The amending process is so slow and the safeguards so secure — passage by a two-thirds vote in two

[14] Bredo Morgenstierne, *Lærebok i den norske statsforfatningsret* (Oslo, 1927), II, 78–79.

sessions of the Storting with an intervening election — that the possibility mentioned in Paragraph 112 of the Constitution (that amendments should not be inconsistent with the principles of the Constitution) has small chance of arising.

Both the substantive and procedural aspects of administrative orders may be reviewed by the courts. In fact, this kind of judicial review is of much more practical significance at the present time than is review of parliamentary enactments.

After a court has decided that the whole or any part of a law, resolution, order, or decree is in conflict with the Constitution, it may simply refuse to accept the offending provisions of the measure as binding law. Invalidation applies only to the pending action before the court; permanent nullification is definitely not contemplated.

It requires only a perfunctory examination of the powers and activities of the courts to establish the fact that judicial review is not extremely important in Norway. It is generally agreed that the courts should allow actions of the parliament and the executive to remain unchallenged unless flagrant violations of constitutional provisions can be established. In attempting to reduce the possibility of passing invalid law, the Storting may demand the opinion of the Supreme Court on perplexing questions of constitutional law before it legislates. Through the use of these advisory opinions, most constitutional questions are settled before laws and resolutions are passed, and this reduces significantly court review of legislation after passage by the Storting. Certainly the Court plays no political role comparable to that of the Supreme Court in the United States.

Judicial Procedure

Civil Cases

Civil procedure in the lower courts in Norway is similar in many respects to the practices prevailing in Great Britain and the United States. If the case has not been settled in the conciliation council, the plaintiff takes it to the local court in the community where the defendant has his residence. The counsel for the plaintiff and the counsel for the defendant give opening statements which are followed by examination and cross-examination of their respective witnesses. If the presiding judge wishes, he may personally question witnesses, and he is generally required to question the two litigants. If the court deems it necessary, it may visit locations or areas which figure in the dispute. In addition to the opening statements, each counsel may twice address the court, the last time summing up his case.

There is a good deal of freedom in the presentation of evidence in a civil case in Norway; the court is not bound by elaborate rules. Within reason anything that may throw light on the dispute will be admitted as evidence. After hearing the evidence and the concluding arguments the presiding professional judge and his lay or professional colleagues will confer, and they will render a decision, usually without undue delay. Should one of the parties have failed to contest the action, the court will automatically render a judgment by default. As has been indicated, appeals from local courts usually go to the court of civil and criminal appeals but may, under certain circumstances and if allowed by the Committee on Appeals of the Supreme Court, go directly to the highest court.

Though Norwegian civil procedure is not unlike that employed in Great Britain and the United States, one point of variation from American procedure should be underscored. The judge plays a much larger role in Norway than he does in the United States where he is often relegated to the role of umpire. The Norwegian judge, not perhaps as aggressively as the French judge, may actively participate in questioning the witnesses.

Criminal Cases

Criminal procedure in Norway shows fewer similarities to Anglo-American practice than does civil procedure. But one does find certain rules, practices, and institutions that are reminiscent of experience and practice in Britain and the United States, as, for example, the formal indictment process, an institution that resembles the grand jury, and the presumption of innocence rule.

The chief officer responsible for prosecuting criminal cases is the State Public Prosecutor (*riksadvokaten*). He is appointed by the King in Council and is directly responsible to the King with no intervening responsibility to the Minister of Justice and Police, an arrangement which makes his office independent of the police administration. This separation was designed to prevent "collusion" between prosecutor and police, which might result in improper arrests or faulty procedures. At present the police and the office of the State Public Prosecutor do not work independently but engage in a significant amount of cooperation.

The country is divided into nine districts for prosecution purposes with a state advocate (*statsadvokat*) in charge of each. This is the office responsible for prosecuting criminal cases at the local court level and also most of the cases that come originally to the court of civil and criminal appeals. It should be recalled that the local courts deal with misdemeanors and minor felonies while the court of civil and criminal appeals handles the major criminal cases (involving penalties of five years imprisonment or more).

Indictments are prepared for presentation to the local courts by the prosecutor in the district where the case will be heard. This is done after the prosecutor has made a thorough investigation of all facts and determined whether or not a trial is warranted. He is assisted in this undertaking by the police in the district. If the witness lives at some distance from the location of the court, testimony will be taken in advance by the local court in the district where the witness resides. This latter court will, for the purpose of taking this testimony, be constituted as an examining and summary court (*forhørsrett*). A court of this type may also have a part to play in determining whether or not a person should be held for trial — that is, indicted — since it not only has power to gather evidence, but also to have the evidence submitted to it by the public prosecutor. Although in local court proceedings the prosecuting officer can, on his own initiative, issue a final bill of indictment, in serious cases to be tried in the court of civil and criminal appeals he must seek the advice of the examining and summary court (staffed by judges from the local court). As a matter of fact, he is generally required to obtain formal consent from this body before even undertaking the arrest and detention of the accused. And, after the person has been arrested, he must be brought before the examining and summary court without delay in order to determine whether he shall remain in detention. Under certain circumstances, the examining and summary court can dispose of a case forthwith, providing the crime in question comes within the jurisdiction of the local courts (punishment less than five years imprisonment). This type of action is possible only if the accused confesses and requests the court to pass sentence immediately. Bail is seldom granted, and, when granted, does not involve money. A man's pledge to appear is honored by the judge.

In cases that go to trial, the procedure in the local court and in the court of civil and criminal appeals is similar, except that a jury is practically always used in the higher court and this necessitates certain procedural rules for hearing evidence, instructing the jury, obtaining the verdict, etc. In both courts the indictment is read by the chairman of the court after arrangements have been made to provide defense counsel, who is either court appointed and serves at state expense or privately employed by the defendant. The trial is opened by the prosecutor who introduces the state's case. Early in the trial, the defendant is asked whether he wishes to testify in his own defense; he may legally refuse to do this, but, unlike American practice, his refusal can be taken into consideration by the judges and jury in deciding the case. Witnesses are then examined and cross-examined. At this stage of the proceedings, the judge, like his counterpart in a Norwegian civil case, plays a more important role than does the judge in most state courts in the United States. If the accused is to testify, the presiding judge, not the prosecutor, will open the questioning. After all evidence has been heard, the two opposing counsels present closing summations. If the case is being tried in a local court, the judge or judges (one professional and two lay judges) will deliberate and render a decision. If the case is being tried in the court of civil and criminal appeals, a jury of ten will most often have responsibility for deciding the facts, while the judge or judges decide questions of law. Impaneling a jury is simple in Norway; fourteen prospective principal jurymen and a number of alternates (*varamenn*), who will serve in the event the principals become disabled, are drawn by lot from a list selected in advance by the communal council. It is obvious from the small number of potential jurors that each counsel has a very limited right of challenge.

After the jury has been impaneled and the evidence presented by both the prosecution and the defense, the judge gives formal instructions to the jury. He may review the entire case, and he certainly will explain the legal rulings that have been made in the course of the trial. On closing his instructions the presiding judge will submit to the jury a set of questions which have usually been drafted by the prosecutor and always carefully examined by the defense counsel. These are put in final form by the presiding judge in such a way as to permit simple "yes" or "no" answers. It will be recalled that a jury may reach a binding verdict if seven of the ten jurors agree.

The procedure in Norway gives the judge certain discretionary powers in dealing with the decision of the jury. He may, after the jury has decided that the accused is guilty of a given offense, ameliorate the situation by sentencing the accused for a less serious offense. It is even possible for the judge to disregard the verdict entirely, if it is unfavorable to the accused and, in the opinion of the judge, improper. If this is done — and it should be emphasized that it is done infrequently — the judge will order a new trial.

Throughout the entire procedure in a criminal case, the burden of proof rests with the prosecution; the defendant must be presumed innocent unless proved guilty beyond any doubt. Great stress is laid on decorum and fair play in the Norwegian criminal courts, and even the smallest deviation may result in criticism not only from members of the legal fraternity, but in press reports and editorials.

Individual Rights

The courts of Norway, like those in other democratic countries, have as one of their principal responsibilities the protection of individual rights. As in other countries, these are generally of two kinds: political (right to vote, to hold office, etc.) and civil (guarantees of freedom, privacy, economic rights, etc.). The political rights have been enumerated in preceding chapters and will not be repeated here. The nonpolitical rights can only be listed without extensive comment.

If one were to search Norwegian history for the foundation of liberty, equality, the rule of law, and like protections to the individual, he could find their roots without much difficulty as far back as the Saga period. Certainly by the time the Constitution was written in 1814 there was a clear consensus on certain inviolable individual rights to which the constitutional framers could give clear expression. Some of these came from old Norse experiences with a kind of primitive democracy; others came from the teachings of philosophers like Locke and Rousseau. Also, without serious doubt, the content and the form of Norwegian statements of rights were influenced by the British experience and by the provisions of the Bill of Rights in the American Constitution.

The following list includes the most important guarantees to the individual found in the Norwegian Constitution:

1. No titles of nobility may be created [after 1814] and no hereditary privileges may be granted. [All titles of nobility were abolished in 1821.]
2. Conviction of a crime must be by law [due process] and punishment may be meted out by established judicial institutions; torture must not be used in the interrogation of prisoners.
3. No law may be given retroactive effect.
4. No one may be arrested and detained in custody except through legal processes, and officers shall be held responsible personally for any illegal arrests.
5. Military force shall not be used against citizens except to prevent breach of the peace and then only after public notice has been given in a prescribed way.
6. Freedom of speech and freedom of the press shall be guaranteed.
7. Privileges shall not be given by the State which will restrict freedom of trade and industry.
8. The search of homes shall not be made except in accordance with established rules. [This has been elaborated: search, seizure, and arrest can be made, with certain obvious exceptions, on authority of a court.]
9. Private property can only be taken for public use after just compensation.
10. The State authorities are required to create conditions so that everyone who is able may earn his livelihood by his work.[15]

[15] *Constitution of Norway,* Paragraphs 23, 96–105 inclusive, 107–110 in-

The above statements have been defined and elaborated by statute and court decisions. It is safe to say that few democratic societies protect their citizens from arbitrary state actions any better than does Norway. Any infractions are usually promptly dealt with by the courts, but should there be any delay in the enforcement of civil rights, the press and the public can be counted on to raise enough clamor so as to bring official action rather promptly.

The Norwegian Bar and Bench

In order to be licensed as a practicing lawyer in Norway a person must be at least twenty-one years of age, be possessed of good character, give evidence of financial responsibility, and have passed the examinations set by the Faculty of Law of the University of Oslo (the University of Bergen does not as yet have a Faculty of Law). The time normally required for completion of the study of law, if pursued on a full-time basis, is five years after graduation from the *gymnasium*, considered equivalent to graduation from junior college in the United States.

After two years of certain prescribed legal experience, the young lawyer may obtain a license to practice in the court of appeals with the title of *overrettssakfører*. To be licensed to practice before the Supreme Court, as a *høiesterettsadvokat*, he must have passed his University examination with first-class standing, have had three years of prescribed court practice, and have passed the tests prescribed by the Supreme Court. These tests usually include an evaluation of the candidate's experience as a courtroom lawyer. All practicing lawyers in Norway are supervised by the Department of Justice which has power to revoke individual licenses.

A great many graduates in law do not become actively engaged in the private practice of law. A number go into the state and communal civil services; a substantial percentage of the higher public service positions is filled by lawyers. Others become associated with various other enterprises, public or private.

The Norwegian judges are appointed by the King in Council on the recommendation of the Minister of Justice. Vacancies in the judiciary are publicly announced, candidates apply, and the competition is judged in the last analysis by the Minister of Justice and, for the more

---

clusive. No description of the history and content of civil rights in Norway is available in English. Some appreciation of the significance of civil rights can be obtained from a book written during World War II by Halvdan Koht and Sigmund Skard, *The Voice of Norway* (New York, 1944). By all odds the best scholarly treatment of the subject is found in Frede Castberg, *Norges statsforfatning* (Oslo, 1947), II, 231–249.

important positions, by the Cabinet in plenary session. The minimal qualifications for a Supreme Court judge and for a presiding judge of the court of civil and criminal appeals is: thirty years of age and a first-class law examination. Lower court judges may be appointed if they have reached the age of twenty-five and have passed a so-called second-class examination. A candidate must in every case be a Norwegian citizen and possess good character and financial solvency. In practice, any lawyer may compete for a judgeship, but judges are usually chosen from members of the practicing bar, the inferior magistracy, the public prosecution authority, or the civil service. In past years the average age of first appointees to lower court judgeships has been about forty-five and to the higher posts slightly over fifty.

By comparison with other civil servants, Norwegian judges are well paid. The local judge receives NK 30,000 ($4,275) annually and the Supreme Court justice may receive as much as NK 50,000 ($7,140) annually. In addition to salaries, other perquisites are available, such as expense allowances and often official residences. The Norwegian judge is also reasonably well taken care of by a pension plan on reaching the compulsory retirement age of seventy.

9

Local Government

Introduction: History and Geography

Norway has a unitary form of government; all power resides finally in the state, and local units have only the power granted them by national legislation. The country is divided into twenty counties (*fylker*), eighteen of which are rural and two — Oslo and Bergen — are urban. The smallest regular unit of local government is the commune, of which there were 732 by the census of 1960; 62 of these were urban and 670 rural (*herred*).[1] In the last two years a serious movement has been undertaken looking toward consolidation not only of small rural communes, but also of fair-sized towns located in close proximity. Without doubt, the number of communes will continue to decrease as it has during the last two years (from a total of 743 to 732). The consolidation is accomplished by administrative action under enabling legislation.

Besides the two regular units of local government — counties and communes — there are special districts which have limited, particularized jurisdiction. Only three types of these need to be mentioned in this discussion: fire districts, harbor districts, and building districts (*bygningskommuner*). The functions of the first two are clear from their names, and they are established either if special problems exist in the commune which call for transference of these normal municipal functions to a special district or if the area to be served is larger than any one regular commune. The building district is responsible for planning and administering affairs essential to a residential building program. The district has power to make provisions for roads and

[1] The urban communes are divided into two classes: *kjøpstader* (market towns) and *ladestader* (port or loading towns). Most of the large cities and towns are *kjøpstader* (there are forty-three *kjøpstader* and only nineteen *ladestader*) and once a degree of prestige was attached to this classification. At present the division is more or less formal.

streets, water supply, sewage disposal facilities, and related services.

Before special districts are created by the appropriate department[2] of the national government, the governing boards of the regular communes, as well as the residents of the area, must be consulted. The law is not clear on the extent to which the regular communes and their citizens may legally obstruct the creation of a special district. It is rather generally assumed that, after proper consultation, the department in question has final authority to establish the district.

Besides the special districts, two or more regular communes may agree to cooperate in undertaking a specific activity, often economic in character. By so doing they may obligate themselves financially within limits of law and departmental regulations, but since this is a voluntary arrangement they are under no compulsion to do so. Each of the cooperating communes may withdraw its support from the enterprise after discharging its financial obligations, and no separate governmental entity is created by this kind of intercommunal cooperation.

Although Norway is a unitary state, it should not be inferred from this that its history or even the present temper of its people is cordial to a high degree of centralized control. In the Saga period and even after the establishment of a national kingship, a significant degree of local autonomy prevailed. The fact that local and provincial affairs were handled by all qualified residents of the areas through the *tinger* (not unlike the town meeting in New England or the *Landesgemeinde* in Switzerland), and not through an established representative assembly and elected officers, made it easier for the King to assert control over local affairs; there was no council or set of officers, with acknowledged responsibility, to resist him. After the Dano-Norwegian King had established himself as an absolute monarch in 1661 all traces of local self-rule disappeared in Norway. Government at every level was carried on by officers appointed by the King. But a degree of popular supervision of the King's agents in town and cities did develop in the late seventeenth and eighteenth centuries; a small group of burghers was designated to serve as a kind of complaint board, and these men exercised a restraining influence on the officials appointed by the King. Rural areas remained under arbitrary royal control, and the restiveness caused by this experience, as well as the fear of domination by the towns, may explain some of the subsequent agitation among the farmers that led to demands for certain safeguards in the Constitution of 1814. The so-called *bonde* (farmer) paragraph in the Constitution assured the rural areas of two-thirds of the seats in the Storting. But, even

[2] In the case of building and fire districts the Department of Communal and Labor Affairs has jurisdiction and in the case of harbor districts, the Department of Fisheries.

under this rule, because of the predominantly nonurban nature of the population, the rural areas were underrepresented during much of the nineteenth century. Changes in districting led to the repeal of the *bonde* paragraph in 1953.

No provision for change in local government was included in the Constitution of 1814. It was apparently assumed that with a democratic central government, the onerous aspects caused by the absence of local self-government would be overcome. Fortified by vocal, if not always proportionate, representation in the Storting, the farm group continued to agitate for more democratic control over local affairs. In 1833 a law was passed establishing a measure of local control over communal affairs, but this act was vetoed by the King. Four years later (1837) the first step was taken toward democratic local government with the passage of a law establishing, at the local level, an executive board (*formannskap*) and endowing it with limited, somewhat ill-defined power. The law did not delineate the area of competence of the local unit or its board, but by practice a limited degree of fiscal control came to be vested in the board; for example, it became impossible, without the board's consent, to levy new taxes on local residents unless specifically authorized by the Storting. But from the point of view of the modern advocate of municipal home rule, the power given the local governmental unit in Norway by the law of 1837 was fragmentary indeed.

During the course of the nineteenth century the functions of the communes expanded and came to include restricted policy-making activities and administration in the following fields: elementary and secondary education, poor relief, church affairs, and roads. By 1900 communal affairs had expanded further and, during the years that followed, municipal water supplies, electric utilities, public housing, and related functions were placed under local control to a lesser or greater degree. Some conception of the extent of the expansion of the activities of communal government can be obtained by examining the rise in the total of the public debt of the communes after 1900. In that year the total municipal indebtedness was NK 22.7 million as compared with NK 1,507.1 million in 1926. Though this substantial increase was due in large part to increased local government activity, it also represented somewhat the effects of inflationary pressure during World War I. The communal debt in 1946 (NK 746.5 million), which is perhaps less affected by post-World War II inflation, was about seven times as large as in 1900.[3]

[3] These figures, as well as certain other factual data in this chapter, are taken from K. M. Nordanger and Arnljot Engh, *Kommunal kunnskap* (Oslo, 1960).

Communal Electoral Rules and Procedures

All Norwegian citizens, twenty-one years of age or over, who have resided in Norway for five years and are residing in the commune in which they wish to vote, may vote if their names are properly included on the voters' register and if they have not under the law been deprived of their suffrage rights.[4] These rules are similar in almost every respect to those in force for national elections; Norway does not recognize any special kind of communal citizenship distinguished from national citizenship. But differences do exist between the state and the commune in matters of residence.

Not unlike the situation in other countries, questions concerning residence can become complicated in Norway. For election purposes, the residence rule requires the prospective voter to demonstrate that he has lived more or less permanently in the commune in which he wishes to vote. For certain nonelectoral purposes it is important to distinguish between his voting residence (*bostedskommunen*) and two other types of communal attachments: the place where he can be said to be at any given point in time (*opholdskommunen*) and his home commune (*hjemstavnskommunen*), the place where he was born or where he lived for at least two years uninterruptedly between the ages of fifteen and sixty-two.

All Norwegian citizens (and resident aliens who have all the rights of citizens except the right to vote and to hold office) have equal rights regardless of their communal residence with one exception: those eligible may receive special treatment in their home commune, particularly if this depends for fulfillment on the communal budget. At present, with national social security legislation so comprehensive, these special rights are confined largely to the areas of public housing, governmental employment, communal vacation and recreational facilities.

Another purpose served by the regulations setting up home communes is related to the disbursement of certain kinds of state financial aid to local governments. Communal services such as poor relief (as distinguished from old age pensions), care of the insane, child welfare activities, and education of abnormal children are supported in part by the state under formulae based upon the number of residents claiming home commune status in each of the local governmental units.[5]

Because the procedure used in Norwegian local elections is roughly similar to that used in national elections, it will not be described in detail at this time. Each commune has an election committee made up of the registrar of voters and the members of the executive board

[4] See pp. 59–60 above and *Lov om kommunevalg av 10 juli 1925*.

[5] The Norwegian home commune is somewhat similar to the Swiss commune of origin.

(*formannskapet*) of the commune. It is the responsibility of this committee to administer the election; the registrar of voters prepares the list of eligible voters for communal elections in much the same manner as he does for national elections.[6]

Communal elections are, as a rule, party affairs; there is scant opportunity for independent candidates and, unlike the practice in some rural areas and small towns in the United States, little use is made of strictly local parties, whether permanent or temporary. In most local elections several of the nationally recognized parties compete, and consequently the normal procedure is to use somewhat the same type of proportional representation as is used at the national level.[7] Parties nominate, usually at general meetings, more candidates than there are places to be filled on the communal council. This is done for two reasons: to make certain that an adequate number of alternates will be available should the party be unusually successful in the election and to give wider interest and geographical representation as well as to allow more people the prestige that comes from being nominated. In many situations the latter reason is not important, and this is evidenced by the fact that the nominee is required by law to serve unless he is over sixty years of age or has served in the position for which he has been nominated during the last four years. It will be recalled that a similar requirement to serve is also imposed upon nominees for the Storting.[8]

The procedure at the polling place is similar to that used in Norwegian national elections and not unlike that generally in use in other democratic countries. The secrecy and integrity of the balloting is safeguarded by close supervision by the election committee. Voting places are numerous enough and located conveniently so that all eligible voters have no difficulty casting their ballots. As is the practice in national elections, anyone unable to appear at the polling place may use an absentee ballot. In brief, the local election in Norway is a party list system with provision for preferential voting. Voters may "accumulate," i.e., they may give more than one vote to someone on the party list or they may add the name of a person not on the list and give him two or three votes. Though there are no official figures or studies available, it seems evident that the voters make little use of their rights to indicate preferences or add names; most people vote the list as prepared by the party. In fact, the ballot can be valid even without names of any individuals if there is a clear, unmistakable indication that the voter is casting his ballot for the candidates in the order nominated by a given party.

[6] See pp. 62–63.
[7] *Lov om kommunevalg av 10 juli 1925,* No. 6, Paragraph 13.
[8] See p. 74.

If two or more parties present candidates, the election results must be calculated according to the formula provided for proportional elections; only if there is no contest between the parties can the proportional system be avoided. Although the calculation process may seem complicated and perhaps unduly technical for this discussion, it is sufficiently different from that used in parliamentary elections to warrant a brief examination. This can best be done by an illustration.

In a given communal election the results of the balloting (not considering preferential voting within party lists) were the following:

Conservative	869
Liberal	1825
Labor	4050
Christian People's	580
Communist	255

In calculating the outcome, the total vote cast for all party lists is added and this total vote is divided by the number of seats to be filled plus one. (In our illustration there are 37 members of the council.) In the given case the result of this operation will be the following: $869 + 1825 + 4050 + 580 + 255 = 7579$. Dividing 7579 by 38 we obtain 199. Each of the individual list totals is then divided by this quotient plus one $(199 + 1)$ with any remainders disregarded. The resulting figure will be the number of seats won by each party and the calculation will take the following form:

Conservative	$869 \div 200 = 4$
Liberal	$1825 \div 200 = 9$
Labor	$4050 \div 200 = 20$
Christian People's	$580 \div 200 = 2$
Communist	$255 \div 200 = 1$
Number of seats allocated	36

Since there are 37 seats to be filled, a second operation is made necessary. Each of the party totals is, at this stage, divided by the number of seats obtained through the first calculation plus one. In this division the remainder is not disregarded. In the example under consideration the calculations in the second operation will be done in the following manner:

Conservative	$869 \div (4 + 1) = 173\frac{4}{5}$
Liberal	$1825 \div (9 + 1) = 182\frac{5}{10}$
Labor	$4050 \div (20 + 1) = 192\frac{18}{21}$
Christian People's	$580 \div (2 + 1) = 193\frac{1}{3}$
Communist	$255 \div (1 + 1) = 127\frac{1}{2}$

The remaining seat will go to the Christian People's party since it obtained the largest quotient. If the results had been close in this second operation or if other seats were to be filled, a third operation might have been necessary. This would have involved dividing each of the party totals by the number of seats obtained through the first calculation plus 2. If this were done in the present example the results would not be changed as will be seen from the figures given below. The Christian People's party still has the largest quotient, considering both calculations.

Conservative	$869 \div (4 + 2) = 144\frac{5}{6}$
Liberal	$1825 \div (9 + 2) = 165\frac{10}{11}$
Labor	$4050 \div (20 + 2) = 184\frac{2}{22}$
Christian People's	$580 \div (2 + 2) = 145$
Communist	$255 \div (1 + 2) = 85$

If there had been four additional seats to be filled, the second would have gone to the Labor party ($192\frac{18}{21}$), the third to Labor ($184\frac{2}{22}$), and the fourth to the Liberals ($182\frac{5}{10}$).

One remaining process remains to be described: the designation of the specific candidates on the several lists who are to take the places allocated to each of the parties. This process is complicated by the fact that each party may "accumulate" votes for certain candidates on its list. This means that certain names may appear twice or even three times on the list. Thus, if a person votes the list, he is in reality giving more than one vote to those candidates having multiple listings. Also, the voter may, if he wishes, exercise preference by the process of "accumulation." Thus, to oversimplify, if there are twenty names on the list, he could give two votes to each of ten, rather than voting for the list of twenty. Most voters do not make use of the privilege of accumulating their votes for preferred candidates, but generally vote the list as prepared by the party. Parties, on the other hand, often put favorite candidates on the ballot two or three times. For example, in the last municipal election in Oslo with eighty-five seats on the council to be filled, the Conservatives nominated sixty-nine, giving sixteen preferential positions entitling them to two votes. This procedure was followed by most of the other parties in this election.

Once the number of places to which each party is entitled has been determined, the lists are canvassed and those candidates with the largest vote (including, of course, accumulations) are declared elected. In the Oslo election referred to above the Conservative party was entitled to thirty-five seats and all sixteen men whose names appeared twice were elected. In the same election the Labor party had placed twenty-two names on its list twice, and all of these were elected while only seventeen of the candidates whose names appeared once on the Labor list were elected.

Structure of Local Government

The County (Fylke)

In each of the twenty counties the chief executive officer is the *fylkesmann* who is appointed by the King in Council on recommendation of the Department of Communal Affairs and Labor for an indefinite term. The position and power of the Norwegian *fylkesmann* is roughly similar to that of the prefect in the French Department. Though significant variations exist, both of these officers represent the national government in their localities and are responsible for interpreting provincial problems to central authorities. The *fylkesmann* perhaps has less real power and does not have the same political role as does his French counterpart. Nevertheless the Norwegian county executive occupies a central position in local administration and commands substantial respect and compensation. He receives at present NK 39,000 per year, which places him at a salary level not much lower than cabinet members.[9]

The primary policy-making organ in the county is the *fylkesting,* made up of all the mayors of the rural communes (*herreder*) and the *fylkesmann* who, though possessed of substantial power in the county, has no vote in the *fylkesting.* Since the *fylkesting* meets seldom — once a year in ordinary session and only occasionally in extraordinary sessions — a smaller group, the *fylkesutvalg,* is provided to handle day-to-day policy questions. This group is made up of the *fylkesmann,* four members and four alternates, chosen for two-year terms by the *fylkesting* from its own membership. The *fylkesutvalg* is summoned into session by the *fylkesmann* when two of the members request it or when the *fylkesmann* considers it necessary to secure group advice or action. Normally the important decisions concerning appropriations, tax levies, and general policy questions are handled by the larger policy-making group, although situations and problems requiring immediate or emergency action can be disposed of by the *fylkesutvalg.*

In some respects the Norwegian county should be considered a secondary type of local government; the commune is both by law and in fact the primary unit. According to the law, the rural communes within a given geographic area "establish" the county.[10] Also the cen-

[9] To obtain some idea of the prestige attached to the *fylkesmann* position one has only to look at the list of present (1963) incumbents. Trygve Lie, after his retirement as Secretary-General of the United Nations, became *fylkesmann* for Oslo and Akershus.

[10] *Lov om styret i kommunene av 12 november 1954,* Paragraph 62.

tral government (i.e., the Department of Communal Affairs and Labor) exercises closer supervision of county affairs than it does over communal affairs. For example, the budget of the county must be approved by the Department, and certain matters not receiving a required two-thirds majority in the county assembly (*fylkesting*) are referred to central authorities for final disposition. Also, the range of function enjoyed by the county is narrower than that exercised by the commune. But in spite of these limitations, certain organs of county government have significant special responsibilities, e.g., the school committee, the agricultural committee, and the forestry committee. The five-man county school committee has particularly important responsibilities, not only for the county schools (there were seventy-two in 1960, most of which were folk high schools), but also in an overall planning and supervisory capacity in relation to the schools of the communes. The members of this committee and others that may become necessary are chosen by the *fylkesting.*

In general the county undertakes functions that are too burdensome or too large for individual communes. Besides providing certain kinds of educational facilities and engaging in forestry and agricultural projects, the county may establish hospitals, hydroelectric installations, build roads, etc. In so doing the county operates to equalize the tax burdens among the rural communities. The county tax resources are drawn from the several constituent communal areas and, as a result, the more fortunately situated communes will assist those whose people are not so well off.

The Commune (Rural: herred; *Urban:* by*)*

Prior to 1954 the machinery of government in urban and rural communes was differentiated. In that year a comprehensive local government act was passed, the provisions of which applied generally and somewhat similarly to both kinds of communes. Dissimilarities between the rural districts and the towns and cities still exist; these are based now not on different laws, but rather on the extent and nature of the functions performed. In distinctly rural areas the structure will be simple with little need for professional administrators; in cities like Oslo, on the other hand, a sizeable bureaucracy is required to provide the necessary municipal services.

With some modifications the institutions of government in most Norwegian communes will include the following:

1. A Communal Council (*Kommunestyre*)
2. An Executive (or Presidential) Board (*Formannskap*)
3. Secretary to the Executive Board (*Formannskapssekretær*)
4. A Mayor (*Ordfører*)

5. Standing Committees of the Council and Board
6. Special Committees and Boards with particularized functions (*Særskilte styrer*)
7. Communal Treasurer
8. Civil Servants

In large communes a general municipal manager (*rådmann*) or specialized managers for certain sectors of communal administration, such as finance, public works, schools, etc., are appointed.

The communal council is the primary policy-making body and varies in size from thirteen to eighty-five, depending upon the population of the commune. Its members are elected for four-year terms, usually under a system of proportional representation. Anyone who is eligible to vote in local elections is qualified to serve on the council, providing he is not serving as a salaried officer or employee of the county or the commune. For the disposition of any given matter, a council member can become disqualified to participate for a number of reasons, chief of which would be a financial interest in the outcome.[11] The members of the council, even in the cities, receive no salary, although they may be given allowances to cover travel and other expenses.

The executive board (*formannskapet*) is chosen by the council from its own membership by a system of proportional representation, if this is requested by any member of the council. One-fourth of the council serves on this board for four-year terms. Members chosen to sit on the executive board, like council members generally, are required to serve unless they are over sixty years of age, have served during the last four years as members of the communal council, or can demonstrate compelling personal disabilities, such as ill health. Two other demands are made of councilors and executive board members: they must attend meetings unless they are formally excused, and they must vote in meetings unless considered disqualified for the reasons mentioned above. The obligation to meet is generally taken seriously; the law authorizes the council to levy fines (NK 10) on members absent without proper excuses. The practice of electing alternate members (*varamenn*), so general in Norway, is also followed in the commune.

The mayor (*ordfører*) and vice-mayor of the Norwegian commune are elected from the executive board by the communal council for two-year terms. The responsibility and actual power exercised by the mayor depends not only on the law, but on the practical political situation in the locality. If there is no communal manager (or managers), his role becomes that of chief executive as well as chief administrator.

[11] There are other reasons for disqualification of the council member in given cases. For example, a dissenter cannot participate if the matter under consideration is concerned with the State Church.

But if a managerial system has been installed, he has no final coordinating administrative responsibility. In every case he is the legal and ceremonial head of the commune, chairman of the council and of the executive board, ex officio member of all committees, the officer responsible for communal records, and the representative of the commune in its relations with the state, other communes, and the public. From a strictly legal point of view the mayor has no sphere of authority that he can defend against the communal council or the appropriate organs of the national government. But he often has a strong political position. Usually he is a well-respected member of the community; often he has served as mayor for several years (though he may be excused from service after one term), and in most communities he is the leader of his party. All of this can result in the exercise of more real power by the mayor than would seem possible from a strictly legal point of view.

The responsibility exercised by the other organs of local government should be clear from the nomenclature of office. The secretary to the executive board is primarily a record-keeper, and the communal treasurer collects, keeps, and disburses, on proper authorization, communal moneys. There are two kinds of committees: standing committees and special committees. The responsibility of the standing committee is similar to comparable groups in any democratic government. The special committees are responsible for particular activities (e.g., education) which are usually provided for by special laws and regulations and not covered in the general legal authorization accorded municipalities. The responsibilities of the manager (or managers) and civil servants will be considered in the subsequent discussion of communal administration.

Policy-Making in the Communes

It should be recalled that Norway is a unitary state and that certain functions which in other countries are given to local governments, such as police, are administered in Norway by central authorities. Others, such as education, are administered in part locally, but under the careful supervision of the national government. If the unitary character of the state brings on a fairly high degree of national supervision, it does not seem to curtail the scope of activity undertaken by local governments. This may be due in part to the total extent of all governmental activity in Norway. The Norwegian commune, and to a less extent the county, is engaged in a wider sphere of activity than is the case in less socialistic countries. Two illustrations of the extent of function at the local level should be noted: the communal ownership of hydroelectric installations and socialized cultural operations, particularly municipally owned cinemas, which are found rather generally throughout Norway. Though these and other socialized activities are under central supervision, the fact of communal involvement in a wide range of activity, even though restricted by the unitary principle, gives the policy-maker and administrator in the local units really significant responsibilities. It is impossible to make a complete list of all the functions carried on by all the units of local government in Norway, but the following are areas in which most communes would be involved to a lesser or greater degree:[12] streets and highways, fire protection, water supply, sewage and garbage disposal, education, health protection, relief activities (including administration at the local level of old age insurance as well as supplementary activities), cultural activities such as provision of libraries, adult education facilities, cinemas, etc., sports and athletics, housing programs, and assistance to the state in the administration of justice, police, and the several parts of the social insurance program. In addition many communes are involved in hydroelectric enterprises and those along the coast generally have responsibilities for harbor installations.

In order to provide for the above services the commune and the county have the right to levy taxes — on property and on income — and borrow money within the limits set by law and subject usually to the supervision of the Department of Communal Affairs and Labor.

The actual process of policy-making in the communes cannot be described in detail in this discussion.[13] For the most part the procedure is essentially similar to that used in local governmental units in the United Kingdom and the United States. Only a few of the deviations from the Anglo-American pattern will be considered in the following paragraphs.

Three types of organs have a share in making policy in the Norwegian commune: the communal council, the executive board, and the committees, standing and special. Of these, the council is primary, but has the power to delegate its policy-making authority to the other groups. Certain matters cannot be delegated by the communal council, e.g., election of the mayor and members of the executive board, transfer or sale of real property, installation of a wholly new program or significant expansion of an old one, negotiation of concessions and leases that bind the commune for more than five years, borrowing money regardless of the amount, control over the communal treasurer, accounting and auditing procedures, establishment of rates for water and electricity, approval of the budget and appropriations procedures, and the establishment of a managerial system in the communal gov-

[12] For the sphere of jurisdiction of the county, see pp. 170–171.

[13] A complete description of policy-making in communal government can be found in Nordanger and Engh, pp. 75–135.

ernment. This rather comprehensive list would seem to place most policy questions in the hands of the communal councilors and give little responsibilitiy to the executive board and the committees. And in some rural communes such is the case; the executive board in these communes exercises limited power and the committees, particularly the special committees, such as the school committee, have only the barest responsibilities given them by law.

But in the larger communes the executive board performs really significant functions. It prepares policy proposals, often submits a draft budget to the council, and approves appropriations within certain limits. Perhaps the most important responsibility of the board is not in the area of policy-making but in administrative supervision. As a collective body it exercises general supervision with particular attention to fiscal accounting; and, as individuals, members of the board assume responsibility for specific administrative activities. Thus, somewhat like members of a small town council or city commission in the United States, each board member is in charge of a given municipal activity. And it is in the exercise of this supervisory function that executive boards make their greatest contribution. Of course, if the commune employs a municipal manager, the board delegates to him the job of final administrative control.

As was indicated above, the standing committees have powers delegated to them by the communal council; the special committees may have, in certain instances, additional responsibility conferred by special laws. Any matter that the communal council is authorized by law to delegate to the executive board can be delegated, at the council's discretion, to committees. The practice varies from commune to commune; in some the committees play a vital role, in others, particularly in small rural communes, they have little to do.

Communal Administration

Not a great deal more needs to be said about the administrative responsibility of members of the executive board. In many communes, particularly the smaller ones, the supervision of administrative services is well performed by these boards. But the serious disadvantage of the system lies in the absence of the integration essential to efficient administration. No one person has overall, final responsibility. Unlike the situation in some cities in the United States, the Norwegian mayor is not, by law at least, given power to act as chief administrator in the commune. To be sure, as has been indicated, his political position may place him in a strategic position where he can exercise a good deal of influence, but this usually affects policy proposals much more than the day to day administrative tasks in the commune.

There has been a general recognition of the fact, not only in Norway but in other democratic countries as well, that the managerial tasks facing local governments are most important; the municipality is primarily engaged in administration with the really important policy decisions made, at least in large part, at higher governmental levels. As a result of this view, even prior to the passage of the most recent general law on local government in 1954,[14] Norwegian cities had been required to install some kind of managerial system — either a single city manager or, in the case of the larger cities, a series of managers with responsibilities in the various administrative areas, e.g., finance, public works, education, etc. Under the law of 1954 this requirement has been strengthened; at present all communes with a population of 10,000 or more are required to establish some kind of managerial system, unless the communal council has specifically disapproved and this action has been supported by the Department of Communal Affairs and Labor. Communes with a population of less than 10,000 may install a managerial system with the approval of the Department.

The appointment of the communal manager (or managers in the case of a few large cities) is made by the communal council which also determines salary and responsibilities. The manager serves at the pleasure of the council, but dismissal by the council must be approved by the Department.

In general, the municipal manager has the following responsibilities:

1. To serve as chief administrator of the commune, supervising all managerial activities with particular attention to fiscal accounting.

2. To prepare a composite preliminary draft of the budget and act as the chief advisor to the council and the executive board in fiscal and economic matters.

3. To examine and approve all requests for disbursement of money.

4. To meet with and advise generally the council and executive board.

5. To undertake such other activities as are authorized by the council.

In the large cities with several managers (*rådmenn*), the finance manager (*finansrådmannen*) usually assumes the task of coordination implicit in the functions listed above. The other managers are in charge of the specialized administrative activities.

In some communes (particularly small cities and rural areas) a degree of administrative integration has been achieved through the establishment of central municipal offices in charge of an office manager (*kontorsjef*). In many respects this officer serves in much the same role as does the communal manager, but with somewhat less power: e.g., he normally would not have the authority to approve expenditures.

[14] *Lov om styret i kommunene av 12 november 1954.*

Sometimes this office is combined with the secretaryship of the executive board.

Since Norwegian communes are often engaged in the administration of social legislation and in certain economic activities, such as generation and distribution of electric power, the task of municipal management may be both diverse and burdensome. Frequently separate agencies or offices are established to manage the economic and social services of the communes. But, except in cases where they are responsible to state authority directly, these offices come under the surveillance and control of the regular municipal authorities.

No administration is better than the civil servants who perform the day to day tasks. The processes of recruitment, selection, placement, and promotion of municipal employees are crucial in any well governed municipality. Like the arrangements at the national level, these processes are not as centrally regulated in Norway as they are in the United States. There are no civil service commissions in Norway at any level of government, and no unified system of personnel administration is found even within individual counties. The process of selecting personnel is simple: the executive board or the manager advertises the vacancies, indicating the general qualifications desired, such as completion of a primary commercial school, *gymnasium,* or a given course of study in one of the institutions of higher learning. Applicants submit their credentials and the executive board, municipal manager, if there is one, or the committee in charge of a special activity makes the selection from the list of qualified candidates. As a rule, the selection authority is free to make its own decision; only occasionally will it be bound by specific local or national legislative prescription or subject to supervision by the appropriate national department. At present, special national legislation covers only the following types of municipal personnel: assessors, fire chiefs, foresters, business managers of local social insurance offices, personnel in local labor offices, and public school teachers.

The board or the committee with authority to employ civil servants also has the power of dismissal, subject to local regulations and often to a specific contract of employment. There is no national legislation regulating either dismissals or selection, but through its generalized control over local government the Department of Communal Affairs and Labor does exercise some indirect supervision of personnel practices. Communal servants have since 1956 been protected by a general law[15] which regulates for all employees — public and private — working conditions, hours of employment, and certain related matters.

Salary and wage scales are generally established by the communal council. Unlike the situation in some countries, civil servants in Nor-

[15] *Arbeidervernloven av 7 desember 1956.*

wegian communes have the right to strike and presumably the communal authorities could resort to lockouts. Such drastic steps are seldom taken, since mediation machinery is readily available and has proved adequate to settle most conflicts before they become critical. The Association of Cities (*Norges byforbund*) and the Association of Rural Communes (*Norges herredforbund*) have taken significant steps to rationalize salary and wage negotiation procedures. This has been helpful not only in eliminating, or at least softening, conflict, but has also provided a measure of common practice in this area of communal administration.[16]

There is no specific academic program in Norwegian institutions of higher learning organized with the aim of preparing general public administrators, national or communal. Specialized personnel, such as teachers, engineers, nurses, and physicians, are of course required to pass examinations in their respective fields. Although probationary periods for persons entering the civil service are usually provided, no program of inservice training has as yet been established. The entire area of training specifically for the public service has until only very recently been very much neglected.[17] A beginning was made in providing training for communal civil servants in 1949 when a special school, *Norges kommunal og sosialskole,* was established. This is a modest undertaking, but may in time assist in developing a more professionalized administrative class in the communal service.

No attempt will be made in this discussion to outline in any detail the personnel classification systems that prevail in Norwegian communes. As has been pointed out, there are substantial variations in the several parts of the country. But a threefold classification based upon the degree of responsibility and nature of work undertaken can be found in most communes. At the highest level is the "public" servant (*offentlige tjenestemann*) who enjoys not only a superior status and better compensation, but also a degree of freedom from legal responsibility in the performance of his duties. In the second category are the ordinary civil servants and secretarial personnel and in the third, the manual workers.

The communal civil servant in Norway is specifically protected in one important respect: he cannot be held liable for damages suffered by any person as a result of accident or miscalculation in the management of communal affairs unless it can be demonstrated that the civil servant was definitely exceeding his legal responsibilities or acting contrary to

[16] These two organizations do much more than provide machinery for salary negotiation. Their research activity and studies have been extremely useful both to administrators and students of local affairs.

[17] For a discussion of recent proposals at the national level, see pp. 114–116.

specified authorization. If the civil servant was acting according to rule, the person damaged has no recourse against him; whether the injured person can recover in a suit against the state or commune depends on circumstances. The present tendency in Norway is to protect the individual who has suffered damages by allowing him to obtain some form of redress from the state or the commune. Though Norway has no administrative court system comparable to that of France nor any similar system of law defining the liability of the state for the torts committed by its servants, the present trend in Norway seems more in line with the French pattern than in the direction of traditional Anglo-American practice, which in the past, if not at present, has given the individual scant protection, at least in the regular courts, against wrongs suffered at the hands of public servants.

In general, communal administration in Norway is reasonably good. There are, of course, the same complaints against bureaucracy, red tape, and undue delays that can be heard in any country where free speech prevails. The fact that the Norwegian commune has such a wide range of function, engaged as it is in economic and social service activities on a much wider scale than is the case in many countries, gives opportunity for more contact between citizens and their local government, and this naturally leads to more opportunities for discontent. But most criticisms are not really serious, and they usually relate to the irritations caused by rules, regulations, and bureaucratic practices that seem unavoidable in large public operations and, incidentally, are not always absent in private sectors of economic and social activity. There have been few instances of graft and corruption in Norwegian communal administration. Generally speaking, the Norwegian cities, towns, and rural districts are operated efficiently and with proper regard for the total welfare of all the people.

10

The Norwegian Social Security System

The Norwegian system of social security is perhaps the most elaborate in the world today. It covers all the people by general legislation against hazards of old age, sickness, unemployment, accidents, and disability; it provides family benefits to all; and protects certain classes in the society, including fishermen, forestry workers, and sailors, in particular ways through special legislation. It is a well established system and has long since passed the stage of political conflict. All parties and most groups, even on the political right wing, support the welfare state idea, not only in principle but, for the most part, in its present form.[1]

Most of the Norwegian social security legislation, with one significant exception, has been passed in the twentieth century. The first of the social security acts, providing for compensation in the event of industrial accidents, was passed in 1894 after other parts of a rather comprehensive plan proposed at that time were rejected. Also as early as 1845 a poor relief act was passed by the Norwegian parliament, but this did not contemplate any national program; it only provided for the collection and disbursement of funds by the communes for the relief of the poor. Throughout most of the nineteenth century, relief activity, whether relating to the aging, the unfortunates, or cripples, was provided by families, churches, and embryonic private relief societies.

[1] The material in this chapter has been adapted from several sources, but principally from an excellent survey in English by Dorothy Burton Skårdal, *Social Insurance in Norway* (Oslo, 1960). Also helpful were Karl Evang, *Health Services in Norway* (Oslo, 1960), and *The Norwegian System of Social Insurance* (Oslo, 1960).

It was in the first decade of the twentieth century that the real beginnings in the present comprehensive social security program were made. In 1908 the provisions of the Industrial Accident Insurance Program, enacted fourteen years earlier, was applied to fishermen, and three years later it was extended to seamen. In 1909 the first comprehensive health insurance act was passed, but it was not until 1936 that a national program of old age pensions was established.[2]

Listed below are the principal programs currently in operation with the date of first enactment of enabling legislation. In most cases there have been significant subsequent amendments to the original acts.[3]

Health Insurance — 1909
Old Age Pensions — 1936
Unemployment Insurance — 1938
War Pensions — 1941
Family Allowances — 1946
Pension Plan for Seamen — 1948
Pension Plan for Forestry Workers — 1951
Pension Plan for Fishermen — 1957
Survivors Benefits for Children — 1957
Occupational Injuries Insurance — 1958
General Disability Insurance — 1960

Special Programs

The three special pension acts for seamen, fishermen, and forestry workers and the general War Pensions Act can be dismissed with little comment. These special pension acts are similar in principle, but vary somewhat in detail and, in the case of seamen, disability payments in addition to pensions are provided if funds are available. All of these programs provide old age and survivors benefits and are financed by employers and employees and, in the case of forestry workers and fishermen, through supplementary special taxes. Other limited membership groups in Norwegian society besides fishermen, sailors, and forestry workers having special pension plans include civil servants, employees of the State Railway System, government manual workers, members of parliament, cabinet ministers, certain high level government officers who are not eligible under other plans, and pharmacists.

The general War Pensions Program, established first on December 9, 1941, by the government in exile in London and reinvalidated and

[2] There was some legislation passed during the 1920's and early 1930's, but this was not a particularly productive period for social welfare legislation in Norway. A new law protecting fishermen against occupational accidents was passed in 1920; in 1923 a law revising the Old Age Pension System was passed by the Storting, but not put into operation due to the unfavorable economic conditions existing at the time. In 1931 a new law was passed protecting seamen and fishermen against the hazards of occupational accidents.

[3] The provisions of these acts with subsequent amendments can be found in the Norwegian collection of laws, *Norges lover 1682–1960.*

expanded after the liberation, is limited to those persons — military or civilian — who suffered disabilities during the war. It provides disability payments, pays all costs of medical treatment, and covers expenditures in connection with rehabilitation and retraining. The amount of disability compensation depends upon the extent of the disability; a man with a 100 per cent disability receives 75 per cent of the estimated earned income he might have had if he had not been disabled. These basic amounts vary today from NK 4,700 to NK 11,200. This program will be liquidated as soon as the present list of eligibles has been served.

Health Program

Norway has, without question, been a pioneer in the development of programs for the protection of health and the care and cure of disease. It became obvious very early that a system of private medicine could not effectively cope with the health problems in a country as rugged in topography and as sparsely settled as Norway. A system of state-employed district physicians seemed the only method of insuring minimal medical attention for all people, regardless of where they lived. These physicians from the very beginning had two chief responsibilities: to take care of the sick and to administer a developing public health program. At the present time (1963) there are 425 district physicians operating in 418 districts. These men, representing about 11 per cent of the medical profession, are appointed by the King in Council and compensated by the state. In addition to their salary they may also earn fees as practicing physicians which, as will be clear from what follows, are paid in large part through the Health Insurance Program.

There is at present no intention to reduce the number of district physicians even with constantly improving transportation facilities. On the contrary, the office of the Director General of Health Services, to which the district physicians are responsible, has plans to expand the program in an attempt not only to offer improved curative services but, perhaps more important, to improve and enlarge the programs of preventive medicine and public health. In addition to the district physicians, about 30 per cent of Norway's 4,200 doctors are attached to hospital staffs and about 59 per cent are engaged in private practice. With few exceptions, Norwegian doctors are educated in one of the two medical schools located at the universities in Oslo and Bergen.

National Health Insurance

The system of health insurance in Norway is simple and easily understood; it allows the physician to be independent in his practice and permits patients to go to any doctor they choose. The doctor's fees are fixed by his professional association, and the patient normally pays the doctor and obtains a refund of from 60 to 100 per cent of the fee from the local insurance office (*Trygdekasse*). In certain instances the doctor may bill the *Trygdekasse* directly. This, then, is the essence of the system broadly conceived; the details are slightly more complicated.

By the amendments to the Health Insurance Program passed in 1956, all persons are required to be associated, either as independent members or as family members. Independent members of the program include unmarried persons who are past the age of eighteen and wives or husbands who are more or less independent of their respective spouses. Family members include children below the age of eighteen and dependent spouses. Two kinds of benefits are provided: reimbursements for medical care (in the broadest sense) and cash payments to compensate the sick or injured for loss of earning power. As has been indicated above, an average of approximately 75 per cent of the cost of treatment carried on outside of the hospital is paid for under the plan. Hospital costs are covered in their entirety; this includes all expenses incurred, such as medical and surgical treatment, drugs and medicines, X-rays, and the like. The cost of dental services, other than those intimately associated with general health problems, are not included in the Health Service Program.

Besides ordinary medical expenses and hospital expenses, transportation costs are also paid by the *Trygdekasse*. Often the cost of transportation from a remote district to a town or city may be substantially more than the cost of the medical treatment itself and, consequently, these expenses have to be met if any kind of equalitarian system for providing health services is to be maintained.

All employees are entitled to a daily compensation for time lost as a result of sickness or accident. These payments vary in amount from a minimum of NK 3 to NK 15 per day depending upon earned income. An additional grant of NK 2 per day is allowed for each dependent. Self-employed people can make voluntary contributions which will enable them to draw corresponding cash allowances. No payment is made for the first three days of each separate case of illness and the payments are limited to 104 weeks for any one illness.

Two other special grants available under the health program should be noted. A maternity benefit of NK 150 is paid unless the local administration of the Health Insurance Program makes provision for prenatal and postnatal treatment in a maternity clinic. To help cover funeral expenses a cash grant of NK 300 is given to the family of any deceased person.

The Health Insurance Program is financed by premiums paid by members and contributions made by employers, the state, and the municipalities. The total of these contributions amounts to slightly less than the premiums paid by members. At the beginning of 1960 the average weekly premium paid by the members in the lowest income class was NK 2.10 for employees and NK 1.05 for self-employed persons. The average premium for the highest income class for both groups was at that time NK 7.50. Self-employed persons were required by the 1960 rate schedule to pay on the average about NK 2 per week in addition to regular premiums to cover the program of supplementary cash grant allowances. In the 1960 budget for health insurance the premiums from the employees amounted to NK 417 million and the contributions from employers, the state, and the municipalities to NK 375 million.

The administration of the Health Insurance Program is in the hands of the local public insurance offices (*Trygdekasser*) mentioned above. These organizations have a significant degree of autonomy and are governed by five-man boards selected for four-year terms by the communal councils. A professional manager supervises the day to day administration of the local office and nation-wide supervision is provided by the National Insurance Institution (*Rikstrygdeverket*). This central authority appoints and supervises local managers as well as auditors and the appeal boards attached to the system. The National Insurance Institution also serves as the final appeal body in the event of disputes.

At the present time (1963) there are over 1,850,000 regular members of the Health Insurance Program and approximately 1,750,000 family members. Though the program is compulsory, there are still a few people not covered. This comes as a result of the continuing operation of private sickness insurance plans and certain particular arrangements for special classes of individuals. In a few years, when the compulsory plan becomes fully operative, all citizens and most resident aliens will be enrolled under the program.

Many of the arguments advanced against socialized medicine (or compulsory health insurance, if that is more pleasing to the ear) in the United States have little relevance and are given scant attention in Norway. The three arguments most frequently heard in American discussions are: any socialized system destroys the intimacy of the doctor-patient relationship; the doctor loses his initiative, since he is limited in the monetary rewards he can expect; and the patient has a tendency to abuse his privileges. Since patients may select their own doctors and this choice often results in a long term acquaintanceship, the doctor-patient relationship is essentially no different in Norway from that found in countries operating under a nonsocialist system. Respecting the second argument, it can safely be said that the average Norwegian physician stands in about the same comparative position in relation to members of other groups in his society as does his American colleague. Many people — both in Norway and the United States — refuse to take the "initiative" argument seriously; surely, they argue, men dedicated to science and healing are not significantly motivated by financial rewards beyond the acceptable standard of living level. And doctors in Norway live well. Finally there seems to be little evidence to support the contention that the Norwegian patient abuses the system. In 1958, the latest year for which figures are available, only about 41 per cent of the members were in receipt of some kind of benefit under the program; of these, 32 per cent received medical treatment outside of hospitals and 9 per cent were hospitalized.

Old Age Pensions

All Norwegian citizens, irrespective of income, are entitled at the present time to an old age pension on reaching the age of seventy, providing that they have lived in Norway during the five years before making application.[4]

At the present time (1963) the annual pension for single persons is NK 3,348 and for married couples NK 5,028. If the recipient supports any children under the age of eighteen, he receives a supplementary grant of NK 900 for each such person.[5] Resident aliens, as well as citizens, are entitled to old age pensions, provided they fulfill the stated residence requirements.

Since the amounts provided by the national pension program are modest at best and since in some communities the cost of living is higher than in others, municipalities are permitted to give supplementary grants to persons receiving old age pensions. Unlike the regulations governing the national program, the pensioner may be required to submit to a means test in order to qualify for a supplement from municipal sources. At present about 150 municipalities give supplementary old age allowances, and 125 of these require a means test.

Prior to January 1, 1959, old age pensions were financed by special taxation. In 1959 the plan was placed on an insurance basis, partly because this was thought to be financially more secure and also because it seemed wise to require some contributions from the recipients. At present all premium paying members of the Health Insurance Program also pay regular premiums for old age insurance and disability insurance, ranging in amounts from NK 3 to NK 18 per week. Premiums are not paid by persons over seventy years of age since in al-

[4] The Old Age Pension System, established in 1936, contained a means test which was removed by the Act of 1957.

[5] The amount of pension has increased as the cost of living has gone up, although there is no automatic escalator clause in the law.

most all cases they are receiving old age pensions. Regular premiums are supplemented, as they are in the Health Insurance Program, by contributions from employers, the national government, and the municipality, and the total of these contributions accounts for slightly less than the amount paid by the premium paying members. The supplementary grants provided by some of the communes referred to above are financed by regular taxes.

The same authorities that administer the Health Insurance Program also administer the Old Age Pension System. The local organ is the *Trygdekasse* and in this case it is also supervised by the National Insurance Institution. During the first year of operation (1959), the new plan of old age pensions showed a deficit of NK 15 million after paying pensions to 275,000 people. It is expected that a balanced budget can be attained after more experience has been had with the rate structure.

Survivors Benefits for Children

By an act of April 26, 1951, any child under eighteen years of age is entitled to a payment of NK 900 annually if his father is dead or if his mother, who had been his chief means of support, has passed away. Similarly, payments are made to children born out of wedlock if no legal means of support have been established. No means test is required to qualify for benefits under this plan.

The Survivors Benefits Program is financed by a small premium (NK 0.15 per week) paid by all persons under seventy who are members of the Health Insurance Program. This is supplemented by an equal amount from employers, the municipality, and the state. The program is administered in much the same manner as is health insurance. In 1959 over 25,000 people received benefits under the program.

Family Allowances

A program of family allowances was established shortly after the close of World War II (October 1, 1946) providing payments to parents for every child, excluding the first. At the present time the parents receive NK 360 annually for each eligible child until he reaches the age of sixteen. The program is applicable to citizens and resident aliens alike, the only qualification being that one of the parents or the child must have been in residence in Norway six months prior to the application for the cash grant. Benefits may be paid for the first child in certain cases: if the parents are divorced or if one or both are dead or if they are not at the time of application married to each other. Also allowances are given for all children supported in children's homes or in special schools irrespective of the size of the family. The Family Allowance Program is administered jointly by the National Insurance Institution and the local insurance office (*Trygdekasse*) and is financed by the state and the municipalities under, at present, a respective ratio of seven to one. On January 1, 1960, 315,000 families with 550,000 eligible children received benefits under this program.

Unemployment Insurance

The original program providing payments to the unemployed, inaugurated in 1938, was replaced in 1959 by new legislation. At present all persons under seventy years of age with an annual income of over NK 1,000, with the exception of certain agricultural and domestic workers employed by close relatives, most government employees, fishermen, forestry workers, salesmen working on a commission, and self-employed persons, are covered by compulsory unemployment insurance. The program is financed by matching premiums paid by employers and employees, varying in accordance with income from NK 0.50 per week to NK 1.90 per week. The administration of the program is provided by the municipal labor boards under the supervision of the National Directorate of Labor. To be eligible for benefits the employee must normally have been a premium-paying member of the plan for a minimum of forty-five weeks during the last three years or for thirty weeks during the last year.

Several kinds of benefits are available: daily payments, transportation allowances incurred in seeking employment, expenses of vocational training, and supplementary allowances in certain cases for families. Daily payments are made for a maximum of twenty weeks in any one year and vary in amount depending upon the income of the recipient. Because supplementary allowances are given for dependents, a man with a wife and three children in one of the higher wage categories could, for example, receive as much as NK 24 per day. To be eligible for this payment, a person must demonstrate that he is seeking employment and that he is willing to accept a job offered to him by the state or communal employment office. In 1959, with over 820,000 employees insured, the income of the fund was approximately NK 104 million and the disbursement NK 90 million.

Occupational Injuries Insurance (Workman's Compensation)

The Occupational Injuries Insurance Program, covering all regularly employed persons and certain other specifically defined categories, such as fishermen, sealers, and students, went into effect on January 1, 1960. In addition to the above special classes, the act also covers seamen on board Norwegian vessels, employees of whaling companies, and employees of civilian airlines, even while serving abroad. Self-employed persons are not covered by the compulsory workmen's compensation program, but may join on a voluntary basis. The benefits provided under the program include: medical, hospital, and rehabilitation costs, as well as weekly cash payments.

All medical and hospital expenses made necessary by the occupational injury are cared for in accordance with rules laid down in the Health Insurance Program. If the injury makes necessary some type of vocational retraining, a supplementary grant which can run to as much as NK 8,400 may be paid.

During the time the injury is being treated, an allowance of from NK 5 to NK 15 per day (depending on wage level), plus NK 2 for each dependent, is paid to the employee. If, after treatment is completed, the degree of invalidity is determined to be less than 15 per cent, the employee receives no further cash grant. But, if incapacity is judged to be more than 15 per cent but less than 30 per cent, he will be paid a lump sum corresponding in amount to three years of the regular daily cash payments mentioned above.[6] If the disability is judged to be more than 30 per cent, the recipient may receive as much as 60 per cent of his previous earned income as a disability pension and in addition to this, NK 900 annually for each child under eighteen years of age. He may also be granted a supplement for nursing care up to NK 2,400 per year, if this is necessary. If the injury results in death, his spouse (if more than forty years of age) will be paid an annual pension of no more than 40 per cent of his previous earned income. But this could be supplemented if the widow is responsible for the support of children under the age of eighteen; most widows, even though under forty, applying for pensions receive them if they demonstrate the need and have children under eighteen years of age. A widow forfeits her pension on remarriage, but if she is subsequently divorced the pension may be restored.

That part of the Occupational Injuries Insurance Program covering employees is financed totally by premiums paid by employers. These premiums vary from NK 0.60 to NK 9.00 per employee per week depending primarily upon the risks involved in the occupation of the employees. The premiums for students are paid totally by the state

[6] From 15 to 30 per cent of the claimants under this program are paid a lump sum equivalent to three years of regular payments. In computing the payments due the minimum annual income reckoned with is NK 6,800 and the maximum NK 14,000.

and the premiums for fishermen are paid by the insured workman with supplementary payments made by the state.

The Occupational Injuries Insurance Program is administered in about the same manner as is the Health Insurance Program. Over 1,500,000 persons are at present insured under the Occupational Injuries Insurance Program and the budget for 1960 was approximately NK 120 million.

General Disability Insurance

On January 22, 1960, a comprehensive program of disability insurance was passed by the Norwegian Storting. Prior to this time, under legislation passed in 1936, aid had been provided to the blind and to certain special classes of physically handicapped persons. In accordance with the new legislation, all physically handicapped persons are entitled to rehabilitation, retraining courses, daily cash grants, as well as the supplementary allowances described below, without the imposition of any restrictions on the cause of the disability or of any means test.

There were three distinct acts passed in establishing this new program, one of which made significant changes in the act of 1936 which had given aid to the blind and certain classes of crippled persons. It is impossible in this connection to recite all the details; a brief description of the General Disability Act will have to suffice.[7]

The General Disability Insurance Program covers all persons resident in Norway who become handicapped from whatever cause.[8] Every disabled person is entitled to a basic annual cash grant of NK 600 which can be increased from NK 900 to NK 1,200 if his disability results in certain demonstrable added expense. He receives this grant whether or not he has an income from a job or from some other source. Besides this basic grant, the disabled person who requires special nursing services or other help receives an allowance of NK 720 per year. He may also receive through loans or grants such money as is necessary to promote a program of rehabilitation which may make possible improved income-producing possibilities for the disabled person.

If a disabled person is unable to work, he will receive, providing he can demonstrate that he is at least 66 per cent disabled, over and above the basic grant and applicable allowances for nursing services, an an-

[7] For details of the entire new program, see Skårdal, pp. 77–95.

[8] Certain groups, such as alcoholics, delinquents, and maladjusted persons, are excluded, but most of these — particularly alcoholics and people suffering from psychological maladjustments — are cared for under the Health Insurance Program.

nual pension of NK 3,348 which is equivalent to the amount paid old age pensioners. This payment can be increased by 50 per cent if the recipient supports a spouse over sixty years of age or if the spouse is also disabled. The pension is paid regardless of past employment; thus if a nonemployed wife supported by her husband becomes disabled, she will receive the disability pension. Additional grants of NK 900 per year are allowed for each child under eighteen years of age that the disabled person supports. As has been indicated, no means test is required; a person will receive his allowance or pension regardless of the amount of his personal income. Disability allowances are not given to persons under eighteen years of age nor to persons over seventy. These people are cared for by other programs: Family Supplements for the youth and Old Age Pensions for the people over seventy. Since the disability allowance and pension are small in comparison with the average annual earnings of male industrial workers (NK 13,500 in 1960) the law permits municipalities to provide supplementary grants and, to date, a substantial number of municipalities have done so.

Like most of the other insurance programs, this one is administered locally by the communal insurance offices (*Trygdekasse*) under the supervision of the National Insurance Institution. The cost of the plan is covered by premiums paid by members of the Health Insurance Program.[9] The employer, the municipalities, and the state pay in the same proportion as they do to the Old Age Pension Fund.

International Cooperation in Social Security

A good measure of cooperation in the area of social security has been established in Scandinavia in the last decade. At present, the nationals of each of the five countries (Norway, Denmark, Sweden, Finland, and Iceland) enjoy the same rights if they reside in one of the other Scandinavian countries as do the natives of that country. Norway has special agreements with Denmark, Sweden, and Iceland permitting the transference of health insurance membership between local offices in the four countries.

A convention between Norway and the United Kingdom extends the protection of the health programs to British citizens while residing in Norway. (The British program, it will be recalled, extends automatically to all resident aliens.) This agreement also allows the British citizen, temporarily employed in Norway, to continue payments to his own social security program without obligation, at least for the first twelve months, to participate in like Norwegian programs.

More limited agreements have been concluded with France and The

[9] See pp. 185–186 for amounts.

Netherlands. The agreement with France guarantees citizens of one of the countries resident in the other the same social security rights as natives, subject of course to the terms of the convention. The agreement with The Netherlands extends the benefits of the Occupational Injuries Insurance Plan to citizens of each of the countries whenever they are residing temporarily or permanently in the other. A reciprocal agreement on certain aspects of social security has recently been negotiated with Italy.

Norway has been active in cooperating with the other European states, the International Labor Organization, and the United Nations in working out other types of international cooperation in the social security field. For the most part these are agreements in principle and do not have, as yet, significant operational character.

Evaluation

The Norwegian social security program is most assuredly comprehensive in that it provides, as the above sketch indicates, cradle to grave protection. There is general acceptance of the program by nearly all people in Norway and little or no controversy even on the details. Most people express real appreciation and a complete understanding of the way the state and the commune protect them against the hazards of old age, sickness, accident, unemployment, and the like. This general acceptance is noticeable among all classes in the society. There are no active saboteurs of the system, and the cooperation of the professional people involved — physicians, nurses, social workers — is generally complete and enthusiastic.

To be sure, there are certain critics who argue that the Norwegian people are too well protected and have become too reliant on the state and, as a result, they may be unwilling to assume responsibility for their own problems. But this type of critic would find it difficult to suggest specific curtailments in the program. Others criticize the program because of its alleged inadequacies: the old age pension is too small, the sick allowances are inadequate, hospital facilities are insufficient to meet pressing demands, nurses are underpaid, and facilities for the care of convalescents and permanently handicapped persons do not meet the legitimate demands. There are also some critics who call for a reorganization of the administration of the system; there are without question at the present time too many different laws and too many individual programs. An attempt was made in 1948 to create an integrated system which would simplify administration and premium collections, but only minor steps have been taken to implement these proposals.

An evaluation of any social security system depends obviously upon one's individual political and social philosophy. An extreme individualist would be shocked at the degree to which the Norwegian people are protected by the community, while the left-wing socialist would, as some Norwegians do, point to the need for expanding the social security system. It is difficult to argue from an "objective" point of view about any system which becomes so related to one's assumption concerning the proper role of the state. But, in spite of this hazard, one cannot but conclude that the Norwegian system fits the situation and the needs of the Norwegian people and operates on the whole effectively. The private practice of medicine, reliance on charity, savings, and private security plans to care for the aging would be as impossible in Norway as would private ownership of the railroad system. The topography, the climate, the limitation of resources, the dependence on relatively few types of economic activities, and the consequent austerity that this has brought to certain classes in society, as well as the uneven spread of the population, all have contributed to make a modest system of state ownership of transportation lines and certain industrial facilities and a fairly elaborate system of social security inescapable in Norway.

11

The State and the Economy

Introduction

Several years ago Marquis Childs wrote a book entitled *Sweden: The Middle Way,* and ever since certain intelligent commentators have characterized all of the Scandinavian countries somewhat as Childs did Sweden at that time; for them there is no real conflict of economic philosophies within these countries. Other observers, particularly in the United States, on viewing Norway — and, for that matter, other parts of Scandinavia — have difficulty understanding the relationships that exist between the state and the economy. They see in Norway a socialist government which has been in undisputed control since 1946. And at the same time they observe a considerable amount of free private enterprise. Quite obviously what they are observing is a mixed system operating with certain socialistic principles and at the same time allowing a significant degree of free enterprise. If there is confusion in the mind of the observer, it probably comes as a result of his failure to understand that in no country in the world today, not even excepting the Soviet Union, is there a socialist system operating with complete purity. Certainly under the Labor government in the United Kingdom and under socialist regimes in Scandinavia, some dating back before World War II, there was no attempt on the part of the ruling party to install full-dress socialistic programs. To do so would have called for an enormous job of expropriation to be undertaken by the state and the municipalities, which obviously would have been utterly impossible from a political point of view. What really happened in the northern countries was that the state took over certain sectors of the economy, as this seemed unavoidable, managing them directly under government departments or through public corporations. But after this was done, a great deal of the economy still remained in private hands, subject, of course, to varying degrees of government control.

In Norway, even before World War II, the state owned and managed, besides such enterprises as the post and telegraph system, the railroads, some of the hydroelectric installations, the liquor dispensary, and the public corporation responsible for the importation of grain. Since 1945 certain of the iron and steel installations have been put under state ownership, as well as additional hydroelectric operations, but the larger share of the Norwegian economy remains under private control. In 1962 about 16 per cent of the gross national product in Norway was created in the public sector of the economy and roughly 84 per cent in the private sector. Enterprises owned directly by the state or by municipalities are managed in much the same way as are private corporations. And since these are managed in a similar fashion as they are in the United States and the United Kingdom, nothing much need be said about their internal governance. To be sure, the relationship of the state to the private sector of the economy is different in Norway from that found in certain other countries, and this will be examined in more detail later.

Certain Norwegian commentators, particularly those of the non-socialist persuasion, take great pains to point out that Norway is in no real sense a socialist country. Professor Ole Myrvoll, in his Tallman Lectures given at Bowdoin College in 1962, emphasized this point with vigor.[1] And there is ample evidence to support this contention. Norway has for centuries had an individualistic tradition. Much of the early legislation protecting and promoting the welfare of the individual was passed before any organized socialist group had appeared in Norway. The first proposal for legislation to protect labor was advanced by the Conservative party in the 1870's and the factory control law of 1892 was sponsored by a Liberal government. Respecting the ideological background of the present-day relationship of state to economy in Norway, Professor Myrvoll has this to say: "The so-called welfare state is not a socialistic, pre-engineered experiment based on Marxist philosophy. It cannot be called 'socialism' without stretching the meaning of that word so far that it becomes meaningless. It is a product of

[1] Ole Myrvoll, "Profile of Scandinavian Economic System," *Tallman Lectures*, mimeographed (Brunswick, Maine, 1962). The author is indebted for some of the material in this chapter to Professor Myrvoll's analysis as presented in these lectures as well as in personal conversations. He is also indebted to E. Brofoss for much statistical material which was taken from the scholarly presentations made by Mr. Brofoss to the students of the International Summer School of the University of Oslo in 1960 and 1961.

Western political and social philosophy, developed gradually and formed by the heritage of history and tradition." [2]

There is unmistakable evidence that even Norwegian liberals of the nineteenth century, unlike their cousins in certain other countries, did not fear the state, but rather welcomed some state intervention if this were necessary to protect the individual. And the present-day leaders of the Labor party are perhaps more accurately called political pragmatists than they are doctrinaire socialists. As a matter of fact, they have been criticized by some of their left wing associates for lack of enthusiasm for the socialist party line. But having said this, the fact remains that despite a good deal of private control of the economy and the disclaimers by nonsocialists there is operating in Norway a set of institutions and practices that for the sake of accuracy must be called socialistic, because the guiding principle is state ownership and control. It goes without saying that all of these socialist enterprises are democratically established and popularly controlled. It should also be clear that because part of the economy is managed under socialist principles, this does not make the *entire* system socialistic. It may be, as Marquis Childs suggests, a middle way.

Nature of Resources

In Chapter 1 of this book the point was made that Norway is a country poor in natural resources with a very limited amount of arable land and plagued by economic and social complications due to its peculiar size and shape. Although the agricultural part of the population has decreased notably in recent years, two-thirds of the Norwegian people still live in rural and suburban districts. Principally because of the topography, about two-thirds of the population can be found within twenty to thirty miles of the coast. The heaviest concentration of people is in eastern Norway in and around Oslo and some of the other larger cities.

The main resources besides agricultural produce, it will be recalled, include timber, fish, and water power. There is some iron ore, but this is of rather low grade, and some nonferrous ores, but these are not found in large quantities. Norway proper has no coal and no oil.

Because of its location Norway has always been a maritime country and has relied heavily upon its merchant marine to provide foreign exchange for use in paying for essential imports, many of which have been extremely important to the Norwegian economy. Roughly 85 per cent of the bread grain and 50 per cent of animal fodder concentrates,

[2] Myrvoll, I, p. 4.

all sugar, coffee, tobacco, cotton, rubber, hides, and most of the iron ore used in manufacturing have to be imported. Exports (including shipping) and imports each account for about 40 per cent of the entire Norwegian gross national product. Because of this dependence upon foreign trade, Norway constantly has to take steps to improve her export position. Since there is a limit to the wood pulp and fish available for export, and since price fluctuations on the international markets are always a hazard, Norwegians must look not only to increasing the bulk of exports, but also changing the form, if by so doing higher prices can be commanded. For example, rather than export raw or dried fish as has been done in quantity in the past, increasing the fish freezing and canning facilities will without doubt bring significantly improved export markets and prices. Also, rather than continuing to export wood pulp in quantity, the Norwegian economic planners have encouraged the expansion of paper manufacturing and related processing facilities.

Since income from shipping is crucial to closing any gap between exports and imports, it is not difficult to understand the concern of the Norwegians with any problem or policy that might disrupt any given shipping situation. In recent years one particularly difficult problem has been caused by the fact that some ships owned by Americans and others have been given certain advantages, particularly respecting taxes, by registering under the flags of other countries (e.g., Liberia, Panama). This the Norwegians deem unfair competition. But Norwegian shipping continues to expand (about 20 per cent of all additional capital expenditures in Norway is now going into shipping) and, as a result, newer, more efficient ships are being added to the fleet. This would seem to indicate, as well as promise, that Norway can remain in a good competitive position in the shipping business.[3]

One dramatic way of demonstrating the dependence of Norway on foreign trade is to examine the effect that price increases or decreases have on her balance of payments. Assuming an average increase in export prices of 10 per cent, with the price of imports remaining constant, the net increase in national income would be about 4 per cent or the equivalent of one year of national economic growth. If, on the other hand, export prices were to drop by 10 per cent or import prices advance by the same amount, an entire year of economic growth could be wiped out. Because the number and variety of exports are limited, it is not unrealistic to suggest that price variations of the kind used in this illustration are quite possible.[4]

[3] *The Norway Yearbook* (Oslo, 1962), pp. 355–359.
[4] Myrvoll, III, p. 5.

Post-World War II Economic Trends

World War II had a devastating effect on the Norwegian economy. Industrial production in 1945 was down 55 to 60 per cent from the level of 1938. Shortages of all kinds resulted in a reduction in consumption running perhaps as high as 65 per cent of the prewar level. Though the Germans had employed a scorched earth policy in North Norway, direct war damage did not account for great losses of capital equipment in other parts of Norway. However, no attempt to replace worn machinery was made during the war, and as a result in 1946 the Norwegian government found itself with a formidable task of rehabilitating industry. Roughly 19 per cent of the national wealth had been lost during the war. Also the cost of occupation in Norway was significantly higher than that in some of the other occupied countries.

Perhaps the most important problem facing the government in 1946 was inflation. The Germans had financed some of the war expenditures by increasing the notes in circulation by five times during the interval between 1939 and 1945. Thus at the end of the war there was a serious imbalance between money and goods available; there was too much money and there were too few goods.

To meet this problem the government could have taken several different courses. They could have simply let the spiral of rising prices go unchecked until a crash occurred and then have awaited a slow recovery. Or they could have engaged in a radical monetary devaluation process, exchanging the old *krone* for one worth significantly less.

The government rejected both of these courses and decided upon a policy of price controls, credit controls, monetary controls — all of which, it was hoped, would keep prices at a stable level after 1946. To implement this program the government continued the system of controls and rationing of consumers' goods that had been in effect during the war. They also imposed strict import restrictions and provided for allocations of all raw materials. All prices, profits, rents, and interest rates were regulated by the state. To keep wages in step with prices and to attempt to avoid inflationary increases in labor costs, an escalator system for wages was installed. As a result, during the period from 1945 to 1950, with the cost of living index rising by only 2 per cent, wage increases were kept at a minimum. To further stabilize the monetary situation, the exchange rate was fixed at NK 20 = one pound (U.K.). To meet the effect of rising prices on certain indispensable imported goods a subsidy system was established. Thus the state was able to assist through direct monetary payments those enterprises that found themselves faced with increasing costs of imports. Subsidies were also employed to aid domestic agriculture, and in line with that policy producers of milk, butter, cheese, meat, and pork received direct grants from the government. This policy had the effect of holding down the cost of living, since some of the most essential food products could be sold to the consumer at lower prices than would have been possible if a free market system had been operating.

In an attempt to freeze the potential purchasing power, restrictions were imposed upon the free use of bank deposits by individuals. This was essential if price stability was to be maintained. Two other methods of reducing the inflationary pressure were instituted: increasing national taxes and borrowing more money than was needed to cover the budgeted expenses.

A more long-range program of the Labor government was announced soon after it came to power in 1946. The principal objectives of this program were full employment, improvement in the standard of living, and redistribution of incomes among the social groups in the society.

It was assumed that these objectives could not be reached through private initiative, and it was at this point that a decision was made to install a planned economy with the objective of stimulating and controlling industry, agriculture, fishing, and shipping. The long-term objectives mentioned above were to be spelled out and an annual plan, called the national budget, was to be established. The national budget should not be confused with the state fiscal budget; the former is in reality nothing more than an annual economic plan with objectives to be realized, in various parts of the economy, through legislative and administrative action — either direct or indirect. Examples of direct instruments employed were price controls, rationing, and import regulation. The chief types of indirect instruments used were monetary and credit regulations.

Shortly after 1945 all major consumer goods were rationed, but as supplies improved, rationing was gradually abolished. By 1952 the last two commodities, coffee and sugar, were removed from the ration list, although there still remained regulations affecting certain imports which for all practical purposes constituted a kind of rationing. With the removal of the regulation of the sale of private automobiles in 1960, the last remnants of consumer controls through the rationing process were eliminated. But there remained a significant control of certain kinds of consumer expenditures through the requirement of building permits and the maintenance of general control of building and construction imposed by the permit system and publicly supported lending institutions; all of these have been made more elastic in the last two years.

It should be re-emphasized that the Labor party, in control of the government since 1946, is dedicated in principle, if not always in practice, to gradualistic socialism. But it has made little use of nationalization or socialization as a means of extending the influence of the state on the economy. Only a few state-owned enterprises have been established since 1945, e.g., a state monopoly for procurement and distribution of fishing equipment, a state monopoly for medicine and drugs, a steel plant at Mo in North Norway, aluminum plants in Årdal and Sundal, and the expansion of certain hydroelectric installations. As is obvious, the state has not expropriated privately owned industrial establishments, but has rather gone into new areas not thought to be adequately serviced by private ownership. By 1960 employment in public industries had accounted for only about 6 per cent of the total employment in manufacturing.[5]

Economic Planning and Organization

It should be clear from the discussion thus far that the activities undertaken by the Labor Government have been, and remain, essentially middle-of-the-road programs. Attempts have been made to allow the privately owned sectors of the economy to remain in private hands and to limit the expansion of socialized industries. It will be recalled that some critics within the Labor party point to the fact that the Labor government has not been socialistic at all, but has been altogether too friendly to capitalistic enterprise. They argue that the government, particularly in the early years after the war, was inclined to give advantages to old, well-established private firms rather than launch into new state-owned enterprises. It is doubtful that many American observers would agree with this criticism because they view the Norwegian economy as being rather tightly controlled by the state regardless of the fact that much of it does remain under private ownership. And, compared with American practice, the Norwegian state does intervene to a substantial extent in private business affairs.

Before considering the objectives, techniques, and the more specific goals of national economic planning, it might be useful to examine briefly certain features of the organization of the Norwegian economy.

Both the trade unions and the employers have national organizations. The Federation of Labor was formed in 1899 and the Norwegian Employers Association in 1900. The Federation of Labor has a membership of over a half million, and the Employers Association includes most employers except those operating on extremely small scales. All wage rates of any importance are fixed after negotiations between

[5] Per Kleppe, *Main Aspects of Economic Policy in Norway* (Oslo, 1960), pp. 6–9.

these two national federations. Usually the negotiators reach acceptable terms, but, if this becomes impossible, the case is referred to a national mediator who is a government official. In the unlikely event that the negotiator fails to secure agreement, the case may be submitted to compulsory arbitration.[6]

Agricultural producers in Norway, not unlike their counterparts in most countries, are faced with inelastic demand and seasonal price fluctuations. To meet these problems the Norwegian farmers have organized producers cooperatives which are called "marketing centrals." To a significant extent these "centrals" were sponsored and promoted by the government under provisions of legislation passed in the 1920's and 1930's. At present the producers cooperatives (or "centrals") cover 99 per cent of all milk production, 70 per cent of the wholesale business in meat and eggs, and 50 per cent of fruit sold at wholesale. In every case, except the fur "central" in which prices are determined by auction, prices are fixed by the board of the appropriate "central." Since each organization is obligated to accept everything delivered to it by the producers, prices cannot be fixed at arbitrarily high levels. Also the state price control mechanism has in the past operated to keep prices within a reasonable scale.

Besides marketing centrals for agricultural products, there are comparable organizations for the marketing of fish. If the fisherman were to operate independently, he would be at the mercy of the small number of wholesalers who could take advantage of the fact that much fishing is seasonal in character. According to the plan now in operation, fishermen sell their fish to the appropriate "central" (for cod, herring, etc.) at predetermined prices. The authorities of the "central" sell the fish, receiving differentiated prices for the form in which it is sold (fresh, frozen, dried, etc.). At the close of the year each participating fisherman shares in the profits of the operation of the "central."

Other areas of the Norwegian economy which are organized in strong national associations include retail and wholesale merchandising, shipping, banking, and insurance. Certain groups, such as manufacturers and farmers, have separate organizations from those described in the preceding paragraphs. In summary, it can be said that the Norwegian economy is not atomistic, but, rather, well and responsibly organized.

In developing the economic plan and in preparing the document (national budget) which incorporates the details of the plan for any given year, the following will need to be given consideration:

1. What has been the economic development to date and what resources are available for future development?

[6] Herbert Dorfman, *Labor Relations in Norway* (Oslo, 1958), pp. 76 ff.

2. What are the political objectives to be accomplished? These may be general, such as full employment, equalization of income among workers, or they may be specific as, e.g., development of given regions or given industries.

3. What are the economic variables which may be out of the control of any planning mechanism? These would include, among other things, price fluctuations abroad, consumer demands, and degree of expected foreign investment. In as far as possible these variables should be identified and reasonable guesses made concerning their effects on the plan.

4. What instruments should be used in implementing the plan? The following have all been used: tax rates, public spending, rationing, licensing, and the discount rate.

After these questions have been answered, the details of the plan are prepared by the civil servants in the appropriate governmental departments, and the resulting document, the Norwegian national budget, is submitted by the Cabinet to the Storting for its scrutiny. Once accepted by the Storting, the national budget becomes the economic blueprint to be followed by the Cabinet and the appropriate government agencies in determining economic goals and procedures for the ensuing year.

Although highly centralized economic planning like that employed in Norway is often advocated by left-of-center political groups, there seems no lack of agreement on the need for economic planning even among the more conservative elements in Norwegian politics. Though there is rather general agreement on the need for a plan, there is often serious disagreement among the political groups on the specific political and economic instruments to be used in implementing the plan. Thus, for example, all may agree on increasing production in certain areas, but some would oppose violently price controls as a way of accomplishing the objective.

The mechanisms and instruments used to implement economic planning in Norway vary in scope and specificity; they may be general or quite particularized. In the general category taxation would no doubt be of most importance and associated with it would be procedures for transferring wealth from the prosperous to the less prosperous segments of society. And, as is the case in other countries, this redistribution of wealth is accomplished through taxation followed by direct or indirect subsidies of one sort or another. The Norwegian income tax rates are progressive and, compared with the United States, high. A person with an income of $15,000 would be taxed at a 60 per cent rate. Besides income taxes, there are excise taxes on many commodities, e.g., spirits, beer, wine, tobacco, chocolate, and gasoline. In addition to these there is a national 10 per cent sales tax.

Some of the tax money collected by state and county governments is returned to certain segments of the population in the form of subsidies, grants-in-aid of insurance programs, and in other ways. For example, a program of family allowances has been in effect since 1946, and this has been financed from tax revenues.[7] All families receive these allowances, irrespective of income, but the low income groups benefit most since they have paid little, if anything, in taxes to support the program. Other types of payments made to effect a redistribution of wealth include disability pensions, survivors benefits to children who have lost their means of support, pensions to the blind, etc. Also, most of the social security programs are supported in part by taxation and, to the extent that they are, they help implement transfer of wealth from one segment of society to another.[8]

As an example of specific types of devices used to implement national economic planning, one might cite the means used to influence investments at various times in the period after the war. By all odds the largest part of increased investments has been provided in the private sector of the economy, especially in manufacturing, shipping, and housing. Encouragement to investment has been given through certain monetary and credit policies of the government as well as by licensing regulations, favorable tax concessions, and through a program of government guarantees to lending agencies. If interest rates are kept low and if certain kinds of investments are encouraged by government guarantees of loans, private investors can be encouraged to borrow money and take risks. To encourage investments in North Norway after 1951 the national government offered preferential tax treatment which proved very effective in encouraging the flow of capital into the three northern counties.

The Economic Plan in Operation

In order to show more clearly the specific objectives of an annual economic plan, a brief summary of some of the provisions in the national budget for 1960 is included below.[9]

One of the first matters considered in the plan for 1960 was the

[7] See p. 187.

[8] The entire program of social insurance, covering hazards of health accident, old age, unemployment, and the like, is in a certain sense part of any economic plan. No separate discussion of the relationship of benefits under these programs to the economy generally will be undertaken in this chapter. The programs are described in Chapter 10. Obviously a welfare program like the one in operation in Norway has the effect of providing income stability which in turn makes less catastrophic the impact of unemployment and accidents on the purchasing power of the consumer.

[9] The 1960 plan is used largely because it seemed to the author to offer better illustrative material than more recent ones.

public expenditure program for the coming year. Increases in past years in appropriations for educational facilities, roads, and airports were noted with the comment that continuing pressures in these areas would lead to increased appropriations. A plan was proposed to eliminate the 8 per cent tax on reserve funds and to reduce the excise duty on chocolate to 60 per cent as compared to 90 per cent in 1959. Other excise duties were manipulated up and down. Note was made of the fact that the duty-free import of machinery had been eliminated as of January 1, 1960, and the rationing of automobiles was to be eliminated in October 1960.

The total budget for the several state banks (manufacturing bank, municipal bank, government bank for fishermen, loan fund for students, post office savings bank) was to be increased in 1960 by NK 70 million from the figures of 1959. Each of these was treated separately, and the presumption was that their additional credit facilities would improve the situation in certain sectors of the economy. The activities of the Bank of Norway (roughly comparable to the Federal Reserve System in the United States) in the area of the kind of credit allowed for improvement of the export situation was considered in some detail in the national budget. One difficult problem in this area had been the financing of the purchase of ships abroad. Ship owners have objected in the past to the requirement imposed by the Bank of Norway and the government that all such purchases be covered to as large an extent as possible by loans raised abroad. This policy was re-examined in detail in the national budget of 1960 but continued for the year to come.

Provision for changing building regulations was made in 1960 to eliminate some of the previous restrictions on size of living units. Increased allocations of material were continued for industrial buildings.

The quotas for imports, remaining regulated, were to be increased in accordance with the provisions of the convention of the European Free Trade Association. Negotiations were also opened to readjust other tariffs consistent with bilateral and multilateral agreements. The hope was expressed that further tariff reductions could be made, particularly in the area of raw materials and semimanufactured goods.[10]

[10] No account is included here of the experience of Norway as a member of the European Free Trade Association which was established in 1959 with Denmark, Norway, Sweden, the United Kingdom, Switzerland, Austria, and Portugal as members. The first reduction in import duties within EFTA of 20 per cent became effective on July 1, 1960. Subsequent reductions were to be made in the hope that all customs barriers would be eliminated by January 1, 1970. The future of EFTA depends now upon its relation to the European Economic Community after unfavorable action on the application for membership filed by the United Kingdom. If the United Kingdom were finally to be admitted, Norway would without question also join the Common Market. (See pp. 217–218.)

It was the expectation that economic expansion in 1960 would increase the volume of total exports by about 7 per cent from the average in 1959. About half of the anticipated increase would no doubt be in metals and minerals while about one-fourth might be represented by pulp and paper products. It was anticipated that the gross foreign exchange earnings of the merchant fleet would increase by 8 per cent in 1960, and this would be roughly in proportion to the increase in the active merchant tonnage. It was anticipated that total earnings of wage earners would increase in 1960 from the 1959 figures by about 1.5 per cent. Higher earnings were expected in agriculture, the fisheries, and in certain of the self-employed enterprises.

It was the expectation that the total gross fixed asset formation, excluding ships and inventories, would increase by 6 per cent in 1960. The number of new industrial buildings started in 1959 was less than in 1958 and consequently an increase in industrial investments in building and construction by perhaps as much as 14 per cent in 1960 over the 1959 figure was anticipated. Investments in machinery was also expected to increase during 1960, hopefully by 9 per cent. Investments in agriculture would remain constant, but investments in forestry and power development were expected to increase.

It was hoped that construction of housing would increase slightly in 1960; work should be started on about 27,000 housing units in 1960 compared to 26,500 in 1959.

According to plan, total investments in transport other than shipping should increase by 14 per cent and investments in air transport by perhaps as much as 100 per cent. This should permit a considerable expansion in much-needed airport facilities.

It is perhaps unnecessary to detail further the specific items in the national budget of 1960. Enough illustrations have been given to demonstrate the specific nature of certain areas of economic planning. It can be assumed that when figures are indicated "predicting" an expansion of 3 per cent in a given area that the administrators in charge of allocations, credit extension, and the like will usually confine themselves to the anticipated planned figure in making their decisions.

One of the usual criticisms heard in connection with the economic planning activities of the Norwegian state is that it is too highly regimented, with too many regulations, too much red tape, too much bureaucracy, and consequently undue delays in decision-making. There may well be some truth in these allegations, but it must always be remembered that a completely free economy in a country of the size and nature of Norway would perhaps be out of the question. Also it should be borne in mind that bureaucracy and red tape are not absent in large corporations in a completely unplanned economy.

There are certain noticeable trends, not only in Norway, but in certain other semi-socialistic countries that might lead one to expect a liberalization of the control of the state on the economy. This has been especially evident in Germany in the last several years. It is doubtful that any significant liberalization can occur in Norway due to the paucity of natural resources and the relative poverty of the country in comparison with the larger industrial countries like Germany, the United Kingdom, and the United States.

In spite of the criticism that is inevitable whenever the state impinges upon men's freedom of action, the mixed economy of Norway seems to have worked quite well. The standard of living is high, the expenditures for non-economic things, such as educational and recreational facilities, are increasing, and the level of culture is certainly on a par with any of the European countries. Not all of this can be ascribed to the operation of a planned economy, but there is ample evidence to support the conclusion that much of the progress made, particularly since 1946, would not have been possible without the effective intervention of the state in the economy. But, having said this, one should recognize that all problems have not been settled, nor has any economic millennium been reached. Currently (1963) the government is concerned about the inflationary pressures caused by wage increases somewhat out of line with planned objectives. The Prime Minister in his New Year's Day address (1963) indicated that the government might be forced to tighten monetary and credit controls in order to curb inflation.[11]

[11] *News of Norway*, January 10, 1963, p. 1.

12

Norway in the World Community

Norwegian Policy and Experience Before World War I

Although modern Norwegian independent statehood dates from 1814, it was not until the dissolution of the Norwegian-Swedish Union in 1905 that Norway was complete master of its own destiny in international affairs. It will be recalled that the breakup of the union was precipitated by the desire on the part of Norway to be completely independent in its relations with other states. Before 1905 Norway and Sweden had been represented abroad by a single set of diplomatic and consular officers, usually Swedish. This situation became intolerable to the Norwegians, not only because they thought that Swedish agents could not adequately represent Norway due to certain conflicts of interests between the two countries, but also because this degree of dependence upon Sweden placed Norway in a distinctly inferior position in the society of nations. It was this, perhaps as much as the economic issue, that led the Storting to pass, over the veto of the King, a law establishing an independent consular service in 1905. This led to a crisis which culminated in the establishment of a new Norwegian dynasty with Haakon VII as its first King.

Except for the internal conflicts which led to the dissolution of the Norwegian-Swedish Union, the period between 1814–1905 had been quiet and peaceful. It was in these years that neutralism and the emphasis on pacific settlement of international disputes — cornerstones of Norwegian foreign policy until 1939 — had their origins. At no time during the period were the military forces of the union King on the field of battle in spite of difficulties and irritations resulting in war in nearby places, notably in Denmark in the 1860's. The great powers, perhaps for their own selfish purposes, seemed to give at least de facto recognition to Norwegian-Swedish neutrality and, at the very least, agreed to the maintenance of the status quo on the Scandinavian peninsula. In 1855 a treaty was concluded whereby Great Britain and France agreed to guarantee the territorial integrity of Sweden and Norway against Russia, providing these states in turn agreed not to cede any of their territory to Russia. This agreement was not neutralistic in character; Oscar I, the Swedish King, definitely favored Great Britain and France in the Crimean War and might even have joined the conflict on the side of the Western powers had an expected invasion of Russia in the Baltic area had been carried through. Having thus antagonized the Russians, Oscar felt the need for territorial security in the uncharted northern areas of his kingdom which bordered Russia. Although the treaty of 1855 annoyed the Russians and had been brewed in the caldron of power politics, it did have the effect of underscoring the desire for noninvolvement which became such an integral part of Scandinavian foreign policy in the first part of the twentieth century.

The Norwegians were not vitally concerned with the intrigues and negotiations of the 1850's because of their preoccupation with asserting the independent identity of their own country against the Swedish King. But not long after the important battle against royal domination had been won in 1884 with the establishment of cabinet responsibility, the Norwegian government turned more of its attention to international affairs, particularly to the development of a formal neutralistic position. In 1902 this movement culminated in a resolution by the Storting urging recognition by other powers of a status of neutrality for Norway somewhat similar to that enjoyed by Switzerland. No international agreement of the kind requested by parliament developed, but in 1907 a multilateral treaty signed by Great Britain, France, Germany, and Russia did guarantee the territorial integrity of Norway. By the time war broke out in 1914 the neutralistic feelings within Norway had developed to a significant degree and, though not recognized formally, many European states had given evidence of respect for the Norwegian policy of noninvolvement.

Norwegian neutrality in World War I was not inexpensive. Direct military involvement at home and abroad was avoided, but shipping losses amounting to about one-half of the Norwegian merchant tonnage and economic crisis brought on by the war proved costly. Because of the size and importance of her shipping fleet, Norway found she could not in fact avoid involvement in the conflict. It is clear that there was, even in 1914, a certain paradox in Norwegian policy which is somewhat similar to the inconsistency of American foreign policy of the same period. Both countries insisted on a policy of noninvolvement, but at the same time pursued trade and maritime activities calling for complete freedom of the seas. This duality of policy was made more difficult by the development of new weapons, notably torpedoes shot from submarines. Both belligerents early in World War I found it difficult, in pursuing their own military objectives, to allow freedom of the seas to neutrals, since to do so might directly or indirectly damage their causes. As a result, both Norway and the United States became involved in the war; the United States as an active participant and Norway as a neutral with heavy economic stakes. For both it may also have been a dramatic demonstration of the impossibility of reconciling wide participation in international trade with neutralistic political and military positions.

Norway and the League of Nations

A full year before hostilities ceased — in November of 1917, to be precise — plans for a world organization based upon a draft submitted by Christian Lange[1] of Norway were being discussed by representatives from the Scandinavian countries. And in January of 1919 the Norwegian League of Nations Association under the presidency of Fridtjof Nansen drafted a rather detailed set of principles, which were thought to be essential if pacific settlement of disputes were to be undertaken by an international organization. Though based primarily on the assumption that disagreements between states could be settled by arbitration and adjudication without resort to economic or military sanctions, these Norwegian proposals were well conceived and demonstrated a fervent hope that war in the future might be avoided. Nansen, who later became an outstanding figure in the humanitarian work of the League, was tireless in his advocacy of the Norwegian proposals. He traveled to London and later to Paris and was well received wherever he went, although it soon became obvious that the statesmen in the large powers did not share his idealism. Nonetheless, these early efforts did give the smaller nations some opportunity to influence the course of negotiations that led to the establishment of the League.

Norway's position after the war was again not without a paradoxical character. Norwegians had become convinced that more formal international machinery was essential to peace, but at the same time their nationalistic — perhaps one might even say chauvinistic — feelings had been intensified. They were firmly convinced that disputes between states could be settled at the arbitration table or in the international courtroom, but they were not willing to permit economic or military

[1] Christian Lange, the father of Halvard Lange who has been the Norwegian Foreign Minister since 1946, was Secretary of the Interparliamentary Union from 1909–1933.

sanctions. They were so certain that the type of collective security they advocated would work that they saw no further need for armaments and defense establishments. In a word, they were relying on morality and good will to enforce the law of nations they wished to enlarge and perfect, failing to realize that even within the most civilized countries man's perversities make necessary less idealistic sanctions in the form of police establishments equipped with force and weapons.

If the Norwegian leaders can be criticized for being overzealous in their idealism, they cannot be condemned for failure to compromise. They did accept a League covenant which to them seemed less strong than it could have been since it retained questionable features based upon past practice, e.g., provision for economic and military sanctions against violators of its provisions. But in spite of some dubiety, the Norwegian representatives at Geneva and the government in Oslo worked assiduously in an effort to make the League work. The contributions of many men were noteworthy, but two — Fridtjof Nansen and C. J. Hambro — were particularly effective in dramatizing the need for world peace and order. Nansen, as High Commissioner of the League, was responsible for the repatriation of a half million war prisoners and the administration of extensive relief activities, principally in the Near East. He was highly respected and enjoyed the full confidence not only of the League officials at Geneva, but also of the responsible officers of all governments concerned. Hambro was a frequent member of the Norwegian delegation to the League and in its last years served as President of the Assembly.

Although the incorporation of sanctions in the League covenant had been accepted reluctantly by Norway, no attempt was made by the Norwegian Foreign Ministry to escape obligations imposed by membership in the League. In fact, forceful pressure was brought even by Nansen, the principal humanitarian in the League, to secure reluctant agreement of the large powers to compel withdrawal of Italian forces from Corfu, occupied in 1923. And every effort was made to comply with League sanctions imposed in 1936 against Italy after that country had occupied parts of Ethiopia. An attempt had been made to soften the League's position, but when this failed Norway went along loyally with the then agreed-upon League policy. After it became evident that the United Kingdom and France were not really serious in applying sanctions against Italy, Norway felt no longer obligated to do so. Also since the large powers had given no serious support to disarmament efforts within the League, the Norwegian government concluded that if the provisions of the covenant respecting disarmament were to be, for all practical purposes, avoided, other articles, notably Article 16 on sanctions, could also be disregarded. By the summer of 1937 this view was made official through a statement by Foreign Minister Halvdan Koht indicating that his government would no longer feel impelled to apply military sanctions against an aggressor.

The complicated background and the extended discussions in Norwegian political circles that preceded this simple statement of policy cannot be discussed at length in this connection.[2] But because it dramatizes once more the difficult position facing Norway during the interwar period, the internal political conflict on foreign policy cannot be completely ignored. Simply stated, the problem posed was whether Norway should remain an active member of the League (there were those who talked of complete withdrawal, but they had no large following) committed to sanctions, military and economic, or remain in the League in a semineutralistic position with no obligations to impose sanctions. The issue came to a head in the national convention of the Labor party in 1936. The party, it will be recalled, had been in power about a year and had early been faced by not only the crisis brought on by the Italo-Ethiopian affair, but also by the aggressive thrusts of the new fascist movement in Germany. In addition, ideological factors within the party proved to be complicating. For one thing the Labor party had been for a few years in the early twenties affiliated with the Communist International and, though formal ties had been broken, sympathy for the Soviet Union remained strong in Labor ranks during the late twenties and into the thirties. Before 1933, while the Soviet Union was outside the League, there was a good deal of anti-League sentiment in some circles of the Labor party which evaporated once the U.S.S.R. joined the League and inaugurated a policy of collective security. In brief, the position finally accepted by the Labor Government abandoned sanctions and opened the way to a neutral status if this should seem desirable; at the same time the need for disarmament and other measures designed to prevent war were re-emphasized.

In the few years that followed before Norway was involved in World War II, i.e., from 1937–1940, the government under the leadership of Prime Minister Johan Nygaardsvold and Foreign Minister Koht pursued a policy of neutrality in spite of warnings and the overt threats of expanding fascism.[3] To supplement neutrality, representatives of the Norwegian Cabinet continued to argue for disarmament in the League and at international conferences and undertook arms reductions in their own country. As a result, by the time the German invasion took

[2] For a careful historical account of the conflict within Norway, and particularly in Labor party circles, see Nils Ørvik, *Sikkerhetspolitikken, 1920–1939* (Oslo, 1960), I, 259–288.

[3] Finn Moe, who is at present (1963) chairman of the parliamentary committee dealing with foreign affairs, had unsuccessfuly argued in the convention in 1936 that Norway could not take a neutral position in the face of an expanding, belligerent Nazi Germany, but this warning was not heeded by the government.

place in April of 1940, the military establishment of Norway was weak and ineffective.

By the fall of 1939 Europe was at war. During the months that followed, Norway pursued a policy of meticulous neutrality attempting to avoid involvements with Germany on the one hand and England and France on the other. This was not easy because the indented Norwegian coast created problems, both legal and strategic. It was not always easy to police effectively all parts of Norwegian territorial waters; isolated sections of the fjords and inlets offered excellent cover for small naval craft. But even as late as March of 1940, Foreign Minister Koht was administering a policy aimed fully as much at British as at German excursions into Norwegian territorial waters.

This policy failed to keep Norway free of international entanglements; on April 9, 1940, in a large-scale operation extending from Narvik in the north to Oslo in the south, the Germans invaded Norway. Even today there are differences of opinion on the question of whether the invasion could have been anticipated, but this discussion seems now fruitless. More important, it would seem, is the general lesson that could be, and for many Norwegians has been, drawn from the experience with neutrality and a grossly inadequate defense posture. As in 1914, Norway was again forced into the conflict between the large powers against her will, this time as an active military participant. It seemed to be evident once again that no small nation could remain neutral in a contest between powerful neighbors if it occupied a position thought strategic by the belligerents or if it was involved in economic operations, such as shipping and trade, which the antagonists in the conflict thought might affect the outcome. Norway in 1940 was in an exposed position in both these respects.

Occupation of Norway, 1940–1945

On the day of the invasion, April 9, 1940, the Norwegian King, Cabinet, and Storting left the capital city and established temporary headquarters at Elverum. The German ambassador in Oslo, Curt Bräuer, in an audience with the King, demanded the resignation of the Nygaardsvold government and the appointment of Vidkun Quisling to the prime ministership.[4] This the King steadfastly refused to do. Though the Germans continued to insist that they intended to support a friendly native regime and that they had come as liberators, not

[4] Quisling led the small fascist party (*Nasjonal Samling*) in Norway which was never taken seriously by his fellow Norwegians. In the election of 1936, although the party nominated candidates in all electoral districts, it polled only 26,577 votes and was unable to elect a single member to the Storting.

conquerors, it was evident early that a dedicated, courageous King and Cabinet had no intention to compromise. Makeshift military arrangements were made, and a delaying action was fought for nearly two months. While this was taking place, the King and Crown Prince, together with the Cabinet, were moving from place to place in order to avoid capture by the Germans. By June 7, 1940, after the British had withdrawn naval and air support, the position of the Norwegian forces had become untenable. The King, his Cabinet, other political leaders, and, incidentally by good fortune, the gold supply of the country, were brought aboard the British man-of-war *Devonshire* and taken to London where a government in exile was established.

Norway's contribution to the allied war effort was out of all proportion to its size and wealth. Particularly important was the role played by the merchant marine, which for the most part was on the high seas or in friendly ports when the war broke out in April. Not only did these ships provide much needed cargo space for the allied cause, but income from their operations gave the government in exile the revenue needed to finance its operations. The leadership provided by the government in exile was of a high order; and King Haakon, through his steadfastness and dedication, became not only a symbol for the resistance movement at home and abroad, but a genuinely influential chief of state. If there had ever been any doubts about the royal position before, they were completely dispelled during the war.

Soon after the establishment of the government in exile in London, an organized resistance movement began operations in Norway itself. And close liaison was maintained between the government in London and the resistance leaders at home. Day by day the intensity of the antagonism against the occupying forces grew, as the individualistic, freedom-loving, patriotic Norwegians went about the task of making life difficult for the Germans. Though forceful resistance against the Nazis and the puppet Quisling regime was not unimportant, political and psychological weapons were more devastating and more difficult to cope with for the German occupying force. This certainly is an interesting period for the student of national psychology, since most of the so-called Norwegian traits were dramatically exposed during the occupation years. Subtle obstructionism, dogged individualistic enterprise, stubborn resistance to the invasion of privacy, disregard for personal safety (sometimes manifested even today by motorcyclists in Norway), and a passionate love of country, both as a geographic and a spiritual entity, all came out in sharp relief during the years from 1940–1945. Many illustrations of tactics employed by the Norwegians could be cited but perhaps the most interesting were related to the sabotage of minor rules and regulations imposed by the Germans. Norwegian men were forbidden to wear flowers in their lapels as was their custom on ceremonial occasions and especially on the King's birthday. So, instead of flowers in their lapels, the men wore paper clips! They refused to sit beside Germans on the street cars and when forced by rule to sit, if seats were available, they ceremoniously pushed the buzzer, got off the car and made their way on foot rather than share seats with Germans.

Norway and the Establishment of the United Nations

By the end of the war Norway had become so deeply committed to the cause of an embryonic United Nations that large-scale participation by its leaders in peacemaking and planning for a new world organization to replace the League had become inescapable. And the participation, both in planning and later in helping to operate the United Nations, was based on an entirely different set of principles from those prevailing in 1919 or those in practice after 1936. Norway was now willing to see established a world organization with wide scope and sufficient power, and was not going to press further a neutralistic policy that had led only to involvement in two costly world wars. The birth of the United Nations as a world organization at San Francisco in 1945 was greeted by the Norwegians with a mixture of relief and rejoicing. At long last it seemed an age of international cooperation was at hand.

The expectations of the Norwegians, as well as those of many other peoples, built on the "spirit of San Francisco" were short-lived. It soon became obvious that the cooperation between the Soviet Union and the Western powers was destined to deteriorate. Norwegian leaders, like those from certain other small powers, worked hard to try to make the United Nations a really important organization with a universal membership. It was their hope, despite the ideological and strategic differences between East and West, that through the United Nations a bridge between the two antagonists might be built. Most Norwegians had by now realized that the fate of their country was involved, whether they liked it or not, in the struggles between the great powers. If the U.N. could not mediate these conflicts, the small nations would be forced to take sides, and the realization of this simple political fact caused the Norwegian government to redouble its "bridge-building" efforts.

The conflict between East and West reached a climax as far as the Norwegians were concerned in the coup in Czechoslovakia in February, 1948. It became apparent to the government in Oslo that the fate that had overtaken the Czechs might, in the years to come, possibly also engulf Norway. Moreover, it had also become increasingly clear, through the establishment of satellite regimes in other countries —

Albania, Bulgaria, Poland, Rumania, and Hungary — that the Soviet Union had no intention of permitting self-determination and independence among its small neighbors. If they were not to be incorporated into a Soviet bloc, they most certainly would be subject to pressure to conform, as Finland had discovered in March of 1940 when she was forced to sign a "mutual assistance" pact with the Soviet Union. Although not willing to give up attempts to make the U.N. a vital instrument for peace, the Norwegian government became convinced that these efforts within the U.N. might not suffice. In line with this change of view, Norway was prepared to take yet another step away from neutrality and noninvolvement by seeking an outright military alliance.

Norway joins NATO

The events leading to Norway's membership in the North Atlantic Treaty Organization can be sketched briefly. About the time of the crisis in Czechoslovakia, the Nordic foreign ministers meeting in Oslo agreed to arrange for discussions of a possible Scandinavian defense pact, and in September of 1948 a commission was established to undertake these discussions. In the meantime the position of the Norwegian government had been clarified by statements of Foreign Minister Halvard Lange, who in a public lecture in Oslo said, "We are a part of Western Europe, geographically, economically, and culturally, and . . . we are and will continue to be a West European democracy."[5]

The negotiations looking toward a joint Scandinavian defense union broke down in early 1949. Essentially this was caused by differences between the states on the matter of political and military orientation. Sweden insisted that the proposed Scandinavian alliance be characterized by strict neutrality, while Norway and, to a somewhat lesser degree, Denmark, insisted on a definite pro-Western orientation. In addition, the question of financial and economic support for rearmament in Norway and Denmark became troublesome. Sweden was unable to guarantee the aid necessary to bring the military establishments of the other two countries to a standard consistent with adequate defense. Only the United States could do this but, if American aid was accepted, a pro-Western commitment would be the *quid pro quo*.

Even while negotiations were in progress in Scandinavia, the United States approached Denmark and Norway to ascertain whether or not they would be willing to join a projected North Atlantic alliance. The Norwegian government was receptive, but loyal enough to the idea of

[5] Tim Greve, *Norway and NATO* (Oslo, 1959). Certain of the factual details in this section are based upon Greve's account of the events leading up to Norwegian membership in NATO.

a separate Scandinavian defense unit to insist that its answer be delayed until all problems in connection with the more limited Scandinavian pact had been fully explored. On becoming convinced that no agreement with Sweden could be reached on satisfactory terms, the Norwegian parliament approved Norway's ascension to the North Atlantic Treaty on March 29, 1949, by a vote of 130 to 13.[6]

Although many of the leaders — notably Foreign Minister Lange — had long been convinced that Norway, or even Scandinavia for that matter, could not stand alone in the world of 1949, and though most Norwegians had a Western orientation, it was not without misgivings that the decision to join NATO had been taken by the Cabinet and Storting. This attitude was based not so much on ideological considerations surrounding neutrality as a principle, but rather on the recognition of the hard facts of Soviet power. If the Soviet Union became sufficiently irritated by Norway's action, serious, perhaps immediate, consequences could be expected. It must be recalled that Norway borders on the Soviet Union in the north and that this area would be difficult to defend. The Soviet Union had in fact evidenced its intense displeasure even before the pact was finally accepted by Norway. The upshot of an exchange of notes between Norway and the Soviet Union and conversations with other signatories of the pact was that the Cabinet announced that at no time except in war or immediate threat of war would foreign troops be stationed on Norwegian soil. This proved enough to quiet the Russians and assuage in part the fear noticeable in some Norwegian quarters. It did not silence a small but vocal opposition in Norway which has carried on an anti-NATO campaign down to the present day.[7] Despite insignificant internal differences Norway remains a strong member of NATO; although it continues to enforce the restriction against the stationing of foreign troops on its territory.[8]

In the preceding discussion no mention was made of the Norwegian participation in the Marshall Plan and the European economic cooperation accompanying it. Most American observers of the operation of these programs have agreed that Norway's cooperation was complete in every respect. It is doubtful that any recipient country made better use of the funds (approximately NK 2.5 billion), and this can be demonstrated by observing the expansion of productive facilities well begun as early as 1950.

[6] Of the thirteen voting against the pact, eleven were members of the Communist party.

[7] The principal opposition to NATO is provided by two organizations: *Orientering* and the Socialist Peoples Party.

[8] This does not mean that NATO planning contingents are excluded from Norway. One encounters on the streets of Oslo American and British military personnel, but there are no massed units to compare with those seen in Germany, France, and other western European countries.

Present Norwegian Foreign Policy

It should be obvious by now that the foreign policy position of Norway changed abruptly with the German invasion of 1940. A policy of noninvolvement in international affairs was no longer consonant with the political facts of life that Norway's location made inescapable. However much he might like to be allowed to go his own way regardless of what his neighbors might do or say, the situation today makes this impossible for the responsible Norwegian political leader.

The pre-1940 policy was neutralistic, but it was not clearly a policy of noninvolvement. In fact, it was not really a clear policy at all; there was always the implied commitment to the United Kingdom, the United States, and the West generally. For generations the Norwegian economy was dependent on Britain, and for a hundred years sentimental ties, secured by the emigration of nearly a million people, bound Norway to North America and particularly to the United States. If one adds the complications operating on a neutralistic position brought about by a merchant marine sailing all the seven seas, it becomes clear that the Norwegian neutralist of the 1930's had really impossible problems to face.

The present policy, though perhaps not as comfortable as the old one, is certainly more precise and consistent. It can be summarized under six principal headings.

Conscientious Adherence to the Principles and Present Practices of the U.N.

All parties in Norway, with the exception of the Communists, agree to this. Norway has given concrete, visible support to the negotiating and policing processes undertaken by the U.N. in the dispute between Israel and Egypt and in the Congo after its liberation from Belgium. There is no support in Norway for far-reaching revisions of the U.N. Charter except in ways that may strengthen the force of U.N. action. Suggestions for enlarging the role of the Assembly are approved, but the proposal to install a three-member secretariat has never had serious support in Norwegian circles.[9] In spite of the fact that the Norwegian delegation has opposed the Soviet Union in its plan to reorganize the

[9] It will be recalled that the first Secretary-General of the United Nations was Trygve Lie, Norwegian Foreign Minister during World War II, and the next incumbent Dag Hammerskiold was a Swede, well respected in Norwegian government quarters. This personal note should not be interpreted to mean that the Norwegians view the question of reorganizing the Secretariat from the limited perspective of nationality and neighborliness. Rather they recognize that any form of "representation" in an executive agency does not permit sound execution of policy.

Secretariat, as well as on other substantive issues, the hope remains that the United Nations can in time become a cohesive, potent force for world peace. On a lower level of aspiration, it is hoped that the U.N. will provide Norway with the means of solving some of the petty, but annoying, problems it may encounter as a result of its strategic position and proximity to the Soviet Union.

An Atlantic Rather than a Strictly European Orientation

Time and again in the last several years responsible Norwegian statesmen have emphasized that Norway is a member of the Atlantic community and not limited to a European viewpoint. This stems from the close association with the United States and the United Kingdom referred to above. But there is also inherent in the attitude an emphasis on a nationalistic integrity that might be sacrificed by too close a relationship with powerful neighbors. The distrust of Germany remains in spite of the fact that the Nazis who invaded Norway in 1940 have long since been liquidated. Uncertainties respecting the future of French democracy and the fear that conservative regimes in that country and Germany would dominate any European union that might develop has also caused proposals for closer European cooperation to be met with skepticism, if not distrust, in Norway. As a result, Norway fears specifically closer economic ties with the continent because she is convinced that economic collaboration will lead to political collaboration. Though perfectly willing to cooperate economically with the small European states and the United Kingdom in the European Free Trade Association, Norwegian authorities have in the past hesitated to join any common market arrangement that would include the more powerful European states. Besides this political reason, which may be more important than admitted, there are certainly strong economic reasons that can be advanced in support of noninvolvement in an enlarged European common market. But in spite of protestations, political and economic argument, Norway may be forced into a European common market if Great Britain joins any such organization. The fact of close economic dependence on Great Britain is completely understood by intelligent Norwegians.

Certain steps were taken in 1962 looking toward negotiations with the European Economic Community. In March of that year an amendment was made to Paragraph 93 of the Constitution clearing away any constitutional objection to Norwegian affiliation with EEC. In April 1962 the Storting authorized the Cabinet to open conversations with representatives of EEC looking toward possible full membership for Norway. At the present time (1963) the negotiations are at a standstill because of problems in connection with the status of the application for membership of the United Kingdom; the Norwegian Cabinet is content for the present to adopt a "wait and see" policy. Without much question if the United Kingdom joins the Common Market, Norway will also join.

Cooperation Within Scandinavia

In spite of past differences and a certain amount of peripheral antagonism, the ties among the Scandinavian countries remain strong. Even before World War II there was a good measure of informal consultation carried on among representatives of the Scandinavian countries, but in 1953 a more formal type of mechanism for consultation was established — the Nordic Council. This body is made up of parliamentarians from each of the countries: sixteen representatives from each of the four large states — Norway, Denmark, Finland, and Sweden — and five from Iceland. In addition, cabinet ministers, not regular members of their respective parliamentary delegations (it will be recalled that members of the Norwegian Cabinet are not voting members of the Storting), may attend sessions of the Council with the right to debate but without vote. Sessions of the Council are held annually, and decisions taken must subsequently be approved by the national parliaments. The specific accomplishments of the Council include: abolition of the passport requirement for travel within Scandinavia by citizens of the five countries; establishment of a common labor market permitting easy migration of workers from one country to another; and the establishment of a system of reciprocity of social security benefits to take the place of a rather complicated network of bilateral and multilateral treaties. A great many other matters have been discussed, including common fundamental economic problems, possibility of a Nordic common market (which, incidentally, Norway did not actively favor, and the question was shelved after the European Free Trade Association was established), cooperation in establishment and maintenance of institutions of higher learning, control of radio and television, study of transportation, and other related problems.

The organization of the Council can only be described in barest outline in this connection.[10] There is no common secretariat; each delegation selects its president, who presides over the Council when it meets in his country. The five presidents of the national delegations make up the presidium which supervises the work of the Council generally and the activities of the national secretaries specifically. Preparatory work is undertaken by five council committees — legal, economic, cultural, social, and communications — and also by the several ministers for foreign affairs, trade, and commerce.

[10] For an elaborate description of the Nordic Council, see Franz Wendt, *The Nordic Council and Cooperation in Scandinavia* (Copenhagen, 1959).

Besides considering matters concerned with Scandinavia, the Council provides an informal setting for discussions of broader scope. It is well known that the Scandinavian foreign ministers in the sessions of the Council, as well as at other times, engage in preliminary discussion of matters that will be coming up later in the United Nations.

Common economic and social problems as well as cultural and linguistic ties provide an atmosphere for easy communication in the Nordic Council not always found in other international associations. Norwegians, Swedes, and Danes have no language difficulties; they understand one another. Although Finnish and Icelandic are not generally understood by the other Scandinavians, most of the Finnish delegates (although by no means all Finns) speak and understand Swedish and all Icelanders are able to speak and understand Danish.

Encouragement of Disarmament and the Limitation of the Use of Atomic Weapons

It is needless to recite in detail the steps taken by the Norwegian government and its delegation to the U.N. to secure consideration of genuine disarmament on a large scale. Several proposals have been made by the Norwegians, but never for propaganda purposes; they have always taken into account the realities of the current world political situation. Norway would like to go much further and much faster with disarmament than now seems possible in view of the continuing tension between East and West.

In the area of atomic weapons the present government has insisted that no atomic weapons be stationed on Norwegian soil except in time of war. This policy is fairly clear, was reiterated in the program of the government party (Labor) in 1961, and is consistent with the reservation respecting bases and the stationing of troops in Norway attached to its membership in NATO.[11] On the international stage the Norwegian delegation in the U.N. has worked diligently for strict control of atomic weapons. When cessation of production seemed impossible, Norwegians turned their attention to proposals that would eliminate further testing of nuclear weapons. Resumption of testing by the Soviet Union in 1961 followed by subsequent resumption by the United States caused real concern among the Norwegian people.

Expansion of Aid to Underdeveloped Countries

Though limited as to resources, Norway has expanded in recent years its program of aid to the new nations of Asia and Africa. This is a popular program among Norwegians generally; they not only recognize their obligation to less fortunate people, but are convinced that they have something more to offer than grants and loans. They are proud

[11] See p. 215.

of their way of life as well as their educational and technological accomplishments and are convinced that their background of experience can be useful to the more youthful countries of the world. Limited programs have brought Africans and Asians to Norway for study, but these programs have not always been successful; the language problem has caused at least some of the difficulty.

Certain projects in the underdeveloped countries have been undertaken, the most important of which is one in India designed to aid the fishing industry. This has only been reasonably successful, although in 1961 India requested its continuation.

President Kennedy's objective for the United States — allocation of one per cent of the gross national product for aid to the underdeveloped countries — was not only applauded in Norway, but a real attempt is being made to duplicate it. In a speech given to the students in the International Summer School in Oslo in July 1961, Foreign Minister Lange indicated that Norway might aspire to a one per cent contribution in about three or four years.

Conclusion

In implementing its foreign policy the Norwegian government faces certain difficult problems. The delicate situation caused by close proximity to the Soviet Union and the strategic position occupied by Norway have been mentioned in another connection. Also it should be clear that Norway, like other small countries, is not the master of its own destiny; it may well be drawn willy-nilly into economic and political affiliations which are not of its making or even in its own best interests. This has always been cause for real fear among Norwegians, but it has grown especially strong in late years. And there are adequate grounds for apprehension. Certainly Norway may be forced to accept closer economic and political ties with Europe, for example, than are consistent with her past and present inclination.

A similar problem arises in connection with Norway's membership in NATO. It has always been the hope of Norwegian leaders that this organization might develop into something more than a defensive alliance; e.g., it might well undertake economic and cultural activities. Even if it were not to do this, the internal character of the states making up NATO has always been of more than passing interest to Norwegians, both in the ministries and on the streets. Norwegians feel uncomfortable when they view the antidemocratic practices evident in a few of the member states and become agitated when they hear occasionally that the United States is not adverse to extending membership to yet another undemocratic country — Spain. The Angolan episode was particularly provocative to the Norwegians and the Foreign Ministry took formal steps in the spring of 1961 to inform Portugal, a fellow member of NATO, of its intense displeasure.

Generally the present Labor Government in Norway is supported in its foreign policy, not only by an overwhelming majority in its own party, but by the other parties as well. There is little disagreement in principle among the people (except, of course, the Communists) on foreign policy. This is true in spite of the fact that the newly organized Socialist People's party, campaigning on an anti-NATO program, won surprising victories in two election districts in the Storting election of September, 1961.

Despite the solidity of this support, the government has been subjected to irritations from a small group which until recently has generally been considered within the Labor party ranks. This group, *Orientering,* has kept up a constant campaign of opposition to Norway's membership in NATO, rearmament, and lately it has been very outspoken in opposition to the stationing of nuclear weapons in Norway. Though not large, not well organized, and characterized by a kind of schoolboy idealism, *Orientering* has been somewhat of a thorn in the flesh of the Labor government. Before 1961 it could be said to agitate for so-called nonpolitical objectives and in so doing provided a corrective to the more "realistic" positions taken by certain right-wing elements in the Labor party. But it lost this constructive function when it virtually joined forces with the newly established Socialist People's party in the last election.

Whatever can be said about the external and internal problems facing Norway in its relations with the rest of the world, the fact remains that its present policy is more clear-cut, less paradoxical than it has been in a long time; neutrality and noninvolvement has given way to commitment and international cooperation. Though not completely eliminated, isolationist tendencies are recognized as no longer possible in the world of today.

SELECTED BIBLIOGRAPHY

Andenæs, Johan. *Statsforfatningen i Norge.* Oslo: Johan Grundt Tanum, 1945. A short (320 pp.) description of the organs of Norwegian government viewed from the legalistic point of view.

Arneson, Ben A. *The Democratic Monarchies of Scandinavia.* New York: Van Nostrand, 1939. One of the first descriptions in English of government in Scandinavia. Useful for comparisons, but obviously not up to date.

Bull, Edvard, Keilhau, Wilhelm, Shetelig, Haakon, and Steen, Sverre. *Det norske folks liv og historie gjennem tidene.* 11 vols. Oslo: H. Aschehoug & Co., 1930–1938. The most complete history of Norway. What it may lack in scholarly paraphernalia it makes up in interest and readability. Anyone familiar with Norwegian, Swedish, or Danish will find this a fascinating account of the history of Norway from the day of the Sagas to the period immediately preceding World War II.

Castberg, Frede. *Norges statsforfatning,* 2nd ed. 2 vols. Oslo: Arbeidernes Aktietrykkeri, 1947. This is *the* authoritative book on constitutional government in Norway.

Castberg, Frede. *Norway and the Western Powers.* Oslo: Oslo University Press, 1957. A short (24 pp.) study of comparative constitutional law.

Castberg, Frede. *The Norwegian Way of Life.* London: William Heinemann, 1954. One of the Way of Life Series prepared under the auspices of the International Studies Conference supported by UNESCO. A delightful little book covering government, education, role of the home and the church and related matters. A good short introduction to Norway.

Christensen, C. A. R. *Norway, A Democratic Kingdom.* Oslo: Royal Ministry of Foreign Affairs, 1959. A brief (47 pp.), popularly written introduction to Norwegian political, economic, and social life written for the casual observer.

Derby, T. K. *A Short History of Norway.* London: George Allen and Unwin, 1957. One of the latest short histories of Norway written by a respected English scholar.

Dorfman, Herbert. *Labor Relations in Norway.* Oslo: The Norwegian Joint Committee on International Social Policy, 1958. This book, written by an American Fulbright scholar in Norway, describes organization of trade unions and Employers' Association, means of settling disputes, role of the government, and like matters. It is readable and reliable.

Evang, Karl. *Health Services in Norway.* Oslo: The Norwegian Joint Committee on International Social Policy, 1960. An excellent, comprehensive description of the organization of health services written by the Director General of Health Services, who has not only had long experience in the position, but has contributed substantially to international health organizations.

Gjerset, Knut. *History of the Norwegian People.* 2 vols. New York: Macmillan, 1915. The most comprehensive history of Norway written in English covering the period before World War I.

Greve, Tim. *Norway and NATO.* Oslo: Oslo University Press, 1959. A good, brief summary of steps leading to Norway's affiliation with NATO written by a professional diplomat and former secretary to the Norwegian Minister of Foreign Affairs.

Haffner, Vilhelm. *Om Stortingets lovbehandling og Stortingets voteringsordning.* Oslo: Universitetsforlagets trykningssentral, 1960. The best technical treatment of legislative procedure in Norway.

Koht, Halvdan, and Skard, Sigmund. *The Voice of Norway.* New York: Columbia University Press, 1944. An excellent statement of the historical, literary, ideological background of Norwegian life written during World War II by a distinguished professor of history and former Minister of Foreign Affairs (Koht) and a professor of American Literature and present director of the American Institute at the University of Oslo (Skard).

Larson, Karen. *A History of Norway.* Princeton: Princeton University Press, 1948. The best short history of Norway written in English.

Lauwerys, J. H., ed. *Scandinavian Democracy.* Copenhagen: American Scandinavian Foundation, 1958. Contains several essays on the development of democratic thought and institutions in Norway.

Lindgren, Raymond E. *Norway-Sweden: Union, Disunion and Scandinavian Integration.* Princeton: Princeton University Press, 1959. The best single volume description — in English or Norwegian — of the breakup of the Swedish-Norwegian Union in 1905.

Lyche, Ingeborg. *Adult Education in Norway.* Oslo: Royal Norwegian Ministry of Foreign Affairs, 1959. A good description of formal (folk high schools) and informal (rural cinema, etc.) institutions providing education for adults.

Løchen, Einar, and Torgersen, Rolf N. *Norway's Views on Sovereignty.* Bergen: John Griegs Boktrykkeri, 1955. A scholarly treatment of past and present legal problems in international relations faced by Norway with some account of their resolution.

Morgenstierne, Bredo. *Lærebok i den norske statsforfatningsret,* 2nd ed. 2 vols. Oslo: O. Christiansens Boktrykkeri, 1927. One of the classic treatments of modern Norwegian constitutional law, now somewhat dated.

Nielsen, Yngvar. *Norge i 1905.* Horten: C. Andersens Forlag, 1906. The best Norwegian account of the breakup of the Norwegian-Swedish Union in 1905.

Norges lover, 1682–1959. Oslo: Grøndahl & Søns, 1960. A codification of all Norwegian laws. Usually revised biennially.

Norges statskalender. Oslo: H. Aschehoug & Co., 1963. A handbook, published annually, listing in detail personnel and organization of all national and some communal organs of government in Norway.

Norway Yearbook. Oslo: Johan Grundt Tanum, 1962. A handbook of general information revised periodically.

Royal Ministry of Justice, ed. *Administration of Justice in Norway.* Oslo Ministry of Justice, 1957. An adequate, though not completely reliable, translation of *Domstolene og rettspleien i Norge,* Oslo: Justisdepartementet, 1955.

Shirer, William L. *The Challenge of Scandinavia.* New York: Little Brown, 1955, pp. 28–109. A popular, carefully prepared description of the occupation (1940–45) and post-occupation periods.

Skodvin, Magne. *Striden om okkupasjonsstyret i Norge.* Oslo: Det Norske Samlaget, 1956. The most scholarly and thorough account of the early months of the German occupation in 1940.

Skårdal, Dorothy Burton. *Social Insurance in Norway*. Oslo: The Norwegian Committee on International Social Policy, 1960. The best single volume, in Norwegian or English, describing the present day social welfare program in Norway.

Statistisk årbok for Norge. Oslo: Statistisk Sentralbyrå, 1963. This handbook, published annually by the Central Bureau of Statistics, contains a wealth of information useful to the student of public affairs. Pertinent sections include English translation. The book is invaluable to the student of Norwegian politics and economics.

Steen, Sverre. *Det frie Norge*. 3 vols. Oslo: J. W. Cappelens Forlag, 1951–53. A comprehensive, thoroughly scholarly treatment of the period immediately before and after Norway received her independence in 1814.

Wiley, George M. *The Organization and Administration of the Educational System in Norway*. Oslo: Royal Ministry of Foreign Affairs, 1955. A complete description of the educational system from the elementary school through the University written by a former Associate Commissioner of Education of the State of New York.

THE CONSTITUTION OF NORWAY

A. Form of Government and Religion

1. The Kingdom of Norway is a free, independent, indivisible and inalienable realm. Its form of Government is a limited and hereditary monarchy.

2. The Evangelical-Lutheran religion shall remain the public religion of the State. The inhabitants professing it shall be bound to bring up their children in the same.

B. The Executive Power, the King, and the Royal Family

3. The Executive Power is vested in the King.

4. The King shall always profess the Evangelical-Lutheran religion, and maintain and protect the same.

5. The King's person shall be sacred; he cannot be blamed nor accused. The responsibliity shall rest with his Council.

6. The order of succession shall be lineal and agnatic, whereby only male, born in lawful wedlock, may succeed male; the nearer line shall pass before the more remote, and the elder in the line before the younger.

Among those entitled to the succession shall be considered also an unborn child, who shall immediately take his proper place in the line of succession the moment he is born into the world after the death of his father.

When a Prince entitled to succeed to the Crown of Norway is born, his name and the time of his birth shall be notified to the first Storting thereafter held, and be entered in the record of its proceedings.

7. If there is no Prince entitled to the succession, the King may propose his successor to the Storting, which has the right to elect another candidate if the King's nominee is not acceptable.

8. The age of majority of the King shall be fixed by law.

As soon as the King has attained the age of majority fixed by law, he shall make a public declaration that he has arrived at his majority.

9. As soon as the King, being of full age, assumes the authority of Government, he shall make to the Storting the following oath: 'I promise and swear that I will govern the Kingdom of Norway in accordance with its Constitution and Laws, so truly help me God, the Almighty and Omniscient!'

If the Storting is not in session at the time, the oath shall be made in writing to the Council of State, and be repeated solemnly by the King at the next ensuing session of the Storting.

10. (Repealed)

11. The King shall reside in the Kingdom and may not, without the consent of the Storting, stay outside the Kingdom for more than six months at a time; otherwise he shall have forfeited, for his person, his right to the Crown.

The King may not accept any other crown or government without the consent of the Storting, a majority of two-thirds of the votes being required.

12. The King himself chooses a Council of Norwegian citizens, who must not be under thirty years of age. The Council shall consist of a Prime Minister and at least seven other members.

More than half the number of the members of the Council of State shall profess the public religion of the State.

The King shall apportion the business among the members of the Council of State, as he deems suitable. On extraordinary occasions, the King may summon other Norwegian citizens to take a seat in the Council of State, beside the ordinary members of the Council of the State, but no member of the Storting may be summoned thus.

Husband and wife, parents and children, or brothers and sisters, may not, at the same time, have a seat in the Council of State.

13. During his travels within the Kingdom, the King may leave the Government to the Council of State. The Council of State shall conduct the Government in the King's name and on his behalf. They shall inviolably observe the provisions of this Constitution as well as the particular constitutionally valid directions which the King may give by Instruction.

The matters of business shall be decided by vote; in the case of an equality of votes, the Prime Minister, or, in his absence, the next highest ranking member present of the Council of State, shall have two votes.

The Council of State shall make a report to the King of the matters of the business which have been dealt with thus.

14. (Repealed)

15. (Repealed)

16. The King shall give directions for all public Church services and public worship, all meetings and conventions dealing with religious matters, and shall ensure that the public teachers of religion follow the rules prescribed for them.

17. The King may issue and repeal Ordinances concerning commerce, tariffs, trade and industry, and police; they must not, however, be at variance with the Constitution or the laws passed by the Storting (as hereinafter prescribed in sections 77, 78, and 79). They shall be in force provisionally until the next Storting.

18. The King shall, as an ordinary rule, cause the taxes and duties imposed by the Storting to be collected.

19. The King shall watch over the management of the estates belonging to the State, and its privileged controls and monopolies, to ensure that they are administered in the manner determined by the Storting and to the best advantage of the community.

20. The King in the Council of State shall have the right to pardon criminals after sentence has been passed. The criminal shall have the choice whether he will accept the King's grace or submit to the punishment imposed.

In the actions which the Odelsting causes to be brought before the Constitutional Court of the Realm [*Riksrett*] no other pardon than exemption from capital punishment may be granted.

21. The King, with the advice of his Council of State, shall choose and appoint all civil, ecclesiastical, and military officials [*embedsmenn*]. Such officials shall swear, or, if by law exempted from taking the oath, solemnly declare obedience and allegiance to the Constitution and the King. The Royal Princes must not hold civil offices.

22. The Prime Minister and the other members of the Council of State, as well as officials attached to the Government offices or to the Diplomatic or Consular services, Chief civil and ecclesiastical officials, Commanders of regiments and other military forces, Commandants of forts and Officers Commanding warships, may, without any preceding judicial sentence, be dismissed by the King, who shall previously have heard the opinion of the Council of State on the subject. Whether pensions should be granted to officials thus dismissed, shall be determined by the next Storting. In the meantime they shall receive two-thirds of their previous pay.

Other officials may only be suspended by the King, and shall then at once be prosecuted before the Courts; but they may not, unless judgment has been pronounced against them, be dismissed, nor may they, against their will, be transferred to another place.

All officials [*embedsmenn*] may, without any preceding judicial sentence, be dismissed when they have attained an age-limit determined by law.

23. The King may confer decorations on whomsoever he pleases as a reward for distinguished services, which must be publicly announced; but he must not confer any other rank or title than such as each office carries with it. The decoration exempts no one from the common duties and burdens of the citizens, nor does it carry with it any preferential admission to the offices of the State. Officials who are released from office with the King's favour, retain the title and rank of the office they have filled. This does not, however, apply to the members of the Council of State.

No personal or mixed hereditary privileges must henceforth be granted to any one.

24. The King chooses and dismisses at his own discretion his Royal household and Court attendants.

25. The King is Commander-in-Chief of the Army and the Navy of the Kingdom. These forces may not be increased or reduced without the consent of the Storting. They may not be transferred to the service of foreign powers, nor may any military forces of foreign powers, except auxiliary forces against hostile attacks, be brought into the Kingdom without the consent of the Storting.

The territorial contingent [*landevern*] and the other troops that cannot be classed as belonging to the line troops may never, without the consent of the Storting, be employed outside the borders of the Kingdom.

26. The King shall have the right to assemble troops, to commence war in the defence of the Kingdom and to make peace, to conclude and denounce treaties, to send and to receive diplomatic envoys.

Treaties on matters of special importance, and, in any case, treaties the implementation of which, according to the Constitution, necessitates a new law or a decision on the part of the Storting, shall not be binding until the Storting has given its consent thereunto.

27. All members of the Council of State shall, unless prevented by lawful impediment from attending, be present in the Council of State. No decision must be taken in the Council unless more than half the number of its members are present.

Members of the Council of State who do not profess the public religion of the State, do not take part in the consideration of matters which concern the State Church.

28. Proposals regarding appointments to offices [*embeder*] and other matters of importance shall be presented in the Council of State by the member to whose department they belong, and the matters in question shall be dispatched by him in accordance with the decisions of the Council of State. Matters strictly relating to military command may, however, to the extent determined by the King, be excepted from being dealt with in the Council of State.

29. If a member of the Council of State is prevented by lawful impediment from attending the meeting and from presenting the matters belonging to his department, these may be presented by another member whom the King may depute for the purpose.

If, by lawful impediment, so many members are prevented from attending that not more than half of the fixed number are present, other men or women shall, to the number required, be deputed to take seats in the Council of State.

30. All the proceedings of the Council of State shall be entered in the records of the Council. Diplomatic matters which the Council of State have decided to keep secret shall be entered in a special record. The same applies to matters relating to military command which the Council of State has decided to keep secret.

Everyone who holds a seat in the Council of State is in duty bound to express with frankness his opinion, to which the King is bound to listen. But it remains with the King to make a decision according to his own judgment.

If any member of the Council of State is of the opinion that the King's decision is at variance with the form of government or the laws of the Kingdom, or is prejudicial to the Kingdom, it is his duty to make strong remonstrances against it, and also to have his opinion entered in the record. A member who has not thus protested, shall be deemed to have been in agreement with the King, and shall be answerable in such manner as may be subsequently decided, and may be impeached by the Odelsting before the Constitutional Court of the Realm [*Riksrett*].

31. All decisions made by the King shall, in order to become valid, be countersigned. The decisions relating to military command shall be countersigned by the person who has presented the matter; other decisions shall be countersigned by the Prime Minister or, if he has not been present, by the next highest ranking member of the Council of State present.

32. The decisions made by the Government during the absence of the King shall be drawn up in the King's name and be signed by the Council of State.

33. (Repealed)

34. The nearest heir to the Throne, if he is the son of the reigning King, shall bear the title of Crown Prince. The other persons entitled to succeed to the Crown are to be called Princes, and the daughters of the Royal House, Princesses.

35. As soon as the heir to the Throne has completed his eighteenth year, he is entitled to take a seat in the Council of State, but without vote or responsibility.

36. No Prince of the Royal House may marry without the consent of the King. Nor may he accept any other crown or government without the consent of the King and the Storting; to obtain the consent of the Storting, two-thirds of the votes are required.

If he acts contrary to this rule, he, as well as his descendants, forfeit their right to the Norwegian Throne.

37. The Royal Princes and Princesses shall not be answerable personally to any other than the King, or to such person as he may appoint to sit in judgment on them.

38. (Repealed)

39. If the King dies, and the heir to the Throne is still under age, the Council of State shall immediately summon the Storting.

40. Until the Storting has assembled and made provisions for the Government during the minority of the King, the Council of State shall be responsible for the administration of the Kingdom in accordance with the Constitution.

41. If the King is absent from the Kingdom, and not in the field, or if he is prevented by illness from attending to the Government, the Prince next entitled to succeed to the Throne shall conduct the Government as being temporarily invested with the Royal power, provided that he has attained the age fixed for the King's majority. If that is not the case, the Council of State shall be responsible for the administration of the Kingdom.

42. (Repealed)

43. The election of guardians to conduct the Government on behalf of the King during his minority shall be made by the Storting.

44. The Prince who in the cases mentioned in section 41 conducts the

Government, shall make to the Storting in writing the following oath: 'I promise and swear that I will conduct the Government in accordance with the Constitution and the Laws, so truly help me God, the Almighty and Omniscient!'

If the Storting is not in session at the time, the oath shall be delivered to the Council of State and afterwards be transmitted to the next Storting.

The Prince who has once made the oath shall not repeat it later on.

45. As soon as their conduct of the Government has ceased, the guardians shall submit to the King and the Storting an account of the same.

46. If the persons in question neglect to summon the Storting immediately in accordance with section 39, it becomes the unconditional duty of the Supreme Court of Justice [*Høyesterett*], as soon as four weeks have elapsed, to cause this summons to be issued.

47. The superintendence of the education of the King during his minority shall, if his father has left no written directions, be determined by the Storting.

48. If the male line of the Royal family has become extinct, and no successor to the Throne has been designated, then a new King shall be chosen by the Storting. Meanwhile the Executive Power shall be exercised in accordance with section 40.

C. Citizenship and the Legislative Power

49. The people shall exercise the Legislative Power through the *Storting*, which consists of two divisions, the Lagting and the Odelsting.

50. Those entitled to vote are Norwegian citizens, men and women, who have completed their 21st year, who have been domiciled in the Kingdom for five years, and are living there.

Norwegian civil servants holding positions in the Diplomatic and Consular Services, and members of their household, are, if otherwise meeting the above-mentioned requirements, entitled to vote in the electoral district in Norway where they last had their domicile.

51. The rules concerning the electoral registers and the registration of the persons entitled to vote shall be determined by law.

52. (Repealed)

53. The right of voting shall be lost in the case of any person who:

(a) is sentenced for criminal offences, subject to such provisions as may be laid down by law;

(b) enters the service of a foreign power without the consent of the Government;

(c) (*repealed*);

(d) is found guilty of having bought votes, or sold his/her own vote, or of having voted at more than one poll;

(e) is declared incapable of managing his or her own affairs.

54. Elections shall be held every four years. They shall be completed by the end of September.

55. Elections shall be conducted in such manner as shall be determined by law. Disputes as to the right of voting shall be settled by the polling officers, against whose decision an appeal may be brought to the Storting.

56. Before the elections commence, sections 50–64 of the Constitution shall be read out aloud by the presiding officer of the poll.

57. The number of representatives to be elected as members of the Storting shall be one hundred and fifty.

58. Every province with its town shall be a constituency.

Representatives from the Kingdom's constituencies shall be divided as follows:

The province of Østfold shall elect eight; the city of Oslo thirteen; the province of Akershus seven; the province of Hedmark eight; the province of Opland seven; the province of Buskerud seven, the province of Vestfold seven; the province of Telemark six; the province of Aust-Agder four; the province of Vest-Agder five; the province of Rogaland ten; the province of Hordaland ten; the city of Bergen five; the province of Sogn og Fjordane five; the province of Møre og Romsdal ten; the province of Sør-Trøndelag ten; the province of Nord-Trøndelag six; the province of Nordland twelve; the province of Troms six; and the province of Finnmark four.

59. Every town and, in the country districts, every municipality, as well as every non-chartered town [*ladested*] possessing a municipal council of its own, shall constitute a separate polling district. The towns may, by law, be divided into several polling districts.

The elections shall be held separately for each polling district. At the poll the votes are cast, by the method of direct election, for the representatives in the Storting of the whole electoral district and their substitutes.

The system of election is proportional. The rules to be applied hereunto, as well as the particular regulations concerning the elections, shall be determined by law. subject to the provisions laid down in the Constitution.

60. How far and in what manner qualified voters may be allowed to deliver their ballot papers without going personally to the poll, shall be determined by law.

61. No one shall be qualified for election as a representative to the Storting unless he is 21 years old, has been domiciled 10 years in the Kingdom, and has the right to vote.

62. Officials employed in the Government offices and attendants or servants and pensioners of the Court are debarred from being nominated as representatives. The same applies to persons attached to the Diplomatic or Consular services.

The members of the Council of State must not attend at the Storting as representatives as long as they have a seat in the Council of State.

63. Everyone who is elected as a representative shall be in duty bound to accept the election, unless elected outside the electoral district in which he has the right to vote, or is prevented by an impediment which the Storting judges to be valid. If any one has attended as a representative at each ordinary session of the Storting following one election, he shall not be obliged to accept election at the next election for the Storting.

If anyone is elected as a representative without being obliged to accept such election, he must, within the time and in the manner prescribed by law, make a declaration stating whether he accepts the election or not.

The time within which a person returned for two or more electoral districts shall state which election he accepts, and the manner in which this shall be done, shall likewise be fixed by law.

64. The representatives elected shall be furnished with certificates, the validity of which shall be submitted to the judgment of the Storting.

65. Every representative and every substitute called to the Storting shall be entitled to receive, as fixed by law, reimbursement from the treasury for travelling expenses to and from the Storting, and from the Storting to his home and back again, during vacations lasting at least fourteen days, and also for expenses for medical treatment in the case of illness.

He shall further be entitled to receive compensation, as determined by law, for attending sittings of the Storting.

66. The representatives shall be exempt from personal arrest while on their way to and from the Storting, as well as during their stay there, unless they are apprehended in public crimes; nor shall they be called to account outside the meetings of the Storting for the opinions they have expressed there. Every representative shall be bound to conform to the rules of the Storting.

67. The representatives elected in the aforesaid manner shall constitute the *Storting* of the Kingdom of Norway.

68. The Storting shall as a rule assemble on the first weekday in October every year in the capital of the Kingdom, unless the King, by reason of extraordinary circumstances, such as hostile invasion or infectious disease, shall appoint for the purpose another town in the Kingdom. Such an appointment must then be publicly notified in good time.

69. In extraordinary cases the King shall have the right to summon the Storting at a time other than the ordinary one.

70. Such an extraordinary Storting may be dismissed by the King when he thinks fit.

71. The members of the Storting shall act as such for four successive years in extraordinary as well as in ordinary Storting held during that period.

72. If an extraordinary Storting is still sitting at the time when an ordinary Storting is due to open, the former shall be dismissed before the latter assembles.

73. The Storting shall nominate from among its members one-fourth to constitute the *Lagting*; the remaining three-fourths shall constitute the *Odelsting*. This nomination shall take place at the first ordinary Storting that assembles after a new general election, and thereafter the Lagting shall remain unchanged at all Storting that meet after the same election, except in so far as any vacancy which may occur among its members has to be filled by special nomination.

Each Ting shall hold its meetings separately, and nominate its own President and Secretary. Neither of the Ting may hold a meeting unless at least one-half of its members are present. Bills concerning amendments to the Constitution may not be dealt with unless at least two-thirds of the to which he particularly desires to call the attention of the Storting. No members of the Storting are present.

74. As soon as the Storting is constituted, the King or the person he appoints for the purpose shall open its proceedings with a speech, in which he shall inform it of the state of the Kingdom and of the subjects deliberations may take place in the presence of the King.

When the proceedings of the Storting are opened, the Prime Minister and the members of the Council of State have the right to attend at the Storting, as well as at both of its divisions, and have the same rights as the members of the Storting to take part in the proceedings in so far as these are conducted in open session, without, however, having the right to vote. They may take part in matters which are discussed in private session only in so far as permission is granted by the Ting concerned.

75. The duties and prerogatives of the Storting are:

(a) to enact and to repeal laws; to impose taxes, duties, customs, and other public charges, which, however, shall not remain operative longer than 31 December of the following year, unless they are expressly renewed by a new ordinary Storting;

(b) to open loans on the credit of the Kingdom;

(c) to control the finances of the Kingdom;

(d) to appropriate the sums of money necessary to meet the expenditure of the State;

(e) to decide how much shall be paid annually to the King for his Royal household, and to determine the apanage of the Royal family, which may not, however, consist of real property;

(f) to have laid before it the records of the Council of State, and all public reports and documents; the records of such diplomatic matters and of such matters relating to military command as, in pursuance of a decision to that effect, are to be kept secret, shall, however, be laid before a committee consisting of at the most nine members chosen from among the members of the Odelsting, and may further be brought before the Odelsting if any member of the committee moves that the Odelsting give its opinion on the subject, or that an action be brought in the Constitutional Court of the Realm [*Riksrett*].

(g) to have communicated to it the treaties and agreements which the King, on behalf of the State, has concluded with foreign powers; the provisions contained in paragraph (f) concerning such matters as are to be kept secret, shall apply equally to secret clauses which, however, must not be at variance with the public ones;

(h) to have power to summon anyone to meet before it in matters of State, the King, and the royal family excepted; this exception, however, does not apply to the Royal Princes if they hold any public office;
(i) to revise the lists of salaries and pensions temporarily granted, and to make therein such alterations as it finds necessary;
(k) to appoint five auditors, who shall annually examine the accounts of the State and publish extracts of the same in print, which accounts shall for this purpose be delivered to the auditors within six months of the expiration of the year for which the appropriations of the Storting are made; and to provide for the organization of an office to approve the accounts of the State accountants;
(l) to naturalize aliens.

76. Every bill shall first be introduced in the Odelsting, either by one of its own members, or by the Government through a member of the Council of State.

If the bill is passed, it is sent to the Lagting, which either approves or rejects it, and in the latter case sends it back with comments appended. These are taken into consideration by the Odelsting, which either lets the bill fall or again sends it to the Lagting, with or without alteration.

When a bill from the Odelsting has twice been laid before the Lagting and has been a second time rejected by it, the whole Storting shall meet in joint session, and the bill is then disposed of by a majority of two-thirds of the votes.

Between any two of these deliberations there shall be an interval of at least three days.

77. When a bill passed by the Odelsting has been approved by the Lagting or by the Storting in joint session, it shall be sent to the King, with a request that it may receive the King's assent.

78. If the King assents to the bill, he shall attach to it his signature, whereby it becomes law.

If he does not assent to it, he shall return it to the Odelsting with the declaration that he does not for the time being find it expedient to give his assent to it. In this case the bill must not again be submitted to the King by the Storting then assembled.

79. If a bill has been passed unaltered by two ordinary sessions of the Storting, constituted after two separate successive elections and separated from each other by at least two intervening ordinary sessions of the Storting, without any divergent bill having been passed by the Storting in the period between the first and the last passing, and it is then submitted to the King with the petition that His Majesty shall not refuse his assent to a bill which, after the most mature deliberation, the Storting considers to be for the benefit of the country, it becomes law, even if the Royal assent is not accorded before the Storting dissolves.

80. The Storting shall remain in session as long as it may find necessary. When, having finished its business, it is dismissed by the King, he shall at the same time communicate his decision with regard to the bills that have not already been disposed of (see sections 77–79), either by assenting to them or by rejecting them. All such bills as he does not expressly assent to, are considered as having been rejected by him.

81. All Acts (with the exception of those mentioned in section 79) shall be drawn up in the King's name, under the seal of the Kingdom of Norway, and in the following terms: 'We, X, make it publicly known that the following decision of the Storting of (such and such a date) in the following terms has been laid before Us (here follows the decision). In consequence whereof We have assented to and confirmed, as We hereby assent to and confirm the same as a law under Our hand and the seal of the Kingdom.'

82. (Repealed)

83. The Storting may demand the opinion of the Supreme Court of Justice [*Høyesterett*] on questions of law.

84. The Storting shall meet in open session, and its proceedings shall be published in print, except in those cases in which a majority decides to the contrary.

85. Any person who obeys an order the purpose of which is to disturb the liberty and the security of the Storting, shall thereby be guilty of treason against the country.

D. The Judicial Power

86. The Constitutional Court of the Realm [*Riksrett*] shall pronounce judgment in the first and last instance in such actions as are brought by the Odelsting against members of the Council of State, or against members of the Supreme Court of Justice [*Høyesterett*], or against members of the Storting for criminal offences which they may have committed in that capacity.

The particular rules concerning impeachment by the Odelsting, according to this section, shall be determined by law. The period within which a prosecution may be instituted in the Constitutional Court of the Realm shall not, however, be fixed at less than fifteen years.

The ordinary members of the Lagting and the permanent members of the Supreme Court of Justice shall be judges of the Constitutional Court of the Realm. The provisions contained in section 87 shall apply to the constitution of the Constitutional Court of the Realm in each particular case. In the Constitutional Court of the Realm the President of the Lagting takes the chair.

A person sitting in the Constitutional Court of the Realm as a member of the Lagting does not vacate his seat in the Court if the period for which he is elected a member of the Storting should expire before the Constitutional Court of the Realm has terminated the trial of the case. If, for any other reason, he ceases to be a member of the Storting, he shall resign as a judge of the Constitutional Court of the Realm. The same shall apply if a judge of the Supreme Court of Justice, sitting as a member of the Constitutional Court of the Realm, retires as a member of the Supreme Court of Justice.

87. The accused and the person prosecuting on behalf of the Odelsting have the right to challenge members of the Lagting and the Supreme Court of Justice [*Høyesterett*], provided that fourteen of the members of the Lagting and seven members of the Supreme Court of Justice remain as judges in the Constitutional Court of the Realm [*Riksrett*]. Each party has the right to challenge an equal number of the members of the Lagting, the accused having, however, the preferential right of challenging one more, if the number to be challenged is not divisible into two equal parts. The same shall apply to the challenging of the members of the Supreme Court of Justice. If, in an action, there are more than one accused, they shall exercise the right of challenge collectively in accordance with rules to be determined by law. If challenge is not made to the extent permitted, members of the Lagting and of the Supreme Court of Justice in excess of fourteen and seven respectively shall withdraw as determined by ballot.

When the action comes up for judgment, the members of the Court in excess of fifteen shall withdraw from the Court, the selection being made by ballot; the remaining judges who are to pass judgment, shall number ten members at most of the Lagting and five of the Judges of the Supreme Court of Justice.

The President of the Constitutional Court of the Realm and the President of the Supreme Court of Justice shall not in any case retire as a result of a ballot.

If the Constitutional Court of the Realm cannot be constituted so as to contain the number of members of the Lagting and the Supreme Court of Justice prescribed in the preceding paragraphs, the case may nevertheless be tried and judgment be passed provided that the Court numbers at least ten judges.

Further provisions as to the manner in which the Constitutional Court of the Realm shall be constituted shall be laid down by law.

88. *The Supreme Court of Justice* shall pronounce judgment in the last instance. The right to bring an action in the Supreme Court of Justice may, however, be limited as determined by law.

The Supreme Court of Justice shall consist of a President and at least four other members.

89. (Repealed)

90. The judgments of the Supreme Court of Justice may not in any case be appealed against.

91. No one may be appointed a member of the Supreme Court of Justice before he is 30 years of age.

E. General Provisions

92. To official posts [*embeder*] in the State shall be appointed only Norwegian citizens, men and women, who speak the language of the country, and who at the same time

(a) were born in the Kingdom of parents who at that time were subjects of the State;

(b) or were born in a foreign country of Norwegian parents who were not at that time subjects of another state;

(c) or shall hereafter have resided ten years in the Kingdom;
(d) or are naturalized by the Storting.

Others may, however, be appointed as teachers at the University and the secondary schools, as physicians and as consuls in foreign places.

93. In order to secure international peace and security, or in order to promote international law and order and cooperation between nations, the Storting may, by a three-fourths majority, consent that an international organization of which Norway is or becomes a member, shall have the right, within a functionally limited field, to exercise powers which in accordance with this Constitution are normally vested in the Norwegian authorities, exclusive of the power to alter this Constitution. For such consent as provided above at least two-thirds of the members of the Storting — the same quorum as is required for changes in or amendments to this Constitution — shall be present.

The provisions of the preceding paragraph do not apply in cases of membership in an international organization, the decisions of which are not binding on Norway except as obligations under international law.

94. The first, or if this is not possible, the second ordinary Storting, shall make provision for the publication of a new general civil and criminal code. In the meantime the laws of the State now in operation shall remain in force, provided that they are not at variance with this Constitution or the provisional ordinances that may be issued in the meantime.

The existing permanent taxes shall likewise continue in operation until the next Storting.

95. No dispensations, protections, postponements of payments or redresses must be granted after the new general code has come into operation.

96. No one must be convicted except according to law, or be punished except according to judicial sentence. Interrogation by torture must not take place.

97. No law must be given retroactive effect.

98. When special fees are paid to officials of the Courts of Justice, the payer shall be exempt from further payment to the Public Treasury in respect of the same matter.

99. No one must be arrested and committed to prison except in the cases determined by law and in the manner prescribed by law. For unwarranted arrest and illegal detention the officer concerned shall be responsible to the person imprisoned.

The Government is not entitled to employ military force against subjects of the State, except in accordance with the forms prescribed by law, unless any meeting should disturb the public peace and not immediately disperse after the articles of the Statute-book relating to riots have been read out aloud three times by the civil authority.

100. There shall be liberty of the Press. No person must be punished for any writing, whatever its contents may be, which he has caused to be printed or published, unless he wilfully and manifestly has either himself shown or incited others to disobedience to the laws, contempt of religion or morality or the constitutional powers, or resistance to their orders, or has advanced false and defamatory accusations against any other person. Everyone shall be free to speak his mind frankly on the administration of the State or on any other subject whatsoever.

101. New and permanent privileges implying restrictions on the freedom of trade and industry must not be granted to any one in future.

102. Search of private homes shall not be made except in criminal cases.

103. Asylum for the protection of debtors shall not be granted to such persons as hereafter become bankrupt.

104. Forfeiture of lands and goods shall be abolished.

105. If the welfare of the State requires that any person shall surrender his movable or immovable property for the public use, he shall receive full compensation from the public treasury.

106. The purchase-money, as well as the revenues of the landed property constituting ecclesiastical benefices, shall be applied solely to the benefit of the clergy and to the promotion of education. The property of charitable institutions shall be applied solely for their own benefit.

107. The Odel and Åsete rights shall not be abolished. The further conditions under which these rights shall continue for the greatest benefit of the State and the best advantage of the rural population, shall be determined by the first or second Storting following.

108. No earldoms, baronies, majorats or fideicommissa must be created in the future.

109. Every citizen of the State is in general equally bound to defend his native country during a certain time, without any regard to birth or fortune.

The application of this principle and the restrictions it may become subject to, shall be determined by law.

110. It is incumbent on the authorities of the State to create conditions which make it possible for every person who is able to work to earn his living by his work.

111. The form and the colours of the Norwegian Flag shall be determined by law.

112. If experience proves that any part of the Constitution of the Kingdom of Norway ought to be changed, a proposal to this effect shall be submitted to the first, second or third ordinary Storting after a General Election, and be published in print. But it shall be left to the first, second or third ordinary Storting after the following General Election to decide whether or not the proposed amendment shall be adopted. Such amendment must, however, never contradict the principles embodied in this Constitution, but merely relate to modifications of particular provisions which do not alter the spirit of this Constitution, and should receive the support of two-thirds of the members of the Storting.

An amendment of the Constitution adopted in the manner aforesaid shall be signed by the President and the Secretary of the Storting, and be sent to the King for public notification in print, as forming an integral part of the Constitution of the Kingdom of Norway.

(The English text of the Constitution is that published by the University Press, Oslo, Third revised edition, 1962. Translation by Tønnes Andenæs. The footnotes of that edition have been omitted.)

INDEX

SCIENCE FICTION AMERICA

SCIENCE FICTION AMERICA

Essays on SF Cinema

Edited by David J. Hogan

McFarland & Company, Inc., Publishers
Jefferson, North Carolina, and London

Also by David J. Hogan

Dark Romance: Sexuality in the Horror Film
(McFarland, 1986; paperback 1997)

Library of Congress Cataloguing-in-Publication Data

Science fiction America : essays on
SF cinema / edited by David J. Hogan.
p. cm.
Includes bibliographical references and index.

ISBN 0-7864-2149-5 (illustrated case binding : 50# alkaline paper) 

1. Science fiction films—United States—History and criticism.
I. Hogan, David J., 1953–
PN1995.9.S26S275 2006 791.43'615—dc22 2005004743

British Library cataloguing data are available

Manufactured in the United States of America

McFarland & Company, Inc., Publishers
Box 611, Jefferson, North Carolina 28640
www.mcfarlandpub.com

For Kim

Acknowledgments

I would like to thank Chuck Anders, Ron Borst of Hollywood Movie Posters, Bob Burns, Tom Conroy of Movie Still Archives, David Del Valle, J.D. Lees and G-Fan, Donnie Pitchford, Mike Vraney and Lisa Petrucci of Something Weird Video, and Dr. Chet Walker for all of their help. Thanks also to the contributing writers who provided photographs and other images.

Table of Contents

Introduction: Science Fiction and the Actual

DAVID J. HOGAN

Science fiction illuminates our public faces and our secret lives.

All right: Here's a visual narrative that comes to me occasionally, not as a dream and not even as an idle daytime fantasy, but as specific images that unspool as if I observe them on a movie screen: A shadowed suburban street on a summer night, viewed from 20 or 30 feet above ground level. No people are about. The houses are dark. One, perhaps two, cars are parked at the curbs. A sigh of wind rustles the branches and leaves of a mature maple tree.

My camera "eye" begins to descend, looking rightward, toward the quiet houses, then left, toward a thin shaft of light that falls across a patch of grass and onto a sidewalk. We're looking at a school — old brick and of substantial size, probably a high school. We begin to move toward the yellow light.

The scene dissolves, and we are inside the school, our vantage point eye level or lower, moving slowly through the dim corridors. There is no sound, and once again there is no light. Classroom doors are closed. We round a corner. At the end of the corridor is the gymnasium.

The gym doors open before us and as we move forward we see the horror inside: townspeople of every age and gender, gathered in knots dotting the corners and side walls, attended to by terrible tentacled things in bubble helmets. Aliens. Extraterrestrials. Invaders. Gross features and puckered, pitted limbs; creatures that suggest words like *cilia*, *pedicle*, *bulbous*, and *mucous*. The gymnasium is dim but the clear helmet worn by each creature gives off a sickly green glow, so the vast room has the quality of an undersea environment where phosphorescent fishes light the murk.

In one corner a gathering of monsters toy with a terrified middle-aged man, snaking their limbs around his body, pushing and shoving him between them. In a dimmer corner a clot of monsters surround three teenage girls, one of whom has lost half her T-shirt. The young women react to their alien suitors with open fear.

Nearby, a visitor gently turns a human baby in its tentacles with evident curiosity, regarding the child the way a bibliophile examines a rare book — or perhaps the way a hungry man anticipates a piece of lunch meat.

Two or three aliens on a slightly elevated band platform confer with a group of middle-aged men, the apparent power brokers of this town. Together, the men and the aliens are arriving at some sort of understanding. One man, dressed in the uniform of a police chief, lies dead on the floor next to the platform, but the other men seem not to notice, or care.

Another uniformed man, a patrol officer, has been hoisted to the basketball hoop, his arms taut behind him and looped over the rim, his body pierced with an array of sharp instruments. Two or three extraterrestrials regard him with interest, and whether the officer is alive or dead, we cannot be sure. Other uniformed officers flank the group on the platform. They seem willfully unconcerned with the fate of their comrade.

The side door of the gymnasium opens with a whang and locks itself to heavy latches set in the concrete block of the inside wall. The captive townspeople jump at the sudden noise. Somewhere in a corner crisscrossed with shadows, a man begins to cry softly.

At the side door, uniformed human soldiers sharply push a group of civilians into the room. One of the soldiers, a captain, detaches himself from the group and strides to the elevated platform. He acknowledges the aliens, then quietly addresses the entire group. Once or twice, he gestures to the people he has helped to herd inside.

Then a sickly yellow light flashes from outside — once, twice. The explosions of color are followed by the hum of precision machinery, and then a deep, ugly ratcheting that suggests machinery of another sort: heavy, biting, brutal. The occupants of the gym, human and alien alike, note the light and noise with a variety of reactions: impatience, satisfaction, fear. One of the middle-aged men standing with the invaders looks at his wristwatch.

"People," he announces. "People, it's time. Time for Bellville to step into the future." When he raises his face to one of the high windows, his features are bathed in the unwholesome yellow gleam.

A woman inhales sharply but before she can scream a tentacle whips across her face and mouth.

The middle-aged man points outside, toward the light and the ugly noise. "It's the future," he says, "and it begins outside."

▪ ▪ ▪

My "movie" tableau is an unpleasant one that suggests many things: military adventurism developed by another culture, and exported over a great distance for the purpose of conquest; human greed and collusion; misapplied science; unwholesome sexuality; the primal, perhaps inbred fear of "the other"; the destruction of families; resistance, and its price; ugly aspects of high technology; institutionalized coercion and torture.

If a lot of this suggests elements of the world we live in, it should. And so this is what I like about science fiction movies: the stark realism.

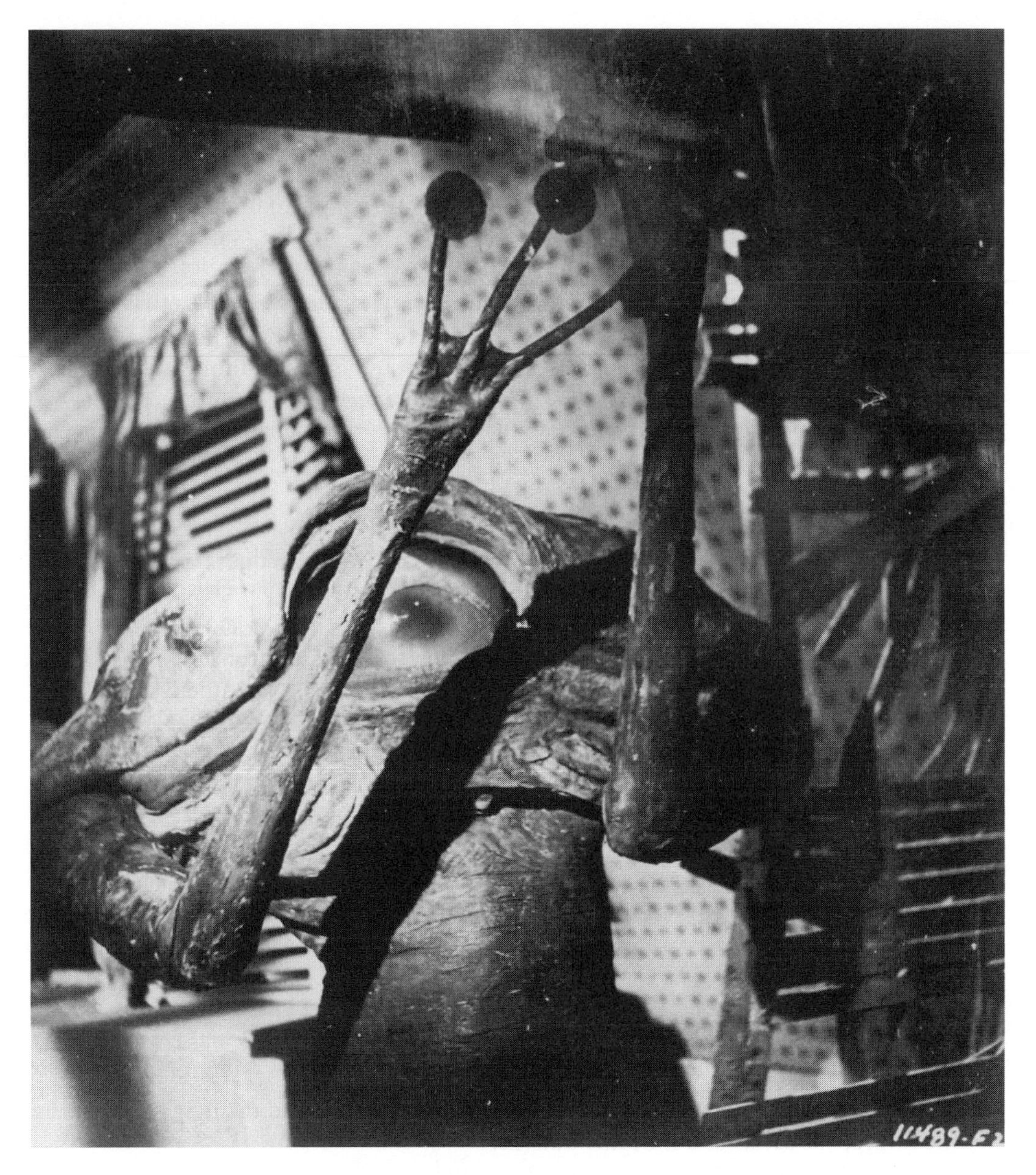

Science fiction cinema: our fears, secrets, and desires made "real." This is the predatory but inquisitive Martian (Charles Gemora) in *War of the Worlds* (1953).

I use the word "stark" advisedly. Rod Serling, creator of *The Twilight Zone* and a prominent genre practitioner, understood that because SF is taken seriously by so few people, it's an ideal vehicle for social comment that, in other contexts, might be unacceptable to audiences.

Explorations of gender issues, war, xenophobia and other difficult topics are more easily accepted by viewers if the tales' protagonists exist in future times or alien places with discernable, but not too literal, links to our own world. If the protagonists are only vaguely human a writer can achieve especially pointed comment because audiences will nod and absorb the lesson without having been made to feel morally deficient or unfairly put upon. It's the scaly alien who dislikes his neighbor because of the color of the neighbor's scales— the person watching the story doesn't dislike anybody.

Serling was a social progressive who was upset with the rich catalogue of human mischief and its concomitant misery. Like many who were his contemporaries in film and print — Kornbluth, Vonnegut, Beaumont, Ellison, Spinrad, Rotsler, Merril, Roddenberry — Serling viewed science fiction as a vehicle for social comment and, he hoped, enlightenment. The rocket ships, the ray guns, the Martians— all of these were *tchotchkes* that entertained audiences, but also functioned as the horse that the message rode in on.

It's true that those in the SF-film audience who have the inclination and capacity to "get it" will get it, and those who can't (such as studio executives and other meddlers) won't realize they've been fed a spoonful of liberal polemics. For example, critical reaction to the 1997 film *Starship Troopers* (a movie discussed in this anthology) almost invariably missed the film's bitter satire of military adventurism, xenophobia, and political agitprop. More than one professional critic dimly dismissed *Starship Troopers* as a "big bug movie."

Now: Has every filmed SF thriller been produced with the purpose of moral and intellectual uplift? Naturally not. SF films and television programs (excepting those rarities produced by zealous amateurs or underwritten by foundations or national film boards) are produced to show a profit, and as far as most producers and studio executives are (not unreasonably) concerned, profit is paramount.

Science fiction creators with agendas larger than profit and the superficial conventions of the genre have the entire canvas of human experience from which to draw inspiration. Government malfeasance, sexism and voyeurism, the sorry consequences of war, corporate avarice, biological weaponry, ageism, institutionalized violence as entertainment, the difficult search for personal identity — these are vivid, very real concerns of modern life.

Individual explications of social issues in SF cinema often are overstated, even clumsy. The classic mantra that closes too many uninspired SF thrillers—"He tampered in God's domain"— is the movie equivalent of a sash weight laid roughly against one's temple, and isn't the only sort of hamhandedness one is likely to encounter in the worst of the genre. *Okay, okay, we understand! We get the idea!* If Serling and others frequently brought heavy hands to their material, they can be forgiven because, in the main, what they offered was good rather than pointless.

Satisfyingly, the messages of many SF films, while integral to the plot, do not *drive* the plot, so viewers have the luxury of absorbing them or regarding them merely as part of the scenery. Audiences are free to absorb, or ignore, as much of a film's polemics as they desire.

More than 30 years ago, as a very young man, I wrote a detailed article about the 1958 Paramount release *I Married a Monster from Outer Space*. The film's hugely exploitable title has "profit motive" written all over it, yet screenwriter Louis Vittes and director Gene Fowler, Jr. (a onetime editor for Fritz Lang who had already demonstrated considerable thoughtfulness and a visually and emotionally dark sensibility with another risibly titled thriller, *I Was a Teenage Werewolf*), made *I Married a Monster* into not just a top-flight thriller, but a smart rumination on the war between the sexes. As a college student I picked up on the picture's well-executed subtext of male exploitation of the female body (in the film, extraterrestrials wish to mate with human women), but I missed another of the movie's undeniable subtexts that is nicely explicated in another of this book's essays: domestic abuse.

If there's a lesson here for cultural historians, it's that SF films, like other sorts of movies, pick up added resonance not simply as society changes with the passing of time, but as the viewer changes with the years. The oldest film discussed in *Science Fiction America, High Treason*, was released in 1930. Factor in the subsequent Depression, two world wars, increased urbanization, affluence and poverty, plus other historical factors post-1930, and you have a film that speaks to us differently today than it did on original release. Likewise, a person who saw *High Treason* in 1930 would have reacted to it differently when the picture turned up on *The Late Show* in 1965.

The most recent film discussed in this book, *The Iron Giant*, was released in 1999, making it a contemporary picture, to be sure, but one that — given its subtext of the nature and responsibilities of government, armies, and warriors— has acquired a fresh layer of meaning as, at this writing, the United States trundles toward the third year of its adventure in Iraq. A look back, then, to a movie released in 1999 — or to one made in 1965 or 1958 or 1930 — is inevitably fruitful.

By its nature, film appeals to our voyeurism, but the film-to-audience relationship is considerably more participatory than the mere act of looking. As (arguably) the most accessible and vivid of the lively arts, film springs almost directly from our heads and hearts. Filmmakers are as invested in and shaped by the larger culture as the rest of us. What they observe, we observe. There is nothing elite about film (or any art); the artist and his or her sensibilities always are shaped by the same realities and concerns that affect and model all of us. Movies entertain us, but they also tell us who and what we are.

Given the strictures of drama, films exaggerate aspects of human experience, but even that exaggeration reveals a great deal about the society, and is often predictive. Two films discussed in the book, *Death Race 2000* and *Rollerball*, take spectator sport as their metaphor for societal sickness. The former is a burlesque, the latter a grim rumination on human weakness, but both take a hard look at the causes and hazards of violence as entertainment. This was a concern when the films were made in the 1970s ("I went to a fight and a hockey game broke out") and is even more pointed today, as expressed by big-money professional "wrestling," Tough Man competitions, bloodthirsty video games, the mercifully short-lived XFL, and TV's reality programs, where contestants are placed in (seemingly) deadly peril for our amusement. The exaggerations of the 1970s are considerably less fanciful today. Again: a look back is always fruitful.

A note about the inclusion in *Science Fiction America* of an essay that discusses a British film, *High Treason* (sound version, 1930): Although predicated on war fears that had obvious, special resonance for Britain and the rest of Europe, *High Treason* proposes a high-tech urban milieu that is considerably more suggestive of the United States, and that nation's burgeoning economy, than it is of Britain. If ideals of military power, technological innovation, and urban growth were already embodied, in the decade after the Great War, by New York City, then *High Treason* is as much American as it is British.

We make a related sort of distinction with the inclusion of an essay about the Japanese Godzilla. Although Godzilla (or *Gojira*, as he's known at home) is a virtual mascot of that island nation, his influence and popularity have been so great Stateside that he has become an adopted — if frequently ill-tempered — son. More significantly, the first Godzilla film (one of two discussed at length in the essay) was made in response to a uniquely American invention, the atomic bomb. In this respect, the giant lizard is nearly as American as he is Japanese.

Each essay in *Science Fiction America* was solicited and written expressly for this book. None has appeared in print before. Sixteen contributors have produced 22 essays that discuss 27 feature films, three serials, a pair of Depression-era cartoons, and a vintage television series. The contributors' backgrounds encompass academia, film history, publishing, painting, religious studies, filmmaking, and TV production.

Like the people who make movies, the contributors are different, and they are the same — like you, and me, and everybody who calls America home.

Arlington Heights, Illinois
Fall 2005

1

High Treason: Great Expectations

JOHN T. SOISTER

Michael Deane:	"Hullo! Hullo! Hullo!"
Evelyn Seymour:	"Hullo, darling."
Both:	"Hullo! Hullo!"
Evelyn:	"I say, isn't it dreadful?"
Michael:	"No, I think it's delightful that you are dining with me tonight."
Evelyn:	"Tonight! You're mad."
Michael:	"Only about you, darling. I'll call for you in my car, as usual."
Evelyn:	"But you can't. It's impossible. Don't you realize that we may be on the verge of declaring war?"
Michael:	"And I am on the verge of declaring something much more important than war, if you will only dine with me tonight. Hullo! Hullo! Oh, damn! Hullo! Hullo! Hullo!"
Operator:	"Isn't your wavelength working all right?"
Michael:	"Of course it is. Fade away, Miss Interference. I'm not talking to you."
Operator:	"Sorry you've been troubled."

The year 1929 found Western civilization ten years removed from the Great War, and four (and counting) before Adolf Hitler would be named chancellor of Germany. As Charles Dickens wrote (in another age, about another era), it was both the best and worst of times.

In the Great War of 1914–18, the Old World had been destroyed in one fell swoop. Despite the staggering magnitude of her losses, Britain would remain an empire, but her Austro-Hungarian, Russian, and Ottoman sisters fell victim to both the violence of the time and to Time itself. War could no longer be viewed as an exercise in gallantry, with man against man, *mano a mano*, and all combat strategies chess-like and aboveboard. Tanks supplanted horses, planes took military advantage into the third dimension, and poison gas dealt with foes who were unreachable by bayonet or pistol. As honor fell, widespread espionage and sabotage arose in its place. The 1914 assassination of Archduke Ferdinand rent countries and disrupted cultures as no cold-blooded murder of pope or king ever had before. Nearly 10 million soldiers died as a result of the war, and 21 million others were wounded. The Great War's five years transformed Europe more profoundly and completely than had the five centuries that preceded them.

The war had been "great," of course, in terms of scope, not grandeur, and not only Britain suffered greatly. Still, that country counted some 750,000 killed between 1914 and 1917—many of the 300,000 troops who died at Passchendaele in August and September 1917 had *drowned in mud*, following cataclysmic rains in Flanders—with another 2.5 million wounded or permanently disabled. The "flower of English manhood" that had been celebrated in fact and lauded in myth since the latter half of the first millennium had either been interred with ceremony, entombed by ruins, or left to rot in countless Continental battlefields and trenches. Class distinctions that had reached their apex during the Victorian era divided officers from the rank and file with devastating results. This lack of communication doomed military operations from Loos to Gallipoli. Combat veterans returned home forever changed: incapable of staying focused and on task; unable to maintain relationships, sire families, or care for the families they had left behind; unwilling to dwell on the horrors of war so as to effect therapy, yet powerless to put the terrifying images out of their minds.

Pacifists—whose presence had been ubiquitous if ineffectual before and during the hostilities—grew angrier and more vociferous. Year after year of bloody conflict had led to increased war-weariness on the part of many, and although—thanks largely to the rhetoric of David Lloyd George—the British masses saw the war (which they viewed as necessary and just) to its bloody conclusion, few would have argued then that the changing face of the world made peace the ultimate end in itself. By 1917, the Union of Democratic Control (peace through negotiation) and the No-Conscription Fellowship (a Christian pacifist movement) were making themselves heard with increasing success.

It seemed as if the war would last forever, as important objectives seemed never to be seized, nor crucial locales secured. After nearly four years, the ceaseless struggles that centered on the trenches in France resulted in almost no troop advancement. Hundreds of men would die to gain 50 feet of scarred and pitted wasteland, and hundreds more would perish soon after when the enemy retook the position. Civilians were in turn frustrated by the failure to inch the hostilities toward a conclusion, and appalled by the incredible number of casualties incurred merely to maintain the status quo.

On the propaganda front, Britain's literary arm cramped badly as the endless slaughter obscured sides that had earlier been clearly drawn, and undermined opinions that had been previously held as unimpeachable. The effort to speak up for or to rail against the Great War had fact and myth battling for the public's ear. Britons who had greeted the onset of combat with righteous anger and a steely resolve found themselves weary of war and words long before the armistice was signed.

If any positive notes were sounded during those long war years, they may have been the widening of the woman's role in day-to-day life, and the narrowing of the chasm that divided the moneyed (and frequently titled) class from the working class. With virtually every able-bodied man of conscriptable age (18 to 45 years old) off fighting the Germans somewhere in Europe, Africa, or the Middle East, the trade unions that had earlier held the Island Empire in a stranglehold eased their grip out of base necessity: there were no men to be had. By 1917, then, nearly three-quarters of a million women had been put to work in munitions factories and shipyards, and this move—born of dire need and not by design—resulted in recognition by a grateful empire and a frank reappraisal of women in British society. The Victorian mores that had been slow to die out on their own were cut down with the troops in the trenches, and by the beginning of 1918, almost five million women had found gainful employment in some field other than desperate prostitution. As a coda, shortly thereafter the Representation of the People Act was passed, and women (aged 30 and older) were finally given the right to vote.

"The Peace Picture": How many theater patrons of 1930 bought tickets hoping to get away from war and mindless violence?

The Great War saw a growing role (and grudging respect) for Parliament's House of Commons, which, at the outbreak of hostilities, had been in the control of the Liberal Party and the Unionists. The former, which represented wealthy merchants and industrialists far more than the workers who toiled for a pittance, were divided over the perceived economic stringencies of the war. Some were concerned that their bottom lines would suffer if individual (and corporate) liberties fell victim to governmental war-fever. Others worried how to profit from the conflict without appearing to be disloyal, while still others—those whose fortunes were *not* tied to munitions—were opposed to war on the sort of general principle that was based in self-interest rather than in ethics.

The latter had nearly brought Britain to a halt in mid–1914, when the railwaymen, the transport workers, and the miners threatened a nationwide strike unless demands were met. The resulting chaos—it was a veritable certainty that widespread violence would have followed—would have crippled England. The army, alert to the incipient outbreak, was simultaneously casting a collective wary eye at Ireland, where nearly a quarter of a million armed men, Catholics and Protestants alike, were on the verge of starting a civil war. The Unionists were betting that Parliament would accede to their demands, caught as that august body was between the Irish crisis and the hostilities that snowballed following Franz Ferdinand's assassination. Although the union leaders were as patriotic as the next man, it was hoped that opportunism would once again win the day.

British blood proved thicker than British blather, and the Great War pushed the Irish and union concerns onto back burners. With neither issue having been resolved by the end of 1916, though, the dogged persistence of both was undermining the war effort. Somehow, Lloyd George manipulated the Unionists and about half of his own Liberal Party—together (via a *one-vote* majority) with the Labour Party—into one cohesive unit, and the war was successfully enjoined by a British "united front" for the first time. At the end of the fighting, however, the Liberal Party was perhaps the most notable casualty of the cooperation. Victory had come on the shoulders of the common man (and woman), and the unions saw growth in membership, power and prestige almost immediately. While the sterling combat performance of titled officers caused snifters of brandy to be raised in private clubs, many more mugs of beer were drained in the memory of pub mates who never came home from the Dardanelles. The renovated House of Commons now was truly common in the lords' eyes, but none could deny that the British working man had won the right to raise his voice in Parliament.

In the decade that followed the armistice, British sensibilities gradually adjusted to the empowerment of women, the swelling influence of the rank-and-file worker, and the snail-like pace of the return to economic stability. The appalling number of casualties had left no disinterested parties in its wake: jingoism and pacifism drew the largest numbers of adherents as survivors sought alternatives to depression and madness. The chief themes that ran through the period's literature and drama were honesty vs. deceit, rebellion vs. subjugation, expansion vs. isolation, and bravery vs. cowardice, all of which were subsumed into innumerable disquisitions on peace vs. war.

Not much improvement could be made on Britain's natural defenses, but elsewhere, national borders were ordered secured (the French installed the largest artillery pieces they could construct along theirs), and national pride, in England and elsewhere, grew in inverse proportion to international tolerance. The works of Shakespeare and Dickens were snapped up in cheap editions in record numbers, as Britons took refuge in the undeniably brilliant Britishness of their literary forebears. The British film industry, which had achieved notoriety for its remarkable stolidity almost from its very inception, spent much of the 1920s producing bowdlerized versions of the masterworks of the aforementioned writers (and of many other native authors and playwrights) and paeans to the country's ironmongers, shepherds, greengrocers and such, without whom England would have been a damn sight less British in the first place. Apart from the (even then) intriguing visions of a young Michael Balcon and an even younger Alfred Hitchcock, the country's cinematic crème was as watery as the soup was, the day before payday. Shiploads of Hollywood Westerns filled the local flickers' seats, as loyal Brits whooped and hollered at the main feature, were edified by the second attraction (produced domestically), and then stood and sang along with the piano player as he invoked God's benediction on the king.

The panoramic London of the future: a great metropolis in the service of military adventurism.

The American motion picture was as lustily welcomed (and as mildly resented) as the Yanks themselves had earlier been when they came steaming across the Atlantic to help put things aright. Far less easy to take was the cinematic incursion of the Germans, who, via a succession of mesmerizing silent features, were vanquishing the British citizenry far more successfully than the kaiser could have ever dared hope. From almost the moment the war had ended, Germany had begun to craft a *kino* that displayed an astonishing beauty, maturity, and intelligence. The common Englishman could still despise the Germans and the British critic could still pooh-pooh the more haunting aspects of the films, but no one could *ignore* the German films. Fritz Lang's epic *Metropolis* (1927) saw the imported art form at its apex, and although H.G. Wells mocked it and any number of English filmmakers went on record to decry it, the heavily cut prints that made their way to the larger movie palaces put as many arses in seats as Hoot Gibson or Tom Mix.

It took a couple of years, but the British film industry finally came up with a *Metropolis* of its own. Based on a rather indifferent play by Noel Pemberton-Billing, Tiffany/Gaumont-British's *High Treason* was cause for the sounding of the trumpets and the raising of the Union Jack. Under the direction of prolific veteran Maurice Elvey, the picture, released in both silent (1929) and sound (1930) versions, may have trotted out the line of depressingly familiar themes that had led to the Great War, but it served them up *en masque* in a science-fiction milieu. Set either in 1940 or 1950 (the publicity materials and the dialogue continuity script for the sound version swear to the first date—which would make the Gaumont gang eerily prescient—while the extant silent version of the film itself avers it's the second), *High Treason* constructed its futuristic drama on the foundations of the recent past.

The scenario opens amid mounting tension between the Atlantic States and the Federated States of Europe. A title informs us that "secret forces are driving the great continents into war as surely as they did in 1914." The film takes great pains to reveal that the most secret of those forces are the munitions dealers.

An altercation at a border leads to sundry acts of sabotage, and war—the Ultimate War—appears imminent. Dr. Seymour (Basil Gill), president of the World Peace League, is beside himself, trying to prevent the coming slaughter. Joining in the good fight is his daughter, Evelyn (Benita Hume), who is torn between her commitment to peace and her love for Michael Deane (Jameson Thomas), redoubtable warrior and officer in the European Air Force. Despite any number of angst-filled meetings of the European Council, the fate of the world appears to hang on the decision of the president of Europe (Humberston Wright). As the isolated acts of violence and sabotage (instigated by the armaments chiefs) continue, the president of Europe decides to broadcast his declaration of war via radio and television at midnight.

Evelyn goes to one of the female conscription centers (both sexes have been called into service) and appeals to the white-uniformed women to prevent the airplanes from taking off. A soldier through and through, Michael orders his black-uniformed airmen to open fire on the rebellious women, but the men refuse to do so.

At the broadcast studios, the president offers Dr. Seymour a chance to make some preliminary remarks before war is officially declared. When Seymour announces that there will be no war, the president reaches for a pistol. Seymour shoots first, however, and the president falls dead, sacrificed to save civilization.

Back at the hangars, Michael instructs his airmen to start revving their engines. Evelyn rallies the women and faces Michael with a bomb in her hand, ready to destroy men and machines if any attempt is made to carry out the president's orders.

War is averted, but Seymour is arrested, tried for murder, and found guilty. As his daughter—reunited with her newly peaceable lover—looks on, her father is sentenced to death. "I am content," Seymour replies.

Neither very good, technically, nor very cathartic, dramatically (the chilling murder of the European president reminds one of the cold-blooded killing of doctors who consented to perform abortions by armed practitioners of the "Right to Life" movement some years back), *High Treason* is a mirror in which the tragic absurdities of any sort of fanaticism are held up for inspection and condemnation. Almost every action and nuance of the film reflect England's variegated stances on World War I; the picture speaks so clearly of the sundry hypocrisies, deceptions, and ironies that mark politics in our own day and age that one notes with great regret that the film is virtually unavailable for public consumption.

It's never made completely clear just where the Federated Atlantic States leave off and the United States of Europe take up on this Earth of tomorrow, and this in itself may serve as wry commentary on the relative liquidity of a country's borders and the sheer happenstance of a nation's identity in times of war. (In the script for the picture's sound version, The *Federation of Europe* is squaring off against The *Atlantic States*, so this casual attention to nomenclature isn't even maintained between the two versions of the same motion picture!) A brief insert of a crudely crafted world map is of no help, as it lacks identifying labels of any kind. The viewer is left uncertain as to whether Britain is a member of the Atlantic contingency or the European. About the only geographical fact we can seize on is that New York is the headquarters of the Atlantic States, while London is the seat of the World League of Peace.

This time round, war clouds begin to gather following an incident involving rumrunners (driving a futuristic "car" that must be seen to be believed) at a national border. The guards interrupt their card game to check the driver's papers and property. When the liquor-mobile makes a dash for it, it's blown to kingdom come by a highly unlikely hand grenade, thrown with unerring skill by one of the guards on one of the sides of the gate; which guard, on which side of the gate, is really not important. What is important, though, is that the guards immediately begin shooting point-blank at *each other*— lots of inserts of odd-looking pistols make their way into the sequence here — in what rapidly becomes a scene of violence taken to the nth level of ludicrousness.

The bellicose bravado snowballs in the picture the same way violent instances took off in the weeks prior to the start of the international hostilities in 1914. In both cases the posturing and swagger reached proportions that had never been seen until then and would not be seen again until the *next* World War was in a holding pattern. The pattern then continued over the years; the most recent example of the unlearned lessons of history coming back to haunt us may be the wedge driven between the, may we say, Atlantic states and the federation of Europe by the circumstances surrounding the 2003 invasion of Iraq.

Like the rank-and-file workers of Britain during the Great War, the rank-and-file airmen of *High Treason* compose a faceless force led by individuals of greater military and social standing. That these common airmen cannot bring themselves to fire upon the women may signal that they are truly men and not merely soldiers— or it may indicate the solidarity that came to grow during the war years among both genders.

"Old" England's stubborn unwillingness to abandon the Victorian class system, even as armored vehicles replaced horses and biplanes dropped explosives from appalling heights, was cited time and again for the failure of battlefield strategies in France and elsewhere. Major Sir John So-and-So, who never once flinched at the thought of sending other men to their deaths— even when those men were hopelessly outnumbered, already injured, or without adequate supplies— was loath to entrust to the conscripts under his command any messages or directives that might have averted disaster. Heavy were the responsibilities of noblesse oblige, but heavier still were the number of casualties that resulted from them.

Not all of the pacifists who opposed the Great War were women, of course, and not all took the high road in their quest to be heard. Still, Evelyn's success at turning the white-clad female tide against the war effort in *High Treason* pretty much splits

The eleventh hour, plus.... Evelyn Seymour's (Benita Hume) magic violin weaves its spell on the female pacifist clones in *High Treason* (1928). Unmistakable in the crowd are black-clad, warmongering males.

the ticket right down the middle. An Evelyn-like diatribe, launched wherever the distaff side of the population is gathering, presumably would produce a like result. Although a good proportion of the sundry World Peace League debating squads is male, the picture itself, purposefully or not, reinforces the notion that women are from Venus, and men, from Mars. Men may not fire on their countrywomen, especially at point-blank range, but indoctrination and a black leather–induced testosterone rush will see them ready to drop bombs on anyone at all. And, mind you, they remain ready to savage the enemy *after* the announcement is made that there will be no war.

That playwright Pemberton-Billing set his drama in the indeterminate future allowed him to make with impunity comments that might otherwise have been considered inflammatory or even politically treacherous. For all that, the science fiction elements that survived the transition from stage to screen remained picturesque (to say the least), imaginative, and not a little prophetic. (Dramatically, they are also quite superfluous.) The idea that the shift in everyday technology could be effected to the degree the scenario depicts in scarcely a decade (1929–1940, per the sound version) or even two (1929–1950, per the silent), staggers the imagination much more than do the onscreen fantasies.

The ubiquitous "teleradiograph," for example, provides instantaneous worldwide communication, but only for the wealthy and powerful; the masses are kept in the know via radio broadcasts and linear word crawls. When Michael Deane and that assembled body of champing–at-the-bit airmen are denied the teleradiograph's visual dimension (thanks to bullets whizzing about the European president's studio), they can only suspect—as did the entrenched conscripts on the Western Front, sent to die to retake 12 yards of blood-soaked soil—that there is more to the story than the part they're getting. Moneyed Britons in the future past also have showers in their offices, and full-body blowers instead of towels.

Entertainment for the ruling class reflects the collective social consciousness, as musicians are discorporate, dance moves turn on hesitation, and nightclub revues feature fencing matches between beautiful and provocatively attired women: the antithesis of feminine pacifism! Crowds are readily seduced by flowery rhetoric, even when such rhetoric is displayed, dispassionately, in ticker-tape fashion. Opinion is as last opinion heard, and loyalties rise and fall in the face of facile pronouncement, not on the shoulders of informed thought. (Some things never change, do they?)

High Treason was in many ways an "answer" film to Fritz Lang's *Metropolis*, much in the same way that certain pop songs in the 1950s and '60s were recorded and released in response to earlier hits, yet the Gaumont production touched on points that the German film did not. The British prided themselves on their reserve, averring that they would never exaggerate the Manhattan skyline to the point of impossibility, as had Lang. If anything, their Anglicized New York would be just a tad more angular and a shade broader than the real thing.

Of greater interest is that not a little transatlantic resentment resurfaced as *High Treason* was transferred from stage to screen. The film's New York is the center of international business, industry, and commerce, as well as a hub of armaments, greed, deceit, and hostility. Americans, the film seems keen to point out, are crass, selfish, and materialistic. Because many Yanks who had spilled their blood in squalid French trenches had also spilled their seed inside compliant Englishwomen, this future New York is clearly a metaphor for British irritability.

What's more, there are no completely guileless human beings populating *High Treason*'s tomorrow. Despite her white garb, Evelyn is no kin to Lang's angelic Maria; rather, she's an inch from turning suicide bomber in order to keep the planes on the ground. She and Michael, the drama's requisite juveniles, are subject to such intense mood swings that, in more normal times, both would be prime candidates for psychoanalysis. On the very eve of war, they banter romantically (and worse, insipidly). Following a series of encounters in which he de facto orders her to be shot down in cold blood, they cuddle guardedly as her father hears he is to be executed. At its nadir (cited at the outset of this essay), their dialogue brings fresh meaning to the word "banal." The audience suffers greatly.

With only four principal characters, the rest of the picture's hefty cast is comprised of a handful of sketchily drawn types and legions of anonymous human wallpaper. The transformation (at the mobilization center) of crowds of fashionable women into rows of dispirited, white-clad automatons is a begrudging homage to Lang's semirobotic workforce, but because the zombie-like women are easily reinvigorated by

Evelyn's eloquence and a chorus of the "Peace Song," one is left to wonder at how shallow and malleable we are meant to perceive the public to be. What's more, *High Treason* denies its viewers the hope of a union of heart and hand that *Metropolis* closed with, chiefly because no one undergoes any sort of conversion. There are no epiphanies here. Roll call votes and emergency sessions notwithstanding, the film's brace of leading intellectuals are totally swayed by rampant emotion, not logic. This is a failure of the scenario, not an irony of the argument, and the result is that the European president's call for war never seems anything but the most foregone of conclusions, while the Peace president's solution to the problem of the imminent declaration of war — assassination — smacks more of expedient hypocrisy than dedication to principle.

As a drama, *High Treason* is replete with facile characterization, specious reasoning, improbable sequencing, and cardboard heroics, and it is capped by a most unlikely denouement. It trivializes both war and the events leading up to war, panders to both sides of the pacifist position without satisfying either one, and reduces legitimate concerns about self-defense to paranoid displays of arrogance and ill-considered acts of retribution. Its main players do not act from the courage of their convictions; rather, in a series of individual dramatic climaxes, they abandon those convictions and act as though they were the very people they had opposed throughout the picture. Forget war; there is no higher treason than to thine own self to be untrue.

As a mirror of the times, however — no matter which times— the film successfully reflects the lack of vision, patience, and understanding that might very well lead to holocaust. Sandwiched between the War to End All Wars and the one that came next, *High Treason* sought to make the simplest of points: while the technology of the future would doubtless show great growth and creativity, the human spirit that spawned the technology might not. Man would remain the only animal that killed his own kind for profit, and there would always be the danger that his creativity, if fueled mainly by greed and shaped chiefly by the whim of the highest bidder, would ultimately lead, not to glory, but to destruction.

Film Discussed

High Treason Tiffany/Gaumont-British/British Acoustic Film (sound version). Released September 9, 1929 (silent); March 13, 1930 (sound). 90 min. (silent version); 100/95 min. (sound versions). Producer: L'Estrange Fawcett. Director: Maurice Elvey. Screenplay: L'Estrange Fawcett, based on the play by Noel Pemberton-Billing. Cinematographer: Percy Strong. Art Director: Andrew Mazzei. Theme song "March on to Peace": Patrick K. Heale and Walter Collins. Dance number "There's Nothing New in Love," and incidental music: Louis Levy, Quentin Maclean, and Desmond Carter. With Jameson Thomas, Benita Hume, Basil Gill, Humberston Wright, Henry Vibart, James Carew, Hayford Hobbs, René Ray.

2

Dr. Jekyll and Mr. Hyde (1931): Science, Society, and Sexuality

Bryan Senn

> It's the things one *can't* do that always tempt me.
> — *Fredric March as Dr. Jekyll*

How many times a day does the average American male think about sex? Forty, sixty, *more than one hundred*? Though various articles and surveys over the years have generated differing numbers, all agree on one thing: sex is definitely of prime importance to the human animal.

Apart from the obvious issue of species propagation, sex has been linked to the very formation of modern society itself. Most mammals copulate only during intermittent periods of ovulation, whereas humans indulge incessantly (albeit some more successfully than others). Sigmund Freud, among other scientists, postulated that it is this constant sexual drive that gave rise to the family structure (since animals that breed cyclically have no impetus to form a strong familial bond) and consequently to the very framework of the civilized world itself. So if we have sex to thank for our modern civilization, it's little wonder that art, including cinema, has found it such an intriguing topic.

With all their attendant anxieties, the themes of sex and death have become two of the principal topics explored (and exploited) by the horror/science fiction genre. Both of these issues generate a great deal of apprehension (I'm sure even Valentino felt his fair share of performance anxiety, and I know of no one who hasn't had some qualms about his or her own inevitable demise); and fear is what this genre is (mostly) about. The horror/SF film lets us explore these two powerful subjects within the safety of fantasy, and the best ones bring some insight and build (dare I say?) a bridge over these troubled waters.

Even in the 1930s, sexuality was an important part of motion pictures, particularly in the pre–Production Code days (prior to 1934). The burgeoning horror/SF genre provided viewers with a particularly intriguing avenue of exploration. The sound horror film was born awash in the themes of Eros and Thanos. Much of *Dracula*'s (1931) appeal can be seen as outright sexual attraction. The mesmeric presence of Bela Lugosi as Count Dracula ("Ah, what letters women wrote me," declared the actor, "...letters of horrible hunger") provides the ultimate figures of confidence to the uncertain males in the audience as he unfailingly conquers his swooning objects of desire. Alongside Dracula stand his three beautiful wives, who descend en masse on the hapless Renfield, intent on draining him of his life-giving fluids—perhaps the ultimate heterosexual male fantasy.

The genre's follow-up entry, the SF-tinged *Frankenstein* (1931), with its doppelganger motif, can be seen (using an admittedly elastic imagination) as a homoerotic struggle between Dr. Henry Frankenstein (played by Colin Clive) and his creation. One can interpret the conflict caused by Frankenstein's creation of a man as the conflict arising from homosexual love and its subsequent rejection. In light of director James Whale's open homosexuality (and Clive's reported closeted bisexuality), this theme becomes particularly intriguing. The discord arises when Henry rejects his creature out of hand, feeling it ugly and brutal. Is this what happens when one disavows one's own sexual instincts? "There can be no wedding," announces Henry, "while this horrible creation of mine is still alive." Frankenstein cannot consummate "normal" love while his homosexuality lives to assert itself.

But the third sound film offered by the fledgling genre proved to be the ultimate erotic thriller of its generation. Released on the last day of 1931, *Dr. Jekyll and Mr. Hyde* unleashed the literal "Monster from the Id" upon an unsuspecting moviegoing public.

The story of Robert Louis Stevenson's *The Strange Case of Dr. Jekyll and Mr. Hyde* has become so ingrained in our popular consciousness that detailing it here would be a waste of space. Suffice it to say that, given only seven weeks and less than $500,000 (only slightly more money than *Dracula* and less than half the amount needed to make MGM's inferior 1941 Spencer Tracy version of *Dr. Jekyll and Mr. Hyde*), director Rouben Mamoulian took Stevenson's classic work on the duality of man and created a brilliant cinematic study of man's struggle to control his primitive instincts—with lust being foremost among them. In Mamoulian's own words (quoted in *Cinefantastique* magazine), "Mr. Hyde is the exact replica of the Neanderthal man, so he's our ancestor. We *were* that once. The struggle or dilemma is not between evil and good, it's between the sophisticated, spiritual self in man and his animal, primeval instincts."

Mamoulian chose to extend the metaphor even further and explore the conflict of society vs. the individual, positioning Dr. Jekyll as the representative of the repressed Victorian "proper" society, and Mr. Hyde as the personification of individual gratification. While Hyde does not live by society's rules (his actions are governed only by the cravings and whims of his own id), Jekyll is restrained—and frustrated—by the dictates of societal mores. Mamoulian daringly explores this theme of repressed desires and pent-up sexuality, intimating that it is these unfulfilled longings that lead Jekyll to destruction, causing him to seek relief in the "evil" form of

Mr. Hyde. And this release *is* evil, as Stevenson's story and the screenplay by Hoffenstein and Heath take great pains to point out. In the best tradition of the morality play, one of the major messages of *Dr. Jekyll and Mr. Hyde* is that just as repression can lead to dangerous risks, so can unbridled self-gratification lead to self-destruction.

Dr. Jekyll and Mr. Hyde **(1931): One man, two personalities. Fredric March as the gentle Jekyll and his rapacious alter ego, Hyde.**

The movie becomes a cautionary tale balancing the two extremes of repression and self-gratification, which, via the SF device of splitting one personality into two, become personified in the same individual. And when Jekyll fails to strike a balance between the two, his destruction ensues. So Mamoulian's (and Stevenson's) *Dr. Jekyll and Mr. Hyde* tells us that moderation in sexual matters, as in most things in life, is best.

Such a message undoubtedly reflected, at least in part, the climate of the times. In 1931 the Great Depression was still arcing toward its desperate peak, with the American economy on the brink of collapse and millions of men out of work (emasculated economically, so to speak). As a prelude to this calamity, the 1920s saw the American woman come into her own at least partially, earning not only the vote, but some measure of sexual liberation as well, as witnessed by the rise of the flapper subculture. While one cannot ascribe a cause-and-effect relationship to these two developments, their proximity on the cultural timeline (not to mention basic human nature, which generally resists change) surely helped cast women's sexual liberation in a negative light, generating a backlash against the burgeoning sexuality of the American female and the diminishment of male control both in the workplace and in the bedroom. But, cleverly, Mamoulian demonstrates that in order to regain such control, the male (Jekyll) must literally become a sexually controlling monster (Hyde). Again, the film demonstrates that a balance, a happy medium, must be found.

On the technical side, Mamoulian paints his sexually charged canvas with strokes both bold and subtle, using a plethora of techniques and themes to create one of the most cinematically alive films ever shot in any genre. Even something as simple as a dissolve becomes a fluid purveyor of thought and emotion. For instance, during a scene change in which Jekyll has just left Muriel, his chaste fiancée, her fading image is superimposed for a few seconds onto the next scene of Jekyll walking with his friend Lanyon, demonstrating that her image is embedded deep within Jekyll's mind, and thoughts of her fill his head. Later, after Jekyll's first rather steamy encounter with chorus girl–prostitute Ivy, Mamoulian superimposes a shot of Ivy's swinging naked leg as the scene dissolves to Jekyll walking down the stairs. This second image serves a dual purpose. Not only does it expose what lingers beneath the surface of Jekyll's mind, it also distracts the viewer just as Jekyll himself is distracted, and so allies our thoughts and feelings with Jekyll's own. This serves to further cement the bond between the character and the viewer, which Mamoulian has taken such pains to forge with his various point-of-view shots at the film's opening.

Mamoulian even employs the split screen technique as a method of changing scenes and emphasizing conflict, allowing the audience to see one scene as it finishes while at the same time viewing the next as it begins. In one transition we see both Ivy and Muriel at the same time — before Ivy is finally "wiped away" as Jekyll meets with Muriel. This split image underscores Jekyll's inner conflict between the Good Woman, Muriel (society's daughter and as such unattainable), and the Fallen Woman of the streets, Ivy (willing and able and very tempting). Thus we see simultaneously the two women in Jekyll's life — and the two very different aspects of his romantic interest. The duality of the male (and his desires) is again emphasized.

One sequence in *Dr. Jekyll and Mr. Hyde* stands out as the most erotically charged scene in the film — indeed, of the entire decade — thanks to the alluring presence and seductive playing of Miriam Hopkins, and the astute and involving direction of Mamoulian. It occurs when sexy saloon singer Ivy Pearson (Hopkins) receives the mild medical attentions of Dr. Jekyll (Fredric March) after she's roughed up by a tavern rogue. "Now you're the kind a woman would do something for!" she tells the good doctor as he gallantly tends to her bruised thigh. Her eyes flash wickedly and her lips curve enticingly. Undressing for bed after the good doctor prescribes rest, Ivy looks at Jekyll — and directly into the camera — and smiles, delicious and inviting. This point-of-view shot transforms the viewer from a detached voyeur into an involved participant in Ivy's game of coquettish seduction. We *become* the bemused (and aroused) Dr. Jekyll, to whom this beauty beckons so delectably. Reaching down slowly, Ivy pulls her petticoat up to expose her long, shapely legs. Gracefully, she removes her stockings and garters and playfully tosses them to Jekyll — to us — with a delightful laugh. Now naked in bed, Ivy reaches up impulsively and draws Jekyll to her. With a muffled, ecstatic "mmfff," she kisses him passionately. Throughout it all, the only flesh we actually see is her exposed back and a bit of leg, but oh does it fire the imagination! After all, eroticism begins in the mind, and the enticing glimpses and inviting glances provided by the sexy Ms. Hopkins give one plenty of food for thought. She's not through with us yet, however. As Jekyll takes his leave ("I'll call that kiss my fee," he laughs), Ivy sits up in bed. Clutching the rumpled bedclothes to (barely) cover her nude body, she looks at Jekyll (at us again) and whispers seductively, "Come back sooooon," while her naked leg swings saucily to and fro over the edge of the bed. Mamoulian then superimposes this shot of Ivy's swinging leg over the scene as Jekyll makes his exit — the lingering sexual image revealing that the seed of lust has been planted. For a full 25 seconds this arousing image of beautiful flesh

Hyde forces himself on Ivy (Miriam Hopkins), an experienced but essentially guileless prostitute, in an act of unrestrained animalism that will bring the destruction of both people — and of a third as well.

is transposed over the sight of Lanyon (Jekyll's friend) chiding Jekyll about controlling his instincts. Controlling instincts be damned; we know what the good doctor is thinking about — and what we are pondering as well. The implied promise of erotic delights to come has set Jekyll's libido racing.

After this dose of highly charged eroticism, Mamoulian goes on to explore the other side of the erotic coin through the unbridled character of Mr. Hyde, who ultimately turns a natural sexuality into hateful, bestial lust. One scene in particular embodies both the picture's horrific content and height of emotional and sexual power. In it, Hyde is at his most loathsome — a sadistic satyr who subtly plays on his victim's (Ivy's) mounting fears to build her emotional agony into a crescendo of terror. It begins as Hyde tells Ivy that he is going away. The sneering brute quickly dashes her ill-concealed hope, however, by asking, "You wouldn't have me go tonight, would you? Of course not; quite unworthy of our great love, hmm?" Clutching her, he forcefully presses his lips to her bosom. Reveling in the loathing and fear this inspires in her, he continues his verbal torture: "That's right, my little bird. The last evening is always the sweetest, you know." Trapped in his arms, struggling to control her dread of the sexual horrors to come, Ivy nearly collapses in panic. Enjoying her torment, Hyde continues his mocking taunts: "And what a farewell this one will be. What a farewell! I don't know whether I shall be able to tear myself away from you at all. In fact, I shall only go as far as the door and the sight of your tears will bring me back. Does that please you, my dear?" March (utterly convincing in his role of tormentor) and Miriam Hopkins (the embodiment of barely suppressed horror) create one of the most chillingly cruel scenes ever filmed. Mamoulian has shown us male sexuality at its most predatory.

Through the scenes with Hyde and Ivy, *Dr. Jekyll and Mr. Hyde* deftly turns the tables and places the male (in the brutish form of Mr. Hyde) in the sexual driver's seat. Stereotypically, sex is viewed as a woman's tool — a velvet device employed by the female to obtain (even extort) what she wants. This leaves the hapless male at the mercy of his partner. *Dr. Jekyll* neutralizes this particular feminine weapon by making the evil Hyde the sexual controller. This can be a very powerful and appealing premise to the males of the audience (particularly in 1931, when millions of unemployed men felt a general sense of powerless due to their precarious economic positions). Mamoulian, however, shrewdly shows us that in order to achieve this brutal power, Jekyll must become a vile, ruthless creature, whose ugly physical appearance mirrors the savagery of his behavior. While one may wish for such a position of power, few wish to be the hideous, depraved creature Jekyll has become in the form of Mr. Hyde.

Fredric March's performance as Jekyll and Hyde was rewarded with an Academy Award. Hyde, as interpreted by March, is a beast, a brute in the form of a man (though Hyde's "form" is not altogether human, thanks to Wally Westmore's wonderfully simian makeup). March excels in the physical aspect of the role, his quick, animal movements showing his impatience to wring every possible pleasure from his newfound freedom. As Hyde stretches with an almost animal delight after his first release, or lifts his face to the rain in an exuberant display, March shows him to be the id incarnate, determined to revel in every sensation. Later, when Hyde becomes a bit more "sophisticated" (i.e., sexual) in his pleasure-seeking, March adds to his brutal physical performance a dimension of subtle cruelty — namely, his sadistic delivery of dialogue. In the scenes in which Hyde verbally taunts Ivy, March's sarcastic and double-edged emphasis (coupled with his abrupt physical movements and quick shifts in demeanor) creates a terrifying picture of unpredictability. While he at first confines himself to the verbal torture of Ivy, it is a certainty that uncontrollable physical violence lurks just beneath the surface. March's brilliant mannerisms and mocking tones reveal the depths of mental as well as physical cruelty that this evil creature is eager — perhaps hardwired — to inflict.

March is well supported by a cadre of fine actors. Miriam Hopkins matches March's Mr. Hyde with a flawless performance as the streetwise Ivy Pearson. At ease singing bawdy songs in a tavern or coquettishly lifting her skirt, her unpolished charm and good humor make of her a very likable and sympathetic figure. Ivy's brazen sexuality is not a dirty thing, not a secret to be hidden away behind locked doors, but a breath of fresh air amongst the stuffy Victorian attitudes portrayed in the film.

While Rose Hobart (*Tower of London*, 1939; *The Mad Ghoul*, 1943; *Soul of a Monster*, 1944) is given the rather thankless role of Muriel, her earnest and intelligent performance manages to make her character real. Ms. Hobart admitted that playing the "good" half of Jekyll's romantic interest (the straitlaced Muriel) was not entirely satisfying. "I would have given anything to play the Miriam Hopkins part. That's why Ingrid Bergman chose it in the [1941] remake." Ironically, Hopkins initially wanted Hobart's role, and it took a persuasive Mamoulian to convince her otherwise. Ms. Hopkins later realized the allure of playing the bad girl, admitting in *Bad Girls of the Silver Screen*, by Lottie Da and Jan Alexander, "I enjoyed playing that sort of woman. They have the courage of the damned. They know what they want and go right ahead."

Yes, indeed: With the alluring "bad girl" Ivy at his beck and call, Hyde is an undeservedly lucky monster. And within the science fiction framework of *Dr. Jekyll and Mr. Hyde*, Rouben Mamoulian demonstrated how such luck comes with a steep price, and that stifled repression and unbridled sexual excess are simply two sides of the same coin — the coin of extremism that ultimately buys disaster.

Film Discussed

Dr. Jekyll and Mr. Hyde Paramount Pictures. Released December 31, 1931. 97 min. Producer/Director: Rouben Mamoulian. Screenplay: Samuel Hoffenstein and Percy Heath. Based on the novel by Robert Louis Stevenson. Cinematographer: Karl Struss. Art Director: Hans Drier. Editor: William Shea. Makeup: Wally Westmore. With Fredric March, Miriam Hopkins, Rose Hobart, Holmes Herbert, Halliwell Hobbes, Edgar Norton, Tempe Pigott and Arnold Lucy. Available on Warner VHS home video and Warner DVD.

3

Cartoons and Technocracy: Disney's *The Mad Doctor* and Fleischer's *Dancing on the Moon*

LEONARD J. KOHL

Science will overcome all things. Even the human emotion!
—*Emperor Ming the Merciless in* Flash Gordon

Most historians would agree that 1933 was the worst year of the Great Depression, and that more people than you might think took a long, hard look at our capitalistic society and wondered if the time for fundamental change had come. Some people looked to communism as the solution to what was ailing the country—the utopian variety that economist Karl Marx theorized nearly 100 years before. Other doctrines of various degrees of fantasy or intelligence were proposed and toyed with by theorists around the country. In his article "*Of Mouse and the Man: Floyd Gottfredson and the Mickey Mouse Continuities*," Thomas Andrae speculates, "At this time, America was plagued by riots, looting, strikes, and even pitched battles with police—mostly in industrial areas and its larger cities. There were, among those in the country who were the nearest to these unhappy events, officials who found that a swelling revolutionary fervor could lead to a possible attempt by the masses to overthrow the government and seize power."

As a result, any theories of how the government should be run—without the use of revolutionary violence—were listened to politely. One theory was called Technocracy and was put into practice (on a small scale) by economic theorist Howard Smith. By 1933, Smith had set up headquarters for his group of scientists and economists at Columbia University in New York City. He called his think tank Technocracy, Inc. These men had earlier formed a group called the Technical Alliance and for years they had studied technological growth in the United States and how it affected economic growth, or the lack of it.

Technocracy, as proposed by Smith and others, posited that America was moving from an agrarian nation where farming had been the main source of income to an industrial and service entity. Advocates of Technocracy argued that as time went by, people would run and service machines designed to take the place of farming and other kinds of physical labor. For maximum efficiency, the government should be run in a technological or scientific manner, with tasks conceived and executed on a scientific basis. Rather than operate society in a democratic manner, the founders of Technocracy, Inc., argued that the society should be a bureaucratic organization, where technicians would use their scientific and industrial know-how to keep things running smoothly.

Technocracy's followers argued that the Depression was the natural result of a technologically produced abundance of goods—food, clothing, and so on — and that unemployment was created because machines displaced workers. The problem, apparently, was the current price system of what goods and services cost the producer and the consumer. This, the Technocrats argued, had to be changed.

The idea of society in the hands of technicians was radical in 1933. Today, of course, some of the concepts of Technocracy are no longer far-fetched. Ways in which science and technology have become parts of our everyday life would startle — and vindicate — dedicated Technocrats. Think of it! Personal computers, portable cell phones, TV monitors in banks. Ultrasound pictures of babies yet unborn. Robot workers on assembly lines. As the general public would have exclaimed in 1933, "It's right out of *Buck Rogers*!"

Technocracy never caught on as a form of government in North America, and by the middle of 1933 it was considered a joke by many, just one more crackpot scheme to coax the American economy back on track. Educational Pictures, probably the lowest of the low-budget movie studios to make two-reel comedy shorts, made one in 1933 called — what else?—*Techno Crazy*—featuring former Mack Sennett Keystone Comedy star Billy Bevan. While I haven't been able to see the short, the plot apparently revolves around what happens when Billy gets mixed up with a fanatical group that proposes a scheme by which machines will do all the work, allowing people the leisure of sleep and other sloth. And in *International House* (1933), comics Stoopnagle and Bud propose a harebrained scheme called Stoopnochracy.

Short subjects included comedies, serials, newsreels, travelogues, and cartoons. They helped lure people into movie theaters from just before World War I to about the beginning of U.S. involvement in Vietnam. Comedy shorts starred the Keystone Kops, Our Gang, Buster Keaton, Charlie Chaplin, Laurel and Hardy, Edgar Kennedy, Leon Errol, and of course, the Three Stooges. Newsreels featured highlights of noteworthy events that had taken place the week (generally speaking) before. Specialty shorts revealed the allure of exotic faraway lands, the wonders of science, and unusual people.

However, some of the best and longest-lasting of all the short subjects were the animated cartoons, featuring Bugs Bunny, Betty Boop, Popeye, Superman, Mighty Mouse, Mickey Mouse, Donald Duck, Goofy, Heckle and Jeckle, Tom and Jerry, Woody Woodpecker, and many others.

Cartoons drew audiences into studio-owned theaters, and contributed immeasurably to the studios' survival. In the early 1930s moviemaking was perceived as one of the few legitimate businesses in America that was profitable. The late animator Gordon Sheehan saw this firsthand. He told me,

> I majored in magazine illustration at the School of Fine Arts, Pratt Institute in Brooklyn, New York, with the hope of becoming another Norman Rockwell or James Montgomery Flagg. However, after graduation in 1932, I soon became shockingly aware that the Great Business Depression, which I hadn't paid much attention to while in art school, was for real. Old established magazines were folding up like flies, and scads of famous, well-experienced magazine illustrators were pounding the pavements of New York City, looking for work. Jobs for green ex–art students were practically nil.
>
> I wore out plenty of shoe leather in the fall and winter of 1932/33, hounding New York City art agencies, advertising agencies, publication offices, etc. in search of *any kind* of an art job ... art jobs were practically zilch for a rank beginner like me. The only industry that seemed to be thriving during those severe Depression days were motion pictures, and particularly the new sound animated cartoons. Many people evidently went to the movies to escape from reality for a few hours.

When a friend told Gordon Sheehan that the Fleischer Studio was hiring artists and cartoonists, Sheehan quickly headed over to check it out. Sure enough, the studio was looking for talented artists, and Sheehan showed the production manager samples of his artwork. A couple of months later, the young artist was hired to "opaque" animation cels, which meant that he had to paint gray, black, and white tones on the back of a series of traced inked drawings on clear sheets of cellophane (animation cels). Completed cels—thousands of them in a single cartoon—were photographed over a series of painted backgrounds for one or two frames of film at a time, to create the illusions of place and movement.

For all this monotonous labor, Sheehan was paid 15 dollars a week—Monday through Friday, and half a day on Sunday. Sheehan could not live in New York City on his salary so he had to find odd jobs to survive until he rose through the studio ranks. Still, at a time when so many people were without work, the modest pay was better than nothing.

From a creative point of view, the directors, artists, writers, and voice actors who worked on cartoon shorts seemed to have had more of a free hand because they had to worry little about front-office interference in what they were doing. Executive meddling usually was restricted to prestige projects and was something that even great live-action directors like John Ford, Frank Capra, and Alfred Hitchcock could never completely escape.

While Chuck Jones's *Duck Dodgers in the 24th and a Half Century* (1953) and other classic science fiction-themed cartoons have been discussed in other movie book anthologies, I'm going to go back much earlier, to a pair of SF cartoons from the Depression era: *The Mad Doctor* (Disney, 1933) and *Dancing on the Moon* (Fleischer, 1936). Both are atypical in the sense that *The Mad Doctor* is noticeably different in tone from other Mickey Mouse cartoons, even in 1933, when Mickey was a considerably more scrappy character than the bland Mr. Nice Guy he eventually became. *Dancing on the Moon*, as well, is not what one would expect from the likes of Max

Fleischer, for its sweet, almost saccharine sentiments are quite at odds with the bizarre, pre-psychedelic tone that typified the Fleischer product.

Paramount, Fleischer's distributor, pushed the studio to make wholesome, family-oriented cartoons; this led to the Color Classics series, which mimicked the worst of the innocuous, offend-no-one Disney cartoon shorts. *Dancing on the Moon*, a Color Classic, is a cute cartoon with similarities to the Disney style, and yet it has the surreal quality that is a Fleischer Studio hallmark. Generally speaking, the Fleischer bunch was more apt to sink its teeth into a tale of mad doctors and weird experiments— science gone bad — while the Disney artists were more inclined create a cute fantasy of honeymooning animal characters on a romantic ride to the moon. Yet here, the opposite is true: It was Disney that took a dark view of technology, while Fleischer chose the other road. Science, according to these cartoons, will open up a brave new world of wonders and undreamt-of delights (*Dancing on the Moon*), or will explore the perils of playing God and delving into things "Man is not meant to know" (*The Mad Doctor*). Let's look first at Disney's *The Mad Doctor*.

By the 1950s, Mickey Mouse was the Mr. Nice Guy or rather, Mr. Nice Mouse, of Disney cartoons, and there were far too many funny things that, by this time, the mouse just wouldn't do. As Walt Disney said around that time "Mickey's our problem child. He's so much of an institution that we're limited to what we can do with him.... Mickey must always be sweet and lovable. What can you do with such a leading man?"

But in the 1930s Mickey was a tough, reckless little guy, funny and fearless, miles away from the goody-goody mouse he later became. Had *The Mad Doctor* been made in 1953 rather than 1933, I suspect it wouldn't have quite the same feeling of genuine terror and suspense when Mickey battles several malevolent creatures to rescue his beloved dog.

In his introduction to the Disney comic strip anthology *Walt Disney's Mickey Mouse in Color*, writer Geoffrey Blum hits upon what was appealing about the animated cartoons and especially in the daily newspaper comic strips that featured Mickey Mouse, particularly in the '30s:

> Children have a remarkable ear for hypocrisy, far keener than ours; they can tell when adults are using Bucky Bug or Practical Pig to preach at them. Mickey may be upbeat, but he does not make a habit of dispensing moral sentiments. What's better, he combines his good cheer with guts, for he is encouraging not only himself but also a whole nation. America desperately needed that encouragement in the wake of The Great Depression. We can use it no less today.

The Mad Doctor opens during the archetypal dark and stormy night. Mickey's dog, Pluto, has been kidnapped. A frantic Mickey hears his dog's frightened cries of distress and follows the sounds to a mysterious, sinister-looking castle. Mickey is greeted by an assortment of creepy skeletons that lurk in stairways and darkened passages. As he tries to locate Pluto, the skeletons bite, strike, and choke him. In his desperate retreat, Mickey falls through several trap doors and passageways until he meets one of the maddest of all mad doctors, a fellow called Dr. XXX (a clear spoof of Warner Bros.' recent horror film, *Dr. X*). XXX wants to graft the wishbone of a dog onto a chicken, which isn't just Technocracy run amuck but a thinly veiled reference to vivisection and eugenics, the latter a pseudoscience then popular with Social Darwinists in Germany, the United States, and other developed nations. XXX has obviously been following the works of Dr. Moreau, whose faux-eugenics misadventures are chronicled in the 1933 horror film *Island of Lost Souls.*

Island of Lost Souls was censored in some American cities and was banned outright in England. *The Mad Doctor* apparently was censored as well, but this seems to have been done either for later theater reissues or when the cartoon was released to television. Some of the scenes where Mickey is attacked by the skeletons are cut from later prints, as well as the scene where the mad scientist cuts the shadow of Pluto's insides with a sharp instrument. Luckily, the cartoon has been restored, and is—as of this writing—available on DVD.

Dr. XXX explains his crazy scheme to Pluto, who is chained to an operating table, and X-rayed. The dog is helpless to do anything but whimper in terror. Mickey suddenly enters the laboratory through the last of the trap doors, but before he can do anything heroic, he's strapped onto a table and about to be sliced to death by a circular saw. "Pluto! Pluto!" Mickey cries out. Everything looks hopeless. Luckily for our friend the mouse, it all has been a nightmare, and Mickey's cries cause Pluto to dash into Mickey's room, happily letting them both know that everything is all right.

The cartoon's finish is typical of the happy "dream endings" of horror comedy that Hollywood was making at the time. In the Laurel and Hardy short *Oliver the Eighth* (1934), for instance, Ollie falls asleep and dreams he's about to be dispatched by a female serial killer who hates all men named Oliver.

Dream ending or not, *The Mad Doctor* is one of the darkest and most frightening of all the early Disney cartoons. Possibly because some felt it was too intense for children, *The Mad Doctor* was seldom revived for retrospectives. The cartoon is one of the very few Disney films exiled to the vaults and forgotten. When copyright renewal came around, the studio forgot to take care of it.

The cartoon has very little quotable dialogue, outside of the anguished cries of our protagonists and the maniacal threats made against Pluto by Dr. XXX. The cartoon is startlingly visual—a nightmare full of wonderfully weird shadows of solid blacks and some of the most sinister-looking skeletons you'll ever see in an animated cartoon. Mickey's wild ride through the trap doors and passageways is particularly well done, and—especially when you see a good print of this cartoon in a theater—the viewer takes a frightening roller coaster ride along with the mouse.

While research has not shown who exactly was responsible for the original story, David Hand, newly promoted at the time from his position as one of Disney's key animators, was assigned to direct the cartoon. Because Disney animation directors worked very closely with the animators in their units, it wouldn't be unfair to say that Hand was responsible for most of the cartoon's gruesome atmosphere. Walt himself, who vetted every cartoon, obviously approved.

Although, in later years, Walt Disney cultivated a grandfatherly kind of image via his *Wonderful World of Color* TV show, the benevolent "Uncle Walt" had not been as benevolent in earlier days. He brutally quashed a 1941 animators' strike, cooperated with Red-baiting HUAC investigators, and assisted J. Edgar Hoover and the FBI in clandestine operations to prevent labor activism and alleged Communist infiltration of Hollywood. All of that was probably service above and beyond what was necessary, but Walt Disney felt a great debt to the American public that had embraced his work, made him wealthy, and provided employment for thousands of people.

Although Disney's handling of the strike was classic punish-the-proles stuff, it should be noted that the studio's fortunes, especially during the Great Depression, rose and fell on the success and failure of each of Mickey Mouse and Silly Symphony cartoon. Walt brooked no disruption of the cartoon process. He was a perfectionist, and he drove himself and his artists to go beyond anything they had done before.

Most of the Hollywood animation studios had a weekly quota of animation footage, and a set number of cartoons to be produced each year. However, Walt Disney — at least before the devastating 1941 strike — didn't believe in time clocks and pushed for quality, not quantity. Many Disney animators would later say that there was a tremendous freedom to experiment during the thirties.

David Hand had enough faith in his own capabilities as an animator — and later as a director — to stand his ground and not knuckle under to Walt Disney's demands. In his book, *Memoirs*, Hand recalled a time when, as an animator at the Disney Studio in the early '30s, he was on the verge of quitting:

> This particular scene I shall never forget. Walt kept denying the beautiful quality I put into [a sequence] and sent me back to my desk, I seem to remember, seven times. Actually, six times. He kept shaking his head, "Not right, needs more zip." I became boiling mad. I, a top New York animator-director being treated this way. So, I went over to my corner and pouted. Thought I to myself, "This guy is a sadist. I'll fix him." So, I planned to do just that. I'd show him. I'd teach him a lesson or two. The trick I had up my sleeve you wouldn't believe. I secretly (radically) changed the whole basis of the animation. I decided I would make extreme key poses — way out — I'd really make him squirm. I decided he wouldn't have to fire me — I would be happy to up and quit. He deserved it. Was I being too hard on him? I hoped so! The seventh time — oh boy, just you wait till he gets a load of this animation! So, the test came back and was threaded into the machine. I stood back with a strong inner expression.
>
> He stood staring at the movieola. I thought I heard him let out a gasp. He snapped around, faced me with a happy grin, said, "There Dave, that's exactly what I've been wanting."

Hand's short autobiography covers his career as an animator and director in America and England and is a fascinating read, but it's too bad that animation students hadn't interviewed him extensively before the end of his life. It would have been more than interesting to find out just how a cartoon as radically frightening as *The Mad Doctor* came out of the Disney animation studio back in 1933. I can only speculate that Hand, the story men in his unit, and his key animators had a special fondness for the new cycle of Hollywood horror that included *Dracula, Frankenstein,* and *Dr. Jekyll and Mr. Hyde* — each of which was a box-office sensation.

Those and other seminal Hollywood horror films proposed that science and rational thought might open doors to horror as easily as to new worlds of wonder. Drs. Frankenstein and Jekyll, absorbed with the nature of life and death, make cru-

cial missteps that lead to their undoings, but *Dracula*'s Van Helsing, the rationalist who defies the undead count to win the day, suggests that cool intellect has its place. The visceral horror that is Dracula is defeated by ordered, systematized thought, which is at the foundation of technology and Technocratic thought. Granted, technology had created the bombs and poison gas of the Great War, but it also had improved agricultural production, given us the motorcar and airplane, and forged great advances in medicine and surgery. Americans looked at both sides of the technology coin and weighed the pros and cons. Technocrats hoped to tip the scale of opinion in their favor.

Walt Disney probably would have been ambivalent about Technocracy. Although born in Chicago, Walter Elias Disney spent many of his young years on a farm in Muscatine, Iowa. Although eventually anxious to return to big-city life to make it as a cartoonist, he never outgrew his love of rural living and life's simple pleasures. As suggested, he had an inherent streak of conservatism. Yet by 1933 Disney's own animation studio was becoming a finely tuned factory of various departments— story, layout, animation, special effects animation, inking and painting, music scoring and sound effects, voice recording, editing, and so on. The animation departments were controlled so tightly that certain animators and directors developed recognizable styles. As a consequence, animators who were great at sight gags or dramatic scenes, or knew how to animate characters speaking dialogue, were assigned to specific portions of various shorts and cartoon features. In a sense, the Disney Studio *was* a type of Technocracy, with "Uncle Walt" and his key personnel in firm command. (Later, defecting animators who headed to cartoon studios in New York City called the Disney Studio— with satiric black humor —"Mousewicz," after Auschwitz, the Nazi death camp.)

As mentioned, it's not too much of generalization to say that Walt Disney distrusted modern technology, unless he was able to understand it and force it to his own will. His studio, the great gamble he called Disneyland, and finally, the beginnings of Walt Disney World were creative and technological expressions of that will.

In *The Mad Doctor* Mickey Mouse confronts science that has veered out of control. The mad doctor here has no moral values, no compassion for what harm he might do in the course of his bizarre experiment. The scientist feels that he is more intelligent than other people and, of course, in this case, the animals around him. He assigns himself the right to do whatever he feels, all in the name of science. The cartoon's parody of surgical grafting, and a demented kind of hybridization, suggest not only eugenics but anticipates Nazi medical experiments and modern-day issues of cloning and other genetic fiddling. Walt Disney, as the figurative voice (and the literal voice for nearly 20 years) of Mickey Mouse, would argue that science is not to be trusted on its own. Society needs benevolent watchdogs to keep a constant eye on scientific activity. The qualities that are most celebrated and cherished in *The Mad Doctor* are the very human values of home, family and friendship, even between an oversized talking mouse and his pet dog.

It's worth noting that the splendid newspaper cartoonist Floyd Gottfredson did a superb, but very different, adaptation of *The Mad Doctor* in his daily *Mickey Mouse* newspaper comic strip. The adaptation was called "Blaggard Castle," and ran as a

Monday-through-Saturday serial from November 1932 to February 1933. (The Sunday strips told completely different stories.)

In the strip, Mickey and his pal Horace Horsecollar investigate mysterious goings-on at the supposedly haunted Blaggard Castle. Mickey and Horace discover that the castle is occupied by a pair of mad scientists who plan to hypnotize people to kill and steal, and deliver to them the riches of the world.

Gottfredson modeled his two ape-like scientists, Professors "Ecks" and "Doublex," on Boris Karloff's brutish butler from *The Old Dark House* (1932). In several scenes the scientists observe Mickey and Horace through a strange closed-circuit television device. Apparently Floyd Gottfredson's young son Norman thought the television device was too outlandish, but the elder Gottfredson had done his homework, and later showed his son that television was indeed more than a possibility. This 1932 look at the exotic and mysterious TV in a gothic or unusual setting probably influenced feature films, including *International House* (1933), *Trapped by Television* (1934), and the disappointingly bad *Murder by Television* (1935). After that, it seemed that every mad scientist or extraterrestrial despot had such a device.

Writer Thomas Andrae saw something else that was significant in Gottfredson's story:

> Films like *King Kong*, with its climactic scene in which Kong symbolized what audiences most feared (and perhaps secretly enjoyed): the liberation of lawless, primitive and bestial forces that were presumed to be dormant within the collective subconscious. So the comic strip image of the scientist as a power mad tyrant who could transform the masses into a murderous mob who would seize the country's resources was deeply meaningful.

During the climax of "Blaggard Castle" Mickey rescues his friend Horace, uses the electrical equipment to un-hypnotize his friend, and turns the electric rays on the scientists. Henceforth, the pair will be useful scientists who serve humanity. As Mickey explains, the two professors have gone to "a big laboratory where they'll still be inventing things ... but they'll be *for* people instead of *against* 'em!" It's interesting, too, that Floyd Gottfredson turned the anti-science tale that was his source material into one that is marginally pro-science. Once again, however, the message is clear: Science and technology must be monitored.

Well, I worked for Max Fleischer. I did animation. I was about seventeen and a half. I was an in-betweener. I worked along a row of tables about two hundred to three hundred yards long. It was like a factory. I began to see the studio as a garment factory. I associated the garment factory with my father and I didn't want to work like my father. I love being an individual. I suppose the second generation sees things differently than the one before it. My father's generation all worked in shops at long rows of machines, and they turned out pieces for finished garments. That was my father's job.

–animator Jack Kirby

> *Animation was more than a job. It was a creative venture, and to get paid for doing this was like "icing on the cake."*
> —animator Gordon Sheehan

Far away from sunny California, deep in the heart of New York City, the animators and artists of the Fleischer Studio were serious rivals to their Disney counterparts through most of the '30s and early '40s. The Fleischer Studio (at 1600 Broadway) was home to famed cartoon stars Betty Boop and Popeye and had caused a sensation in the '20s with the Out of the Inkwell series featuring Koko the Clown. In later years, the Fleischer brothers, Max in particular, insisted that the studio find its own style and refrain from copying Disney. The late animation director Shamus Culhane told me that Max Fleischer wanted to keep the "loose comic strip" style intact. Culhane criticized this, and thought that in this respect, the Disney Studio was light-years ahead of what was being done at Fleischer's.

The late cartoon animator Gordon Sheehan also had a few things to say about the late head of the studio, Max Fleischer:

> Max Fleischer was a practical businessman as well as a skilled cartoonist. As a pioneer in the early motion picture development era, he found a thriving market for his "cartoony" films, built up an efficient producing studio and gave hundreds of cartoonists and artists their opportunity to make use of their creativity.
>
> Meanwhile, over the years, he observed several animation cartoon studios, long since forgotten, who tried to become "arty," go into bankruptcy. Walt Disney was an exception. So in my opinion, Max cannot be faulted too severely because he stood firm on producing the type of animation which had been successful for him. And in spite of Shamus [Culhane's] criticism, Fleischer's animated product did improve steadily in quality, year after year.

By the late '20s Max and Dave Fleischer had signed on with Paramount Pictures, which would distribute their cartoons. It was a generally happy arrangement for over ten years, but budgets were considerably tighter at Fleischer than at Disney. Because Fleischer was on a strict schedule to produce a certain number of cartoons (generally one every six weeks), the idea of starting over from scratch in the middle of an unsatisfactory production was unthinkable. Disney could do it with its cartoon shorts, and even did so with *Pinocchio* (1940). The Fleischer production staff didn't have that luxury. Gordon Sheehan told me that the so-called "golden days of cartoon animation" weren't always so golden. In later years, Gordon would still cringe when looking at some of the old cartoon animation on the screen, wishing that he and his colleagues had had the time and money to do it over again.

At the time Fleischer did *Dancing on the Moon*, several of the studio's animation units were at work on Popeye, Betty Boop, Screen Songs (the "bouncing ball" series of sing-along cartoons), Color Classics, and other animated productions.

While the Fleischer artists didn't have their own training program, which by this time Disney offered to his people, Gordon Sheehan recalled that the Fleischer animators carefully studied the work of Disney and other competitors. Many Fleischer animators ate a quick lunch and then caught an hour of cartoons at the Trans-

Lux Newsreel Theater across the street. Another nearby theater showed an hour of cartoons for a quarter. In these ways, the animators could study the newest trends in animation and humor. Live-action comedies were studied, as well. The curious animators were akin to scouts who watch the plays of a rival football team. This scouting, Gordon Sheehan told me, was not done on company time, which really says something about the Fleischer staffers. They wanted to learn and do better at their jobs.

The quality of a Fleischer animated sequence was tested when the animator flipped the drawings by hand. This was presumed to be adequate for an animator to learn how to time the speed of the movement. At Disney, rough penciled animation was shot quickly on negative film and studied. This "pencil test" footage and the use of rotoscoping, which traced live-action movement to get a feel for how the cartoon characters should be animated, were considered crutches by the Fleischer regime—even though Max Fleischer had invented the rotoscope process several years before.

Like Walt Disney, Max Fleischer was a technical innovator who was, if anything, even more hands-on than Walt. In addition to the rotoscope, Max invented the cartoon "set-back" system (cutout elements used for dimensional effects), and experimented with the synchronization of animation with sound—all of this in the mid '20s, years before Disney did it. Further, Max and Dave invented the mechanical claw used in penny arcades, and the conveyor-belt system still used at supermarket checkouts. Fleischer knew, at least as well as his rival, that technology meant livelier, more exploitable cartoons.

Despite the wishes of the Fleischer brothers, Paramount Pictures eventually pushed hard for the studio to copy the more profitable Disney style. So, somewhat reluctantly, the Color Classics series was launched, beginning with *Poor Cinderella,* the only color Betty Boop cartoon the studio made. Fortunately, the best of the Color Classics films retained the familiar and wacky Fleischer-esque charm. One of the best was *Dancing on the Moon,* which was released in 1935.

As the cartoon opens, a strange rocketship squats on a launch pad; a sign identifies the ship as the "Honeymoon Express." Another sign says, "TONIGHT: DANCING ON THE MOON. ONE DOLLAR PER COUPLE." The owner, a friendly lion, steps from the hatchway of the ship to welcome a group of honeymooning animals. Music swells and the lion warbles a song about sweet romance "above the silvery clouds." Happy animal couples march along in pairs and enter the ship. They join the song, anticipating "dancing on the moon" following a wondrous flight that will take them near Venus, Jupiter, and Mars. Finally, "hearts will hum a tune when we're dancing on the moon!"

As the animals sing on the launch pad a male and female cat in wedding attire run frantically toward the ship as it takes off. "Hey! Wait! Wait! Hey!" they cry out. The boy cat makes it as the door closes, but the girl does not, and she's angry: "You left me on purpose, you alley cat!" The sad husband calls out, "Don't worry, wifey! I'll be back!" He's one sad character all right, as he spies romantic couples all around him: elephants, giraffes, bears, penguins, even houseflies. He ends up playing solitaire.

And there is the moon ahead. It turns into the happy face of singer Kate Smith

A simplified explanation of the Fleischer "set-back" system of dimensional animation. Not just a producer of exceptional (and eccentric) cartoons, Max Fleisher was a technical visionary and innovator.

(well known for her song "When the Moon Comes over the Mountain"). She greets the travelers with a cheery "Hello, everybody!"

In no time at all, the ship plops down on the moon. "All out!" says the owner, and the animal couples head for "Honeymoon Lane."

"This is a great place for necking!" says a giraffe groom. His wife agrees. She

Top: **Mr. and Mrs. Kittycat are separated as the rocket leaves for the Moon. This will have repercussions when the Mister returns to his frustrated bride.** ***Bottom:*** **Touchdown on the Moon, and romance!**

entwines her elongated neck around his and says, Mae West–style, "Why don'tcha come up and see me sometime?" And he does. Their kiss untangles their necks, and they snuggle together. A female cow happily jiggles her cowbell as she and her hubby playfully kiss. Mr. and Mrs. Seal mischievously slap each other, saying, "Koochie, koochie, koochie coo!" and almost get carried away as the slaps get a little rougher each time. Before war has a chance to break out, a bear husband and wife begin to sing about heavenly love among the stars. In a moment, all the couples are dancing.

Even the forlorn tomcat joins in, dancing sadly alone in time to the music. When the ship lifts off for the trip home, the animals, now glimpsed through portholes, sing of heaven's "Pearly Gates," and dancing on "the Milky Way."

With that, the little rocket speeds to Earth. Storks appear on the launch pad, bringing "bundles of joy" to the happy honeymooning animals. No such luck for the unhappy cat, sad to say. His wife is understandably miffed, and clobbers him good as the cartoon ends.

The tomcat's predicament aside, *Dancing on the Moon* offers an extremely sanguine view of science and technology. (Remember that the cat's pickle is the result of his own pokiness, not any fault of science.) The rocket ship epitomizes technology dedicated to the pursuit of happiness and, as the storks suggest, healthy propagation and happy family lives.

Marriage, home, family. These basic values were promoted with particular urgency during the Depression, when many Americans looked at life and wondered *What the hell is the point?* If the stitching of the American fabric was to hold, America's family life had to be vibrant, and sufficiently content so that people felt they had a purpose that transcended the battered economy.

Like *The Mad Doctor*, *Dancing on the Moon* revolves around issues of some interest to Technocrats, but with no hint of eugenics or other unscrupulousness. As Fleischer interpreted things, technology creates a device (the rocket) that encourages traditional marriage, commitment, and parenthood. It's the ultimate expression of Technocracy's benevolent social side. And when the social contract (i.e., family) is fulfilled, can economic health be far behind?

The delightful animation of *Dancing on the Moon* is credited to Seymour Kneitel and Roland "Doc" Crandall. Kneitel had been one of Fleischer's head animators for years, along with Crandall, who had been at the studio since the silent-movie days of Out of the Inkwell. Kneitel, the head animator on *Dancing on the Moon*, did his best to hide his talent for cutting costs. Look carefully at the cartoon and you'll spot "cheating." Animation of the dancing animal couples is recycled, and the animation of the rocketship's landing on the moon is the same as when it lands on Earth. Here, corner cutting is carefully done, but Kneitel would get more blatant about it as the years passed. In the early part of his career, though, Kneitel had a real knack for musical cartoons. *Brotherly Love, Little Swee'pea, Me Musical Nephews,* and *Dancing on the Moon* are just a few.

While he's not credited on screen, William Henning probably animated portions of *Dancing on the Moon*. Henning was regarded by his peers at Fleischer as one of the best animators of animals, particularly horses.

The other outstanding attribute of this musical cartoon is the dancing. Both Gordon Sheehan and animator Dave Tendlar remembered the talents of writer, cartoonist, and former vaudeville dancer Jack Ward. Tendlar said, "He could draw. He drew all the [dance] steps for us. He drew everything out. The positions of the feet. He was a professional dancer. He drew out all the steps in very great detail, and we could follow the feet movements that he drew. He was not an animator. He worked in the Story Department. In his early days, he and his wife were vaudeville actors; they danced."

Technocratic principles set to dance — what could be more persuasive?

Music was equally important. Soundtracks for Fleischer cartoons were made after the animation was finished, completely unlike the Disney method, where the soundtrack was recorded first and used as a guide for the finished animation. Gordon Sheehan explained to me,

> Before the middle 1930s, most of the animation was drawn first, then recorded later. To visually guide the recording musicians on the tempo, cartoon characters were animated to bend their knees, wave their arms or perform some other obviously repetitive action in time with the "beat." Usually the tempo of the movement would start out slow, pick up speed as the film progressed, and end up fast at the climax.
>
> Around the mid–1930s, the Fleischers expanded their music and sound department and initiated a system whereby music, voice and sound effects were pre-recorded and marked on "lead sheets," which were very much music sheets, and informed the animator exactly what frame of film the cartoon character moved on, how long the action should be, and where to place the accents on the action.
>
> This made for more refined synchronization between cartoon action and the soundtrack, but some animators complained that this system allowed less freedom to animate. I believe that all in all, it improved the quality of animated films.

The credits of every Fleischer cartoon, *Dancing on the Moon* included, named Dave Fleischer as director. However, the true director of individual cartoons was the head animator. So, then, what *did* Dave Fleischer do? According to Gordon Sheehan,

> Dave and Max Fleischer were equal partners in Fleischer Studios as far as I know. At least, they took equal salaries out of the company's profits. Max got producer's credit. Dave got director's credit on all cartoon productions, but this was an honorary credit. He didn't draw so he wasn't actively involved in the laying out or animating of the films. However, he did check over every script before it went into production, made changes and offered suggestions, usually in the line of supplementary gags or humorous situations....
>
> Dave had the authority to make changes in the rough films but I doubt he ever used it. In respect to Dave's contribution to the studio's animation output, although he appeared to take very little active part in the drawing end of the animation, he was credited with having a keen sense of timing and pacing of a cartoon; and the head animator consulted him frequently on this very important subject and on general animation problems that might pop up from time to time. Dave also sat in on most animated cartoon recordings, and played a big part in selecting the music and sound effects that helped make Fleischer films an important contribution to the theatrical animated cartoon industry.

A completed storyboard made of 11"-by-14" sheets was put on a bulletin board. Storyboards allowed for notations of timing, dissolves, and other camera effects. The entire animation staff studied the story, acted out scenes, and was invited to contribute story ideas, gags, and other bits of business. Layouts were followed by a week's study of music sheets. Notations of action and dialogue were made on the sheets, a process that consumed another week. Two or three weeks were spent on animation, more if the cartoon involved a new or otherwise challenging character.

In fine Technocratic fashion, production of Fleischer cartoons was staggered so that as one was wrapping, another would come down the pipeline. Production schedules were tight, and animators despaired of front-office memos that notified the unit that it was running late. Efficiency came with a price, for the pressure was always on.

We describe much of the Fleischer process here to emphasize the technological craft of cartoon making. Max and Dave Fleischer honed their system so that the studio was able to produce about 40 cartoons a year during the '30s. Although intensely creative, the cartoon process must also be mechanized if the films are to be produced with maximum efficiency. The Fleischers understood this as well as anybody who ever contributed to the art. *Dancing on the Moon*, which is predicated on the happy wonders of science and invention, illustrates how the studio turned technology to warm, humanistic ends.

Of all the animation studios of the thirties, Fleischer was most likely to be sympathetic to principles of Technocracy. Perhaps this was due to the urban backgrounds of Max and Dave, and the brothers' gift for innovation and invention. In another Fleischer Color Classic, *Christmas Comes But Once a Year* (1936), benign Professor Grampy runs his world via the buttons and levers of '30s-style high tech. The cartoon's futurist vision is wacky and fun. Walt Disney, a product of rural America, would have displayed less enthusiasm.

Today, in a society linked and managed by computer, and when increasing amounts of farmland are purchased for development as high-tech industrial parks, we seem to have achieved a kind of Technocracy. Whether it will help us or harm us depends on how we control and understand it. What was considered the notions of crackpots in the thirties now mark our present as well as our future. Will it be a benign future, as the Fleischers would have it, or will it be sinister, as envisioned by Disney? Stay tuned!

Films Discussed

The Mad Doctor Walt Disney Productions/United Artists. Released January 21, 1933. Approx. 7 min. Director: David Hand. Music: Frank Churchill. Available on Walt Disney Home Video DVD.

Dancing on the Moon Paramount Pictures/Max Fleischer. Released July 12, 1935. Approx. 7 min. Director: Dave Fleischer. Animation: Seymour Kneitel and Roland Crandall. Music and lyrics: Charlie Tobias and Murray Mencher. Not presently available on home video.

Sources

Andrae, Thomas. "Of Mouse and the Man: Floyd Gottfredson and the Mickey Mouse Continuities," in *Walt Disney's Mickey Mouse in Color: 1930s Disney Comic Strip Classics*, edited by Geoffrey Blum.
Blum, Geoffrey. *Walt Disney's Mickey Mouse in Color: 1930s Disney Comic Strip Classics*. New York: Pantheon Books, 1988.
Culhane, Shamus. Interview with author.
Dancing on the Moon, not presently available on home video.
Hand, David. *Memoirs*. Cambria, Calif. Lighthouse Litho, no date.
The Mad Doctor. Available on Walt Disney Home Video DVD.
Sheehan, Gordon. Interview with author.
Tendlar, Dave. Interview with author.

Special thanks to "Uncle Donnie" Pitchford, Chuck Anders, and Steve Stanchfield for helping me find graphic materials for this article! As Wimpy would say in a Popeye cartoon, "Thank you too much!"

4

Flash Gordon Conquers the Great Depression and World War Too! The *Flash Gordon* Serial Trilogy

LEONARD J. KOHL

A lot of us TV-bred baby boomers grew up watching—and immensely enjoying—vintage movies of our parents' time: features, cartoons, and serials. For a lot of us, television was a time machine, bringing us a wonderful helping of old delights. Until TV stations could rely on the networks to supply great quantities of new programs, they bought up whatever they could find, and a lot of it was terrific. Many of us have watched at least one chapter of an old *Flash Gordon* serial.

My father was our Catholic parish's grade school football coach, and I can recall several late Saturday mornings when fellow coaches and friends would congregate in our living room with my brother and me to watch *Flash Gordon* on Chicago's WGN, channel nine. Imagine a group of people, adults and youngsters, absorbing vintage, epic adventure on a black-and-white TV screen in the middle 1960s. And then imagine a bunch of kids in a darkened theater in the late 1930s, when money was tight, and decently paying jobs—or any jobs at all—were frighteningly scarce. Somehow, although I understood it only vaguely, the *Flash Gordon* serial sagas offered kids and fun-loving adults the idea that there was hope for the future, when there seemed to be little hope at all.

Cartoonist Leonard Starr, who created the comic strip *Mary Perkins*, remembered the time well: "My family was distinctly affected by the Depression. My father was out of work, savings were dwindling, and there were no harbingers of better times coming. I'm sure there was desperation all around me, but I was somehow unaware of that part of it. I can recall only that those years were totally gray. I know that the sun never once shone in all that time. Only on the planet Mongo was there any color; only there could there be found any vitality, any life."

I once asked my aunt Dolores what my grandfather—her father—earned during the Great Depression. She recalled that in 1931 my grandfather made about $7 a week as a meat butcher. If this is true, that was a very low wage for anyone in Chicago at that time. Actor Buster Crabbe told me that while going to college in the early '30s, he worked at Silverman's, a men's clothing store in California, for $8 a week. It wasn't nearly enough to live on, so he found other jobs to support himself.

When cartoon animator Gordon Sheehan got out of art school in New York City in the spring of 1933, he was lucky enough to get a job as a cel inker at $15 a week. He had a room at the local YMCA, but said that no one could live in New York on that salary alone. Sheehan had to find odd jobs to supplement his cartoonist's wages. So, despite the fact that standards of living were cheaper in Chicago than New York and California, my grandfather had to stretch mightily to make seven bucks a week cover the rent and food for himself, my grandmother, my aunt, and my father. Seven dollars a week—I don't know how he did it! Yet, as author Laura Hillenbrandt notes in her wonderful *Seabiscuit: An American Legend*, the average per-capita income for an American family in 1935 was a meager $432 a year.

Back then a gallon of milk averaged about 35¢. You could buy a hamburger sandwich at the local lunch counter for a dime and make a phone call for a nickel. If you could find a way to finance it, you could buy a new car for about $500. Pontiac offered an easy payment plan of "15 cents a day," but many Americans didn't have 15¢ to spare. Many of them had good jobs before the stock market crash of Black Tuesday, October 29, 1929. Afterward, the American landscape was darker and more menacing. The Depression was the worst economic epidemic America would ever endure. The fact was that the giddy prosperity of the Roaring Twenties had been partly illusion, a tissue of heedless optimism and risk-taking. Now it was over. People who loved to play the stock market had over-invested borrowed money that they suddenly couldn't pay back. As companies began to go bankrupt, and valuable shares became suddenly worthless, the formerly wealthy heads of business corporations went on reduced salaries, or became jobless. Many men really did sell apples on street corners in order to survive. Farmers were starving because there was an abundance of produce but no real market to accept it. The money just wasn't there.

"Looking back on it now," my dad said, "most of our neighborhood was poor, but we didn't realize it." Because my grandfather was a meat butcher and later owned his own grocery store, my dad never starved. Yet there were people in the neighborhood who lost everything. Strangers would knock on back doors to ask for a handout. But nobody begged. People were willing to do some kind of work for food.

In 1933, the worst year of the Depression, my maternal grandfather lost his wife, shortly after losing his mother. He lost his sign-painting business and suddenly found himself with five mouths to feed—himself and his four daughters. My grandfather's mother-in-law and her husband came to live with them and help out, when they could. There was a time when it looked as if my mother and her sisters might live with other relatives rather than together as a family. But my grandfather got a job running a tavern and kept his family together.

An outing to the movies, as my mom remembers it, was not a weekly treat but a special event. *Snow White and the Seven Dwarfs* or *The Wizard of Oz* were something special for her and her sisters. No regular Saturday matinees of cartoons, comedy shorts, features, and movie serial chapters for them!

But many kids *were* able to scrape up a dime — and perhaps a bit more for candy or a soda pop — for their weekly visits to the movies. John Wayne, Buck Jones, Tarzan, Charlie Chan, Bugs Bunny, Daffy Duck, Popeye and many other movie favorites kept the kids who could afford it on a rich diet of movie fantasy — every week. Movie serials were a valued part of that diet. For 12 to 15 weeks, kids enjoyed cliffhanging episodes often featuring their favorite comic strip heroes or heroines. At the end of one serial, crafty theater owners ran a teaser for a new one, or unspooled the first chapter. The kids were hooked.

For many Americans, entertainment was a necessary escape. Movies, radio, comic strips, pulp magazines — all of these transported people to other places and helped them to forget the terror of the breadline. Fantasy was particularly appealing. So it was that the writers, production people, directors, and actors adapted Alex Raymond's immensely popular *Flash Gordon* comic strip and made a classic serial. Imagine sitting in a darkened theater in the spring of 1936. You've plunked down your dime for the Saturday matinee, and you're expecting a good show for your money. After the little airplane flies around the globe to announce "A Universal Picture," booming music announces the serial, and pictorial credits introduce the cast. Then you witness a scientific observatory that shudders beneath a raging storm. Inside, a group of scientists debates the future of the world; a rogue planet has suddenly appeared in close proximity to Earth, and is causing mayhem. Two middle-aged men, professors Gordon and Henslon, look at telegrams from scientists located all over the world while we see newsreel clips of panicked people. Professor Henslon has hope that the great scientist Dr. Hans Zarkov will understand and correct the problem. Indeed, Zarkov believes that the mysterious planet is inhabited, and hopes to reach it in his rocket ship and reason with whoever is causing all the disturbances. Professor Gordon, however, believes Zarkov is mad and that his theory is ridiculous. The last telegram that Professor Gordon receives is from his son, nicknamed Flash, a collegiate athlete who's "given up his polo game" to be with his family "before the end."

Alex Raymond self-portrait. The *Flash Gordon* cartoonist's rich imagination and elegant draftsmanship gave the serials plenty to draw from.

We then cut to a swirling sky, which seems to be exploding apart, as if a gigantic fireworks display has gone horribly, horribly wrong. Inside a wildly swaying Ford Tri-Motor airliner, a terrified young lady and a young man prepare to parachute into the maelstrom. As the plane crashes to earth, the pair lands near a weird-looking rocket ship. When the beautiful woman — Dale Arden — remarks on the craft, the young man — Flash Gordon — says, "Yeah, some fool trying to fly to Mars."

The "fool's" name is Zarkov (Frank Shannon), and he quickly strikes up an alliance with Flash (Buster Crabbe) and Dale (Jean Rogers).

"Your father thinks I'm mad," Zarkov laments. "They all do. But I know there's a way to save Earth. I believe the planet rushing upon us is inhabited. It is also intensely radioactive. If I can reach the planet in my rocket ship, I may be able to control its power, and avert it from its course toward the Earth."

"It's worth trying," says Flash.

Zarkov replies, "For four hours I have waited for my assistant, but he has turned coward. I need a man to help me! Will you go? It's the only chance to save the Earth!"

Flash agrees, but only if Dale accompanies him. A deal is struck. And so, as actor Buster Crabbe noted many years later, "three crazy people in a rocket ship" set out on a series of adventures to the planet Mongo in one of the greatest movie serials of all time. For 13 weeks, on theater screens all across America, the adventurers interacted with Ming the Merciless, Ming's sexy daughter Aura, flying hawk men, shark men, lion men, deadly giant lizards, and other weird creatures. The saga began in the middle of March 1936. It was boggling.

The first four Sunday *Flash Gordon* comic strip pages of 1934 are virtual blueprints for the first episode of the 1936 serial. Yet, the scriptwriters at Universal did something unique to these comic strip characters: they made them as human and down to earth as possible. Here, I think, is a key reason these serials resonated with Depression audiences. In Raymond's strip, Flash is a "Yale man"— a superb athlete and a participant in the "good life" that only the privileged few in America were able to enjoy. There's a touch of East Coast snob in Raymond's conception of Flash. The serial writers, however, downplayed Flash's wealth, and turned the character into a "regular guy." Flash never suggests he feels he's better or smarter than anybody else. Although he wears a stylish sport coat and tie at the start of the serial, the Universal version of the Flash Gordon character makes him a likeable guy that anybody might want to be friends with. More significantly, Crabbe suggests that he'd be pals with you, too. Somehow, Crabbe was able to give the elegant but emotionally remote pen-and-ink Flash flesh and blood, and an all–American personality. In Raymond's defense — if he really needs one — his adventures were seen on Sunday newspaper "funny pages" that had to engage readers quickly. Raymond had neither the physical space nor the time needed to lavish his characters with believable human traits and richness in characterization, especially in the context of a rip-roaring fantasy-adventure strip.

Despite the subtle yet important changes made by the Universal scriptwriters, much of Alex Raymond's soap-opera plot elements remain. As in the comic strip, the serial version of Princess Aura (Priscilla Lawson) lusts after Flash as zealously as Emperor Ming covets Dale Arden. Prince Barin sees only the good in Aura and truly loves her, despite the fact that her father, Ming, is one of Barin's most bitter enemies. Aura later befriends Flash and Dale — too abruptly in the first serial version — but

Flash Gordon **(Buster Crabbe) and Dale (Jean Rogers) set foot on the planet Mongo for the first time. The place will turn out to be an allegory for the myriad real-life challenges faced by America and the world during the interwar years.**

Lawson conveys a sexy sultriness not often found in female characters in serials designed for children; Flash can hardly resist.

Alex Raymond's conceptions of the kingdoms of Mongo are a fascinating hodgepodge of old Egypt, Greece, and Rome, with futuristic sky cities, and interior design and costumes that suggest great personal and institutional power. Much of this, too, was retained for the serial. The blend of adult emotion and a fantasy landscape is intriguing and invigorating.

The Depression diminished many qualities of American life, but it couldn't kill romance or people's desire for it. The Mongo of the comic strip and the serial is an essentially romantic place, an idealized milieu of privilege and comfort, populated (narrowing the definition of "romance" a bit) not just by masterful men but by gorgeous women, against whom Earth's own all–American representative, Dale Arden, more than holds her own. Mongo is a place so crammed with technological and human beauty that the inhabitants are free to cultivate a mindset far removed from mundane issues of rent or new shoes. Mongo is an enclosed, self-defined reality, populated by archetypes of good and bad. And no one is "badder" than Emperor Ming.

It's not clear if it was Alex Raymond or newspaper mogul William Randolph

Ming the Merciless (Charles Middleton), the antithesis of the faintly self-congratulatory, Christian American value system of the Depression years.

Hearst who wanted Ming the Merciless to personify the racist Yellow Peril stereotype that had flourished since the nineteenth century. Fortunately, the concept seemed to get muddled and lost over time in the wild outer-space adventures, which in these politically correct times is probably just as well. It probably helped that Charles Middleton's conception of Ming was not so much as an Asian but as sheer, cold-blooded evil, with no allegiance to any real race on Earth. The cold, clipped, almost Midwestern voice, the icy stares, and the malevolent sneers and snarls in Middleton's tone and manner suggest a nightmare vision of Grant Wood's farmer in the famous painting *American Gothic.*

Middleton was a Shakespearean actor with a gift for imperiousness. It's no stretch to assume that Depression audiences regarded him not simply as Ming, but as a personification of all the bosses, speculators, bankers, land swindlers, loan officers, and bill collectors who made life frustrating and miserable for so many Americans. Ming wasn't just a malevolent, extraterrestrial despot — he was the dark, heartless face of the nation. Because he was an individual, Ming could be dealt with psychologically and, in imaginary serial terms, physically. He personified the arrogant, intimidating elements of Depression life, but he made them manageable, as well. You couldn't punch the nose of every stuffed shirt at the local bank, but you took immense satisfaction whenever Ming absorbed a smack in the chops. As Flash dealt harshly with Ming, audiences took vicarious swings at a system of government, ethics, and economics that seemed to have failed them.

Some Americans wondered if the concept of democracy was a passing fad. Some thought that other systems of government might pull us out of the depths of the Great Depression. Some wondered if communism was such a bad thing. Others wondered if Mussolini or Hitler might actually know what they were doing. Still others believed in Technocracy, under which scientists should run the country. The flirtation of some intellectuals and the disenfranchised with communism was very real, but Technocracy never found a wide audience. Early on in *Flash Gordon* Ming declares to Zarkov, "Science will conquer all things, even the human emotions." Like Zarkov, Ming is a scientist, or at least one who understands the destructive potential of how science might be bent to serve his needs. In this respect, Ming represents the misuse of science. Zarkov is his philosophical opposite, a man who lives for science's positive, ethical side.

When Flash, Dale, and Dr. Zarkov learn that Ming has been causing all the catastrophes on Earth, Ming smugly admits it. "I control absolutely the movement of this planet, and I will destroy your Earth in my own way!" Thinking quickly, Dr. Zarkov asks, "Why destroy the Earth? Why not conquer it?"

"Why not?" ponders Ming. Learning that Zarkov invented his own rocket ship to make the heroic trio to Mongo, Ming says with admiration, "You are a remarkable man! I can use you." He orders his guards to take Zarkov to the laboratory and "give him everything he requires ... except his freedom." And of course, when all men are in danger of losing their freedom, they realize that freedom is what they prize the most. Zarkov is no exception. From that moment on, he is dedicated to defeating Ming and saving, as he once put it, "old mother Earth." Dr. Zarkov here becomes the most benign of what comic strip fans and serial-goers first assumed would be yet another mad scientist.

Universal was reasonably faithful to the physical appearances of Alex Raymond's characters. The most easily distinguished difference is actress Jean Rogers's Dale Arden, who is innocently blonde rather than the sophisticated brunette of Raymond's imagination. Perhaps the scriptwriters reasoned that a blonde Dale would appear

"Science," Ming (Charles Middleton) informs the captive Dr. Zarkov (Frank Shannon), "will conquer all things. Even the human emotions." This sentiment underscored Americans' vague awareness of what was brewing in Germany and Italy.

more exotic to Emperor Ming, just as Fay Wray's Ann Darrow was the "golden woman" to the Skull Island natives, and to King Kong. In *Flash Gordon*, Ming leers at the frightened Dale and sighs, "Your hair, your eyes, your skin.... I've not seen one like you before! Ahhhh, you are beautiful!" With that, Flash reaches for Ming and nearly chokes him to death: "You keep your slimy hands off her!"

Flash's violent reaction underscores part of the dark psychology of the Depression. The blonde Dale is prototypically all–American: Midwestern-sexy but virtuous, plucky, and unfailingly loyal. Ming recognizes these characteristics, and although he desires Dale, he hates her with even more fervor, and contemporaneous audiences knew why. Viewers absorbed Ming's faux–Asian aspect in a primal, frankly prejudicial way, but on a more meaningful level they regarded him as an "other" whose depredations transcended race. Yes, he was exotic but also a creature of considerable power, shielded by vassals and holding lives in his hands—much like those aforementioned bankers and predatory farm agents.

Flash Gordon was budgeted at about $350,000, making it perhaps the most expensive serial up to that time. Serials produced at rival Republic Pictures generally cost less than half of that amount. While producer Henry MacRae, Universal's "Serial King," was called on the carpet for the expense of *Flash Gordon*, and later demoted to associate producer on later serial productions, it must be noted that Universal was a major studio, geared for making decently budgeted horror films, musicals, dramas, and Westerns. Republic was set up to focus on lower-budgeted Westerns and serials. So Republic's top directors, stuntmen, editors, musicians, writers, and technicians could turn out superior-looking serials and films in record time and with smaller budgets. At Universal the studio's top special-effects technician John P. Fulton and his staff were working on the intricate special effects of *The Invisible Ray* while *Flash Gordon*'s technicians had to produce their effects in camera, as they lacked the time and money to do otherwise.

Buster Crabbe recalled that the first *Flash Gordon* serial was a lot of hard work. He could be easily called into the studio at 7:00 in the morning, and was lucky to be able to quit by 10:00 at night. On the average, 80 to 90 camera set-ups were required every day from director Frederick Stephani and (uncredited) director Ray Taylor. With a rigid six-week shooting schedule and a script the size of a small phone book, there was more than enough work for cast and the crew. Producer Henry MacRae did his best to keep the cast and crew at their best by supplying "jungle juice"—a concoction of gin and fruit juice—and serving caviar sandwiches when needed.

There was little time for retakes of flubbed lines, and apparently no budget for "looping"—re-recording necessary lines of dialogue—by the cast. The late writer and film historian George Turner told me that he suspected that the person doing most of the obvious re-dubbing of various lines in the serial was film's editor, Saul Goodkind. In any case, one can reasonably surmise that the *Flash Gordon* cast and crew were delighted to have a place to go where they could be worked into the ground. Unemployment levels among actors are always horrifyingly high, so performers are happy to work at any time, and were particularly pleased during the Depression, when close to 25 percent of the American workforce wasn't working at all.

Despite budget limitations and a tremendously tough production schedule, the serial was a triumph for the studio. Despite the sets borrowed from other Universal productions—*The Mummy, Dracula's Daughter, Bride of Frankenstein*, and others—and props of rocket ships and footage lifted from Fox's peculiar science-fiction musical *Just Imagine*, the serial was a real-life version of Raymond's strip. While the musical score had some original material by composer Clifford Vaughan, it was chock full of cues from other Universal films, including *The Black Cat, The Invisible Man, Destination Unknown*, and *Werewolf of London*. However, the music editing seemed flawless, and many of the themes—themselves reworked from classical pieces by Brahms, Liszt, Chopin, and others—remain timeless and exciting to this day. (Music from *Bride of Frankenstein* was not heard in the serial, despite popular legend, but some themes were incorporated later when a feature version of the serial was edited for theaters that showed no serials.)

However it happened, everybody involved seemed to give the first Flash Gordon serial much more than their normal share of energy. In this way, they hoped that the film would turn out not to be a total disaster. In later years, Jean Rogers told me in a letter, "Buster and I thought *Flash Gordon* was preposterous when we made it!" Somehow it all worked out. When *Flash Gordon* was released, the cast and crew were amazed at what they had accomplished. Work on the sequels was probably easier, but even so, that feeling of having made the unreal seem real was never lessened or diluted. That optimistic feeling shines through to this day. Buster Crabbe later remarked that the serial was a real gamble for the studio, but Universal made a small fortune from it. Crabbe later claimed that *Flash Gordon* was the second biggest moneymaker for Universal in 1936; a Deanna Durbin musical, *Three Smart Girls,* was the first.

However, the serial's initial profits were not enough to save Universal Pictures, which had been on the verge of bankruptcy for years. At the end of 1935, Universal showed a loss of $475,053. The Depression had come home to roost at Universal City. As a result, the studio's founder, Carl Laemmle, was forced to turn studio operations over to one Charles R. Rogers and lawyer J. Cheever Crowdin of Standard Capital over payment of a loan of $750,000. The contract had an option for Standard Capital to assume operations if the loan was not paid on time — and that's exactly what happened. (More than one person thought this was unfair, and J. Cheever Crowdin was later lampooned by one of MGM's scriptwriters in the 1939 Marx Brothers comedy *At the Circus.* In that film — really only memorable because of his rendition of "Lydia, the Tattooed Lady" — Groucho Marx plays a slightly devious attorney by the name of J. Cheever Loophole.)

Thanks to the "Horror Ban" in Great Britain, Universal suspended production of its very profitable horror films for a few years and generally devoted itself to making family films like the moneymaking musicals with perky Deanna Durbin. Yet by late 1937 or early 1938, somebody decided that a sequel to *Flash Gordon* should be in production. A script with a heavy focus on Azura, the Witch Queen of Mongo, was accepted. This script was not quite as faithful to Alex Raymond's comic strip as before. Further, the budget was cut in half, to a reported $175,000, in spite of the fact that *Flash Gordon's Trip to Mars* ran two additional chapters—15 in all. And in an odd touch, the serial was released on an eerie, green-tinted film stock. Directed by serial and Western vets Ford Beebe and Robert F. Hill, *Flash Gordon's Trip to Mars* made a tidy profit for Universal. Sadly, this serial sequel was nowhere near as sexy or as lavish-looking as the first *Flash Gordon* serial, and it was clearly geared for youngsters. However, despite continuity errors and unwelcome comedy relief by Flash's new sidekick, reporter Happy Hapgood (Donald Kerr), many fans consider *Flash Gordon's Trip to Mars* to be the best of them all.

Certainly, Charles Middleton was as terrifically good as ever — or "bad" as ever — as Ming. Jean Rogers (now a brunette Dale to keep continuity with the comic strip) was absolutely fine, along with Frank Shannon as Zarkov, and Richard Alexander as Prince Barin. Besides Happy, the most important new character in this sequel was Azura (Beatrice Roberts), ruler of Mars.

This time, Ming pretends to befriend Queen Azura in her war against the Clay People, a humanoid race that, by virtue of one of Azura's magical spells, has been turned into living clay. But what really interests Ming is an explosive element called nitron, and to that end he develops a machine that will suck nitron from Earth's atmosphere; undreamt-of disasters are sure to follow. Naturally, Zarkov discovers what Ming is up to, and Zarkov, Flash, Dale, Happy, Prince Barin, the Clay People,

Flash (Crabbe) and Ming (Middleton) in a decisive moment from *Flash Gordon's Trip to Mars* (1938).

and eventually even the Martians turn on Ming, who becomes so power-obsessed he goes temporarily insane.

The editing of *Flash Gordon's Trip to Mars*, as well as the musical score (this time including loads of cues from *Bride of Frankenstein*), are not as smooth as in the first serial, and in some cases, the skimpiness of the budget really shows in the rocket ships and the sets. On the other hand, some of the special effects are fine, including the eerie scenes in which the miserable Clay People seem to ooze out of the walls; statues disintegrate in death rays; and characters walk across Martian "light bridges."

Finely crafted characters are a real asset. Lovely Beatrice Roberts is terrific as the slightly villainous and more than slightly sexy Queen Azura who, in time, realizes how much cruelty she has set in motion, and tries to mend her ways before it's too late. Dying, she tells Flash how to lift the curse from the Clay People. "That was the finest thing you could have done," says Flash, his voice almost breaking with emotion.

The liberation of the Clay People has special piquancy. Victimized long-distance by a powerful, completely unsympathetic force, they had been slaves to a corrupt system of governance. To be unhuman in appearance is no treat, but isn't nearly as awful as to be turned into slaves, mere chess pieces, by (admittedly exotic) bureaucrats. Again, parallels to the ongoing Depression are obvious. The Clay People are

Queen Azura (Beatrice Roberts) commands a moment of attention in *Flash Gordon's Trip to Mars*. From left, Prince Barin (Richard Alexander), Dale (Rogers) and Zarkov (Shannon) observe. The Clay King (center left) is C. Montague Shaw; next (center right) is Flash's sidekick, "Happy" Hapgood (Donald Kerr).

liberated by magic, but, alas, no such magic would free America's unemployed. Only the New Deal, building conflict in Europe, and concomitant American rearmament, would do that.

In 1939, Universal released *Buck Rogers* to serial fans, but despite good work from Buster Crabbe in the title role, and solid support from actors Henry Brandon and C. Montague Shaw, the serial paled in comparison to the *Flash Gordon* epics. Some of the sets and special effects were a tremendous improvement over the first two *FG* serials, but the serial's story, plainly put, just wasn't as good. Buster Crabbe thought that *Buck Rogers* was an uninspired knockoff of *Flash Gordon*, despite the fact that the *Buck Rogers* comic strip appeared in 1929, preceding *Flash Gordon* in the funny pages by about five years. Crabbe thought of Buck as not much more than a do-gooder, and that's as good an explanation as any for why this serial has never captured anyone's passionate admiration. Generally, the whole feeling of fun and excitement, of actors enjoying the characters they were portraying, just is not there. Despite having some of the same cast and crew as the *Flash Gordon* serials, the spark is missing. So later in 1939 plans were made to make another *Flash Gordon* serial, this one called *Flash Gordon Conquers the Universe*, which was released early in 1940.

While this last serial of the *Flash Gordon* trilogy was called a "cheater" by Buster Crabbe in later years, he still enjoyed his character and did his best with the material. Despite the fact that it was full of stock footage from previous *Flash Gordon* serials and a 1929 German-produced docudrama called *The White Hell of Pitz Palu*, and ran the standard 12 chapters this time, it looked and had the feel of a lavish production. For this reason, some — including onetime *Flash Gordon* comic strip artist Al Williamson — prefer this serial to the other two. Sexy Carol Hughes assumed the Dale Arden role this time out, and is a real-life version of the character as drawn by Raymond.

Slender, muscular Roland Drew now played Prince Barin, a sleek figure in keeping with Alex Raymond's slightly changing conceptions of his comic strip characters. By this time, Raymond's draftsmanship had become superb, in the manner of top-level magazine illustration. Further, he grew increasingly preoccupied with expressing a sophisticated, urbane tone (which he would explore more fully in his later, non-fantasy strip, *Rip Kirby*). This tonal shift made Raymond's *Flash Gordon* a brilliantly drawn strip, but one philosophically far removed from 1940 America, where millions of people lacked indoor plumbing, telephones, and access to basic services. "Urbanity," as far as most Americans were concerned, was not part of the national vocabulary. "Isolationism," however, had become a very popular word. Brutal, mechanized war had come to Europe in the late summer of 1939, when Hitler's *Wehrmacht* and *Luftwaffe* laid waste to western Poland, and when Hitler's new ally, Joseph Stalin, attacked Poland from the east. Many Americans, disillusioned by the United States' 1918 participation in the Great War, had no truck with another stab at intervention. Many citizens viewed President Roosevelt, for all his popularity, as an internationalist who was scheming to involve the U.S. in the European conflict. Those Americans were right, of course, and although FDR did the only sensible thing, the fact remains that "right" was unpopular with an enormous segment of the American population.

Hollywood's film industry was founded and still controlled in 1940 by New York progressives who had a keen awareness of intolerance, so although many in movie audiences wanted no part of "Europe's war," film executives subtly pushed for intervention. In *Flash Gordon Conquers the Universe*, directed by Ford Beebe and Ray Taylor, Emperor Ming is back on Mongo, with a new kind of peril for Earth and Flash. Ming's Nazi-like troopers drop particles of "Death Dust" from rocket ships near Earth. The deadly particles cause a purplish spot to appear on the victim's forehead, and instant death. Called the "Purple Death," it understandably causes panic on Earth. Once again, Dr. Zarkov (a returned Frank Shannon) sets out with Flash and Dale to pull the plug on Ming's scheme. (The most insidious feature of the Death Dust is that it kills people of intelligence and spares those who are suited for roles as mindless slaves. One can imagine Hitler dreaming of such a weapon.)

Beyond Alex Raymond's increasingly fashion-like illustrations, the *Flash Gordon* strip kept pace with the changing world. Now, Ming was no longer a mere emperor but a dictator, and his outfits and the uniforms of his soldiers look very Nazi-like. Flash knows that Ming has to be stopped. If Americans still were generally loath to join former allies Britain and France to fight against Germany, Japan, and Fascist Italy,

Flash Gordon Conquers the Universe (1940), with help (left to right) from Roland Drew, Frank Shannon, Carol Hughes, and Lee Powell. The "Robin Hood" costumes worn by Crabbe and the others reflect the stylistics of Alex Raymond's concurrent comic strip.

American factories were building weapons for the British, for distribution under FDR's Lend-Lease program. It was only a matter of time before America joined the conflict. Raymond's *Flash Gordon* comic strip and Universal's third serial version were in a very real sense preparing us for the responsibilities and horrors of war.

With the success of *Flash Gordon*, Universal contracted with King Features Syndicate for *Jungle Jim* and *Secret Agent X-9*, and licensed *Red Barry* from King. Other studios put together such *Flash Gordon* imitations as *Undersea Kingdom* and *The Fighting Devil Dogs*, or turned to other characters from comic strips, pulp magazines, and radio shows to gain rights to *Zorro, The Shadow, Dick Tracy, Mandrake, Chandu*, and *The Spider*. But the *Flash Gordon* films remained the most popular of the strip-derived serials.

Universal had the rights to the *Flash Gordon* property for 15 years, and the serials and feature film versions (of the first two serials) were kept in constant re-release. When the rights reverted to King Features Syndicate, the property was licensed to television, where a mildly successful syndicated series (with former photographic model Steve Holland as Flash) was broadcast in 1957. An animated cartoon version aired on Saturday morning TV during 1979-80 and 1982-83. Film producer Dino

Dale (Carol Hughes), Flash (Crabbe), and a product of the arsenal of democracy, from *Flash Gordon Conquers the Universe.*

DeLaurentiis offered a ham-fisted camp version of *Flash Gordon* in 1980, and most have agreed with Buster Crabbe that it was a misconceived turkey.

No remake or imitation has diminished the power of the original *Flash Gordon* serial trilogy. With greater ease than any other movie serial shown on TV, the films created several more generations of fans. With the advent of home-use videotape and

DVD, the serials remain popular. Even after all these years, they have lost little of their magic. Buster Crabbe, Jean Rogers, Charles Middleton, and others in the casts gave the characters a dimensionality that their comic strip counterparts only hinted at. The optimism of Flash, Zarkov, Dale, Prince Barin, and the other heroic characters encouraged youngsters to feel positive about themselves and the future of this country. No obvious flag-waving or sugary-sweet messages were necessary. The *Flash Gordon* serials showed us that it's a love of others that is important, and taught us to never give up on the future, no matter how bleak it seems.

Circumstances of the Great Depression made many adults feel that the economic hard times were somehow their fault. The 1920s— the Jazz Age — had brought a level of prosperity to Americans in general that had never existed before. Suddenly, due to economic factors both simple and complex, all this was taken away. People who had never known hunger or had to do without the basic necessities now found themselves without work or a true sense of purpose. To the youth of America, though, *Flash Gordon* showed that the American Dream might still be attainable. The comic strip and serials suggested that the disasters befalling Earth were not our fault, and that instead of feeling punished and subdued, we should press on. Flash and his companions showed us that determination and cooperation could solve enormous problems. For kids and imaginative adults it was just the kind of medicine to help swallow the bitter reality of a wrecked economy and impending war, make the best of it, and survive for another, better day. Even now, in a jaded and hardly more optimistic time, the *Flash Gordon* adventures have the power not just to excite and entertain us, but also to encourage us to hope, and do what it takes to create that better tomorrow.

Films Discussed

Flash Gordon; aka Rocketship Universal Pictures. Released April 6, 1936. 245 min. (13 episodes). Producer: Henry MacRae. Directors: Frederick Stephani and Ray Taylor (uncredited second unit). Screenplay: Basil Dickey, Ella O'Neill, George H. Plympton, Frederick Stephani, based on the comic strip by Alex Raymond. Directors of Photography: Jerry Ash, Richard Fryer. Art Director: Ralph Berger. Editors: Saul A. Goodkind, Louis Sackin, Alvin Todd, Edward Todd. Music: Clifford Vaughan. Electrical Effects: Norman Dewes. With Buster Crabbe, Jean Rogers, Charles Middleton, Priscilla Lawson and Frank Shannon. Available on Image Entertainment DVD.

Flash Gordon's Trip to Mars; aka Rocket Ship; Space Soldiers' Trip to Mars Universal Pictures. Released March 21, 1938. Approx. 260 min. (15 episodes). Producer: Barney A. Sarecky. Directors: Ford Beebe, Robert Hill, Frederick Stephani (uncredited). Screenplay: Herbert Dalmas, Norman S. Hall, Wyndham Gittens, Ray Trampe. Based on the comic strip by Alex Raymond. Director of Photography: Jerome Ash. Art Director: Ralph M. DeLacy. Editors: Joseph Gluck, Saul A. Goodkind, Louis Sacken and Alvin Todd. With Buster Crabbe, Jean Rogers, Charles Middleton, Frank Shannon, Beatrice Roberts, Donald Kerr and Richard Alexander. Available on Image Entertainment DVD.

Flash Gordon Conquers the Universe; aka Perils from the Planet Mongo; Purple Death from Outer Space Universal Pictures. Released March 3, 1940. Approx. 245

min. (12 episodes). Producer: Henry MacRae. Directors: Ford Beebe and Ray Taylor. Screenplay: George H. Plympton, Basil Dickey and Barry Shipman, based on the comic strip by Alex Raymond. Directors of Photography: Jerome Ash, William A. Sickner. Art Director: Harold H. MacArthur. Editors: Joseph Gluck, Saul A. Goodkind, Louis Sackin and Alvin Todd. With Buster Crabbe, Carol Hughes, Charles Middleton, Anne Gwynne, Frank Shannon and John Hamilton. Available on Image Entertainment DVD; VCI Home Video DVD.

5

Atomic City, Atomic World

DAVID J. HOGAN

The message was relentless, and it went this way: you are not safe anywhere. It could happen while you sleep, or as you splash with your family at the beach. It could happen at the minute of your birth, or as you fail from terminal illness. It could happen to your wife, your husband. It could happen to your children, your innocent children.

If luck is with you, you will barely be aware of it as it happens. A millisecond of yellow-white flash, perhaps, and then your body is vaporized and it will be as if you and the world you knew never existed. But if you are unlucky enough to be farther removed from the explosion, you will see the flash, hear the blast. You will be seared like an egg in a kiln. Your death will not be instantaneous, and it will be unbearably painful. The flesh will hang from your limbs in strips. If you are standing next to a streetlight, its shadow may be burned into your flesh. Your ears or fingers may melt. Your eyes may run down your face. You will enter hell.

Or perhaps you will be farther away still, and you will believe you have escaped, that you and your family will survive. And then, in a day or two, will come the nausea, the retching of blood, the hair falling from your head. Your very blood will become poison. If luck and mercy have ignored you altogether, you will have time to witness and contemplate the deaths of your loved ones.

Welcome to the Cold War.

The Real 1950s

The carefully tooled nostalgia offered by film and television of the past 25 years suggests that 1950 through 1959 — in fact, everything until November 22, 1963 — was a happy mélange of hot rods, roller-skating car hops, rock 'n' roll, letter sweaters, sturdy boys in crew cuts, and understanding, if amusingly square, parents. Politicians were benevolent. Estes Kefauver wore a coonskin cap. Adlai Stevenson was an intellectual, an egghead, and we still don't like that sort very much, but Stevenson at least had the easy grace to campaign with a hole in his shoe.

If you liked Ike—our avuncular, perpetually golfing president—you liked the system. You were protected. There was evil afoot elsewhere in the world, but your leaders looked out for you because they cared about you. The decade of real love, we're told today by the New Right, wasn't the 1960s, but the '50s. It was love that was honest and decent and American, in a decade of smiles and goodness. What did television's Superman stand for if not "truth, justice, and the American way"?

If you believe all of that, you've had your head in a hole. Nostalgia is sweet, but it's pernicious, too, because it distorts the historical record.

Eisenhower was a smiley kind of guy, and a considerably better president than is generally acknowledged. But he also came of age in the military tradition, which leavened his essential humanity with a nerveless pragmatism. When he addressed the troops on the eve of the Normandy invasion in 1944, he spoke of God and country and duty and nobility, but as he spoke he knew he was sending thousands of young men to gruesome deaths on a foreign beach. Ike exhorted them, he mourned for them—and he knowingly sent them to their doom. He was a practical man, and practicality exercised in the world of warfare and geopolitics looks a little chilly when viewed from the outside.

Eisenhower also was a good man, uncorrupted except by the menaces he had to face as a general and as president. He was decent enough even to disdain his vice president, Richard Nixon, a man who exemplified the opportunistic, unprincipled side of American political life.

Nixon came to Congress in 1946 by beating the incumbent, a straight arrow named Jerry Voorhis, with the "soft on Communism" club. Four years later, Nixon gained a Senate seat by describing his opponent, Congresswoman Helen Gahagan Douglas, as "the pink lady," referring not to her wardrobe but to her alleged Communist sympathies. In both of these elections, voters fell for Nixon's calumnies. They allowed themselves to be frightened. They voted for Nixon because he told them what they had already been told by others: the bogeyman was out there. He lived in Russia, and he had missiles.

HUAC Spooks Hollywood

Aggressive snooping by the House Un-American Activities Committee (HUAC) into Hollywood political activity and alleged Communist infiltration began in 1947, and scared the hell out of the film colony. The studios' business was to manufacture entertainment at a profit, and so to have top stars and executives called before the unsmiling homunculi of HUAC was pure misery. Larry Parks and other actors who did not answer questions about their pasts to the committee's satisfaction were blacklisted. Likewise Edward Dmytryk and other directors, and Dalton Trumbo and other screenwriters.

A few figures, such as Humphrey Bogart, were powerful enough to resist the committee and, in essence, tell it to go to hell, but even Bogie's power was limited, and he was later coerced into a public retraction of much of his criticism of the committee's motives and methods. And for every Bogart or Edward G. Robinson or Danny Kaye, there was a major star (the committee loved cooperative "major stars," because of their useful visibility) who spoke freely about "pinks" he had known. Robert Taylor, Gary Cooper, Adolphe Menjou — they ratted out coworkers and acquaintances, and were publicly thanked for their patriotism.

Studio executives, by nature experts at survival, knew what they had to do. No more pro–Russian pictures like 1943's *Mission to Moscow* (which got Jack Warner into trouble later with HUAC, and frustrated him no end because he had promised never to reveal that he had made the film at the request of President Roosevelt). Henceforth, Hollywood would take a firm, anti–Red line.

So the pictures came to American (and Allied) screens: *I Was a Communist for the FBI*, *I Married a Communist*, *Walk East on Beacon*, *My Son John*, *Big Jim McLain*, *Blood Alley*, *The Red Menace*, *The Iron Curtain*, and the delirious *Red Planet Mars*, in which God speaks from the red planet to denounce bolshevism.

No Laughing Matter

These are pretty amusing films (or disheartening, if you're in a philosophical frame of mind), artifacts that we now perceive as paranoiac. The 1991 dissolution of the Soviet Union only encourages our dismissal of the period's anti–Red hysteria. But that dismissal is too easy, and deeply misleading. HUAC was crass and opportunistic, but the fact remains that the postwar Communist threat was very real — not in the sense that the Soviet Union intended to destroy or even take over the USA (it had no such ambition), but in the sense of the covert and illegal wartime and postwar transfer of highly sensitive information that would allow the Soviets to quickly achieve military and political parity with the U.S.

The U.S.-USSR alliance of World War II existed strictly for convenience's sake. The two nations had a common enemy in Germany, but little else united them. Autocratic bolshevism had taken hold in Russia in 1917, and before that the nation had no tradition whatsoever of democracy. It had been a relatively minor player on the world stage in the early years of the twentieth century, losing a war to Japan in 1905, and bailing out of the Great War in 1917, soon after its radical left overthrew Czarist rule. The collectivist philosophy that came with the Communist revolution made a shambles of the USSR's already backward economy. This, coupled with an exhausted military, placed Russia at a potentially disastrous disadvantage.

Joseph Stalin's rise to Communist Party prominence and finally absolute power culminated in massive, murderous purges of teachers, intellectuals, clerics, military leaders, and scientists throughout the 1930s. Even as Stalin claimed to strengthen the USSR, he was weakening it and shaping its institutions into instruments of his own power.

Russia's surprising, thoroughly cynical 1939 alliance with Hitler's Germany went south two years later, when Hitler launched vast armies against the Ukraine and drove for Moscow. From 1941 until the spring of 1945, the Soviet Union shouldered the greater part of the Allied war effort against Germany. At places like Leningrad, Kursk, Rostov, Khimki and other Moscow suburbs, the Caucasus, and Stalingrad, the Red Army fought ferociously and sustained staggering losses. Soviet civilians, too, died in astonishing numbers. By the time Germany capitulated, at least 20 million Soviet soldiers and civilians had perished in what is still referred to in the former Soviet Union as the Great Patriotic War. In dramatic contrast, American deaths in Europe and the Pacific combined amounted to about 405,000, the vast majority of them military personnel.

The Alliance Ends

Stalin was resentful about the disparity of loss and also was keenly aware that the United States came out of World War II infinitely stronger than it went in. The country's vast natural resources, and skilled workers available to maintain and enlarge a sophisticated industrial sector, invigorated the U.S. economy, and returned money to workers' pockets. At war's end, those workers began to spend. America's industrial might, which had so recently produced tanks, planes, and bombs, now devoted itself to automobiles, washing machines, furniture, appliances, and housing materials. The American economy was reasonably robust in 1945; by 1950, it bestrode the world like a colossus. But Great Britain, a key U.S. ally and one of the war's winners, had bankrupted itself for the war effort. Rationing continued in Britain into the 1950s. The situation was no better on the Continent. And in the Soviet Union, where an entire generation of young men had been erased, and where bridges, factories, rail lines, and housing had been blown up or smashed flat, no relief was in sight. Stalin looked at the seemingly limitless—and growing—wealth of the United States, and he worried. America had the Bomb and he did not. The Soviet scientists sacrificed to purges in the 1930s were a significant loss, but then, Stalin knew something that Harry Truman didn't.

Espionage

In the early '40s a highly talented expatriate German physicist named Klaus Fuchs went to work in Britain on that nation's infant A-bomb program (which was shortly betrayed by Donald MacLean and other spies in the employ of the Soviets). By 1944 Fuchs had received security clearance to transfer to the American atomic-research facility at Los Alamos, New Mexico. There, in the midst of drum-tight security, Fuchs set to work, becoming privy to crucial secrets about the U.S. program to develop an atomic bomb. Fuchs did his work well and earned the respect of his peers.

Klaus Fuchs was a spy working for the Soviet Union.

Because of Fuchs and others at Los Alamos and in New York—David Greenglass, Harry Gold, Julius and Ethel Rosenberg—the Soviet Union had gained, by 1948, extensive knowledge about the Bomb program and the particulars of the weapon's theory and design. Throughout the war the U.S. worried about Japanese and German A-bomb programs (both of those belligerents had such programs, but were woefully off the mark); the real danger, the machinations of our Soviet "ally," went unrecognized.

Only when the Fuchs spy ring began to be uncovered in 1948–49 did the U.S. grasp the implications of what had happened. And then, in remote Kazakhstan on August 21, 1949 the Soviet Union successfully test-exploded an atomic device. The headlines sprouted blackly on front pages across America: REDS HAVE A-BOMB!

America and the rest of the free world understood that the war had not ended after all. It had simply taken a new form and a new direction, with a new enemy nation. Suddenly, Stalin and the USSR were more frightening than anything Hitler and Germany might have aspired to. Through connivance, and help from captured, second-rank German physicists, the Soviets had achieved apparent parity with the United States.

Atomic Cities

After 1945, all urban Americans lived in atomic cities. If your home was near a metropolis of any consequence, that city was on the USSR's target list. The list lay next to a red button, and the Reds, Washington wanted us to understand, would not hesitate to look at that list and press that button. But a nationwide panic — you know: looting, suicide, rape, murder, drunkenness, people literally running for the hills— would be bad, so although Americans had to be warned, they had to be reassured, too.

Of course, Washington knew that there was no practicable protection from atomic attack for masses of civilians but, in one of those governmental gestures that is at once calming and grotesquely misleading, Washington oversaw a glut of A-bomb safety films. (Many of these are collected in the intriguing 1982 documentary, *The Atomic Café*.) "Duck and cover," the exhortation of a peppy cartoon turtle, is one of the most famous and often-quoted. "When the bomb comes, do like Bobby does! Duck! And cover!" Bobby flings himself from his bicycle, does a tuck-and-roll into a gutter, and lives to watch *Howdy Doody* another day — that is, if Mr. Doody had the presence of mind to duck and cover.

The conclusion of what is perhaps the most absurd of these films finds the Average American Family in the basement shelter after the bomb has fallen. The shelter's a little dusty, but everybody's okay. Dad issues some calming, dad-like instructions, and adds, "Well, we can go upstairs in two or three hours and clean up."

Ponder on that for a moment. Your government was telling you to leave whatever pathetic shelter you may have devised and expose yourself to enough roentgens to give your *cancer* cancer.

The Atomic Movie

Given this level of deception, it's a matter of no small amazement that Paramount released *The Atomic City* (1952), a film that, in key ways, hews to the government

Mexican lobby card from *The Atomic City* (1952). Smiling from Los Alamos in the central image are (from left) Gene Barry, Lydia Clarke, Lee Aaker, Nancy Gates, and Michael Moore. Peripheral images suggest the danger and violence that will shortly germinate in and around the atomic city.

line, but that in others defies it and brings unexpected honesty to atomic politics. A lot of people seemed to have been inspired on this one: journeyman director Jerry Hopper; likeable journeyman actor Gene Barry; and a generally unheralded but top-flight screenwriter, Sydney Boehm, who had earlier scripted *The Undercover Man*, *Side Street*, *Mystery Street*, and *Union Station*, and who would go on to write *The Big Heat*, *Rogue Cop*, *Violent Saturday*, *Hell on Frisco Bay*, *Black Tuesday*, and *Seven Thieves*. Boehm's story and screenplay for *The Atomic City* was nominated for an Academy Award.

We're meant to understand from the film's earliest moments that atomic war is a poor option because, well, because we'll be killed. Tommy (Lee Aaker), young son of Los Alamos physicist Frank Addison (Gene Barry), is excited when a new television is delivered to their home on this tightly secured government facility. (Hopper filmed his exteriors on location at Los Alamos.) Suddenly, Tommy wants to be an electrician, and blurts, "If I grow up, I know what I'm going to do!" Delivered quickly, the line doesn't register with you for a beat, and when it does, you're instantly sobered. Here is an archetypal American ranch house, with a new TV and a happy boy, and the kid understands he may not grow up. Although his mother (Lydia Clarke) is concerned about the remark, to the boy it's natural, a no-brainer. His dad, a key contributor to the first Los Alamos bomb, carries on with his work, perfecting bigger and more apocalyptic bombs. Tommy's remark is an explicit reflection of the boy's understanding that he may one day be killed because of what his dad does for a living.

Later, Addison comes home in an agitated state because another physicist has been accidentally overexposed to gamma rays. Addison claims he can't say whether it's serious or not, but his expression and tone of voice spell doom. His colleague is a walking dead man. Addison knows it and so do we. The Los Alamos scientists perform dangerous, sensitive work, which is why the facility is patrolled by armored personnel carriers, horse-mounted soldiers, and sentries with dogs, and why even a face as familiar as Addison's is carefully checked against his ID as he enters the research area each morning.

For Tommy, the guns and soldiers are part of normal life. He happily waves to the MPs and they wave back. The soldiers' presence reflects reality, of course, but also is Cold War Hollywoodese for *Don't worry, you're safe, we're all safe.* But here's Tommy, aware at age six of his own possible extinction. Dialogue given to the mother reveals that 4,000 children live at Los Alamos. It's easy to make the connection: 4,000 kids know they are at a place that makes death, and that they may die. The subversive nature of this point of view, politically and dramatically, is eye opening.

The engine that propels *The Atomic City* is Tommy's kidnapping by Communist agents while the boy is on a school field trip to Santa Fe. Addison's subsequent encounters with a pair of gimlet-eyed FBI agents (Michael Moore and Milburn Stone) establish what is, ostensibly, the film's overarching theme: it is morally wrong to place millions of lives at risk in order to preserve the life of a single boy. The agents' priority is to flush the spies, not save Tommy. This is one of the most unsentimental observations of any Hollywood film of the 1950s. It assuredly is not part of the fantasy decade we know from *Happy Days* and *Grease.*

The agents will do what they can, in an incidental sort of way, to rescue Tommy, but they're not going to allow the enemy operatives to extort atomic secrets. Fortunately for Tommy, and our peace of mind, the spies are undone because of a fluke (a clever stroke by Boehm, which will go unrevealed here).

Boehm's script is smart and tight, clipping along in the brisk manner of his other films, mingling human drama with moral and philosophical issues. Dr. Addison's world was complex during the war; now, with his son in enemy hands and Addison's awareness that the atomic ransom will not be paid, the world is ugly and profoundly unforgiving. Because Addison applies his gifts to A-bomb research, he has made a deal with the devil (another quite subversive notion), and now must face the consequences. The reality of what he has devoted himself to hits him like a sledge, and he suddenly grasps the difference between abstract theory and reality. When he tries to explain his wife's feelings to one of the FBI investigators, he says, "To her, Tommy counts more than the millions. They're just numbers, but Tommy is very real." Spare and eloquent, the lines simultaneously condemn American selfishness and lack of empathy, and affirm the preciousness of life.

The subversive nature of *The Atomic City* continues. Although the FBI agents clearly state that their first loyalty is to the government (or, in Cold War parlance, the State), Addison is bound by no such constraints. Never once is he portrayed as anything less than an exemplary American, yet when he has an opportunity to beat information from a captured Commie stooge — information that will allow him to act recklessly and on his own — he takes it. Where the FBI will not act to save his boy, Addison will.

Stark Realism

The film's final third was shot on location at abandoned Puye (poo-yay) Indian cliff dwellings in the rocky New Mexico desert. It is here that the spies (among them blocky character player Bert Freed) have secreted Tommy, whom young Aaker plays as a stoic realist. He's not been mistreated, but he senses his life is drawing to a conclusion because the spies have realized that equations sent by Addison (without knowledge of the FBI) are useless. In a moment of small brilliance from Boehm and director Jerry Hopper, Addison and the FBI *see* the immediate danger to the boy when they burst into an empty Santa Fe house and discover a blackboard with Addison's garbage equations written out, erased, written again, and revealed as useless.

Leads are thin, and running out. In a lengthy, particularly effective sequence that recalls *Undercover Man* and many other police procedurals, agents in Los Angeles trail a petty criminal to the ballpark, where he passes information to a Communist spy without the FBI noticing. After it finally dawns on the G-men what has happened, the go-between is in the parking lot at his car, which explodes beneath him in a gout of flame when he turns the key. It's a fine, jump-in-your-seat moment that illustrates the harsh consequences of realpolitik.

The climax at the cliff dwellings is sharply effective, constructed from the blithe heartlessness of the spies (who are shown to be little different from the FBI in attitude and tactics); the rush to the site by Addison and the authorities, who are for a long time helpless to reach the top of the mesa; and Tommy's courage in the face of being entombed alive and, minutes later, hanging for his life from a cliff edge.

Hopper, whose career was mainly undistinguished and who did his best work for episodic television, made his feature-film debut here. It was a challenging assignment, particularly the enormous logistics involved in the cliff shoot. It's never easy to carry equipment to rugged locations, and Hopper also had to choreograph his cast, dozens of extras, and even a helicopter. Much of what precedes the climax is documentary-like, with a smart but purposely subdued visual style. When the FBI joins the investigation, the film's documentary feel increases, marked by much surveillance activity and radiophone talk between cars. The film comes to full dramatic and visual life at the cliff dwellings. Lighting by cinematographer Charles Lang is alternately fully sunlit and darkly noir-ish. Scenes inside the very tight, cave-like dwellings, where a novice director might be expected to falter, are excellent, with dramatic camera angles, judicious use of close-ups, and spot-on editing (by Archie Marshek) that Hitchcock would have envied.

The Atomic City was made during a period of intense political propaganda. What sort of propaganda does the film represent, and does it achieve its goal? Is it successful propaganda?

The Propaganda of Fear

The essence of effective political propaganda is twofold. First, it is just true enough that we take it seriously. Granted, propaganda is cheap shorthand that reduces complex issues to slogans and atrocity cartoons. It appeals to fear, xenophobia, and the brainless sort of pride that arises from the geographical accident of our births. We look at propaganda's grain of truth and see a boulder.

The second aspect of effective political propaganda is the demonization of the enemy. "They" are not like you. They do not look like you. If your life and nation exemplify the light, theirs exist in darkness.

They do not share your moral code. They do not honor your God. They have no God. They kill easily, without compunction or reason. They are accomplished torturers, more animal than human. They regard you as an obstacle in their path to conquest. They will rape your women and enslave your men. When they turn their dark gaze upon you, they see prey. They are monsters.

Naturally, there is a certain wisdom in destroying them before they destroy you.

And so we come to the nasty nub of propaganda and the emotions it engenders: it kills reason. It turns you into precisely what it claims the enemy to be. It coarsens your emotions and hardens your heart. Because it depicts the enemy as a thing, an abstraction, you are relieved of moral culpability. You become prepared to deal with the enemy with as much assurance of purpose as when you strike down a hornet's nest that hangs too close to your children's sandbox.

But even more significant is the way in which effective propaganda encourages you to abandon your personal interests, and the interests of your family, in order to elevate the interests of the State. This is known as "the greater good." You and yours, the propagandists tell you, are expendable. You can vanish with no harm done except to you, but the State must go on. It must be protected. You must do whatever you can to ensure the State's survival.

This is known as self-sacrifice.

The End Run

When *The Atomic City* was released, Hollywood was, as noted, good and scared. Ironically, it was the bullies of HUAC, not Communists, who were of immediate concern to studio bosses. Hollywood had always entertained, but now it had to placate, and it could do that easily. It had to calm HUAC and calm whichever citizens had swallowed HUAC's line and grown angry with the movie colony. HUAC's bullying, then, inadvertently produced an industry of toadies, rather than self-motivated patriots.

On the face of it, *The Atomic City* is just what HUAC wanted. It posits atomic extortion by Communist spies. The spies are thwarted. Yet as we've seen, there is some trickiness afoot.

Addison takes it upon himself to send junk equations to the kidnappers, hoping to buy time for his son. But junk to Addison may not be junk to the enemy. How does Addison know which sorts of information the enemy lacks? Bomb research is an intricate puzzle, and a key piece — dross to Addison but gold to the Communists— may be among Addison's figures. In essence, Addison puts the nation at risk for his son. A fine and dramatically sound sentiment, but hardly one that would please HUAC or the rest of Washington.

The film establishes that our national law-enforcement arm, the FBI, will not beat a suspect in order to gain information. This is successfully propagandistic because it allows us to believe that we are nobler than the enemy. On the other hand, it suggests a weakness that runs counter to Washington's pose of being on top of things. When crucial information about the kidnapping is needed, the FBI is useless; the information is gleaned by a decision made by a single citizen. Addison's aggressive action runs counter to the FBI agents' message about single lives being insignificant in the context of millions. In the dim interrogation room, the FBI and the symbolic millions it represents are absent, ineffectual. It is the Man Alone (a recurring figure, by the way, in films written by Boehm) who makes the difference.

The FBI won't mess up a Commie's face, but the agency and the Communists exist on the same intellectual plane. The FBI men are efficient automatons, bereft of emotion, functioning only with cold reason. If the pod people of the later *Invasion of the Body Snatchers* had entered government service, they would have been these FBI agents.

Emotionlessness isn't the American model, and if anyone had looked at *The Atomic City* carefully, Boehm and Hopper's agenda would have been exposed.

That the FBI shows up at the cliff dwellings at all isn't due to solid investigative work or thinking outside the box or anything like that. They show up because of sheer happenstance, a freak (but perfectly logical) tip-off that tells them where the boy is being held. In this way, too, the film subverts the national propaganda agenda, suggesting that the FBI is staffed not by geniuses, but rather by well-meaning dimwits who make too many fundamental mistakes (such as failing to notice the passed paper at the ballpark), and whose bacon is saved by dumb luck.

The military comes off looking no wiser, for although Los Alamos is ringed with sturdy, heavily armed soldiers, the sons and daughters of scientists are permitted to have a holiday in Santa Fe accompanied only by a slender young schoolteacher. Addison is examined like a stranger every morning at the entrance to the lab, but his kid is allowed to disappear more easily than a set of car keys. Clearly, the possibility of kidnapping, extortion, and subsequent atomic doomsday had occurred to no one.

Finally, the script explicitly paints the Los Alamos community as an unpleasant place to live. When Addison's wife frets about the fences and gates, the constant presence of soldiers, and the treeless isolation, Addison lamely counters with something about the community grade school, and the shopping in Santa Fe. Even the man who delivers the Addisons' TV at the beginning of the film remarks on the creepiness of the place.

Barry, Aaker, and Clarke: The nuclear family threatened by nuclear technology and the heartless machinations of the Cold War.

What does Mrs. Addison's unhappiness signify? Well, it signifies the self-sacrifice we talked about, the notion of giving over comfort and convenience in order to serve the state. However, it also signifies the state's dearth of emotional values and its expectation that people live like captives. In a more realistic film, Mrs. Addison would drink vodka and pop Valium all day, and the professor would drag himself home at night and get quietly looped in front of that new television. Tommy would be a nervous wreck, worriedly listening to his parents' arguments when their angry voices cut through his closed bedroom door.

None of that happens in this movie, but it's clear that, with a push, it could; and not the big push of kidnapping, either, but the small push of the grind of everyday life in an alien, inhospitable place.

In the end, we must return to the TV deliveryman, who is played by comic actor Jerry Hausner with a neat edge of apprehension and confusion. If a surrogate for the audience exists in *The Atomic City,* it is this plain fellow who brings the television — that is, the larger, outside world — to the Addisons. Blinded by neither zealotry nor expediency, he sees the atomic city for what it is. You can read it on his face: *How can they live like this?*

He eyes the fences and soldiers and guns and he sees the accoutrements of life as practiced by the Soviet Union. This is the ultimate, subtly brilliant inversion of this ostensibly HUAC-friendly film: it tells us that we are destroying ourselves and are in freefall to the level of the demons our propaganda has created for us.

Film Discussed

The Atomic City Paramount Pictures. Released May 1, 1952. 85 min. Producer: Jerry Sistrom. Director: Jerry Hopper. Story & Screenplay: Sydney Boehm. Director of Photography: Charles Lang. Editor: Archie Marshek. Music: Leith Stevens. Art Directors: Hal Pereira and Al Roelofs. Special Effects: Gordon Jennings. Process Photography: Farciot Edouart. With Gene Barry, Lydia Clarke, Lee Aaker, Michael Moore, Nancy Gates, Milburn Stone, Bert Freed, Jerry Hausner, Frank Cady and Olan Soule. Available on Paramount/Gateway VHS home video.

6

Where Do Little Green Men Come From? A Speculative Look at the Origins of a Pop Culture Icon

VINCENT DI FATE

Your darkened bedroom, usually a place of familiar comfort, takes on a strange and ominous aspect on this night as you descend slowly into sleep. You doze off briefly, then feel a sudden surge of wakefulness prompting you to rise out of bed. But you are somehow powerless to move. As you lie there in an odd state of paralysis, you see a dark presence moving about the room. It is a fearsome humanoid creature of diminutive size and, as it creeps up to your bedside, it extends slender, prehensile fingers toward you, clutching at your throat. You find yourself gasping for breath, as though a terrible weight has been placed on your chest. By morning the creature will have fled, but you will be left with the terrible impression of some horrific event that you now only half remember.

For increasing numbers of modern persons, these events can only be rationalized as alien abductions—a bizarre but growing phenomenon that seems to have taken root in American popular culture sometime in the latter half of the twentieth century. If the statistics offered by a controversial 1992 Roper poll can be believed, an astonishing 4 million residents of the United States alone claim to have been abducted by inquisitive, furtive extraterrestrials.

Strange visitors from outer space and the fabulous vehicles in which they ply the skies of planet Earth have, like many other fantastic concepts, long been fixtures of science fiction literature. Their ships—what are popularly known in our time as flying saucers or UFOs (for Unidentified Flying Objects) may well have initially become a component of our mass consciousness through the motion picture serials, which were the first broadly popular venue for them beyond the medium of print.

In 1950 the Columbia serial *Atom Man Versus Superman* introduced a flying saucer into its thirteenth episode — albeit by means of cartoon cel animation. At about the same time the first feature-length film to deal with the subject, Mikel Conrad's independently produced *The Flying Saucer* (1950), went into limited release. In both instances the craft in question were of local manufacture and were not of otherworldly origin, reflecting a widely held opinion about UFOs at the time.

There are earlier examples of disc-shaped craft in the serials, of course: the gyroships of the lion men in the 1936 Universal serial *Flash Gordon*; the bat-winged planes of Republic's *G-Men Versus the Black Dragon* (1943) — in this instance they were attributed to America's wartime foe the Japanese, but the same bat-winged props resurfaced in 1950 as objects of alien fabrication in another Republic serial entitled *Flying Disc Men from Mars*. Before 1950, however, these unusual ships were never referred to in the movies as flying saucers, because the term simply didn't exist prior to June 25, 1947.

The term "flying saucer" is attributed to journalist Bill Bequette, then a reporter for *The East Oregonian*, a newspaper based in Pendleton, Oregon. Bequette used the term while reporting a UFO sighting made the previous day by businessman and pilot Kenneth Arnold. It was the first such sighting of the post–World War II era to receive national attention and it fired the popular imagination. At about 3 PM Pacific Time on June 24, 1947, Arnold saw nine silvery discs flying at a tremendous speed in a reverse echelon formation over the peaks of Mount Rainier, Washington, while he was en route by plane from Chehalis to Yakima. Reports of the event made the national newspapers the following day and touched off a wave of UFO sightings that became a subject of controversy throughout the late 1940s and well into the 1950s. Arnold described the motion of the objects as that of "a saucer ... if you skipped it across water."

In his 1952 book *The Coming of the Flying Saucers* (Palmer and Arnold, self-published), coauthored with *Fate* magazine editor Raymond A. Palmer, Arnold clarified further that the objects were not completely round like saucers, but were actually crescent shaped. Whatever shape they were and whatever their purposes may have been, flying saucers were among the hot topics of the day. Early speculation favored their being secret experimental aircraft of either the U.S. government or of another earthly power.

That was indeed the theme of the feature-length motion picture *The Flying Saucer*, actor Mikel Conrad's low-budget film that began a protracted two-year gestation shortly after the Arnold sighting made headlines. Conrad came up with the idea, coauthored the script with Howard Irving Young, and produced, directed, and starred in the film as secret agent Mike Trent. It is ultimately revealed in the film that the extraordinary craft has been specifically designed to deliver the atomic bomb and is the invention of reclusive scientist Carl Lawton (Roy Engel), who at one point is abducted by Soviet agents eager to appropriate the technology for their own sinister purposes. In a publicity stunt intended to promote the film, Conrad claimed that the feature contained actual UFO footage that he had photographed himself sometime earlier during a junket to Alaska, but that had been censored by the U.S. government. This was duly reported by the press, then retracted by Conrad in late 1949, just prior to the film's limited theatrical release in January 1950.

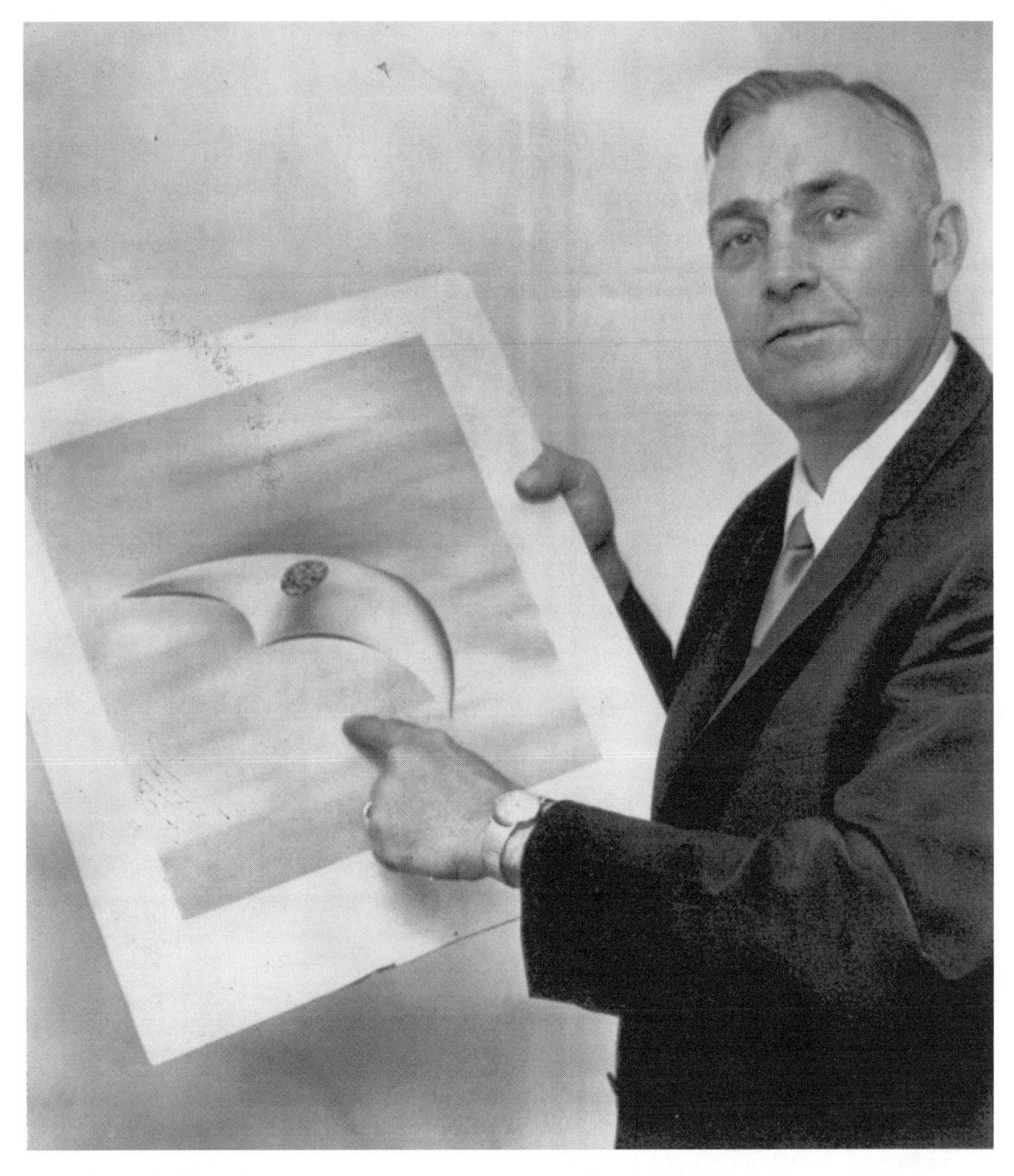

Some 19 years after his history-making 1947 sighting of nine silvery discs flying in formation over Mount Rainier in the Cascade Mountains of Washington, pilot Kenneth Arnold shows a detailed drawing of a crescent-shaped craft. "Flying saucers," fears of subversive infiltration, and other Cold War anxieties were preoccupations of SF films of the mid-twentieth century.

The coalescing of the American science fiction movie into a distinctive genre with its own unique iconography began in 1950 and was largely a matter of coincidental timing and the assimilation of topical ideas and icons from other media—especially print. UFOs, for example, and the idea that they might be interplanetary craft under intelligent, nonhuman control, were quickly absorbed into the subject

Playboy and secret agent Mike Trent (Mikel Conrad) lets loose with a double uppercut to get free of Communist spies intent on using a flying saucer to deliver an atomic bomb, in Conrad's vanity production *The Flying Saucer* (1950).

matter of these films. Regardless of the realities of the so-called flying saucers, many psychologists saw a link between them and the broader scheme of global affairs at the end of World War II. In an effort to account in part for the flying saucer phenomenon, government spokespersons offered the possibility that some UFO witnesses were suffering from a form of mass hysteria induced by anxiety over international tensions.

Immediately following the end of World War II relations began to deteriorate between the United States and its wartime ally, the Soviet Union. Ideologically the two nations were at odds, and disagreements over the disposition of postwar Europe, and particularly of Germany, led to a series of confrontations. The conflict crystallized with the Berlin airlift in 1948 and culminated in the building of the Berlin Wall in 1961, which symbolized what had long been a reality, the division of Germany into two nations, East and West. This preoccupation with Germany was part of a broader strategy by the Soviets to limit their vulnerability to invasion from the west by creating a buffer of client states throughout Eastern Europe.

Further heightening international tensions was the fact that the U.S. (with some early assistance from Britain) had developed the atomic bomb in secret, which it used against Japan in the closing days of the war and which it was unwilling to share

Red spy Col. Marikoff (Lester Sharpe) is about to be crushed in an Alaskan ice cave at the climax of *The Flying Saucer.*

with some of its allies— particularly the Soviets. With the detection of radiation from the test detonation of the Soviet Union's first atomic device in the summer of 1949, it had become clear that the Soviet nuclear arms program had been built on an elaborate network of espionage to steal atomic secrets from the United States. This tension between the two postwar superpowers resulted in the precarious Cold War, which lasted for more than 40 years.

Even before the existence of the Soviet spy network was known, Wisconsin senator Joseph R. McCarthy (1909–1957) leveled accusations against the U.S. State Department, the army, and other government agencies alleging that they'd been infiltrated by individuals sympathetic to the Communist cause. Beginning in 1950 and spanning a period of a little more than four years, McCarthy succeeded in exercising personal veto power over the hiring and firing of employees at the State Department. He also influenced U.S. foreign policy, drove many of his political foes out of office, accused presidents Harry S Truman and Dwight D. Eisenhower of treason, and succeeded in creating an aura of distrust within American society that led to the ruination of thousands of innocent lives. Thus, UFOs, the Cold War, and the Communist witch-hunts became the grist for a new era of Hollywood movies in which the SF genre was to play a pivotal role.

The most significant component of Kenneth Arnold's 1947 UFO sighting was the speed at which the reported objects were traveling. During the incident Arnold noted the time of day on his flight map, the location of his plane, and the apparent position of the discs as they soared among the snow-clad peaks of Mount Rainier. In the minute and 42 seconds of the sighting the discs had apparently traveled a remarkable 47 miles. Arnold was reasonably certain of this as, at one point, the objects passed behind a mountain peak, thus establishing a reliable land reference.

For the discs to be visible to Arnold at a distance of 20 to 25 miles, as he believed, they would have had to occupy at least two degrees of arc; less than that and they would have been too small for the naked eye to perceive. Based on this fact, investigators established the minimum size of the objects as 210 feet in length (at the time of his initial report, Arnold incorrectly estimated that they were between 45 and 50 feet long).

Given his distance from them, the span covered in their flight and the short duration of the sighting, the speed of the discs was calculated to have been an astonishing 1,700 miles per hour. In 1947, and unknown to the world at large, the fastest-moving piloted, manmade vehicle was the Bell X-1. On October 17, nearly four months after the Arnold sighting, U.S. Air Force captain Chuck Yeager flew the X-1, a rocket-powered airplane, to a speed of 760 miles per hour — approximately 20 miles per hour faster than the speed of sound.

Further characterizing the unusual nature of the Arnold sighting was the objects' ostensible maneuverability. Capable of veering and banking at high speeds, the aerodynamic resistance to which the discs were subject would have caused earthly metals to disintegrate; not to mention the effect these same forces would have exerted on a human occupant. Although the idea of secret experimental aircraft seemed at first to be the most likely explanation, it eventually became clear that this interpretation was inadequate to explain the Arnold encounter and the rash of similar sightings that soon followed. By 1950 the notion that UFOs were the spacecraft of visitors from other worlds, though seeming plausible to relatively few, had become entrenched in the popular culture.

Alien visitors were not new to SF literature. As far back as just before the turn of the twentieth century, through the works of artists such as Warwick Waterman Goble (1862–1943), Paul Hardy (1862–?), and John Frederick Thomas Jane (1865–1916), even the cultural mainstream had been afforded a glimpse of visiting armadas from outer space in the form of numerous magazine and book illustrations. With the 1923 release of W. W. Hodkinson's three-dimensional film *Radio-Mania* (also known as *M.A.R.S.*, *The Man from Mars,* and *Mars Calling*), the mass audience was further exposed to what seemed a new archetype — the large-headed, humanoid alien. The 1938 Universal serial *Flash Gordon's Trip to Mars* would, however briefly, also show us native Martians similarly endowed with enlarged craniums.

Three feature-length films about visiting aliens were released in 1951, very near the start of the 1950s science fiction movie cycle. All of these extraterrestrials arrived on Earth via spaceships of one sort or another during a time when flying saucers were much in evidence in the national headlines. Two of them, Howard Hawks's *The Thing from Another World* and Robert Wise's *The Day the Earth Stood Still,* were immediately lauded for their quality and are remembered today as classics. The third, Edgar Ulmer's minutely budgeted yet atmospheric *The Man from Planet X,* was quickly dis-

This impressive early depiction of large-headed, big-eyed humanoids living on Mars was painted by W.R. Leigh to illustrate a speculative article by H.G. Wells in a 1907 issue of *Cosmopolitan*.

missed by critics. Yet in spite of its relative obscurity it is far more historically significant and influential on American popular culture than has been previously acknowledged.

Despite the fact that it was the last of the three films to go into production, *The Man from Planet X* was the first to find its way into theaters. Its screening in San Francisco in March 1951 (fully a month before the premiere of Hawks's *The Thing*

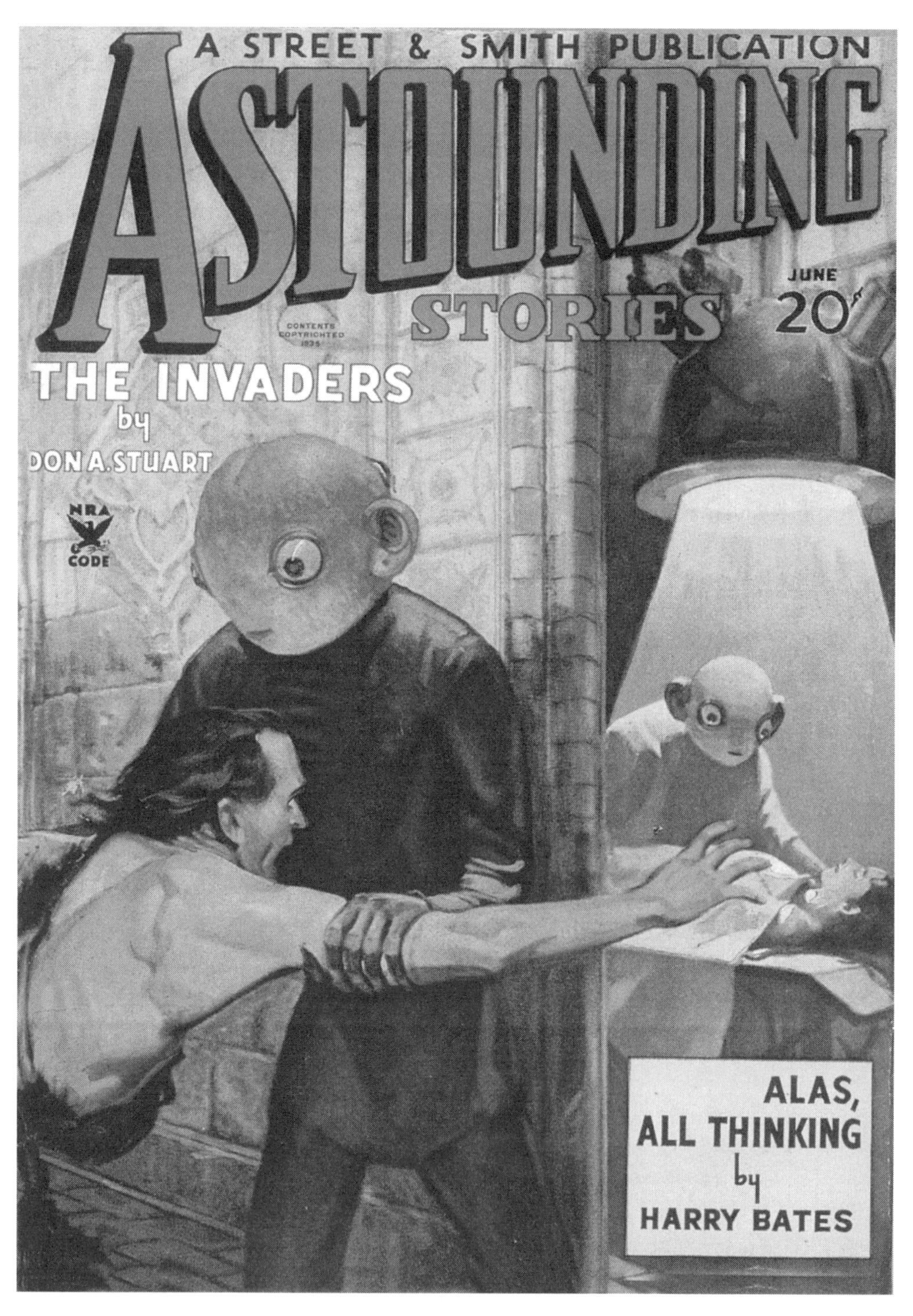

During the 1930s and '40s, SF pulps had a fascination with bug-eyed aliens with large heads. This Howard V. Brown cover painting for the June 1935 issue of *Astounding Stories* illustrates a scene from "The Invaders," a story written by John W. Campbell, Jr., under the author's "Don A. Stuart" pseudonym. As Stuart, Campbell wrote "Who Goes There?" which inspired Howard Hawks's 1951 thriller, *The Thing from Another World*, and a 1982 adaptation directed by John Carpenter.

and a month prior to its own general release) established it as the world's first feature-length alien invasion film. Its alien, with its large, distorted head, swollen eyes, and childlike body, is one of the seminal film portrayals of a "gray," and further establishes these physical characteristics of the alien archetype. Although the creature's face is actually green, its skin is described in the on-screen dialogue as being "shiny as a new shilling." The fact that the movie was photographed in black and white makes its skin color ultimately irrelevant for the man from Planet X is, quite literally, a "gray" in the minds of those who've seen it. David Annan takes this idea a step further in his book *Movie Fantastic: Beyond the Dream Machine*:

> Because Mexico is, indeed, the nearest country with an ancient civilization close to Hollywood, the art of the pre–Colombians has much influenced the look of fantasy films. It may be rare to find the most famous of the jade Mayan death masks actually reproduced. But the fetal look of the early civilizations of Veracruz and the jaguar-gods of the Olmecs have come back to haunt our science-fiction. The art of old civilizations often embodies the archetypes of mankind now reproduced for mass fantasies.*

As to the idea of extraterrestrials possessing childlike physical characteristics, UFO researcher Michael Grosso suggests that anxiety about the impending New Age haunts Western society. He notes that UFO abductees consistently describe their captors as appearing fetus-like, with enlarged heads, bulging eyes, and sickly, emaciated bodies that resemble the news photographs of children from countries ravaged by war and famine. He further suggests that the Western world, with its prodigality and its excesses, might harbor guilt over its failure to care for the children of the world.† For whatever motives, conscious or otherwise, the gray has been elevated to a cultural icon. *The Man from Planet X* is almost certainly the first example of this archetype to emerge from motion pictures during the flying saucer craze of the 1950s, thus making the unequivocal connection of the archetype to the concept of UFOs and visiting aliens.

The Man from Planet X was directed by Edgar G. Ulmer (1904–1972), a now-celebrated auteur who labored at the most disreputable end of Hollywood's notorious Poverty Row. Many of his most interesting films were made during the 1940s for Leon Fromkess at the Producers Releasing Corporation (PRC), the lowest of the low-end studios, and were typically shot in a week or less, with budgets that seldom exceeded

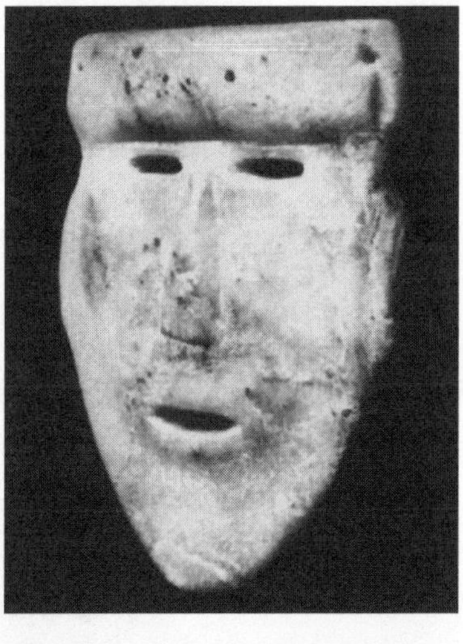

This pre–Columbian stone mask created c. AD 900 in Vera Cruz, Mexico, is offered by writer David Annan as evidence of the influence of Native American mythology on modern fantastic cinema. The features bear an unmistakable resemblance to the face of *The Man from Planet X* (1951).

*David Annan, *Movie Fantastic: Beyond the Dream Machine* (Bounty Books, 1974), 16–17.

†Michael Grosso, "UFOs and the Myth of a New Age," *Revision, Journal of Consciousness and Change* 11, no. 3 (winter 1989), 1.

$10,000. Though still something of an acquired taste, Ulmer's dark visions have been embraced by a small but avid cult following, mainly for his disturbing PRC film noir classic *Detour* (1945) and for the historically significant *The Man from Planet X*. His most legitimate film, *The Black Cat* (1934), was made for Universal Pictures as a vehicle for the teaming of Boris Karloff and Bela Lugosi. It claims some connection to the famous short story by Edgar Allan Poe but is in actuality a grim though artfully told tale of Satanism and murderous depravity.

The Man from Planet X is a creepy, atmospheric little film that in some ways is more gothic horror than SF. An unknown planet enters the solar system on an alarming path toward Earth. Newspaperman John Lawrence (Robert Clarke) heads for the fog-bound island of Burrey in the Orkneys to cover the story because the island will be the location to which the fugitive planet will come closest in its passage through space. Lawrence, his wartime acquaintance Professor Elliot (Raymond Bond), Elliot's pretty daughter Enid (Margaret Field, the mother of Academy Award–winning actress Sally Field) and Elliot's associate, the ambitious and sinister Dr. Mears (William Schallert), soon come face to face with a grotesque, gnome-like creature (Pat Goldin) who has arrived on Earth from Planet X via a spherical spaceship.

Mears attempts to communicate with the creature using mathematics but, when

Enid (Margaret Field) comes face to face with an inscrutable space alien (Pat Goldin) in Edgar Ulmer's moody and atmospheric *The Man from Planet X* (1951). Note the facial resemblance of the alien to the Mexican stone mask on the previous page.

unobserved, resorts to physical cruelty to extract information about the rogue world's advanced science. The creature eventually escapes, kidnaps Enid and professors Elliot and Mears, and begins hypnotizing the villagers in order to create a workforce to prepare the desolate moors for the arrival of an invading army from his home world.

The theme of alien-controlled human hosts had surfaced for the first time some eight years earlier in the Republic serial *The Purple Monster Strikes* (1943), but *The Man from Planet X* is the first feature-length film to make use of the idea. Ulmer's picture played in theaters through the late winter and early spring of 1951, concurrent with the U.S. House Un-American Activities Committee (HUAC) investigations into Communist infiltration of American society. It would be in circumstances like these, the somewhat comforting insulation of a fantasy, that film audiences would consider the unthinkable, while on the screen actors would symbolically play out the audiences' worst fears of the Cold War.

Although a United Artists release, *The Man from Planet X* was shot on small but impressive sets situated on the RKO-Pathé sound stage that were left over from the 1948 production of *Joan of Arc*. To achieve many of the atmospheric scenic views of the fog-bound moors, a miniature was constructed based on a design by Ulmer and executed by Howard Weeks, who, with Andy Anderson, created the film's limited special effects. Ulmer also produced a charcoal sketch showing an upward-angled view of the broch, a medieval turret in which much of the action takes place. The drawing, presumably intended as a guide for an eventual matte painting, was used as an insert in the completed film and was never replaced. The insert is perhaps the movie's weakest and least convincing visual element — and this, in a film about little green men and an invasion from a runaway planet.

Ulmer flooded the sound stage with fog to camouflage the Spartan sets and to generate atmosphere. In an interview appearing in *Filmfax* some 46 years after the film's release, actress Margaret Field recalled,

> The sets for *The Man from Planet X* were quite small, but were very impressive to work on. In the scenes that had us walking out to the spaceship and on the moors, they built large rocks and put them around to disguise the smoke or mist machines they were using. They laid in a lot of this mist and I remember clearly that it was difficult to work because it would get into your throat and irritate us all. It was also hard to see where you were walking. It was so bad that we would have to stop at times and all go outside and take deep breaths.
>
> ... The spaceship that was built was one complete structure and was closed all around. It was not just a facade. I remember my scenes where I'm lured out onto the moors and I walk completely around it; it was an interesting prop and unique to the other spaceship-styled flying saucers that came after it in other science fiction films.*

J. Hoberman, a film critic for *The Village Voice*, had this to say about Ulmer's visual style: "Ulmer infused his productions with a surplus of craft. Far from being artless, Ulmer was, if anything, too arty. He cluttered his backgrounds with shrewdly

*Paul and Donna Parla, "The Woman from Planet X: An Interview with Margaret Field," *Filmfax*, no. 58 (1996), 72.

Enid on the desolate moor with her father (Raymond Bond), who has been exposed to a hypnotic ray emanating from the alien's bathysphere-shaped ship. The notion of alien subversion of human will is common to many alien and alien-abduction stories.

placed bric-a-brac, contrived to dapple the most barren set with shadows, varied angles and forced perspectives and created 'atmosphere' with a vengeance — no director ever made more adroit use of smoke pots and fog machines."*

Like so many others in the motion picture industry who played a defining role in the development of fantastic films, the Vienna-born Ulmer had an extensive background in art. Prior to assuming responsibilities as a director he worked in art departments on such silent classics as *Das Kabinett des Dr. Caligari* (1919), Paul Wegener's *Der Golem* (1920), F.W. Murnau's *Nosferatu* (1922), Lang's *Metropolis* (1927) and the Universal productions of *The Hunchback of Notre Dame* (1923) and *The Phantom of the Opera* (1925), both starring the legendary Lon Chaney, Sr.

Ship and creature designs seen in *The Man from Planet X* were created collaboratively by Ulmer and the film's art director, the Italian-born Angelo Scibetta. Scibetta had worked on several of Ulmer's earlier films. The 12-foot-tall spaceship was built under the supervision of head prop man Rudy Butler in the Hal Roach Studio's prop department. Construction of the creature mask and costume was overseen by Howard Weeks in the studio's prop and effects shop. Weeks would later design, build,

*J. Hoberman, "The Films of Edgar Ulmer," *The Village Voice*, August 5, 1980, C-5, 1.

and operate the notorious rat-bat-spider-crab creature, a scowling marionette, for Sid Pink's ultra-low budget SF outing *The Angry Red Planet* (1959).

The story and script for *The Man from Planet X* were the work of the film's producers, Jack Pollexfen and Aubrey Wisberg, and were inspired by the then-current rash of UFO sightings. Pollexfen and Wisberg would also work collaboratively as writers and producers of SF movies over the next two years, cranking out *Captive Women* (1952), *The Neanderthal Man* (1953) and *Port Sinister* (1953). Creative differences caused the partnership to dissolve. Pollexfen, on his own, later produced and directed *The Indestructible Man* (1956), a vehicle for the aging Lon Chaney, Jr., and an unofficial remake of Chaney Jr.'s first feature-length SF/horror film, *Man-Made Monster* (1941). As with Pollexfen's collaborations with Wisberg, *The Indestructible Man* was produced independently and at very little cost.

Once casually dismissed as just one among many low-budget science fiction films of the 1950s, *Invaders from Mars* (1953) now enjoys a large cult following and is regarded by many psychologists and social historians as a mirror of the cultural anxieties of its time. Dr. Kenneth Ring, a professor of psychology at the University of Connecticut and one of the world's foremost researchers in the field of near death experiences (NDEs) and UFO encounters (UFOEs), notes the strong similarities between the events depicted in the film and the now famous 1961 UFO abduction case of Betty and Barney Hill. Under hypnosis the Hills recounted that they had been taken aboard a flying saucer and subjected to a rigorous physical examination by big-eyed, humanoid aliens. Betty claimed that at one point during their encounter a sharp metal object was inserted into her body. Since the publicizing of that famous case in the late 1960s, many individuals who believe that they've been abducted and taken aboard alien spacecraft have described experiences that are virtually identical to that of the Hills. Although there is little physical evidence to support these claims, most purported abductees describe having small metal devices implanted in their bodies during a rigorous physical examination. In the motion picture *Invaders from Mars*, humans are taken aboard a flying saucer against their will, placed on an examination table and implanted with small metal control devices that are inserted at the base of their skulls. According to Dr. Ring, since all UFO abductions share these essential details with little deviation and the Hill case itself so closely follows the events portrayed in *Invaders from Mars*, it is reasonable to believe that the film may have initially suggested the basic alien abduction scenario.

The Hill case received national attention with the publication of John G. Fuller's account of the abduction, *The Interrupted Journey* (Dial Press, 1966). Extracts were serialized in *Look* during 1966–67. There also was a 1975 made-for-TV movie about the case titled *The UFO Incident.* After it aired, the number of alien abduction claims rose sharply. According to Dr. Ring, it might also be possible that the film reflects some deeply seated racial memory — one that may ultimately have nothing whatever to do with visiting extraterrestrials. Whatever the merits of these observations, there is little question that at the time of its release, *Invaders from Mars* tapped into a number of topical anxieties.

The main plot of *Invaders from Mars* is bracketed by a framing device, the beginning and end of which are virtually identical. On first viewing, the film seems deceptively naïve and childlike; the entire production possesses a dreamlike quality. It also presents a spare stylization in its overall production design. These elements of unreality become progressively more evident as the story unfolds. This is mainly the doing of the film's director, William Cameron Menzies (1896–1957), who was a revered figure in motion picture production design, and of its original screenwriter, John Tucker Battle (1902–1962). Angered by the addition of the story frame and a significant change to the script's ending making it all a dream, Battle had his name removed from the screen credits. Sole credit for the screenplay was given to writer Richard Blake, who did, at most, only minor revisions to Battle's text and added the story frame in collaboration with Menzies.

Prior to his involvement in film, Menzies was trained as a painter by the illustrious Robert Henri at New York's Art Students League and by the noted artist and illustrator Harvey Dunn at his private art school in Leonia, New Jersey. Menzies directed only a handful of films over his 30-odd-year career, all of which contain strong elements of fantasy and which he designed as well as directed. Perhaps his best-known achievement purely in the role of production designer was for David O. Selznick's *Gone with the Wind* (MGM, 1939), for which he received a special Academy Award. This was not his first Academy Award; he'd received another — the first

The parents who are not parents: David (Jimmy Hunt) knows that his folks (Leif Erickson and Hillary Brooke) are under alien control in William Cameron Menzies's stylish and disturbing *Invaders from Mars* (1953). The boy's ally is Dr. Blake (Helena Carter).

A detail of a drawing by Hans Wessolowski for the Oliver Saari story "Two Sane Men," which appeared in the June 1937 issue of *Astounding Stories*. The illustration inspired John Tucker Battle, the screenwriter of *Invaders from Mars*, when he described the film's "Martian Intelligence" and the interior of the alien spaceship.

ever given for production design—for two films, *Tempest* and *The Dove*, both released by United Artists in 1927.

Invaders from Mars begins with 12-year-old David MacLean (Jimmy Hunt) witnessing the landing of a flying saucer in a sand pit behind his home. David's parents and other trusted members of the community are subsequently dragged underground and implanted with control devices. As alien surrogates, they engage in the sabotage of a secret government project to develop an atomic-powered rocket ship.

Mars is a dying world and the highly evolved but physically feeble Martians have taken to living in space-borne mother ships. The Martians have bred a race of synthetic humanoids—powerful, mindlessly obedient minions—to do their physical labor. These blank-faced, bulbous-eyed creatures of great size lope about in subterranean passageways built beneath the sand, supplementing the efforts of the controlled humans above.

At the film's conclusion, David and Dr. Patricia Blake (Helena Carter), a psychologist who has taken a kindly interest in the boy, are dragged into the Martian netherworld of subterranean tunnels. The two earthlings are later interrogated aboard the hidden ship, but are uncooperative. Dr. Blake is brought before the Martian Intelligence, a being with an immense, brontocephalic cranium and an atrophied body with frail, tentacle-like appendages. The creature is so physically feeble

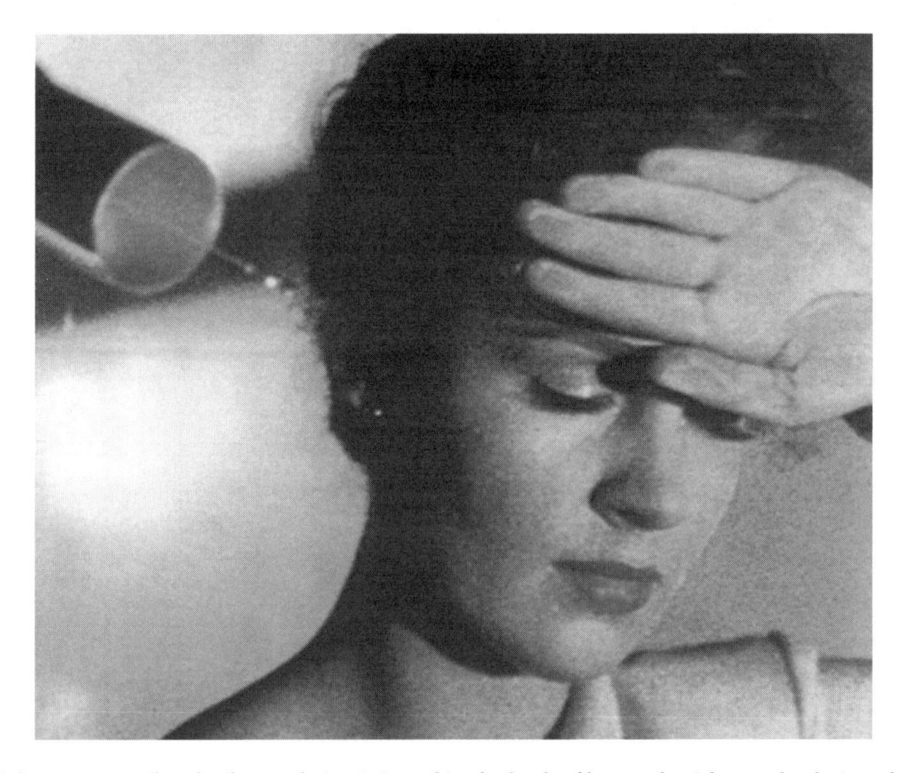

Blake comes perilously close to being injected in the back of her neck with a probe designed to strip her of her personality and force her will to that of the invaders. Intrusive, often horrifically painful violations of the human body are elements of many tales of alien abduction.

that it must live in a protective bubble. The Martian telepathically instructs its minions to prepare Dr. Blake for the insertion of a control device. The mutants place her face down on a glass table. A gleaming X-shaped needle descends, spinning toward the base of Dr. Blake's skull. Before the device can be implanted, however, army troops above locate the saucer and blast their way underground to rescue the captured humans. Explosives are hurriedly placed in the ship and the humans flee. Key events of the story are replayed in sequence in an accelerated montage, then repeated in reverse order as David runs for safety against this streaming tapestry of images. When the explosives detonate, David awakens suddenly to find that it has all been a horrible dream. Tucked safely back in bed by his parents, the boy awakens a few hours later to again observe the landing of the flying saucer, signaling that the nightmare is about to become real.

Despite its popularity during the 1950s, it was nearly two decades before SF cinema was taken seriously enough for film historians and critics to note the parallels between the Red Scare of the 1950s and the recurrent theme of alien possession in these films. *Invaders from Mars* was among the first SF movies to use the theme (the first, as noted, was Ulmer's *The Man from Planet X*), but it should be noted that Don

Don Siegel's terrifying, philosophically dark tale of alien takeover, *Invasion of the Body Snatchers* (1956), proposes that although there are no little green men, displaced humans do come from big green seed pods. Here, one of the infernal vegetables is about to be torched by Kevin McCarthy.

Siegel's *Invasion of the Body Snatchers* (1956) is almost certainly the best known and most well regarded of what is ultimately a sizable science fiction subgenre.

Earthly politics and alien possession are central to the historical importance of *Invaders from Mars* and the film's influence on popular culture, but what of its images? The original release prints were unusually high in color saturation, giving its eccentric view of small-town America a subtle aura of unreality. It also contains barren, nearly abstract sets that transform the comfortably familiar features of the everyday world into bleak places of sterile menace. Film historian Vivian C. Sobchack offers these insightful observations:

> Whether an image [in these films] evokes a sense of strangeness—a sense of wonder — or whether it seems familiar is not always dependent upon the inherent strangeness or familiarity of its actual content. In *Invaders from Mars* ... a small town police station becomes a setting as visually jolting and alien as any other-worldly planet.*
>
> The setting of nearly all such films is ... a community, which is as familiar, predictable, snug, and unprivate as a Norman Rockwell magazine cover for *The Saturday Evening Post.* In such a world, against such a background, the smallest deviation from the norm, from ritual and habit, from warm, friendly, social — even eccentric — Americana will carry the visual force of a Fourth of July fireworks display.... What is chilling about the films, what causes our uneasiness, is that they all stay right at home threatening the stability of hearth and family, pronouncing quietly that nothing is sacred — not even Mom or Dad, nor the police chief, not even one's own true love.†

There are, as well, iconic forms in this particular film that seem to hearken back to the works of Bosch and before: the mannequin-like mutants with their blank faces and ominous manlike forms; the Buddha-like, omnipotent Martian Intelligence; the flying saucer, a luminous disc in which the alien creatures descend to earth. These images are much like Jungian archetypes and their resonance is unmistakable. Carl Jung identified the concept of the *universal unconscious*—a vocabulary of forms, which he call archetypes, that are common to all people regardless of nationality or of life experience, and from which images can emerge into our awareness. Of special interest to him late in his life was the mandala, a disc-shaped religious artifact containing geometric shapes, depictions of deities and other forms that symbolize the universe. Jung believed that the mandala was accountable for many of the UFO sightings that occurred during the 1950s. In its religious context the mandala represents the wholeness of the self; the supreme integration of mind, spirit and body. In the era of the Cold War, with the fate of humanity hanging precariously in the breach, this desire for wholeness became a matter of widespread, if largely unspoken, wishful thinking. He also believed that these sightings were a portent of some significant transformation that was about to take place.‡ In this respect, all works of science fiction, regardless of medium, purport to proclaim the coming of change.

*Vivian Carol Sobchack, *The Limits of Infinity: The American Science Fiction Film* (A.S. Barnes & Co., 1980), 87.

†*Ibid.*, 121.

‡Anthony Storr, Ph.D., *The Essential Jung* (MJF Books, 1983), 229–35.

Whatever these images mean, if they indeed have any meaning at all, they seem to tap into something deeply rooted in the human experience. Michael Grosso, the noted UFO expert, echoes Jung's belief that these types of images, emerging in our culture at this time, express our concerns about the troubling conditions that prevail in our world and are part of a growing awareness that civilization is about to experience a period of transformation — a New Age. Whatever meaning these images possess, they seem to have manifested mainly through the visual arts and through our religious iconography.

Invaders from Mars was produced independently by Edward L. Alperson, Sr., and released by Twentieth Century–Fox in May of 1953. Although its reviews were generally favorable and it quickly recovered its modest investment, it was soon lost in the glut of similar movies. For those of an impressionable age, it became a source of nightmares. In addition to its inherent xenophobia, the story worked on yet another level — the fear of surreptitious infiltration. The thought that people in the everyday world might not be what they seem had clearly found an outlet in the highly specialized medium of the American science fiction film. In that same year, Universal-International's *It Came from Outer Space*, released in June, struck the same jarring note of subversive penetration.

Interestingly, the young star of *Invaders from Mars*, Jimmy Hunt, now a salesman and long separated from his motion picture career, was not frightened by the film, but did find other science fiction movies of the period to be especially affecting. In a recent phone conversation, Hunt stated, "I was 12 when we filmed [*Invaders from Mars*]; 13 when they released it. That movie did not scare me as much as *The Thing* [*from Another World*] — that scared the heck out of me. Another one was *The Man from Planet X*, that scared the — I mean, really, I lay in bed one night and didn't move the whole night. I just laid there stiff as a board just knowing that guy was coming down the hall to get me."

Rounding out this survey of cinematic Little Green Men is Fred F. Sears' *Earth vs. the Flying Saucers*, a 1956 Columbia release that employs the stop-motion artistry of animator Ray Harryhausen. Loosely based on Major Donald E. Kehoe's non-fiction book, *Flying Saucers from Outer Space* (Henry Holt, 1953), it deals with an invasion of Earth by renegade aliens from a disintegrated planetary system. Harryhausen's climactic invasion is waged against humanity at the nation's capital in Washington, D.C., where such recognizable landmarks as the Washington Monument and the rotunda of the Capitol Building are laid to waste. In many respects, this is perhaps Harryhausen's purest SF film of the 1950s and it follows many of the basic setups originated in George Pal's *War of the Worlds* (1953), perhaps the foremost alien invasion movie of the period. *Earth vs. the Flying Saucers* is more notable today, however, for its seemingly prophetic representation of a "gray" — the kind of diminutive, large-domed, big-eyed alien that would be consistently described in countless UFO abduction cases nearly two decades later. Thus, in 1956, long before the near-epidemic outbreak of alien abductions, this otherwise unimposing and largely derivative film accurately depicted the appearance of the aliens that would be consistently described in the overwhelming majority of abduction cases. Could this be another example of

The greatest of all SF-movie flying saucers were created by stop-motion animator Ray Harryhausen for Fred F. Sears' competent and entertaining *Earth vs. the Flying Saucers* (1956).

motion pictures planting an image in the mass mind? Or does it instead mark the timely emergence of an image that has long resided deep in the human psyche?

According to an article published in the July 6, 1999, edition of *The New York Times*, a growing number of scientists are beginning to connect the alien abduction phenomenon to an ancient but little-known sleep disorder called sleep paralysis. During the onset of REM sleep (for Rapid Eye Movement—the stage of sleep during which dreams are likely to occur) the brain disconnects from the nervous system as a safety mechanism, least we act out our dreams and do ourselves serious harm. If awakened suddenly at this point, people can experience temporary paralysis and many suffer bizarre hallucinations—usually involving diminutive humanoids. In ancient times these phantoms were described as witches and gnomes and many of them have made their way into works of art (Hieronymus Bosch's "Hell," the third panel of his triptych *The Last Judgment*; his well-known masterpiece, *The Garden of Earthly Delights*; and John Henry Fuseli's *The Nightmare* spring readily to mind).

In the *Times* article, associate professor of psychology Al Cheyne of the University of Waterloo in Canada is quoted as saying, "People will draw on the most plausible account in their repertoire to explain their experience.... Trolls or witches no longer constitute plausible interpretations of these hallucinations. The notion of

Removed from the protection of their ships' force fields, the armored aliens are vulnerable to bullet hits. Here (from left) Maj. Huglin (Donald Curtis), Carol Marvin (Joan Taylor), and Dr. Russell Marvin (Hugh Marlowe) examine a visitor who strayed too far in *Earth vs. the Flying Saucers.*

aliens from outer space is more contemporary and somewhat more plausible to the modern mind."*

Still, UFO adherents are quick to note that sleep paralysis cannot account for all alien abduction claims, particularly not those that occur in the daytime and during which the victim is presumably wide awake. It would seem more likely that all of the factors suggested herein combine to produce the complex phenomenon that we now identify as the alien abduction experience—just as there is no single explanation adequate to account for all UFO sightings. Clearly, people see objects in the sky that they can't identify; thus there is no question that, in the most literal sense, Unidentified Flying Objects do exist.

Even those who would want nothing more than to believe in the existence of visiting extraterrestrials have reason to doubt the experiences reported thus far.The late astronomer Carl Sagan rightly observed of the subject of UFOs that extraordinary phenomena require extraordinary evidence. To date, there has been too little

*Nicholas D. Kristof, "Alien Abduction? Science Calls It Sleep Paralysis," *The New York Times*, July 6, 1999, F1–2.

tangible evidence that UFOs are the vehicles of otherworldly visitors, or of the reality of alien abductions and their related surgical implants. True, there are some such incidents that defy conventional rationalization and that cannot—*and should not!*—be dismissed. Serious scientific study of these cases is warranted. Claims of government cover-ups, however, while entirely plausible, and perhaps even likely, are simply too convenient a rationale to explain away the nearly complete absence of hard physical evidence, given the extraordinarily high number of UFO sightings and alien abductions reported over the past half century. There is also a very fundamental difference between believing in the possibility of extraterrestrial life (something any self-respecting science fiction fan would probably embrace) and believing that those ETs are traversing the trackless light-years of space with the frequency with which they are reported, for the bewildering purposes of cutting crop circles in wheat fields, mutilating cattle, and impregnating the female residents of remote, rural American communities.

Perhaps a key to better understanding the popularity of these phenomena lies in acknowledging how extensively they have been embraced in motion pictures, and in a better comprehension of the power of films to affect us. For many of us, exposed to movies in childhood, we've vicariously experienced a range of emotions in a variety of normally unfamiliar contexts. Having seen the Civil War drama *Glory* (1989), for example, one can live in the skins of black men who have suffered the deprivations of slavery and who, in spite of this, have given up their lives in defense of freedom for a system whose greater virtues are denied them. In countless other films we've "seen" empathetically through the eyes of the blind, the poor, the infirm, and other unfortunates, taking comfort in what little we ourselves have and wishing, however fleetingly, that all peoples could know freedom, comfort, understanding, love, peace, solace, and wisdom. To sit in a darkened movie theater and to connect emotionally and intellectually with the events portrayed on the screen is strikingly similar to lying in a darkened room on the verge of sleep. Like our dreams, we have no real control over the direction of the narrative that unfolds before us, making us, in a sense, emotionally defenseless and vulnerable. Such is the power of the motion picture to so thoroughly engage the senses as to rule, however briefly, the mind, the heart, and the psyche.

Movies are informative and richly entertaining, yes, yet in hindsight many of the SF films, particularly of the mid–twentieth century, reveal the principal anxieties and concerns of their day. In personal interviews with actors such as Jimmy Hunt and Kevin McCarthy (*Invasion of the Body Snatchers*), who appeared in films now widely associated with the apprehensions of the McCarthy era, it is surprising to learn that much of what has come to be regarded as the historical significance of these motion pictures is largely the result of coincidence with parallel events in the real world. The somewhat abstract and detached nature of the science fiction story makes possible a kind of natural assimilation of real world anxieties into the fantastic

Opposite: **This detail entitled "Hell," from the third panel of Hieronymus Bosch's triptych, *The Last Judgment* (painted c. 1504), is typical of work that placed Bosch among the giants of Renaissance painters. It may well depict events inspired by an episode of sleep paralysis. Immobility, often during slumber, is yet another familiar component of alien-abduction claims.**

narrative. By happenstance, dumb luck or cunning design (and in most cases, by virtue of all of these factors combined), the SF cinema holds a mirror to us and to our culture that is at times far more illuminating of the human condition than in contemporary movies set in the familiar world we all share.

It is my belief that the works of all visual artists operate on this deeper level— that beyond the manifest nature of all art there is a latent content that enriches the human experience and is, in fact, art's most durable virtue, particularly when the topicality of its more apparent subject matter has faded from memory. In the case of the science fiction film, however, its most fundamental iconography may address the very issues of species survival and is not so far removed from the more palpable concerns of the stories and concepts that it supports. Science fiction stories lie largely in the future and on distant worlds, making obsolescence unlikely, but they are invariably rooted in the human experience, and deal ultimately not with the alien and the exotic but instead with our own fundamental humanity.

And of these strange humanoids who glance back at us from the silver screen, looking deep into the very essence of who we are with their mysterious, glistening, obsidian eyes—they are not beings other than ourselves, looking outward to the far reaches of the cosmos, but rather are us looking inward in a restless search to better know ourselves.

Films Discussed

The Flying Saucer Colonial Productions. Released January 4, 1950. 69 min. Producer: Mikel Conrad. Director: Mikel Conrad. Story: Mikel Conrad. Screenplay: Mikel Conrad and Howard Irving Young. Director of Photography: Philip Tannura. Editor: Robert Crandall. Music: Darrell Calker. Art Director: Murray Waite. With Mikel Conrad, Pat Garrison, Hantz von Teuffen, Lester Sharpe, Russell Hicks and Denver Pyle. Available on Englewood Entertainment VHS home video; Image Entertainment DVD.

The Man from Planet X Sherrill Corwin/United Artists. Released April 7, 1951. 70 min. Producers: Jack Pollexfen and Aubrey Wisberg. Director: Edgar Ulmer. Screenplay: Aubrey Wisberg and Jack Pollexfen. Director of Photography: John L. Russell. Editor: Fred R. Feitshans, Jr. Music: Charles Koff. Art Directors: Angelo Scibetta and Byron Vreeland. Special Effects: Andy Anderson and Howard Weeks. Visual Effects: Jack R. Glass, Jack Rabin and Edgar Ulmer. With Robert Clarke, Margaret Field, Raymond Bond, William Schallert, Roy Engel and Pat Goldin. Available on MGM/UA VHS home video; MGM/UA DVD.

Invaders from Mars National Pictures Corp./Twentieth Century Fox. Released April 22, 1953. 78 min. Producer: Edward L. Alperson. Director: William Cameron Menzies. Story: John Tucker Battle. Screenplay: Richard Blake. Director of Photography: John F. Seitz. Editor: Arthur Roberts. Music: Mort Glickman. Art Director: Boris Leven. Special Effects: Jack Cosgrove. Visual Effects: Irving Block, Jack Rabin and Howard Lydecker. With Helena Carter, Arthur Franz, Jimmy Hunt, Leif Erickson, Hillary Brooke, Morris Ankrum and Luce Potter. Available on Englewood Entertainment; United American Video VHS home video; Image Entertainment DVD.

Earth vs. the Flying Saucers Clover Pictures/Columbia. Released July 1956. 83 min. Producers: Sam Katzman and Charles H. Schneer. Director: Fred F. Sears. Story: Curt Siodmak, based on *Flying Saucers from Outer Space* by Donald E. Keyhoe. Screenplay: George Worthing Yates and Bernard Gordon (latter credited as Raymond T. Marcus). Director of Photography: Fred Jackman, Jr. Editor: Danny Landres. Music: Mischa Bakaleinikoff. Art Director: Paul Palmentola. Special Effects: Russ Kelley. Special Photographic and Animation Effects: Ray Harryhausen. With Hugh Marlowe, Joan Taylor, Donald Curtis, Morris Ankrum, John Zaremba, Thomas Browne Henry, Harry Lauter and Paul Frees (voice). Available on Columbia Tristar VHS and DVD.

7

In Them We Trust? Fear, Faith, and *It Came from Outer Space*

JERRY YAMAMOTO

Amateur astronomer John Putnam peers into the dark recesses of the mine. He strains his eyes, but he can not see the alien who spoke to him. He feels vulnerable, helpless. The alien from another world clearly can see him, but Putnam has no idea what the alien looks like. Whenever the Xenomorphs had appeared, they had taken the form of humans they had abducted, and now they had taken Ellen Fields, Putnam's fiancée. It was her beckoning physical form that lured him to this cave in the barren mountains of the Arizona desert.

Roused to action by the beautiful image of his beloved, Putnam desperately wants to know if she is alive and unharmed. He dares not stir the alien's anger, but he insists on knowing Ellen's whereabouts. The alien tells Putnam that he and his otherworldly companions had not intended to land on Earth, and that they now need time to repair their spacecraft. Most importantly, the time is not right, the alien declares, for earthlings and them to meet in friendship. But the alien's words don't assuage Putnam's anxieties. How could they? They had acted secretly and suspiciously. The visitors had kidnapped several people. Perhaps they had even murdered them, including Ellen. The time the aliens need may be not to repair their ship but instead to organize a local or even global attack.

"We have souls and minds," the Xenomorph protests, "and we are good." *Words! Just words!* Putnam tells himself. *How can I believe the alien if it refuses to reveal itself?*

"You would be horrified at the sight of us," the Xenomorph warns.

"Had you fallen on our world, it might have been different. We understand more."

More words! How can I trust this thing from outer space?

If you were John Putnam, would you believe this alien? If strange visitors had abducted the person you loved most, would you place your faith in their assurances? If they refused to show their real selves to you, could you do as they requested? And if you were living in 1953, having the mindset of a typical middle-class American, could you put aside your fears and prejudices?

That Bradbury Touch

It's hardly a surprise that *It Came from Outer Space* is among the most intelligent American SF films of the 1950s. The basic treatment and much (or most, according to many sources) of the screenplay are the work of SF giant Ray Bradbury, who had exploded onto the national literary scene with his story collections *Dark Carnival* (1947) and *The Martian Chronicles* (1950). His deep imagination and poetic language had won him many thousands of followers, and he rightly viewed *It Came from Outer Space* as an entree into the motion picture business. The film was a box-office success and boosted the careers of Universal-International staff producer William Alland and director Jack Arnold, who would have other fruitful SF/horror collaborations during the decade, most notably *Creature from the Black Lagoon* (1954) and *The Incredible Shrinking Man* (1957); the latter gave another talented SF writer, Richard Matheson, a toehold in the film industry.

The positive impact of *It Came from Outer Space* on the SF crowd can't be debated, but the film also spoke to general audiences and to society in general. Today, it reveals much about American fears and longings of more than a half century ago.

Ironically, Ray Bradbury has an intense fear of flying. Instead, he lets his imagination soar through the sky and among the stars. His wonder about what's "out there" and what could happen if "it" came to Earth bore fruit in a pair of detailed story treatments, "The Meteor" and "Atomic Monster," which journeyman screenwriter Harry Essex adapted into screenplay form. The basic story idea came from producer Alland, who hired Bradbury to take his idea and fashion a film from it. Although Harry Essex later claimed that *It Came from Outer Space* was his original story and script, nothing else in Essex's filmography approaches the quality of *It Came from Outer Space*; certainly nothing else with Essex's name attached to it has the wistful poetry of this film. Nearly every scene and a preponderance of the dialogue are Bradbury's.

It Came from Outer Space began production in February of 1953. Shooting went swiftly but was started up again after completion because U-I executives insisted that the Xenomorphs be shown on screen. That accomplished, final shooting wrapped in April. Alland and Bradbury had wanted the Xenomorphs to remain off screen and in the imaginations of the viewers. A philosophical, rather than physical, alien presence, Bradbury felt, would have the greater dramatic effect. That Universal overruled his wishes remains Bradbury's chief complaint about the film.

Alland enlisted Jack Arnold to direct the movie, and Irving Gertz, Herman Stein, and Henry Mancini to score it. Casting included Richard Carlson in the role of John Putnam; Barbara Rush as his love interest, Ellen Fields; and Charles Drake as Sheriff Matt Warren. (The handsome, quietly authoritative Carlson, like Alland and Arnold, would become a mainstay of the genre, appearing in *Creature from the Black Lagoon, The Magnetic Monster, Riders to the Stars,* and others.)

It Came from Outer Space was first of many SF films in the '50s to use the desert as a backdrop. Although the story's setting is Arizona, exteriors were shot in California, with many scenes filmed in the Mojave Desert near Victorville. Desert pedigree aside, *It Came from Outer Space* was the first SF film to use subjective camera to show the point of view of an alien, and the first shot in wide-screen 3-D. The dimensional effects avoid the gimmickry of most other 3-D productions and don't detract from the story. 3-D has never been used more judiciously.

As they watched the alien spaceship crash in the Arizona desert outside the small town of Sand Rock, moviegoers had no idea whether the aliens in this film would be friendly or hostile. Only two years earlier, two groundbreaking SF films had amazed

While driving alone in the desert, Ellen (Barbara Rush) is startled by the figure of Frank (Joe Sawyer), a local telephone lineman, in Jack Arnold's *It Came from Outer Space* (1953): is he human or Frank's alien duplicate?

audiences: *The Thing from Another World* and *The Day the Earth Stood Still* (both 1951). If you were John Putnam and you thought the blood-drinking "Thing" was in the mine, you would have run like hell. But if you thought the diplomatic Klaatu was speaking to you, your fears would have subsided considerably. Both films reached deep into our subconscious fears and longings; but where one horrified us, the other ennobled us. A faithful disciple of SF would have seen both films, possibly several times.

John Putnam, an amateur astronomer who looked at space with awe and wonder, would probably have been more trusting—and certainly more curious—than most people. In fact, his reactions were far more rational than the behavior of the sheriff and townspeople of Sand Rock, and for that reason, the aliens placed their trust in him by informing him of their innocuous intentions via the physical form of two linemen they had abducted earlier. By this time, the aliens no longer merely intrigued Putnam but had seemingly become a menace to society. Too many people had disappeared, and he feared the worst. Instead of exposing them, however, something in Putnam persuaded him to believe the aliens and let them carry out their plans. Apparently he wanted to believe that these creatures, who were technologically superior to humankind, were morally superior as well, and that therefore their intentions were benign.

The same can't be said for Sheriff Matt Warren and his vigilantes. Their instinctive reaction was to shoot first and ask questions later. And so they did toward the end of the movie. They set up a roadblock, and as soon as they saw one of the aliens driving a truck toward them, they gunned down the Xenomorph with their rifles and sidearms. No time to talk. No time to reason. No time for mercy. The only good alien was a dead alien.

Putnam not only had to deal with frantic aliens; he also had to contend with an angry and panic-filled mob. If an alien civilization is smart enough to know how to travel millions of miles through space, then they might be smart enough to know that paranoia dominated intelligent life on Earth in the early '50s. So which advanced civilization from another planet could expect to visit us at that time on friendly terms? Either the Xenomorphs had landed on Earth to obliterate humankind or had come by accident. In either case, most of us would have been terrified.

Director Jack Arnold once said the basic premise of *It Came from Outer Space* is that "we are prone, all of us, to fear something that's different than we are — whether it be in philosophy, the color of our skins, or even one block against another in a big city. Because your form is different than theirs, you want to hate, you want to kill — that is your first reaction. Until we are mature enough to meet something different than ourselves on a higher level without being afraid of it and without recoiling in horror, only then will we be worthy to meet whatever else is out there in the cosmos."

What is Arnold saying about us? Why do we instinctively fear that which is different from us? Surely our paranoia can't be attributed to disturbing SF movies. Those are good for thrills, but alone they do little more than entertain us. Nor can we blame it primarily on the Cold War and the McCarthy Senate hearings of 1953. There are inherent elements in our social consciousness that have given birth not only to our fear of the unknown but also to our longing for the transcendental. Prevalent religious attitudes and assumptions are two such elements. They have contributed significantly to how we channel our primal urges—both to the bad and to the good.

How We See Wrongly

> The scrawny, five-year-old boy squeezed his mother's hand tightly and snuggled against her leg as he stared up at the two men standing on the steps leading to the front door of the church. Although she was shorter than five feet, and although the boy had never heard her raise her voice, his mother seemed like the safest place in the world. The men continued to glare at his parents as they told them that they were not welcome and that they should worship at a church with people of their own kind. The boy felt his mother's hand tighten until his fingers hurt. As his family walked away, the boy turned and saw eyes filled with hate, and he couldn't understand why.

For the next several decades I still could not comprehend why that white man looked at me with inexplicable loathing. I have learned a lot about racial bigotry, and I have experienced many of its cruelties, but I still can't understand why people hate without cause. At times I have even seen the same response to me as the Xenomorphs saw when people looked at their real selves—of course, not with the same fright at my appearance, but with the same fear of who I am. What is even more baffling is that my deepest wounds of this kind were afflicted within the Christian church. And yet, it should not have been surprising to me. I had often heard that the most segregated time of the week is Sunday morning, and that was certainly true in the '50s and to some extent in the '60s, when I attended churches that were mostly white.

Still, why did many white Christians hate me? I was a Christian, too. I believed what they did. I placed my trust in the same Bible they did. I worshiped the same God they did. The only difference I could find was that I looked different from them. But why should that cause them to fear me? Of course, their fears were most evident as I grew older and when opportunities to date their daughters appeared. Even the most socially progressive, the more spiritually enlightened, the friendliest and nicest of them were not immune to this one dread. So elders and parents in the church often told me to stay clear of their daughters when it came to dating. A girl like Ellen Fields would certainly have been off limits to me.

American society has matured considerably during the past 50 years. Much of the racism I endured in my youth has not been experienced by my own children. Even in the church, there has been much healing. But is racism gone? Not by a long shot. For many years after World War II, we thought that what had happened to Japanese-Americans would never occur again in the United States. Most of us know that interning loyal Americans in concentration camps for years was one of the most serious criminal acts perpetrated by the United States government. Of course, such injustice would never be repeated. And then came the Patriot Act, and like my grandfather, who was sent to prison without any trial because he was an elder in a Buddhist church, American Muslims have been incarcerated for months without due process of law — in the United States in the twenty-first century! And where has the Patriot Act received its strongest support? From the conservative Christian church. And why? Because of fear of those who are different from us. It's ironic, but sadly telling, that one of the State Department's spokespersons who justified the Patriot Act on the news networks was a Japanese-American.

When *It Came from Outer Space* was released in 1953, the justices on the United States Supreme Court were listening to arguments for and against the *Oliver Brown et al. v. Board of Education of Topeka* decision, which had been brought to their court in the fall of 1952. In their historic ruling in the spring of 1954, they ended racially segregated public schooling. Of course, judges can rule and make laws, but time is needed for people's hearts to change. Even now the most segregated time of the week is still Sunday morning.

Having little exposure to people who are different from us, it is easy to create caricatures of them and form judgments about their value as human beings. And if we think that those people threaten us in any way, we will fear them — often irrationally. Because the church has had a long history of doctrinal disputes that have divided congregations and denominations, we desperately want our church to stay united, and so we want nothing new and nothing different to disturb the comfort and security that we believe the church should offer us as we retreat from the daily struggles of being in the world. Of course, this is true not only within Christianity but also within every religion. People become so upset about theological issues that they either have to eliminate the opposing views as heresies or separate from the people who disagree with them. The more passive avenue is what has usually occurred in American society.

Thus the church becomes an ideal breeding ground for fears of those who are different. Because most people regularly attended church up through the '50s, and because that's where they learned to stereotype and accept the preconceived notions of previous generations, the church was largely responsible for instilling a deep distrust of anyone unlike themselves in most people's minds. Everything else in society simply reinforced those perceptions and inclinations. Then, during the Korean War of 1950–53, people were even more on edge and xenophobic, and they often heard from the pulpits throughout the country that God was on their side and against unbelievers.

If there is anything that stands out to a racial minority about SF films in the '50s in general and *It Came from Outer Space* in particular, it is the absence of anyone who is not white. The townspeople of Sand Rock represented American society. I and others like myself were excluded. We did not belong. Like the aliens, our presence would have caused suspicion and the desire for us to leave immediately. The two men who stood on the front steps of the church and the townspeople of Sand Rock shared something in common — the impulse to react immediately to protect what they believed to be their sacred territory, which had been bestowed upon them by God and sanctified by their own cultural beliefs.

John Putnam no doubt would have harbored many of the same fears as the townspeople of Sand Rock. He probably would have attended an all-white church. All his friends were probably white. When he watched the evening news, he saw only white, male newscasters. When he watched sports, most of the players were white. If he had married Ellen and had children, he might even have told his daughter not to get interested in that black kid in her high school class. But then again perhaps not. Perhaps that's why the aliens watched Putnam and chose him as their liaison with the rest of his community. Perhaps they saw in Putnam an earthling who could overcome his cultural inclinations and his fear of that which is different.

There is no doubt that Putnam's encounter with the visitors has a transforming effect on his character. The alien in the mine horrifies Putnam when it finally reveals itself to him, but Putnam's decision to aid the aliens despite what he sees denies bigotry and racial fear. Even after the Xenomorph in the physical appearance of Ellen tries to kill him, and when the alien leader talks of self-destruction, Putnam argues against violence. He becomes a stronger, better person because he does not let his understandable apprehension about something strange and possibly danger-

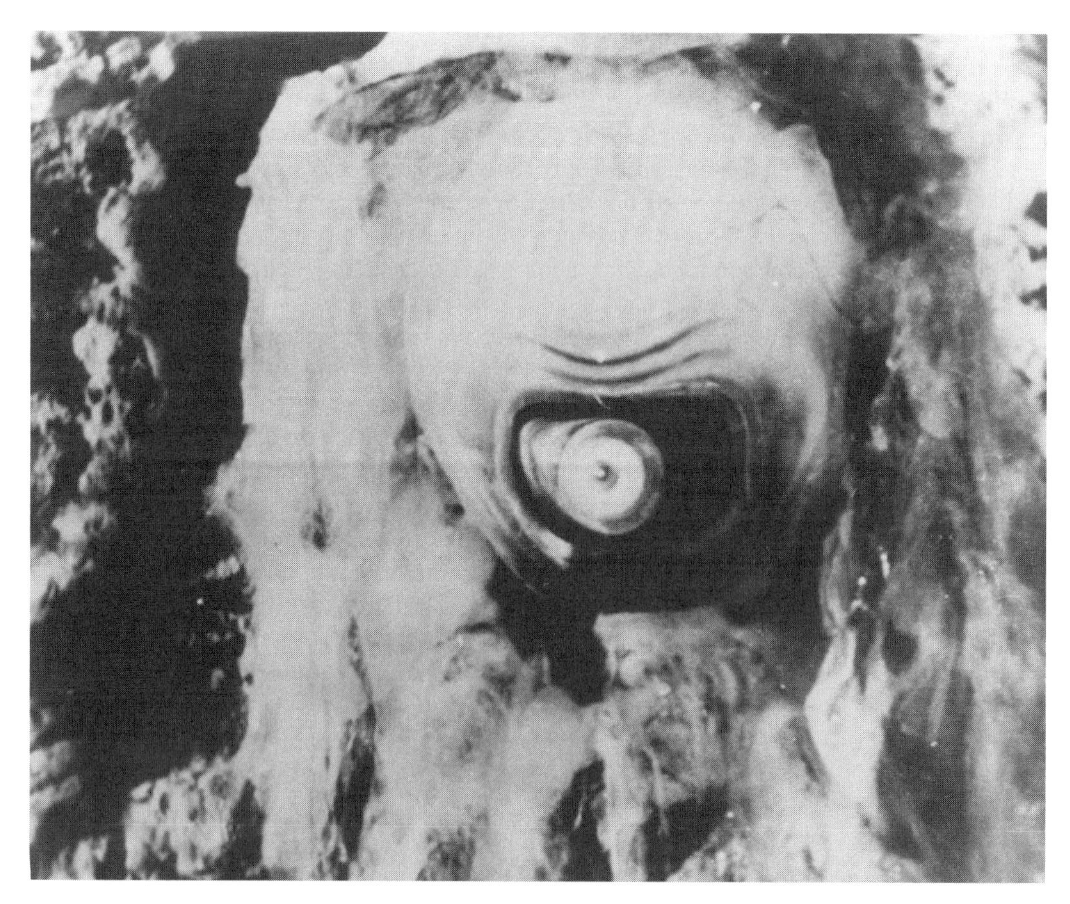

The fearsome yet essentially benign "Xenomorph" greets Putnam in the cave. Hideous to human eyes, it and its companions are merely sidetracked travelers.

ous take hold of him. I wish Putnam had stood on those church steps more than 50 years ago. I think he would have stretched out his hand toward my family, and he would have looked at me with a smile.

A Transcendental Tale Retold

The ritual of baptism is a hallowed sacrament of the Christian religion. Christianity, however, cannot claim to be the founder of this rite. This ceremonial act of purification and initiation was common among the Jews as far back as Moses' day. Nevertheless, the earliest Christians endowed baptism with another meaning by symbolically attributing the death, burial, and resurrection of Christ to the new believer who is baptized into Christ's church. "We were therefore buried with him through baptism," said the apostle Paul, "into death in order that, just as Christ was raised from the dead through the glory of the Father, we too may live a new life" (Romans 6:4).

In all probability it is incidental that we find correlations between *It Came from Outer Space* and the Christian account of Jesus' last days. People in our society, however, are so well acquainted with the story of Jesus' death, burial, and resurrection that Christian symbols in this film register in our minds whether or not they have been intentionally absorbed. The most unmistakable correlation is evident twice: when the alien spacecraft crashes on Earth and is buried beneath an avalanche of rocks; and at the conclusion, when the ship finally bursts from its terrestrial tomb on its journey back to the heavens. During the time the spacecraft is buried, a fear of death is the prevailing mood of earthlings and Xenomorphs alike. By the time the spacecraft breaks free of Earth, the human witnesses have acquired a new understanding of life. It's as if those who have hope for a future meeting and subsequent friendship have been reborn.

This theme is underscored at various times in subtle images that appear throughout the film. The opening scene of Putnam and Ellen, for example, contains several religious images that invite many possible meanings. The romantic pair sits before a fireplace, facing each other lovingly. We view them from a point at the back of the grate. The foreground is dominated by dancing flames. Ellen is partially framed by one end of the grate, which has the shape of a cross. Between the couple, in the background, are three burning candles. After Putnam and Ellen rise, and before they step outside, Putnam blows out the candles and says, "Let's see what the stars have to say" about their future. This scene not only reveals the warmth of their relationship, but also foreshadows what is to come. While flames are common imagery for hell, the three burning candles have been symbols in Christian worship of the Trinity — that is, God the Father, God the Son, and God the Holy Spirit. With the extinguishing of the candles, flames burn only in the fireplace, suggesting that death — not as an end to life but rather as the absence of the Life as God embodies it — will set the tone for much of what follows.

The cross is a recurring image, primarily in the guise of telephone poles that march across the lonely desert. Shortly before Ellen's abduction, the camera pans upward from the base of a pole and finally to the cross beam. As clouds pass in a dark background, the telephone pole appears as an ominous wooden cross. A moment later a Xenomorph in the physical form of the lineman Frank stops Ellen's car and abducts her.

There are many other purposeful glimpses of phone poles, but the most intriguing is when the real Frank (Joe Sawyer) works at the top of one, using a handset to listen to the wires and remarking that he can hear strange sounds, as if something alien were using the wires to communicate. Just as the message of the cross was incomprehensible to people prior to Christ's resurrection, the intentions of Xenomorphs baffle the people in and around Sand Rock.

One hint of the aliens' inherent goodness, however, is delivered when Putnam and Ellen discover the other lineman, George (Russell Johnson), in the desert. When he stares longingly at the sun without blinking or injuring his eyes, he speaks of the comfort and succor of that star — and also tips off Putnam and Ellen that this is not George at all, for what human could stare unblinking at the sun? Here again light plays an important role. To the Xenomorphs, the sun is beautiful. They are obviously more accustomed to light than humans are.

After Putnam and Ellen nervously depart, the alien tells George and Frank, "Don't be afraid. It is within our power to transform ourselves to look like you or anyone. For a time it will be necessary.... Don't be afraid."

The aliens are very much like "Christ Jesus: Who, being in very nature God ... but made himself nothing, taking the very nature of a servant, being made in human likeness" (Philippians 2:5–7).

Later, one of the visitors tells Putnam that it and its companions are good. And then, at the end of the film, the aliens depart without having harmed anyone, even though humans have killed two of their company. All of this suggests that the aliens are not only wiser than we but are morally superior as well. It can be argued that they are archetypes of the Christ.

As the Xenomorphs' spacecraft hurtles out of sight, Sheriff Warren pronounces, with evident relief, "Well, they're gone." Ellen asks, "For good, John?"

Putnam stares into the heavens. "No—just for now," he answers. "It wasn't the right time for us to meet. But there'll be other nights, other stars for us to watch. They'll be back."

Just as Jesus promised his followers that he will someday return, the notion of fear is absent in the expectation of the Xenomorphs' return. Although the creatures claim to have come to Earth by accident — unlike Christ, who made it clear that he intentionally came to Earth to be one of us—both events precipitate life-changing encounters that reveal the tragic consequences of fear. Thus, using the Christ story as an inadvertent but logical analogue to strengthen the subtext of *It Came from Outer Space*, we see that the film urges us to abandon our fear of those who are different from us, and not to allow our judgment to be poisoned so that we act out of mindless rage. Patience and understanding — these are two keys to our humanity.

Bradbury and Arnold are clearly sympathetic to the Xenomorphs, and to the two that died unnecessarily, so that Putnam and the others can grasp the sorry consequences of animal fear. Perhaps their sacrifice, along with the untimely burial and eventual resurrection of the alien spacecraft, was necessary for us to realize that trust is more noble than fear, and that with trust people can step into the future morally improved, and ready to meet other intelligent life — including our neighbors — in friendship.

Film Discussed

It Came from Outer Space Universal-International. Released May 25, 1953. 81 min. Producer: William Alland. Director: Jack Arnold. Story: Ray Bradbury. Screenplay: Ray Bradbury (uncredited) and Harry Essex. Director of Photography: Clifford Stine. Editor: Paul Weatherwax. Music: Irving Gertz, Herman Stein and Henry Mancini. Art Directors: Robert Boyle and Bernard Herzbrun. Special and Visual Effects: Roswell Hoffmann and David Horsley. With Richard Carlson, Barbara Rush, Charles Drake, Joe Sawyer, Russell Johnson and Kathleen Hughes. Available on Universal VHS home video and Universal DVD.

8

Secret Identity, Fragile Identity: TV's Superman in "Superman on Earth," "The Stolen Costume," "The Face and the Voice,"and "Panic in the Sky"

DAVID J. HOGAN

Key words in the opening voice-over narration to episodes of *The Adventures of Superman* (brilliantly read by announcer Jack Narz) are these: "Strange visitor from another planet who came to Earth with powers and abilities far beyond those of mortal men!" In a single sentence the first of the two most important elements of the Superman mythos is established: He is not of this earth, and thus is not, strictly speaking, human. He is a visitor, a stranger, and although he will grow to adulthood among us, he can never truly be one of us—or even, simply, *of* us. His genetics, his familial history, his race memory—all of these are fundamentally alien.

In the narration a few moments later, Narz adds of Superman, "and who, disguised as Clark Kent, mild-mannered reporter for a great metropolitan newspaper, fights a never-ending battle...." This establishes the second crucial element of Superman's existence on Earth: He lives and works among us in a secret identity, in the guise of a man who, though existing on legal records (he is, after all, the adopted son of Ma and Pa Kent), is nevertheless a fabrication, for he is not Kent at all, but Kal-el, orphaned survivor of Krypton and son of Jor-el and Lara.

Further, Superman behaves precisely as the small-town Earth culture that molded him expects him to: as a selfless savior. We invest in him not just our nobler virtues (empathy, altruistic imagination, gentleness, courage), but our fears, as well. Even as we assume him to be an expression of us, so too must he be our protector. In practical terms, he defends us (the law-abiding masses) from ourselves (the criminal element).

George Reeves as Superman.

The topper, of course, is that Superman is the most powerful being on Earth. Other than God himself, this man from another planet is our ultimate protector. Clearly, all of this involves a great deal of responsibility and, one would assume, emotional pressure. To be Superman is an enormous job, and a "never-ending" one.

To be Superman is also to be Clark Kent, and to be human, and to be a lot of other things that Kal-el is not. When does Superman get to be Kal-el? What are the limits of his capabilities and his patience vis-à-vis his secret identity? What happens when the lines between personal reality and fabrication blur, or are erased? *The Adventures of Superman* never explored the psychological implications of our hero's double life, and never suggested that he was conflicted by it; that was left to the dark and nihilistic Superman comic books of the 1990s, in which, for a brief (and ill-considered) period, Superman became a brooding, emotionally ambivalent figure, a man unhappily aware of the vast differences between himself and the earthlings with whom he has been forced to throw in his lot. The television series (filmed in 1951 and 1953–57) was created for children, so although American movie audiences had had exposure to antiheroes (Bogart, Jimmy Stewart in the cycle of Anthony Mann Westerns, Brando, and others), *The Adventures of Superman* was neither prepared nor obligated to go down that road.

Possible answers to questions of Superman's identities can be found in standard, well-regarded literature of the behavioral and social sciences, chiefly Erik Erikson and Abraham Maslow. The German-born psychoanalyst Erikson (1902–94) recognized the existence of a gap between the science of psychoanalysis, which studies the nature and effects of internal emotions, and the larger issues of environment's consequence on character and personality development. He was particularly interested in the influence of family dynamics and the cues a person picks up from one's peers. Maslow (1908–70) is best known for establishing a credible theory of needs, a pyramid with basic needs (food, physical safety) at the bottom; the needs must be fulfilled, in steps, if one is to progress to the pyramid's summit, which Maslow called self-actualization.

Like Maslow, Erikson regarded personality development as a process of ascension, though Erikson tied his progression more closely to chronological development. He regarded life's chronological milestones as obstacles to be challenged and overcome. Erikson isolated eight of them, and posited that each came with a critical question.

Erikson's Stages of Psychosocial Development Through Challenges

Stage 1

Neonatal
Trust vs. Mistrust

- The world should be predictable as well as safe. The nature of cause and effect should be regular.
  Question: *Is my world predictable and supportive?*

Stage 2

Toddlers, ages 1 to 3
Autonomy vs. Shame and Doubt

- Body control, particularly coordination and potty use, are vital.
  Question: *Can I do things for myself or must I always rely on others?*

Stage 3

Preschool, ages 3 to 6
Initiative vs. Guilt

- The child learns he can manipulate his environment and has influence over others and his own learning.
  Question: *Am I good or bad?*

STAGE 4

School age, ages 6 to 12
Competence vs. Inferiority

- The child explores and expands his physical and psychological parameters. He learns from his own errors.
  Question: *Am I competent or am I worthless?*

STAGE 5

Adolescence, ages 12 to 18
Search for Identity vs. Role Confusion

- This is a search for identity, during which the child tries on a variety of qualities of character, choosing some and repudiating others.
  Question: *Who am I and where am I going?*

STAGE 6

Young adulthood, ages 18 to 35
Intimacy vs. Isolation

- Relationships are central during this stage. We learn to communicate effectively, and come to believe that validation comes from others.
  Question: *Shall I share my life with another, or elect to live alone?*

STAGE 7

Middle adulthood, ages 35 to 60
Productivity vs. Self-absorption

- Productivity and creativity are the means by which the individual becomes a responsible, contributing member of society. He may become altruistic, and share his insights with others.
  Question: *Will I produce something of lasting value?*

STAGE 8

Old age, ages 60+
Integrity vs. Despair

- During this period of introspection, the individual reviews his life and assesses whether it was lived well and fruitfully. Depending on the answers, peace or anxiety result.
  Question: *Did I take the paths that led to a full life?*

Abraham Maslow believed that people are motivated by unfulfilled needs; further, certain lower needs must be satisfied before higher, more sophisticated ones can be realistically contemplated. Because Maslow studied accomplished people (such as, in a fictional world, Superman), he took a tack radically different from Sigmund Freud and B.F. Skinner, the leading lights of psychology of Maslow's era. Freud, although admitting that human beings are rational, argued that we seldom behave that way, and that in fact our actions are more closely linked to the animal than to the human. Maslow was prepared to disregard many of Freud's conclusions because Freud preoccupied himself with the study of the mentally ill, a nonrepresentative sample of the population.

Skinner conducted ornate experiments with white rats and other lab animals, and applied his conclusions about the results to human beings. Many of his experiments were constructed around simple action-vs.-reward scenarios, and a great deal of his professional regard for people came from statistical analysis. Maslow agreed that the study of animals could be fruitful, but only if the researcher focused on the creatures' sense of play and affection.

Maslow felt that people are essentially good and trustworthy, with naturally altruistic tendencies. The pyramidal structure of his theory was no accident; he believed that human beings, by their nature, strive toward an elevated generosity of spirit and motive as they ascend the hierarchy of needs.

Maslow's Hierarchy of Needs, Bottom to Top

Physiological

Air, food, water, sleep, sex. Without these needs being satisfied, we may feel ill, fearful, irritated.

Safety

We wish to achieve stability and consistency in a chaotic world. Without a feeling of general safety, we cannot love or feel as if we belong to something larger than ourselves, such as a family or society.

Love

Humans naturally incline toward groups: family, organizations, gangs, and other bodies that allow us to feel loved in nonsexual ways. We have a need to be needed.

Esteem

Self-esteem results from mastery of a task. A second kind of need comes from the admiration of others. It boosts self-esteem, like our competence at a task, but is far more closely tied to a need for power.

SELF-ACTUALIZATION

Maslow described this as "the desire to become more and more what one is, to become everything that one is capable of becoming." People who have achieved the earlier stages of the hierarchy can seek knowledge, aesthetic experience, inner peace, and spiritual fulfillment. They know they are admired by others, but they take that admiration in stride, and do not regard it as an expression of personal power. The person at the summit of Maslow's pyramid exists unto himself. He is self-actualized and self-validated.

Given the essentially alien nature of Superman's origins, it is useful also to cite the ethno-psychologists Jose Guanipa and Carmen Guanipa-Ho. They acknowledge that identity is a tricky path for every adolescent, but particularly rocky for a young person who belongs to an ethnic group that constitutes a minority among the larger group. Such a status brings with it a built-in potential conflict: allegiance to the parents' ethics and value systems, and a desire to integrate oneself into the larger society. The adolescent usually resolves the conflict by developing more than one ethnic identity. Thus positioned, he or she can assume or (literally, as in the case of the adult Clark Kent) "put on" the identity that is most appropriate to particular situations. Psychologically healthy minority adolescents acknowledge that they are multicultural, and are comfortable and proud. But for others, the task of melding ethnic identity with personal identity is difficult.

Guanipa and Guanipa-Ho note that an accent, for instance, may stand in the way of easy integration of the ethnic and personal identities. Physical appearance is another factor that may be a hurdle. For Kal-el, who has no accent (colloquial American English is, after all, his first language), and whose physical appearance is (attractively) human, ethnic identity would seem not to be an issue. His value system has come from the simple, altruistic Kents. He is an American, and from the heartland, no less. But although Kal-el/Clark has no accent, he has extraordinary mental and physical powers that set him apart from others. He inherited these not from the Kents, but from Jor-el, Lara, and the generations of Kryptonian ancestors that preceded his parents. As we will see, the young Clark is confused and troubled by his abilities, and it is left to his adoptive parents to tell him that is he not of this earth. These and other issues of ethnicity and formative identity begin to be explored at the outset of *The Adventures of Superman*.

Although George Reeves had played the Man of Steel for the first time in the 1951 Lippert feature film *Superman and the Mole Men*, "Superman on Earth" is the initial episode of the television series. (A recut version of *Superman and the Mole Men*, with a few moments of added narration, became episodes 25 and 26 of *The Adventures of Superman*.) "Superman on Earth" is an anomalous episode, neither as assured in tone and execution as later ones, and, further, neither as grim as episodes from season one nor as lighthearted as later installments. Reeves appears considerably younger than his 37 years, giving an appropriately callow performance suggestive of a young man who is still a newcomer in more ways than one, and who can be dazzled by a big city after a childhood spent on a farm with his adoptive parents.

Voice-over narration at the beginning of the episode invites us to, "come with us now on a far journey" to the planet Krypton. The announcer's tone is reverential, almost awed, and we're meant to understand that this is at once a fable and a story of great weight. Young scientist Jor-el (Robert Rockwell) is mocked by the planet's ruling council when he warns of impending quakes that will rend Krypton apart. His language is equal parts petulance and apocalyptic joy: "You'll be sorry you failed to heed my warning ... when you and your families are swept from the face of this planet like dust!"

Jor-el has hoped to have time enough to create a fleet of rockets to carry Krypton's inhabitants to another, safer planet called Earth. (Apparently, Jor-el and Krypton not only have terrific telescopes, but limitless R&D budgets.) When the final, destructive quake comes, Jor-el has only a small prototype rocket. He insists that his wife, Lara (Aline Towne), ride in it with their infant son, Kal-el, but Lara insists that she belongs with her husband on the doomed planet. So it is that baby Kal-el (with help from some clumsily inserted V-2 footage) rockets to Earth alone.

A particularly clever aspect of the original Superman story as imagined by the character's teenaged creators, writer Jerry Siegel and artist Joe Shuster, is the marked contrast between the sophisticated, technologically advanced Kryptonians and the ingenuous, *aw shucks* nature of the Kents (called Eben and Sara in "Superman on Earth"), the middle-aged couple who witness the tiny rocket's crash as they rattle past in their burping flivver. Sara (Frances Morris) is properly impressed: "Land sakes alive!" Eben (Tom Fadden) rushes to the burning craft and pulls out the unharmed baby. How could the infant have survived — and without a scratch? "Land o' Goshen!" Eben exclaims.

Granted, Eben and Sara's dialogue is a Hollywood TV writer's lazy notion of guileless middle Americans, but there is a simple honesty and warmth about the Kents that makes them instantly appealing. You know right away that they'll instill fundamental American values in their adopted son. From his first moments on Earth, then, Kal-el begins to absorb a culture quite different from the one of his origin.

Later in the episode the adolescent Kal-el (Joel Nestler), who has been given the name Clark, asks, "Ma, why am I different from all the other boys?... Why can I do things that no one else can do?" As Ma Kent begins to explain, the narrator notes, "The boy listened, and he understood."

Ah, but does he? As suggested by Guanipa and Guanipa-Ho, Clark is struggling to come to grips with his innate sense of otherness. His unique gifts set him apart from his peers. When he approaches his mother his attitude is sober and confused, suggesting that his uniqueness has been made clear to him not simply by circumstance, but by others, and probably not always in supportive or approving ways. Healthy ethnic identity, according to Guanipa and Guanipa-Ho, arises from the youngster's integration of ethnicity into self-image. Clark is unable to perform that trick of integration. It's not merely that he's part of an underrepresented ethnic group — he's the *only* member of his ethnic group. He has no counterpart on Earth, and must exist in unique and occasionally unpleasant isolation.

(It should be noted that the Superman line of comic books inaugurated a discrete title, *Superboy*, in 1949, two years before the onset of the television series. Superboy is Superman as a boy, and his costumed adventures take place about 20 years before Superman's. Superboy, like the young Clark of "Superman on Earth," is an inevitably isolated figure in the ethnic or genetic sense, but he is a hero to the people of his small town, and receives the approval and validation that the adolescent Clark of the television series is denied. In the world according to *The Adventures of Superman*, there never was a Superboy.)

After the natural death of Pa Kent, Clark leaves for Metropolis, where he "assumes a guise of mild-mannered timidity." He has reasoned that if he's to help earthlings he must live among them, hiding his capabilities until the powers are needed. Still, Kal-el's ego must surely feel the sting of having to live as a mouse.

A montage sequence shows Clark, suitcases in hand, walking the streets of Metropolis, perhaps awed by the place; perhaps subconsciously unimpressed because dim memories of the splendor that was Krypton flash in his mind. In a logical move, he looks for employment at a place that will allow him access to breaking crises: a great newspaper. (In the comic books of the 1970s Clark left print journalism for TV, which had by that time superseded newspapers as the preeminent source of information.)

Clark drops by *The Daily Planet* but irascible editor Perry White (John Hamilton) refuses to see him. In a cute moment, Clark simply steps through a window hundreds of feet above the street and strolls the narrow ledge around a corner and into White's office; White turns and Clark is just *there*. Veteran reporter Lois Lane (Phyllis Coates) later regards Clark with a jaundiced eye, and practically gloats with anticipated triumph when cub reporter Jimmy Olsen (Jack Larson) rushes in to announce that a dirigible has broken free of its moorings with a worker clinging to a rope a thousand feet above the airfield. It's a great story. "Mr. White," Clark blurts, "if I get an exclusive with the man, will you give me a job?"

The deal is made, and Clark rushes from the office, with Lois—determined not to be outdone by a turnip-green novice—quickly following.

From here, "Superman on Earth" assumes a familiar shape: Clark changes to Superman and streaks through the air to rescue the hapless worker (Dabbs Greer) seconds after he has lost his grip on the rope; Clark returns with the story *and* an exclusive interview with the survivor; and Lois looks at Clark to ask for the first time what she'll spend the rest of her career asking: "How did you get there before every experienced reporter in town?" George Reeves gives the grin that endeared him to millions of fans. "Maybe I'm a superman, Miss Lane."

That's a cute comeback, but it skirts the essential issues raised by "Superman on Earth": Who is Superman? *What* is Superman? Why is he here? What are his responsibilities? Who is Kent? How important is Kent to Superman? How attached has this alien visitor become to his earthly guise? Is Kal-el gone, or merely hidden? Is Superman a creature now of one world or two? Shall he love the people of his adopted planet, or despise them for their relative weakness? After all, humanitarianism doesn't necessarily imply respect for the people being served.

As noted, "Superman on Earth" raises the issue of validation. According to Erikson, people in young adulthood (ages 18 to 35) experience self-validation when it comes from others. Not yet fully formed at these ages (Superman is at the outer edge of the age span), young adults feel most whole when they receive the approval and respect of others. The adolescent Clark receives no validation for his uniqueness because he does not function as a hero figure. Years later, in Metropolis, people are suitably impressed by Superman. His positive validation begins immediately after the dirigible rescue, but that validation is on Earth terms. Kal-el/Clark/Superman must accept approval as it's defined and offered on Earth. The accolades come with no appreciation of Superman's unique origins. The more love people give to Superman, the stronger their assumption that he is human — one of them. Given Superman's singular psychology, public approval is like an eraser that wipes a blackboard clean. As Kal-el/Clark becomes increasingly successful and revered as Superman, the further his origins recede.

Without complete inclusion into the larger group, an individual's psychological state is unfinished, perhaps unhealthy, and possibly dangerous— to the individual, and to others. Our hero, lacking complete identity integration, is an altruist with a dark streak of self-absorption.

These issues are evident in "The Stolen Costume." In this episode, the most visible accoutrement of Kal-el's double life is filched by a badly wounded "rope burglar" who lowers himself into Clark's apartment via the balcony and inadvertently opens a hidden closet. Clark is mortified by the theft of his spare costume, and recruits a sympathetic private detective, Candy (Frank Jenks), to track down the missing item. The trouble is, Clark won't tell Candy precisely what has been taken. "What'd he steal?" Candy inquires. "The family jewels?" Clark scowls at him: "Something a lot more valuable to me!"(Of course, the situation makes us wonder, *Why does Clark need Candy at all?*)

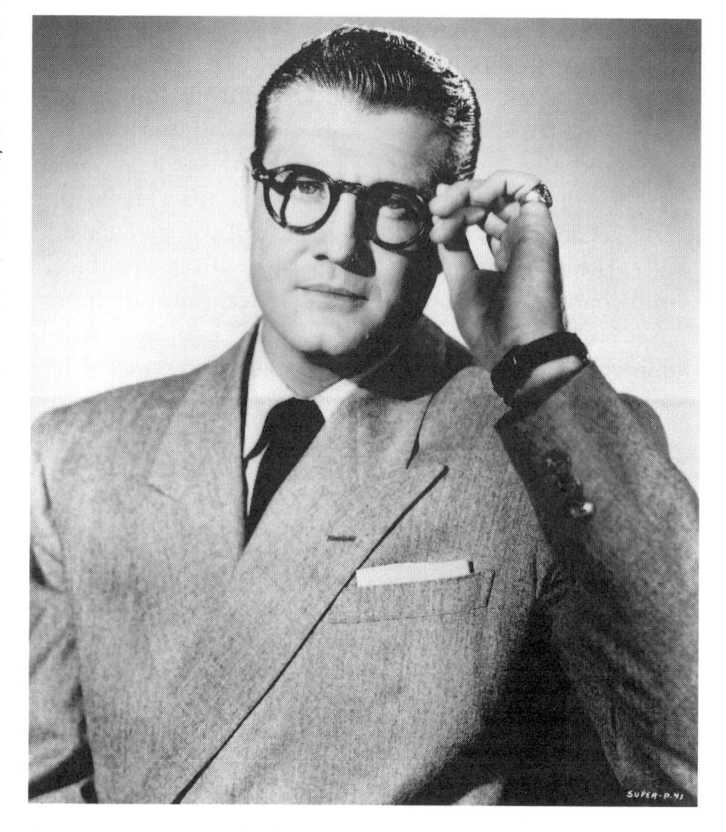

Reeves as Superman's alter ego, Clark Kent. Earthlings never glimpse the hero's true identity, Kal-el of the planet Krypton.

Meanwhile, the rope burglar and the costume have fallen into the hands of a pair of criminal lowlifes, Ace (Dan Seymour) and Connie (Veda Ann Borg). Connie presses the dying burglar for the name of the costume's owner, but the best the thief can come up with is, "Apartment. Fifth floor. 5-H."

Ace is unimpressed by the whole situation. "Just because a guy's got a costume hanging in his closet doesn't mean he's Superman."

Connie, though, grasps the concept of Superman's secret identity, and thinks a step ahead: "Maybe he took it off on account of he wanted to be the other guy." This is pretty metaphysical when you think about it; *the other guy*, and yet *the same guy*. Connie is sharper than she appears but, as we shall see, nevertheless overestimates her leverage and underestimates Superman's determination not to be revealed.

When Connie snoops out the apartment, Clark is out but Candy is inside. Naturally, Connie assumes that the horse-faced private dick is Superman. "He don't look like Superman to me," she tells Ace later, "but I guess when he gets the costume on he looks different."

Just to be sure, Ace rigs the hidden closet with a motion-activated bomb. Candy trips the device but is saved by Clark. However, the bomb makes a splendid noise, and when Ace phones the apartment, Clark answers, suggesting to Ace that somebody in the apartment is Superman. Following a bit more folderol involving Ace's misapprehension about Candy, Superman (clad in his primary costume) confronts Ace and Connie.

"Now where's my costume?" he demands. He sounds ferocious, but Ace isn't buying. After all, he knows that Clark Kent is Superman, and he can gum up our hero's career (and psyche) by telling the world. "How you gonna stop us?" Ace smirks. "Everyone knows Superman don't kill people."

Well, no, he doesn't, but when his secret identity—his carefully cultivated layer of Earth-type humanness—is threatened, he *is* capable of Machiavellian behavior. He scoops up the criminal couple and flies them to the summit of a frigid mountain in Antarctica. It's not a death sentence, but kidnap and exile. There's a warm, well-stocked cabin nearby; Ace and Connie will stay on the mountain *for as long as they live.*

At this point the alert viewer will ask a few questions: *Is Ace going to put up with this new, enforced lifestyle? Is Connie going to let Ace put up with it? These two are creatures of the city; are they going to be content to rough it on this mountain?* And then the viewer is likely to realize that Superman knows that these two sneaks will never stay put in the cabin. Whether out of greed, or fear that Superman never will return to replenish their supplies, they're going to try to escape that mountain.

Sure enough, Ace announces his belief that Superman is gone for good. In bulky overcoat and wingtips, he begins to negotiate a shaky descent on the sheer, icy slope. Connie, stepping gingerly in her alpine-friendly high heels, follows. In a moment she slips and falls on top of Ace. Both plummet to their deaths.

To which the dismayed viewer can only say, *Yow!*

No, Superman doesn't kill people, but he won't hesitate to let people kill themselves when they threaten the tissue-thin reality of his human existence. He doesn't kill Ace and Connie but, then again, he does.

The accolades directed upon Superman by a grateful Metropolis are easy for him to accept, and vital to his veneer of psychological well-being. If his secret identity were to be exposed, his entire mélange of roles, however selflessly created, will cause him to be perceived as a sort of fraud, a cheat. The validation by others may stop. Social and emotional abandonment, issues tied to Erikson's Stage One and Maslow's Love and Esteem developmental levels, are possibilities. In such a situation, Kal-el/Clark Kent/Superman would be, as the fellows in the Vandykes like to say, conflicted.

The inevitable outcome of "The Stolen Costume" is that Ace and Connie must die. Their deaths will 1) make Superman feel better, and safer, and 2) ensure that the validation he enjoys from others will continue. Ace and Connie die in order that Superman can continue to feel good about himself.

"The Face and the Voice" explores impersonation, i.e., the hijacking of Kal-el's public identity for criminal purposes. In a comically Runyonesque turn, George Reeves doubles up in this episode to play the imposter, a slightly punch-drunk pug called Boulder. The big lug's Svengali is Fairchild (Carleton Young), a smooth crook who looks past Boulder's mashed nose and cauliflower ear and sees possibilities. Following plastic surgery and the agony of elocution lessons, Boulder, clad in a fake costume, becomes a Superman look-alike and sound-alike. (A minor and perhaps intentional joke here is that Boulder's elocution teacher, Hamlet, is played by elderly character actor Percy Helton, a whiny-voiced fellow who could not properly pronounce his *r*'s. Hamlet is as much a fraud as his pupil.)

For all the expenditure of time and capital, Fairchild's plan to utilize Boulder in an armored car heist is disappointingly pedestrian — even with the added fillip of Fairchild's intention to murder his cat's-paw when the robbery is complete. First, though, Fairchild has to be sure that his faux Superman can cut the mustard. The initial test takes place after dark at a small corner grocery, where Boulder-Superman sticks out a hand and says to the startled clerk, "May I have all the money in your cash register?" He walks away with the grand sum of $165.

The next day, a Metropolis charity receives an anonymous donation of $165. The pattern is repeated following the imposter's brazen nighttime theft from a jewelry store: amazed owner, and a charity donation the next day in the amount of the stolen goods.

Daily Planet editor Perry White reluctantly concludes that Superman is acting out a warped Robin Hood complex. Police inspector Henderson (Robert Shayne) feels the same way. Even Clark Kent experiences a tremor of uncertainty: "I don't *think* he [Superman] walks in his sleep!"

He doesn't think so, but he's not sure, either. Suddenly, the safety and consistency of Maslow's second stage is undermined. The possibility that Clark may be acting contrary to the expectations of others gnaws at him, and brings out his dark side in a meeting (as Superman) with Inspector Henderson. The cop backs away from Metropolis's hero, keeping a desk between the two of them. Superman is impatient for access to clues. "Bill," he says, "we've been friends for years. I'd hate to use you for a volleyball in your own office!" Cowed, Henderson agrees to help uncover the presumed imposter.

The robbery of the armored car goes off, and Fairchild shoots the person he thinks is Boulder. Interestingly, Boulder wears a bulletproof vest during his criminal misadventures; in the climactic moment, Fairchild happily declares his intention to shoot Boulder in the head, implying that he'll not simply kill his stooge, but obliterate his "Superman" face. Destroy the face, and whatever it is that is perceived to be Superman also is destroyed. Of course, Fairchild is unknowingly facing off against the real Superman. His bullet bounces from our hero's face and zings into the underbrush, and the costumed Boulder is easily collared. In the episode's coda, Boulder pouts, "I shoulda known it takes more than a face and voice. There's only one Superman!"

With Erikson's hierarchy of psychosocial development as a model, we see that Fairchild guides Boulder through the early stages of human growth. A preschooler (ages three to six) learns to manipulate his environment (Metropolis), as well as the adults in it (store clerks, White, Henderson, even Clark). At school age (six to 12), the child expands his physical and psychological boundaries. He becomes goal-oriented (to rob successfully, and in disguise). But Boulder, unlike Kal-el/Clark, stumbles at the adolescent stage of development (12 to 18), during which a healthy youngster develops an appropriately moral character after sampling various value systems.

Kal-el/Clark, influenced by the Kents and the simple morality of his small hometown, develops the altruistic character needed to best serve society. Boulder, however, has no character at all. He is not the exemplary, trustworthy sort whom Maslow felt typified human beings, but a creature whose motivations are as much animal as human, a la Freud and Skinner's views of the human species. Boulder isn't simply unintelligent, but completely self-absorbed. Although he has been made to look and sound like Superman, he is Superman's opposite.

More significantly, of course, is that Boulder threatens to overturn the validation Superman gets from others. Perception, even of self, is reality, and when positive perception is jeopardized, the individual will fight to retain self-worth — hence the deaths of Ace and Connie in "The Stolen Costume," and the apparent willingness of an edgy and frustrated Superman to turn Inspector Henderson into a piece of sporting equipment. One's positive sense of self-worth — and thus, of self — must be preserved.

The Adventures of Superman may never have offered an episode to top "Panic in the Sky," in which Kal-el forgets he is Superman during a time when Earth urgently needs him. Like other episodes in the series, this one is modestly budgeted, but particular care was taken with script, direction, and casting. It's a revelatory installment, suggesting that Superman's dark streak does not define him, after all, and that this immensely powerful visitor from another planet will remain Earth's selfless protector even after losing all concept of his identity.

It's evening in Metropolis, and the sky is illuminated by the false daylight of an asteroid, five miles in diameter, that hurtles toward Earth. A leading astronomer, Professor Roberts (Jonathan Hale), tells Superman that an awful collision is inevitable. But Roberts has devised a briefcase-sized bomb of incredible power. If Superman can fly to the asteroid and detonate the bomb, disaster may be avoided.

Superman successfully makes the journey and arms the bomb, which explodes moments after Superman has left the asteroid's surface. We learn only later that the asteroid is shot through with Kryptonite, irradiated pieces of Kal-el's exploded planet, and the only substance that can harm and kill him.

Stunned by the blast, Superman makes a shaky landing in an isolated area near Metropolis. He's been physically weakened but the real damage seems to be mental. Although he has sufficient presence of mind to put on the Clark Kent disguise he finds in the pouch of his cape, his memory has been wiped clean. Except for the wallet that identifies him as Kent, he has no ability to recognize himself. For the moment, Superman — and Kal-el, too — no longer exist.

Metropolis and the world grow alarmed when Superman doesn't reappear. Did the bomb kill him? In the city, Clark sits dumbly in his apartment, struggling with puzzle pieces that elude him. He knows he's Kent, but there's something more, too. If only he could remember....

His friend Jimmy Olsen stops by to commiserate about Superman's disappearance. In one of the great moments of this lively series, Clark turns away from Jimmy and unbuttons his shirt, tugging it free of his slacks to reveal the Superman tunic, and its splendid "S," beneath. In a great irony, Superman's secret identity may be revealed when Clark has no notion of having one.

Fortunately, he keeps his back to Jimmy, who helps steer him toward the bedroom. Alone, now, Clark accidentally trips the door to the hidden closet. The spare costume is inside; Clark examines it. If only he could remember....

A minute later the apartment is split by a terrible crash. Clark has fallen through the glass shower door and lies unconscious on the floor. Later, he awakes in his bed surrounded by Jimmy, Perry, and Lois (Noel Neill, who succeeded Phyllis Coates in the role). Jimmy marvels that Clark came away without a scratch. And getting him into bed wasn't easy: "He must weigh a ton!"

Conversation with his friends confirms his amnesia. Clark doesn't recall any of them, and has only a vague notion of Earth's missing hero. "Superman? I seem to have heard of him somewhere before. Who *is* Superman?" (Amusingly, Clark lies in bed without his glasses; he's clearly Superman and yet, because of the wonderfully childlike suspension of disbelief that's central to the series, no one, not even the maniacally snoopy Lois, notices.)

Word comes from Professor Roberts that the bomb merely sidetracked the asteroid. It's still drawing closer to Earth, causing terrible natural disasters (courtesy of de rigueur stock footage). Roberts has even worse news: "That thing might disturb the balance of the entire solar system!"

Shortly, Clark gazes again at the spare costume. In the living room he says to Jimmy, "I've been thinking about Superman. Do you suppose it's his costume that gives him his peculiar powers?"

Jimmy considers. "No, no, that's not right. His costume has no particular powers. Only Superman can do super things."

When Jimmy leaves, Clark puts on the tunic. He sits in frustration, thinking, and when he suddenly levers his fist onto an end table, the piece of furniture is reduced to flinders. With that, some small piece of the puzzle falls into place in Clark's mind.

In costume now, Clark returns to the observatory. Roberts hands him another bomb. Clark still hasn't sorted out his identity, but he knows the moment is a serious one. He looks at the group: "Goodbye, Professor, Miss Lane, everyone."

On the asteroid for a second time, Clark pauses. "Well, whoever I am, here goes." He arms the bomb.

This time the asteroid is split asunder (expressed via cartoon animation). Superman returns to Earth. Yes, *Superman*, for Earth's greatest hero has regained his memory, and sense of self.

"Panic in the Sky" is a visual treat. Despite the stock footage and climactic cartoon explosion, its belies its very low budget with Reeves's fabulous springboard takeoffs directly into the camera and matted flying sequences that shoot down on Superman as he soars above Metropolis, and follow as he tilts upward, flies at us, and then gracefully soars out of frame. A phalanx of upturned faces at the beginning of the story, as the asteroid casts its weird light, is effective, and the asteroid itself is suitably convincing, smoking and spitting like an angry, illuminated Christmas ornament.

All of that is great fun, but the real power of "Panic in the Sky" is its explication of the nature of Superman. The amnesia frees Kal-el of identity conflict, and we understand beyond any doubt, for perhaps the only time in the series, that Superman

Earth's greatest hero, Superman (Reeves), and Lois Lane (Phyllis Coates), prepared to sustain a self-actualized life without love.

is truly and deeply altruistic. He deals with the asteroid a second time not because he unconsciously seeks approval and validation; he has no "Superman" persona who might desire such validation. Issues of ethnicity, as identified by Guanipa and Guanipa-Ho, no longer are factors in Kal-el's behavior. Further, the amnesia allows Kal-el to escape the role confusion described in Erikson's Stage Five (who am I and where am I going?), and the self-absorption that can accompany Stage Seven (will I produce something of real value?). Indeed, Kal-el, though only about 35 years old (as noted, at the upper level of what Erikson terms Early Adulthood), is able to progress to Erikson's final level, Stage Eight, during which the elderly individual ponders, *Have I lived a good life?* Kal-el answers that question for us and for himself with action. He is filled with integrity of the sort that, according to Erikson, marks the self-image of the aged who have lived good, meaningful lives.

Further, in development according to Maslow, Kal-el has reached the summit: self-actualization, or, as Maslow expressed it, "to become more and more what one is, to become everything that one is capable of becoming."

The splendid psychological success of Kal-el/Clark/Superman as expressed in "Panic in the Sky" has but a single shadow. For all his humanity, Superman is not truly human. He is a son of Krypton, not a child of Earth. As noted earlier, he is one of us, but not *of* us. Although he attains the highest levels described by Erikson and Maslow, he must, by virtue of his origins, skip a key developmental landmark, the level Erikson calls Intimacy versus Isolation, and what Maslow terms Love Needs. Superman is devoted to his adopted planet and its inhabitants, but he distances himself from deep personal relationships. If he has love needs, or desires for (nonsexual) intimacy, *The Adventures of Superman* never reveals them. To the contrary, the series makes clear that Superman, in his Kent disguise, lives alone and sleeps alone. He usually eats alone. He has no favorite recreations and no confidantes. Throughout the series' run, George Reeves played Kent/Superman with wit, but with an undeniable coolness, as well. Clark is loved by others (most fiercely, perhaps, by Jimmy), but Clark reveals his innermost selves to no one.

Erikson posited that in early adulthood people must ask, *Will I share my life with another or live alone?* Kal-el has answered, *I will live alone.* That's not a tragedy because Superman is capable of living a self-actualized life *without* love. A lamentable situation to our minds, perhaps, but a triumph for Superman. The amnesia of "Panic in the Sky" demonstrates that Earth's greatest hero, though he must consciously juggle the histories and responsibilities of Kal-el, Clark Kent, and Superman when in full possession of his faculties, is at his core a congenial gestalt of all three. He lives inside his skin easily, comfortably. The amnesia temporarily frees him of issues of ego, identity, and subterfuge. Kal-el is, psychologically speaking, stripped naked. We see that he is a pure altruist who needs no intimacy. This fact is a measure of his fundamentally alien nature, but also a gauge of his greatness.

Television Episodes Discussed

"Superman on Earth" First broadcast September 19, 1952 (episode #1, filmed 1951). Approx. 25 min. Producer: Robert Maxwell and Bernard Luber. Director: Thomas Carr. Teleplay: Richard Fielding, Robert Maxwell and Whitney Ellsworth. Director of Photography: William Whitley. Editor: Al Joseph. Music: Leon Klatzkin (opening and closing themes); MUTEL Music Service/Capitol "Q" Library. Art Director: Ralph Berger. Special Effects: Danny Hayes. With George Reeves, Phyllis Coates, John Hamilton, Robert Rockwell, Aline Towne, Tom Fadden, Frances Morris, Dabbs Greer and Joel Nestler. Available on Warner DVD.

"The Stolen Costume" First broadcast December 12, 1952 (episode #13, filmed 1951). Approx. 25 min. Producer: Robert Maxwell and Bernard Luber. Director: Lee Sholem. Teleplay: Ben Peter Freeman. Director of Photography: William Whitley. Editor: Al Joseph. Music: Leon Klatzkin (opening and closing themes); MUTEL Music Service/Capitol "Q" Library. Art Director: Ralph Berger. Special Effects: Danny Hayes. With George Reeves, Phyllis Coates, Jack Larson, John Hamilton, Frank Jenks, Veda Ann Borg, Dan Seymour and Norman Budd. Available on Warner DVD.

"The Face and the Voice" First broadcast November 21, 1953 (episode #36, filmed 1953). Approx. 25 min. Producer: Whitney Ellsworth. Director: George Blair. Teleplay: Jackson Gillis. Director of Photography: Harold Stine. Editor: Harry Gerstad. Music: Leon Klatzkin (opening and closing themes); MUTEL Music Service/Capitol "Q" Library. Special Effects: Thol Simonson. With George Reeves, Noel Neill, Jack Larson, John Hamilton, Robert Shayne, Carleton Young, Percy Helton and Hayden Rorke. Note: This episode is part of the 20th Century–Fox compilation feature, *Superman in Exile* (1954). Not presently available on home video.

"Panic in the Sky" First broadcast December 5, 1953 (episode #38; filmed 1953). Approx. 25 min. Producer: Whitney Ellsworth. Director: Thomas Carr. Writer: Jackson Gillis. Director of Photography: Harold Stine. Editor: Harry Gerstad. Music: Leon Klatzkin (opening and closing themes); MUTEL Music Service/Capitol "Q" Library. Special Effects: Thol Simonson. With George Reeves, Noel Neill, Jack Larson, John Hamilton, Jonathan Hale and Jane Frazee. Note: This episode is part of the 20th Century–Fox compilation feature, *Superman and Scotland Yard* (1954). Not presently available on home video.

Sources

Erikson, Erik H. *Erik Erikson Reader*. New York: W.W. Norton, 2001.

_____. *Identity, Youth and Crisis*. New York: W.W. Norton, 1968.

Grossman, Gary. *Superman: Serial to Cereal*. New York: Popular Library, 1976.

Guanipa, Carmen. "Ethnic Identity and Adolescence." <http://edweb.sdsu.edu/people/Cguanipa/ethnic.htm#develop>.

Maslow, Abraham. *Motivation and Personality*, second ed. New York: Harper and Row, 1954.

Maslow, Abraham A. *Toward a Psychology of Being*. Princeton: Van Nostrand Reinhold, 1968.

Pazsaz Entertainment Network. "The Adventures of Superman." <http://www.pazsaz.com/super.html>.

9

The Atomic Kid: Radioactivity Finds Andy Hardy

Ted Okuda

When you're in the first grade, there are certain things concerning school rules and regulations that you accept on good faith. For instance, you don't question the need for crossing guards or fire drills; surely, the fact that they exist proves there's a very real need for them. The same held true for air raid drills.

Though the average person under the age of 50 has no idea what I'm referring to, for a generation that attended grade school (or grammar school, as we called it back then) during the late '50s and early '60s, the memory of these drills should strike a familiar chord. At the sound of a blaring air raid siren, we'd dutifully leave our desks, go to the classroom wall farthest from the big plate glass windows, then cover our faces with our hands. Other schools had varying procedures; some former kids I've spoken with recall crouching under their desks, while others remember finding a safe haven in the cloakroom. (If you don't know what an air raid drill is, then a cloakroom must have you completely stumped.) Regardless of where you sought succor, however, the message was always the same: Protect yourself from bodily harm in the event of an atomic attack.

If we had the misfortune of being caught in an atomic bomb blast, we were told, the consequences would be no less than grisly. Although we were largely spared the gruesome details, it was easy to conclude that the old adage "that's me all over" would become a literal truism. Yet this dire scenario could easily be avoided if we just got our butts off our desk chairs and huddled by a wall every time we heard the air raid siren. *Thank goodness we have a safety plan that actually works!*

What wasn't so clear to us was why we would be attacked in the first place. We had some notion there was an evil European Empire overrun with these folks called Communists who were intent on total annihilation (ours). But one thing school taught us was not to question the system — all we had to know was that we had to be prepared for an attack. This was for our own good, so we trusted the messengers implicitly, even if the rationale behind their messages eluded us.

The Cold War wasn't pitched to seven year olds in the same manner it was presented to older students and adults, who were fed a steady diet of government-approved data about the Red Menace. At our lowly first-grade level, the closest thing to political coverage we were exposed to was the photos of our ever-smiling (and hand-waving) president that were printed in *My Weekly Reader*. By all appearances, he seemed to be a pretty confident leader; if we had to play by his rules, so be it.

Of course, we were also shown such now-legendary A-bomb safety films as *Duck and Cover* (produced by the Federal Civil Defense Administration in 1951) which instructed us on what to do in the event of an atomic blast ("Duck! And cover!"). However, the safety tips were delivered by an animated turtle named Bert. So the urgency of the message was undermined by its conceptual conceit; we weren't watching a safety film, we were watching a cartoon, and a rather bland one at that.

Whatever knowledge we had regarding world events was gleaned from television and movies. (A situation that, regrettably, hasn't changed much.) Whether the subject was handled in an ultra-earnest manner or simply as a lark, of this we were certain: Nuclear weapons in the hands of foreign powers would only be used for heinous, world-domination purposes—unlike the altruistic agenda of the good ol' U.S. of A. After all, as depicted in one Hollywood motion picture after another, those dirty Commies, contemptuous of our liberty and freethinking lifestyle, wouldn't hesitate for a moment to press the little red button that would wipe us off Rand-McNally's maps. America, on the other hand, merely "gathered" information and "tested" nuclear weapons, using prop buildings and mannequins as targets. Heaven forbid that we'd actually have to use an atomic bomb on real people ... again.

We'd see bomb shelters on television programs like *The Twilight Zone*, although they were a plot device to address social conflicts (*screw the neighbors, there's only enough room for us*) rather than political issues. Whether by design or unconscious omission, the scripts deftly pirouetted around the political ramifications of an atomic cataclysm. *Never mind the reason why, just hurry up and get into that shelter.* So, like Mafia wives, we did what we were told and didn't ask questions.

Besides, as movie-loving youngsters, we favored escapist fare. Anything that remotely smacked of being educational or conveying a lesson was avoided like ... well, like an atomic blast. Who wanted to spend a Saturday afternoon listening to Gregory Peck ponder the end of the world in *On the Beach* when we could watch the Three Stooges being chased by an oversized, fire-breathing tarantula in *Have Rocket—Will Travel*? (Ask a kid if he'd like to see a movie that's an emotionally enriching life experience and you'll really see him duck and cover.)

Fifties SF cinema was rife with cautionary tales concerning atomic power. Through the miracle of stock footage, A-bombs brought about World War III in *Invasion, U.S.A.* Doomsday survivors were depicted in *Five*, *Day the World Ended*, and *The World, the Flesh, and the Devil.* The dread of atomic warfare was addressed seriously in Akira Kurosawa's *I Live in Fear* (aka *Record of a Living Being* and *Fear*) and comically in the little-seen *Run for the Hills*. Other films used their nuclear themes as gimmicks to unleash an assortment of beasts (*Them!*, *The Beast from 20,000 Fathoms*, *Godzilla*, *Attack of the Crab Monsters*) and mutated human beings (*The Amazing Colossal Man*, *The Incredible Shrinking Man*, *The H-Man*).

In retrospect, a comedy about radiation poisoning would seem to be in the worst taste imaginable. And yet Jerry Lewis thought he was dying from it in *Living It Up*, one of the best of the Martin and Lewis pictures. Early on, Jerry learns he's perfectly healthy but uses the publicity he's received as a way to wrangle an all-expenses-paid trip to New York City. *You can relax, folks. Jerry's okay; it's just a harmless prank.*

Paramount Pictures released *Living It Up* to theaters in July 1954. Five months later, Republic Pictures released its own radioactive comedy; only this time, in a dubious attempt to increase the laugh quotient, the lead character was actually contaminated. *Laugh? I thought I'd die!*

Mickey Rooney is the titular victim in *The Atomic Kid*. One of the most versatile entertainers of all time — and one of the screen's most underrated actors— Rooney was a huge box office draw during the late thirties and early forties, in lavish musicals with Judy Garland and in the ongoing *Andy Hardy* series. It was as Andy, an average American small-town teenager, that Rooney endeared himself to the movie-going public. Honest, fun-loving, and irrepressible, Andy may not really have been an average youth, but he did typify the ideal of an all–American youth. During the World War II years, it was Andy Hardy (and icons like him) that helped entertain and reassure an anxious nation.

The postwar era brought about changes in the national mood. We became more cautious, more cynical, less sentimental. As a performer, Rooney was awkwardly caught in the gears of shifting tastes. Though still a tremendously gifted talent, he was no longer a youth, and his earlier persona exemplified a sort of naïveté that had fallen out of fashion. Tellingly, *Love Laughs at Andy Hardy*, the first postwar Hardy picture, was a resounding flop at the box office.

By the early '50s Rooney began producing his own movies in an effort to secure a new screen persona (or retool his old one). After dabbling in film noir and musicals, he turned to a topical subject with *The Atomic Kid*. Andy Hardy finally confronted the Cold War, though it was strictly on his own terms.

In the atomic movies of the era, certain themes surface repeatedly:

- Americans are good, Communists are rotten
- America's greatest weapon is the inherent decency of its people
- Nuclear research is our friend
- Atomic bombs are no match for your faith in God (*our* God, the real one)
- Even the most unrepentant citizen becomes a super-patriot when the American way of life is threatened
- You're lucky to be an American

While many films touched on one or more of these themes, *The Atomic Kid* contains them all. (In fact, it was distributed in some U.S. markets under its alternate title, *Call Me Lucky*.)

For a movie aimed squarely at the kiddie market, *The Atomic Kid* begins on a strangely ominous note as stock footage of atomic mushroom clouds fills the screen under the opening credits, accompanied by Van Alexander's doom laden music score. Documentaries on the devastation of Hiroshima have had cheerier beginnings.

This somber mood is shattered immediately, however, as we see the figures of Barnaby "Blix" Waterberry (Rooney) and Stan Cooper (Robert Strauss) wandering through the Nevada desert. A Mutt 'n' Jeff pair of would-be prospectors, Blix and Stan's dream of finding a uranium deposit has left them broke—financially and spiritually. Just as all seems lost, the hapless duo stumbles across an oasis in the form of a modern tract home smack dab in the middle of nowhere. "Maybe this is one of those families who moved way out here in the desert to get away from the atom bomb," Blix muses. As their Geiger counter starts clicking away, Stan immediately assumes the property is loaded with uranium. Pay dirt at last!

What these two Fortune 500 wannabes don't realize is that the model home is part of an A-bomb test site. Finding a car (another target) conveniently parked outside, Stan heads to town to file a claim, leaving Blix behind to guard their discovery. A short time later, an atom bomb levels the house, with poor Blix trapped inside. To the amazement of government scientists and the military brass, Blix survives the blast; overnight, he's thrust from obscurity into the international spotlight, bringing him to the attention of a foreign spy ring.

The Atomic Kid (1954), Blix Waterberry (Mickey Rooney) and pal Stan (Robert Strauss) discover something amiss in the fully furnished house they discover in the middle of the Nevada desert.

At times, *The Atomic Kid* has the feel of a feature-length newsreel, as it incorporates stock footage of an actual A-bomb test. The target site includes military equipment and a tract home filled with mannequins, furniture, and household appliances, so that "scientists can determine what an atom blast would do to Mr. and Mrs. Average American" (the ones who haven't seen *Duck and Cover*, evidently).

While the military is depicted as a humorless, by-the-book operation, the scientific community is shown in the most humane terms possible. Moments before the detonation, chief physicist Dr. Rodell (Bill Goodwin) remarks forlornly to his assistant Dr. Pangborn (Whit Bissell), "Strange, isn't it? The most powerful atom bomb yet developed and it's already outdated." "Yes," observes Pangborn, "Right now in some secluded laboratory they're already putting on paper a weapon that'll make this look like a firecracker." *Sure, nuclear research is a dirty business, but that doesn't mean we're not human.*

But the film is, first and foremost, a comedy, so there's plenty of knockabout, pre-blast humor as Blix and Stan fumble their way through the abandoned house, shrieking in terror at their first sight of the target mannequins.

When Stan leaves to file their claim, a starving Blix discovers a pantry full of food and promptly whips up his favorite meal: a peanut butter, sardine, and horseradish sandwich. (Since these items are on the premises, does this mean the government wants to evaluate the effect an atom blast has on condiments and canned seafood?) After the bomb is detonated, a smoky, blackened Blix emerges from the rubble, jabbering a mile a minute (the result of his accelerated metabolism, we're told) and still holding onto the now-toasted sandwich.

Dubbed "Operation Miracle" by the press, Blix is checked into the Atomic City Hospital, where he's quarantined and undergoes a battery of tests. For a guy who was caught in an atomic blast, Blix cleans up remarkably well — well enough to attract the attention of a pretty nurse named Audrey Nelson (Elaine Davis).

Stir-crazy after a month of isolation, Blix is anxious to get out of the hospital, if only for one night, to hit the town with Audrey. He has an incredibly sympathetic ally in Dr. Rodell, who helps stage an escape, instructing two FBI agents (Hal March, Peter Leeds) to keep Blix under surveillance: "It'll do him good to have some recreation. I can't see that he'll get into any harm." *Sure, doc, what harm would there be in allowing a patient festering with radioactive toxins to roam freely among the general public? Besides, isn't it worth risking widespread contamination so we can cater to the romantic whims of a sympathetic little ragamuffin?*

Even in a film as frivolous as this, the image of our scientific community as friend-parent-protector is reinforced. They may have developed weapons of mass destruction that can wipe out millions of lives in an instant, but they are still genuinely concerned about the needs of the common man. And if it takes endangering countless innocent bystanders for one lone American to get his freak on, well, that's a chance they're willing to take, *dagnabbit*. Is this a great country or what?

Yet any rational fears are unfounded. In stark contrast to those atomic safety films, Blix's condition turns out to be more embarrassing than lethal. When he catches up with Audrey at a Las Vegas casino (he hitches a ride with those friendly FBI fellas), Blix's radioactivity triggers a jackpot in every slot machine he passes. Later, in

HERBERT J. YATES presents
The ATOMIC KID
starring
MICKEY ROONEY ROBERT STRAUSS
"STALAG 17"
introducing ELAINE DAVIS (Mrs. Mickey Rooney)
WITH
BILL GOODWIN · WHIT BISSELL · HAL MARCH · FAY ROOPE
Screen Play by BENEDICT FREEDMAN and JOHN FENTON MURRAY
Directed by LESLIE H. MARTINSON · Associate Producer MAURICE DUKE
A MICKEY ROONEY PRODUCTION · A REPUBLIC PICTURE

Kaboom! Blix (Rooney) is seared by an A-bomb, which fries him (and his peanut butter sandwich) to a golden brown, giving uneasy Atomic Age audiences something to think about.

a private moment, Blix's amorous feelings result in him glowing in the dark. That darn ol' radiation poisoning — why, it's just like a bad case of acne.

For a nurse who works so closely with atomic scientists, Audrey is amazingly unperturbed by the contagious nature of Blix's deadly condition. Love really does conquer all.

One aspect of the film that is credible is its cynical view of hype and commercialism. Though grief-stricken when he thought Blix was killed in the blast, Stan Cooper quickly reverts to his avaricious self. Capitalizing on his pal's newfound celebrity by becoming his "agent," Stan engineers endorsement deals with Mother Goose's Homogenized Peanut Butter ("The peanut butter with the built-in atomic protection!") and Snyder's Atomic-Proof Pants. Cashing in on someone else's misfortune in order to make a quick buck — now, *that's* the American Way in action!

Stan's blind greed provides the perfect entrée for enemy spies to contact Blix. A certain "Mr. Reynolds" (Robert Emmett Keane) approaches Stan and proposes a tribute to Blix in the form of a biography, for which Reynolds and his "associates" would need classified information — to make the story authentic, mind you. At one point Reynolds slips up and calls Stan "comrade," to which the inattentive oaf responds, "My name isn't *Conrad*."

HERBERT J. YATES
The ATOMIC KID
starring
MICKEY ROONEY ROBERT STRAUSS
"STALAG 17"
introducing ELAINE DAVIS (Mrs. Mickey Rooney)
WITH
BILL GOODWIN · WHIT BISSELL · HAL MARCH · FAY ROOPE
Screen Play by BENEDICT FREEDMAN and JOHN FENTON MURRAY
Directed by LESLIE H. MARTINSON
MAURICE DUKE
A MICKEY ROONEY PRODUCTION · A REPUBLIC PICTURE

In the tradition of U.S. government denials of harmful effects of atomic testing, Blix (Rooney) hasn't been lethally dosed because, well, because the atomic bomb is our friend. The situation even brings romance, as the malingering Blix falls for pretty nurse Audrey (Elaine Davis).

However, in keeping with the theme of every American being a patriot at heart, the cowardly Stan puts the needs of his country ahead of his own well-being when he learns he's been duped. Attempting to expose the spies, Stan becomes an inadvertent hero when he accidentally knocks Blix out of an open window and onto a fleeing "Mr. Mosley" (Peter Brocco), the leader of the spy ring.

The film's characterization of an enemy spy is as perfunctory as you might expect. Though never identified as a *Russian* spy, Reynolds is obviously a foreigner and more obviously a Communist. The powers he represents are hell-bent on getting their hands on Blix, who is "the only living nuclear chain reaction." They believe he holds the key to a new scientific discovery and intend to poke, prod, and, if necessary, dissect him. Bastards! Hey, wait a minute — isn't that essentially what the U.S. government is doing here? Although our leaders would never go so far as to chop Blix up into little pieces (would they?), they still want to unlock the mystery as much as our enemies do, and employ these secrets to further their own political agendas. Clearly, the difference is that *we* are motivated by unquestionably good intentions, while *they* are incapable of anything but evil. Ergo, your morality is directly linked to which side of the map you're on. If you're in America, you're obviously in the right. If you're one of those darn foreigners, you're inherently sinister. Even when things look identical, we know there's a difference. As George Carlin facetiously observed, detestable Lenin, a Russian, had a beard while lovable Gabby Hayes, an American, had whiskers.

A hallmark of the Andy Hardy films were the heart-to-heart "father and son" talks in which Andy turns to the stern but compassionate Judge Hardy (Lewis Stone) for solace and advice. A comparable scene turns up near the end of *The Atomic Kid*. When informed he's no longer radioactive and therefore of "no further importance to your government," Blix becomes melancholy. "Why so solemn?" asks Dr. Rodell. "You're a normal human being again." "It's a funny thing," Blix replies. "When I was a nobody, I used to dream of the day when I'd be somebody. When I became somebody all it meant was just a lot of examinations and being cooped up in a room. I'd have given anything to have been nobody again. Now that I'm nobody again, I don't know what I want." (It's a requisite of movie comedians like our hero to run the gamut from Frantic Buffoon to Soulful Everyman.)

"There's a great many people like that," Rodell reassures him. "You know the old saying: There are only two types of people in the world — those who are unhappy because they haven't got what they want and those who are unhappy because they have." Taking advantage of the physicist's philosophical bent, Blix inquires, "Perhaps you could tell me, how did I survive the atom bomb blast?" Rodell responds, "I only hope you can remember the prayers you said when the bomb went off because five months of careful research have shown us that only a miracle could have saved you."

In this scene, Blix is essentially an Atomic Age Andy Hardy. But Dr. Rodell becomes more than just a stand-in for the elder Hardy; he's a reassuring, all-knowing government figure. Forget all that stuff you may have heard about searing pain and burning flesh; Blix Waterberry survived intact because he's a decent God-fearing American — which is, ultimately, the best defense against any adversity.

None of this is meant to imply that *The Atomic Kid* is a cunningly crafted piece of propaganda. It was and remains nothing more than an example of silly, disposable entertainment made for undemanding audiences. And being a knockabout farce, it's ludicrous for us to expect an incisive look at science and politics. But the film's plot points and narrative choices undeniably reflect the attitudes of its era: For the good of mankind, America must continue its atomic testing, if only to keep our enemies at bay. Just put your faith in God and your government, though not necessarily in that order.

In later years, Mickey Rooney would collectively dismiss his movies of the late '40s and early '50s as failures. No doubt he was looking at them in terms of box office success because, creatively speaking, some of his finest, most compelling work comes from this period: *Quicksand*, *The Strip*, *Drive a Crooked Road*, and *The Bold and the Brave* showcase bravura Rooney performances.

The Atomic Kid can't be ranked among Rooney's greatest achievements, although it's entertaining enough for the audience it was primarily intended for: children. It certainly isn't the painfully unfunny experience critics would have you believe it is. (You want real pain? Try sitting through *Corky Romano*.) Rooney gives a sincere if somewhat schizophrenic performance, as he wavers from manic funster (think Jerry

Lewis at his best) to bathetic loner (think Jerry Lewis at his worst). But he's always in there pitching, even with a paucity of good material.

The film is aided and abetted by a sturdy supporting cast. Brawny, lumbering Robert Strauss, best known as "Animal" in *Stalag 17* (he was nominated for an Academy Award), proves to be a perfect foil for Rooney. Bill Goodwin made a career out of playing soft-spoken nice guys (*The Jolson Story*, *Jolson Sings Again*), so he was the ideal choice to play a soft-spoken nice-guy scientist. Whit Bissell was one of Hollywood's most reliable character actors, appearing in films ranging from *The Creature from the Black Lagoon* and *I Was a Teenage Frankenstein* to *The Caine Mutiny* and *The Manchurian Candidate*.

Leading lady Elaine Davis was Mrs. Mickey Rooney at the time; she's even billed that way in the credits (this was, after all, a Mickey Rooney production). She's pleasant and attractive here, although later, as Elaine Devry, she would give more memorable performances in *The Cheyenne Social Club* (as one of the "bawdy house" girls), *The Boy Who Cried Werewolf* (as a lycanthrope's unsuspecting spouse), and *A Guide for the Married Man* (tantalizing as Walter Matthau's would-be mistress).

Benedict Freedman and John Fenton Murray concocted the screenplay for *The Atomic Kid* from a story by Blake Edwards (*Peter Gunn*, *The Pink Panther*, *Days of Wine and Roses*, *The Great Race*, *Victor/Victoria*). Edwards had also written the superior *Drive a Crooked Road* for Rooney; later, when he turned director, Edwards gave Rooney a supporting role in *Breakfast at Tiffany's*. The direction by Leslie H. Martinson (*Hot Rod Girl*, *PT-109*, 1966's *Batman*, *Fathom*) is workmanlike, no more, no less, given the limitations of this kind of B-level filmmaking.

The special effects were handled by Republic Pictures' in-house geniuses, the Lydecker brothers (Howard and Theodore), who were responsible for the eye-popping visuals in such vintage serials as *The Adventures of Captain Marvel*, *Spy Smasher*, and *King of the Rocketmen*. Unfortunately, *The Atomic Kid*'s slender budget didn't afford them much opportunity to strut their stuff.

I can't recall exactly when I first participated in an air raid drill, just as I can't recall exactly when the practice was terminated. One day they just called it quits, and I never noticed. But the memory of the era comes rushing back to me whenever I watch *The Atomic Kid*. It may not be anyone's idea of exceptional cinema, but it's a time capsule that's both nostalgic and fascinating, with a few laughs thrown in for good measure.

I used to scoff at the concept of air raid drills, but in light of these increasingly volatile times, they're not such a bad idea after all. We really do need to be prepared. I know I plan to have a peanut butter, sardine, and horseradish sandwich on hand, just in case my prayers go unanswered.

And if I survive — as I know I will — I'll owe it all to Blix Waterberry, the Atomic Kid.

Now, where's that pretty nurse?

Film Discussed

The Atomic Kid (Alternate release title: *Call Me Lucky.*) Republic Pictures. Released December 8, 1954. 86 min. Producer: Mickey Rooney. Director: Leslie H. Martinson. Screenplay: Benedict Freedman and John Fenton Murray. Story: Blake Edwards. Director of Photography: John L. Russell, Jr. Editor: Fred Allen. Music: Van Alexander. Art Director: Frank Hotaling. Special Effects: Howard and Theodore Lydecker. With Mickey Rooney, Robert Strauss, Elaine Davis, Bill Goodwin, Whit Bissell, Joey Forman, Hal March, Peter Leeds, Fay Roope, Stanley Adams, Robert Emmett Keane, Milton Frome and Peter Brocco. Formerly available from Republic Pictures Home Video; currently out of print.

10

Godzilla vs. the Military-Industrial Complex

ALAN DIRK LESTER

> When I returned from the war [in China] and passed through Hiroshima, there was a heavy atmosphere, a fear that the world was already coming to an end.
>
> —*Toho Company director Ishiro Honda*

Maybe you're completely unaware of how it really all began. Or maybe you've only heard one or more of those *Reader's Digest* abridged versions of the tale. Either way, if you'll be kind enough to sit back for a short while, I'll be more than happy to tell you everything I can about his story. (Cue ominous Akira Ifukube score.) In the early morning hours of March 1, 1954, the 23-man crew onboard a fishing trawler called the *Fukuryu Maru* (*Lucky Dragon*) inadvertently cruised to within range of one of America's nuclear weapon test sites. The "Bravo" hydrogen bomb set off that day at Bikini Atoll produced a blast equivalent to about 12 million tons of TNT. It was an explosion 750 to 1,000 times more massive than those produced by the atomic weapons that'd been dropped on Hiroshima and Nagasaki a decade before, and more importantly, it was at least twice as powerful as scientists in the United States had led the rest of world to believe it would be.

From somewhere close to 85 miles away, the *Lucky Dragon*'s fishermen looked on, believing God-only-knows what had occurred: "The sky in the west suddenly lit up and the sea became brighter than day," crew member Yoshio Misaki would later recall. "We watched the dazzling light, which felt heavy. Seven or eight minutes later there was a terrific sound; like an avalanche. Then a visible multi-colored ball of fire appeared on the horizon." For hours afterwards, a rain of white ash fell, gathering in drifting piles across the *Lucky Dragon's* deck. Some of the fishermen collected bags of it as souvenirs. By nightfall, everyone onboard the vessel was ill. All 23 were hospitalized after returning to Japan, and at least one of them, radio operator Aikichi Kuboyama, died seven months later of kidney failure reportedly caused by the radiation.

Ironically, Kuboyama's death was later determined to have been caused by unrelated hepatitis. Still, the erroneous perception of the nature of his passing assumed greater cultural and political weight than the facts—so much so, in fact, that when *Gojira* was released in 1954 the Japanese press accused Toho of profiteering from the *Lucky Dragon* tragedy.

If the story of the *Lucky Dragon* sounds even vaguely unfamiliar, it shouldn't at all. An incident, quite intentionally comparable, opens the 1954 film *Gojira* (re-edited and released in the United States in 1956 as *Godzilla, King of the Monsters*), and easily more than a dozen parallel scenes have been prominent features of the 25 sequels that followed. There can be little doubt that the fate of the *Fukuryu Maru* and its crew helped inspire the Toho Company to make its first movie monster a radiation-mutated dinosaur, reanimated as a veritable force of nature, out to terrorize mankind. The event planted a seed in harried producer Tomoyuki Tanaka's mind as to how he could replace his proposed war epic, *In the Shadows of Glory*, a film project he'd only recently been forced to abort due to irreconcilable differences with its supposed coproducers, the Indonesian government. He quickly shared his nightmare visions of "a monster that invades Tokyo the way King Kong attacked New York," with director Ishiro Honda and special effects supervisor Eiji Tsuburaya. Together, the three men went on to create both a cultural icon and what is now the longest-running film series of all time. Godzilla towers over his nearest competitor, the fabulous James Bond, by five installments.

But it's not the how or even the why that concerns us today; it's the what. That's a little something I've been going on and on about for years, ever since I was challenged to explain my reverence for the Godzilla films to the *uber*-pacifist and doctorate-certified intellectual masquerading as my brother-in-law. He was upset because I'd dared to show a violently militaristic slice of cinema—namely the 1964 masterpiece of "suitmation" known Stateside as *Godzilla vs. the Thing*—to his then three-year-old son.

Having been addicted to the King of the Monsters' exploits since I was about that age, my response was just as immediate as it was previously unarticulated: "Godzilla is a living embodiment of the greatest folly of the industrial age, the atom bomb; armies are always absolutely powerless before him and his victims are mostly capitalist exploiters or members of the military industrial complex." My brother-in-law, being no great fool, recalled that I had once defended Bugs Bunny during a similar exchange by arguing that on account of his relative nonviolence as compared to his adversaries, and consistent plus successful use of brains-over-brawn tactics, Bugs was indeed a positive role model for children.

However, my brother-in-law demanded immediate and definite proof of my new Godzilla-based claims. To provide such, I first went over much of the same character history I've recounted for you here; then we sat down and re-screened *Godzilla vs. the Thing* with an eye toward either disproving or firmly establishing Big G's credentials as a radical environmentalist and all-out enemy of "the Man."

Implacable and devastatingly destructive, Godzilla is the evil genie loosed by the atomic bomb. This is the original Gojira of 1954, captured by the modeler's art and displayed at a Godzilla fan convention (J. D. Lees).

(Note: My nephew didn't mind this development at all.)

Just as I was starting to worry that maybe I should've stacked the deck in my favor by showing the spoilsport 1971's *Godzilla vs. the Smog Monster* instead, the *Thing*'s storm-tossed opening credits came to an end. A horrible typhoon has struck Japan, ruinously flooding the beachfront industrial area of Nagoya where a cleanup effort, headed by a stereotypically venal politician, has begun. While that bureaucrat is busy berating her reporter partner for writing negative articles, one of the photographers chronicling the devastation discovers a strange object amongst the debris that later turns out to be a sort of companion piece to a "monster egg" floating off nearby Karada beach.

Much of this provided me with the ammunition I was looking for. In just the first several minutes of this film we're introduced to a clearly negative portrayal of a weasel-faced public servant immediately assaulting the right to free speech; and a pair of positive (by virtue of being set in opposition to the bureaucrat) journalist heroes, one of whom scores extra PC points for progressive gender-modeling by virtue of being a competent, single career woman. And then there's the storm itself. Storms have served as metaphoric stand-ins for Godzilla since the Odo Island sequence featured in G's first film, and so we can read "Hurricane A's destruction of the industrialization project" as having been accomplished by the King of the Monsters himself. Is there a tree-hugger who could ask for more?

Next up, we're introduced to the aforementioned village of Karada, where the local fishermen, under the protection of a Shinto priest, have taken possession of the "monster egg" and dragged it ashore. By the time our two crusading journalists, Sakai (Akira Takarada) and Yoka (Yuriko Hoshi), arrive on the scene eminent scientists are already studying the egg. Luckily for me, the "traditional setting slash benign study" portion of the film's day doesn't last very long. Those scientists are quickly shooed away from their work by the appearance of a pig-faced man named Kumayama (Yoshifumi Tajima), a representative of a concern called Happy Enterprises, which has purchased the "monster egg" from this village of simple fishermen for the equivalent price of 150,000 chicken eggs and intends to exhibit it solely for profit.

Here's where I first really had to branch off into the accepted internal reality of the series to better make my point, because both new characters' archetypes pop up again and again in the Godzilla films. First off you have the scientist, Professor Miura (Hiroshi Koizumi), whom we may safely assume is a good guy because he's interested only in pure research. Why? Because, just as the world can rest assured that James Bond will eventually bed any female with a double entendre for a name, you can bet your last dollar that any scientist who invents something functional in a Godzilla picture is in for some serious troubles; and anyone in a white coat who is responsible for making any sort of weapon is out-and-out dead meat. From the first film's suicidal Dr. Serizawa to the ill-fated creator of the Titanosaurus in 1975's *Terror of Mechagodzilla*, they all meet gruesome ends. Much the same can be said of Kumayama's greedy businessman and his ilk. No such individual has ever made it out of one of the Big G's adventures alive. In one film, 1965's *Godzilla vs. Monster Zero*, our gargantuan hero even goes out of his way to stomp down a group of hostile aliens "merely posing" as corrupt businessmen. He hates businessmen just that much.

As *Godzilla vs. the Thing* moves on we discover that the piggish Kumayama is little more than a walking-talking front company puppeteered by a much slicker businessman identified by Sakai as Torahata (Kenji Sahara), a notorious moneyman. "He hides behind the scenes. He has influence. He is well acquainted with all the big politicians in the city." To which Yoka actually replies, "I see, an exploiter." A clear echo of my earlier statement. We're also introduced to the Cosmos (the *Shobijin*), a pair of diminutive female fairies (Emi Ito and Yumi Ito), who try unsuccessfully to convince the businessmen to return the giant egg. Frustrated, the Cosmos contact our three good guys. They explain that the egg belongs to the Mothra (the Thing, the star of her own 1961 film and monster guardian of Infant Island). "I've heard of your island," Professor Miura offers during this exchange. "Weren't atomic tests conducted there after the war?"

It was at this point that I realized that I had my brother-in-law right where I wanted him. Scenes of those vile capitalists scheming about how to best exploit the Thing's egg (a clear representation of the natural wealth of the Pacific), then actually trying to *buy* the Cosmos girls, speak for themselves. Add to that all the talk of disastrous nuclear testing and we find ourselves on ground that even the most zealous Greenpeace activist would be pleased with.

After their new allies try but fail to get Happy Enterprises to give up on their nefarious plans, the Cosmos split. Their departure apparently allows the project to proceed—well, at least until Professor Miura gets his hands on that mysterious object Yoka found in the debris at the beginning of the film. It's revealed to have been radioactive, so the three head back to the Nagoya waterfront to search for its source. Ah, and the source turns out to be none other than Godzilla himself. The Monster King surges up out the mud of the industrial project's now drained beach and promptly begins a brutal assault on the city that neither the Japanese nor the American militaries are able to slow much less stop. Left without any other options, our three human protagonists decide to head to Infant Island and beg Mothra for assistance. A brief but reflective trek through the bone-littered desolation left behind there by nuclear testing leads to a parlay with an irate native elder who angrily declares that "the gods are punishing you because you have defied them. Our island has been cruelly used. Our people stricken with disease. And you ... you who played with the fires of the gods. Your people are being punished. Their time has come. May your land be ruined like ours!"

Not what I would call a subtle indictment.

Of course, after listening to a suitable amount of groveling, the Cosmos agree to ask the Thing for her help, and soon enough that giant representative of the natural world is in Japan battling Godzilla to the death. It's during this small setback in Mothra's efforts to stop his rampage that Big G takes a familiar detour to engage one of his favorite pastimes by squishing both Kumayama and Torahata—who, we're pleased to note, have been too busy fighting over money to escape. In due course, the Thing's egg hatches and—circle-of-life style—her vengeful progeny attack and drive the King of the Monsters back into the sea. The End.

Pretty clear-cut antiestablishment stance for a giant monster movie, right?

Another Godzilla model roars at a Godzilla fan convention (J.D. Lees).

Still, I hasten to point out that most Godzilla films follow this formula precisely. I'll mention not only the self–explanatory *Godzilla vs. the Smog Monster* (1971) and its overwrought "save the earth" message but also the less often seen 1972 release *Godzilla vs. Gigan*, wherein the Big G defends Earth from an invasion of mutant alien cockroaches (yes, you read that correctly) who have decided that our earth, because of its ruined environment, would be an ideal home.

What I don't bother to bring up is a fact not widely known outside of Japan: Godzilla clearly represents more than just the dangers of the atomic age; Godzilla is the United States itself. His very name emphasizes a foreign nature. "Gojira," as our friend is called in Japan, is spelled in Katakana, the written characters used in that country to represent foreign words. Since this rendering could easily have been written using traditional Hiragara characters instead, it's definitely possible to interpret much of the above as an allegory condemning the West for its perceived attempts to crush nationalist business movements represented therein by ambitious and hard-working Japanese such as Kumayama and Torahata.

But why ruin a good time with such negativity?

Meanwhile, confronted by what seemed like a mountain of evidence (and late for work besides), that brother-in-law of mine conceded my point and dutifully left his son and me to better enjoy the unparalleled cinematic experience of watching a small man in a big rubber suit step on itsy-bitsy model tanks.

In the end, what more can one really ask of life?

Godzilla signage and other displays in Japan. After more than 50 years, the monster's stardom, and cultural significance, are undiminished. New 35mm prints of the original, Japanese-release version of *Gojira* (1954) played across the United States in 2004 (J.D. Lees).

Films Discussed

Gojira; aka Kaiju-o Gojira; Godzilla, King of the Monsters Toho/Embassy Pictures. Released November 3, 1954 (Japan), April 27, 1956 (U.S.). 98 min. (Japan), 81 min. (U.S.). Producer: Tomoyuki Tanaka (Japan), Joseph E. Levine and Richard Kay (U.S.). Director: Ishiro Honda (Japan) and Terry O. Morse (U.S.). Story: Shigeru Kayama. Screenplay: Takeo Murata and Ishiro Honda (Japan), Al C. Ward (U.S.). Director of Photography: Masao Tamai (Japan) and Guy Roe (U.S.). Editor: Yasunobu (Kazuji) Taira (Japan) and Terry O. Morse (U.S.). Music: Akira Ifukube. Art Directors: Satoshi Chuko and Takeo Kita. Special Effects: Eiji Tsuburaya. Special Effects Art Director: Akira Watanabe. Optical Effects: Hiroshi Mukoyama. Sound Effects: Ichiro Minawa. With Raymond Burr (U.S. only), Takashi Shimura, Momoko Kochi, Akira Takarada, Haruo Nakajima and James Hong (uncredited voice actor, U.S.). Available on Simitar Home Video DVD *Gojira*); Sony Music DVD (*Godzilla, King of the Monsters*).

Godzilla vs. the Thing; aka Mosura tai Gojira; Godzilla vs. Mothra; Godzilla Fights the Giant Moth; Godzilla vs. the Giant Moth; Mothra vs. Godzilla; Mothra vs. Gojira Toho/American International Pictures. Released April 29, 1964 (Japan); September 17, 1964 (U.S.). 89 min. Producers: Sanezumi Fujimoto and Tomoyuki Tanaka. Director: Ishiro Honda. Screenplay: Shinichi Sekizawa. Director of Photography: Hajime Koizume. Editor: Ryohei Fujii. Music: Akira Ifukube. Art Director: Takeo Kita. Special Effects: Eiji Tusburaya and Akira Watanabe. Visual Effects: Teisho Arikowa. With Akira Takarada, Yuriko Hoshi, Hiroshi Koizumi, Yu Fujiki, Emi Ito, Yumi Ito, Yoshifumi Tajima, Kenji Sahara and Haruo Nakajima. Available on Columbia/TriStar home video VHS; Sony Music DVD.

Sources

Unpublished Sources

Honda, Ishiro. Interview (1986) with Guy Mariner Tucker.
Milner, David. Interview (2000) with John Rocco Roberto.
Nakajima, Haruo. Interview (2000) with John Rocco Roberto.
Saperstein, Henry G. Interview (1995) with John Roberto and Guy Tucker.

Published Sources

Biondi, Robert. "Godzilla vs. The Thing: A Film Book." *G-FAN* 1, no. 12 (November 1994).
Cerasini, Mark, and J.D. Lees. *The Official Godzilla Compendium.* Random House, 1998.
Godziszewski, Edward. *The Illustrated Encyclopedia of Godzilla.* Daikaiju Publishing, 1995.
Marrero, Robert. *Godzilla: An Illustrated Guide to Japanese Monster Movies.* Fantasma Books, 1996.
Ragone, August, and Guy Tucker. "The Legend of Godzilla." *Markalite* 1, no. 3 (November 1991).
Roberto, John, with Robert Biondi. "Godzilla and the Second World War." *KAIJU-FAN* 2 (March 1994).
Rovin, Jeff. *The Encyclopedia of Monsters.* Facts on File, 1989.
Tucker, Guy Mariner. *Age of the Gods: A History of the Japanese Fantasy Film.* Daikaiju Publishing, 1996.

11

Cosmic Frames and Cover-ups: *Invasion of the Saucer Men* and the UFO Conspiracy of Silence

LYNDON W. JOSLIN

> If it is true that the [Air Force] or the Government withholds telltale facts, then one can only say that this is the most unpsychological and stupid policy one could invent.
> — *C.G. Jung, letter to Major Donald E. Keyhoe, 1958*

The Discovery

> "We've found a flying saucer!"
>
> The voice of reporter Ned "Scotty" Scott rang through the Arctic air. A group of military men and scientific researchers stood in a circle, their outstretched arms defining the size — and the *shape*— of a downed craft dimly seen through the melted and refrozen ice.

In 1951, when the movie featuring this scene, *The Thing from Another World*, was released, these men weren't the only ones looking for answers. Government officials, military brass, scientists, and ordinary citizens all wanted to know more about the strange things that were appearing in the skies worldwide. Some people wanted to tell the world; others were prepared to see to it that the world would never know.

In the midst of the political, scientific, and pop-culture furor that spun around the subject of UFOs, a crummy little movie was made in 1957. *Invasion of the Saucer Men* is no classic — at best, it might be a guilty pleasure — but as an artifact of its times, it's hard to top.

Before considering this artifact, let's have a look at those times.

The Onset

June 1957: *Invasion of the Saucer Men*, a low-budget release from American International, opens under the starry summer skies at a drive-in theater near you. For the purpose of putting this inconsequential B-film into its social and cultural context, our story starts exactly ten years earlier, in the summer of 1947. That was when the "flying saucers" first started showing up in earnest.

Two events in summer 1947 were to have widely differing influences on what was becoming an international mania for unidentified flying objects. The first, on June 24, was the sighting of nine shiny, disc-shaped objects flying near Mount Rainier, Washington, by pilot Kenneth Arnold. He later told the newspapers that the objects were saucer-shaped (by which one presumes he meant round), and the term "flying saucer" was born. The term has enjoyed staying power in the ensuing half-century-plus.

The second incident was the reported crash of at least one, and possibly two, strange airborne craft in the desert of New Mexico near the town of Roswell, in the southeastern part of the state. The *Roswell Daily Record* announced on July 8 that pieces of a wrecked "flying saucer" had been recovered by a local rancher and handed over to a nearby Army Air Corps base. That evening, the Air Corps (which would become the separate Air Force later that year) claimed that the wreckage was nothing but the remains of an experimental weather balloon. That story has never satisfied the numerous locals who say they saw, handled, and collected pieces of the craft, only to be bullied by the military into giving them up. The official story is also unconvincing to those who say they saw the occupants of the craft, several diminutive creatures described as dead, or dying, but definitely not human.

These two incidents—the Arnold sighting and the Roswell crash (and its subsequent alleged cover-up)—were just two of literally hundreds of sightings from across America and around the world at the time. But whereas the Arnold sighting gave UFOs a catchy and amusing name, the Roswell incident, after the explanation offered by the Air Force, sank into obscurity for a long time. Frank Scully's 1950 book, *Behind the Flying Saucers*, made only vague and inaccurate references to the crash and its recovery.

At an almost subterranean level, the Roswell mystery lingered, debatably for a dark reason. In the immediate postwar world, it seemed to give Americans reason to be suspicious, even fearful, of their government, and worse, of their military, which had so recently rescued them and the rest of the world from the Nazis and the Fascists and the Japanese warlords. With the dawning realization that the Soviet empire represented a huge bit of unfinished business, it was a nervous time to be unable to trust your own elected representatives.

In the modern world as it was understood to have developed since the (self-named) Age of Enlightenment — the world of Darwin and Freud, of Edison and Einstein — it had become widely accepted, certainly in the West, that science held the answers to all observable phenomena. And flying saucers were being observed everywhere, as often as not by people who weren't looking for them, weren't interested in them, and didn't even believe in them. Science's seeming inability to explain them, and its growing willingness to ignore or dismiss them, was hardly reassuring.

Toss in the development of the atomic bomb (which was first tested in New Mexico, fewer than 100 miles from the Roswell crash sites), the fear of the Red Menace, the development of the hydrogen bomb, and finally the word, in 1949, that the Soviets had the A-bomb, and it was an especially fearsome time. People were watching the skies, not only for alien craft, but also for Russian bombers. In fact, the initial widespread belief was that the saucers were secret weapons developed by the Reds, or covertly by our own military.

All told, the UFO or flying saucer phenomenon became a defining aspect of the American mind of the 1950s. It was as much a hallmark of the era as was the Red Scare, rock 'n' roll, and the nation's growing love affair with the car, along with the car's popular gathering place, the drive-in theater.

So, of course, it wasn't long before the American dream machine, Hollywood itself, saw a chance to make a buck by telling a tale or two to an anxious, ready-made audience.

The Movies

As is often the case when the film industry sees a chance to cash in on a craze, the early results were a mixed bag. The very first film to use the term "flying saucer" was the aptly titled *The Flying Saucer* (1950), a plodding, travelogue-style cheapie shot in Alaska. Our hero, a government agent, travels there to investigate persistent saucer sightings. There's never a hint that the thing is from space; it turns that out a local scientist invented it, and the Russians, right next door to Alaska, are trying to steal it.

The first "alien visitor" film was *The Man from Planet X* (1951), again a low-budget project, but one with foggy atmosphere and style. By this time, UFO witnesses had long been seeing the occupants or pilots of the strange craft, often describing them as "little men" (or "little green men," if you prefer). A typical "visitor" tended to be three to four feet tall, slight of build, with a disproportionately large head, and dressed in a shiny suit with a helmet and what appeared to be a breathing apparatus of some sort; in short, a space suit, which would allow him (it?) to survive Earth's unfamiliar atmosphere. This description fits the Planet X denizen perfectly. (This alien, by the way, isn't overtly hostile until he finds he has to defend himself from earthlings.)

A different sort of visitor arrives in the aforementioned *The Thing from Another World*, also released in the spring of 1951. No "little man," this alien (six-foot-six James Arness) is a humanoid plant (an "intellectual carrot," as Scotty puts it), and is reflexively hostile and dangerous. The title of *The Thing*'s source novel, *Who Goes There?* by John W. Campbell, Jr., refers to the shape-shifting abilities of the creature in the story, which allow it to imitate any living thing — and any*one*. This paranoia-inducing trait, unused in the movie, turns up in numerous other alien-invasion (or, more commonly, alien infiltration) thrillers of the '50s. Conventional wisdom sees this plot device as allegorical of a Commie takeover. In any event, the novel's alien and its spacecraft are found frozen in the Antarctic ice, where they've been preserved for untold ages. By contrast, the film's craft is observed as it goes down in the Arctic, prompting an expedition to seek it out. *The Thing* is the earliest crashed-saucer movie.

In the fall of 1951, *The Day the Earth Stood Still* hit movie screens. The film's alien emissary, Klaatu (Michael Rennie), though essentially peaceful, arrives nevertheless with an intimidating robot bodyguard that brooks no resistance from earthlings. Klaatu warns the earthlings that our apparent willingness to launch nuclear weapons into space has made the galactic community nervous. His message addresses the international tensions endemic in the early '50s—the face-off between the free world and the Soviet bloc; the arms race; the Cold War. Klaatu isn't shy about making an entrance, for his saucer lands in Washington, D.C. An early image in the movie, and no doubt a jarring one at the time, was the sight of this glowing saucer kiting past the Capitol Building and other D.C. landmarks.

Then, in July and August of 1952, less than a year after the release of the film, dozens of saucers appeared over Washington, D.C. As Frank Edwards reports in *Strange World*, "Sixty-eight of these strange glowing objects were over Washington, D.C., all at one time—on the night of August 13." Edwards adds, "From 1947, when they first appeared, to the summer of 1952, reports on flying saucers were carried openly by the news services; newspapers front-paged many of the sightings." But despite documentation by the Civil Aeronautics Administration, Edwards continues, "the August 13 incident was so well suppressed it was not even mentioned by the news services."

What the hell was going on?

The Air Force

The primary concern of the young Air Force during these five years was whether UFOs constituted a threat to the security of the United States. But according to some UFO theorists, there was another agenda: the possibility that a downed or captured saucer could yield advanced alien technology that would prove militarily useful. There were already rumors that the Nazis' development of jet fighters, the V-2, and other superweapons late in World War II had been made possible by technology salvaged from a UFO crash. Once the USSR demonstrated that it, too, had atomic weapons, the U.S. military, it was reasoned, was looking for the next leg up, from whatever source available. This theory explained the hush-hush and cover stories that had descended on the Roswell crash sites. (And indeed, according to retired U.S. Army Col. Philip J. Corso in *The Day After Roswell*, alien hardware salvaged from the Roswell wreck later led to the development of lasers, integrated circuit chips, and fiber optics.)

The Air Force's official UFO investigation, dating to 1947, was given the name Project Blue Book early in 1952. Continuing into the mid–'50s, periodic Air Force statements routinely said that there was no evidence of the existence of UFOs, flying saucers, or alien spacecraft. Project Blue Book was understaffed and overworked. A major, a sergeant, and a clerk were tasked, in those pre-database days, with checking a backlog of thousands of sightings against available weather and astronomical data (and, in later years, the paths of all known satellites). Little or no actual fieldwork was done in most cases, since the resources to do so weren't made available. Blue Book's dismissive explanations of most UFO reports were, if anything, the result of doing a cursory rush job on them, the best that could be expected under the circumstances.

Still, believers in UFOs, or people at least willing to entertain the possibility of their existence, were already claiming that the Air Force and Blue Book were engaged in a cover-up. So in 1956, a rival investigative body was formed. The National Investigations Committee on Aerial Phenomena (NICAP) was a civilian group made up of scientists, physicists, and retired military officers dissatisfied with the Air Force's official skepticism. NICAP's director and spokesman, Maj. Donald E. Keyhoe, USMC, retired, had already written two books on the subject by this time. Their matter-of-fact titles—*Flying Saucers from Outer Space* (1953) and *The Flying Saucer Conspiracy* (1955)—make his position clear enough. The former book receives a "suggested by" credit at the beginning of the 1956 film *Earth vs. the Flying Saucers*, another unambiguous title.

The sightings continued. And the accusations and denials did, as well. And nobody knew what the hell was going on.

The Short Story

By the mid–1950s, there was nothing left to do but greet the confusing situation with a nervous laugh. Paul W. Fairman's 1955 short story "The Cosmic Frame" featured an alien encounter of a darkly ironic kind.

> "Just saw a flying saucer," a teen says early in the story.
>
> "Only one?" somebody replies. "Nobody's got a right to brag these days unless they see at least six. And they've all got to spout at least five colors."
>
> "This one was blue."
>
> Small-town teens Johnny Carter and Joan Hayden are out on a heavy date; Johnny's even borrowed his dad's Packard, apparently for the occasion of popping the question. Late that night, Johnny calls home in a panic and tells his father, Sam Carter, that there's been an accident, but he's unable to describe what happened. Sam wakes his neighbor, Lee Hayden, who is Joan's father, and they drive out to see what the problem is.
>
> Johnny, while driving down a lonely country road, has hit and killed, sure enough, a little green man. "It was not more than four feet long and had a head far too large for the thin body. Its skin was green."
>
> Lee Hayden, seeing an opportunity to cash in on the discovery, persuades the Carters to store the body in their deep freeze. But later that same night, the dead alien's crewmates turn up, recover the body,

and severely damage the front end of the Packard with some tubular weapons they carry. Sam Carter observes, "They think the Packard did it; they're punishing the car for killing their comrade." Lee asks, "How can they be smart enough to invent and use space ships, and yet...?"

Their mission accomplished, the aliens vanish into the night. Almost immediately the police arrive and start asking questions. Seems somebody driving a Packard hit and killed the farmer whose phone Johnny had used. "A car smashed him into a tree and killed him," the trooper says. The officers demand to see the Packard so they can check it for damage. And as soon as Sam tries to explain, in terms of a "little green man from Mars or someplace," and sees the look the cop is giving him, he knows they're all screwed.

The cosmic frame has worked. So has the cover-up, pulled off by the aliens themselves: they've departed, leaving no trace behind.

The Film

"The Cosmic Frame" is a scant dozen pages long, just enough to form a germ of an idea for a movie. *Invasion of the Saucer Men* is a short film, running only 69 minutes, but even still, it pads Fairman's story considerably. Possibly because the aliens in the story play, in effect, a practical joke on the earthlings, the film has a decidedly tongue-in-cheek tone. Despite an ad poster that yelled "CREEPING HORROR ... from the depths of time and space!," *Invasion of the Saucer Men* is a comedy, or an attempt at one.

The story unfolds in Hicksburg, which could be anywhere, as opposed to Fairman's fictional Kensington Corners, which is said to be in the area of Sioux City, Iowa. Early action includes a scene straight from Fairman's story, featuring the dialogue about having just seen a blue flying saucer. Added to this scene is a new character, a Lieutenant Wilkins of the Air Force (Douglas Henderson). His entire comment, upon being told of the sighting, is, "Oh?" He then hurries off. That's the full extent of his interaction with the kids in the story.

Johnny and Joan (Steve Terrell and Gloria Castillo) go to Lovers' Point, unaware that the blue saucer has landed in nearby Pelham Woods, a location from Fairman's story. Later, on their way out of the woods, Johnny's car strikes and kills one of the aliens. (Whereas Fairman's story gets us to the scene after the fact, the movie depicts the accident as it happens, which is, of course, the more cinematic way of handling it.) Flat tire, no spare; they walk. They use the phone at the home of comically cranky Farmer Larkin (Raymond Hatton), whose farm, much to his chagrin, encompasses Lovers' Point. Naturally, the cops laugh at the call about a little green man, and hang up.

Meanwhile, Lieutenant Wilkins has awakened his superior officer, a blustery Colonel Armrouge (Sam Buffington), with the news of the sighting. We learn immediately what course of action they plan to take. "Our job," the colonel says, "is to prevent a possible nationwide panic by keeping the information from the public."

"The cosmic frame" is begun when Johnny (Steve Terrell) and Joan (Gloria Castillo) run over and squash one of the little men.

The Air Force was believed by conspiracy buffs to be trying to prevent a repeat of the panic caused in 1938 by Orson Welles's Halloween Eve radio dramatization of H.G. Wells's *The War of the Worlds.* The colonel warns Wilkins, who was a PR man in civilian life, that he'll be "court-martialed and shot" if anything leaks out.

The colonel clearly isn't kidding, but the light, comic music that underscores the scene indicates that we're to dismiss him as a buffoon. Wilkins, who is obviously humoring Armrouge, grins as he turns to leave the room. Comic or not, it's interesting to see to what extent an acknowledgment — indeed, an assumption — of Air Force cover-ups had become accepted by 1957, and in a youth-oriented entertainment at that. And it's clear that the Air Force has supposedly been behaving this way for some time: "The general was pretty sore at us for letting the last one get away," Wilkins says.

From this point, we watch two parallel stories. One involves the kids in the woods. Johnny and Joan, and ultimately the other teens, see the aliens amid the trees, but not the landed saucer. The other storyline — which, for our purposes, is of more interest — involves the Air Force at the landing site. The airmen see the craft, but never come into contact with the aliens.

The only point at which the two stories overlap is via another non–Fairman character, Joe Gruen, a vagrant who, like Lee Hayden in the story, sees a chance for a quick buck. Joe (played by Frank Gorshin, a comic actor who gained larger fame as the Riddler on the *Batman* TV series in the 1960s) sees the saucer land, and later finds the dead alien wedged under the front bumper of Johnny's abandoned car. When Gruen runs into the surviving aliens, they kill him by pumping him full of alcohol injected via retractable needles in their fingertips! They then substitute him for their dead comrade under Johnny's car, thus setting up the cosmic frame.

The Cover-up

As befits a low-budget movie, the Air Force "surrounds" the landed craft with only a handful of men: the two officers, a couple of sergeants, and a few enlisted men. The colonel, in a dead-giveaway line, says, "Amazing! One of them actually landed intact!"

As opposed to what?

As opposed to crashing. As opposed to Roswell. (Not, I would argue, as opposed to the downed saucer of *The Thing*, since it's described by that film's Captain Hendry as "intact, embedded in the ice," before being destroyed by ill-advised attempts to recover it.) *Invasion of the Saucer Men* was released only ten years after Roswell, and the ongoing interest in the flying saucer phenomenon had evidently kept the little-known story of the crash from fading completely from the public's mind. The mythology of alien touchdowns and Air Force cover-ups was already in place. Silly trifle though it is, *Saucer Men* deals with that aspect of the public mind as directly as any science fiction movie of its period.

The airmen make several unsuccessful attempts to establish contact with the aliens. A bullhorn brings no reply from within the saucer; neither do gunshots. Apparently the entire alien crew is out chasing Johnny and Joan through the woods. Finally, engineers try to cut the saucer open with acetylene torches. That triggers a reaction and the craft explodes, with a blast seen and heard from Lovers' Point to Hicksburg.

When the police check it out, Lieutenant Wilkins is ready with the cover story: "Everything's under control, officer," he says. "One of our jets crashed." The police buy it and leave. The Air Force, in a popular entertainment created during the Eisenhower years, has lied to the local police. Subversive though it may be, it's treated in this lightweight comedy as a joke.

The Air Force officers send for a team of "camouflage boys," who spend the rest of the night picking up the debris and making the landing site look as though nothing has happened. "Makes you proud, doesn't it?" Armrouge asks Wilkins. "Being part of a show like this. Protecting our country from alien invaders. Just think of it: only this special unit and the president of the United States will know what happened here tonight."

Wilkins retorts, "You mean you think *we* know what's happened?... Did it ever occur to you, colonel, that there might be other units just like ours, covering up other things?" The colonel's befuddled silence is meant to be amusing. But it's a good question especially since, during the Truman administration, the National Security Council had supposedly created the *uber*-secret panel known as Majority. Also called MJ-12 (for the number of its members-for-life), Majority, according to conspiracy theorists, oversaw every counter-alien operation, under various code names such as Pounce, Aquarius, and Sigma. Majority was answerable only to the president, leaving the likes of Colonel Armrouge far down the food chain indeed.

Wilkins' question also predates government lies that were to come to light in later years in the wake of Vietnam and Watergate, to say nothing of lingering suspicions about the JFK assassination. Clearly, by the mid–1950s, the stage was already being set, largely via growing suspicion over the Air Force's handling of the UFO question, for massive public cynicism about governmental motives and covert military operations. At the time, though, the possibility of such deceptions still had to be laughed off as far-fetched, seen only in contexts such as this silly teen exploitation film.

How had earlier alien-encounter movies handled the question of the public's right to know? In *The Day the Earth Stood Still*, Klaatu's in-your-face arrival is worldwide news, impossible to conceal or to explain away. In *The Man from Planet X*, our hero smugly and outrageously asserts that hushing up the whole incident is the right thing to do for the greater good: "Knowledge would only bring more fear in a world already full of it." Even if such a secret can't ultimately be kept, he says, "it can be reduced to gossip." In *The Thing*, a middle ground is reached: Scotty is kept from telling the world of the alien visitor until the peril is past, and then he's handed an open mike. "Keep watching the skies!" he famously warns.

The Aliens and the Alienated

In keeping with Fairman's description of the aliens, which was in turn apparently inspired by actual sightings, the visitors are little green men with oversized heads. What that means, in a low-budget movie, is diminutive adults fitted with huge head masks. The masks are the work of Paul Blaisdell, a magazine illustrator and a prolific monster-maker for low-budget movies of the mid-to-late fifties. As is often the case with films with which Blaisdell (and wife Jackie) were involved, the creature work in *Saucer Men* is the movie's most striking and memorable aspect.

These aliens remain utterly alien throughout the movie. They're a complete mystery: we don't know, and never learn, who they are, where they're from, what they want, or why Hicksburg is their landing site. We don't know whether they would have been hostile regardless of whether Johnny had killed one of them, but we can guess, for their glaring, immobile faces hint at nothing other than hostility, except maybe anger.

They don't even seem to be particularly intelligent. In addition to allowing themselves to be trapped at the film's finale, they leave their craft unguarded. When it's destroyed, they seem unaware of, or indifferent to, being stranded on Earth. Nor do they seem prepared to call for backup, since they have no evident communications gizmos. They have no zap guns; they have no other sophisticated gadgetry. In set-

A pair of ill-tempered alien visitors, from *Invasion of the Saucer Men* (1957). The scowling, perfectly archetypal creatures were designed and executed by Paul and Jackie Blaisdell.

ting up the frame, one of them damages Johnny's fender with what looks like a handheld jackhammer! (Johnny, reasoning as his father did in Fairman's story, thinks they're punishing the car.) Even their attempted frame of Johnny fails, because Gruen's death is found to have another cause. All told, the aliens are an aimless gang, and more of a nuisance than a menace. For all we know, they could be escaped (or exiled) criminals, or even children.

Speaking of whom: At least as much as it's a satire of the Air Force's response to UFO incidents, *Invasion of the Saucer Men* is a commentary on youth culture and what would later be called the generation gap. Johnny and Joan are sore beset by virtually every adult they encounter.

Larkin threatens them and their friends with a shotgun. The police, who find Gruen's body under Johnny's car when they investigate the explosion, don't want to hear anything from Johnny except a confession. Joan's father, an unsuccessful entrepreneurial schemer in Fairman's story, is the town attorney here; he's prepared to help her, but he's equally prepared to throw "this roughneck" Johnny to the wolves.

Even after an autopsy reveals that Gruen died of alcohol poisoning, the police are useless. Telling Johnny that he's no longer being sought (impossible: he's escaped from custody *and* stolen a squad car by then), they still refuse to check out his story about the alien peril in the woods.

Help ultimately comes from "the gang" down at Lovers' Point, as a fleet of jalopies surrounds the aliens in a clearing. Light, we've learned, is their enemy, and the teens' headlights vaporize them. In this youth-oriented product — released as the bottom half of a double feature with *I Was a Teenage Werewolf*— it had to happen.

The Livestock

Farmer Larkin has a bull named Walt. Walt tends to hang around Lovers' Point and annoy the kids. The kids like to get Walt drunk. That's one of the movie's big jokes.

Walt the bull charges one of the saucer men; the alien defends himself by jabbing the bull repeatedly with his alcohol-spouting needles. It's an astoundingly unconvincing scene, edited together from shots of the real bull trying to shake off a strapped-on alien dummy, intercut with shots of one of the tiny actors jabbing at a dummy bull.

What makes this scene interesting here is what Bruce Rux has to say about it in his 1997 book *Hollywood vs. the Aliens.* That book's subtitle — *The Motion Picture Industry's Participation in UFO Disinformation*— sums up Rux's premise, which is, as he puts it, that "the entertainment industry has been and continues to be exploited by agents of military intelligence and the CIA for purposes of ... confusing ... the public at large on UFO facts." This objective is brought about, Rux claims, by including in science "fiction" films details about UFO encounters before they're known to the general public. If someone later comes forth with a UFO story similar to something that's already been filmed, the public will think the witness got his idea from the movie(s).

Rux points out that abductions, for example, were featured in UFO-related movies (e.g. 1955's *This Island Earth* and 1956's *Earth vs. the Flying Saucers*) well before Barney and Betty Hill's first abduction, in 1961, was publicized in John G. Fuller's 1966 book *The Interrupted Journey.* Likewise, aliens perform medical procedures on an Earthling in *Killers from Space,* a particularly cheesy 1954 release, prior to the time abductees started describing similar experiences. The cheesier and sillier the movie, Rux claims, the better, "if the intent [of the disinformation campaign] was to make people not take such accounts seriously."

What better way, he reasons, to make light of cattle mutilation than to put it into a silly teen comedy? The first cases of mysterious livestock mutilation were reported in the 1960s, and there was an apparent outbreak during 1974–75. UFO enthusiasts have long tied the gruesome phenomena to saucer sightings. Never mind that Walt isn't mutilated, nor even attacked; he charges the saucer man, who defends himself with the only weapon available. The saucer man, in fact, is on the receiving end of the mutilation. In an "ick factor" moment of the type that was becoming a staple of drive-in movies at the time, Walt gores the alien in the eyeball. The bull ends up drunk from the injected alcohol, and Larkin blames the kids.

And the incident, Rux suggests, is close enough to a cattle mutilation to serve as foreshadowing — and preemptive ridicule — of the later reports.

The Aftermath

Following the release of *Invasion of the Saucer Men*, the Air Force continued to investigate UFO reports. UFO enthusiasts continued to suspect a cover-up.

Invasion of the Saucer Men was remade, ruinously, as *The Eye Creatures* in 1965. One wonders if the original movie wasn't bad *enough* to fulfill Rux's theory of disinformation.

In 1969, the Air Force officially closed down Project Blue Book because of insufficient scientific evidence as to the existence, origins, or threat level posed by UFOs.

That same year, Jimmy Carter, while running for governor of Georgia, saw a UFO. He didn't report the sighting until 1973.

Widespread reports of cattle mutilations started in 1974–75. They continue sporadically to this day.

In 1978, the Roswell story resurfaced in a big way. Jesse Marcel, former intelligence officer with the 509th Bomb Group, claimed in a series of interviews that the "weather balloon" explanation was an Air Force cover story. A 1980 book, *The Roswell Incident*, by Charles Berlitz and William Moore, told the world.

Since that time, books, movies, and TV shows dealing with Roswell, and with different aspects of the UFO mystery, have become a growth industry. A complete list of titles could fill another whole essay, so to mention only the most germane:

Kevin D. Randle and Donald R. Schmitt based *Roswell*, a 1994 made-for-cable movie, on the 1991 book *UFO Crash at Roswell*. In 1995, the Fox network broadcast a short film purporting to be actual footage of an autopsy of one of the Roswell aliens. In 1998, Fox aired a program that said the autopsy footage had been faked. And in the UPN series *Roswell* (1999–2002), contemporary teens living in the New Mexico town are descendants of the aliens.

Roswell itself still remembers. Home of not one but two competing saucer-crash museums, the town was the site of a 1997 gathering of UFO enthusiasts commemorating the fiftieth anniversary of the crash — or whatever the hell it was that happened that summer night in 1947.

Whatever it was, it ultimately, if indirectly, inspired a silly but strangely subversive movie that made its debut on another summer night, ten years later.

Film Discussed

Invasion of the Saucermen Malibu Productions/American International Pictures. Released June 1957. 69 min. Producers: James H. Nicholson and Robert J. Gurney, Jr. Director: Edward L. Cahn. Screenplay: Al Martin, based on "The Cosmic Frame" by Paul W. Fairman. Cinematography: Frederick West. Editors: Charles Gross, Jr., and Ronald Sinclair. Music: Ronald Stein. Art Director: Don Ament. Special Effects: Howard Anderson and Alex Weldon. Makeup and Props: Paul and Jackie Blaisdell, with Bob Burns. With Steve Terrell, Gloria Castillo, Frank Gorshin, Lyn Osborn, Raymond Hatton, Douglas Henderson and Sam Buffington. Previously released on VHS home video by Columbia/Tristar.

Sources

Alexander, David. *Conspiracies and Cover-Ups: What the Government Isn't Telling You*. New York: Berkeley Books, 2002.

Corso, Col. Philip J. *The Day After Roswell*. New York: Pocket Books, 1997.

Edwards, Frank. *Strange World*. New York: Bantam Books, 1969.

Fairman, Paul W. "The Cosmic Frame." 1955. Reprinted in *They Came from Outer Space: 12 Classic Science Fiction Tales That Became Major Motion Pictures*. Jim Wynorski, ed. Garden City, N.Y.: Doubleday, 1980.

Jung, C.G. *Flying Saucers: A Modern Myth of Things Seen in the Skies*. New York: MJF Books, 1978.

Nesheim, Eric and Leif. *Saucer Attack! Pop Culture in the Golden Age of Flying Saucers*. Los Angeles: General Publishing, 1997.

Randle, Kevin D., and Donald R. Schmitt. *UFO Crash at Roswell*. New York: Avon Books, 1991.

Rux, Bruce. *Hollywood vs. the Aliens: The Motion Picture Industry's Participation in UFO Disinformation*. Berkeley, Calif.: Frog, 1997.

Warren, Bill. *Keep Watching the Skies! American Science Fiction Movies of the Fifties*. Jefferson, N.C.: McFarland, 1998.

White, Dale. *Is Something up There?* New York: Scholastic Book Services, 1969.

Worth, D. Earl. *Sleaze Creatures: An Illustrated Guide to Obscure Hollywood Horror Movies 1956–1959*. Key West, Fl.: Fantasma Books, 1995.

12

The Cold War in Orbit: Two Films of Aliens, Arsenals, and Interventions

LYNDON W. JOSLIN

We Are Not Alone, Whatever That May Mean

"No one would have believed, in the last years of the nineteenth century," wrote H.G. Wells at the time, "that human affairs were being watched keenly and closely by intelligences greater than man's and yet as mortal as his own." Half a century later, when the Wells novel in question, *The War of the Worlds*, was made into a movie, its story was updated to contemporary times. An opening voiceover paraphrased Wells to say that "in the middle of the twentieth century" earthlings were still unaware that they were being studied by extraterrestrials.

But in fact, by the time of the film's 1953 release, a great many people were convinced that the Earth was not only being watched by alien intelligences but was being visited by them. The UFO craze was in full swing and was spinning off tales of landings, crashes, cover-ups, visitations—and apparent surveillance of military bases by the strange flying discs. Given that the world was dotted with military installations, guesswork was growing as to what an alien intelligence would make of human nature, especially our warlike habits. And since we didn't yet know what the aliens' motives were—whether they came in peace or as potential conquerors—the question was all the more troubling.

Science fiction films of the period played upon various possibilities. *War of the Worlds* itself presented an invasion by Martian hordes who were invulnerable, and therefore indifferent, to terrestrial arms. Their attack on the entire world united the human community against the common foe, but to no avail. The slightly earlier film

The Day the Earth Stood Still (1951) posits the existence of an interstellar community concerned about the danger presented by the entry of earthlings into the atomic age and the space age simultaneously. "It is no concern of ours how you run your own planet," says Klaatu, the alien emissary, "but if you threaten to extend your violence, this Earth of yours will be reduced to a burned-out cinder." The aliens' invitation — join our club or die — sounds rather like that of a protection racket.

Nor were these two well-known American films the only ones of the 1950s to explore the question of alien attitudes toward Earth's international hostilities. Among the long parade of SF films of the period, two lesser-known titles offer their own unusual takes on the matter. Both, as it happens, involve benign alien intelligences that are nonetheless inclined to throw the Prime Directive right out the window. But beyond that, *The 27th Day* (1957) and *The Space Children* (1958) bear little resemblance to each other.

Geopolitics and Human Nature: The 27th Day

When *The 27th Day* was released in the summer of 1957, alien abductions weren't the growth industry they were to become later in the twentieth century. Crackpots like George Adamski had been reporting since 1952 that they'd accepted invitations to board the spacecraft of Martians, Venusians, and other visitors. The first abduction, as such, was reportedly that of Barney and Betty Hill in 1961.

Yet *The 27th Day* starts with a raft of them. Five earthlings, from various places around the world, are simultaneously whisked away aboard a flying saucer. There, a smooth-talking alien (unpretentiously calling himself "the alien") gives each of them a small, transparent container. Each container holds three capsules; each capsule, the alien explains, can destroy all human life (and only human life) within a circular area 3,000 miles wide. Together, the capsules can depopulate the world. Each container can be opened only by the person to whom it's been given, but once it's opened, anybody can "launch" the capsules. If any of the five recipients dies, his or her capsules are deactivated. And all the capsules, if not used by midnight of the twenty-seventh day, become inoperative.

What does this alien (Arnold Moss) have in mind? It seems his home planet is about to be destroyed by supernova. Interstellar law prevents his race from conquering or destroying another, or invading their world. But if the human race should destroy itself, as history indicates it seems destined to do sooner or later, then Earth is up for grabs. The alien's gift is a nudge intended to speed up the process of global suicide, unless the earthlings can figure out some way of rising to the occasion. "The choice is not new," the alien says — one thinks of the ape-men braining each other with bone clubs in *2001* — "only the weapons."

The alien informs the abductees that they've been chosen "as representatives — not of your particular countries, but as representatives of the human race." In John Mantley's 1956 novel, which Mantley adapted for the screen, the alien makes the oxymoronic statement that the subjects have been "selected almost entirely at random from several of the greater earthly nations." This "random" assortment is made up of one person apiece from the United States, England, Germany, the USSR, and China. One sees the significance at a glance: it's the permanent members of the United Nations Security Council, with the significant substitution of Germany for France. We're not surprised to learn, as the novel's alien says, that his people have been observing the Earth for some time, since they clearly grasp who's wearing the pants in the postwar world.

And who are the individual lucky winners? The American is Jonathan Clark (Gene Barry, late of *War of the Worlds*), an L.A. newspaperman. Jonathan's experiences as a combat veteran and a beat reporter have left him deeply cynical about human nature.

The Brit is Eve Wingate (Valerie French), abducted (swimsuit and all) from a seaside resort in the south of England. Mantley seems to be implying that Britannia, once the empress of the sea, is now just a chick at the beach.

The German is Professor Klaus Bechner (George Voskovec), the only one of the five who is world famous. Given the role of German scientists in the development of the nuclear missile programs of both the U.S. and the USSR, it hardly seems random that Bechner is a physicist.

The 27th Day **(1957) and the victims of alien abduction (from left): Eve (Valerie French), cynical American newspaperman Jonathan Clark (Gene Barry), Chinese peasant Su Tan (Marie Tsien), German scientist Klaus Bechner (George Voskovec), and Soviet foot soldier Ivan Godofsky (Azemat Janti). Each will be given small devices with the power to destroy the world.**

The geopolitically minded alien (Arnold Moss) observes as his guinea pigs take the doomsday capsules that only they can open. But once unsealed, the terrible weapons can be used by anyone.

The Soviet is Ivan Godofsky (Azemat Janti), a young soldier. The aliens' bland indifference to earthly weaponry is illustrated insofar as Ivan is beamed aboard still carrying his rifle. Ivan is refreshingly depicted, not as a scowling exponent of the Red Menace as one might expect in an American novel and film of the fifties, but as both a cog in the Soviet military machine and as a victim of it.

But crowning victim status belongs to the Chinese "delegate," the unfortunate Su Tan (Marie Tsien). What a day she's been having. She has already seen her family killed and her home burned by marauding soldiers, an unexplained incident that may have something to do with forced collectivization, and that in any case is a Western-style indictment of Communist brutality. The novel adds the detail that Su Tan had been beaten and raped. Next comes abduction by an unctuous alien who places a fifth of the fate of the world onto her slender shoulders, then drops her and the others back on Earth. Good luck!

Barely more than a child — the novel gives her age as 18 — Su Tan is the first of the five to take decisive action. She re-enters the smoking ruins of her house, finds a knife, pays her respects at a Buddhist shrine, and fatally stabs herself. As the alien said they would, her capsules disintegrate.

How do the others handle the alien's gift? Jonathan pragmatically decides that the obvious thing to do is sit tight and keep his mouth shut about the incident for 27 days. It runs counter to his every newsman's instinct to sit on the biggest story of his life — but who would believe it anyway?

Eve flings her container into the sea and flees, not just to America, but to Jonathan's side. Mantley seems to be drawing a (rather unflattering) parallel between Eve's behavior and the relationship between the United Kingdom and the United States in the world wars.

Professor Bechner, stunned by another alarming development, wanders into traffic and is injured by a car. Bechner's distracted state is brought on by an unexpected broadcast: the alien interrupts every radio and TV signal in the world and spills the beans about the abducted five, though he says only that they were given important "information."

Naturally, the world erupts in a panic — especially since, in the book, the broadcast is visually enhanced by a brief appearance of the alien fleet in the skies the world around. (Whereas the novel describes ships of *Independence Day* proportions—"a great shimmering disk ... grew until it blotted out most of the sky"— this moderately budgeted film presents, at the time of the abductions, only a brief shot of a craft from 1956's *Earth vs. the Flying Saucers*. Similarly, the vast interior of the craft is reduced to a cramped waiting room with translucent walls and a porthole in the floor.) As rioting and unrest spread, Jonathan and Eve take it on the lam. Being young, white, Anglo-American heterosexuals in a movie made in the 1950s, they naturally fall for one another. Ivan, too, tries to run, but ends up in the unsympathetic hands of the Kremlin.

Bechner, meantime, is recuperating in the hospital. His capsules have long since been discovered by the authorities, though he's been glib about their nature. Soviet agents soon make an attempt on his life. Hearing the news on a radio, Jonathan and Eve decide it's time to come out of hiding. They also fear what could happen with two of the containers in the hands of the Communists (news of Su Tan's death hasn't reached the West).

Unlike some SF films of the fifties, *The 27th Day* doesn't use an alien presence as a metaphor for creeping Communist influence; here, the Communists star as themselves. Jonathan and Eve, having briefly met Ivan and Su Tan, know them to be just frightened persons of no particular importance, much like themselves. Even in an American movie made in the midst of the Cold War, they don't fear Ivan and Su Tan as Commie finks who'll turn the capsules over to their bloodlusting Red overlords at the first opportunity. But they're very much afraid of what the Soviet and Chinese governments may do to Ivan and Su Tan in order to secure their cooperation.

These fears are well founded. When Ivan finally yields to official "persuasion" to tell what he knows about the capsules, and when he relents and opens the container, the USSR demands the immediate withdrawal of all U.S. forces from Europe and Asia. With the world standing by for Soviet takeover, Jonathan, Eve, and Bechner agree to cooperate with the American authorities.

Another German scientist on the American team, Karl Neuhaus (Frederick Ledebur), suggests that the capsules may be an elaborate hoax sprung by the aliens in a self-serving attempt to trigger an atomic war. The only way to be sure is to test one,

Heartsick by developments, an American-affiliated scientist, Dr. Neuhas (Frederick Ledebur), decides to sacrifice himself to save humanity — even if, according to the film, a certain proportion of humanity doesn't deserve to be saved at all.

an impractical suggestion. But it's determined that an unpopulated area big enough to conduct the test can be found at sea, "off the east coast of South America." Neuhaus volunteers to be the test subject, explaining that he's given himself a "fatal overdose of gamma radiation." (In one of the book's weaker moments, Neuhaus claims to have injected himself with a deadly poison with no antidote. The poison goes unnamed, and no one bothers to check his story. Turns out he's lying, though we have no indication that the film's Neuhaus is doing so.)

The test is quickly set up and carried out, though the latitude and longitude given are all wrong: they're the coordinates of a spot in Antarctica, south of the Pacific! Mantley's novel says the test is conducted at "the Pole," though oddly he never specifies which one. Maybe the location in his screenplay was altered by somebody who neglected to change the coordinates. In any case, it turns out that, whatever else the aliens may be, they're honest about their technological capabilities. Dr. Neuhaus becomes, literally, an empty suit, while the test animals aboard the same raft are unharmed.

The U.S. pullback begins. The Soviets prepare to blanket North America with Ivan's three capsules, destroying all Americans at one blow. With hours to spare, Professor Bechner takes the radical step of reading the instructions, which are engraved on the capsules in mathematical code. He then reprograms the operational parameters of the capsules—we don't see him doing so, though Jonathan asks him later how he'd learned the capsules could be altered—and launches his remaining two, and all three of Jonathan's, to coordinates around the world.

The result? As a news broadcast tells us (in Paul Frees's unmistakable voice), every "confirmed enemy of human freedom" is destroyed. Peace, love, and understanding rule. The surviving earthlings invite the alien and his race to share our planet and escape their dying sun. It's the Summer of Love. It's the dawning of the Age of Aquarius. It's a cop-out letdown of what had been an interesting and intelligent movie.

Problems: Who, exactly, did the "confirming"? Professor Bechner? Not likely, since he's presented all along as an humble man reluctant to wield the Godlike power of the capsules. This sort of judgment call is the last thing he'd want to undertake, especially since a "naughty and nice" list would have to be conjured up on such short notice, and with insufficient data for most of the several billion people of the world.

So Bechner evidently makes use of an existing operational template within the capsules' program. Even then, who makes the cut? To name one specific issue (more of an issue today than it was in the '50s), is a pro-lifer an "enemy of freedom" for wanting to prevent a woman from exercising control over her body? Or is an abortion advocate an "enemy of freedom" for seeking to deny an unborn person the right to draw his (or her) first breath?

The book sheds a good deal more light on the question of how this artificial Shangri-la has been brought about, though its explanations are downright chilling: Noting that the alien radiation caused migraines and shock among a great many people who survived it (including Jonathan), Bechner posits the existence of a chemistry of evil, a hypothetical substance analogous to the adrenaline that floods the bloodstream of a frightened or angry person. "Now," he says, "supposing that the evil man ... has a higher percentage of this malignant secretion [in his body] than the average. The alien power certainly could be set to attack those cells where the secretion index was above a certain level. With those high above the basic norm, so many cells would be destroyed that the attack would be fatal. With those with somewhat less, it would be highly painful." In other words, the entire human race has been subjected to a lobotomy—or an exorcism—by radiation therapy.

"On the other hand," the professor continues in the novel, "perhaps what we call 'evil' in men is only the instinct of aggression developed to an abnormal degree.... It may be that the capsules merely attacked ... and killed our aggressive instincts. It's too soon to tell, but we may discover we now live in a world where competitive sports do not exist any longer." Bang goes a billion-dollar segment of the economy, as we learn that the alien treatment may be not only a lobotomy but an emasculation. One is reminded of the satirical British film *The Monitors* (1969), in which meddlesome do-gooders from deep space set up an efficient bureaucracy to run Earth's affairs. They solve all social ills and make the trains run on time—until the human race revolts out of sheer boredom.

There is little chance of that happening here, at least as the situation is spelled out in Mantley's novel. An epilogue set in the future year of 1973 observes, "We still have occasional cases committed to the hospitals where the symptoms are spastic collapse preceded by a hollow roaring in the head. We call it Power Sickness." Another British dystopian satire comes to mind: Anthony Burgess's *A Clockwork Orange*, in which antihero Alex is "cured" of his criminal tendencies by a treatment that makes him ill every time he tries to act on his "natural" (i.e., criminally violent) impulses.

But Alex's treatment, which deals only with his violent actions and leaves his criminal motives intact, is a type of conditioning that is known to wear off after a while. By contrast, the wonder-drug radiation of *The 27th Day* purges the *internal* wellspring of violence — and provides occasional "booster shots" as needed, making it endlessly efficacious. The warning of the prison chaplain in *A Clockwork Orange* is even truer here: "He ceases to be a wrongdoer. He ceases also to be a creature capable of moral choice."

It's been observed that the best fiction is that which is honest about human nature. The feel-good conclusion of *The 27th Day*, both book and movie, is what makes it ultimately, and unfortunately, dishonest. However it's phrased — whether in terms of original sin or the idea that nobody's perfect — the human condition is one of perpetual imperfectability. A brief shower of alien radiation would be highly unlikely to fix the human psyche, and in pretending that it could, *The 27th Day* crosses the line from morality tale to fairy tale, from "What if" to "Wouldn't it be nice if." Like other utopian visions, it requires the rewiring of the human mind in order for it to work, and in so doing, it requires human beings to become something other than, and debatably less than, fully human.

By contrast, the aforementioned *The Day the Earth Stood Still* maintains its classic status precisely *because* it purveys no illusions about human nature, even among human beings (which Klaatu clearly is) from other planets. That film's interplanetary community has created an army of robo-thugs and given them irrevocable power in matters of aggression: if somebody dares start something, Gort and the boys will be there in a hurry to bust things up. Granted, it's inadvisable to give a machine such total power over human affairs, as any number of cautionary SF films have warned: *Colossus the Forbin Project* (1970), *Zardoz* (1974), *WarGames* (1983), and the *Terminator* series, not to mention the passive-aggressive HAL of *2001*. But the point here is that Klaatu's race harbors no pretense that a jiffy miracle of science can cure what ails the human soul.

The 27th Day— which is well made, low key, unusual, mostly intelligent and well worth seeing — unfortunately gives way in the end to wishful thinking. That being the case, it's perhaps appropriate that the film's final image is a shot of the United Nations building.

And a Little Child Shall Lead Them: The Space Children

The Space Children presents a scenario about extraterrestrial intervention in warlike human affairs that's much different from that of *The 27th Day*. For one thing, *The Space Children* is far more limited in scope: It unfolds over a frenzied period of

PARAMOUNT PRESENTS
THE SPACE CHILDREN
STARRING MICHEL RAY · ADAM WILLIAMS · PEGGY WEBBER · PRODUCED BY WILLIAM ALLAND · DIRECTED BY JACK ARNOLD · SCREENPLAY BY BERNARD C. SCHOENFELD

Title card for Jack Arnold's slow but intriguing *The Space Children* (1958). Among the cast are Adam Williams and Jackie Coogan (center), and Peggy Webber (far right).

two days and nights, and all in one local area, unlike the weeks-long, globe-spanning tale of *The 27th Day*. The nature and apparent motivation of the extraterrestrial intelligence are also dissimilar.

We open at the beach — not a spring break party zone, but a desolate, deserted stretch of seaside wilderness. Chubby science nerd Dave Brewster (Adam Williams), his wife Anne (Peggy Webber), and their two preteen sons Bud and Ken (Michel Ray and Johnny Crawford), cruise along the lonely highway in a station wagon (of course), nearing the end of their journey. Brewster, we soon learn, has been assigned to work on a secret weapon at the Eagle Point Missile Project: a multistage rocket designed to boost a nuclear launching platform into orbit. The project is taking place within the context of the arms race: "Is ours the only one?" Anne asks at one point. "We don't think so," Dave replies.

As they near the base, the alien intelligence makes its impending presence known, if indirectly: the car stalls, a classic symptom of a UFO in the area. But there is no UFO — only a shimmering band of light in the sky, focused on a point on the beach. Another odd (and foreshadowing) manifestation: the boys hear something strange, but their parents don't. Nor do we, but the eerie music on the soundtrack serves as a surrogate. (Van Cleave's consistently weird and ominous score is one of this slight movie's strengths.) Brewster is able to restart the car and move on; the alien has yet to arrive.

The trailer park where the Brewsters take up residence reminds one of the Spartan accommodations endured by the test pilots and their wives in *The Right Stuff*. Anne, who dislikes the beach, ambiguously gripes about "living so close to the end of the world." As the boys explore a seaside cave, they meet and easily mingle with the other kids in the neighborhood. After a quick look at the rocket (depicted, in a handsome if not quite convincing matte painting, between a pair of gantries with a backdrop of cliffs), the kids return to the beach—just in time to see the arrival of the alien.

The visitor descends to Earth via the aurora-like band (which may be iridescent; the movie's in black and white, so it's impossible to say); a tiny ball of light rides down the shining path and disappears behind some seaside cliffs, where the kids quickly find it. The alien is in the form of a brain-like glob, roughly the size of a football. It pulsates and glows. It makes no audible sounds, but Bud evidently is "hearing" what it tells him. The other kids may not "hear" the alien as clearly, but they have an understanding that Bud is now their leader in their dealings with whatever it is. "From now on," Bud tells the other kids, somehow without a trace of bossiness, "when I ask you to do something, we'll do it together." The kids agree, regarding the alien with reverent awe.

Despite their comic-bookish names, Lieutenant Colonel Manley and Dr. Wahrman (Richard Shannon and Raymond Bailey), the brass and the brains at Eagle Point, are depicted sympathetically. Caught in a candid moment on the beach, both casually dressed as Manley fishes in the surf, they chat about the upcoming launch in terms of preserving the world and protecting their own kids. We're given no indication that we're to see them as being cynical, hypocritical, or maniacal; they clearly believe in what they're doing. Whether they're right or misguided is another question. As they chat, their own respective children, a boy and a girl in their teens, cheerfully hurry past on their way back from a swim. To them, these men are just their dads.

That evening, the new family on the block meets the neighbors, among whom fans of vintage TV will spot a couple of familiar faces. Hank Johnson is played by Jackie Coogan, later Uncle Fester on *The Addams Family*; Joe Gamble is played by Russell Johnson, later the Professor on *Gilligan's Island* (and a veteran of several other fifties SF films, as well). Joe is a hard-luck case: unemployed, drunken, irritable, and abusive of his wife Peg (Jean Engstrom) and her son Tim (Johnny Washbrook); even Joe's last name is a vice. When he later tries to lay violent hands on Tim, Joe becomes the only human casualty of the story: he turns up dead in his trailer, without a mark on him. The alien is clearly protective of its chosen ones.

Apparently guided by the alien, Bud and Ken let their parents in on the secret, and Dave brings the alien back to the trailer. Anne is aghast at the sight of it, but the kids persuade her to let it stay the night. It grows slightly during the night (we aren't told why, since it doesn't seem to be draining anyone of anything), and the next day Bud and Ken stash it in the cave. They explain that it needs to be kept "safe and warm until tonight." When Brewster learns that the rocket is scheduled for launch that night, he fears the worst.

Children of the Space Age willingly serve the alien intelligence that wishes to destroy the Thunderer, an American rocket probe. The youngsters include Sandy Descher and Michel Ray (third and fourth from left) and Johnny Crawford (far right) (courtesy Ronald V. Borst/Hollywood Movie Posters).

Although even the ads for *The Space Children* refer to the kids as being under the alien's control, such is not the case. They cooperate with it willingly, though the Brewsters think their kids are being controlled. And what is the alien up to? As Dave suspects, it seeks to prevent the launch of the Thunderer, as the rocket is clumsily known (why not "Thunderbolt" or "Thunderhead"?). To make a short story even shorter (the movie is only 69 minutes long), the alien succeeds.

The children somehow act as its agents, or perhaps more accurately, its conduits. Strange things happen whenever the kids are present, though they don't actually seem to be doing anything to cause the problems. (Tom Filer, who wrote the story on which this film was very loosely based, had used a similar device a couple of years earlier in his script for *The Beast with 1,000,000 Eyes*, in which an alien uses local animals and birds as its eyes and ears.) A truck delivering fuel for the rocket runs off the road near Bud on his bicycle; its brakes and steering have failed, something Bud clearly hasn't actively caused. (Tampering thus with a truck labeled DANGER—INFLAMMABLE makes the alien seem quite cavalier about human life, unless it somehow is also responsible for stopping the truck in the dunes.) A sentry tries to answer a phone in his booth, only to find that it won't work; two kids nearby simply lick ice cream cones and trade knowing smiles. Brewster tries to tell his superiors that he fears that the launch will fail, but he can't because he loses his voice, can't even write his message down, and collapses—all shortly after Bud mysteriously appears in the room, in a secured area of the base.

Finally, the kids enter the base on the evening of the launch, exiting again a short while later. Both coming and going, a padlock on the gate opens for them. We don't see what they do on the base, but shortly afterwards, the Thunderer, at the end of its countdown, explodes on the pad.

The inevitable confrontation then takes place as the adults face off against the children down at the cave. The grown-ups are distraught because they think the alien has left the United States defenseless against enemy nations working on similar projects, but the kids tell them that the same thing has happened to these weapons the world over, "in Moscow, Prague, and London."

The alien — which has grown much larger now, to about the size of a car — emerges from the cave and rides the beam of light back into the sky. Nukes will not be launched into space — not today. Earth has dodged a bullet of its own making.

As noted, *The Space Children*'s approach to alien intervention is different from that of *The 27th Day*— and, for that matter, of most other SF films. No flying saucer here, no spaceman in a shiny suit, no robots or ray guns; this visitor is less like an alien than an angel. But unlike, say, 1952's *Red Planet Mars*, in which God himself speaks from space to denounce communism, *The Space Children* reflects anxieties about the arms race and the Cold War in terms of more generic, if no less overt, religious symbolism.

The alien itself descends from the heavens, as gods of various mythologies are said to have done; Jesus is described as having descended to Earth from God. The alien returns to the heavens, again as both Jesus and Muhammad are said to have done at the end of their respective missions. Its appearance as a brain is no coincidence, since the form indicates pure intellect; then again, St. Paul exhorted Christians to put on "the mind of Christ" and to "be of one mind." In their unity of purpose, the kids mount a veritable children's crusade, though its aim is shrouded in secrecy. (Bud, who has big soulful eyes and insists on wearing long-sleeved black shirts, looks the part of a junior cult leader.)

If the alien is, in H.G. Wells's words, not a supernatural being but an intelligence "greater than man's but as mortal as his own," then it must be assumed that

The Space Children protect the alien, and its intentions. Two of the youngsters are the sons of rocket scientist Dave Brewster (Adam Williams, second from left); an alien agenda has trumped fatherhood.

its advancement beyond human capabilities is immeasurable. Not only does it need no physical tools, it also has outgrown the need of a physical body. Christ has no hands or feet but ours, St. Teresa of Avila said. And as SF author Arthur C. Clarke has observed, "Any sufficiently advanced technology is indistinguishable from magic"—or, in this case, from miracle. Certainly the alien's psi capabilities appear to be miraculous; what disturbs us is that we don't know at first what its motives are.

Its origins and nature, too, are such a mystery that "outer space" seems a simplistic answer. An interesting possibility is that the alien may in fact be a creation of the children—either as a startling example of psychological projection or as a manifest prayer for peace. The film's title to the contrary, these "space children" are *Earth* children. In the opening credits, their awestruck faces appear in sequence, superimposed on a series of star fields. They're "aliens" from planet Earth! "The children—all over the world," Bud explains at the end, "they did what we did, in every country." Did what, exactly? Cooperate with the alien only, or generate it as well? We aren't told, and it may not be knowable. Is a "second coming" possible? "I don't know," Bud says. It depends, apparently, on whether we try to orbit nukes again.

For those in the audience who may not have been paying attention, the film's religious implications are spelled out at the conclusion. There, against another starry backdrop, appears the text of Matthew 18:3: "Verily I say unto you ... except ye become as little children, ye shall not enter the kingdom of heaven." "Is there any man on this earth who has the wisdom and innocence of a child?" an exasperated Dr. Wahrman asks the alien during a brief encounter earlier in the movie. But is it "wisdom and innocence" the alien seeks, or is it simply a mind old enough to be curious, yet young enough to be largely unprejudiced? "Empty your cup" is one of the first directives of Zen. Though Wahrman is concerned about the alien's purposes, he doesn't fear the visitor, nor is he hostile to it, so it makes no move against him. But it also has nothing to "say" to him.

Unlike *The 27th Day*, *The Space Children*, despite its arguable tendency to idealize children, has no illusions about human nature. (There is, for example, no pretense that unilateral disarmament is a workable option.) If it, too, indulges in wishful thinking, at least its wish is more attainable: "I wish we wouldn't build stupidly dangerous weapons systems" is a wish more likely to be granted than "I wish everyone, everywhere, were nice to each other forever." *The Space Children*'s message is simply that the human race isn't mature enough to be trusted with nukes in space. And who can argue with that?

It's ironic that children are the agents who, by enabling the sabotage of the space bound nukes, deliver this message about our childishness. Nor is the alien, regardless of its origin — whether deep space or the collective psyche of Earth's children — likely to believe that it has fixed the human race's problems. It's simply forbidden us (to put it again in mythic-religious terms) to make this particular repetition of the hubris of Prometheus, to steal this particular fire from the gods.

The Space Children is a strange little movie with a numinous and oddly intimate atmosphere, not unlike (and not much longer than) an episode of the classic *Outer Limits* TV series of the early '60s. Since the film doesn't rely on spectacle, it isn't much hampered by its low budget, and the location filming, on whatever isolated stretch of beach that may be, is effective. Jack Arnold, director of such classic and near-classic SF films as *It Came from Outer Space*, *Tarantula*, and the first two *Creature from the Black Lagoon* movies, directs here with his usual emphasis on unearthly atmosphere in an isolated setting. The result is a low-key film that is seldom seen today but is worth seeking out for its power to provoke thought.

Films Discussed

The 27th Day A Romson Production/Columbia Pictures. Released July 1957. 75 min. Producer: Helen Ainsworth. Director: William Asher. Screenplay: John Mantley, adapted from his novel. Cinematography: Henry Freulich. Editor: Jerome Thoms. Musical Conductor: Mischa Bakaleinikoff. Art Director: Ross Bellah. Special Effects: Ray Harryhausen (uncredited). Set Direction: Frank Tuttle. With Gene Barry, Valerie French, George Voskovec, Azemat Janti, Frederick Ledebur, Arnold Moss, Marie Tsien and Paul Frees. Released on laserdisc by Columbia/Tristar, 1995; out of print.

The Space Children A William Alland Production/Paramount Pictures. Released 1958. 69 min. Producer: William Alland. Director: Jack Arnold. Screenplay: Bernard C. Schoenfeld, based on "The Egg," by Tom Filer. Cinematography: Ernest Laszlo. Editor: Terry O. Morse. Music: Van Cleave. Production Design: Roland Anderson and Hal Pereira. Special Effects: John P. Fulton. With Adam Williams, Michel Ray, Peggy Webber, Johnny Crawford, Jackie Coogan, Richard Shannon, Johnny Washbrook, Russell Johnson, Raymond Bailey and Jean Engstrom. Not presently available on VHS or DVD.

Sources

Burgess, Anthony. *A Clockwork Orange.* New York: Ballantine Books, 1975. [1962]
Mantley, John. *The 27th Day.* New York: Crest Books, 1958.
Warren, Bill. *Keep Watching the Skies! American Science Fiction Movies of the Fifties.* Jefferson, N.C.: McFarland, 1998.
Wells, H.G. *The War of the Worlds.* Racine, Wisc.: Whitman, 1964. [1898]

13

Scenes from a Marriage: The Sexual Politics of *I Married a Monster from Outer Space*

Mark Clark

Love and marriage, Sammy Cahn wrote, go together like a horse and carriage. For the last hundred years, however, anxiety and controversy have also clung to the institution.

The Massachusetts Supreme Court sparked a firestorm in November 2003 when it ruled that the state's ban on same-sex marriage was unconstitutional. Enraged social conservatives, including President George W. Bush, called for an amendment to the United States Constitution defining marriage exclusively as a union between a man and a woman. Gay rights activists opposed such an amendment and demanded full recognition of homosexual marriage rights. A few maverick mayors, including San Francisco's Gavin Newsom, began marrying gay couples in defiance of state laws. Most Americans found themselves somewhere between these two camps, forced to consider the philosophical and political meaning of a union that buttresses our social structure.

The intensity of emotion on both sides of this issue belies the truth that this sort of disagreement is nothing new. Americans' attitudes about marriage have evolved considerably over the past century, shaped by broader social forces in the way that running water carves out canyons and valleys.

In 1958, in a different time of social change, an unheralded science fiction film examined the roles of marriage and family in American life and ruminated on the sexual politics of its era. True, the film's eminently risible title—*I Married a Monster from Outer Space*—didn't help its credibility. But a funny thing happened on the way to cinematic oblivion. Subsequent generations of film fans and historians realized that *IMAMFOS* (the working title of the picture) is a buried treasure—a well-crafted and surprisingly resonant movie.

Even if it had worn a more respectable title, nothing in the *IMAMFOS* pedigree would have indicated the picture was more than a routine B-budget shocker. The film was shot in eight days, for a modest $175,000, on the Paramount Pictures back lot and at venerable Bronson Canyon. "*IMAMFOS* is ... clearly a low-budget picture, done with care and imagination," Bill Warren writes in his book, *Keep Watching the Skies! American Science Fiction Movies of the 1950s.* "That it's as good as it is, is a tribute to the craftsmen who made it."

Indeed, nearly every aspect of this production proves remarkably well conceived and executed, well above standard for late–'50s genre pictures with similar budgets. Director Gene Fowler, Jr., lends the film the same "atomic gothic" ambiance and fluid, moving camera that enlivened his previous genre entry, *I Was a Teenage Werewolf* (1957). The script by Louis Vittes is unusually sensitive and intelligent. Cinematographer Haskell Boggs drenches the proceedings in evocative shadows. Crisp editing by Hitchcock protégé George Tomasini keeps the pace brisk without sacrificing suspense. The special visual effects, overseen by John P. Fulton, are effective and judiciously employed. The alien costumes designed by Charles Gemora are imaginative and creepy. And Gloria Talbott contributes a career-best performance in the leading role. Not bad for a film that, in its initial release, often played on the bottom half of a double bill with *The Blob.*

"Maybe They're Married or Something."

Science fiction films from the 1950s have become celluloid inkblot tests for critics and viewers with vivid imaginations. Consider the analytical conundrum posed by *Invasion of the Body Snatchers* (1956): Are its politics anti–Communist or anti–McCarthyist? Does it have any politics at all? Like numerous other SF classics, *Body Snatchers* can be read in many different ways. But none of those readings invalidate the others. Nor should these interpretations be discounted because the filmmakers didn't proceed with any sort of overt agenda, other than to entertain audiences and turn a profit. Movies, especially fantasy films, constantly and usually unconsciously reveal the aspirations and anxieties of their times, albeit through the fractured prism of science fiction. Like psychic sponges, they soak up the zeitgeist that surrounds them.

Of course, as Sigmund Freud might have said, sometimes a ray gun is only a ray gun. But in the case of *IMAMFOS*, there's simply too much sexually and politically charged content for this material to be dismissed out of hand. As editor Phil Hardy's *Overlook Film Encyclopedia: Science Fiction* observes, "In retrospect, it is its sexual politics that are ... interesting and disturbing."

The movie opens with a slow pan across the sleepy, seaside village of Norristown, USA. Given the size of the homes and the recent vintage of the cars, we gather that this is an affluent suburban community. The camera fixes on two men and follows them as they enter a nightclub. In a convertible in the parking lot, a young man and his date share a kiss of Production Code–defying length, an embrace that continues as the camera turns away. Inside the bar two frustrated-looking women sip martinis and eye several young men gathered at a nearby table. "Those guys ain't even giving us a hard look," the first woman complains. "Maybe they're married or something," her friend replies. "Well, if we're willing to overlook it, *they* certainly are," the first notes sourly.

This exchange, the first dialogue spoken, immediately establishes the film's preoccupation with gender and familial roles. Author Caitlin Flanagan, in the December 2003 issue of *The Atlantic Monthly*, writes, "There's one bit of power women will never wrest from men: The decision to deem one group of women candidates for marriage and another group candidates for quick and quasi-anonymous sex." *IMAMFOS* reflects this "Madonna/whore" bifurcation: Women in each of these camps not only recognize their roles, but seem curiously content within them, or at least accustomed to them.

The film seems to support functionalist social theory, which was prevalent in the 1950s. Social conservatives believed the rising tide of feminism in America posed a threat to the traditional family structure. Feminism emerged as a political force during the women's suffrage movement in the early twentieth century and gathered new momentum when the percentage of women working outside the home skyrocketed during World War II. Functionalists, who believed that marital success and familial harmony were based on how spouses performed specific functions in support of the family unit, called for a return to "natural" gender roles: men as providers and heads of households, women as homemakers and mothers.

All the women in *IMAMFOS* (except for those clearly identified as trollops unfit for marriage) hold wedlock and motherhood as their highest aspirations. None of them seem even mildly interested in work outside the home, except as something to kill time until the right man comes along. For instance, after her longtime boyfriend finally proposes, aging bride-to-be Helen (Jean Carson) expresses relief: "I'd just about given up hope. I was reading books about Florence Nightingale, Joan of Arc, Madame du Barre—you know, *career women*. But now I've been saved."

Men, meanwhile, seem glumly resigned to the pressures that accompany marriage and their responsibilities as sole wage earners. That's the impression we get back at the nightclub, during the film's opening sequence. The camera tracks away from the two bitter floozies at the bar and toward the table of young men. We learn a bachelor party is in progress, in honor of amiable insurance salesman Bill Farrell (Tom Tryon). His friends soak up liquor and trade jibes about married life. "Every one of us was married, is married or is about to get married," his pal Ted (Chuck Wassil) informs a waiter. "Give us *all* another drink!" This might be shrugged off as typical macho wedding-eve tomfoolery, but the dialogue takes on an unusually bitter tone. For example, Bill's friend Harry (Robert Ivers) proposes "mass suicide" as an alternative to holy matrimony.

Bill leaves the party early to check in on his fiancée, Marge (Gloria Talbott). Walking to his car, he passes the same couple we saw earlier, now writhing against each other as their marathon kiss continues. Suddenly the young woman pulls away and slaps her beau across the face. This, we presume, indicates that she is the marrying kind, rather than the cheap cop-a-feel-in-the-parking-lot kind.

On his way to Marge's house, Bill falls prey to a shopworn ruse. He slams on the brakes when he encounters what he thinks is a wounded pedestrian (actually a dummy) in the middle of the road. When he exits his car to investigate, he's ambushed by the titular Monster from Outer Space, which looks a little like a bipedal elephant. At least it looks that way momentarily. Then a mysterious cloud engulfs Bill's body and the alien assumes the appearance of its victim.

"Bill Isn't the Man I Fell in Love With."

Among other complications, his abduction makes Bill (or, rather, the monster disguised as Bill) late for the wedding. Once he finally arrives, Marge pastes a long, passionate kiss on him. The kiss is so long and so passionate that it embarrasses Marge's mother (Mary Treen). "Marge! Marge, you're not married yet!" she protests. Throughout the film's opening act, Marge's sexual desire for Bill is presented in frank terms.

But the young bride's desire soon turns to fear and suspicion. She begins to realize something is amiss during the couple's drive to their honeymoon hotel. Bill, naturally, is at the wheel. Marge sleeps, cuddled beside him on the car's front bench seat. She awakens when Bill almost causes an accident, driving at night without headlights. Marge asks why he didn't turn the lights on. Bill claims he forgot. When she presses further ("Forgot? Bill, it's dark. How could you see?"), he snaps at her: "I told you I just forgot!" Marge pulls away from her husband. Talbott's face registers a look of shock and pain. Clearly, she is taken aback by her husband's harsh tone.

After this eerily cold wedding night the story flashes forward to the couple's first anniversary. Marge looks forlorn as she writes a letter to her mother: "It has been a horrible year. I'm frightened and bewildered. Maybe it's me but, oh Mama, Bill isn't the man I fell in love with—he's almost a stranger–"

She stops writing, crumples up the letter and sighs heavily. Most of the rest of the film unfolds from Marge's perspective. It was atypical for SF films from this era to assume a woman's point of view, and unheard of for that character to be a disenchanted housewife. We witness her heartache and confusion in literal and figurative close-up. From this vantage point, we also observe parallels to real-world marital issues.

The first of these difficulties exists in the foreground, and represents one of the film's major plot points. Like a good, functionalist housewife, Marge wants children, and she wants them now. None of this "let's enjoy our life together for a few years first" business. Even though she has plenty of childbearing years left, and despite the fact that her relationship with the prospective father seems to be on the rocks, Marge remains steadfastly intent on becoming a mother. So much so that after only 12 months of marriage—and, presumably, since she is the "good girl" marrying type, after only 12 months of sex—she volunteers for a series of invasive medical tests to verify her fertility. She's perfectly healthy, she learns. The doctor suggests that Bill stop in for some tests.

In addition to infertility, the film subtly implies that the couple suffers from another problem: domestic violence. Bill exhibits behavior characteristic of batterers: He is jealous, controlling, resorts to physical violence to solve problems and, as head of the household, believes his authority should go unquestioned. Although we don't see violence aimed directly at her, Bill strangles a puppy Marge buys him as an anniversary gift. At the least, his conduct could be considered emotional abuse.

Moreover, Marge's actions mirror those of abuse victims. She is reluctant to reveal her problem, and blames herself—writing, in that crumpled letter, "Maybe it's me." Once-lusty Marge feigns sleep to avoid sex. (This timeless avoidance tactic has almost become a cliché. It was even immortalized in the lyrics of a Pearl Jam song about domestic violence, "Better Man": "She pretends to sleep as he looks her over.") When at last she seeks assistance, most people—even her girlfriend, Helen, and the local police chief—either ignore her concerns or offer simple platitudes of no real help. This, sadly, remains a common experience for abused women. It was far more prevalent in the 1950s, when domestic abuse was seldom reported.

Talbott's evocative performance goes a long way toward suggesting abuse. In historian Tom Weaver's book *Interviews with B Science Fiction and Horror Movie Makers*, Talbott said, "I did like the role, although in a sense it really was written one-dimensional. I tried my best to put some dimensions into her." Her performance as Marge is convincing and well shaded, forming a multidimensional portrait of the distressed but courageous young wife. It's by far the best of Talbott's several genre portrayals.

In fact, nothing in Talbott's other films—which include *Daughter of Dr. Jekyll* (1957), *The Cyclops* (1957) and *The Leech Woman* (1960)—indicate that she's capable of work this impressive. Clearly, something in *IMAMFOS* inspired her. Might it have been that she understood the film's subtext of domestic violence, and called upon personal experience? Consider that, according to the Center for the Prevention of Sexual and Domestic Violence, domestic violence occurs in at least 28 percent of all marriages (the actual numbers may be much higher, since many incidents still go unreported). Nearly half of all American women experience some form of emotional or physical abuse during their lifetimes.

Eventually, Marge discovers that Bill is a monster in the literal, not just colloquial, sense. When he leaves the house in the middle of the night, she follows him to a wooded area outside town, where his spaceship is hidden. As Marge watches, the alien exits Bill's body (actually, as it's revealed later, a duplicate of Bill's body) and, in its elephant-man form, enters the ship. In a panic, Marge, still wearing her bedclothes and dressing gown, runs into town and pleads for help at the first open establishment she can find—a bar. For her effort, a barfly offers to buy her a drink and tries to pick her up. Once she leaves, a prostitute rolls her eyes and mocks her. So she rushes to the police, not yet realizing that the entire Norrisville PD is also staffed by alien imposters.

For their part, the aliens take their functionalist roles as protectors of the family unit seriously. Too seriously! All who threaten the sanctity of the family must be destroyed. When the lowlife who propositioned Marge at the bar begins hanging out in front of her house, hoping to come between the wife and her husband ("I figure the marriage don't take," he correctly ventures), Bill communicates telepathically

Marge (Gloria Talbott) witnesses the alien's agony when the invasion/impregnation plot begins to unravel. She had been selected for her womb, and her "husband" (Tom Tryon) had abused her physically and psychologically, but now Marge's apparent liberation is at hand.

with two of the alien policemen, who promptly execute the would-be home wrecker. The hooker, who has no compunction about propositioning married men, also runs afoul of the aliens, who disintegrate her with a ray gun. Decades later, the chiller *The Stepfather* (1987) would emerge as a sleeper hit by mining this same conceptual vein — family values gone mad.

"*What* Kind *of Children?*"

Marge learns why the aliens are so protective of family life when she finally confronts Bill with what she knows. "I know you're not Bill," she says, her voice quivering. "You're some *thing* that crept into Bill's body!" "Aren't you afraid to be telling me all this?" Bill asks. "Yes," she answers, sounding anguished. "Does frightening women make you proud?" Talbott's rattled demeanor convinces us that Marge has reached the end, emotionally. She's scared, but can no longer stand the torment of pretending she's unaware of the truth.

Bill freely admits that he's an alien and explains what he and his comrades are doing on Earth. They are from a now-dead planet in the Andromeda system. All the planet's women died along with their world, and the male survivors are trying to discover a way to mate with Earth women in order to perpetuate their species.

"Eventually, we'll have children with you," he states, matter-of-factly.

Marge recoils. "What *kind* of children?" she asks (here, Talbott wrinkles her nose, looking as if an unpleasant odor just drifted into the room).

"Our kind," Bill replies coolly.

Therein lies the central, underlying horror of *IMAMFOS*: that in mating with these monsters from outer space, human beings will lose their humanity. It is fear of miscegenation, on a planetary scale.

Despite the courage and independence she displayed earlier in the film, in the end Marge relies on men to solve the crisis. First, she enlists the aid of Dr. Wayne (Ken Lynch), who she knows is not an alien because he accidentally killed one of the imposters by administering oxygen. "We've got to destroy their ship," Marge pleads. "Otherwise, they'll overrun the earth and we'll be bearing their children!" But they will need help to combat the aliens, and how do they identify men who aren't secretly monsters? Suddenly, Dr. Wayne hits on the answer. "I know where to find the men we need — human men!" he declares, and marches boldly toward a door marked Maternity Ward. So the world is rescued by good, all-American guys who are capable of fathering children — and who, not coincidentally, are fathering purebred, not half-breed, babies.

In these overtones, the film speaks almost directly to the major social upheaval of its day. Just four years earlier, the U.S. Supreme Court, in *Brown v. Board of Education of Topeka, Kansas*, had unanimously ruled that segregation in public schools is unconstitutional, paving the way for desegregation in all walks of life. Just one year before *IMAMFOS*, nine black students were blocked from entering formerly all-white Central High School in Little Rock, Arkansas, on the orders of Governor Orval Faubus. President Eisenhower sent federal troops and the National Guard to intervene on behalf of the students. The Civil Rights Act of 1964 remained six years in the future, and black-white marital unions would remain illegal in 16 states until 1967, when the U.S. Supreme Court, in *Loving v. Virginia*, struck down laws that banned interracial marriage. But already, social conservatives could forecast the political winds, and argued bitterly that mixed race unions threatened the institution of marriage. Fear of miscegenation underpinned all segregationist arguments.

This fear, however, was not uniquely American, or unique to any country or

Alien monsters march from their spaceship in a futile attempt to turn back the normal men whom Marge (Talbott) has summoned to fight on her behalf—and for all the women of Earth.

century. Shakespeare, perhaps the finest observer of timeless human foibles, records this anxiety in *Henry V*. The insidious dauphin cajoles the weak-willed French king into war with Henry with the following taunt: "Our madams mock us and plainly say / Our mettle is bred out, and they will give / Their bodies to the lust of English youth / To new-store France with bastard warriors." It's hardly surprising, then, that the theme of aliens who desire to mate with human women turns up in several science fiction films of this era from around the world, including Japan's *The Mysterians* (1957) and a pair from Britain, *Devil Girl from Mars* (1954) and *Village of the Damned* (1960). Arguably the most notorious of these films, the American-made *Mars Needs Women*, was released in 1967, the same year as *Loving v. Virginia*.

In America, fear of racial mixing dates back to the Colonial era, and accounts in part for the founding fathers' approval of a constitution that perpetuated the horror of slavery. No less a figure than Thomas Jefferson, author of the Declaration of Independence, wrote in his *Notes on the State of Virginia*:

> If the blacks did not intermarry with the whites, they would remain black until the end of time; for it was not contended that liberating them would whitewash them; if they did intermarry with the whites, then the white race would be extinct, and the American people would all be of a mulatto breed. In whatever light therefore the subject was viewed, the folly of emancipation was manifest.

Jefferson's words seem especially ironic since DNA evidence now proves that he sired mulatto offspring with slave Sally Hemmings. Yet, he was right about one thing: After emancipation, with an influx of immigrants of African, Asian, and Hispanic lineage, and without the hindrance of anti-miscegenation laws, the American people have become increasingly mulatto, as well as mestizo and other racial and ethnic blends. Fifty years ago, 87 percent of Americans were white, ten percent were black, and most of the rest were Asian, Latino, or Native American. Multiracial Americans were statistically insignificant. Today, about seven percent of Americans identify themselves as multiracial or multiethnic, a growing percentage.

What's difficult to comprehend, from a twenty-first century perspective, is why this blending was perceived as a threat in the first place. Today, multiracial couples and their children are readily accepted in most American communities. Some mixed-race people have become celebrities, even popular icons. Golf star Tiger Woods, son of an African-American man and an Asian-American woman, is one of the most recognizable people on earth.

Fifty years from now, when young people look back on the current gay marriage controversy, they may find the anti–gay marriage position as puzzling as the old anti-miscegenation arguments now seem. The arguments have an ominously similar ring: mainly, that it's destructive to the social order, and against God's design. In any case, the winds of change seem to be blowing, regardless of how the current controversy plays out. Already, according to the Urban Institute, at least 1.2 million homosexual couples live together in the U.S. as "unmarried partners." The actual number may be considerably higher, since many gay couples remain reluctant to identify themselves as such. More than a quarter of same-sex couples are raising children together. Like straight parents, they have an average of two per family.

Even if fear of homosexual marriage abates, in the future new perceived terrors will almost certainly emerge to "threaten" the integrity of marriage. (Genetic engineering, perhaps?) Whatever those fears turn out to be, they will almost certainly find expression in tomorrow's fantasy and science fiction films. With any luck, at least one of those will prove as fascinating and well crafted a bundle of anxiety as *I Married a Monster from Outer Space*.

Film Discussed

I Married a Monster from Outer Space Paramount Pictures. Released 1958. 78 min. Producer and Director: Gene Fowler Jr. Screenplay: Louis Vittes. Director of Photography: Haskell Boggs. Editor: George Tomasini. With Gloria Talbott, Tom Tryon, Peter Baldwin, Robert Ivers, Chuck Wassil, Ty Hardin, Ken Lynch, John Eldredge, Alan Dexter, James Anderson, Jean Carson, Jack Orrison, Steve London, Max Rosenbloom and Valerie Allen. Available on Paramount DVD.

14

Two Faces of Voyeurism: *Nude on the Moon* and "*X*"— *The Man with the X-Ray Eyes*

Chase Winstead

Former *Esquire* employee Hugh Hefner had a great idea in 1953 and executed it beautifully. Although the earliest issues of *Playboy* were filled with agency pinup art and public-domain fiction, by late 1954 the magazine was shooting its own glamour pictorials and commissioning stories and articles from many of America's finest thinkers and authors. Sex had become, well, casually natural; it had gone legit.

Throughout the '50s *Playboy* was a resolutely saucy magazine, ambling into our lives with a wink and a smile, and with an intelligent, gentle wit that was nothing if not subversive. *Playboy* was the antiestablishment bible for young gentlemen whose revolution was urban, discreetly upscale, and, largely, sexual. (And for many years, those gentlemen were unquestionably assumed to be white, which was not simply a forgivable expression of the times, but Hef's nod to the intriguing idea of sexual liberation for the educated. Later of course, Hefner proved himself a committed progressive, and transformed his baby into one of the most inclusive of all magazines, and a vehicle for much-needed social reform.)

Hef, himself a dedicated voyeur, self-created sophisticate, and lover of women, brought voyeurism out from beneath the counter and laid it on the coffee table. The girl-next-door aesthetic he created for what he called the Playmate of the Month elevated the male urge to gaze from the milieu of strip clubs or worse to the office, the beach, and trendy coffeehouse. Readers happily absorbed the magazine's suggestion that they were surrounded daily by beautiful, willing women. The men worked alongside them at the ad agency, chatted them up at the supermarket, eyed them at the beach, made bank deposits at their windows, and confirmed dental appointments with them. Indeed, Hef found an early (and the magazine's only three-time) Playmate, the fabulous Janet Pilgrim, at work in the magazine's circulation department. The fact that Janet was married was kept secret, and nobody revealed that "Janet Pilgrim" wasn't even her real name; readers didn't need to know any of that.

What would have been served by full disclosure? Hefner understood that voyeurism, though a reality driven by mind and body, must never be completely real because the new urban sophisticates who bought *Playboy* spurned pure reality, not least because many of them had had a bellyful of it during two wars in Europe and Asia. Instead of reality, then, *Playboy*'s readers wanted a pinkly glowing simulacrum of it. The dedicated voyeur desires sexual reality as he defines it, and that means no entanglements, first names only, and the sweet, sensual spark of presumed mutual willingness that leaps from observer to female and back again.

In this regard, *Playboy* spoke with particular urgency to married men who had discovered that romance (which men crave at least as strongly as women) was not necessarily forever. The quilted housecoats, the curlers, the flat slippers, the sanitary pads stored under the sink. For Pete's sake, Janet Pilgrim would never wear a housecoat. Janet knew where it was at; she was put together, she was primed.

Because male voyeurism, as suggested in the previous paragraph, is essentially immature, no matter how willing the object of the male voyeur's desire, final, ultimate control of the game must belong to the male. The object of his gaze must be available, of course, but also perfectly lovely as she brings a cheerful insouciance to her part in the dynamics of the pastime. She's proud of her face (always attractively made up), her breasts (never crisscrossed by the marks of rumpled bed sheets), her mane of hair (never lusterless because of illness or lack of time to look after it), her belly and ass (firm because she has not used her body in childbirth). If the sturdy young fellow in the waxed crew cut and the natural-shoulder wool suit with two-inch lapels (or maybe a tennis outfit) wants to look at her, well, she's not merely flattered, but ready. And that's what the male voyeur demands.

From the mid–'50s throughout much of the '60s *Playboy* was one of the world's greatest magazines. It suggested fresh ways one might think, question, laugh, feel, and, yes, *look*. The magazine's success was so immediate and so great that America's newsstands were soon crowded with imitators. Some of the early knockoffs—*Nugget* (first issue 1955), *Rogue, Cavalier,* and a few others—were well done, certainly not to *Playboy*'s standards but with a pleasing sophistication of editorial content and art direction. The imitators' existences make clear that even as Hefner enthusiastically built a superb magazine and a personal empire, he also forged a new national — even international — sexual philosophy and aesthetic. If he has never been the intellectual he fancies himself, that's forgivable, irrelevant, because his greatest contribution to our liberation has been visceral. Yes, he champions, with great sincerity and effectiveness, such intellectual issues as women's rights, racial justice, educational opportunity, an unbiased legal system, the Bill of Rights. In the end, though, Hef unloosed the primal section of men's brains, and liberated their loins. He was one of our most effective teachers during the '50s and early '60s, elevating his readers with tips on fine wine, imported automobiles, and subtly elegant threads; urging them to think progressively when America still was irrationally spooked by Reds; declaring that it was okay to look, but more than that, it was good to look, because it was natural for a man and natural for a woman to participate in the voyeur's dance. There was no more doubt, no more shame. Sex was natural and it was good, and the male expression of it began with the act of looking. The most desirable women, Hef insisted with his boyish smile, understood this, and played along. Happily, they played along.

Playboy lost its charm years before the turn of the millennium. Now the Playmates have the appearance and attitude of high-priced call girls. Time and taste have passed Hefner by, but he isn't giving up. He has history, he has a rep. He's still Hef.

Now, Jeff, really! Remember what we came here for!
—astronaut to his peeping companion; *Nude on the Moon*

In the late '50s, following a stint in film distribution, a recently widowed Miami woman named Doris Wishman took her cues from film producer Walter Bibo—and from *Playboy*—to write, produce, and direct her first feature, a cheerful nudie called *Hideout in the Sun.* The picture played well in Florida, California, and Texas before the distributor went bankrupt. Never mind: Wishman had picked up the sexploitation bug. Over the next four decades she made 24 films. Like Hef, she had begun her career when men were pleased simply to gaze at pretty girls and their naked breasts. But time passed and Wishman was nullified by the new culture. She tried to keep up: The final film on which she worked was called, discouragingly enough, *Dildo Heaven.*

Small, wizened, and fractious by the time of her death at 82 in 2002, Wishman possessed neither the financial resources nor the gifts needed to allow her to carry on as she might have wished. Because cultists had discovered her, she wasn't forgotten, and she enjoyed appearances on *Letterman* and other attention, but the truth is that she was, in the main, an amusing eccentric from the past.

Wishman's second picture was *Nude on the Moon.* It was released in 1962, by which time photographer-turned-filmmaker Russ Meyer had made *The Immoral Mr. Teas* (1959) and *Eve and the Handyman* (1960), cheerful, brightly colored films that removed women from the nudist camps and placed them into everyday contexts. The girls were still naked, but now they posed prettily behind the lunch counter or in the receptionist's chair. Meyer was a revolutionary, and Wishman followed his lead.

Anything called *Nude on the Moon* is going to be difficult to ignore, but some of Wishman's early films are even more blatantly provocative (the metaphysical nightmare called *Bad Girls Go to Hell* springs to mind), and she made pictures with more amply endowed leading ladies (like the grotesquely equipped Chesty Morgan, star of *Double Agent 73*—inches, that is). But for charm and purity of voyeuristic intent, *Nude on the Moon,* Wishman's science fiction masterpiece, is nonpareil. With it, she demonstrated, Hef-style, that looking is wholesome, it's fun, it's healthy, and a fellow could maybe even be rewarded by coming down with a case of Love.

At a lab in Florida two researchers, Professor Nichols (Lester Brown) and the strapping Jeff Huntley (William Mayer), prepare their secret rocket ship for a trip to the moon. Jeff, though tall, dark, and handsome, perpetually looks right through his smitten secretary, Cathy (Marietta). He's all business: "I'm not interested in marriage or settling down. Science is my life—and nothing else!"

The trip is accomplished, and following a model shot of the ship's touchdown on the dark and barren lunar surface, the astronauts open the hatch and emerge into—paradise. (Wishman shot at famed Coral Castle, located in Homestead, Florida, and built in the 1920s by a Latvian émigré for a fiancée who jilted him.) The sky is bright with sun, the landscape lush and tropical. Jeff muses, "Maybe this is the dark side of the moon, the part nobody's ever seen before." The Professor nods gravely.

Following a few interesting discoveries—air temperature that allows for open faceplates, gold nuggets the size of "Oh Henry!" bars—Jeff climbs an outcrop of rock and discovers that Earth's closest neighbor is an idyllic nudist camp populated by gorgeous women clad only in bikini bottoms. Although definitely mammalian, the women sport curved antennae on the tops of their heads. Sure enough, then, they're moonwomen (or, as the saccharine title song refers to them, moondolls). Jeff is disinclined to stop his surreptitious peeping, and doesn't until the Professor practically drags him to ground.

A pair of muscled but unthreatening moonmen deliver the astronauts to the gals. Although the Professor continues to take careful, studious notes as he and Jeff are greeted and feted by the lunar nudie-cuties, he at least has the presence of mind (or libido) to forget about the gold nuggets.

The queen (Marietta) introduces herself telepathically, and for the remainder of the visit the Professor and Jeff observe a nude council meeting, a nude swim, nude

In Doris Wishman's *Nude on the Moon* (1962), the queen (Marietta) is as uninhibited as she is regal.

sunbathing, nude jogging, nude ball-toss, and some nude horseplay, as two lovelies dribble water on the back of one of their dozing (nude) friends.

As happens in other SF films, the all-business scientist succumbs to extraterrestrial romance. "Don't you understand?" Jeff shouts at the Professor. "I'm in love! For the first time in my life I care for someone!"

The queen, the object of Jeff's interest, telepathically interjects, "Earthman, I too feel strange and wonderful. Is this the love you speak about?"

Well, it's probably just hormones but — it'll do.

Unfortunately, the travelers' oxygen is nearly depleted; it's time to get back to the ship and go home. Worse, traveling weight has been worked out to the ounce, so the queen cannot return with Jeff. Since that's the case, Jeff, stupidly enough, wants to stay on the moon — never mind that his oxygen will run out in a few minutes.

The travelers reluctantly lift off. Back on Earth the Professor discovers that he's left his camera on the moon — the camera with enough nudie shots to fill the sock drawers of an entire male nation and, more significantly, the proof the scientists need to convince their professional colleagues of their journey. Jeff is particularly disconsolate because he doesn't have even a single image of his beloved queen.

The secretary Cathy enters the room. Jeff looks at her, does a double-take, and looks at her again. Naturally, Cathy (who, as you recall, has secretly loved Jeff all along) is a dead ringer for the queen. "I can't believe it!" Jeff exclaims. "You're here on Earth. I didn't lose you after all!" Oh boy! In an instant, Jeff's hormones are doing wind sprints again. Love — and enough nudity to tickle the most dedicated voyeur — have won the day.

The original trailer for *Nude on the Moon* promises "A nature camp on the moon! *See man's secret dreams come true!*" (emphasis added). Indeed. Although our boys don't spy the gals until after 31 minutes of the 70-minute film have gone by (tease 'em, Doris, tease 'em!), Wishman fashioned a true travelogue of the flesh —from a male point of view, and for male pleasure. Top-billed Marietta (a guess is that she worked as a Miami showgirl) is darkly pretty and possessed of breasts that are, well, magnificent. Wishman takes care to see that Marietta and the other good-looking, deliciously endowed women in the cast arch their backs, stretch their arms above their heads, lean over, lie back, and allow their torsos plenty of mischievous side-to-side wriggle. A bathing sequence, in which the women drizzle each other with water, is brilliant in its simple, direct appeal to male scrutiny.

The movie experience is by nature voyeuristic, of course, but the small genius of *Nude on the Moon* is that both astronauts, particularly Jeff, are depicted as unashamed peepers. Long before the moon cuties know the men are there, Jeff and the Professor get an eyeful. That Wishman makes nothing at all of this is a sort of green light for the male members of the audience. Jeff and the Professor take a good long look on the sly — and why not? As the culture had finally admitted, it's in a man's nature. Thus, the voyeurism of the paying customers continues long after the voyeuristic tendencies of Jeff and the Professor have been mitigated by discovery.

Despite a budget too small for synch sound, *Nude on the Moon* is no worse as science fiction than, say, *Cat-Women of the Moon* or *Queen of Outer Space* or *Robot*

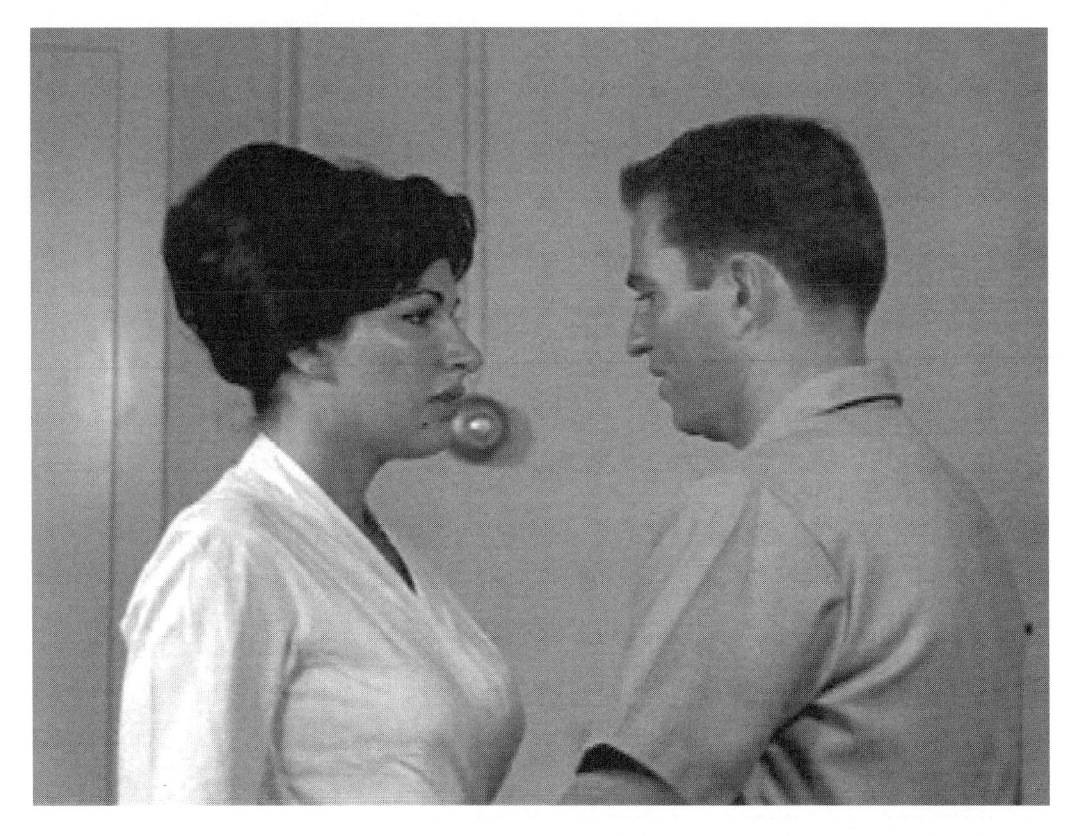

The journey back to Earth safely accomplished, Jeff (William Mayer) is overjoyed to discover that the lab assistant (Marietta) who has secretly loved him, but whom he has ignored, is a dead ringer for the naked queen. Because Jeff hasn't lost his love after all, his peeping isn't merely condoned, but rewarded.

Monster, or any number of other SF pictures of the era that utilize women's bodies for voyeuristic purposes, but that lack the inclination to take us where we go when we see *Nude on the Moon*, i.e., to Epidermis Alley. In this respect, *Nude on the Moon* is more honest than those other films, but to say so and leave it at that is certainly to give Wishman more credit than she deserves. Let's just say she knew her audience.

On *Moon,* Wishman mixed it up adequately well as a director, with professionally timed close-ups, inserts, and cutaways. Model work is primitive but not hopeless, and Wishman earns a few points for having the *chutzpah* to use the undisguised door and fuselage of an airliner for the spaceship exteriors.

Oddly, as her career progressed Wishman lost, or simply lost interest in, her modest feel for the fundamentals of filmmaking. The dialogue in *Nude on the Moon* is dubbed fairly well, but in later films (also shot without sound) Wishman hid actors' mouths behind telephone receivers or their hands, thus eliminating the need to be precise during postproduction dubbing. She indulged a fondness for meaningless, protracted shots of walking legs (no torsos, no faces, just legs); and headache-inducing handheld camerawork. The most peculiar of Wishman's innovations was to lay down dialogue tracks in flopped fashion, so that whenever an actor speaks, we've already cut to the back of the person's head.

But all of that was in Doris's future. *Nude on the Moon* is a goofy treat, and rather like the early *Playboy*: sexy, pretty, and saucy; at home with the culture of the moment and offering a bounty of things to look look look at.

I can't heal. I only look.
—Dr. Xavier; *"X"— The Man with the X-Ray Eyes*

Director-producer Roger Corman, who began his film career in 1954, was, like Hugh Hefner, keenly tuned to the zeitgeist of the '50s and '60s, a period that was, as for Hef, the peak of Corman's creative work. Resolutely independent, he associated himself on a picture-by-picture basis with the most successful of the indie production companies of the era, American International Pictures. AIP had begun life as the American Releasing Corporation in 1954, as a venture of a cynical entertainment attorney named Samuel Z. Arkoff and a former exhibitor and lifelong movie fan named James H. Nicholson. They perceived, helped to fortify, and subsequently rode the teen-culture wave of the fifties and sixties. Corman, who distributed through Allied Artists or his own company, Filmgroup, when not working through AIP, had an instinctive understanding of kid-audience expectations. Like Arkoff and Nicholson, he was a tuning fork who vibrated to the possibilities of trash culture.

Many of Corman's early pictures were Westerns and straight dramas, but he hit the SF boom hard, offering unexpectedly clever, well-acted thrillers the likes of *It Conquered the World (*1956), *Day the World Ended* (1956), *Not of This Earth* (1957), *Attack of the Crab Monsters* (1957), and *Wasp Woman* (1959). A horror comedy called *A Bucket of Blood* did well for Corman in 1959, but when he remade it a year later as *The Little Shop of Horrors*, it died.

By 1960 the teen-horror cycle

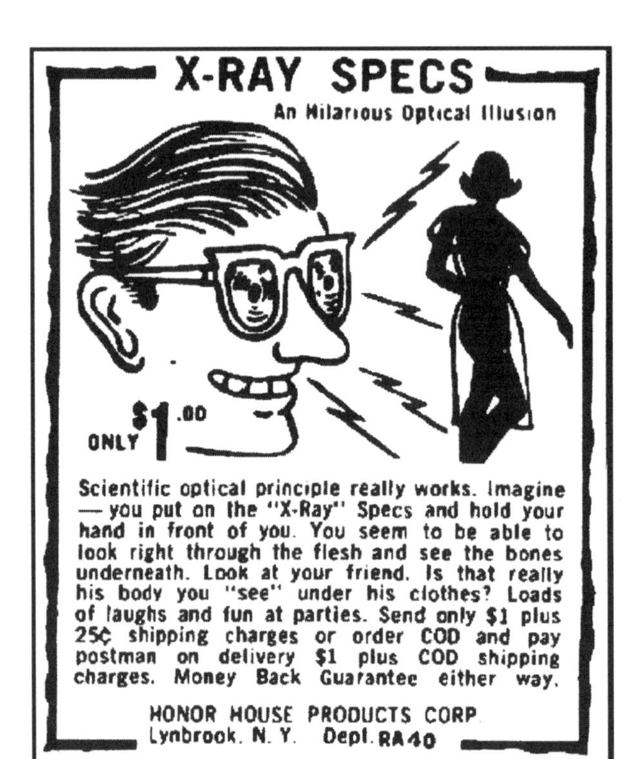

"X-Ray" Specs were the dream of every little boy, and of a lot of big boys, too. Predicated on the male urge to peep without being detected, the toy spectacles produced a layered image of light and dark areas, with a concomitant simulation of X-ray vision (Honor House Products Corp.).

seemed to have run its course. Then Corman went to Arkoff and Nicholson to pitch a retelling of Poe's *The Fall of the House of Usher,* in color and with a name star (Vincent Price). AIP went along with the gag and enjoyed a tremendous box-office hit. The studio and Corman would go on to make a highly profitable, and often worthy, series of Poe films, notably *The Pit and the Pendulum* (1961) and *The Masque of the Red Death* (1964).

Yet, in the midst of this revival of "period horror" (sparked in large measure by the successful gothics from Britain's Hammer Studios), Corman remained a thoroughly contemporary figure who wore khaki pants and sneakers on the set, and who never stopped looking for the next exploitable notion. He found it, and fashioned it into one of his best films, in *"X,"* known from ad art—but not on the film's title card—as *"X"— The Man with the X-Ray Eyes* (1963). *"X"* was scripted by Ray Russell, onetime fiction editor for *Playboy*, and Robert Dillon. It was a color picture shot in 15 days rather than the ten to which Corman had grown accustomed. The cast was solid, led by Ray Milland as surgeon and vision-research scientist Dr. James Xavier.

Underfunded and frustrated, Xavier believes he can enhance human eyesight so that diagnoses of illness will be perfectly accurate, leading to proper and successful surgeries. An urbane, handsome fellow who wouldn't need to do this unless he really wanted to, Xavier just wants to spare people unnecessary suffering and save lives.

When funding is pulled out from beneath him Xavier experiments on himself with ever-increasing doses of a serum he has distilled into eye drops. His colleagues, Drs. Diane Fairfax (Diana van der Vlis) and Sam Brant (Harold J. Stone), are appalled by the risk Xavier is taking.

Xavier's interest quickly becomes obsessive, and by the time he accidentally shoves Brant from a window to his death, he's already seen more than any human was meant to behold. "It's like a splitting of the world," Xavier moans, "more light than I've ever seen!"

The greater part of the film is a fugitive melodrama, during which Xavier works as "Mentallo," a carnival shill, in order to continue his research in secret. During one performance Xavier reads a letter in the pocket of a jeering heckler (Dick Miller). It's "from a girl you deserted," Xavier pronounces flatly. "A girl who loves you." Xavier's crass manipulator, Crane (Don Rickles), is impressed but believes Mentallo has a trick, a gimmick. Crane asks Xavier what he wants to do, what he wants to be. Xavier answers, "Maybe this is all he could be. This and nothing more. And you. What do you want to see? Crane replies, "All the undressed women my poor eyes could stand."

The power of Xavier's sight deepens. Grotesquely large sunglasses jut from his head like the distended eyes of an insect. He looks only barely human. Crane finds a tenement flat and sets Xavier up as a "healer," but Xavier knows that he cannot heal at all, only see, and that to see serious illness while helpless to remedy it is soul crushing. X-ray vision, the dream of numberless boys and men, is nothing but a hurtful curse.

Xavier divorces himself from Crane, is found by Diana, and travels to Las Vegas, where he makes a killing at the blackjack tables (he can see the cards before they're turned over). When casino security gets a look at his silvered eyes, Xavier is pursued into the desert by police.

AMERICAN INTERNATIONAL presents

IN PATHÉCOLOR AND SPECTARAMA

RAY MILLAND

STARRING AS

"X"

THE MAN WITH THE X-RAY EYES

CO-STARRING

DIANA van der VLIS · HAROLD J. STONE · JOHN HOYT and DON RICKLES

Produced and Directed by ROGER CORMAN · Screenplay by ROBERT DILLON and RAY RUSSELL · Story by RAY RUSSELL · Executive Producers: JAMES H. NICHOLSON and SAMUEL Z. ARKOFF · Music by LES BAXTER

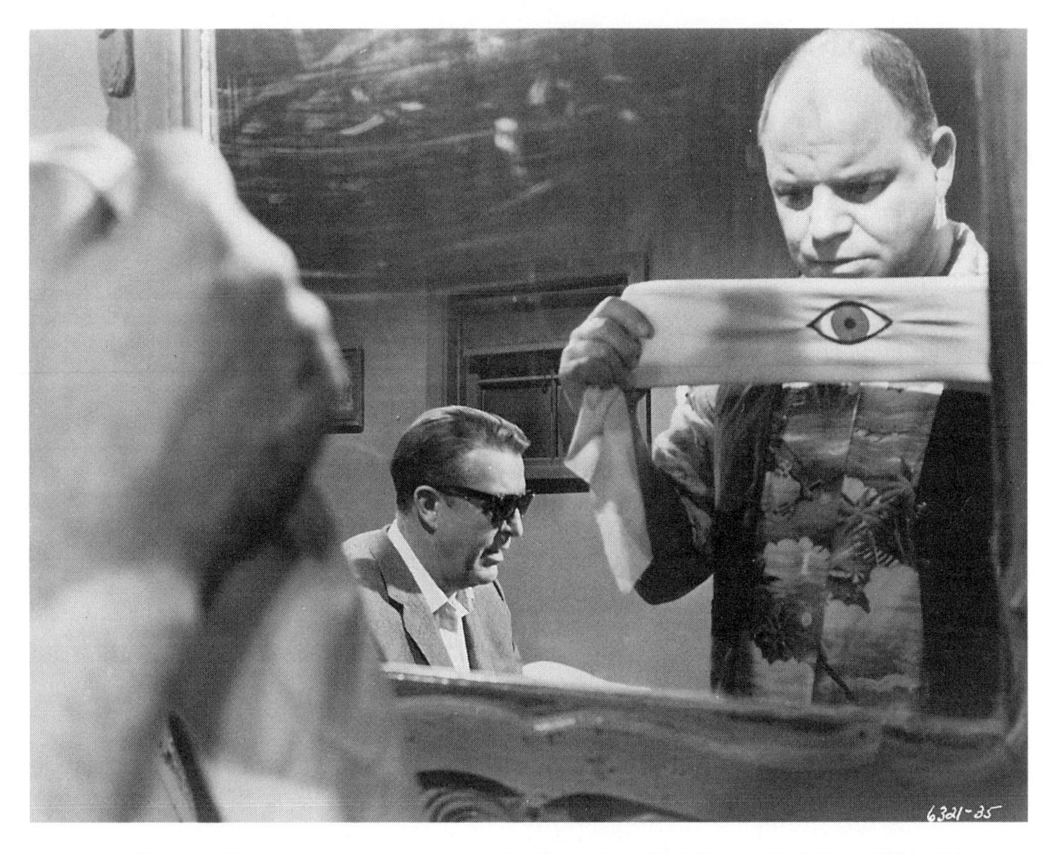

Carny shill Crane (Don Rickles) is convinced that "mind-reader" "Mentallo" (Ray Milland) has a gimmick, but can't figure out what it is. For his part, Xavier's X-ray vision has become a physical and emotional burden that he frantically struggles to reverse.

The world in which Xavier now moves is a surrealist torment. He sees buildings "without their sheaths of brick and stone," and the very flesh seems to fall away from people's bones "in an acid of light." The sun is no longer a source of comfort but a pulsing hole of energy that is part of a maddening vision of the incomprehensible universe, revealed. Xavier sees through his closed eyelids, sees more and farther, until finally he says, "I'd give anything, *anything*, to have dark!"

He finally stumbles upon a revival tent ringed by old, battered cars. This is the last stop of the hopeless, the dissolute. In the heat and sweat of the tent a fundamentalist preacher (John Dierkes) asks Xavier what he sees. Xavier replies, "Great darkness ... and in the center of the universe, the eye that sees us all."

"You see sin and the Devil!" the preacher pronounces. He regards Xavier's eyes, by now a glittering black, and advises, "If thine eye offends thee, pluck it out!"

In one of the fine shock moments of SF cinema, Xavier obeys.

Corman fashioned a cautionary tale, a remonstration to bad boys who like to

Opposite: **The one-sheet poster for Roger Corman's *"X"—The Man with the X-Ray Eyes* (1963) suggests the prurient nature of Dr. Xavier's abilities, and no hint of the terrible punishments that will befall him.**

Xavier (Milland) stumbles upon an evangelical revival meeting, his tortured eyes spheres of obsidian that see to the pulsing core of the universe. In the film's memorable, shock-cut conclusion, the scientist willingly pays the price of his unrestrained desire to *look*.

peep. Although during an early stage of the experiment Xavier gets a voyeur's kick from seeing Diana and the other good-looking women at a cocktail party twist and frug nude beneath their clothing ("Why, you can *see* me!" Diana exclaims), Xavier has limited interest in sex, and none at all in romance. Rather than arouse him, his voyeurism makes him emotionally impotent. His research, like the science cited by Jeff in *Nude on the Moon*, is all that matters to him, but here there's no easy redemption by love — or even lust. Xavier is blind to the fact that Diana adores him, and when he reaches such a low ebb that she may be his only salvation, he is too far gone, emotionally and physically, to be saved.

The intense conservatism of "*X*" is startling, particularly in light of how quickly American society was liberating itself in 1963. Xavier's story could easily have been an adventure of a quite different sort: essentially upbeat, ironic in an amusing way, a journey of nonlethal self-discovery. Instead, Corman and his writers worked from a point of view that Hefner and Wishman would not have cared to explore. "*X*" tells us (and by "us" I mean "men") that not everything is meant to be seen, and that when we level our voyeur's gaze on a woman, we neither know her nor love her. We do not diminish her, but she becomes diminished in our minds, and we almost certainly diminish ourselves.

Films Discussed

Nude on the Moon; aka Girls on the Moon; The Moondolls; Nature Girls on the Moon; Nudes on the Moon Moon Productions/J.E.R. Pictures. Released 1962. 70 min. Producers: Doris Wishman and Martin Caplan. Director: Anthony Brooks (Doris Wishman). Screenplay: O.O. Miller (Doris Wishman), based on story by Jack Caplan. Director of Photography: Raymond Pheelan. Music: Daniel Hart and Doc Severinsen. Editor: Ivan McDowell. With Marietta, William Mayer, Lester Brown, Pat Reilly, Lacey Kelly and Shelby Livingston. Available on Something Weird DVD.

"X"; aka "X" — The Man with the X-Ray Eyes Alta Vista/American International Pictures. Released September 18, 1963. 85 min (with prologue). Producer and Director: Roger Corman. Associate Producer: Bartlett Carré. Screenplay: Robert Dillon and Ray Russell, based on story by Ray Russell. Director of Photography: Floyd Crosby. Art Director: Daniel Haller. Music: Les Baxter. Editor: Anthony Carras. Special Photographic Effects: Spectarama, John Howard. Special Effects: Butler-Glouner, Inc. Makeup: Ted Coodley. With Ray Milland, Diana van der Vlis, Harold J. Stone, John Hoyt, Don Rickles, Morris Ankrum, John Dierkes, Dick Miller, Jonathan Haze, Barboura Morris and Lorrie Summers. Available on MGM/UA DVD.

Sources

Kissell, Ted B. "Screen Queen." *Miami New Times,* September 18, 1997.
Program notes, 5th Annual New York Underground Film Festival.

15

The Satan Bug: Some Nightmares Are Quite Inescapable

ALAN DIRK LESTER

There's no such thing as perfect security.
— *Dr. Hoffman, in The Satan Bug*

I have this many-faced, recurring nightmare; it's one of those that make you feel as if, upon waking, you could pull a wriggling black dung beetle out of your ear. I've had the nightmare ever since I was a kid, I think. The events of the dream always seem to go something like this: A hard guy named Lee Barrett gets himself recruited into duty at his former job as the security head of Station 3, one of those top-secret germ warfare laboratories tucked way down deep in California's red desert. Why? Because Station 3 has just been burglarized and flasks containing the place's *raison d'être*, the "unstoppable Satan Bug," an engineered virus so potent it will destroy all life on Earth when released, has been stolen for reasons and by parties unknown. Barrett quickly realizes that such an audacious theft must surely have been an inside job. He manages to discover that the person behind the scheme is one of those mad-man millionaires, a fellow who, unbeknownst to his pursuers, is posing as one of the facility's scientists. Now said millionaire is threatening to release the Satan Bug in Los Angeles if Station 3 is not immediately shuttered. I tell you, it's some dream.

That the above happens to be an accurate summation of *The Satan Bug*, a medium-budget John Sturges science fiction thriller from 1965, is a fact I attribute to nothing but my astonishing powers of prophecy.

But, let's not get ahead of ourselves.

The filmed *Satan Bug*, as opposed to my nightmare version, was based a novel published by ill-tempered Scotsman Alistair MacLean, author of *The Guns of*

Navarone, Ice Station Zebra, and *Where Eagles Dare.* MacLean published *The Satan Bug* under his Richard Bachman–esque pseudonym Ian Stuart, to prove that his works were popular on their own merits and not merely because his famous name appeared above their titles. MacLean was right, and *The Satan Bug* was adapted for the screen by a young James Clavell, who'd already been responsible the scripts of *The Fly* (1958) and *The Great Escape* (1963). In later years he became well known for sprawling, Orient-themed novels: *Tai-Pan, Shogun,* and *Noble House.*

And as noted, *The Satan Bug* was directed (and produced) by John Sturges, who brought us the classics *Bad Day at Black Rock* (1955), *Gunfight at the OK Corral* (1957), and *The Magnificent Seven* (1960).

The Satan Bug is a tight, smartly plausible thriller. Although one can't say it was a step down for Sturges, the film's cast, though talented, is of the "TV star" variety. Top-billed George Maharis was coming off his considerable success as Buz Murdock on *Route 66,* the Stirling Silliphant series of 1960–64. After studying acting at New York's Actors Studio, Maharis appeared off–Broadway in *Deathwatch* and *The Zoo Story.* He made a number of appearances on the TV series *Naked City* before being cast, with Martin Milner, as one of two friends who search for adventure as they pilot a Corvette along America's most famous highway. The show was a hit and turned Maharis into a momentary teen heartthrob, a fact he quickly capitalized on by heading into the studio to record seven albums, beginning with 1962's *George Maharis Sings!* Although his star has faded, Maharis is a talented, edgy actor who seems at home in the high-stakes intrigue of *The Satan Bug.*

Costar Anne Francis (edgy in her own right) had made strong impressions in *A Lion Is in the Streets* (1953), the aforementioned *Bad Day at Black Rock, The Blackboard Jungle* (1955), *Forbidden Planet* (1956, as Altaira), and *The Crowded Sky* (1960).

Richard Basehart, by this time the star of TV's *Voyage to the Bottom of the Sea,* is joined by Ed Asner, later of *The Mary Tyler Moore Show,* and Dana Andrews, the stolid and appealing leading man of *Laura* (1944), *The Best Years of Our Lives* (1946), and *Night of the Demon* (1957). Even *Star Trek*'s James Doohan shows up in a bit part.

The adventure begins with a jarring, jangling burst of Jerry Goldsmith's score and an overhead image of a rust-and-scrub desert road that says *isolation.* The setting is immediately unnerving, not least because of its remoteness. Anybody who gets into trouble here is going to be on his own.

Our sense of security is further eroded as we pass through Station 3's supposedly secure checkpoints, manned by a lone guard who wouldn't look out of place in front of an old folks' home and protected by a double fence that wouldn't have kept Cool Hand Luke inside for 60 seconds. By the time we're inside Station 3 — specifically, Lab E — and getting an indication that it contains something that "makes the guys back in D.C. nervous," we've noted with some unease that only a single soldier with a machine gun and a German shepherd guards the door outside. The theft that follows is in and of itself unspectacular, as it seems too easily executed. It's only later that we're informed of the nature of what's been stolen.

Because Station 3's acting security chief Reagan (John Anderson) is dispatched by the intruders, the facility feels obliged to re-recruit former security chief Lee Barrett (Maharis). We're introduced to him in a smoky, bongo-beat jazz club that would

Anne Francis and George Maharis warily examine a flask containing *The Satan Bug* (1965).

have said "height of cool" only a decade earlier but that still manages to convey Barrett's mod, antiestablishment tendencies. When Barrett's recruiter describes him as a "superb lone operative who has no master in areas of cunning, secrecy or violence," the script draws a sharp line between Barrett and the more politically oriented (and easily dispatched) Reagan. Our guy is of that individualistic new breed called antihero.

We also should mention that the only person at Station 3 who's trusted by Barrett is a black security guard, Johnson (Hari Rhodes). Interracial respect was not common to Hollywood leading men of the day, and just in case you think I'm exaggerating, recall that two years later no less an honorable personage than Spencer Tracy would require 107 minutes of the 108-minute *Guess Who's Coming to Dinner?* to decide that the peerless Sidney Poitier was to be trusted with his daughter. My point here, like the filmmaker's, is simple: *The Satan Bug* takes us quickly into a new world, with opportunities and dangers that require new heroes.

It's a thought that's as lonely as it is reassuring.

Later, when Station 3's only present-and-accounted-for lab researcher, Dr. Hoffman (Basehart), delivers a veritable ode to the lethality of both the Satan Bug and the less-dangerous botulinus stored in the very same lab and stolen alongside it, a couple of previously innocuous facts take on decidedly sinister aspects. First, as we listen to Hoffman brush aside the other bio-weapons created by his fellow scientists as inconsequential, the very name of the place, Station 3, becomes an ice cube sliding down our spines. Think about it: If there's a Station 3 and a Lab E, doesn't that mean that there are, at the very least, Stations 1 and 2 and perhaps 4 and even more, each one with its very own Labs A through E producing roughly the same amounts of materials? In other words, there are at least 120 poorly guarded bio-weapons in the United States alone. I say "alone" because we're talking about a high–Cold War setting here, in which it can be assumed that whatever the USA has been trying to develop, the Soviets are trying to develop, too.

Secondly, the lackluster security we noticed on our way in starts screaming out a chilling truth: These people are far more concerned with their secrets than they are with their security. What's happened to proper precaution? Only 20 years earlier, people involved with the Norden bombsight were monitored so closely they couldn't go to the bathroom alone. By 1965 we were in an infinitely more challenging environment, but nobody at Station 3 seems to have noticed.

As if we'd require further proof of the lab's intransigent security, we meet General Williams (Andrews), who is unsure whether to preserve or destroy the Satan Bug. Whatever protection he'll authorize, then, is likely to be halfhearted.

Williams has a beautiful, Mata Hari–esque daughter Ann (Francis), who's introduced, like Barrett, to jazz accompaniment. It's important to note that we learn absolutely nothing *and* a great deal about the nature of Ann's character. While it's immediately obvious that she and Barrett will develop a romantic attachment, and may in fact be married to each other, the precise nature of their connection is never revealed. Likewise, though MacLean goes into it in his novel, the filmmakers never pause to explain what Ann does for a living—you know: how she occupies herself to earn money for cocktail dresses and food. It's clear that she's something other than just the hero's girlfriend and that she's privy to a sizable amount of what we've been told is highly classified information. When she tries to head off screen to do girlie stuff she's told not to, which suggests that she has tactical value. The sight of a dead scientist floating in a pool doesn't bother her in the least, and she's able to provide, rapid-fire, the make, model, color, and license number of a mysterious car she's glimpsed in the dark during what the rest of us would consider a moment of great emotional distress. (And at that, Ann shrugs that she didn't get a good look at the car at all.) Fans of SF cinema wouldn't be treated to another heroine quite so steady on her feet until Sigourney Weaver's Ripley showed up 14 years later in *Alien*.

Until the character introductions are over and done with, *The Satan Bug* maintains the kind of measured, realistic tone which, though creepy, could easily be mistaken for drag or padding. But I prefer to think of it as cinematic possum-playing since it lures us into the assault on our collective sense of security that follows.

Mere minutes after our protagonists have assembled they receive an extortion note from the bio-weapon's kidnappers. The perps demand that Station 3 be closed down. Of course, that's just impossible, so much so that not a single character with the U.S. government even suggests it; not even after they've been treated to haunting newsreel footage of the 100 percent fatal aftereffects of the lesser of those two stolen bio-agents, the botulinus, which has been released in a small Florida town; not even as they look at sprawled bodies of its victims (who, let's face it, are inescapable reminders that the carnage is the result of one of 40, and that the Satan Bug itself is a thousand times—*a thousand times* more dangerous). Not even then do these paladins of the U.S. government suggest that Station 3 be closed.

Much of what follows is your standard Hollywood thriller played out against the backdrop of all those horrific consequences my nightmare is made of. The film skillfully sets up standout scenes such as Barrett and two agents trying to survive after a spilt flask of botulinus is thrown into a barn, and a climactic midair fight between hero and villain above Los Angeles in and around a wildly careening helicopter.

Government operative Lee Barrett (Maharis) escapes a botulinus-riddled barn.

All of this is good stuff, but the real piquancy resides in the textual backdrop against which the action is played out. You see, we ultimately discover that the majority of the many murders, betrayals, and counter-betrayals weren't intended to cover up the theft of the virus, but rather to conceal the fact that it has a working antidote. Now, this sounds like a good thing, right? Wrong. Because the only thing that this revelation guarantees is that the same government that started out with mixed feelings about the Satan Bug will put it right back in the same poorly guarded vault where the whole mess started—just in case the Reds decide to get frisky. Or as Barrett says while heading home in the helicopter, seemingly victorious: "I'll give you the flask when we're right back where we started." The remark is smart and funny as well as queasy, and sets *The Satan Bug* apart from the usual run of SF-intrigue thrillers. Back where we *started*? Every time I see the film, I wait for the THE END title card to morph itself into a question mark (à la *The Blob*), but it never happens.

I wonder why?

If you're anything like me (and if you aren't I can't think of a single good reason you'd be taking time out of your life to read this), you've already realized that *The Satan Bug* doesn't belong on a shelf next to the "keep watching the skies 'cause everything'll be all right if we all keep a sharp eye out" SF thrillers that preceded it; or with the Vietnam-era "Soylent Green is made of people!" paranoid futurist visions that followed. In the immediate wake of the Second World War Hollywood's craftsmen went into overdrive to distract a battle-weary populace from the very real Pandora's Box of dangers the late conflict had unleashed: Germany's jets and rockets, America's atomic arsenal, and Japan's super-secret plague weapons. At war's end these goodies (and the people who created them) were divvied up between two immediately hostile states, the USA and the USSR. But while the world geared up to enact selected scenes from the Book of Revelation, our movies were screaming that what we really needed to worry about were carrot men from Venus making trouble at the North Pole, but not to fret too much because if space invaders ever did show up, square-jawed holdovers from Dubya Dubya Two, like actor Kenneth Tobey, would give those evil aliens the same brand of knuckle sandwich they'd only just fed to the Axis.

Now, I wasn't there to see it for myself, but I can't help but believe that this was exactly what folks wanted to believe right about then. Until 9/11 I hadn't given much thought to the propaganda value of films like 1959's *The Atomic Submarine*. They were Cold War riffs that anticipated the Martian translator from Tim Burton's *Mars Attacks* (1996), who says, "Please do not run; the atomic bomb is your friend."

After 9/11 I was possessed by the irrational and let's just say *uncharacteristic* longing for a return of those Ike-era manly men I'd once scoffed at.

The government will handle things. It was a great strategy for the immediate postwar world. It just didn't work for long.

What put an end to our "invincibility" mind-set was so simple I can sum it up with one word: Korea. Between 1950 and 1953, those same near-invincible Allies, whom everyone was supposed to believe would have little trouble fighting off an invasion of saucer men, waged a series of bloody and more or less even–Steven battles against two nations of dirt-poor rice farmers and a handful of Soviet MiGs without achieving anything more decisive than a stalemate (which, as we're constantly reminded, continues to this day).

Also—and to my mind this was the real deal breaker—the UN (read: USA) didn't use the Bomb. Let me be clear here—when a million Chinese stormed across the Yalu River and delivered perhaps the most embarrassing defeat in American military history, we didn't use the Bomb against them ... when Russian MiG-15s swept down out of the high air to shoot down everything with a white star on it, we didn't use the Bomb against them ... when MacArthur screamed to irradiate those Commie bastards, we didn't use the Bomb against them. Even a public as notoriously gullible as America's couldn't help but wonder why on Earth its government would rather get its ass kicked than use its friendly neighborhood ultimate weapon.

Korea, not Vietnam, was the crack in America's consciousness. It turned 1952's duck-and-cover drills into 1962's backyard bomb shelters. All those "what the hell aren't they telling us" questions left the gung-ho "whatever happens we've got it covered" military reassurances of films like *The Thing from Another World* (1951), *Earth vs. the Flying Saucers* (1956), and *The Atomic Submarine* looking thin indeed.

The vague sense of unease informed Don Siegel's *Invasion of the Body Snatchers* (1956), an SF-political allegory that told us—bluntly—that the government didn't know what was going on—or maybe it did, and just didn't give a damn.

By the time the Cuban Missile Crisis percolated in 1962, Hollywood showed a decidedly more ugly political point of view with *The Manchurian Candidate*, in which Washington is clueless about a Communist plot to use a brainwashed cat's-paw to assassinate the U.S. president. Somewhere in the gravitational pull separating *The Satan Bug* and *The Manchurian Candidate* our childish notions about an alert, paternalistic government came to an end.

The films' protagonists, Frank Sinatra's Major Bennett Marco and George Maharis's Lee Barrett, are disgruntled Korean War vets on the edge of burnout, but they're still capable of lone-wolf activity. *The Manchurian Candidate*'s heroine, Janet Leigh's oblique "maybe she's a Soviet spy or maybe she's something else" Eugenie Rose Chaney obviously attended the same charm school as Anne Francis's Ann Williams. And even the pictures' villains, Angela Lansbury's megalomaniacal Mrs. Iselin and Richard Basehart's messianic Dr. Hoffman, share similar mental disorders.

What's more significant is that *The Manchurian Candidate* and *The Satan Bug* work from the same belief system. Both suggest that sheer dumb luck is the only way we might stagger to natural deaths without botulizing ourselves or blowing ourselves up first. Because of that expressed notion, these are films on the cusp. They're determined to worry us, but they still believe in that luck. By the time Vietnam worked its way into the collective psyche, that hopeful sense of luck was dead and gone.

The probability is that none of us have to stew about brainwashed preppie presidential assassins or planets bursting with ill-tempered, colonialist extraterrestrials, but we *should* worry about the world's real-life Satan Bugs. At last count, about a score of nations possessed various biological weapons or the means to manufacture them. And as you might unhappily conclude, security in all of these nations—including our own—isn't exactly infallible. The wealthiest of these states—the USA, Japan, and the UK—have strictly observed policies that locate their "Station 3s" as far away from their own populations as possible. What that means, even though it might sound like a good idea from where we're sitting, is that right at this very moment there's a poorly guarded bio-weapons "Lab E" right in the path of some Kalashnikov-toting South American or Central African or Middle Eastern revolutionary, and the only things between him, its contents, and us are a guy with a German shepherd and that long-dead dumb luck.

Maybe the weapon that kills us won't be called the Satan Bug, but then again, it could. My father, a Korean-era Cold Warrior in his own right, used to say that "some nightmares are quite inescapable," and though he and I often violently disagreed, when that man was right, he was right.

Film Discussed

The Satan Bug Mirisch-Kappa/United Artists. Released April 14, 1965. 114 min. Producer and Director: John Sturges. Screenplay: Edward Anhalt and James Clavell, based on the novel by Ian Stuart (Alistair MacLean). Director of Photography: Robert Surtees. Editor: Ferris Webster. Music: Jerry Goldsmith. Art Director: Herman A. Blumenthal. Special Effects: A. Paul Pollard. With George Maharis, Richard Basehart, Anne Francis, Dana Andrews, John Larkin, Richard Bull, Frank Sutton, Edward Asner, Simon Oakland and John Anderson. The 1997 MGM/UA VHS video release is out of print.

16

"Conclusion of All Our Yesterdays": The Jungian Text of *The Omega Man*

Ryan Baker

Science fiction inevitably has one foot firmly planted in the here and now. Though often wistfully daydreaming of forthcoming wonders, the fanciful is often grounded by the looming reality of the human condition and its innate hardships. There is the caste turmoil of *Metropolis*, the specter of mortality in *Blade Runner*, or the apocalyptic xenophobia of *War of the Worlds*. Terrors and nightmares are rationalized, embodied through science and fact, never simply the offspring of an arcane mythology or supernatural fatuity. Chaotic forces like radiation, communism, apocalypse, and technology spawn the creepy crawlies of science fiction, the man-made fiends embodying at once our greatest triumphs and most profound blasphemies.

We are thus allowed to gaze into the foreboding realities and cautionary tales of society awry, of unbridled human nature in the midst of glorious self-destruction. Science fiction peers into the nebulous realm of the future, constructed by the perimeters of the past, to cast a shadow of the present. In the case of *The Omega Man* (1971), this is especially true; the foreseeable future — a mere seven years following the film's release — serves as a petri dish where the disease of our own fear thrives. These fears can, however, be recognized and approached — it often simply requires looking in the most bizarre of places. A critical look at a film like *The Omega Man* is a sobering experience. Films that may seem of no redeeming quality often contain the most prominent subtexts and outrageous politics. Using the writing of Carl Gustav Jung as a lens through which to evaluate such material, as one will see, can be beneficial in that psychological analysis reveals an entirely new dimension of criticism.

The Alpha of The Omega Man

The road to *The Omega Man* follows not so much the tribulations of main character Robert Neville as the frustrations of author Richard Matheson, on whose 1954 novel *I Am Legend* the film is based. Matheson's work is hardly unfamiliar to the film industry; several of his other works have been adapted including *Hell House* (*The Legend of Hell House*, 1973), *Stir of Echoes* (1999), and *What Dreams May Come* (1998). Matheson also lent his talent to Roger Corman's series of Edgar Allan Poe yarns for AIP, *The Twilight Zone* and the 1980 adaptation of Ray Bradbury's *The Martian Chronicles*. Matheson's genre work — both literary and cinematic — remains visible today, even as a proposed remake of Matheson's *The Incredible Shrinking Man* founders in "development." Yet somehow, *I Am Legend*, perhaps his most singular work, has failed to garner a faithful translation. Not surprisingly, efforts have been made.

Hammer Films bought the rights from Matheson in 1957 but the project died following the script's rejection by the British censors.[1] Soon thereafter, producer Robert Lippert purchased the rights and churned out a reprehensible adaptation christened *The Last Man on Earth* (1964).[2] Dashed promises of illustrious German filmmaker Fritz Lang's directing and brutal script rewrites embittered Matheson, who, in rebuttal, attached his pen name, Logan Swanson, to the script, and publicly denounced the effort.[3] Matheson said of the film, "It was poor ... the film was released and disappeared as it should have done. Maybe someday *I Am Legend* will be filmed as I wrote the book, but I doubt it."[4]

Warner Bros. released *The Omega Man* on August 1, 1971, an even further departure from Matheson's novel. Scripted by the husband-wife duo of Joyce Hooper and John William Corrington, who also were responsible for Corman's *Von Richthofen and Brown* (1971), Scorsese's *Boxcar Bertha* (1972), and J. Lee Thompson's *Battle for the Planet of the Apes* (1973), the plot was only mildly similar to that of *I Am Legend*, even though early drafts bore Matheson's original title. Producer Walter Seltzer handed directing responsibilities to television veteran Boris Sagal, who cut his teeth on *Alfred Hitchcock Presents* and *Peter Gunn*. The resulting amalgamation of Matheson's global cataclysm, the Corringtons' bizarre, thinly veiled politics, and Sagal's cheap, uninspired direction was odd, to say the least. Firmly grounded in the early 1970s, the film is nearly as dated as its fashion sense, proudly taking its place in Charlton Heston's SF trilogy that includes *Planet of the Apes* and *Soylent Green*.

The year is 1977. Los Angeles has become a rotting graveyard, its empty buildings housing only corpses, its highways littered with the long since dead. Three years earlier, a border skirmish between China and Russia elevated to international war, and the horrors of nuclear and bacteriological warfare were realized. A contagion spread across the globe, toppling nations, destroying institutions, murdering continents. The human race saw its doomsday. But Colonel Robert Neville (Heston) survived. Using an experimental vaccine, Neville injected himself mere moments before he would have succumbed to the choking death of the plague. He is now the single man in Los Angeles— but he is not alone.

In some instances, the plague did not immediately kill; it only jumped to the third stage, rendering victims photosensitive, deranged, and drained of their skin

The megalomaniacal Matthias (Anthony Zerbe), leader of the mutants, pronounces judgment on Neville.

pigment. A former newscaster, Jonathan Matthias (Anthony Zerbe), created an order—called the Family—to rebuild society by tearing it down. The Family destroys libraries and museums, all in the attempt to wipe clean the evolutionary slate, to raze the world of all monuments of the civilization that destroyed the world. Their greatest enemy—because he is emblematic of that civilization—is Neville, who must hole himself up at night in his fortified high-rise apartment, replete with generator, surveillance system, high-powered rifles and eight-track cassette player. For all of his weapons and tools, however, Neville's existence is still inevitably a lonely one.

Neville is rescued from the Family by a group of young survivors, including former medical student Dutch (Paul Koslo) and Lisa (Rosalind Cash), whose little brother Richie (Eric Laneuville) is suffering the final stages of the disease. Taken back to their hideout in the hills, Neville finds a small collection of survivors—mostly children—who, though infected, demonstrate some sort of resistance to the bacteria. The group returns to Neville's home, and using his equipment, creates a serum of his own blood to cure Richie. In the meantime, romance blooms between Neville and Lisa.

Following Richie's recovery, the trio plan to collect Dutch and the other children and flee to the mountains, taking the serum with them. Richie secretly goes to Matthias to offer the Family the serum, but is killed; Lisa's plague progresses shockingly, and she becomes one of the Family; Neville is betrayed and ambushed by

Lisa (Rosalind Cash), by now in Stage Three mutation, accompanies Neville (Charlton Heston) on a last, desperate scramble for freedom, and the future of the human race.

Matthias inside his own home. Escaping with the mutated Lisa, Neville is struck down by Matthias, a spear piercing his chest. He falls, bleeding, into the fountain, where he lies until Dutch and the children find him. Giving Dutch the last vial of serum, Neville dies, arms outstretched and feet crossed in Christ-pose, leaving the human race to begin again.

The oft-discussed *I Am Legend* project that floated around Hollywood during the end of the '90s was, at one time, attached to names like Ridley Scott, Michael Mann, Will Smith, and Arnold Schwarzenegger. The script, by Mark Protosevich, was touted as chilling, emotional, and intense, yet studios balked as projected budgets swelled and definite creative forces failed to materialize.[5] The project seems to have found its resting place in the dismal abyss of development hell—perhaps, at least by Matheson's opinion, for the better.

White Shadows and Negative Images

The application of Carl Jung's psychoanalytical concepts may seem outrageous or absurd in dealing with a film such as *The Omega Man*. Understandably, it seems rather far-fetched that the filmmakers were deliberately interpolating the writings of the renowned former student of Sigmund Freud. For this reason, however, Jung's work is particularly potent in that in the avoidance of meaning and deliberate symbolism, the most latent and primitive aspects of the unconscious imprint themselves. Much of Jung focuses on the state of disrepair within, the fracturing of the personality through repression of undesirable or unacceptable thoughts, which he believed stood at the foundation of mental sickness. Through an education in ancient mythology and comparative religion, Jung developed his concept of the collective unconscious, an enormous shared entity containing primitive imprints and concepts that emerge consciously as archetypes. Partially based on Freud's theory of "archaic remnants," the archetypes serve a common purpose in that they embody basic motifs but differ greatly in their representation.[6]

Jung's archetypes are not uncommon in film, though they are more prevalent in certain genres, particularly science fiction and fantasy. Both the *Star Wars* and *Lord of the Rings* films have found themselves consistently analyzed based on Jung's theory, but the archetype is much, much too fluid to be restrained to a single genre. The richness of the psychoanalytical subtext of the horror genre in particular, however, does allow for a proliferation of this concept, and has helped in perpetuating one of the most common and intriguing of the archetypes: the shadow. Similar to the German concept of the doppelganger, the shadow is an aspect of the unconscious that contains thoughts, feelings, and emotions disowned by the conscious self as a result of societal mores or personal development. It is emotional and primitive, capable of a certain level of autonomy that allows it to occasionally lash out into the conscious; as such, it is, on a personal level, a relatively recognizable aspect of the unconscious. However, the shadow exists both intrapersonally as a relic of the self and as a portion of the collective unconscious, in which its power is greatly amplified, reflecting a societal — if not global — series of repressions and negativities rather than individual anxieties.

Specifically, then, the Family is a monolithic shadow to Neville, expressing deep-seated technological and racial anxieties. Neville represents science, civilization, and order, whereas the Family eschews these artifacts of society in lieu of destruction, religion, and mass identity; the conflict stems from the inherent polarity, but the superficial differences belie the salient similarities. Primary is the conflict between the majority and the minority, one trying to relegate the other into insignificance. Neville believes the Family to be a bunch of disorganized lunatics in "Halloween costumes." He dismisses them as "vermin" and makes light of their rampant destruction of educational, technological, and literary bastions. Matthias calls Neville "obsolete" and "part of the dead"; he is "discarded, the refuge of the past." The irony of the Family condemning Neville as anachronism is clear, even as Matthias accuses him in a candlelit, Gothic chamber with a wrought-iron chandelier and pews seating the obedient masses like a congregation, outfitted in flowing black robes like Satanic monks. The Family rejects technology in all of its forms, preferring wooden tools and weapons such as bow and arrows, knives, bats, and hammers. Our introduction to the Family finds them burning books, a pastime evoking both Nazi Germany and the dystopia of *Fahrenheit 451*; the Family discards even high art and other forms of expression, including literature, which are clear symbols of education and civilization.

Strong emphasis is placed on homogeneity of appearance, however. Physical appearance defines the dichotomy of living and dead, sane and insane, creator and destructor. Even the romance between Neville and Lisa, which was reportedly inserted purely for controversy, is marred by Lisa's eventual acquiescence to the pigment-draining disease. As Neville awakens in the Family's grip, Matthias asks his concordant congregation "to look at him — does he have the marks, do you see them ... is he of the Family? Is he of the sacred society? Then what is he?" Their unanimous response: "*Evil.*" When the marks are finally unveiled — the horrible contagion-stricken mutilation of the eyes— the camera glides along the faces of the Family, lingering on their ghostly orbs, and cuts to an extreme close-up of Neville's bright blue eyes nervously surveying the visages of his captors. The contrast is unavoidable. Later, Lisa tells Neville of her involvement with Matthias and the Family in the beginning: "We thought we were alone — just me and Richie with millions of corpses! But there was Matthias and other people. Well, anyway, he gave us the Family—for a while. We helped with the burials, we helped with the burnings, but when it was over, and the worst was past, they began to know how different we were — our skin, our eyes. One day while they were asleep, we just — took off."

The film is highlighting societal divisions within a microcosm; after all, the characters of *The Omega Man* quite simply hate any and all people unlike them. Even in the ravaged post-apocalyptic Earth, racism is the chief impetus for action, a volatile urge to preserve the society from genetic and cultural inferiors. Yet the subtext is not nearly as transparent. A more complex reading of *The Omega Man* arrives from the coupling of historical context and the theories of Carl Jung. While racism has coursed through America's veins since before the nation's inception, the tumultuous era of the 1960s— punctuated by race riots, antiwar demonstrations, and societal upheaval of the civil rights movement — spotlighted race and class, and catapulted the anger and strain into plain view.

The shadow self of *The Omega Man*, then, becomes a manifestation of white America's dread of losing societal supremacy. The entire architecture of the film constructs itself around the concept of Neville, an affluent white man, as the minority besieged by an alien majority. In this particular instance, the majority is not necessarily black, but rather, hyper-white; within the Family, all racial categories have collapsed. In this sense, the Family becomes even more grotesque for it suggests that bogey of every racist: miscegenation. The Family is a monolithic majority and thus assumes control of society, free to mold — or, in this case, destroy — as the Family sees fit. The bigotry in much of white America finds itself the victim rather than the victimizer; the Family, as black America, seems to desire a complete razing of American culture, leaving only Neville's isolated home a sanctuary of art and technology. The notion seems more appropriate to *Birth of a Nation* than a mainstream 1971 science fiction film.

But to invoke D.W. Griffith's clearly racist 1915 film does illuminate the kind of societal anxiety (albeit hyperbolized) about authority wrested from white America. Certainly, the late '60s and early '70s beheld figures like Martin Luther King, Jr., who propounded humanism and peaceful integration, but the emerging Black Panthers—gun-toting and frankly revolutionary—were King's political and philosophical opposites. Obstinacy of the white establishment had prevented blacks from attaining meaningful privileges or rights as citizens. Clearly, the Panthers and other radical black movements were born out of the larger society's consistent refusal to assimilate blacks into the American mainstream.

The subsequent dread of societal destruction and infiltration is what forms and motivates the shadow, molding it into the radical figure of the Family. Here the dread transcends singularity, reflecting a societal fear of white victimization, of being the alien, the stranger, forced to hide and wander alone through once familiar streets now in ruin. The entirety of the film seems to feed off social inversion: the familiar is now unfamiliar, black is now white, white is now black. Even the city, once the symbol of safety and civilization for mankind, becomes a darkened prison. Conversely, the once strange rural area becomes pristine and ideal.

The individuated impact of the shadow self can be found more palpably in both of the distinct characters in the Family: Matthias and his paladin, Zachary. While the whole of the shadow self reflects racial angst, these two characters exhibit their own dynamics of inverted racism. Neville finds a parallel in the violent and anachronistic Zachary, while Matthias is a distortion of the father role Neville finds himself in. Both serve to greater elevate the film's level of racial subtext.

Neville and Zachary: Brothers in Arms

Brother Zachary, played by Lincoln Kilpatrick, is the intimidating right-hand ghoul to Zerbe's commanding Matthias. Zachary is portrayed as bloodthirsty and vengeful, and upon closer inspection, represents an aspect of Neville's repressed self. Both figures bear vestigial mind-sets, unaffected by the cataclysmic event. Neville, obviously, still grasps at civilization, order, and technology; Zachary clings to what Matthias tells him are "the old ways ... all your hatreds, all your pains." It seems his contempt for Neville stems from a racial and economic memory; he refers to Neville's home as a "honky paradise." During Neville's judgment, Matthias asks his congregation if Neville is "of the Family." The camera does not focus on the obedient masses, but on Zachary, seated to the left of Matthias. His response is framed in close-up and even gets precedence on the audio track. Zachary eagerly condemns the outsider, an obvious reversal in a character obviously black (the script describes him as having "features clearly African").

Zachary is the only leading member of the Family to advocate the use of technology to kill Neville. He beseeches Matthias to allow him to use "just a little nitro ... I can get the cannons out of the old Guard armory; we can have him out of there in no time!" Matthias denies him, refuting the use of technology. Zachary counters by insisting that as long as Neville remains, they must all "rot and hide like grubs."

Neville and Zachary are contrasted visually in an action sequence during the latter half of the film. Neville and Lisa find themselves vulnerable when the generator runs out of gas, blanketing the complex in darkness. Fearing infiltration, Neville descends to refill the generator, while Zachary ascends the building walls. Their movements represent their polarity; Neville intends to ensure his safe haven remains unspoiled, even as Zachary means to usurp Neville's power. Zachary also brandishes a pistol, his usage of a forbidden tool accentuating his determination to kill Neville by any means necessary. An obvious embrace of technology again strengthens the parallel between Zachary and Neville; once Zachary is finally felled, he plummets from the top story and crashes to the ground below, upside down in a prophetic variation of Neville's final cruciform pose. Zachary, like Neville, is a martyr, dying for the cause, fallen at the hand of the enemy. (Earlier drafts of the script included Matthias's condemnation of Zachary's use of the pistol, but this remains strangely absent from the final film.) Thus, Zachary, like Neville, dies trying to preserve and protect a familiar way of life, safeguarding his majority, as Neville protects his minority status.

Both men desire to serve as vanguard to their respective group, eliminating the majority or abnormality. The indication of Zachary's lingering racism is the film's most pointed allusion to timely racial tensions. It seems his drive to murder Neville stems from hatred and jealousy rather than from a sincere urge to concretize normality and safety for the Family. Likewise, Neville bears personal hatred for the Family; he's obsessed with a sense of territorialism. When Dutch refers to Neville's home as a "pillbox," Neville calmly replies, "Well, that's where I live. It's where I used to live, it's where I'm going to live, and not Matthias nor his Family nor any other son of a bitch is going to make me leave." Zachary represents the ushering in of a new era, a new society, and Neville is the staunch symbol of the remnants of old society. It is the embodiment of America's fear, societal usurpation through violence—specifically, a black uprising that would "infect" American society. Extremists such as the Ku Klux Klan and neo–Nazis still espouse such philosophy, attempting to protect and maintain white culture, but it is a belief as hideous as it is antiquated. The hatred that infected the real world of 1971 is reflected in the fervent bloodlust—fueled by a singular hatred—of Zachary and Neville, who attempt to preserve or create their own sense of normality, unaware that their goals are reprehensible.

Neville and Matthias: Reflections of Mana

"Are you God?" a little girl asks Neville. His knowledge of science and medicine, coupled with his seemingly inexhaustible capability to survive, clearly builds a case for his deification. The second half of the film finds Neville reconstructing his life and finding meaning through his love for Lisa, his adopted position of leader and mentor to the small band of survivors, and his newfound mission to replicate a medicinal cure for the plague. Neville has become a leader, a father, a superior wise man.

Conversely, Matthias's hypnotic voice resonates through the Family as they follow his every command, never questioning his authority, or even exhibiting enough of an identity to do so. Matthias leads his brothers and sisters down "the long road of truth," granting them positions as cogs in his machinations to reconstruct society. Matthias is a leader, a father, an undisputed authority.

In their dynamic of influence, Neville and Mathias exhibit traits of Jung's *mana-personality*, an individual capable of tapping into the limitless reservoir of the collective unconscious, unknowingly using it to exert dominance and authority.[7] Jung claims that the mana-personality serves the necessity for authority figures, fathers, idols, and leaders. Their inexplicable insight—a sort of psychological third eye—propels them to be gods and kings.[8] This sort of psychic energy, in these examples, manifests itself as complex understandings of medicine and science (a sort of contemporary magic) and oratory influence.

The depiction of Matthias as a sort of warped priest complies with the concept of a dark father figure, a byproduct of the wrong individual's capability to understand the greater unconscious. He relies on his sort of religion, which Jung rightly states "means dependence on and submission to the irrational facts of experience."[9] His vehement espousals are indicative of his own submission to the strength of the mana-personality, a maddening addiction to the wielded power of the father figure role. Jung writes of the danger of allowing the power to stunt one's own identity, thereby supplanting it, eradicating the humanity and replacing it with a sterile role. In this sense, Matthias has advanced upon Neville; Matthias, too far gone, has relinquished himself to the mana-personality, and become lost inside the insanity of the twisted father figure.

Conclusion

Ultimately, Jung points to the dualism within man's self as represented by the shadow: at once the singular reflection, as in Matthias and Zachary, and a reflection of the whole. In this psychological dualism we disassociate ourselves from our own evils, granting them flesh and blood through projection, just as Neville finds his own beliefs and fears staring back at him. We demonize and victimize society's Others—the minorities—because in them we see pieces of ourselves. Man destroys "everything he does not know and does not want to know about himself by foisting it off on somebody else." In this action we empower our fears as they materialize and assimilate the fear we have of them; yet they never stray far from the features of our own face.

This self-duplicity spawns multiplicity, an infinite reiteration of what we fear. This is *The Omega Man*: the final hours in which all we know and hold familiar is suddenly inverted. White America is the victim, the minority, hunted and hated like animals, struggling to preserve its icons of class and civilization. Social change is not the blowing wind, but a cleansing baptism of fire; institutions and technology are rendered useless and meaningless. White America becomes obsolete. The society's intense bigotry has turned upon it, amplified, and threatens to annihilate it.

Neville is the symbol of white America, his shadows in the insidious influence of Matthias, Father of the Family, and the blood-stained vindication sought by Brother Zachary, whose remembrance of isolation now drives his hunger for unity. White viewers find shadows in the Family, the Puritanism, the psychotic delusions of racial contamination and the persecution of our supposed inferiors. The film takes place in Los Angeles, but the true landscape is the collective unconscious; white viewers are satisfied that, although Neville has fallen, his precious blood—"genuine 160 proof Anglo-Saxon"—is left to cure the population, to purify and leave the freakishness of the Family to rot as an antiquated anomaly. Neville endures suffering and becomes the Christ figure, martyred to provide the human race with another tomorrow; Matthias, triumphant, speaks from the balcony of Neville's home: "the bad dream is over, friend Neville—now we can sleep in peace." The shadow figure, then, finally inhabits the *sanctum sanctorum*, the edifice of the self. In the wake of its emergence, two of the three black characters are dead, and the final one conspicuously turned white as a tertiary case of the miasma. The outlook is, to say the least, unsettling.

Such is the fruition of capitulating to the shadow, the stalking figure of barbarism and prejudice lurking inside the unconscious. Failure to face the demons and assert responsibility for one's own inner mechanisms only proliferates projection, which only furthers isolation and divergence, which, of course, breeds hatred. Those unwilling to stare into the baneful planes of the unconscious secrete their phobias just like the contagion of the film, transforming the world into a reflection of their own unease. Mankind's wholesale distribution of self-repressed monsters creates "a cocoon, which in the end will completely envelop him."[10] The global catastrophe of *The Omega Man* warns that our options are few: Either acknowledge and cope with the shadow self and all of its trappings, or continue to cast the shadow upon others and allow our phantasms to guide us toward the destruction of the world, consumed in the inferno of our own hate. Just as Matthias ominously utters to his darkness-clad brethren, speaking of both past and future: "Nothing cleanses quite like fire."

Film Discussed

The Omega Man Warner Brothers Pictures. Released April 1, 1971. 98 min. Producer: Walter Seltzer. Director: Boris Sagal. Screenplay: John William Corrington and Joyce Hooper Corrington, based on *I Am Legend* by Richard Matheson. Director of Photography: Russel Metty. Editor: William H. Ziegler. Music: Ron Grainer. Art Director: Walter M. Simonds. Make-up: Gordon Bau. With Charlton Heston, Anthony Zerbe, Rosalind Cash, Lincoln Kilpatrick, Paul Koslo, Eric Laneuville and John Dierkes. Available on Warner Home Video VHS and DVD.

Sources

1. William Johnson, ed., *Focus On: The Science Fiction Film*. Englewood Cliffs, N.J.: Prentice-Hall, 1972, p. 163.
2. *Ibid.*
3. *Ibid.*
4. *Ibid.*
5. Protosevich's script is readily available on the Internet.
6. Carl Gustav Jung, "The Archetype in Dream Symbolism." *The Collected Works of C.G. Jung*. Trans. R.F.C. Hull. 18 vols. Princeton: Princeton University Press, 1990, p. 108.
7. Carl Gustav Jung, "Relations Between the Ego and the Unconscious." *The Essential Jung*. Ed. Anthony Storr. Princeton: Princeton University Press, 1983, p. 123.

8. *Ibid.*, p. 124.
9. Carl Gustav Jung, "Religion as the Counterbalance to Mass-Mindedness." *The Collected Works of C.G. Jung*. Trans. R.F.C. Hull. 18 vols. Princeton: Princeton University Press, 1990, p. 12.
10. Carl Gustav Jung's "The Shadow." *The Essential Jung*. Ed. Anthony Storr Princeton: Princeton University Press, 1983, p. 93.

17

The Sport of Violence: *Death Race 2000* and *Rollerball*

Bryan Senn

The crunching tackle on the football field, the bloody crack of heads on the soccer pitch, the bone-crushing crash on the motocross or Indy track, the memorable *Wide World of Sports* "agony of defeat" as a ski-jumper tumbles and careens out of control — these are the wince-inducing moments that fascinate and captivate viewers of professional sports. Granted, more than just violence is at work in this and other games. There's the subtle strategy of the gridiron, the sudden adrenaline rush as engines race to pull ahead, the sheer elegance of "the beautiful game" during World Cup competition. But the tantalizing prospect of violence is the icing on the cake, the *pièce de résistance* of the sporting world.

The year 1975 saw two very different science fiction films tackle this topic: *Death Race 2000* and *Rollerball*— one a comedic parody, the other a deadly serious action film, but both intent on exploring the idea of sporting violence taken to the extreme.

In the year 2000 hit and run driving is no longer a felony, it's the national sport!

—*Death Race 2000* ad line

"One of the things a low or medium budget filmmaker can do," espoused *Death Race 2000* producer Roger Corman to interviewer Leonard Maltin, "is experiment, take chances— such as we did with such a zany idea as *Death Race*— because you're not gambling that much money." Said zany experiment was budgeted at about $300,000, which was indeed cinematic chicken feed in 1975.

"The year 2000: America is a vast speedway," begins the film's trailer. "People line the streets to witness the greatest drivers on Earth in a race from sea to shining sea." This is not simply an annual transcontinental road race, however, but a death race — in which running down pedestrians earns you points (with the highest tallies awarded for "scoring" toddlers and senior citizens). A small group of underground rebels intends to sabotage the bloody road race and capture the world's top driver, known only as Frankenstein (David Carradine). To this end, one of their own (Simone Griffeth) has infiltrated the system by becoming Frankenstein's navigator. But unknown to the rebels, Frankenstein, fed up with the carnage, has decided to kill America's dictator-like president after the race and put an end to the sanctioned violence. Only the winner of the contest will get close enough to Mr. President to accomplish this, and Frankenstein must drive and battle his way through the trap-laying rebels and his archrival racer, Machine Gun Joe Viterbo (Sylvester Stallone), for the opportunity.

Coming in the middle of the cinematic exploitation explosion of the 1970s, *Death Race 2000* roars ahead of its questionable competition to offer up something besides the expected sex and violence. In amongst the gratuitous massage scenes and (often wittily staged) hit-and-run gore sequences are healthy dollops of social satire poking pointed fun at everything from hero worship to political rhetoric ("We have

Ace driver Frankenstein (David Carradine), with navigator Annie (Simone Griffeth).

positive proof that it was none other than the treacherous *French* who have been sabotaging our great race," blusters the president, concluding, "Is it no coincidence, my children, that the word 'sabotage' was invented by the French?"). Granted, none of it is particularly subtle (the leader of the patriotic rebel group is an elderly woman named Mrs. Thomasina Paine; and the fawning reporter, whose sycophantic interviews invariably begin with her labeling her subject a "close personal friend of mine," is called Grace Pander), but the film is no less effective (nor less amusing) for its blatancy. Many moviegoers apparently agreed, for, according to *Variety*, the picture grossed $5.25 million in the U.S. and Canada for Corman's New World Pictures.

Given that level of box-office success, it's reasonable to assume that *Death Race 2000* touched a nerve with the American public of 1975.

The mid–'70s saw the nation in transition, moving away from the hopeful, brotherly love mentality of the 1960s toward the unapologetic greed-is-good corporate mindset of the 1980s (a theme which, as detailed later, *Rollerball* explores with considerable prescience). Gone was the optimism of the early sixties, replaced by the cynicism and ennui prompted by such cultural calamities as Watergate, the Energy Crisis, runaway inflation, and America's sorry experience in Vietnam. *Death Race 2000* cleverly incorporates each of these concerns in a palatable, entertaining fashion.

Regarding politics, the movie's "Mr. President" (Sandy McCallum) is corrupt and above the law—just as a certain U.S. president of recent memory had proved to be—at least for a while. (Amusingly, the film's dictatorial president rules America "from his summer palace in Peking"; a backhanded swipe, perhaps, at one of Richard Nixon's most publicized accomplishments—his various trips to, and establishment of relations with, Red China.)

Economically, America was in trouble in 1975, with foreign influences apparently dealing body blows to the U.S. economy. OPEC seemed to be holding the nation hostage—at least that's how it looked to every American who drove up to the gas pump, only to face sudden shortages, long lines, and soaring prices. The film playfully pokes fun at this daily dilemma via obfuscating officials who blame the race's acts of sabotage on "the treacherous French ... just as they and their stinking European allies have undermined and destroyed our great national economy." I mean, really ... the *French*?

Rather than make a realistic—and, consequently, painful—point about these concerns, *Death Race* addresses them via the theater of the absurd, allowing audiences to laugh at outrageous excess, while still supplying a subtext calculated to resonate with the populace of the time. By employing parody, *Death Race* makes its points without preaching, and without alienating the viewer. And its sharpest point penetrates the topic of violence as spectacle—to which the average American in the mid–1970s had grown rather accustomed, courtesy of nightly news coverage of the Vietnam War.

"I have made the United Provinces of America the greatest power in the known universe," boasts the president in his pre-race address. "I have also given you the most popular sporting event in the history of mankind, the Transcontinental Road Race, which upholds the tradition of 'no-holds-barred'.... Once more, I give you what

The drivers have a carefully cultivated knack for killing hapless pedestrians, the *raison d'être* of the competition.

you want." And what the people (and the movie audiences) want is sanctioned, anything-goes violence. There follows incident after incident of bloody mayhem, much of it quite disturbing (such as when Machine Gun Joe "scores" an innocent fisherman in a creek bed by spinning his wheels over the hapless man, creating a spray of red that mingles with the clear, cool water).

But after showing the ugly brutality of the violence, director Paul Bartel goes a step further by revealing the utter absurdity of it all, leavening the savagery with a large spoonful of black humor — thus making it both more palatable and less overtly exploitative. After one nasty score, the peppy commentator (L.A. deejay "The Real" Don Steele) enthuses, "a beautiful kill, a neat kill"; the tearful-yet-appreciative widow of the race's first fatality receives (on national television) "a high-style two-room apartment in Acapulco!" as prize for her (mis?)fortune; the Resistance pulls a *Road Runner* trick involving a detour sign, a false-front roadway, and a cliff. Cheerful silliness such as this points up the innate ludicrousness of the violence and of the entire competition.

Perhaps the most amusingly revelatory moment comes when doctors and nurses at a geriatric hospital situated along Frankenstein's route wheel aged patients onto the roadway for "Euthanasia Day." But as Frankenstein speeds toward the helpless targets, his car suddenly veers off the street and onto the hospital drive to send the callous doctors and nurses sailing into the air like rag dolls. It's a small, subversive victory, as Frankenstein dispatches the professional "healers" and leaves the geriatrics unhurt. "Which only goes to show," observes the race commentator, "that even the fearsome Frankenstein has a one-hundred-percent red-blooded American sense of humor, heh heh heh." (Here Bartel and his cohorts seem to ask: Has the constant viewing of real-life brutality — such as that covered by the nightly news of the early 1970s — so inured Americans to violence that even their sense of humor is now defined by it?)

The movie's closing scene raises further intriguing questions. The denouement begins with Frankenstein, now president(!), and his new bride (his former navigator) announcing the abolishment of the violent race that made him a national hero — and successor to the president he overthrew and killed: "We feel that the country no longer needs this gratuitous display of violence to show the world that its virility is intact." This elicits vociferous protests from the surprised commentator. "The race, sure it's violent," the reporter shouts to Frankenstein, "but that's the way we love it — violent, violent, violent!" Exasperated with the rant, Frankenstein and his bride, by now seated in their killer car, run over the commentator and drive off.

While ostensibly a simple comedic closer, a final throwaway gag, the conclusion opens up that proverbial can of worms. Though in his new guise Frankenstein now condemns violence, he casually commits it yet again; does this imply that attaining the ultimate power (the presidency) has corrupted him, just as it did his predecessor? Or does it mean that you can take the man out of the race, but you can't take the race out of the man (the violence comes from within — and it *will* out)? Or, on a larger scale, does this represent one final knowing wink about what people — and the viewer — really want after all? Though a "mere" exploitation-oriented satire, *Death Race 2000* offers not just food, but a veritable smorgasbord for thought.

Production-wise, the low budget shows through on occasion (the matte paintings of the futuristic city look like something straight out of *The Jetsons*, and the occasional painful synthesizer riff reminds us that Danny Elfman was not within Corman's price range), but the car race scenes are well staged and exciting. And the thematic richness and sheer audacity of the film's concept (not to mention the genuinely funny black humor) help paper over the remaining cracks.

According to co-scripter Charles Griffith, Corman was not pleased with Bartel's comedic approach to the material; he ordered much of the humor removed and brought Griffith on board as a second unit director to shoot additional scenes of action and violence. Corman apparently wanted less exploration and more exploitation of the subject. "There are many times when a Corman picture can only be a comedy," commented Griffith in Mark Thomas McGee's *Roger Corman*. "Roger didn't want [*Death Race 2000*] to be a comedy and felt we were in a conspiracy against him. Actually, we were in a conspiracy *for* him."

Corman himself, however, disagrees. In the same book, Corman claims, "This thing about turning it into a comedy against my wishes is wrong. I told [co-writer] Bob Thom, who'd written *Bloody Mama* for me (which was a serious picture with comedy, insofar as these films can be serious), that what I wanted was something along the lines of *Dr. Strangelove*: a serious comedy about violence. To me, *Death Race* was about gladiator fights in ancient Rome or boxing today — the need the public has to experience vicarious thrills. I wanted to treat it with humor, but what Paul Bartel and Chuck Griffith wanted to do was make it a silly comedy. A farce comedy. I wanted it to be a smart comedy."

In the end, the producer got his wish, for *Death Race 2000* is indeed a smart comedy.

Death Race was based on a serious 1958 short story called "The Racer" by Ib Melchior (*The Time Travelers, Robinson Crusoe on Mars, Planet of the Vampires*). "At first I was appalled," recalled Melchior. "After the first ten minutes, I said, 'My God, what have they done to my story?' Then I started laughing, and by the time the film was over I thought it was one of the funniest things I had ever seen."

Filmmaker George Miller has said that *Death Race 2000* provided the inspiration for his *Mad Max* and *Road Warrior* films. While those Australian classics admittedly "have a slight edge on *Death Race*" (as Corman himself modestly put it), *Death Race 2000* remains a watershed in exploitation cinema, offering broad but biting satire, along with nudity and violence, to create an entertaining and thought-provoking vision of an amok dystopia. So sit back and enjoy the ride, but remember: Buckle up for safety—it's the law.

In the not too distant future, wars will no longer exist. But there will be rollerball.

—*Rollerball* ad line

"I think *Rollerball* is a warning," commented producer-director Norman Jewison during filming, "that possibly in ten or twenty years a game like this will indeed exist and we will indeed be in the hands of a corporate society." One of the classic big-budget science fiction films of the 1970s, *Rollerball* takes the viewer on a veritable roller coaster ride of violence. The movie's brutality proves far from gratuitous, however, for there is meaning behind it, not the least of which is a demonstration of the unsettling acceptability of mayhem within the context of sport.

In the not-so-distant future, the game of rollerball has been created "to demonstrate the futility of individual effort" and to keep the masses in line (a la Roman gladiatorial games) by the global corporations that have replaced individual nations as the governments of the Earth. It is a fascinating world, a sterile world, with major decisions made by the enigmatic "Executives" who control the all-powerful Corporations.

Rollerball is a hybrid of roller derby and football, with elements of hockey and motocross thrown in. It is fast, exciting, and dangerous—often lethal. Jonathan E. (James Caan) is the greatest rollerballer in the history of the sport, surviving ten seasons. He has become too popular and the Corporations want him out. "If a champion defeats the meaning for which the game was designed, then he must lose," states Mr. Bartholomew (John Houseman), a powerful energy corporation executive. Jonathan refuses to retire, and the rules of the game are changed in an attempt to

Opposite: **The Spanish one-sheet for *Rollerball* (1975) graphically contrasts the savagery of the sport with the effete society that produced and nourishes it.**

¿UN FUTURO PROXIMO?
ROLLERBALL
JAMES CAAN en
Un film de NORMAN JEWISON "ROLLERBALL"
con JOHN HOUSEMAN MAUD ADAMS · JOHN BECK · MOSES GUNN
PAMELA HENSLEY · BARBARA TRENTHAM RALPH RICHARDSON
Guion WILLIAM HARRISON Director musical ANDRE PREVIN
Productor asociado PATRICK PALMER Producida y dirigida por NORMAN JEWISON TECHNICOLOR
CB Films

defeat him until, finally, rollerball is no longer a game but a vicious struggle of life and death — and the struggle of the individual spirit.

Jewison builds a realistic and complicated tableau, not only for the game of rollerball itself but for the safe, controlled world in which rollerball serves as a necessary outlet for aggression. With pop culture of the mid–'70s seemingly abandoning the simple, less-is-more lifestyle movement of the '60s in favor of the more-is-simply-not-enough materialism that would fully take hold in the '80s, 1975 was the perfect time for a science fiction film to explore the ultimate corporate dream (or nightmare). "Corporate society takes care of everything," explains Bartholomew. "All it asks of anyone, all it's ever asked of anyone *ever*, is not to interfere with management decisions." The questioning Jonathan, stumbling for words, expresses an important theme when he explains, "People had a choice a long time ago between — havin' all them nice things or — freedom. 'Course, they chose comfort." It's a wistful, regret-filled comment evoking the abandonment of the make-love-not-war idealism of the '60s for the looking-out-for-number-one materialism of the '70s. Small touches, such as women's clothing and hairstyles that subtly suggest those of ancient Rome (conjuring up the power and moral laxity of that decadent empire) say volumes about the world of *Rollerball*, in which luxury is paramount and violence is entertainment.

The three game sequences themselves, about which the film revolves, are masterful set pieces of bloodlust excitement made acceptable via the context of "sport." As the Executives try to induce the too-popular Jonathan to quit the game, they introduce rule changes — abolishing penalties and limiting substitutions; then, ultimately, abolishing *all* penalties, substitutions, and time limits. Each successive match further strips away the veneer, peeling away the game's ostensible acceptability like the layers of a rotting onion to expose the savage violence (the game's true *raison d'être*) concealed within. At the end, rollerball is laid bare for all to see, and it is nothing less than sanctioned gladiatorial combat.

The editing, photography, and soundtrack charge these scenes with a wild energy that's found only in the thrill of violent competition. We, the audience, disturbingly find ourselves caught up in the brutal excitement, cheering as Jonathan knocks a player into the boards or smashes his fist into the face of an opponent. Jewison draws us into the game and then shows us how far this "harmless" exhilaration, this "safe" outlet for aggression, can go. In a particularly vivid and upsetting slow-motion sequence, Jonathan's teammate and friend, Moonpie (John Beck), is crippled when an opponent tears off his helmet and slams a fist into the back of Moonpie's head. The stricken athlete slowly and inexorably falls to the rollerball track. With total silence on the soundtrack, his head hits the floor and you see that his eyes are open and staring — he is brain-dead, a vegetable. It is a sight not soon forgotten.

"I have to be very careful that I don't turn the audience on to the violence," stated Jewison, "but that I turn them *off* to violence." Jewison obviously felt that watching violence can trigger violent behavior (witness the sometimes frenzied, brutal actions of the fans during the game); ergo, a film such as this holds great power — to corrupt as well as enlighten.

Rollerball is not without flaws. A great deal of running time is devoted to the

"It is not a game man is supposed to grow strong in"—yet for all the arrogance of the corporate mindset that produces that pronouncement, star player Jonathan (James Caan) proves that the individual will ultimately triumph over the corrupt group mind in *Rollerball.*

efforts of the rather dense Jonathan to learn why the game's manipulators want to push him out—when the simple answer is obvious to the audience. But the occasional tedious sequence is forgotten by film's end, when we become caught up in Jonathan's struggle against the system that made him and now wants to destroy him. "No player is greater than the game itself," declares Bartholomew when he confronts Jonathan. "It is a significant game in a number of ways—the velocity of the ball, the awful physics of the track; and in the middle of it all—men, playing by an odd set of rules."

Bartholomew then reveals the whole point of rollerball: "It is not a game man is supposed to grow strong in."

At the climax (after a veritable symphony of vicious mayhem and destruction) the crowd is at first silent. Slowly a chant builds. "Jonathan, Jonathan, Jonathan," they whisper, steadily growing louder until their chant becomes a deafening roar of triumph—the triumph of the strength of one man, the strength of the individual. It is an exhilarating release.

Rollerball is dismissed by some of its critics as a celebration of violence. That's a superficial conclusion that misses the point, for the film is not an exploitation of violence but rather an exploration of it—and in the end a condemnation. As Jewison points out, *Rollerball* is about "the absurdity of violence and blood sport."

Each film takes a distinct tack. The lampoonish satire offered by *Death Race 2000* encourages us to laugh at the absurdity of violence; the serious tone and emotional impact of *Rollerball* force us to feel the pain. Both movies intimate that violent sport breeds not only further violence (a catalytic rather than cathartic stance) but also complacency about the true nature of our existences. We will allow self-serving bureaucrats to direct our institutions (and thus our lives) as long as the lethal entertainments continue. While not every viewer will agree with such conclusions, both films, like all good SF movies, embed their concepts within engrossing and entertaining frameworks, creating ideas that will linger in viewers' minds long after the screen images have faded.

Films Discussed

Death Race 2000 (1975) New World Pictures. Released April 1975. 78 min. Producer: Roger Corman. Director: Paul Bartel. Screenplay: Robert Thom and Charles Griffith, based on a story. "The Racer," by Ib Melchior. Music: Paul Chihara. Cinematographer: Tak Fujimoto. Editor: Tina Hirsch. With David Carradine, Simone Griffeth, Sylvester Stallone, Mary Woronov, Roberta Collins, Martin Kove, Louisa Moritz, Don Steele, Joyce Jameson, Carle Bensen and Sandy McCallum. Available on New Concorde VHS home video; New Concorde DVD.

Rollerball (1975) United Artists. Released June 25, 1975. 128 min. Producer and Director: Norman Jewison. Screenplay: William Harrison, based on his story, "Roller Ball Murders." Cinematographer: Douglas Slocombe. Editor: Antony Gibbs. Production Designer: John Box. Art Director: Robert W. Laing. With James Caan, John Houseman, Maud Adams, John Beck, Moses Gunn, Pamela Hensley, Barbara Trentham and Ralph Richardson. Available on MGM/UA VHS home video; MGM/UA DVD.

18

Logan's Run to Relevance

ROBERT TINNELL

In the mid–twenty-third century, the citizens of a domed city lead remarkable lives, wherein every conceivable need is met, every pleasurable urge fulfilled. There's only one catch. At age 30 people who compose this youth-oriented society must enter a ritual known as Carousel. If they survive the ritual they will be "renewed." If not, they die. There are those who would rather run than face Carousel. But these runners face formidable odds in their efforts to escape, in the form of the "sandmen." The sandmen are policemen of sorts. Their only vocation is to kill the runners.

Logan 5 (Michael York) is one such sandman. He's recruited by the Orwellian computer system that runs the city to discover how over a thousand runners have managed to escape. To do this, he is prematurely marked for Carousel. What's worse, Logan discovers that Carousel itself is a fraud: no one is ever renewed. Thus begins his run, aided by Jessica 6 (Jenny Agutter), a member of an underground group dedicated to escaping the certain death of Carousel.

To view *Logan's Run* again after many years validates the notion that regardless of whatever distinguishes a film, intelligent storytelling will trump all shortcomings. And this film's shortcomings are legion. The special effects are laughable in contrast to today's. Truth be told, they are laughable in comparison to *Star Wars*, which was released a scant year later. The models of the domed city are so inadequate that it is difficult to imagine audiences found them in any way convincing; the only thing missing is Godzilla. But let's not insult the fine technicians of Toho with that particular comparison. The sandmen use ray guns that display a peculiar, impotent-seeming flare of light when fired. The various holographic effects seem quaint. The only bright spot, effects-wise, appears toward the end of the film, when Logan and Jessica explore the ruins of Washington, D.C. As realized by the superb matte paintings of Matthew Yuricich, these images retain a real power in their ability to convince the viewer of just how the city would appear after hundreds of years of neglect and decay. The images don't pack the punch of the final, wrenching sequence of *Planet of the Apes*, but they resonate nonetheless. One setup is particularly striking, as the couple wades down the Reflecting Pool toward the Washington Monument. Scenes within the Lincoln Memorial are also oddly moving, especially because Lincoln, with his weary, worn face, is the first person of mature age they've ever seen.

Logan's Run is most assuredly a poster child for the pre–*Star Wars*, groovy SF film with irritating sets; bad wardrobe; primitive, pseudo-psychedelic special effects; and dreadful, droning synthesized music. But for all its faults, it still manages to do what the best SF can do: namely, propose a situation, ideology, or crisis (or any combination of the three); imagine it set against a background of future technologies, cultures, or civilizations; and then resolve (or not) the ensuing dramatics in a way that is entertaining, thought-provoking, and thematically appropriate.

Logan's Run still strikes the viewer as thoughtful. Granted, the screenwriter, David Zelag Goodman, had good source material from which to draw. William F. Nolan and George Clayton Johnson's novel is a great read, and though the movie frequently wanders from the source, it never abandons the ideas that propel the book. What's more, the movie has proved to be remarkably prescient (metaphorically, at least), particularly when it comes to its central theme — its Big Idea.

Before exploring said Big Idea, a few preliminary thematic elements of the film are worthy of examination. Early on we encounter Logan 5 and his best friend, Francis 7 (Richard Jordan), another sandman. Logan 5 has made a visit to a hospital nursery, happily watching the infant Logan 7, his newborn son. Logan has no idea who the mother is, will have no hand in the child's upbringing, and was himself reared to have no concept of a relationship with his biological parents. Their identity is a mystery to him.

Francis chides Logan about his sentimental curiosity. It would seem to be completely out of character for a male in this hermetically sealed society to express such feelings of attachment to a child. A short while later Francis (and Logan) cheerfully toy with a runner before killing him. They have no conscience about it whatsoever. A short while after executing the runner, Logan attempts to have casual sex with Jessica, whom he has just met. He's mystified when she elects not to go through with it, and before she has even left the room he and the newly arrived Francis are sexually engaged with two women. Look at this incident from the perspective of modern-day American society. How can one not be reminded of similar behavior practiced by some of our young males?

And as has become epidemic among many of these same young men, women are, for the most part, nothing more than sex objects, devices. That's certainly the attitude of Logan and his friend. In their off hours they indulge in recreational drugs and casual sex. How dehumanized they are, and how familiar. This is not to say that audiences in the '70s found this portrayal of two self-absorbed, amoral men shocking — the Holocaust, My Lai, and other atrocities were far too fresh in the collective unconscious for that. But had that same audience a clue as to how close in the future this behavior would manifest and spread, and in some cases be celebrated, they would indeed have been shocked.

The nature of the sandmen's violence is also intriguing. While Francis and Logan don't exhibit the killer mentality of, say, the Columbine shooters, they do behave with a similar lack of compassion for their victims. True, their violence differs in that it

The sandman, Logan 5 (Michael York), and Jessica 6 (Jenny Agutter) regard the mall-like setting that is emblematic of the narcissistic, youth-obsessed world of the future in *Logan's Run* (1976).

is government sanctioned (tell it to Rodney King) but that in no way excuses the fact that they deliver it joyfully and without compassion for their prey.

The prescience of *Logan's Run* doesn't stop there, however, nor is it limited to the male. The movie reveals that citizens can pop in for radical plastic surgery, in a mall-like setting, if they're tired of the way they look. Sound familiar? It should, considering we now have television shows that celebrate the dramatic handiwork of plastic surgeons. In our perpetual quest to look younger and more appealing, the surgeons' work has become commonplace in American life. This story device prompts yet another intriguing idea. As we age, we often remark, "I feel like I've lived a few different lives." Perhaps Logan's fellow citizens subconsciously realize they're going to be denied that experience of growth and change, and hope to replicate it by altering their appearances.

Francis is a personification of the rigid belief system that dominates the society defined by the film. He's a religious zealot. His belief in Carousel and renewal is absolute and unquestioning. He will brook no disagreement, no discussion from others. He has no curiosity about Carousel. Like a seventeenth century witch hunter,

Francis does the Lord's (the government's) work — and if he becomes aroused in the act of persecution (in his mind, *salvation*) what of it? He's just doing his job. And by running, haven't the runners rendered themselves less than human anyway? Francis, dogmatic and unshakable, would feel right at home on one of our cable news screaming-head political shows.

George Romero's classic *Dawn of the Dead* would not appear for another two years, but *Logan's Run* foreshadows something of that film's anticonsumerist sentiment. In fact, the whole of the domed city is very reminiscent of *Dawn*'s shopping mall. Romero described his mall as a "temple of consumerism." This description is epitomized by Logan's world. The sterile, pastel city looks like a mall and makes every effort to seduce and indulge the citizen-shopper. A perfect climate, piped-in music, innocuous décor, faux waterfalls, tasteless attempts at public "art" — the worlds of *Logan's Run* and *Dawn of the Dead* are virtually interchangeable, and not just visually. The inhabitants of both worlds behave similarly. *Dawn*'s zombies and *Logan*'s citizenry wander mindlessly through the mall-city searching to fulfill their empty consumer needs. Meanwhile, a small core of enlightened individualists attempts to return to the "way things were before."

The Big Idea of *Logan's Run*, however, encompasses the dangers of hedonism, youth worship, and, particularly, the dangers of government-sponsored euthanasia. It's in these aspects that the film has proved to be terribly prescient.

State euthanasia is an extraordinarily ambiguous issue in our present society. In the aftermath of the German-sponsored Holocaust, the Japanese atrocities in the Pacific during World War II, and Stalin's state-sponsored slaughter in the USSR, we had hoped for more from the world, at least in the developing countries. Excluding for the moment chronically problematic places such as Colombia and North Korea, we still find governments like the one formerly headed in Yugoslavia by that fragmented nation's dictatorial president, Slobodan Milosevic. Government-sanctioned brutality in a "developed European country" — that couldn't happen after all we've learned in the last century, could it?

The rationale behind the euthanization of everyone over 30 is not made clear in the film, although one could guess it to be the result of some formula that deals with food supplies, energy, or similarly limited commodities. It seems a little more civilized than killing folks because of their religious or racial or ethnic identities, doesn't it? But, of course, it isn't.

There are those who might say that government-sponsored euthanasia is, in fact, alive and well in the United States. If they stand on the right of the political spectrum they might say that this dark aspect of *Logan's Run* has already been fulfilled via legal abortion. The Supreme Court's 1973 *Roe v. Wade* decision is a near contemporary of the film, and in its aftermath abortion became much more commonplace in this country. For some women, abortion is a method a birth control. And as we know, many people equate abortion with murder.

Alternatively, supporters of legal access to abortion are likely to note that since *Roe*, there has been a startling and dehumanizing upsurge in capital punishment. They may declare that state-sponsored executions are abominable abuses of power, not simply because of the lives that are taken, but because the practice allows the state to take lives with the presumed approval of the citizenry, many of whom oppose the practice.

Hedonism is another core issue of *Logan's Run*. "Sensualism" may be a more apt word because, as mentioned, the carefree sex lives of Logan, Francis, and the citizenry in general anticipate the behavior of a significant segment of today's American society. However, an even wider comparison can be made, one that encompasses not just individuals but the group mind. Like Logan's fellow citizens we crave comfort. Our homes are evolving into cocoons of self-sufficiency. We can program our heating and cooling systems for maximum comfort. Even members of the middle class own spa-like bathrooms, swimming pools, and home theaters. We listen to satellite radio in our cars, picking and choosing the types of music and information we want. In some cases, our cars themselves are like homes (some cost more than some homes). We are inundated with images of sexual abandon. Fashion spreads, advertising, pop-star performance style — the list goes on. None of this, strictly speaking, is sex. Rather, it's the *lure* of sex. It's sex turned into a commodity, something distant from genuine human experience. We enjoy it because it requires that we make no emotional effort. And anyway, who needs intimacy, especially post–AIDS?

While the above-mentioned examples of "the good life" are (debatably) victimless crimes or simple entertainment choices, most of them make stressful demands of our psyches and the environment. Emotional casualness becomes callousness, and we become incapable of meaningful sustained relationships. In each other's eyes, we become objects. On the physical level, our indulgent homes must be heated and cooled. Waste must be disposed of. Wildlife is dislocated. Our often-oversized vehicles devour fossil fuels and belch toxins. Yet we continue to live in domes of our own making, oblivious to those stresses. We live in a time wherein energy costs are manipulated to rise and fall as the very sources of energy decline, and alternate-energy research is underfunded and even subverted. Extraction of fossil fuels is often economically and environmentally exploitative and even ruinous. Do we then search for ways to conserve? Do we drive more efficient cars, wear a sweater and keep the furnace turned down a few degrees, turn off the lights when we leave the room? No, we turn our backs as our government opens up more and more precious wild places to rampant development, even as we and our elected officials pay lip service to alternative energy sources and increased fuel efficiency.

Although these are weighty subjects, the most resonant idea explored by *Logan's Run* is the allure and power — and anger — of youth. In the wake of the '60s and youth-driven countercultural movements, *Logan's Run* seemed a cautionary tale of the young usurping the old. In their song "My Generation" the Who sang, "Hope I die before I get old." Move to Logan's world and you'll get your wish. To be young is, literally, to be alive. But the dangers of that philosophy are amply illustrated throughout the film, most notably in the longing of Logan and Jessica for something more than an existence that serves only physical needs. They come to understand that their world offers nothing for the heart and spirit.

Societies once revered and looked after the needs of their older members. Elders lived with their children. Family patriarchs and matriarchs were welcomed as sources of stability, wisdom, and advice. Granted, plenty of *bad* advice was handed down

In an ice cave, the fleeing couple confer with Box (Roscoe Lee Browne), a human-robot hybrid who preserves plankton and other life forms on the orders of a long-lost civilization. The irony of Box's essential humanity is not lost on Logan.

from parent to child, and there was plenty of mindless authority that deserved to be flouted. But have we gone too far in our apparent worship of youth?

In the spring of 2004 conservative commentator Bill O'Reilly criticized the older, progressive commentator Andy Rooney, and added that perhaps the time had come for the 85-year-old Rooney to retire. "Elderly people," O'Reilly declared, "can say crazy things." Rooney responded with dignity in a *60 Minutes* broadcast. "That wasn't nice, Bill," he said. "I didn't get old on purpose. It just happened. If you're lucky, it could happen to you."

Movies and television, undeniably, are temples built to revere and exploit youth. America's great economic engine of consumerism is powered by 18 to 25 year olds. A great deal of media leans to even younger audiences. The number-one cable network as of this writing is Nickelodeon, which specializes in highly commercialized children's programming. At this writing, Disney's film production and distribution branch has just had its most profitable year ever. The formula is simple: Kids = dollars.

When *Logan's Run* was released American cinema was enjoying one of its golden ages, with groundbreaking, high-quality films the likes of *The Godfather, Patton, Ser-*

pico, and dozens more. And worthy foreign films, as well, found enthusiastic audiences in America. Many films of the '70s, domestic and foreign, made intellectual demands of viewers. Even the Woody Allen comedies of the period leavened their slapstick with thoughtful satire. They were geared for adults who had mature perspectives on life and living. Three decades later, the climate is different. Woody Allen still makes comedies, but when was the last time one was booked by your local theater? How does Woody's current box office stack up against *American Pie* or *Dude, Who Stole My Car?*

This isn't to suggest that young people don't deserve films geared to their interests, or that only adults deserve good films. What it does suggest, however, is that the studios are chasing after this youthful demographic with considerable vigor, leaving behind a large, dissatisfied audience of grownups. When the Jack Nicholson–Diane Keaton comedy *Something's Gotta Give* became a hit, the former lawyers and accountants who call themselves studio executives were dumbfounded, as if the existence of an audience over the age of 40 had seemed an impossibility.

Television isn't quite as youth-obsessed as cinema; the wealth of channels provides an ability to laser in on a particular demographic to deliver targeted advertising at reasonable rates. The History Channel, A&E, CNN — these and other networks depend on an older viewership to sustain them. But by and large, a significant segment of free and cable programming revolves around the coveted youth demographic. How did this happen? When did Mom and Dad hand over the checkbook?

As a society, our relationship with the young has changed dramatically over the last 150 years. The once-accepted practice of children entering the work force, either as apprentices or as factory or farm labor, has, thankfully, fallen by the wayside, at least in this country. Children are no longer bred as farmhands. But in correcting these cynical attitudes, we've gone too far in the opposite direction, making children kings and queens, and infantilizing the culture in the process.

Children are showered with toys and gifts— often when families can't even afford basic insurance — while corporate America grooms these kids to be eager, brand-conscious consumers. Insipid pop stars use sex to garner millions of acolytes— which would be okay if the singers' target audience was older than 12.

Parents pride themselves on buying their kids new cars and brag about how "I busted my hump to make it so my kid won't have to." I'm not so sure you're doing Timmy a favor, Dad. Delaying Junior's inevitable swim in the deep end of the pool might have its drawbacks.

The turbulent climate of the '60s shunted much of our country into two camps that still exist. One feels that youth activism and the counterculture were heroic and necessary. The other thinks the societal shifts of the period were merely ill-conceived, narcissistic, intellectually shallow antiauthoritarianism. They're both correct. The good that came out of the '60s is embodied in an increasingly diverse society that, generally speaking, has learned to run harmoniously. The bad, however, has manifested itself no less broadly, and is revealed in many of the ills that have been discussed in this essay.

The youth of the '60s asserted their power in an effort to fight injustice (real or perceived). Movements sprouted on college campuses with at least the pretense of intellectual validity. There were very real problems— racism, sexism, voter suppression, the war in southeast Asia, the Bomb — that could be tackled only by direct confrontation with the government and the bureaucrats who oversaw it.

Young people fled their churches, their family structures, the status quo. These now were analyzed, criticized, rejected, and abandoned. No longer bedrocks of society, they became points of departure.

Today, given society's even more permissive climate, kids have been handed the keys— never mind that they have no idea how to "drive." They're not rebelling against anything. To revisit a previously cited issue: given the tremendous environmental concerns we face as a nation and a world, where are the kids? Playing Nintendo!

Admittedly, many of America's young people are bright, discerning, and involved. My purpose is not to slight them or to unfairly criticize their unenlightened counterparts. They didn't set up this situation. Their parents with two jobs, insatiable consumerist appetites, and laissez-faire morals did. My point is to ask why we've thrown grandpa out with the bath water.

I do not worship the '50s or any other past era. I don't believe the world before Vietnam was better. I don't think that somewhere in our near or distant past America or any other country was a Utopia, where ancestor worship was practiced beneath pristine skies. But to encourage kids to call the shots culturally in this country is irrational, and to allow youngsters financial and sexual autonomy is dangerous. And to regard our graying society as unhip, unworthy, and obsolete is foolish and morally wrong.

I can't speak for Messrs. Nolan and Johnson regarding their intent when they wrote the *Logan's Run* novel, but the film's parallels to our present society make me increasingly uncomfortable.

In fact, they make me want to become a runner.

Film Discussed

Logan's Run Metro-Goldwyn-Mayer. Released June 23, 1976. 120 min. Producer: Saul David. Director: Michael Anderson. Screenplay: David Zelag Goodman, based on the novel by William F. Nolan and George Clayton Johnson. Director of Photography: Ernest Laszlo. Editor: Bob Wyman. Music: Jerry Goldsmith. Art Director: Dale Hennesy. Makeup: William Tuttle. Special Effects: L.B. Abbott. Visual Effects: Jim Liles and Matthew Yuricich. With Michael York, Richard Jordan, Jenny Agutter, Roscoe Lee Browne, Peter Ustinov and Farrah Fawcett-Majors.

19

Entropy in B-flat; or, Disordered Thoughts on *The Black Hole*

GARY D. RHODES

As I speed down the highway thinking about this essay, the words "black hole" blare from my car speakers. It's National Public Radio airing a story unveiling the latest news on the subject. Apparently a black hole is swallowing so much material in the Perseus Cluster that it's creating jets of material shooting above and below it. These jets create pressure, which then creates sound waves. The sound waves produce a B-flat. No kidding, a B-flat—a sort of one-note space samba, inaudible to humans because it's 57 octaves below middle C on a piano keyboard. This startling discovery made news far beyond the pages of astronomy journals, showing that public fascination with black holes has clearly rolled onward.

Flashback to the 1970s. Popular interest in black holes grows steadily throughout the decade, beginning with spate of magazine articles in 1971. *Newsweek* and *Time* are among many publications to cover the phenomenon, which moves quickly from academia to popular thought. After all, scientist John Wheeler had coined the term "black hole" only two years earlier, in 1969. As the 1970s progress, so does the stream of black hole publications aimed at the Everyday Joe.

One of the key problems discussed in print during the early 1970s was the topic of black holes and entropy. Entropy, of course, is most commonly defined as a measure of the disorder in a system. Debate sparked over the hypothesis that the area of a black hole's event horizon, its boundary, was equal to its entropy. Physicist Stephen Hawking was among the leaders of the charge to dispute that hypothesis. The argument seemed pedantic to the general public, perhaps, but was of major concern to astrophysicists.

Strangely enough, entropy can be of concern to film theorists, too. Thinking about entropy helps clarify what it is we try to do when we write about a film. Writing about "what a film means" suggests that self-apparent conclusions don't exist; that films have to be thought about, and then those thoughts must be told to others. Films need our help, or at least we think they do. And of course a key aspect of entropic theory is that disorder can be reduced in a system if energy is exerted to create order. Mere emotional responses like joy aren't good enough, so we readily exert energy to reduce the disorder of a given film; to find meaning, or even make meaning. This is not to invent meaning, but make meaning, as we do when we colloquially "*make* sense."

Then the disorder of the film is reduced, even if only in qualitative terms. Well, maybe. After all, some readers might argue that the disorder of meaning *increases* after reading an essay on a film. More essays or books on the same film are subsequently written. More energy is exerted. With a body of work by various authors, the disorder should certainly be reduced, presuming that anybody is even reading the ever-increasing number of essays written about films. Does it really matter what the measurement of an event horizon is if no event — say, reading — is on anyone's immediate horizon? We can't forget that there is no sound in space.

Flashback to the 1970s, Part II. As a youthful filmgoer under the spell of *Star Wars* (1977), I eagerly devour science fiction and horror wherever I can find it in those pre–home video years. I also avoid Disney films with a passion. But the previews of the studio's film *The Black Hole* (1979) pique my interest, and indeed, to see the picture on the big screen at age seven was a thrill. Spaceships, laser blasts, and searing images of a cosmic kind of Hades impressed me greatly. This was the dark side of Disney, even if two overly childish droids spoke with voices belonging to Slim Pickens and Roddy McDowall. Maximilian Schell and everlasting hell more than compensated for them.

We went for ice cream afterward. I remember that distinctly. For reasons both obvious and obscure, *The Black Hole* was one of those perfect viewing experiences. No big-hat women sitting in front of us. No loud, annoying teens. Butter on the popcorn just right, etc., etc. Fade to black.

Of the films I saw with my mother and sisters during the decade, *The Black Hole* is referenced among us more than any other. I've thought about it for years. After having done so much recent research work on my passions, like horror films, Irish cinema, and movie mockumentaries, it was a joy to get to choose a science fiction film to write about for this collection, because the choice was clear. If for no better reason than nostalgia, *The Black Hole* has remained lodged in my mind. And that presented its own kind of disorder because I have random, nostalgic memories of a film that I know was judged harshly by critics in 1979 and has received damning verdicts ever since. Order is now needed in the court.

Unfortunately for the defense, my recent reacquaintance with the film on DVD proved once again the potential danger in revisiting a favorite movie from one's youth. *The Black Hole* was impressive then, but much less so now. Perhaps it's the unfunny comic relief generated by the cutesy robots. Perhaps it's what is assuredly a confused plot. And perhaps it's also the obvious attempts by the film to be perceived as impressive and deep. But that *The Black Hole* stuck so firmly in my memory suggested all the more reason to understand *why*, to make sense of it, and to overcome a degree of disorder much higher than expected.

If entropy can act as a kind of metaphor for this process of analyzing films, it can suggest science as a starting place. Like so many SF films in search of a plotline, *The Black Hole* attempts to synthesize a minor amount of science with a rather grandiose idea. In a small way, the film does show a familiarity with the scientific thought on black holes in the 1970s. *Cygnus*, the name of Commander Reinhardt's ship, is elementary word play on Cygnus X-1, which on the heels of the discovery of neutron stars gave further evidence in support of preexisting theoretical work on black holes. By 1975, Stephen Hawking had become 80 percent certain that Cygnus X-1 was indeed a black hole. As time passed, his belief strengthened.

And yet, like so many science fiction films, *The Black Hole* avoids science when fact proves inconvenient for fiction. Most egregious is the film's conclusion, in which the *Cygnus* spaceship is compromised by meteor hits and the black hole's gravitational strength. This is a dire, life-ending situation, and yet the crew continues to breathe without difficulty, and without even assistance from spacesuits, oxygen tanks, or the like.

Then we come to the fact that black holes aren't visible to the naked eye. The film's special effects, however, make the hole's fancifully swirling shape into a visual trope for all the disorder and perceived evil that exist in the universe. The hole is large (incorrect), black (a misnomer to begin with), and noisy (without even B-flats on the soundtrack). The eponymous black hole defies scientific knowledge readily available in 1970s issues of *Newsweek* and *Time*.

At times, *The Black Hole* does insert scientific terms into dialogue to build an illusive sense of reality and credibility. Words and phrases like "vortex," "antigravitational force field," and "optimum angle of rotation" labor to create an impression of science verisimilitude. Dr. Durant (Anthony Perkins) even asks briefly about whether there might be an "Einstein-Rosen bridge" that should be considered before the ship attempts to journey into the black hole. Sounds good, but it's unexplained, much to the detriment of the film's inconclusive conclusion. After all, the idea of a wormhole through which one could be relocated to another place or even another universe might have clarified the film's climactic voyage.

The ways in which the film's notions of science intersect with religion are more ordered than the unexplored wormhole concept, and definitely more fascinating. Prior to the 1970s, SF cinema generally posed these two topics as dialectical oppositions. They were distinct areas that did not overlap; they were able to clash regularly because of their completely different aims. The Hollywood horror films of the 1930s (and to a lesser degree those of the 1920s and 1940s) were nothing if but a large collection of storylines in which the wayward scientist was mad in part because he eschewed religion or even wished to sweep it aside with science. An unwholesome urge to meddle in what man was meant to leave alone was the obsession of films of this period, leaving *Dracula* (1931) and *The Mummy* (1932) among the lonely few supernatural-themed tales unleashed in those years. Better to know what it feels like to be God and thus replace or displace him. Science fiction plotlines were horrifying in part because of the pressure they placed on religion, just as scientific thought on such subjects as evolution was placing pressure on religion in contemporaneous American life.

That was true during much of the 1950s and 1960s as well, when movie science linked itself to the U.S. government and military. Even if the scientist wasn't totally mad, he wasn't really sane — not with atomic power as a new play toy, which could so easily destroy that which God created. Endangering other people and arguing with soldiers or even generals were now among scientists' chief activities, conducted in service of pursuing what was best (as the scientists saw it) for the alien species. A 1951 *Thing* had more of a right to live than a handful of everyday folks hanging out in the Arctic, so the good doctor told us. But none of his brethren are in sight when the masses flock to church in 1953 during *War of the Worlds*. Church and science in America, like church and state, were separate, at least in SF movies.

Movie science continued to go wrong in the 1960s, showing us yet again that growing scientific knowledge meant more danger to the world than less. *Planet of the Apes* (1968) was formerly a planet of humans, with the "formerly" part the result of nuclear arms. And as much as *2001: A Space Odyssey* (1968) broke with tradition and transcended the confines of genre, the film merely underscored what Fritz Lang had already told the world in 1927 with *Metropolis*: Artificial intelligence created by scientists bodes none-too-well for humans. Once something can think, it can think bad thoughts. Lang's false Maria *was* false: untrue and *incorrect*. And *2001*'s HAL 9000 computer *can* make mistakes. A disinclination to admit that fact encourages HAL to terminate all the human life he can, causing a cover-up worse than the first crime. It's the lie that gets you. But at least turning the computer off and casting aside science allows the surviving astronaut to become the Star Child.

And then there was the late 1970s, a period which belongs for better or worse to *Star Wars* (1977), an elastic film enterprise in many respects, not the least in its generic sensibility. It's a Western, it's a fantasy, and it's a war. The available science was more fact than fiction, meaning that it was more marketing theory than astronomy lecture. To its credit, *Star Wars* did refuel interest in SF films to a higher degree than at any point since the 1950s. And its followers had to decide whether to follow or break from its lead. In an orderly way or not, *The Black Hole* chose the latter path.

This all-too-quick road down 50 years of science fiction's memory lane causes us to invoke the term entropy again. It's indicative of the use of an (admittedly low) amount of energy used to decrease the disorder of a generic system. To make meaning from history is a problematic goal (even when more energy is exerted) that lapses all too often into generalities and oversimplification. History yields none too kindly to precise measurements.

At any rate, *The Black Hole* does break from science fiction film traditions in its treatment of science and religion. And it's this that fascinates me. I remember talking about good guys, bad guys, science, and hell at the ice cream parlor in 1979. To look at the picture in the context of SF-film history only highlights why it's worth discussing, because in *The Black Hole* science is both aligned with and at odds with a Christian faith that seems omnipresent. Some scientists are in keeping with religion's aims; others are not. Though a relatively simple system, this approach still is more complex than depictions of science as completely at odds with religion.

That's not to say there isn't bad science in the film. The discovery of the black hole and plans to enter it are shown as evil; the black hole itself becomes a clear representation of hell. That it is a scientific anomaly — a "rip in the very fabric of space and time," VINCENT (the McDowall robot) tells us—gives us sufficient reason to assume that it isn't proper. It doesn't follow the rules. *Palomino* crewmember Harry Booth (Ernest Borgnine) clarifies that it's like "something out of Dante's *Inferno*." And Charlie Pizer (Joseph Bottoms) mentions that he always expects to "spot some guy in red with horns and a pitchfork" standing at the side of a black hole. The script is leading us, and the destination is obvious.

That fellow in red figuratively and (in the second half of the film) literally is Commander Reinhardt (Maximilian Schell). And that figure is mirrored by his robot creation Maximilian, who is sheathed in red metal. That Maximilian is "no friendlier than Dr. Frankenstein's Monster" initially suggests much the same kind of outlook on science and religion that earlier films commonly gave us. But it's actually through the film's depictions of robots that we most clearly grasp its complex stance on good and bad science and how they square with religion.

When VINCENT and the robot Maximilian face off the first time early in the film, Reinhardt makes one of his various references to the Holy Bible by likening their confrontation to David and Goliath. Along with foreshadowing their later and more violent encounter at the film's conclusion, the David and Goliath reference is one of the first ways we realize that the film's impression of good versus evil helps define who is truly human, a determination that extends to some robots and people and not to others. Science for humans and humanity reaches for the divine, and bad science is the road map to hell.

To begin, artificial intelligence in *The Black Hole* is anthropomorphized in greater or lesser degree depending on the entities in question. The levitating and rotund VINCENT and Bob robots take on very human (and allegedly witty) personalities. On the other hand, Reinhardt's sentry robots show a greater physical likeness to the bipedal human form but can't speak. In most respects, granted, such anthropomorphized qualities draw from *Star Wars* and its legion of predecessors. Indeed, 50 years before C-3PO, the robot of *Metropolis* appears somewhat human even before taking on Maria's fully human appearance.

But robots in *The Black Hole* need more than humanlike form or personality traits if they are to exist with humanity, and not simply on a periphery. They have to exemplify Christian-approved character traits. When the *Palomino* crew first experiences the black hole's gravitational pull, VINCENT saves the ship by risking his own existence. Tethered to the exterior of the ship, he closes a hatch door that threatens to leak the ship's oxygen supply into space. While VINCENT is saving everyone on the ship, Dan Holland (Robert Forster) and Pizer discuss how much a part of the crew he is. "VINCENT is *one of us*," Holland explains. Portrayed as human in spite of a robot form, VINCENT even shares the ability to communicate through ESP to crewmember Kate McCrae (Yvette Mimieux).

Like VINCENT, old Bob exemplifies Christian values. Whether initially turning the other cheek to Maximilian and the sentry robots or later risking his own existence to help the *Palomino* crew, Bob proves that he is "good." When he finally has to fight, he risks everything in defense of his friends. In fact, he ends up sacrificing himself for the humans, "dying" after a final conversation with VINCENT in what is simultaneously the film's most poignant and most ridiculous scene.

While VINCENT and Bob are shown to be essentially human, the film establishes other robots as significantly nonhuman through their inhuman behavior. Pride and anger are what cause STAR, the head of the sentry robots, to overheat after losing a video game to VINCENT. Jealousy and suspicion mark Maximilian's behavior during the first two-thirds of the film; these emotions culminate in murder in the film's final act. These robots are manifestations of the wrong that science can do, of course, and their actions and reactions deny them human status.

The film's questioning of what it means to be human extends more clearly to the nonrobots, of course. Reinhardt himself is in many ways the best example of what the film considers inhuman or nonhuman. He is a liar and an egomaniac. More than even Maximilian, Reinhardt is a calculating murderer responsible for innumerable deaths. Though one-dimensional in most respects, he does seem to fear his destiny. He quietly asks Kate to save him from Maximilian; this is—in essence—a plea to be saved from his own evil deeds. Bad behavior and bad science go hand in hand. It seems at first that his fears—and the Frankenstein reference from early in the film—are more than justified when a wall in the command center falls on Reinhardt after the ship has been hit by a meteor storm that is being pulled into the black hole. When Reinhardt calls for Maximilian's help, the robot simply leaves on the elevator. Before the doors have shut, he has clearly heard his master's plea and chosen to ignore it.

But the narrative isn't that simple. Complex or confused, the story links Reinhardt and Maximilian in a way that transcends the simple creator/master and creation/servant dichotomy. This point becomes clear in an otherwise rather opaque sequence in the minutes leading up to Maximilian's betrayal. The black hole has assumed a blazing red color, making its link to hell all the more obvious. While adrift in space after the *Cygnus* has been ripped apart, Reinhardt and Maximilian encounter one another. They embrace. The image cuts and we see Reinhardt's eyes reflected inside Maximilian's head. The camera pulls back to reveal Maximilian's body standing on top of a mountainside with flames consuming much of the landscape.

It is Dante's Inferno, and the Reinhardt/Maximilian character is apparently in charge, with Maximilian's extended metal arms standing in for Pizer's earlier reference to a pitchfork. As the camera continues to pull back, we see condemned souls, slaves, trudging along land bridges between other, smaller mountains. The flames continue to rise. Reinhardt's inhumanity and his evil use of science have found destiny and fulfillment in hell. "Life forever," just as Reinhardt predicted the black hole would be, even if of a different sort than he may have hoped for.

The Black Hole even differentiates bad science and inhuman acts by degree. For example, Dr. Durant and Harry Booth border close enough to bad science and evil to warrant their own deaths. Durant dies because he's too blind to see Reinhardt's evil until it's too late; he seals his own fate because he wants to stay aboard ship and enter the black hole with Reinhardt. Booth, by turning his back on the crew, dies when he tries to escape alone in the *Palomino*. Bad behavior from both to be sure, but not quite bad enough to merit the eternal damnation that apparently awaits Reinhardt.

Of course, caught in the middle of the human-nonhuman debate are the humanoids, the *Cygnus*'s old crew members. Some years before the *Palomino* had found him, Reinhardt deprived the crew of their free will via an unexplained scientific process. By sending crewmembers to the ship's "hospital," their minds were reprogrammed with laser. The crew's physical characteristics remain, as we can see from one who walks with a limp. And Holland encounters a group of humanoids holding a funeral for one of their own, which actually makes us wonder just how much of their free will has been stolen. Regardless, the hospital's process is irreversible. Death is "their only release," Bob tells us. Human they were, but are no more. And thus the *Palomino* crewmembers don't make much effort to save them. If Bob is correct, the humanoids are saved, or released, not by anything the freethinking humans might have done, but by the sheer destruction of the *Cygnus*. And we have every reason to believe Bob, because in this film there clearly is a God to Make It So.

We know this not only because we see the blazing fires of hell, but also because of the trip Holland, Pizer, McCrae, and VINCENT take through the black hole. They seem transported down a kind of ethereal hallway with a figure leading them onward to safety. God or Jesus or angel, we don't know, but it is reminiscent of images described in near-death experiences. We see white light rather than red. The crew is approaching God's heaven rather than Reinhardt's hell.

The confused narrative I mentioned earlier comes into play here. Once the crew is on the other side of the black hole it's difficult to tell whether the star they are headed toward is heaven or if the hand of God has simply helped them survive the black hole. The final credits begin and explanations end.

The journey through the black hole and the ambiguous ending caused some critics at the time and in the years since to draw unfavorable comparisons to *2001: A Space Odyssey*. Valid, to be sure, but one key difference is worth pointing out. In *2001*, it was not God awaiting Bowman at the end of the Star Gate. It was the alien life form that helped us evolve from ape to man and man to Star Child. By contrast, one certainty at the end of *The Black Hole* is that a Christian God is in control. And he isn't playing dice with the universe.

The Black Hole suggests that God is in control of who and what is human or inhuman, making decisions based on which brand of science the characters are aligned with. Science here is not intrinsically evil or wrong, as it had been in the days of Drs. Frankenstein, Mirakle, and Griffin. It's all in how you use it. And it is at the very intersection of science and religion that *The Black Hole* does stand out as unique, and remains unique even in the wake of several more modern science fiction films. For example, black holes in the 1997 film *Event Horizon* lead to hell too, but the science-versus-religion debate is far less complex than in *The Black Hole*.

Has writing about *The Black Hole* made the film better or more comprehensible? Is the disorder any less chaotic, especially for a film that has all kinds of narrative problems? Order has probably improved only by a meager amount. The entropy of a film is difficult to gauge, and it's actually difficult to measure my own disorder. My fondness for the film continues even after reexamining it, and it's hard to decide whether this is due to the movie's intriguing take on science and religion or if I'm just suffering from a severe case of nostalgia.

Things could be worse. Entropy can be understood by other definitions than the one at stake in the black hole debates. It can also mean the loss of information transmitted in a message. (How commonly that happens in film writing.) Or it can mean the inevitable and steady deterioration of a system or society. Misapplied film writing can actually harm a film. And if so, then maybe perceived disorder should just run amok. Maybe we should just *experience* films and savor that experience alone. Not everything that is meaningful, like a little boy's love of *The Black Hole*, is full of meaning when put under a microscope.

In space, of course, no one can hear you scream, and you have to listen awfully hard to hear the sentimental B-flats produced by *The Black Hole*.

Film Discussed

The Black Hole Walt Disney Pictures. Released December 20, 1979. 97 min. Producer: Ron Miller. Director: Gary Nelson. Story: Jeb Rosebrook, Bob Barbash and Richard Landau. Screenplay: Jeb Rosebrook and Gerry Day. Director of Photography: Frank V. Phillips. Editor: G. Gregg McLaughlin. Music: John Barry. Production Design: Peter Ellenshaw. Art Directors: John B. Mansbridge, Robert T. McCall and Al Roelofs. Special Effects: Ken Speed. Visual Effects: Art Cruickshank, Harrison Ellenshaw and Peter Ellenshaw. With Maximilian Schell, Anthony Perkins, Robert Forster, Joseph Bottoms, Yvette Mimieux, Ernest Borgnine, Roddy McDowall (voice) and Slim Pickens (voice). Available on Anchor Bay VHS home video and DVD.

20

Pets or Meat: *Alien, Aliens,* and the Indifference of the Gods

MARK CLARK

The ancient Greeks believed that the world was ordered by a race of aloof giants who lived among the stars atop mighty Mount Olympus. The self-absorbed, capricious gods were prone to fits of pique, meddling in human lives when it amused them to do so. Mere mortals could only grovel and pray for the benevolence of these remote deities.

Thirty-six hundred years later, the world the Greeks imagined has arrived, only the giants are called corporations.

"The world is eventually, obviously, going to be run by companies and organizations, which seemed exotic [25] years ago, but now it's reality. That's the way we're headed," director Ridley Scott posits during a DVD audio commentary for his 1979 film, *Alien.*

The titular menace of Scott's watershed science fiction chiller burst from the chest of actor John Hurt and leapt onto movie screens and into pop culture mythology. But the true villain of the film is not the unstoppable giant bug from outer space. It's the sociopathic corporation from Earth that, with complete indifference to human life, sends the unsuspecting crew of the starship *Nostromo* to retrieve the alien.

There's nothing speculative about the idea of a company bent on increasing its profits, even if it means destroying the lives of its workers. The nineteenth and twentieth centuries are littered with examples, dating back to the Industrial Revolution and even before. But you need not look any further than recent headlines: the Enron and other energy industry accounting scandals, similar improprieties at WorldCom and other telecommunications companies, insider trading in the mutual fund industry, among many other incidents—corporate crimes that, in some cases, wiped out the life savings of thousands of workaday Americans.

Our modern, globalized economy favors multinational conglomerates and makes life ever more precarious for mom and pop businesses. Free trade agreements have made it easier than ever for corporate behemoths to siphon manufacturing jobs away to developing nations. Blue-collar workers in many American industries have been forced to accept pay cuts and reduced benefits simply to retain their jobs. The plight of those who labor in Third World sweatshops, for pennies on the dollar compared to Stateside wages, is even more dispiriting. The outcry from the Third World against economic globalization reached a horrifying crescendo with the 9/11 attacks on the World Trade Center.

Meanwhile, most white-collar workers spend their days confined to prefabricated, identity-nullifying cubicles, like so many chickens in a coop. They hack away at soul-eating jobs for faceless corporations whose only concern is keeping profits and stock prices on a perpetual climb. Who can blame them if they feel swallowed up like Charlie Chaplin in the cogs of the machine from *Modern Times*?

Filmmakers and recording artists complain that bean counters with MBAs have seized control of their industries. Corporate-sponsored political action committees have government by the pocketbook. Even the funny pages aren't free from this seeping dread of corporate malevolence. America's most popular comic strip, Scott Adams's *Dilbert*, chronicles the frustrations and humiliations suffered by the employees of a nameless company run by a pointy-haired nincompoop and an evil talking dog.

In times like these Ridley Scott's *Alien* seems not only resonant but prescient.

"What About the Money?"

Alien wears its influences on its sleeve. Although no credit is given, the film's scenario bears striking similarities to director Edward L. Cahn's 1958 low-budget classic, *It! The Terror from Beyond Space*, which was scripted by science fiction author Jerome Bixby. Other elements recall *Planet of the Vampires* (1965), *2001: A Space Odyssey* (1968), and *The Green Slime* (1969). The film's working-stiffs-in-outer-space attitude was first expressed in director John Carpenter's *Dark Star* (1975), which was cowritten by *Alien* screenwriter Dan O'Bannon. No wonder, then, that one of the charges most frequently leveled against the film by its critics is that *Alien* is "derivative." Sure it's derivative, although no more so than pictures such as *Star Wars* or *Raiders of the Lost Ark*. Like those films, *Alien* assimilates its influences and reshapes them into an original configuration.

At the center of this realignment nests the concept of a future ruled by an all-powerful company, or perhaps by an oligarchy of monopolies. This may not have been an entirely new idea (something like it was presented in 1975's *Rollerball*, and related concerns are at the core of *Metropolis* [1927]) but it remained pertinent to 1979. This vision informs nearly every aspect of *Alien*, from production design to characterization.

The first shot in the film, after its opening credits, shows the giant, eerie *Nostromo* as it rumbles through space, looking like a cross between an oil refinery and

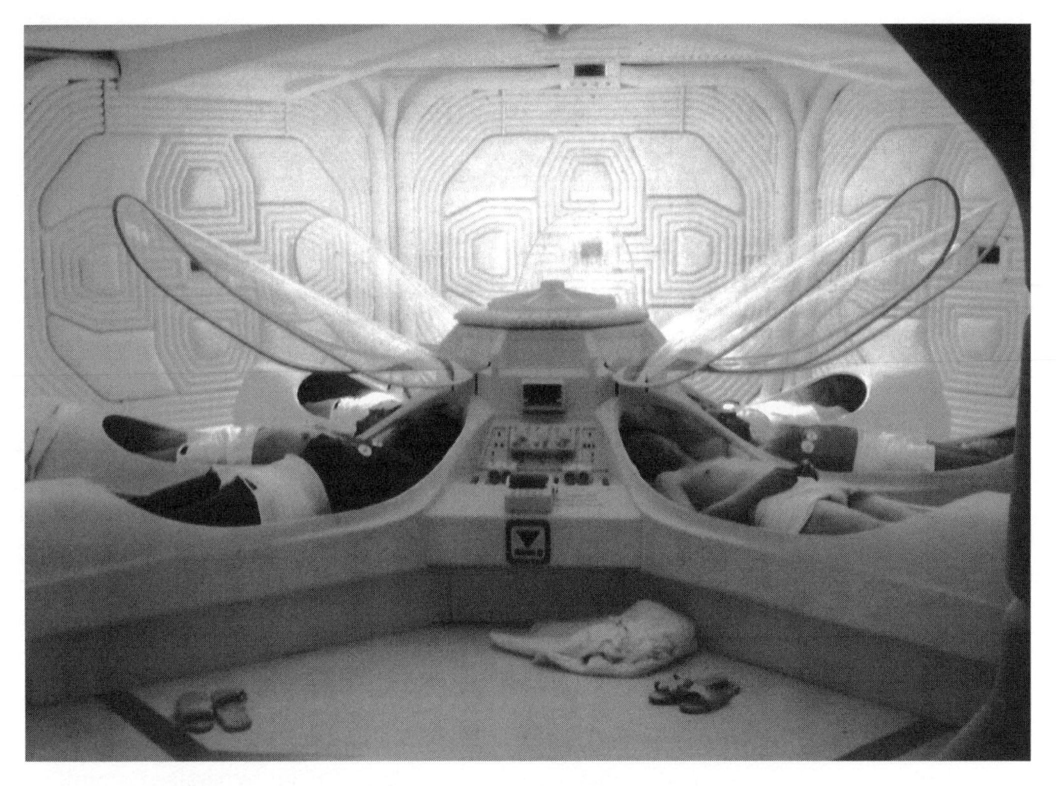

Ridley Scott's *Alien* (1979): Appearing to alien eyes as inviting as soft-shell tacos, the crew of the *Nostromo* awakens from protracted hypersleep during their journey in service of a giant corporation. In the foreground are Yaphet Kotto (*left*) and John Hurt.

a nuclear power plant (probably the two ugliest and scariest industrial complexes the designers could imagine). Titles inform us that the vessel is heading home to Earth, carrying a cargo of 20 million tons of mineral ore and a crew of seven. The *Nostromo*'s cargo connects its crew with some of the most-exploited workers in history—miners.

Coal fed the superheated economic engine we now call the Industrial Revolution. But digging for coal was difficult and dangerous work. Miners, including boys not yet 15 years old, worked up to 12 hours a day for near-starvation wages and were forced to buy overpriced goods from company-owned stores. With no meaningful safety regulations, deaths from cave-ins or other mishaps were common.

Eventually, following a series of protracted strikes, the United Mine Workers union wrested concessions from mining companies, including a wage increase and a reduction of their regular working day from ten to eight hours. However, tension and unrest continued in the mining industry for decades, as chronicled in the Oscar-winning 1976 documentary, *Harlan County, USA*—all of which lends a texture of believability to *Alien*: It is easy to imagine the struggle between miners and mining companies continuing even hundreds of years from now.

Although *Alien* is set in the future, the *Nostromo* seems almost Dickensian. Unlike the spaceships from most classic science fiction films, which have gleaming silver hulls and antiseptic white interiors, the *Nostromo* is dreary rust and gray, with exposed cables and grungy instrument panels. Everything looks as if it's been smeared with grease and streaked with oil. Dirty laundry hangs in the hallway and boxes clutter the floors. Instead of boasting a clean-cut crew in spiffy uniforms, the *Nostromo* is crewed by scruffy-looking malcontents in mismatched outfits: a Hawaiian shirt, a headband, a pair of Chuck Taylor high-tops. There's even a cat on board. The crew doesn't behave like typical science fiction characters, either. They bicker with one another, smoke, drink beer, curse, make sexually explicit jokes at the expense of female crewmembers. *Forbidden Planet* this ain't.

Earlier science fiction films tended to depict the future as either a veritable Utopia or a post-apocalyptic hell. The thinking seemed to be that if mankind could keep from blowing itself to smithereens, everything would be peachy in the end. The negotiations and compromises required to avert Armageddon would somehow turn the human race into one, big happy family. *Alien* foresees a future much closer to our present. Technology may change, the film argues, but human nature does not. Our petty preoccupations and prejudices will persist.

Chief among these will be greed. Above all, the *Nostromo*'s crew seems preoccupied with money. The first dialogue in the film is a discussion of "the bonus situation," initiated by technicians Parker (Yaphet Kotto) and Brett (Harry Dean Stanton). Captain Dallas (Tom Skerritt) tells Parker flatly, "You'll get what you contracted for, like everybody else." Parker complains, "Yeah, well, everybody else gets more than us."

When the crew learns that they have been awakened from hypersleep months distant from Earth in order to investigate a signal of unknown origin from a nearby planet, Parker takes the opportunity to lobby again for more cash. "It's not in our contract to do this kind of duty," he says. "What about the money? If you want to give me some money to do it, I'd be happy to. Let's go over the bonus situation."

But company regulations state that the crew must investigate all signals of possible intelligent origin or forfeit all shares. So Parker and Brett have little choice.

"Standard Procedure Is to Do What the Hell They Tell You to Do."

The first half of *Alien* is pure science fiction, as the crew investigates the planet and discovers—to the particular horror of crewman Kane (John Hurt)—the film's famous face-hugging beastie. Ripley (Sigourney Weaver) grows suspicious when science officer Ash (Ian Holm) seems more concerned with preserving the alien than with saving Kane's life. This sparks a heated, and revealing, argument between Ripley and Dallas:

DALLAS (exasperated): Look, I just run the ship. Anything that has to do with the science division, Ash has the final word.

RIPLEY: How does that happen?

Deep within the planet, Ripley (Sigourney Weaver) and other crewmembers unexpectedly discover evidence of an advanced and frighteningly alien civilization.

DALLAS: It happens, my dear, because that's what the company wants to happen.

RIPLEY: Since when is that standard procedure?

DALLAS: Standard procedure is to do what the hell they tell you to do.

This exchange tells us a great deal about the culture of the company. It also suggests that Dallas has risen in rank not only because he is a capable officer, but because of his willingness to toe the company line and refrain from asking difficult questions—tendencies third officer Ripley does not possess.

Soon Kane, freed from the grip of the face-hugger, enjoys a last supper and then dies, shockingly and by now famously, when a baby warrior alien bursts from his chest. Afterward, the crew gathers to watch as Kane's lifeless body is jettisoned into outer space. "Anybody want to say anything?" Dallas asks. No one speaks.

Even though they have spent an undisclosed, but presumably lengthy, time together in the loneliness of outer space, the crewmembers remain in their own metaphoric silos. There are no meaningful connections between them, except perhaps between Parker and Brett, who share a common bond of envy and resentment against their better paid coworkers.

From the chest-bursting scene forward, *Alien* becomes less pure science fiction and more a body-count horror film. It keeps viewers off stride by playing against their expectations. Audiences probably expect Captain Dallas to be the film's hero, but he is killed with a third of the film remaining. They probably don't anticipate that Ripley, a woman, will emerge as the story's sole survivor. (Keep in mind that, when *Alien* premiered, its ensemble cast was composed of virtual unknowns.) In some instances, the film establishes expectations and then defies them. For instance, Brett meets his fate when he wanders off by himself in search of the cat, Jones. Given this setup, audiences expect the same thing to happen when, later, Ripley wanders off by herself in search of Jones. But the film double-crosses us: Ripley survives, while the alien kills two other crewmembers.

During all this, the idea of the greedy company as the source of evil creeps ever forward in the narrative, eventually stepping into the forefront when Ripley decodes a secret special order from the *Nostromo*'s onboard computer, ironically known as "Mother":

> NOSTROMO REROUTED
> TO NEW COORDINATES.
> INVESTIGATE LIFE FORM. GATHER SPECIMEN.
> PRIORITY ONE
> INSURE RETURN OF ORGANISM
> FOR ANALYSIS.
> ALL OTHER CONSIDERATIONS SECONDARY.
> CREW EXPENDABLE.

Ripley also discovers that Ash has been in on this scheme from the beginning. Then the crew learns that Ash is not even human, but a robot. "How come the company sent us a god-damned robot?" Parker asks. "All I can think of is they must have wanted the alien for the weapons division," Ripley answers.

Mother and Ash rank among the film's most poetic expressions of its theme. To communicate with Mother—and through her, with the company—the crew must pass through a secure door into a cramped, bright white chamber (the only clean, white space on the ship) illuminated by thousands of tiny lights. It looks much like a shrine full of votive candles, and the name Mother connotes the Blessed Virgin. That's only appropriate, since the crew is expected to follow the company's orders as if they were the word of God.

Ash, the walking embodiment of the company, is literally inhuman. He follows his programming without question and without pity. When Ash talks about the alien, he does so reverently. He calls it "a perfect organism ... unencumbered by conscience, remorse or delusions of morality"—words that might also describe the company.

Given all this, *Alien* risks coming off like some Maoist manifesto from Jean-Luc Godard. But its message isn't anti-capitalist. It's anti-materialist.

In this regard, *Alien* shares a kinship with the work of director Mario Bava. Regarded as the maestro of Italian horror, Bava orchestrated numerous films in many genres with a single theme: that those who value material wealth more than human life consign themselves to misery (and usually death). This dynamic plays out in film after film, but is most pointedly expressed in *Bay of Blood* (aka *Twitch of the Death Nerve,* 1971). In this blackest of black comedies, the inhabitants of a secluded rural community kill each other off, one by one, in all manner of gruesome ways, to try to gain control of a valuable piece of coastal real estate. In *Alien*, too, the greedy are punished.

Although Ripley's decision to sign on with the *Nostromo* must have been at least in part a financial one, she seems less concerned than her crewmates about money. She values people more than cash. One illustration of this is Ripley's emotional connection with the cat, Jones. That may sound superficial, but it's a stronger connection than exists between anyone else on board, and the only one based on simple affection. In fact, Ripley's concern for Jones saves her life. Because she takes time to search for the cat, she isn't present when the alien kills Parker and Lambert. Also, Ripley is the only crew member who consistently questions the authority and motivation of the company. In short, she's the only one who hasn't fully bought the company line: "If you want money, then shut up and do as you're told."

"I Work for the Company, but Don't Let That Fool You. I'm Really an Okay Guy."

Director James Cameron's 1986 sequel, *Aliens*, differs from Scott's original film in many significant respects. Whereas *Alien* was an SF film that felt more like a horror movie, *Aliens* is SF that feels more like a war picture. The sequel plays like *Sands of Iwo Jima* crossed with *Them!* It's also a bigger film in every respect, boasting a larger cast, richer budget, and longer running time. More significantly, where *Alien* at times bordered on the deconstructionist in its assault on audience expectations and genre clichés, *Aliens* is a far more conventional, formalist work. Instead of playing bait and switch, it simply delivers the goods. No wonder many filmgoers prefer the sequel to the original film. Because it demands less of the audience, *Aliens* is far easier to like.

Yet, as different a film as *Aliens* is, it manages to not only carry forward the theme of the original film but to embellish and deepen that message.

For starters, Cameron envisions his story through the lens of the Vietnam War. "To me the whole Vietnam experience was almost science fictional, in the sense that it was the first real high tech war that was waged against an extremely low tech enemy—and lost. Which, to me, is a very strange thing," said James Cameron, in an interview included on the *Aliens* DVD. "It showed how technology didn't work and there's an aspect of that in the film. It's like, why are we losing?"

By invoking Vietnam, Cameron also brings into play the bogeyman behind countless Cold War– and Vietnam-era conspiracy theories: the military-industrial complex. As editor Phil Hardy's *Overlook Film Encyclopedia: Science Fiction* puts it: "The film presents its marines ... as cannon fodder thrown away by conscienceless corporation men back on Earth."

Aliens picks up precisely where *Alien* left off, with Ripley and Jones in hypersleep on their way back to Earth. A passing space freighter hauls in Ripley's shuttle. As in the original film, the first lines of dialogue are an expression of greed. "Bio readouts are all in the green. Looks like she's alive," one of her rescuers reports in an annoyed voice. Another disappointed crewman sighs, "Well, there goes our salvage, guys."

Ripley's shuttle has been meandering through space for 57 years. The company—finally identified by name as Weyland-Yutani Corp.—sends smarmy Carter Burke (Paul Reiser) to help Ripley adjust to her new life. "I work for the company, but don't let that fool you," Burke says. "I'm really an okay guy." That's the first of Burke's many lies. Although less perfectly symbolic of the company's inhumanity than the robot Ash, Burke remains an enlightening personification of Weyland-Yutani Corp. and its attitudes. He is a brown-nosing, backstabbing sycophant who will stop at nothing to further his own career; Burke is a study in what Hannah Arendt called "the banality of evil."

One of Burke's duties is to guide Ripley through an inquest into the fate of the *Nostromo* and its crew. Clearly, the Weyland-Yutani suits are more concerned about the vessel than the people. "You freely admit to detonating the engines of and thereby destroying an M Class star freighter, a rather expensive piece of hardware," one of them intones gravely. "Forty-two million dollars in adjusted dollars," another company man chimes in. "That's minus cargo, of course." As the inquest ends, Ripley learns that the company has founded a settlement on the planet, now identified as LV-426, where the *Nostromo* discovered the alien. When she asks how many people are there, she's told there are 60 or 70 families. "Families?" Ripley gasps. "Jesus!" Her first thought is about the safety of all those men, women, and children.

Cameron's DVD "director's cut" of *Aliens* offers 17 minutes of additional footage not included in the original theatrical release, including some illuminating new scenes. One of those takes place on LV-426 before the discovery of the aliens. During this sequence, supervisor Al Simpson (Mac McDonald) complains about the lack of communication from the company: "I don't ask because it takes two weeks to get an answer out here and the answer is always, 'Don't ask!'"

Weyland-Yutani's ironic slogan ("Building Better Worlds") refers to terraforming, and Simpson and his coworkers are indeed terraforming LV-426, a task that suggests the company cares as little or perhaps even less about the environment than it does about people. After all, what could be more ecologically abhorrent than to destroy and refashion a planet's entire ecosystem to turn a profit? It's the equivalent of strip-mining on a global scale.

Burke calls Ripley and informs her that the company has lost contact with the colonists. He recruits Ripley to join him and a team of Colonial Marines for a mission to LV-426 to investigate. Ripley is reluctant at first, but signs on once Burke assures her the mission is to destroy the aliens. In her words, "not to study, not to bring back, but to wipe them out." "That's the plan," Burke lies again. "You have my word on it."

Ripley returns to space accompanied by a platoon of 13 marines, a battle-hardened group of men and women with a new commanding officer, green Lt. Gorman (William Hope). At first, the marines are supremely confident. "Me and my squad of ultimate bad-asses will protect you," Private Hudson (Bill Paxton) assures Ripley. The unit also includes a robot, Bishop (Lance Henriksen). "I prefer the term artificial person," the mild-mannered Bishop clarifies. The antithesis of Ash, Bishop seems to yearn for the approval of the humans on board. Cameron's characterization of Bishop makes Burke seem even worse in contrast. Robots may be programmed for evil, the film suggests, but only humans can choose it freely.

On the planet, the soldiers discover a ten-year-old girl named Newt (Carrie Henn). Ripley immediately bonds with the girl, tenderly feeding her and washing her face. Like Ripley, Newt is the sole survivor of a devastating alien attack. In the director's cut, Ripley also has a more profound reason to connect with Newt: She was a mother herself, with a daughter who was about Newt's age when she shipped out with the *Nostromo*. During Ripley's 57-year hypersleep, her daughter grew old and died.

At first, only Ripley and Newt fully comprehend the gravity of the situation the platoon faces. The rest catch on after their first encounter with a nest of alien warriors, which wipes out all but four of the Marines—Gorman, privates Hudson and Vasquez (Jenette Goldstein), and Corporal Hicks (Michael Biehn). In the wake of this debacle, Ripley suggests they return to their spaceship and nuke the site from orbit. Burke balks. "This installation has a substantial dollar value attached to it," he says. Burke, and by extension the company, values profits more than human life—even his own. Ripley does not. "They can bill me," she replies.

James Cameron's *Aliens* (1986): Half a lifetime removed from the horrors of her first clash with the Aliens, Ripley (Weaver) comes to grips with a bad situation made worse by the machinations of corporate sneak Carter Burke (Paul Reiser, far right). Ripley is flanked by Cpl. Hicks (Michael Biehn) and the orphaned Newt (Carrie Henn).

"You Don't See Them Fucking Each Other Over for a God-Damned Percentage"

Ripley develops a warm friendship with Hicks, who helps her look after Newt. When Hicks attaches a locator device to Ripley's wrist, he jokes, "It's just a precaution. It doesn't mean we're engaged or anything." But this moment carries much symbolic weight. Together, Ripley, Hicks and Newt form a makeshift family. The union between the adults is consummated, emotionally speaking, during an intimate moment later in the film when the two call each other by their first names, Ellen and Dwayne. In the meantime, Ripley grows fiercely devoted to Newt, promising ("cross my heart and hope to die") not to leave the girl behind.

Ripley's suspicions are confirmed when she discovers that Burke has ordered Bishop to preserve two live face-huggers for shipment back to the company labs on Earth. When Ripley explodes at Burke, he tries to buy her collaboration with a share of the millions he will make by delivering these specimens to the company's weapons division. The bribe only makes Ripley more furious.

"You sent them to that [alien] ship," Ripley says. "Directive dated 6-12-79 signed Burke, Carter J. You sent them out there and you didn't even warn them. Why didn't you warn them, Burke?" Burke says he didn't want to make "a major security situation out of it" and screw up his exclusive rights. Clearly, he's dismayed that Ripley doesn't share his interest in profiting from the aliens. "I expected more from you," he says. "I thought you'd be smarter than this." "I'm happy to disappoint you," Ripley counters.

Next, Burke tries to eliminate Ripley, and Newt in the bargain, by turning the two face-huggers loose on them. After his plan is foiled, Ripley explains Burke's duplicity to the marines:

> He figured he could get an alien back through quarantine if one of us was impregnated, or whatever you call it, and then frozen for the trip home.... The only way he could do it was if he sabotaged certain freezers on the way home, namely yours. Then he could jettison the bodies and make up any story he liked.

When Burke mounts a halfhearted defense, Ripley lambastes him with lines that encapsulate the moral center of the film as eloquently as any: "You know, Burke, I don't know which species is worse. You don't see them fucking each other over for a god-damned percentage."

Like *Alien*, *Aliens* expresses its theme through its choice of survivors. However, the sequel broadens the scope of its indictment to include not only the greedy, but also anyone who values manmade constructs more than human life. In this, *Aliens* echoes the work of humanist director Jean Renoir, who explored this theme in several pictures but perhaps best in his immortal *Grand Illusion* (1937).

Renoir's classic chronicles the travails of three military officers—two French, one Prussian (one from the bourgeoisie, one from the proletariat, and an aristocrat)—at a World War I prisoner-of-war camp. The film's title refers to all the self-imposed barriers men create to separate themselves from one another: national borders, class distinction and military rank, languages, governments and economic systems, and on and on. The story's heroes (Jean Gabin and Pierre Fresnay) escape and survive because they are able, temporarily, to ignore these illusory walls. The aristocratic Prussian (Erich von Stroheim) holds steadfast to these beliefs and pays with his life.

Aliens presents a similar dynamic. Those who put their faith in natural, primal human affiliations (like the nuclear family forged by Ripley, Hicks, and Newt) survive. Those who strive to connect with and be accepted by other people (such as, ironically, the android Bishop) survive. Those whose primary concern is financial gain (Burke), personal promotion (Gorman), or whose allegiances lie with man-made constructs (such as the Colonial Marines or, in the case of the terraformers, their settlement) die.

Even Ripley's mistakes underscore her humanity. For instance, she needlessly provokes the alien queen by destroying hundreds of face-hugger eggs (an alien "family"). Her actions are totally uncalled for, since the whole area is about to go up in a mushroom cloud anyway. Worse, they delay her escape and prolong the danger to Newt (who she's come to rescue). Since she uses up all her ammunition, she leaves herself practically defenseless against an enraged monster-mother. Nevertheless, we understand why Ripley does what she does. The aliens have hurt her deeply, and she can't resist the urge to hurt them back. Ash would simply follow the program: retrieve Newt and leave. Ripley cannot. Her emotions place her in danger, but also give her the will to triumph in the end.

Two more sequels, *Alien*^{3} (1992) and *Alien: Resurrection* (1997), followed *Aliens*. Both those pictures strayed from the anti-materialist message of the first two films. *Alien: Resurrection* contained at least one good idea, namely that Weyland-Yutani's biogenetics division attempts to clone a human-alien hybrid. Unfortunately, the corporate ethics issues raised by this plot point remain unexplored.

Many subsequent science fiction films integrated an *Alien*-like vision of the future, from *Robocop* (1987) to *Minority Report* (2002). Ridley Scott returned to the concept for his 1982 SF noir, *Blade Runner*. Other, non-genre films have addressed directly the issue of heartless corporate behavior and its impact on human lives, none more pointedly than director Michael Moore's acclaimed documentary *Roger & Me* (1989).

With a wickedly amusing sense of irony, *Roger & Me* captures the devastating economic and psychological impact the closure of a General Motors plant has on the community of Flint, Michigan. One jobless Flint resident raises rabbits to supplement her income. A handmade sign outside her home advertises, "Bunnies or rabbits—pets or meat." The woman explains that if the bunnies aren't sold as pets by the time they reach a certain age, she kills, skins, and guts the animals and sells them as "fryers" or "stewers." The film suggests that corporate giants like GM apply the same ruthless logic to their relations with employees. They feed us and keep us in our cages so long as it's advantageous for them to do so. But if the day arrives when it's more profitable to slaughter us (figuratively speaking), then we become meat instead of pets.

The first two *Alien* films make this same argument. In a strange coincidence, the red-and-white checkerboard corporate logo emblazoned on the bulkheads of the *Nostromo* looks remarkably like the logo of the Ralston Purina Company—a manufacturer of pet food.

Ripley nearly doesn't make it out alive.

Films Discussed

Alien 20th Century–Fox Pictures. Released May 25, 1979. 117 min./116 min. (director's cut). Producers: Gordon Carroll, David Giler and Walter Hill. Executive Producer: Ronald Shusett. Director: Ridley Scott. Story: Dan O'Bannon and Ronald Shusett. Screenplay: Dan O'Bannon. Director of Photography: Derek Vanlint. Editors: Terry Rawlings and Peter Weatherley. Music: Jerry Goldsmith. Production Design: Michael Seymour (additional designs by H.R. Giger). Special Visual Effects Supervisor: Nick Aller. With Tom Skerritt, Sigourney Weaver, Veronica Cartwright, Harry Dean Stanton, John Hurt, Ian Holm and Yaphet Kotto. Available on 20th Century–Fox home video and DVD.

Aliens 20th Century–Fox Pictures. Released July 18, 1986. 137 min./154 min. (director's cut). Producer: Gale Anne Hurd. Executive Producers: Gordon Carroll, David Giler, and Walter Hill. Director: James Cameron. Story: James Cameron, David Giler, and Walter Hill. Screenplay: James Cameron. Director of Photography: Adrian Biddle. Editor: Ray Lovejoy. Music: James Horner. Production Design: Peter Lamont. Special Visual Effects Supervisor: John Richardson. With Sigourney Weaver, Carrie Henn, Michael Biehn, Paul Reiser, Lance Henriksen, Bill Paxton, William Hope and Jenette Goldstein. Available on 20th Century–Fox home video and DVD.

21

The Brave New World of *Starship Troopers*

Ken Weiss

In *Brave New World*, Aldous Huxley predicted a society in which human beings are genetically engineered for commercial and industrial purposes. They don't protest because they are designed "to love their servitude."

All propaganda, as every advertising and public relations professional knows, requires several ingredients—comprehensibility, consistency of message, and repetition being the three most important ("Keep it simple, keep it straight, and keep it coming"). In public relations, when dealing with large national issues, an added fillip is the demonization, real or created, of the intended enemy. The rules are timeless: In *Mein Kampf* (1925) Adolf Hitler made the same points when he noted that "all propaganda must be popular and its intellectual level must be adjusted to the most limited intelligence among those it is addressed to," and that propaganda "must confine itself to a few points and repeat them over and over."

The subtext for these rules, rarely admitted by those in the business, is the belief that the public in general is ignorant and easily duped. Recognition that "a lie repeated often enough over time will be believed as true" is probably as old as civilization itself and remains the basis of many advertising and public relations campaigns. Julius Caesar warned against leaders who bang "the drums of war to whip the citizenry into a political fervor, for patriotism is indeed a double edged sword. It emboldens the blood, just as it narrows the mind." And when the populace has been properly motivated, "the leader will have no need in seizing the rights of the citizenry. Rather the citizenry, infused with fear and blinded by patriotism, will offer up all their rights unto the leader and gladly so." Two thousand years later, Nazi Hermann Goering told a friend, "Of course the people don't want war. But after all, it's the leaders of the country who determine policy, and it's always a simple matter to drag the people along whether it's a democracy, a fascist dictatorship, or a parliament or a communist dictatorship. Voice or no voice, the people can always be brought to the bidding of their leaders. That is easy. All you have to do is tell them they are being attacked, and denounce the pacifists for lack of patriotism and exposing the country to greater danger. It works the same in any country."

When *Starship Troopers* was released in 1997 it was generally dismissed as just another "sci-fi bug movie." Produced on a healthy $95 million budget, the picture managed a domestic box-office take of just $54.7 million. The director, Paul Verhoeven, had claimed the film's goal was to "evoke old Westerns, World War II movies and adventure tales"—and carefully avoided mention of its political content. Janet Maslin, demonstrating typical perspicacity in *The New York Times*, said it was "about the cute young co-ed army and the big bugs from space"—which it is. It also has a lot of comic-book blood and gore, the cast is ridiculously gorgeous, and there's no dearth of violence, humorous and otherwise. But there is also much more. As would be expected, almost all the mass-media reviewers missed the issues raised by the film: its cynical, satirical, and scary predictions of things to come; its observations about militarism and war; and its "don't trust authority" signals. They also missed what the film was saying about a society totally influenced by media that march in lockstep with government. They missed all these things back in 1997. It's doubtful they'd miss them today. *Starship Troopers* serves as a predictor of the future, most notably by demonstrating the timelessly effective techniques of propaganda. The movie serves as a warning, in the grand tradition of Aldous Huxley's *Brave New World* and George Orwell's *1984*, in which the authors used the device of a future society to comment on the world they saw evolving around them. The film is based on the novel by science-fiction legend Robert A. Heinlein, who probably would have been delighted with Hollywood's adaptation of his book.

The novel, set thousands of years in the future, is a first-person account by Juan "Johnny" Rico, a mobile infantryman in the Terran-based Federation Army, at war with the "Bugs," an insectlike race from another galaxy. Johnny takes us through his last semester in high school, his enlistment in the Federation Mobile Infantry, basic training and, primarily, his various adventures in combat, fighting the Bugs on far-off planets. The novel can be divided into two unequal parts: The larger one is a detailed look at the mobile infantry, its equipment, weapons, rules, traditions and battles. Heinlein, a brilliant storyteller, loves that stuff. He can go on for pages explaining the ins and outs of future legalities and protocols on other planets. A trainee punches an officer in the face—there are ten pages detailing his military trial and his punishment. Mobile infantry troopers wear "powered armor," a suit that "isn't a space suit" but can serve as one, that isn't a tank, although a suited trooper could easily defeat a squadron of tanks, and isn't a ship, although "it can fly a little." Heinlein devotes five pages to a description of the suit's various features.

The novel's other part, equal in significance though not as lengthy, is an exploration of the meaning of personal civic responsibility and a citizen's obligation to the state, a la Heinlein. As always, he offers an enormous menu of viewpoints to choose from, each presented and defended or demolished brilliantly. Everything from "inalienable rights" like life, liberty and the pursuit of happiness (he's against 'em), "communal entities," social workers, and child psychologists (he doesn't like them either), to corporal punishment and self-sacrifice (he's for them). He seems to posit the view that personal sacrifice for the state is the highest form of virtue, the individual sacrificing for the good of the many — the mobile infantryman being a prime example. Late in the book, Johnny's businessman-father, who had been vehemently opposed to his son's signing-up, joins the MI, and explains why: Johnny had exposed the father's cowardice. "You had done something that I knew, buried deep in my heart, I should have done. I had to perform an act of faith. I had to prove to myself that I was a man. Not just a producing-consuming economic animal, but a man." It is difficult not to hear Heinlein speaking.

Readers might remember the Federation (the government that followed the collapse of twentieth century society) from *Stranger in a Strange Land* and many other Heinlein novels. It's the same old mind-numbing Federation, although the satisfied populace would never recognize it as such. In Heinlein's *Starship Troopers*, as in *Stranger*, the Federation is depicted as untrustworthy and deceptive. It's clear that the people of the Federation are being lied to, and that the whole point and direction of the war are questionable. Johnny's first combat drop is a disaster. Most of the men and officers are killed, but the Federation calls it a "strategic victory."

Johnny isn't overly bright. He tells us he hadn't intended to join the MI, but his best friend, Carl, had decided to join up, and cute Carmencita Ibanez, his sort-of girlfriend, was joining up, too, and, well, it seemed the thing to do. And besides, military service was the only way to achieve full citizenship and the right to run for public office. As always, Heinlein is merciless in his disdain for the brainwashed. A one-armed, legless enlistment sergeant does his best to discourage the new recruits, pointing to himself as a product of service. Undeterred, they join up anyway. During the physical Johnny asks the examiner if he'd been a doctor before joining the military. The man is shocked. "Do I look that silly?" he says, and assures Johnny he's a civilian. "No offense," he continues, "but military service is for ants." This makes no particular impression on Johnny.

Although there are few signs of media in the novel, we know from Johnny's narrative that the information he's getting reinforces the belief that while the Federation is winning the war, victory is still a long way off. The obliteration of Buenos Aires is noted offhandedly by Johnny, except for its effect on him (his mother is killed in the attack). The destruction of San Francisco and the San Joaquin Valley is referred to after the fact, with no details. Johnny mentions that the last thing he suspected was that they were actually *losing* the war. Everyone is led to believe the Bugs operate almost entirely on instinct. Gradually we realize that the Bugs, while organized differently, are probably as intelligent as Terrans. It's made clear that the Worker and Warrior Bugs follow orders and have little imagination. Brain Bugs are the heavy thinkers and leaders, but no Brain Bug has ever been caught. Heinlein doesn't mention the similarity of organization between the two forces. He doesn't have to.

Nor does he address the question of personal responsibility when one's cause happens to be wrong, although his contempt for the Federation is obvious even while he's idealizing the men who fight and die for it, and apparently sees no contradiction in this. The absence of media in the novel is matched by the almost total lack of information about Terran existence outside the military. There are several flashbacks of Johnny in high school, particularly his class in History and Moral Philosophy, whose teacher, Mr. Dubois, pointing his "stump of a left arm," reinforced the notions that violence and force are the ultimate arbiters of what is right, and a soldier is the prime example of civic virtue because he defends the body politic with his life, while the civilian does not. There is little sign of specific commerce or other aspects of civilian society. We know that Johnny's father is a businessman, but that's all. Economic interests do not seem to exist. Heinlein does provide his always-convincing picture of a population totally and willingly dominated by big government, but, as usual, there is no exploration of motives (who is doing this and why?), no reasons given for the war (how did it start?), and never a vision of what he himself might consider a just, equitable and workable society. Despite considerable railing about personal freedom, self-sacrifice, and responsibility (concepts with little objective meaning), in the end Heinlein offers a philosophy of hopelessness. Despite an obviously vibrant imagination and enormous knowledge, perhaps he felt that a just society was not possible, in itself a useful wake-up call to anyone who values democracy.

The movie version of *Starship Troopers* removes some of the novel's ambiguities. It attempts to be true to Heinlein's vision of hegemonic subjugation, with a few additions to satisfy box-office needs, like romantic complications. The movie creates a society in which all information comes from one source, to the complete satisfaction of the populace, who enjoy every luxury except individualism and the ability to think critically. The young people in the movie might have stepped out of a Guess or Calvin Klein commercial — visual symbols of their vacuity. As science-fiction historian Paul Sammon explained, "This is a right wing group of empty-headed beautiful people doing exactly what they're told to do."

The novel and movie differ most in their handling of male and female relationships, and the influence of media. The film's take on gender differences probably would have displeased Heinlein. In the novel the mobile infantry is strictly male and macho. Troopers sometimes go for many months without seeing a woman. For female companionship they head for Sanctuary, an Earth-like planet used for R&R. This is typical Heinlein, whose "wise" characters are, by today's standards, hopelessly chauvinistic. (See the all-knowing Jubal Harshaw, in *Stranger*, and his harem of beautiful women.) Although Heinlein's novels are set in the far future the societies are pretty much the same sexist ones we're familiar with. In the film, the mobile infantry is completely co-ed. Men and women train together, share the same quarters, take showers together and fight side by side. In a happy combination of political commitment and box office savvy the producers present a prolonged nude shower scene involving a lot of very attractive young people that offers considerable T&A to make a political point. For despite the ribald talk and abundance of bare breasts and buttocks, there is no condescension, no leering, nor groping, nor wise-ass comment regarding nudity. Instead, it is handled matter of factly, as something so normal it's unnoticeable to the characters. The training and combat scenes are no different. The women are equals, as tough and resourceful as the men, sometimes more so.

Practically invisible in the novel, media are prominent and set the desired tone for the movie, which opens with a Federation Network television news broadcast that instantly establishes the level of public awareness and the form of government that prevails. In this first broadcast (and all others) the Federation's decor and architecture, its logo—an angular, wings-spread bird of prey, its officers' uniforms, its army training ground scenes, all clearly authoritarian in nature and design, were, in fact, inspired by close study of Leni Riefenstahl's Nazi propaganda masterpiece, *Triumph of the Will*, which provided the tone the producers were trying to establish. *Troopers*' director of cinematography, Jost Vacano, wanted to show "what would have happened if Hitler had won. What would the world look like?" Despite this in-your-face blatancy, most film critics missed the point completely, and a few even thought director Verhoeven was *endorsing* fascism.

The film's opening shot is the Federal Network logo, followed by a long shot of a training field with hundreds of fully uniformed and armed troopers in formation. The visual and sound techniques are those of a slick television commercial. "Join up Now!" a title declares, as the camera zooms in on individual troopers, each young and attractive, and a voiceover tells us, "Young people from all over the globe are joining up to fight for the future." "I'm doing my part," a female trooper says to the camera. "I'm doing my part," a male trooper adds. "I'm doing my part, too," a uniformed, gun-toting preadolescent boy pipes in, to the amused laughter of the troopers. "They're doing their part. Are you?" A caption asks, "Would you like to know more?," and the screen is filled with a Federation Mobile Infantry flag waving in the wind as the voiceover exhorts, "Join the mobile infantry and save the world. Service. Guaranteed citizenship." The inspirational music fades and turns ominous as a headline, "Bug Meteor," appears over a giant meteor hurtling through space. "Klendathu sent another meteor our way. But this time we're ready. Planetary defenses are better than ever." We see a huge Federation starship fire its cannons at the meteor and blast it to space dust. "Would you like to know more?" a caption asks, as another segment titled "Why We Fight" shows a simulation of a deadly asteroid belt of meteors launched from Klendathu to Terra as the narrator warns, "To ensure the safety of our solar system Klendathu must be eliminated."

Bold metallic letters flash on screen: "Invasion!," and we see an armada of huge Federation battleships flying toward the enemy planet. A "Live TV" announcement flashes on and off as "FedNet takes you live to Klendathu where the invasion has begun." The sounds of gunfire, explosions, and yelling troopers are almost deafening. Amidst the din a reporter covering the invasion gives us the lowdown. "It's an ugly planet," he shouts into the camera, "a Bug planet, a planet hostile to life." He doesn't notice that all the troopers are fleeing, nor the giant Bug that appears, until it lifts him into the air and rips him to shreds. The cinéma vérité camera weaves wildly, finally focusing on an MI trooper (we'll later recognize him as Johnny) who shouts, "Get outta here now!" One trooper stands his ground and blasts away at a Bug but can't prevent it from killing him. Johnny, trying to help, is impaled through the thigh by a Bug claw, but manages to pull himself free. The TV screen offers a close up of his face in pain as interference terminates the broadcast. The screen goes black and there is silence. A caption says, "One year earlier."

The style of the broadcast is as fast-paced as tomorrow's commercials (whose purpose, too, is to sell things), disturbingly similar to the TV we're accustomed to. As examples of propaganda the Federation broadcasts (which appear every half hour or so) illustrate what can happen when news becomes entertainment. Successful propaganda is not possible without the complicity of media. (At first, Hitler didn't have to take over the German press. Publishers got the message quickly enough, and the ones that didn't found their offices wrecked by patriotic vigilante groups.)

The Bugs are demonized on every broadcast, but let's face it, it's the Bugs who steal the show. These fantastic creatures, created by Phil Tippett, a two-time Oscar-winning special effects, animation, and computer graphics genius (he's the creator of Jabba the Hutt, among others) are wonders to behold — part ant, part roach, nine feet tall, fearless, practically indestructible and entirely fascinating, although witnessing them in action is not for the squeamish. Unlike MI troopers, Bug warriors carry no weapons, depending instead on their greater number, their courage, their chit armory, their mandibles and sharp claws. There's plenty of tongue-in-cheek dismemberment, including a moment when an MI officer (Michael Ironside), his finger probing a hole in the top of the head of a dead trooper, says grimly into the camera, "They sucked his brains out."

The second FedNet broadcast starts with "A World that Works" emblazoned across the screen as an MI trooper holds up a large, "fully automatic Baretta" rifle and asks a bunch of preadolescent children, "Who'd like to hold it?" The kids all yell, "Me!" and grab at the rifle as troopers laugh appreciatively and start handing out bullets. The voiceover tells us, "Citizen rule is people, making a better tomorrow." The familiar "Would you like to know more?" caption appears on the lower part of the screen. "Crime and Punishment" introduces an intimidating courtroom whose style and decor are again strongly reminiscent of the Third Reich. The accused appears helpless and somehow innocent as he hears himself sentenced to death: "A murderer was captured this morning and tried today." A gavel slams. "Guilty," a stern-faced judge declares. The screen shows a glass-enclosed room containing a sleek, futuristic, stainless steel reclining electric chair. "The sentence — death. Execution tonight at six, all net, all channels"— an announcement repeated via onscreen flashing captions. "Would you like to know more?" Eerie music follows as a segment encourages viewers to explore their "psychic power" and to be aware that "Federal studies are being conducted in your community. Would you like to know more?"

A cow is pushed into a steel room with a captured Bug and the door slides shut. "Every schoolkid knows that arachnids are dangerous," the voiceover comments. The Bug rips the cow to shreds, as a "Censored" sign discreetly blocks out the goriest parts. "However, Mormon extremists disregarded Federal warnings and established Port Joe Smith deep inside the arachnid quarantine zone." The camera shows an isolated outpost stained by blood and strewn with mutilated chunks of bodies. They realized too late, the voiceover continues, that the area "had been already been chosen by other colonists— arachnids. Would you like to know more?"

Two requirements of a true democracy are an informed, participative citizenry, and a government that provides adequate, accurate information. The "Would you like to know more?" question at the end of each segment serves as ostensible evidence of the Federation's willingness to provide information. There is little doubt but that the information will simply be more propaganda designed to prevent critical thought. So the movie, like the novel, invites the viewer to consider the nature of a democracy whose government can not be trusted. And like the novel, it offers no solutions.

Buenos Aires is destroyed by meteors launched from Klendathu. Johnny's parents are killed in the attack, which he learns from a FedNet report: "8,764,590 Dead." The city has been wiped off the face of the earth. For Johnny, the war against the Bugs takes on greater urgency. Until the attack the war had been an undeclared one. Now the Federation makes it formal. In the next FedNet broadcast flaming metallic letters announce "War," as footage of the devastated city appears on screen. "Out of the ashes of Buenos Aires comes first, sorrow." A family photograph among the debris. "Anger." A dog buried under large slabs of concrete. "The only good Bug is a dead Bug," an enraged Terran yells. "In Geneva, the Federal Council convenes." Sky Marshal Dienes, the symbol of authority, law and order, appears to be a Hollywood World War II caricature of a Nazi. "We must meet the threat with our valor, with our blood, indeed with our very lives, to ensure that human civilization, not insects, dominates this galaxy now and always," he exhorts. Another segment, "Know Your Foe!," describes how "Federation scientists are looking for new ways to kill Bugs." A military specialist tells us a "basic arachnid warrior isn't too smart, but you can blow off a limb —" he fires an automatic weapon at a Bug in a cage, crippling it, "and it's still 86 percent combat effective. Here's a tip: aim for the nerve stem, and put it down for good." Another blast — in the right spot — kills it. "Would you like to know more?"

"Do Your Part!" a title declares, as we see young schoolkids enthusiastically stomping insects (the common garden variety of beetles and grubs). "Everyone's doing their part. Are you?" The gleeful kids keep squashing the insects till the soles of their boots are covered with mush. "The war effort needs your effort. At work. At home. In your community." An adult woman urges the children on, laughing. Fade to a huge armada of spaceships, each one the size of a city. "We break Net and take you live to Fleet Battle Station Ticonderoga, deep inside the arachnid quarantine zone, where the men and women of the Federal Armed Services prepare to attack." A reporter, followed by a camera, is aboard the *Fort Ticonderoga*. He interviews a few of Johnnie's buddies, all of whom can't wait to take on the Bugs. When the reporter mentions that some people had suggested a "live and let live" approach to the Bugs, Johnnie irately grabs the mike and declares, "I'm from Buenos Aires and I say kill 'em all."

The next time we see FedNet is during the invasion of Klendathu, which returns us to the movie's starting point. There's the reporter, saying, "It's an ugly planet. A Bug planet. A planet hostile to life," and being seized by the Bug while the cameraman moves closer for a better shot. And there's Johnny, getting his thigh pierced by a giant hornlike, needle-sharp claw. (It's okay — he'll be submerged in a liquid healing tank that will have him up and around in a few days.) The scene ends with the MI in full retreat. "100,000 Dead in an Hour" is the leadoff story on FedNet. We see acres of barren terrain littered with bloody body parts. "Crisis for humankind," a voice-over intones. "Fleet officials admit they underestimated the arachnid's defensive capability." We move next to the spacious chamber of the Federation Council, where Sky Marshal Dienes resigns and the new sky marshal, Tahat Maru, explains

(*Top*) A Tanker Bug takes the measure of its human opponents. (*Bottom*) A sniper-scope image reveals the hideous death of Sgt. Gillespie (Curnal Aulisio) beneath the talons of a Hopper Bug.

her strategy. "To fight the Bug, we must understand the Bug. We can ill afford another Klendathu," she proclaims to applause. Then the familiar voiceover, "Would you like to know more?"

"Bugs That Think" is the next segment. A man and a woman sit opposite each other, shouting to make a point, parodying contemporary midday talk shows. "Insects with intelligence?" shouts the man. "Have you ever met one? I can't believe I'm hearing this nonsense."

The FedNet broadcasts frame the film and give it context outside the world of the military. Each broadcast is a fast-paced compilation of Federation-selected scenes buttressed by stimulating headlines and simplistic, manipulative voiceovers. No event is covered in depth and words and images flash by, competing with each other for the viewer's attention. In this regard, the movie is predictive. As a phenomenon of everyday American life, news broadcasts in 1997 had not yet accepted competing onscreen imagery and messages. Hardly more than five years later they had become common on CNN, Fox, and Bloomberg. Content shrinks as viewers are conditioned toward shorter attention spans. In 1997, with most media owned by a handful of multinational corporations, writer Ed Neumeier and director Verhoeven could intuit which way the wind was blowing, and their perception is embedded in the film. With *Starship Troopers* Verhoeven set out to show the world a functioning fascist society, full of attractive people the audience feels compelled to identify with. But Gestapo-type uniforms and the overbearing authority of the State present a disturbing contradiction to the beautiful people we're rooting for, forcing us to consider one of Verhoeven's points: Don't be fooled by appearances.

The final FedNet broadcast appears shortly after a successful battle in which the first Brain Bug is captured. "Know Your Foe" is the lead-off segment. We see orange-cloaked and hooded technicians with the captured Bug, an enormous, slug-like, gelatinous creature with a mucousy hole of mouth surrounded by eight large, soulful eyes. "What mystery will the Brain Bug reveal? Federal scientists are working around the clock to probe its secrets. Once we understand the Bug, we will defeat it." A scientist with a two-foot injection probe sticks it into the creature's side, another pushes a multi-pronged probe into its mouth, a "censored" sign blocking the penetration but leaving the sad eyes visible. It is a tribute to Verhoeven and Tippett's skills that we actually feel sympathy for this otherwise repulsive Bug. "Join up Now!" appears onscreen over an enormous armada of Federation battle ships. "We have the ships. We have the weapons. We need soldiers." Soldiers like Lieutenant John Rico, who is seen leading his men to the drop chamber of a starship and screaming, "C'mon you apes, you want to live forever?" "We need you all," the voiceover continues. "Service. Guaranteed citizenship." A headline declares, "They'll Keep Fighting," as the mighty armada sails through space. "And they'll win!" It's the last image on screen so the movie ends where it began, with an exhortation — to a population that has learned to love its servitude — for support in a war apparently without end.

Starship Troopers is distinctive in that it's the only film to present an American-type democratic society in which all citizens accept the enforced hegemony and are unquestioning believers in the propaganda being fed them. In other films, such as *1984* (1956), *Fahrenheit 451* (1966), or *Soylent Green* (1973), there is always someone, a protagonist or band, who challenges the system. But like the novel, the movie is unsparing. *Everyone is brainwashed.* It is the society that Heinlein anticipated and the one Paul Verhoeven could sense emerging in 1997. The accuracy of their predictions is yet to be determined. The signs are not encouraging.

Film Discussed

Starship Troopers Tri-Star Pictures and Touchstone Pictures. Released November 7, 1997. 129 min. Producers: Jon Davison and Allan Marshall. Director: Paul Verhoeven. Screenplay: Ed Neumeier, based on the book by Robert A. Heinlein. Director of Photography: Jost Vacano. Editors: Mark Goldblatt and Caroline Ross. Music: Basil Poledouris. Production Designer: Allan Cameron. Creature Designer: Phil Tippett. With Casper Van Dien, Dina Meyer, Denise Richards, Jake Busey, Neil Patrick Harris and Michael Ironside. Available on Columbia/Tri-Star DVD.

Sources

Hitler, Adolf. *Mein Kampf*, Boston: Houghton Mifflin, 1971 [1925].
Gilbert, Gustave M. *Nuremberg Diary.* New York: Farrar, Straus, 1947.
Maslin, Janet. "No Bugs Too Large." *New York Times*, Nov. 7, 1997.
Heinlein, Robert. *Starship Troopers.* New York: Ace Books, 1987 [1959].
Production comments by Verhoeven, Tippett, Vacano and Sammon from *Death from Above* and *Paul Verhoeven and Ed Neumeier Commentary. Starship Troopers* Special Edition DVD. Columbia/Tri-Star.

22

The Iron Giant: A Gun with a Soul

JACQUE DAY ARCHER

> He swayed forward, on the brink of a high cliff. And his right foot, his enormous iron right foot, lifted — up, out, into space, and the Iron Giant stepped forward, off the cliff, into nothingness.
>
> — *Ted Hughes, from the book* The Iron Man, *which inspired the motion picture cartoon,* The Iron Giant

Introduction: A Lifetime of Searching

I've spent a lifetime looking for the Iron Giant.

For the first 13 years of my life I existed in a domestic war zone, dodging chickens that bounced off ceilings, plates that crashed to the floor, a plethora of hurling objects— spoons to spatulas to boards to fists.

I needed an Iron Giant.

I escaped, as many children do, into my own fantasies, devouring sometimes a dozen books a week and as many movies as I could come by in pre-cable Carter- to Reagan-era rural Pennsylvania — late night creature features, Vincent Price movies, Abbot and Costello comedies, and the unequaled Godzilla. But since movies meant time spent among others, I stuck mostly to books, plowing through the heady Hemingway collection given me by my paternal grandmother, the only truly human adult member of my family. I tore through the seemingly endless selection of paperback horror novels my father kept around the house —*Amy Girl* and *The Green Ripper* and *The Boogeyman* and *Suffer the Children* and *When the Wind Blows* and *The God Project* and everything Stephen King, and even Robert Bloch's ineffable *Psycho*. When I needed uplifting material, I went for John Gunther's *Death Be Not Proud* and Kin

Platt's *The Boy Who Could Make Himself Disappear*, which I found to be a valuable primer for social skills.

I could definitely be described as a morbid, self-serious kid.

Through these years my Iron Giant lay in wait, an abstract concept whose existence I felt but struggled to define. As a kindergartner I stared longingly at my prized poster of Arnold Horshack, begging him to come to me in the night and take me away somewhere where we could play.

I mastered my séance skills in an effort to resurrect Lou Costello, but out of generosity I asked for him only at night—heaven could have him back in the daytime. Others came and went with the passing years, but still no Iron Giant. So at the launch of my teens I became a cynic, and finally I ceased to care entirely and swallowed enough prescription medication to stop my heart and land me in the intensive care unit.

I woke up in a purple haze surrounded by people in white coats. Still no Iron Giant. I went back to sleep. There is no other way to say this.

A few weeks later, on my fourteenth birthday, my mother made the half-correct declaration that living with my father had caused me to want to take my own life, and thereby announced their divorce. I went upstairs and played the Halleluiah Chorus from Handel's *Messiah*, which I'd bought on vinyl at a garage sale for 25¢. That was a good day, but still no Iron Giant.

Life has an unusual way of peeling our eyes open. For me it was the sight of my younger brother and sister, Jennie and Matt, seven and three, watching tearfully as all the so-called security they'd ever known crumbled to pieces.

So I did the only thing I knew to do. I became *their* Iron Giant.

For the next several years we lived life much like Hogarth Hughes did in Brad Bird's animated feature *The Iron Giant*, with a few exceptions. Our father wasn't dead; just surgically attached to a barstool at the VFW. Our mother worked a lot, but she also drank a lot. And I wasn't a giant metallic creature that ate cars, though if I had been, I'd have had my pickin's from the array of junkers hoisted up on cinder blocks lining Route 982.

But I learned some important skills during those years— like how to make a bag of rice and two chicken legs into a weeklong meal. And at night when the wind blew hard, my door creaked open and Jennie and Matt would stand there in their pajamas, waiting for my permission to climb in. They always asked, as though I might say no.

Those were the best years. Heaven with stomach cramps. And eventually we made it, and I stopped looking for the Iron Giant.

Fast forward to 1999, the year *American Beauty*, *The Insider*, *The Matrix* and *The Sixth Sense* eclipsed the box offices. In 1999 I was 28, divorced, and had managed to keep my head above water working in movies. In 1999 my sister was living with me in my matchbox of an apartment. In 1999 I thought I had things pretty well figured out. So when I saw the ads for *The Iron Giant* by relatively unknown animator-turned-director Brad Bird, I thought, "Looks like a cute movie." It would be another two years before I'd see it. One of my biggest regrets is having never watched the film on the big screen.

Part One: If We Don't Stand Up for the Kooks, Who Will?

The Iron Giant crash-lands on Earth 1958, near a small town in Maine called Rockwell, about which Hogarth Hughes opines, "Welcome to downtown Coolsville! Population ... us."

We meet Hogarth (voice by Eli Marienthal) in a diner as he attempts to convince his single working-waitress mother Annie Hughes (Jennifer Aniston) to let him bring yet another wayward animal home, during which said animal—a wild squirrel—escapes and climbs up the jeans of the local beatnik scrap metal artist, Dean McCoppin (Harry Connick, Jr.), who proceeds to stand up and intone, "Excuse me! I would like to take this opportunity to apologize in advance!" He opens his pants, releasing the frenzied squirrel to frolic about and cause the requisite squirrel-fracas.

Admittedly when I first saw the diner scene, a fit of anger consumed me. Nothing like a warm-hearted and fun-filled moment between a mother and son to incite an abandonment-fueled torrent of wah-wah-wahs and "Who has this kind of relationship with their mother?" But I can't ignore the scene, because this is when we find out some important things.

Hogarth and his mom like each other, a point clearly demonstrated by his comfort level in posing the squirrel question, and by Annie's wearied but aw-that's-my-son reaction to the ensuing squirrel debacle.

Hogarth feels utterly compelled to take in unusual creatures.

Hogarth desperately needs companionship, ergo the squirrel, and a father figure, ergo his almost immediate gravitation toward Dean McCoppin.

Dean McCoppin, an outcast among normal men, is almost certainly going to end up being Hogarth's new dad.

Here we find the simple heart of our story—a lonely boy who lost his father in World War II, an idea communicated by a photograph of a soldier in a house with no dad. Of course, into my cynical mind popped the thought, "Yeah maybe the old man didn't bite it in the Big One; maybe he's surgically attached to a VFW barstool."

But that's for later.

The diner scene also takes a nip at the paranoia that grows and grows and eventually mushroom-clouds into the real enemy.

Frame back to where the squirrel makes busy stalking the denims of Dean McCoppin, who's holding a paper showing the headline "Disaster Seen as Catastrophe Looms," which is allegedly the same headline read by Jim Dear in *Lady and the Tramp* (1955) and Jiminy Cricket in *Fun and Fancy Free* (1947). Next to Dean's table at the diner, Earl Stutz (M. Emmet Walsh), the mad boatman who witnessed the Iron Giant's plummet from space into the sea the night before, regales a skeptical bunch of balding and overweight galoots with the yarn. They laugh it off as drunken foolishness, but Dean sticks up for Earl, which convinces Hogarth that Dean is, like him, a true believer. Dean replies, "Sorry kid. I didn't really see anything, but if we don't stand up for the kooks, who will?"

Part Two: Stranger in a Strange Land

Annie calls. She's working late. She's sorry. He can heat up some cold chicken. "No scary movies, no late snacks, in bed by eight o' clock. Got it?"

Right.

Cut to Hogarth at just before 9:15, stuffing Twinkies with canned whipped cream and watching what appears to be a pretty scary movie. We come wide-eyed to the "No ... no...." scene when the giant monster appears, when the unthinkable occurs—the reception goes out. Enter Moment of Cynicism Number Two. Hogarth climbs out his window and onto the roof. Effortlessly.

Right.

When I was his age, if I climbed anything higher than ten feet off the ground I was reminded more often than not that gravity has a sense of humor. But Hogarth swings up to his roof like Spider-Man and skips along the ridge with perfect balance to the antenna (okay, maybe he doesn't skip, but you get the idea) to overlook the world below, eyes level with the treetops. And from this giant's-eye view, Hogarth discovers that something pretty big has torn up his yard.

After this momentary retreat into my derision-ridden comfort zone, I buck it up and decide once again to run with the story. I rejoin Hogarth as he flips into action like a good war hero, assembling his battle gear while standing beneath a *Forbidden Planet* poster hanging on his bedroom wall, strapping on his helmet and fearlessly stalking past a *Red Menace* magazine into the night to single-handedly take on an invasion by Martians, or the Communists, or a future where retail giants and Freedom Fries reign supreme.

Imagine, for a moment, that you're on a journey through outer space. No wait. Too far out. Let's just say you're on a voyage across the Pacific. Your vessel stumbles into a white squall and you're hurled overboard and tumble into the sea. You wash ashore. You have no idea where you are, or how you're going to get home. You know creatures the size of your thumb have spotted you, and you quickly determine that you're the only one of your kind in this place. You are not Gulliver, and this is not Lilliput.

You're really, really hungry.

So you find something that looks like food and you eat it. You find more of those things and eat them. You pick up another one, bite away half of it, and you toss it. The edible objects are just lying around like apples under a tree, so they must be there for the taking (I've often wondered when I pick up an apple off the ground, if I've somehow encroached on some squirrel's property.)

So you see something that looks like big food, and you lunge at it and immediately try to eat it, but by the time you realize this thing's going to hurt when you pick it up, it's too late. Like a meeting with a rattlesnake.

This is where Hogarth meets the Iron Giant (voiced by then-rising star Vin Diesel). Out on his scout for the invaders, Hogarth barely dives to safety as the Giant lunges for the tasty-looking high-voltage power station. The Giant tears away the structure, sending enough electricity through his metallic body to fry a town. Hog-

Young Hogarth Hughes (left) and the Iron Giant get a good look at each other, and begin what will become a deep friendship.

arth finds the power switch and throws it. The night goes black, and the Iron Giant falls first to his knees, then to the ground.

Given what we learn later about the Iron Giant — this guy's a nuclear-equipped walking gun who can collide with a missile and reassemble in deep space — a little jolt of electricity isn't going to kill him. But at the time, it looks like he's going down in a big way.

Again imagine yourself, the giant stranger washed ashore, holding this rattlesnake, and it's about to sink its big fangs right into you. And this little creature comes along and lops off the rattle, hobbling the snake and saving you from the Big Ouch. Enter yet another classic archetype, the lion and the mouse. The lion can still destroy the mouse, but the notion is out of the question now.

Part Three: Dead Soldiers Don't Die

If she's got a flask hidden in that apron pocket, we never see it.

Annie Hughes, American Single Mom: not an easy thing to be now, decades into the wake of the women's movement and affirmative action, let alone in the postwar era of the 1950s. Annie Hughes leans, at least in that well-adjusted American sense, toward the notion of the wholesome 1950s single mom whose husband bought the freedom of America with his life. Or does she?

After watching the film I said to my husband, "Well, you know, the story doesn't specifically *tell* us that Hogarth's father died in the war. I mean, maybe he was like Dennis Quaid in *Far from Heaven*, you know, the guy who came back from the Big

One and decided he just couldn't be a heterosexual." My husband squinted his eyes in that are-you-bloody-crazy way and replied, "Of course he died in the war! Leave it to you to turn *The Iron Giant* into a dark story."

I argued. "It *is* a dark story — it's a feel-good movie about the Cold War for chrissakes!" I deferred to my earlier points — paranoia, xenophobia. Get the idea?

But after my husband's short monologue marinated in my thoughts, I found the notion irksome on a deeper level. Do we really hold war-widowed single moms to a higher standard? Lots of kids in the 1950s were raised by single moms whose men didn't go down in the blaze of glory. Take for instance, Stephen King, who spent more than one book waxing nostalgic about growing up in the 1950s. By his own testament, his dad went out for a pack of cigarettes one day when Stephen and his brother David were still pretty small, and just never came back. Does that make Nellie Ruth Pillsbury King any less of a mother than Annie Hughes? One particular story Stephen King tells about his mother crawled under my skin many years ago and has since grown into a haunting vicarious memory. His mother, whose life was never easy, secretly went without meals so she could send five dollars a week to her sons while they were in college. You can't see it now, but I'm shivering.

My point is, Annie Hughes is that mom, the kind who does right by her kid, which to me renders irrelevant the ambiguity of what fate befell Hogarth's father.

Okay, get off me about Stephen King. Remember that part where I said I disappeared into books as a kid? I was born in the 1970s, and Stephen King wrote a lot of books during my growing-up years — books about kids with crazy moms (*Carrie*, 1974), kids with crazy dads (*The Shining*, 1977), kids with crazy cars (*Christine*, 1983), and kids who saved the world, or at least as much of it as they could (*The Talisman* with Peter Straub, 1984, and *It*, 1986). He wrote about kids who saw what other people couldn't, or wouldn't, see. He wrote about kids who believed the things they saw. He wrote about kids with fucked-up home lives they couldn't change, who went outside and discovered other fucked-up things they could do something about. His books weren't the best I'd ever read, and truth be told I outgrew them. But the kids he created stay with me because they did the things I wanted to do, whether it be trekking across the country with an oversized wolf boy, setting evil ablaze with the sheer power of mind, or doing battle with a subconscious-lurking terror by simultaneously believing wholly in its existence, and that it can only be defeated by the bonds of true friendship. Put simply, he wrote about kids like me, and Hogarth.

Thank you for the digression.

Annie Hughes doesn't really "get" Hogarth, but she seems to understand she doesn't have to. She and Hogarth understand one another about as much as a single woman raising a son and a fatherless boy can understand one another — which means if they like each other, life can be pretty interesting.

So while Hogarth is out scouting the countryside getting ready to bump into his big metallic friend-to-be, Annie returns home to a dark, empty house and immediately goes looking for her son. By the time Annie finds Hogarth, he's already had the life-changing experience of pulling the thorn from the lion's paw. They come together in a trenchant moment — her with panic melting into frustrated relief, and him with panic rising into the excitement of wanting to share a tale of a hundred-foot-tall robot. He doesn't understand her worry. She doesn't understand metallic men munching on power stations. "Hogarth, I'm not in the mood." But I forgive her for that, because her priority *should* be keeping that boy in one piece.

And hell, she has to be tired.

From the dictionary:

> paranoia: A tendency on the part of an individual or group toward excessive or irrational suspiciousness and distrustfulness of others.
>
> xenophobia: Fear and hatred of strangers or foreigners or of anything that is strange or foreign.

You think this metal man is fun, but who built it? The Russians? The Chinese? Martians? Canadians? I don't care! All I know is we didn't build it, and that's reason enough to assume the worst and blow it to kingdom come!

—Kent Mansley

Enter folly-prone Kent Mansley (Christopher McDonald), the National Security agent who bears the two-dimensional collective paranoid xenophobia that served as a necessary component of classic Cold War consciousness. Mansley is one of the more finely crafted clichés in *The Iron Giant*, largely because his character feeds on a crescendo of ludicrousness that eventually brings about his implosion. He's part vestige, part homage, part comic relief. He also represents something darker, an all-too-familiar affliction of the human condition, like the temptation to punctuate any self-introduction with a resume. "Kent Mansley, United States government." Like the tendency to look upon all things alien with extreme prejudice. "The biggest thing in this town is probably the homecoming queen." Or disdain. "Hogarth? That's an embarrassing name. They might as well have called him Zeppo or something."

Mansley's Sputnik-obsessed McCarthian surface character gives way to some more frightening issues. Let's examine, historically, acts of extreme hatred. Whether on the local level or on a global scale, they all seem to involve a Kent Mansley. He's the person who leads the campaign to drive the "uppity black family" out of the community. He's the person who brings about and enforces book bans. He's the person who transforms "Communist" into a word synonymous with evil. He's the person who tells us that homosexuals are damned sinners at worst, and second-class citizens at best. He's the one who incites people to raise their fists and declare, not in my back yard!

Our Mansley has just enough power to be dangerous, but luckily he's got a boss. Just imagine the ramifications of an *uber*–Mansley with his finger on the button. A Mansley who comes from a dynastic American lot. A Mansley who looks on the world as one big sandbox. A Mansley who says, "People want to know their government has a response. I am that response."

Oops. Too late.

Hogarth and Mansley share a common trait—they both believe the Iron Giant exists. But while Hogarth pursues the Iron Giant in need of a friend, Kent pursues him in need of an enemy. While Hogarth sees only possibilities, Mansley sees only red.

The day after the power station incident, Hogarth seeks out the Iron Giant, who, as it turns out, has been waiting for him. When the giant drops the on-off switch at Hogarth's feet, they go from being curious to being friends. Hogarth also begins to speak, as he does through much of the film, in two distinct and simultaneous voices—impulsive child, and conscience. "I gotta tell someone. I should call someone.... No, they'll panic. People always wig out and start shooting when they see something big like you."

As in any friendship, they've got their challenges, like the language barrier between the English-speaking human and the alien-speaking robot, and, of course, the Iron Giant's appetite for large metal structures. When the giant causes a train wreck by attempting to consume a railroad track, Hogarth starts to see the magnitude of the problem. He fully understands the danger posed to his new friend when Kent Mansley shows up at his door. Knowing Mansley's on to them, and knowing his new friend is really really hungry, he does what any true friend would do. He takes the Iron Giant to where the food is.

There are two kinds of metal in this yard: scrap and art. If you gotta eat one of them, eat the scrap. What you currently have—IN YOUR MOUTH!—is ART!

—Dean McCoppin

Dean McCoppin's junkyard is the perfect haven for the Iron Giant, and it takes only a post-espresso shock and all of 37 minutes of Hogarth cajoling and jabbering for Dean to cave on taking the Iron Giant in. It happens in the nick of time too, because while this is going on, Annie has rented out her spare room to Kent Mansley.

Now this trait of Annie's bothers me a bit. I'd think she'd be a better judge of character. I mean, Mansley is a real scumbag. But she trusts him at first. She even convinces Hogarth to take Mansley around to see the sights. While they're out, as Mansley rants on about national security and getting-them-before-they-get-us, Hogarth devises a plan to ditch Mansley by sprinkling laxative on his ice cream sundae.

He catches up with Dean and the Iron Giant bonding over scrap art creation, and they have something like a fantasy afternoon, three guys together—the kid, the beatnik and the giant robot—doing cannonballs into a lake and just plain hanging out. Hogarth and the Iron Giant go exploring, and they come across a deer. The Iron Giant is perplexed and touched by the creature. Gunfire rings out, and the deer falls dead. Hogarth tries to explain death to his new friend.

"Things die. It's part of life. It's bad to kill, but it's not bad to die."

"You die?"

"Well, yes. Someday."

"I die?"

"I don't know. You're made of metal, but you have feelings ... and you think about things. And that means you have a soul. And souls don't die."

"Soul?"

"Mom says it's something inside of all good things, and that it goes on forever and ever."

"Souls don't die."

I can do anything I want, whenever I want, if I feel it's in the people's best interest.

—Kent Mansley

Kent Mansley is where he needs to be. He's inside Hogarth's home, he's got Annie's trust, and he's watching Hogarth's every move. And when he develops the film swiped from Hogarth's camera, he's got the proof he needs to call in the army—Hogarth and the Iron Giant, together. But Mansley's not that bright, and Hogarth easily slips past him to warn Dean and the Iron Giant that the big guns are on their way. Making Mansley look like an ass in front of the United States military proves an easy task when the Iron Giant poses as one of Dean's sculptures.

The army leaves, and Mansley retreats with them, resolved to redeem his name and convince the world that the Iron Giant isn't a hoax. Meanwhile, Hogarth's idyllic fantasy life is about to change forever.

Victorious and with his secret intact, Hogarth resumes life in his little world where only he, Dean, and the Iron Giant exist. During a game, the Iron Giant plasters a big "S" on his chest and declares, "I'm Superman!" Hogarth points a toy laser gun at his mammoth friend, an act that triggers something. The giant's eyes glow red and from them shoots forth an atomic blast aimed at Hogarth, who unknowingly ducks out of the way of certain death. The Iron Giant comes out of his trance, disoriented. Unaware of any danger, Hogarth again points the toy laser at the Iron Giant, triggering the same red glowing eyes, the same death-ray lasers. Dean leaps to Hogarth's rescue, knocking him out of the laser's path. The red leaves the Iron Giant's eyes, and he again becomes himself to face an accusing Dean, calling him a "weapon, a big gun that walks!"

Part Four: The Epiphany of the Iron Giant. "I Am Not a Gun."

Here begins a series of epiphanies.

The Iron Giant collapses into shame for what he is, and devastation for what he's capable of. He whispers, "I am not a gun," as if trying to convince himself, then retreats into the wilderness. Here, at his lowest, the Iron Giant takes his first human steps.

Up to this point Dean represents the liberal, the open-minded. But after driving the Iron Giant away, Dean learns something important about himself; that upon seeing the red eyes he, too, had falsely judged the Iron Giant. Though he is correct that the Iron Giant was built to be a "big gun that walks," he comes to understand it as

In a moment of marvelous epiphany, the Iron Giant realizes that love and play are better than the pursuit of war. He does not have to be a gun.

a defense mechanism, that the giant attacks only when attacked. Dean gets what Hogarth seems to understand all along: The Iron Giant is more than the sum of his parts.

Hogarth has run after the Iron Giant on foot. Dean catches up with Hogarth on his motorcycle, and together they pursue their fleeing friend.

Two boys on a rooftop in downtown Rockwell spot the big metal man, and in their excitement they fall off and plummet toward the earth. The Iron Giant rushes forth to save them, in full view of all of Rockwell and the U.S. Army. Introducing himself to Annie Hughes and the world at large with an act of heroism, the Iron Giant finds himself facing people who regard him with awe and wonder, but not fear. He smiles at Hogarth. "I am not a gun." Now he knows it to be true. Epiphany continues.

The army's guns fire upon him.

With Hogarth enclosed in his giant palm, the Iron Giant flees. The fighter planes pursue them. They run and run and run. In an effort to dodge a school bus, the Iron Giant trips, slides, and plummets over the high cliffs of Maine. Down they go ... falling ... falling, while Annie watches helplessly from the edge. From the Iron Giant's feet shoot forth flames, and they stop falling.

"You can fly?"

Like a rocket, they rise up from the precipice, past Annie, and soar into the air.

"You can fly!"

Up and up they go, and Hogarth again lives the fantasy. "Try pointing your arm straight ahead ... like Superman!" The Iron Giant does, and for a moment he is Superman, and for a moment Hogarth has reached the pinnacle of glory with his fully realized war-hero father figure.

The fighter planes shoot them out of the sky. They crash-land. The Iron Giant does his best to protect Hogarth from the impact. But when the Iron Giant sees Hogarth lying unconscious, he believes the boy is dead, so when the tanks fire on him next, he unleashes his full power, transforming into the very monster envisioned by Kent Mansley.

Epiphany continues. Grief. Guns spring forth from every part of him, and he becomes a walking weapon of mass destruction. It's a very human reaction when you think about it.

The army lets loose with everything it's got, but can't stop the Iron Giant. Mansley reminds General Rogard (John Mahoney) that they haven't tried the Bomb. They fix on him as a target, and it becomes clear that if fired on by the Bomb, the Iron Giant will wreak destruction such that nobody will survive. Hogarth, alive after all, faces down the Iron Giant at his most frightening visage. Standing before what was once a giant iron arm, and is now a nuclear gun the length of a building with a barrel as big as Hogarth, the boy reaches deep into the Iron Giant.

"You don't have to be a gun. You are what you choose to be."

The Iron Giant's soul rises, almost visible in the animation. His eyes fade from red to green, and his guns disappear into his body. "Hogarth!"

Dean reaches the general. The Iron Giant is defensive. He only fires when fired upon. The general orders the army to hold fire. But Mansley, taking matters into his own hands, gives the order to launch the Bomb. It hurls up into space. When it falls back to Earth it will kill everyone.

Here we come to the final phase of the Iron Giant's human transformation.

The epiphany, which begins with shame, culminates with the understanding that he can choose the method by which to use his great strength. His humanity complete, the Iron Giant bids Hogarth farewell, flies into space and detonates the bomb, safely above Earth. His first and last words spoken as a complete human. "Superman!"

Ka-pow!

The film begins with a prologue and ends with an epilogue. Dean, Annie, and Hogarth are a family. Dean finally finds success as a junk artist with his sculpture of the Iron Giant, which stands tribute in Rockwell with the inscription, "Dedicated in memory of the Iron Giant by the town of Rockwell, Maine."

And the very end, a precious piece of this film, which I'll leave un-described, tickles us with a reminder of an earlier exchange: "Souls don't die." The Iron Giant lives on.

So here it stands. Hogarth loses a father who pays for the future with his life. Hogarth gains a larger-than-life father figure who makes the ultimate sacrifice. Hogarth ends up with a human guy who will never be his father, but who's worthy enough to try and fill the spot. Hogarth had the inclination to be a good person; now he has the information he needs to grow into an Iron Giant himself someday.

Conclusion: The Iron Giant of Ted Hughes

Ted Hughes existed to be punished....

—Germaine Greer, author

Was he an unwitting Prometheus, a scoundrel, or simply the man who drove Sylvia Plath to her grave? In any case, Ted Hughes holds court with the vilified artists of the twentieth century. On their first date, Plath bit Hughes's face hard enough to draw blood. They got married — naturally the next logical step. It was 1957, the same year Hughes published his first poetry collection, *The Hawk in the Rain.* For the next five years, Plath and Hughes continued to forge their way through the ups and downs of the pursuit for a place among the literary elite. They had a relatively typical marriage while it lasted. Hughes picked his nose and went about his business in the most slovenly manner possible, and Plath wove one psychotic episode after another into their daily lives while entertaining elaborate fantasies about Hughes's extracurricular love affairs. Her dreams came true in 1962 when Hughes abandoned her for his mistress, Assia Wevill. No stranger to self-perpetuated tragedy, Plath killed the pain by sticking her head into an oven, asphyxiating herself. She left behind two children, daughter Frieda and son Nicholas, and a desperate Hughes who, by many accounts, never recovered from her death. For the next three years he obsessed over editing and publishing his late wife's work.

He wrote the book *The Iron Man* (1968) supposedly for his children, and oh, doesn't that speak volumes?

I go now to Hughes's incarnation, which inspired not only Brad Bird's film but also a whole album by the Who's Pete Townshend (who also executive-produced the film). Tall as a tall tree, stronger than any creature on earth, the Iron Giant comes into our view by taking a suicidal step over a cliff, quite without explanation. He plummets to the rocky beach far below, breaking to pieces as he crashes down the precipice.

Nobody knew the Iron Giant had fallen.
— Ted Hughes, *The Iron Man*

After pulling himself together with the help of some curious seagulls, the Iron Giant steps into a world that doesn't understand him. The farmers, frustrated at this giant creature devouring their cars and tractors, devise a plan to lure him into a deep pit. The plan comes to fruition by the wit of a small boy called Hogarth Hughes, who is immediately consumed with guilt. He feels so guilty, in fact, that he leaves the Iron Giant buried alive, to rust in a living grave, long enough for everyone to forget he's buried there.

Finally the Iron Giant pushes his way through the surface of the Earth — reborn, or perhaps resurrected — only to face a community with an even more aggressive plan for obliterating him. Plan Number One: call in the army to take care of him once and for all. Hogarth, moving on to active guilt, elects to help the Iron Giant by convincing him to prove to the world that he's one of the good guys by taking on a giant space-bat-angel-dragon, with a head the size of Italy, who's perched on Australia and threatening to gobble up villages and, well, basically everyone on Earth. The Iron Giant defeats the space-bat-dragon, not by might —for the Iron Giant is no match for a space creature the size of a small continent — but by wit.

On the surface, I see at the root of this story a Ted Hughes so tormented by his own sense of inadequacy that he creates a larger-than-life Iron Man to swoop in and take on the role of savior. Underneath, I can only conclude that Ted Hughes was an even bigger whiner than I am. The story reeks of self-pity, of shortfall wrought by self-absorption. Hunted, persecuted, trapped, buried alive long enough to be forgotten, even by the children.

Puh-leaze!

A year after the publication of *The Iron Man*, Hughes's mistress Assia Wevill poisoned their daughter and killed herself in the same manner Sylvia did — asphyxiation via head in oven. Do we discern a pattern here?

So what did Ted Hughes tell me with this story? That it's easier to write an Iron Man than to be one? That may be true. But the mere effort to be one is what makes a good man worth a damn in the first place.

Should I end on such a sour note? I think not. Director Brad Bird used his instincts well. Where Hughes's *The Iron Man* strayed from the relationship between Hogarth and the Iron Giant, Bird stuck with it. In an interview, Bird told *SPLICEDwire* magazine, "The idea I pitched to Warner Bros. after reading the book — when I said that I really liked it but I wanted to do something different with it — was I said 'What if a gun had a soul?'"

Enough said.

Film Discussed

The Iron Giant Warner Bros. Released August 4, 1999. 86 min. Producers: Pete Townshend and John Walker. Director: Brad Bird. Screenplay: Tim McCanlies, based on a story by Brad Bird, from the book *The Iron Man* by Ted Hughes. Director of Photography: Steven Wilzbach. Editor: Darren T. Holmes. Music: Michael Kamen. Art Director: Alan Bodner. Special Effects: Carl Canga. Visual Effects: James Hathcock. With the voices of Jennifer Aniston, Harry Connick, Jr., Vin Diesel, Eli Marienthal, Christopher McDonald, James Gammon, Cloris Leachman and M. Emmet Walsh. Available on Warner Home Video VHS; Warner Home Video DVD.

Sources

Blackwelder, Bob. "A 'Giant' Among Animators." *SPLICEDwire* magazine, July 19, 1999.
Hughes, Ted. *The Iron Giant*, originally titled *The Iron Man*. New York: Random House.
"The Iron Giant (1999)." <http://www.geocities.com/theactionkingsk/ ActionKings-Diesel-TheIronGiant.html>.

For Michael and Christopher Koutaves, my Iron Giants.

Contributors

Jacque Day Archer is a writer, journalist, editor, and TV and stage producer. Among her credits is the Discovery series, *Chicago's Lifeline* (AMA Freddy Award for best medical reality series). Before television she worked on movie crews ranging from Hollywood pictures like *Stir of Echoes* to independent films like *Kwik Stop*. Recipient of the Linda Haldeman Fiction Award, Jacque writes for *Peeks & Valleys*, *New England Fiction Journal*, and *Characters*. She was on the editorial team for the book *Civil Rights Chronicle*, and her articles appear in *Newcity Magazine*, *ReelChicago*, and many other publications.

Ryan Baker is in the University of Oklahoma's film and video studies program. His work has previously appeared in *Monsters from the Vault* and *Video Watchdog*. Despite an intense love for the horror genre, German Expressionism, Roger Corman, and all things Dracula, Baker enjoys rocking out.

Mark Clark is the author of *Smirk, Sneer and Scream: Great Acting in Horror Cinema* (McFarland). He has been a staff writer and film critic for the *Louisville Courier-Journal*, and has written for *The Cincinnati Enquirer* and *Writer's Digest*, as well as *Filmfax*, *Scarlet Street*, and *Monsters from the Vault*. Clark also has contributed essays to *Actors Series: Vincent Price* and *Actors Series: Peter Lorre* (Midnight Marquee Press). He lives with his wife and daughter in Columbus, Ohio.

Vincent Di Fate has for four decades been a premier futurist painter. His science fiction visions are crisp, moody, and painterly. His commercial clients have included IBM, *The Reader's Digest*, the National Geographic Society, and the National Aeronautics and Space Administration. His work has been exhibited across North America, Europe, and Asia. He has won many awards, including the coveted Hugo, and was guest of honor at the 50th World Science Fiction Convention in 1992. Di Fate is an adjunct professor at the Fashion Institute of Technology (State University of New York), where he teaches history of illustration and science fiction and fantasy art. His books include *The Science Fiction Art of Vincent Di Fate* (Paper Tiger), *Di Fate's Catalog of Science Fiction Hardware* (Workman), and *Infinite Worlds: The Fantastic Visions of Science Fiction Art* (Penguin Studio Books).

David J. Hogan is publisher of Legacy Books, a division of Chicago-based Publications International. He is the author of *Who's Who of the Horrors and Other Fantasy Films* (A.S. Barnes), *Your Movie Guide to Drama Video Tapes and Discs* (Signet), and *Dark Romance: Sexuality in the Horror Film* (McFarland). He has written for *Filmfax*, *Outré*, *Moviegoer*, *Photon*, *Cinefantastique*, and other magazines. Hogan has edited and cowritten numerous books of automotive history, and is editor-in-chief and contributing writer to *The Holocaust Chronicle* (Publications International). *Civil Rights Chronicle* (Legacy), and *The Sixties Chronicle* (Legacy). He lives in a Chicago suburb with his wife, Kim, three children, and numerous animals.

Lyndon W. Joslin is a self-described hostile hermit who lives in the wilds of northwest Harris County, Texas, near Houston. He is the author of *Count Dracula Goes to the Movies* (McFarland).

Leonard J. Kohl works for the Code Enforcement division of Chicago Streets and

Sanitation. He also is a freelance cartoonist and writer whose work has appeared in *Filmfax*, *Cult Movies*, *Scarlet Street*, and *Classic Images*. He contributed essays to the anthologies *Lon Chaney, Jr.* and *It's Christmas Time at the Movies*, and is sole author of *Sinister Serials of Boris Karloff, Bela Lugosi, and Lon Chaney, Jr.* (all Midnight Marquee Press). He is currently at work, with Kristin Dewey, on a history of old-time radio and serial hero Chandu the Magician.

Alan Dirk Lester grew up as a State Department brat in various countries in Africa, as well as Great Britain and Washington, D.C. He attended Georgetown and Columbia, and has worked as a Greenpeace fundraiser, childcare specialist, bodyguard, and newspaper reporter. He also worked briefly for Ken Starr's law firm, Kirkland and Ellis. When not working on screenplays, Lester enjoys movies and comic books at home with his wife in Chicago.

Ted Okuda is a prolific film historian whose books include *The Columbia Comedy Shorts* (with Edward Watz), *The Monogram Checklist*, *The Soundies Distributing Corporation of America* (with Scott MacGillivray), *The Jerry Lewis Films* (with James L. Neibaur), all from McFarland, and *The Golden Age of Chicago Children's Television* (with Jack Mulqueen; Lake Claremont Press). A former editor of *Filmfax* and *Outré*, he has also written for *Classic Images*, *Cult Movies*, and *Classic Film Collector*.

Gary D. Rhodes is a documentary filmmaker (*Lugosi: Hollywood's Dracula*), and a professor in the University of Oklahoma department of film and video studies. His books include *White Zombie: Anatomy of a Horror Film*, *Horror at the Drive-In: Essays in Popular Culture*, and the definitive *Lugosi: His Life in Films, on Stage, and in the Hearts of Horror Lovers* (all from McFarland).

Bryan Senn is a prolific horror-film historian whose books include *Fantastic Cinema Subject Guide: A Topical Index to 2500 Horror, Science Fiction, and Fantasy Films* (McFarland), *Golden Horrors: An Illustrated Critical Filmography of Terror Cinema, 1931–1939* (McFarland), and the groundbreaking *Drums of Terror: Voodoo in the Cinema* (Midnight Marquee Press).

John T. Soister is a teacher of modern and classical languages, and the author of *Up from the Vault: Rare Thrillers of the 1920s and 1930s*, *Conrad Veidt on Screen*, *Claude Rains* (with JoAnna Wioskowski), and *Of Gods and Monsters: A Critical Guide to Universal Studios' Science Fiction, Horror and Mystery Films, 1929–1939* (all from McFarland). Soister lives in Orwigsburg, Pennsylvania.

Robert Tinnell has worked in the film industry for 20 years as a writer, producer, and director. He produced *South of Reno* and *Surf Nazis Must Die*, and wrote and directed *Kids of the Round Table*, *Frankenstein and Me*, *Airspeed*, and *Believe*. Recent screenplays include *Sacrifice*, and an adaptation of the French-language hockey comedy *Les Boys*. Tinnell also has worked extensively in television commercials and the music video industry. He and his wife have two children.

Ken Weiss spent 35 years in advertising and public relations, went back to school, and taught college-level communications as an associate professor for ten years. He is the author of *To Be Continued: A History of Sound Serials 1929–1956* (Crown; 3d ed., Cummington), *To the Rescue: How Immigrants Saved the American Film Industry* (Austin and Winfield), and numerous articles and monographs.

Chase Winstead holds a master's degree in film studies from Texas State University at Dallas. When he is not writing or lecturing about science fiction cinema, he runs Winstead Wrecking, operating 40 tow trucks from various locations around Dallas. He shares a home with his wife, Lisa, and a gila monster named Nitro.

Jerry Yamamoto earned an M.A. in New Testament studies from Gordon-Conwell Theological Seminary in 1982. He has done graduate work at Harvard Divinity School and the University of California, Berkeley. He is presently the inspiration editor for Chicago-based Publications International, a consulting editor for the *Christian Research Journal*, and an adjunct professor at Judson College in Elgin, Illinois. He has been on the editorial staff of *Christianity Today* and Cook Communications and cowrote *If Jesus Loves Me, How Do I Know?— Experiencing the Depth of God's Love* (InterVarsity Press). He also has written *Buddhism, Taoism and Other Far Eastern Religions* and *Hinduism, TM and Hare Krishna* (both Zondervan), *Beyond Buddhism* and *The Puppet Master* (both InterVarsity), and several other books. He and his wife have two college-age children, and live near Chicago.

Index

Numbers in ***bold italics*** indicate photographs